MICROCOMPUTERS: developments in industry, business and education

organized by
EUROMICRO

sponsored by
ECI (AFCET, AICA, BCS, GI, NTG, NGI)
ASI, The Netherlands
IEEE (TC Micro)
ACM (Sig Micro)
Bell Telephone Mfg. Co., Belgium
TH Twente, The Netherlands
E.R.O., United Kingdom
ETSIT, COIT, AEIA (Academical Org.), Spain
Secoinsa Hewlett-Packard CTNE, Spain
ADAMICRO, ICL (Spain)

MICROCOMPUTERS:

developments in industry, business and education

ninth EUROMICRO symposium on microprocessing and microprogramming

Madrid, September 13-16, 1983

edited by

D. R. Wilson

Cees J. van Spronsen

1983

NORTH-HOLLAND – AMSTERDAM • NEW YORK • OXFORD

ISBN: 0 444 86742 2

Publishers:

ELSEVIER SCIENCE PUBLISHERS B.V.
P.O. BOX 1991
1000 BZ AMSTERDAM
THE NETHERLANDS

Sole distributors for the U.S.A. and Canada:

ELSEVIER SCIENCE PUBLISHING COMPANY, INC.
52, VANDERBILT AVENUE
NEW YORK, N.Y. 10017
U.S.A.

Library of Congress Cataloging in Publication Data

Euromicro Symposium on Microprocessing and Micropro-
gramming (9th : 1983 : Madrid, Spain)
Microcomputers : developments in industry,
business, and education.

1. Microcomputers--Congresses. I. Wilson, D. R.
(Derek Robert), 1936- . II. Spronsen, Cees J. van,
1941- . III. Euromicro. IV. European Cooperation
in Informatics (Organization) V. Title.
QA76.5.E9 1983 001.64 83-13292
ISBN 0-444-86742-2 (U.S.)

PRINTED IN THE NETHERLANDS

INTRODUCTION TO THE PROGRAM

The theme of the ninth Euromicro symposium - Developments in Industry, Business and Education - has attracted contributions from all the European countries and many others. The programme committee has been able to prepare the scientific sessions with a selection of original papers. All the authors have confirmed that their papers have not been presented previously and the conference should provide a fruitful and meaningful basis for technological progress to be reported.

The call for papers specified special themes of current interest. Software was particularly emphasized as an area in which the programme committee would welcome original contributions. In the event the programme will include a special session on Software Quality Assurance as well as sessions on High Level Language development and compiler construction. European initiatives in Small Business Systems has created the opportunity to mount a panel which will focus on the opportunities in Office Communication, which will be supported by a special session on Office Automation.

Euromicro 83 is proud that the keynote speakers will be able to review areas of paramount importance. From Japan Dr Kani will speak on VSLI Microprocessors. The impact of Japanese technology on all aspects of European manufacturing capability and capacity has created immense respect for Japanese developments. The programme committee is delighted that one of the keynote addresses will be presented by Dr Kani and that he will be able to report on VLSI technology. The second keynote address concentrates on the impact of the technology in the vital area of Education. In the United Kingdom the introduction of small computer systems into all grades of School, starting with primary schools at age 6., is seen as an attempt to orientate society to the impact of Information technology. Richard Fothergill is the Director of the Microelectronics Education Programme in which the U.K. Government has invested substantial funds to stimulate the introduction of the computer into all aspects of the curriculum. The emphasis throughout the School's programme is on the teacher introducing the technology into the subject area for which they are responsible in order that the computer becomes an adjunct to the learning process.

Euromicro's traditional contribution to hardware will be maintained with special sessions on Hardware Design Methods, Computing Structures, Multiprocessor Bus Systems and Local Area Networks.

The Industrial Sessions on the Application of Microelectronic Technology will be supported by an exhibition, and an Industrial Programme of visits. The short note session also provides industrialists the opportunity to make state of the art presentations of recent developments.

In welcoming you to this ninth Symposium I would like to express my appreciation to the deputy programme Chairman, Cees J. van Spronsen, the members of the programme committee and the referees, without whose timely assistance the Scientific sessions would not have been possible.

Have a good Symposium.

Derek R. Wilson
Programme Chairman

LIST OF REFEREES

ALABAU, PROF: A.	SPAIN	PAKER, PROF: Y.	GREAT BRITAIN
ANDERSON, J.S.A.	GREAT BRITAIN	RICHTER, LUTZ	WEST GERMANY
BILLINGSLEY, DR. J.	GREAT BRITAIN	RISPOLI, ING. LUIGI	ITALY
BOUTE, PROF: IR.	NETHERLANDS	SAMI, PROF: M.	ITALY
BRUYNE, IR. P. DE	BELGIUM	SCHECHER, PROF: DR.HEINZ	WEST GERMANY
CHROUST, DR. GERHARD	AUSTRIA	SCHUMNY, H.	GERMANY
DAVID, DR. D.J.	FRANCE	STADLER, K.	AUSTRIA
DAVIES, PROF: A.C.	GREAT BRITAIN	SKARD, TORSTEIN	NORWAY
DAVIES, DR. O.J.	GREAT BRITAIN	SPRONSEN, C. VAN	NETHERLANDS
DOWSING, DR. ROY	GREAT BRITAIN	STRIEN, A.C.G. VAN	NETHERLANDS
FERGUS, P.	GREAT BRITAIN	TABAK, PROF: DANIEL	ISRAEL
GUGGENBUHL, PROF: WALTER	SWITZERLAND	TIBERGHIEN, PROF: J.	BELGIUM
LENT, BOGDAN	POLAND	THOMPSON, L.	GREAT BRITAIN
LEVI, BOZIDAR	YUGOSLAVIA	VAJDA, FERENC	HUNGARY
LAWSON, PROF: HAROLD	SWEDEN	VRIELINK, H.	NETHERLANDS
MARCZYNSKI, PROF: R.	POLAND	WALDSCHMIDT, PROF:DR. KLAUS	WEST GERMANY
MILUTINOVIC, PROF:DR.VELJKO	U.S.A.	WILMINK, J.	NETHERLANDS
MØLGAARD, JOHN	DENMARK	WINKELHAGE, FRIEDRICH	WEST GERMANY
MYHRHAUG, B.	NORWAY	WINTER, S.C.	GREAT BRITAIN
NICOUD, PROF: J.D.	SWITZERLAND	WOOD, DR G.	GREAT BRITAIN

TABLE OF CONTENTS

MICROCOMPUTERS: Developments in Industry, Business and Education
D.R. Wilson and C.J. van Spronsen (eds.) /© EUROMICRO, 1983
Elsevier Science Publishers B.V. (North-Holland)

Trends in VLSI microprocessors

Kenji Kani

VLSI Development Division,
NEC Corporation
Kawasaki, Japan

With the advance of semiconductor device technology, VLSI microprocessors are expected to be introduced into various applications as a key to the microelectronics revolution. In this overview, the future trends in VLSI microprocessors are discussed. In addition to the general purpose microprocessor, dedicated microprocessor is pointed out as a new direction. Technological issues in VLSI microprocessor design are also discussed.

1. Introduction

The rapid evolution of semiconductor technology continues to make possible higher performance and more sophisticated microprocessors. Usually, the term, "VLSI microprocessor" is used to denote a microprocessor which contains more than 100K components. Already a couple of VLSI microprocessors are introduced as practical products. And a number of VLSI microprocessors are now being developed and introduced hereafter into various applications. The microelectronics revolution will be acceralated in a wide range of society.

As shown in Fig.1, the channel length of MOS transistor, used in commercial products, was reduced from 3 ~ 4 μm in 1980 to 2 ~ 3 μm in 1982, and is expected to be reduced 1 μm in 1990. Based mainly on this progress in semiconductor device technology, the number of components in a chip is estimated as shown in Fig.2. Until 1986, it is expected that dynamic random access memory (dRAM) will make 4 times/3 years progress, while microprocessor will make 2 times/2 years progress. That is, 64K bit dRAM (150K components) and 256K bit dRAM (560K components) were introduced in 1980 and 1983, respectively, and 1M bit dRAM (2.2M components) will be available around 1986; high level microprocessors contained 20K ~ 80K components in 1980, and they will contain 160K ~ 640K components in 1986. Beyond 1986, however, even if 1 μm technology can be used in 1990, it will not be easy to attain 4M bit dRAM (8.8M components). In other words, if the progress in Fig.1 and no technological breakthrough are assumed, the growth in complexity will slow down beyond 1986. On the other hand, in the case of microprocessors, it will be possible to attain larger growth rate than in Fig.2. That is, microprocessors which contain very large memories can have similar growth rate as memory chips. A 32bit microprocessor, developed by HP [1], is considered as a typical example. It contains 450K components, and 342K components (76%) of which consist of ROM where microprograms are stored.

2. General Purpose Microprocessors

2.1 Single chip microcomputers

As the most economical solution to realize a computer, single chip microcomputers, which contain program and data memories and I/O circuits in addition to CPU, are used for various applications such as VTR, microwave cookers, cash registers, telephone set and so on. The proportion of the single chip microcomputers to total microprocessor shipmentvolume is 80%. The following trends should be pointed out in 1980s.

(1) Increase in on-chip memory size
As shown in Fig.3, the on-chip memory size continues to be larger. For example, the ROM in which application programs are stored, was 1K bytes in 1975, and now it is 8K bytes in 1983, and is expected to be 64K bytes around 1990. The more the microprocessor applicationsbecome sophisticated, the larger application programs become. Thus, a large on-chip memory as well as an access capability to external memories is strongly required. The architecture in which program memory (ROM) and data memory (RAM) are separated, is suitable for single chip microcomputers, and will also be used in the future besides the standard (non-separated memory space) architecture.

(2) Increase in on-chip functions
Single chip microcomputers are adding more on-chip functions such as serial interface, A/D converters, display control etc.. A variety of desirable combinations of these functions and memory sizes in different application leads to a diversity of products as shown in Fig.4. By 1990, hundreds of single chip microcomputers will be available, ranging from a low end, half dollar 4 bit product for white goods to a high end 16 bit

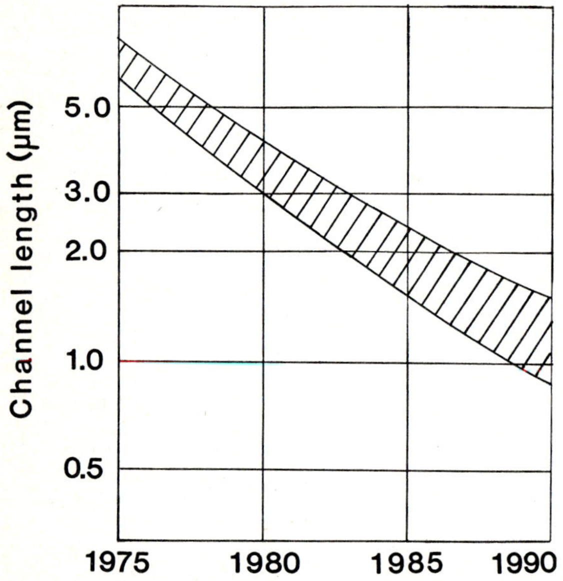

Fig. 1 Progress of MOS technology

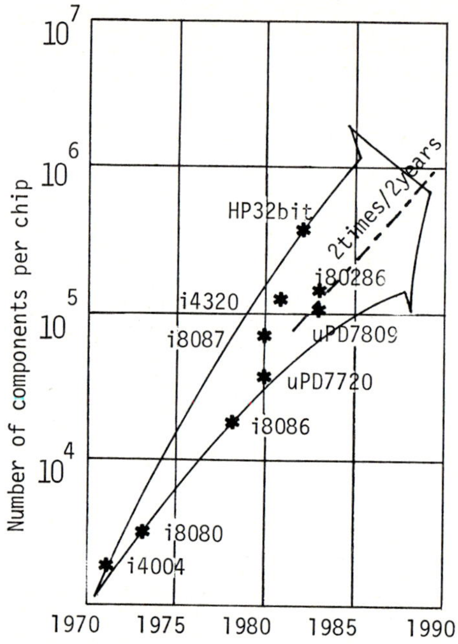

Fig. 2 Growth in microprocessor complexity

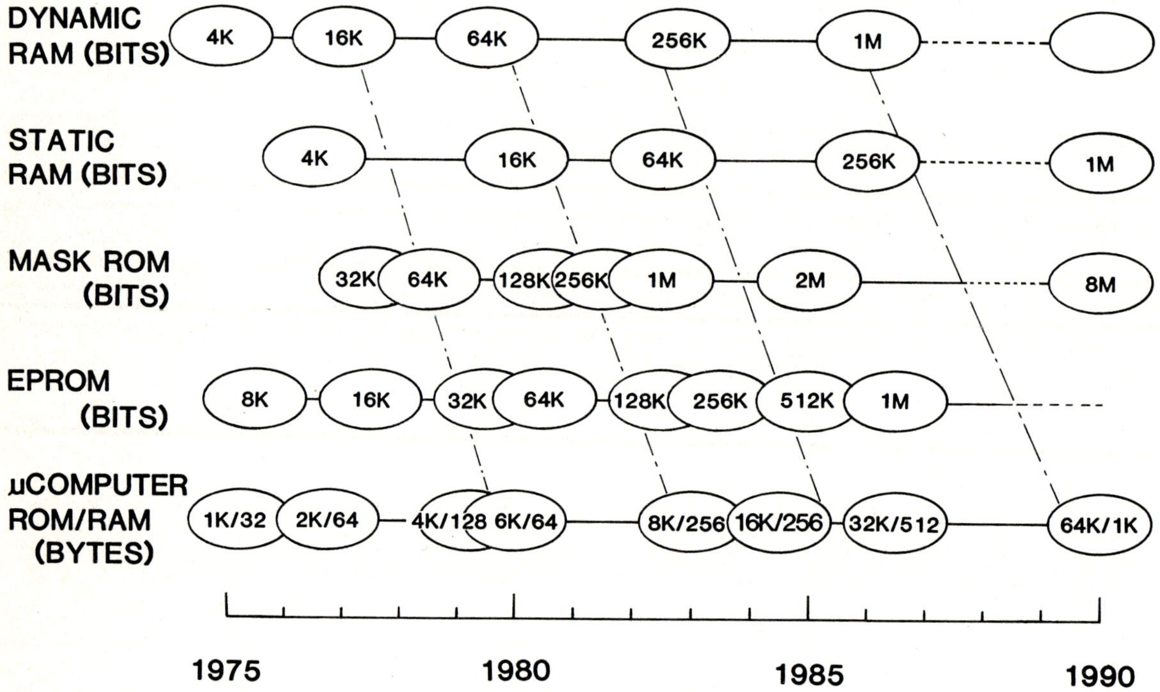

Fig. 3 Progress of memory technology

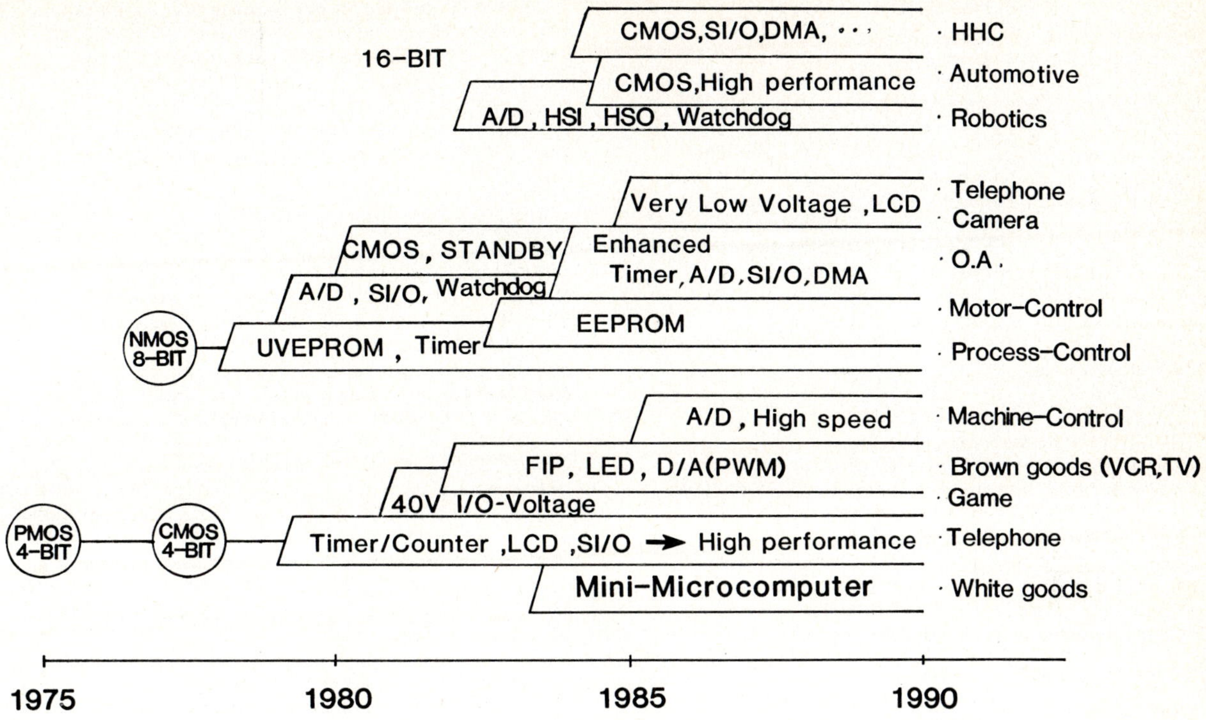

Fig. 4 On-chip functions in single-chip microcomputers

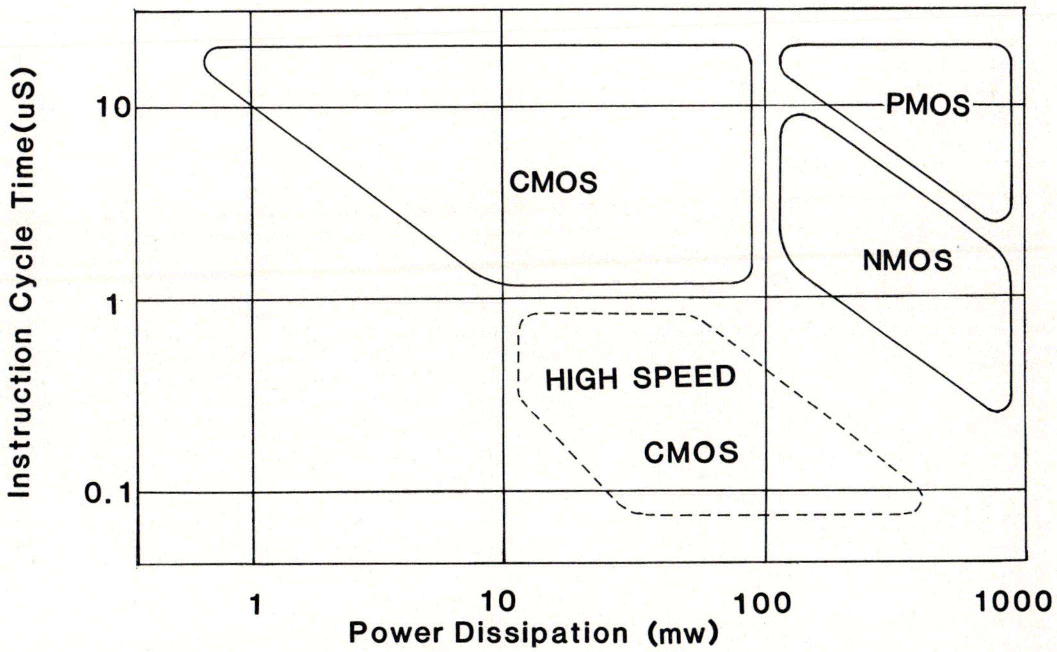

Fig. 5 Speed-power relationship for microprocessor device technologies

product for automotive engine control.

(3) Device technology
In 1970s, pMOS, followed by nMOS, were used. Now in 1980s, CMOS products are dominant because of their lower power consumption and wider voltage range. The CMOS's disadvantage of low speed is now going to be improved owing to architectural improvement such as pipelined processor and advanced device technology. As shown in Fig.5, high speed CMOS microprocessors will be a design target. In addition, when they are applied in small volume production equipment, writable program memory is desirable, and therefore on-chip CMOS EPROM or EEPROM technology will be accelerated.

2.2 High level microprocessors

As the most advanced high level microprocessor, some 32 bit MOS microprocessors were presented at ISSCC in 1981, and now are applied in commercial products. Particularly, in a superpersonal computer or an advanced work station, the high level microprocessor performs a key role. Trends in 32 bit MOS microprocessors are the following.

(1) Architecture
Firstly not only a large addressing space up to 4.3G bytes is available (cf. 1 ~ 16M bytes in 16 bit CPU), but also a virtual address management is supported by paging, segmentation or by these combination. Secondary, a code cache will be introduced to the next generation 32 bit microprocessors. And a data cache will follow. Finally, built in software such as floating point arithmetic and task management (i.e., operating system kernel) are realized by the use of on-chip memory. This trend will be more and more important because the highest integration density is realized in the ROM structure.

(2) Device technology
Currently, 60K ~ 450K components are integrated. And CMOS is used only in BELLMAC32 [2]. However, CMOS will be dominant in the future 32 bit microprocessors by the same reason as described in 2.1.

(3) Performance
Due to the above improvement, high level microprocessor's performance is catching up with 1970s large computer, as shown in Fig.6. Implementation technologies such as pipeline and cache, which were introduced to 1970s large computers, are now being introduced to a silicon chip. Thus a target, 10 MIPS microprocessor in 1990, is not unrealistic.

3. A New Direction: Dedicated Microprocessors

In addition to the general purpose microprocessors described in Section 2, some kinds of dedicated microprocessor will play an important role in the future. Particularly, microprocessors for the speech and image processing are strongly requested, because these two kinds of data are not efficiently processed by the general purpose microprocessors. The general purpose microprocessors will mainly cover the language I/O interface, numerical data processing and text processing, as shown by a hatched circle in Fig.7.

3.1 Speech processor

(1) Speech synthesis LSI
A speech synthesis LSI was successfully introduced in 1978 by TI. They applied it to the "Speak and Spell". After that a lot of speech synthesis LSIs (these have not CPU) were developed. But the market for there products has not yet grown to a significant size. In the future it is expected that the following two types of speech synthesis LSI will be serviceable and meet market needs: the waveform coding product which has on-chip analysis part for such applications as voice mail and high quality voice output; and the so called 'text-to-speech' product for such applications as voice response system, learning aids for the blind and translators.

(2) Speech recognition processor
The speech recognition processors have been introduced by several manufacturers since 1982. Most of them can handle only the speaker-dependent and isolated word recognition, and are used for incoming inspection, warehousing sorting etc.. Recently, a processor for the connected word recognition was introduced [3], and will be used, for example, for computer data entry. As the technology progresses, the recognition chips for the speaker-independent isolated word, the speaker-dependent isolated syllable, and finally in 1990s the speaker-independent continuous speech will be developed as shown in Fig.8. These processors will be useful for telephone service, banking system, voice typewriter or word processor and automatic translator.

(3) Digital signal processor
A digital signal processor, which allows high speed digital signal processing of sampled analog data sequence, such as digital filter and FFT, was first introduced in 1980 by NEC [4]. This type of processor can also be applied both for the speech synthesis and recognition. However, the digital signal processor, the speech synthesis chip and the speech recognition processor will grow separately because the better economical solution is asked for in different applications.

3.2 Image processor

A very high speed processor is required for the processing of binary or grey-scale images. The application of the image processor spreads from sophisticated ones such as computer tomography and picture data processing from satellites, to office use such as copier, image printer,

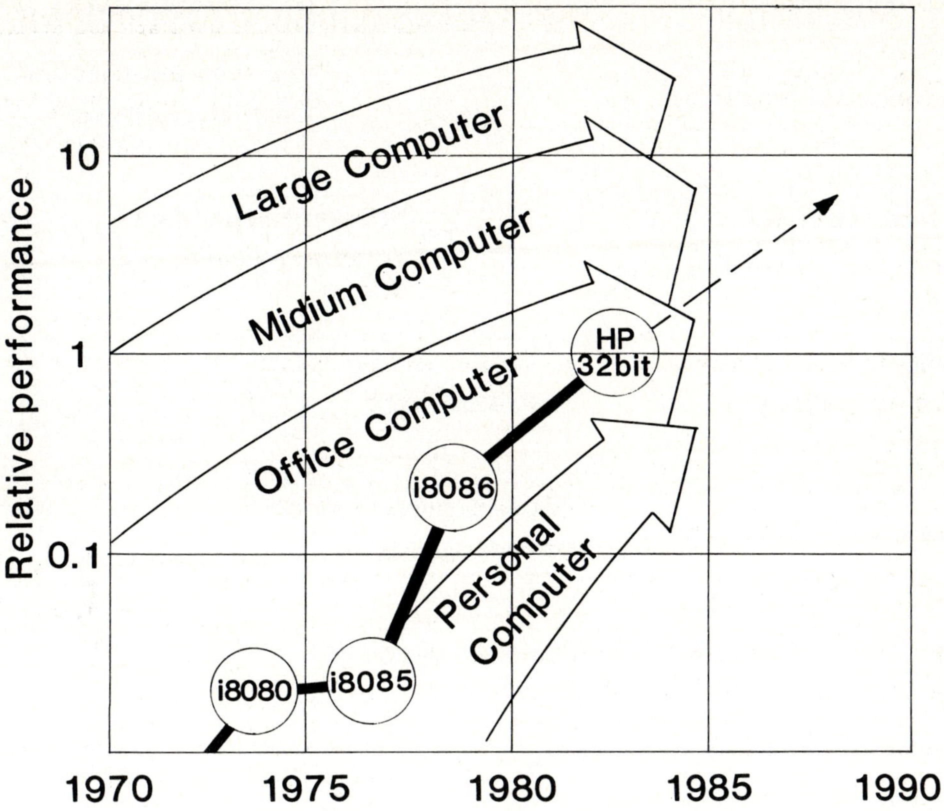

Fig. 6 Progress in microprocessor performance

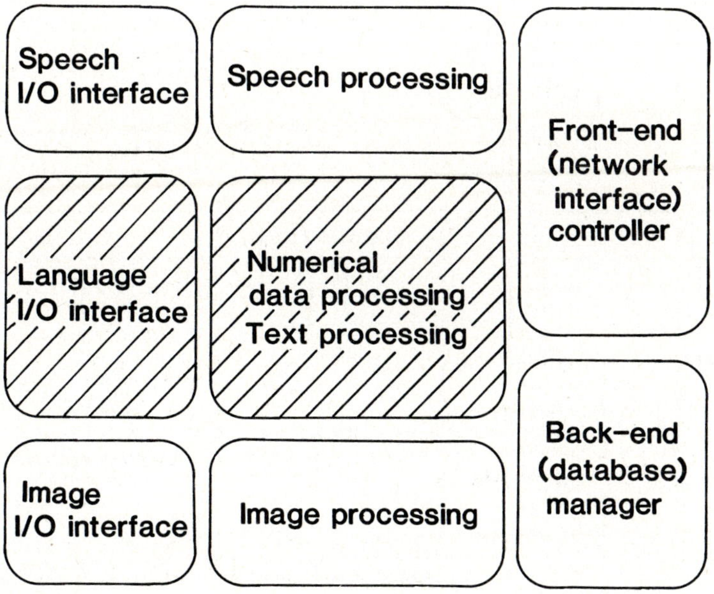

Fig. 7 Main function of next generation office computer

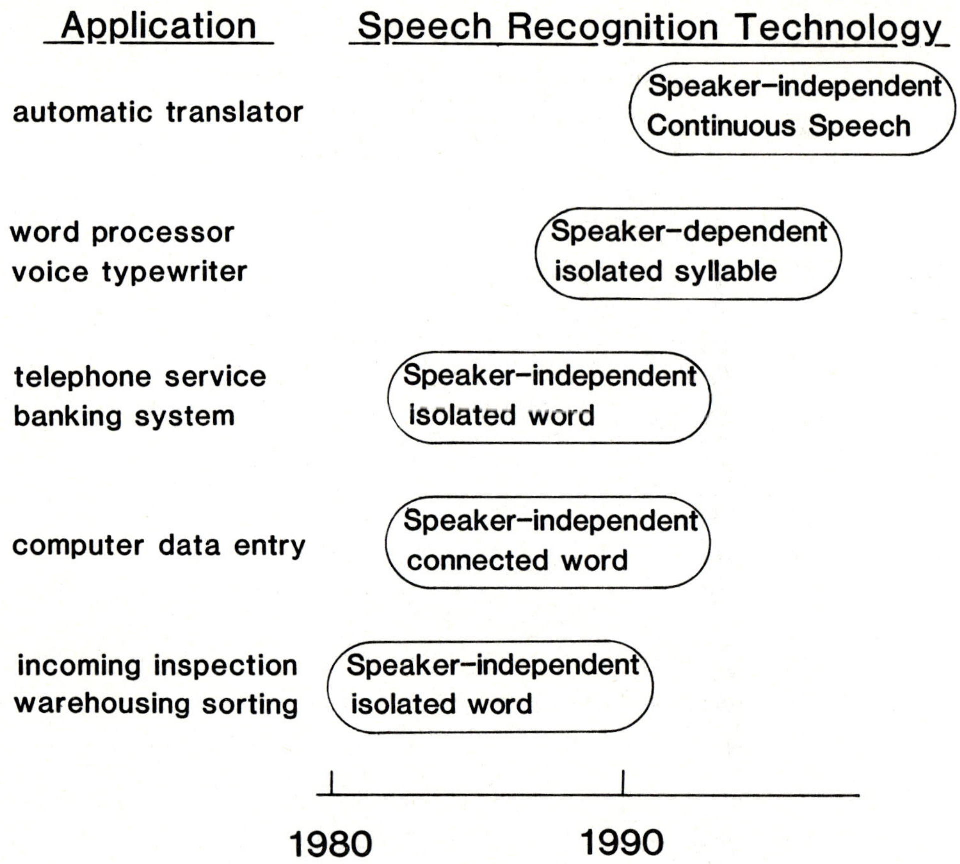

Fig. 8 Speech recognition chips

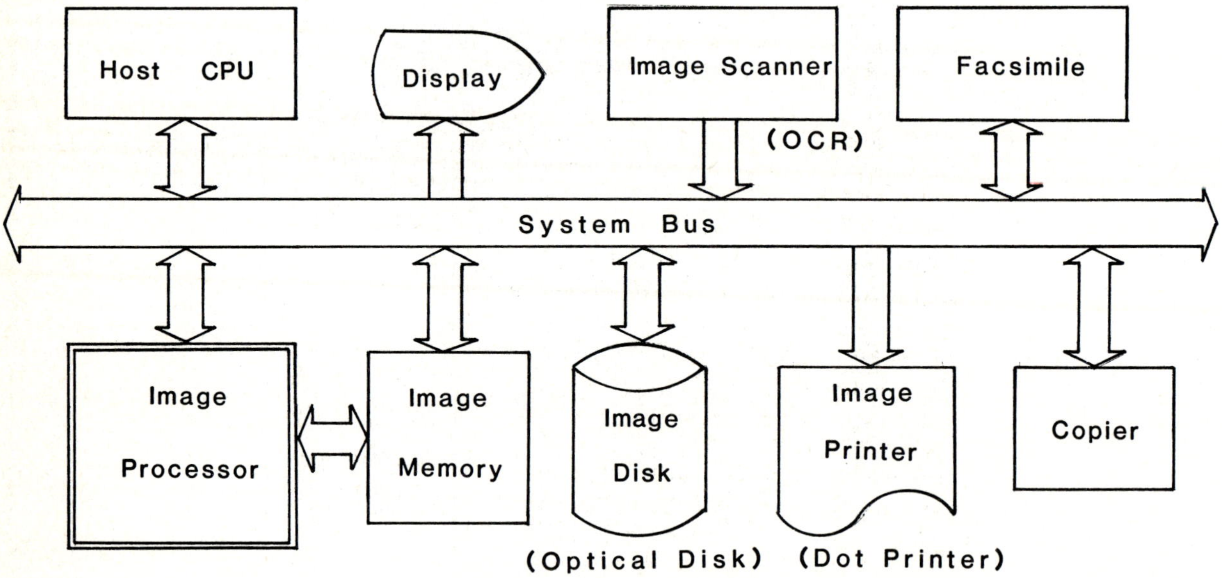

Fig. 9 Image processing in office

facsimile, image display and OCR as shown in Fig.9. The dedicated image processors are now being implemented in a silicon chip [5].

Main features of an image processing are the following.
a) The amount of data is enormously large. For example, a binary image of A4 sized paper, scanned by 8 lines/mm, consists of 0.5M bytes.
b) The program size is small. For example, an affine transformation of a 512 x 512 binary image is described by less than 100 assembly language steps.
c) The iterative operation for a local image is possible. For example, smoothing can be done by operating on every 3 x 3 local image successively.
d) The high speed operations are required. For example, an affine transformation of a 512 x 512 binary image which requires 0.5M multiply, 0.7M add and 0.5M shift operations, is desirable to be processed within a few seconds in the case of the office document processing.

As parallel processing architecture can be applied for image processing, the image processor will progress in a different way from the conventional von Neuman architecture processor.

4. VLSI Microprocessor Design

Technological issues in VLSI microprocessor design are discussed in this section. It is well-known that the VLSI development period becomes longer and longer as the number of components per chip increases [6]. In order to cope with this trend, a VLSI oriented design method and an adequate CAD system for it should be combined and improved [7].

(1) Layout plan
It is clear from the discussion in Section 1 that regularity in the layout pattern is essential to achieve more intelligent device, or high integration density chip. Thus the following layout plan should be considered early in the architecture design stage.
a) Use regular pattern structure as much as possible, such as ROM, RAM and PLA,
b) Use repeatable patterns which include wiring patterns,
c) Use block library for the remained part.

(2) Easy testable structure
The following structure should also be considered early in the architecture design stage.
a) Partition to appropriate sized function blocks,
b) For each block, add enough circuits to increase controllability and observability,
c) For highly complex blocks, use a scan path or a signature method.

(3) CAD for mixed software and hardware system
So far, hardware and software were developed independently. However, the VLSI microprocessor has the built-in software such as operating system kernel and language interpreter, so that unification of hardware and software will further enhance the performance of the VLSI microprocessor. Thus a design and verification tool for these intelligent microprocessor will be more important in the future.

5. Conclusion

Semiconductor device technology progress promises to make a 10^6 components supermicroprocessor in the near future. In order to utilize this highly intelligent microprocessor in human society, the following should be more discussed; what function will be specified on the VLSI microprocessor. The VLSI supermicroprocessor will bring about drastic changes not only in industry and office, but also at home. The curtain rises.

References

[1] J. W. Beyers et al, "A 32b VLSI CPU Chip", ISSCC Digest of Technical Papers, pp 104-105 (Feb., 1981)
[2] B. T. Murphy et al, "A CMOS 32b Single Chip Microprocessor", ISSCC Digest of Technical Papers, pp 230-231 (Feb., 1981)
[3] T. Iwata et al, "A Speech Recognition Processor", ISSCC Digest of Technical Papers, pp 120-121 (Feb., 1983)
[4] Y. Kawakami et al, "A Single Chip Digital Signal Processor for Voiceband Applications", ISSCC Digest of Technical Papers, pp 40-41 (Feb., 1980)
[5] M. Iwashita et al, "Modular Data Flow Image Processor", Digest of Papers COMPCON83, pp 464-467 (Feb., 1983)
[6] K. Kani et al, "CAD in the Japanese Electronics Industry", pp 103-119, "Computer Aided Design of Digital Electronic Circuits and Systems", edited by G. Musgrave (North Holland, 1979)
[7] K. Kani, "Microcomputer LSI Design and CAD", NTG-Fachtung Grossintegration, pp 16-18 (March 1981)

Session B1:

COMPILER CONSTRUCTION

Chairman: B. Myhrhaug
Tandberg Data A/S
Oslo (Norway)

Compiler construction has been an important topic in computer science almost from the time of the first computers. It is only natural that it also is important to professionals working with microcomputers.

This session contains three papers, all dealing with different aspects of compiler construction. The first paper, by J. Lewi, K. De Vlaminch, J. Huens and E. Steegmans from Belgium has the title "The Language Implementation Laboratory LILA: an overview". It describes a methodology for compiler construction.

The second paper is also from Belgium. Written by J. DeMan, M. Peerlinck, D. Genin and V. Goovaerts, it deals with a specific implementation of the language CHILL. This language is widely used in telecommunication programming.

The final paper deals with yet another aspect of compiler construction, namely parser generation. Its title is "ANALIZADOR: An LALR (1) parser generator for micro-computers" and is written by I. Goicoechea and G. Mazario from Spain.

For those not completely familiar with the area of Compiler construction, these three papers will introduce you to different facets of this important area.

MICROCOMPUTERS: Developments in Industry, Business and Education
D.R. Wilson and C.J. van Spronsen (eds.) /© EUROMICRO, 1983
Elsevier Science Publishers B.V. (North-Holland)

THE LANGUAGE IMPLEMENTATION LABORATORY LILA: AN OVERVIEW

J. Lewi, K. De Vlaminck, J. Huens and E. Steegmans

Katholieke Universiteit Leuven
Department of Computer Science
Celestijnenlaan 200 A
B 3030 Leuven, Belgium

This paper describes a programming methodology in compiler construction. This methodology is supported by the translator writing system LILA. LILA and its underlying methodology promote the modular design and implementation of compilers. The main characteristic of LILA, which is responsible for this modularity, is related to the technique of syntax-directed compiler description. Such a description mainly consists of a number of so-called translation syntax modules. Semantic actions, attribute handling, object (constants, variables, types, procedures and functions) declarations and error recovery information can be specified local to each translation syntax module. LILA also supports the development of multi-pass compilers, each pass being described in a syntax-directed way. One of the major design goals was to build a compiler writing system, which can be used in all its generative power, but which also allows a high degree of user interaction.
The methodology and the use of LILA are illustrated by a simple example.

Keywords : compilers, translator writing systems, software engineering, compiler construction

1. Introduction

One of the major problems in software development is the production of programs that meet the software engineering requirements of simplicity, reliability, adaptability, portability and efficiency. The production of such programs becomes manageable by introducing the adequate methodology and the appropriate tools supporting it. Such a methodology will reduce the software production costs not only in the design phase but also in the maintenance phase. Moreover, it will serve as a sound communication means within a software team, resulting in programs that are uniformly documented, commonly readable and maintainable.

This paper describes a programming methodology in compiler construction. This methodology is supported by a software tool, called LILA, standing for Language Implementation LAboratory.

LILA and its underlying methodology promote the modular design and implementation of compilers. The main characteristic of LILA, which is responsible for this modularity, is related to the technique of syntax-directed compiler description. Such a description mainly consists of a number of so-called translation syntax modules. Semantic actions, attribute handling, object (constants, variables, types, procedures and functions) declarations and error recovery information can be specified local to each translation syntax module. LILA also supports the development of multi-pass compilers, each pass being described in a syntax-directed way.

One of the major design goals was to build a compiler writing system, which can be used in all its generative power, but which also allows a high degree of user interaction. This means that in the development of a compiler with LILA, a number of LILA decisions can be overridden, in order to meet very special requirements. In such cases, step-wise overriding of default definitions has turned out to be an adequate design philosophy.

A general problem in the development of compiler writing systems is the production of compilers with error recovery. LILA offers an elegant solution where the error recovery is mechanically produced from the error recovery information in the LILA input.

2. Software development criteria

It is generally agreed upon that program quality is the most important factor to reduce software production costs. One of the most difficult tasks in software development is writing programs of high quality, i.e., programs that satisfy a number of software engineering criteria Our software engineering criteria will be : simplicity, reliability, adaptability, portability and efficiency.

Simplicity is the program property that makes it possible to understand what programs do. It can be achieved by splitting up a complicated task into simpler ones (modules). This technique is called modular design. Obviously, each module must correspond to a specific task. In a modular design, we deal with two types of questions
(1) how does each module work individually ?
(2) how do the modules work together ?
In a program that is modularly designed, each module should be individually verified, compiled, executed, checked and documented.

Reliability is highly related to simplicity, in the sense that both program qualities depend on the degree of modularity of the program. To date, there exist a number of well-known verification techniques, covering different aspects of reliability. Among these techniques are proofreading, compile-time checks, run-time checks, systematic testing and program correctness proofs. Program correctness proofs and the use of compile-time checks are techniques to show the absence of programming errors. These techniques handle properties of programs statically. If such a property is verified or proved to be true, then this holds independently of any program run. The techniques of systematic testing and the use of run-time checks handle properties of programs dynamically. If such a property is verified to be true at a particular program run, then it may be false during the next run.

Adaptability guarantees that programs can be modified and extended at a reasonable cost. It is a programming aspect every software designer has to cope with sooner or later. In most software projects the maintenance phase is much longer than the design and development phases. If no precautionary measures have been taken during the design phase, the maintenance cost may rise beyond proportion. Indeed, a modification of a program part often introduces a number of errors which are difficult to localize, because previously tested program parts may behave differently. Adaptability is also promoted by the degree of modularity of the program. The aspect of individuality of modules guarantees that modification of a module implementation will not affect the other modules. Only the modified module must again be verified, compiled, checked and possibly proved to be correct.

Portability is the property by which programs can be easily moved from one computer environment to another.

Efficiency is related to the amount of time and space needed for a program to be executed.

Obviously, there is always a trade-off to be made in meeting the criteria of high quality programs. In this respect, simplicity, reliability and adaptability have the highest priority.

3. Tools in software development

In large software projects, the construction of programs of high quality is a difficult and tedious task. This task will become manageable by introducing a programming methodology that promotes simplicity, reliability and adaptability in the first place, and portability and efficiency in the second place. Such a methodology can be tuned towards a given application area, such as the development of compilers. An application-oriented methodology is in fact the accumulation of an amount of experience and know-how about the application, gathered by many people and made accessible for any potential user working in that area.

A specific problem in a software team is related to the fact that the members of the team may have different ideas and requirements on program quality because of differences in training and background. This communication problem can be cured by a sound methodology. Such a methodology, commonly used among all the members of a software team, promotes the production of software that is readable and adaptable by any member of the team. This is an important aspect of software maintenance.

If a methodology has been established in a given application area, the next logical step is to design a software tool to support that methodology. The software tool must be such that the user is encouraged and/or forced to follow the underlying methodology. A simple illustration is the use of types in a programming language with strong typing. For example, in writing a Pascal variable declaration we specify a relation between the variable and the domain of values over which the variable is defined. For any applied occurrence of the variable, we are able to verify this relation. The use of types in Pascal can be considered a methodology that promotes reliability. A tool supporting the use of strong typing would be a Pascal compiler systematically checking the consistent use of types in Pascal programs.

4. LILA as a tool in compiler construction

The methodology, described in this paper, is supported by the software tool LILA. With LILA, we claim that one is able to produce compilers meeting the software requirements of simplicity, reliability, adaptability, portability and efficiency.

Let us first introduce a few definitions. A translation t is a set of pairs (x,E), where x is a string of symbols over some alphabet, called input vocabulary, and E is the contents of an environment. This environment may contain e.g. real variables, array variables and print files. We state that E is the translation of x. The set of all strings x for which there exists an E, such that (x,E) belongs to t, is called the input language.

Translations can be described by means of generative devices, called translation syntaxes, and by means of recognizing devices, called transducers ('transducer' is a general term including compilers and interpreters).
The translation syntax is the ideal tool to describe and document translations, whereas the transducer is the automaton that maps input strings x into E, if x belongs to the input language. If x does not belong to the input language, error messages are produced.
Our methodology in compiler writing consists in building the translation syntax F and to produce the transducer B from it in a mechanical way. The translation defined by F, denoted t(F), must be identical to the translation defined by B, denoted t(B). The mapping of translation syntaxes into transducers can be defined by means of a finite set of generation rules, called the generation scheme.
In the literature, there exist translation syntaxes and transducers of different types, each type having different properties. The choice of the type of translation syntax and transducer is very important. In LILA, the translation syntaxes are of the type 'generalized Attributed Extended Context-Free (AECF)', whereas the transducers are of the type 'generalized Attributed Push-Down (APD)'. These formalisms and the use of LILA are explained in [5]. A more theoretical approach can be found in [4]. The heart of LILA is a generation scheme that maps a generalized AECF translation syntax into its equivalent generalized APD transducer (Fig. 1). The transducer is generated in the form of a standard Pascal ([1],[3]) program.

generalized
AECF
translation syntax

▼

LILA

▼

generalized
APD
transducer

Fig. 1.

Two-level structure of modularity

The methodology of LILA supports a two-level structure of modularity. The first level is related to the syntax-oriented method of writing compilers. The translation syntax F is said to be a syntax-oriented description of the transducer B. A translation syntax consists of a number of syntax rules defining the input language. With each syntax rule a number of semantic actions and attributes are associated describing the translation. Such a syntax rule together with the semantic actions and attributes involved, constitutes a translation syntax module. Each such module treats the translation of a specific feature of the input language e.g., there will be modules to treat assignments, expressions, terms and factors. Also, each module can be written and verified independently from the others and the interface between all modules is straightforward. To each module in the translation syntax corresponds a transducer module, called transducer routine. This is schematically illustrated in Fig. 2.

The second level is related to the possibility to describe transducers in several passes, resulting in multi-pass transducers. Each pass of the transducer is described in a syntax-oriented way by means of a translation syntax. The translation syntax of a transducer pass describes a specific function within the translation. It can be designed, verified and tested independently from the others. The interface between the different passes is simple and is part of the input of LILA. This interface is such that the output of one pass will be the input of an other pass. This is illustrated in Fig. 3.

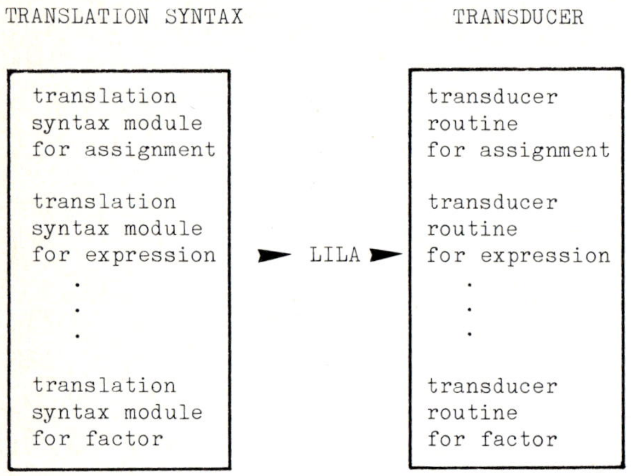

Fig. 2.

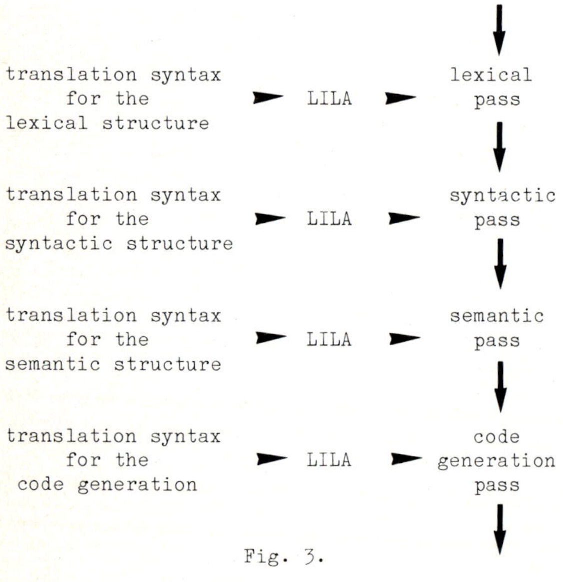

Fig. 3.

Stepwise overriding of default definitions

Many design criteria and aspects of LILA have to do with human engineering. A great effort is made to make LILA flexible.

Let us first explain what we mean by flexibility with respect to LILA. LILA can be used at different levels of sophistication. The lowest level consists in using the defaults for all the generation features. This means that the user agrees with all the decisions taken by LILA in the mechanical production process of transducers. However, in some cases one wishes to override default decisions made by LILA. As an example, the user may redefine the module for reading the input symbols in the generated transducer. The more work the user takes over from LILA, the more know-how is needed about the behavior of LILA.

One of the design principles of LILA is to build a compiler writing system which can be used in all its generative power, but which also allows a high degree of user interaction (a number of decisions made by LILA can be overridden). The highest level of user interaction would be to write the complete transducer by hand. Between the lowest and highest level of user interaction, a whole range of possibilities exists. An interesting aspect of the design philosophy in writing compilers with LILA is as follows. First, LILA is used in all its generative power. The generated transducer can be systematically verified and tested. Then, if necessary, LILA features may be redefined one by one. Each time a LILA feature is redefined, the new version of the generated transducer is tested only for that redefined feature.

Step-wise overriding of default definitions makes it possible to produce several releases of a compiler. This is an important tool in the debugging phase and maintenance phase of compilers. An example of step-wise overriding of default definitions is the implementation of the lexical analyser in a compiler, produced by LILA. In a first step, the lexical analyser can be developed as a separate pass, the other pass being the syntax-semantic analysis. In a second step, the lexical analyser can be implemented as a compiler subroutine by overriding the read module of the syntax-semantic analyser.

5. Description of a translation syntax

This paragraph will demonstrate how a translation syntax must be specified as the input of LILA, thereby illustrating the previous paragraph. This will be done by means of a simple example. The language that will be implemented is called Unit Conversion (abbreviated UC). This language was described in [2]. The implementation described here is not the only possible way to implement language processors with LILA. It was chosen because it is short and yet illustrates some important capabilities of LILA.

The language UC is used for defining new units starting from the base units m, kg and s. Conversion factors can then be calculated between units with the same dimensions. This is an example of a UC program:

```
cm = 0.01 * m, inch = 2.54 * cm,
feet = 0.3048 * m,
how many inch in feet?,

yard = 0.9144 * m,
how many inch in yard?,
how many feet in yard?,

sqinch = inch * inch, sqfeet = feet * feet,
how many sqinch in sqfeet?,

cuinch = inch ^ 3, m2 = m * m, m3 = m ^ 3,
how many sqinch in m2?,
how many cuinch in m2 * m?,

how many m/s in (sqfeet/yard) / s?
```

The language processor for UC consists of two phases: a lexical analysis and a syntax-semantic analysis (Fig. 4). The results produced by the above UC program are :

```
ANSWERS TO THE QUESTIONS
************************

 1.20e+01
 3.60e+01
 3.00e+00
 1.44e+02
 1.55e+03
 6.10e+04
 1.02e-01
```

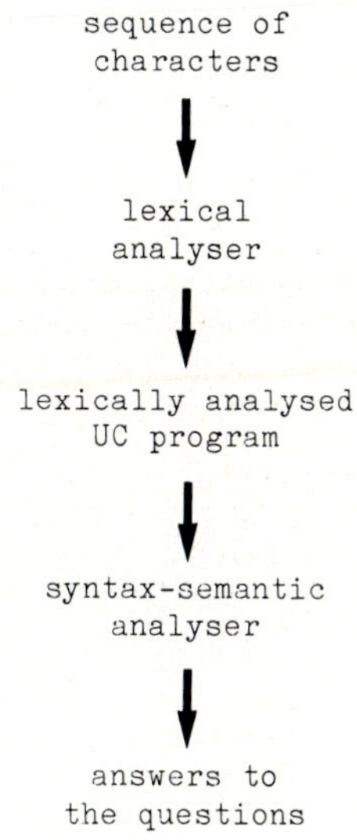

Fig. 4.

5.1. <u>Syntax-semantic analysis</u>

The translation syntax for the syntax-semantic analysis of UC consists of:
1) an input vocabulary,
2) translation syntax modules, containing:
   a) the translation syntax rule, that defines the nonterminal symbol with activations of the semantic actions of that module,
   b) the definition of the attribute type of the defined nonterminal symbol,
   c) definitions of the semantic actions,
   d) the local information, containing the definitions of constants, types, variables, functions and procedures, which are local to a specific syntax module,
3) the global information, containing the definitions of constants, types, variables, functions and procedures, which are global to all translation syntax modules.

All definitions of semantic information are in Pascal, extended with a notation for attribute referencing.

5.1.1. <u>The input vocabulary</u>

The input of the syntax-semantic analyser for UC is a lexically analysed program. This program is a sequence of input symbols, where some of them are attributed. The input vocabulary is

```
###inputvocabulary  rep(integer);

  "identifier" = 2 : name

  "number" = 3 : real

  "how" = 4     "many" = 5     "in" = 6
  "kg"  = 7     "m"    = 8     "s"  = 9

  "(" = 10   ")" = 11   "*" = 12   "+" = 13
  "," = 14   "-" = 15   "/" = 16   "=" = 17
  "?" = 18   "^" = 19
```

The input symbols are represented by integer values as defined above.

The attributed input symbols in UC are "identifier" and "number". Each "identifier" is attributed with a string of characters, which is the name of the identifier. Each "number" is attributed with a real value representing the value of the number. The type of the attribute of "identifier" is 'name' and the type of the attribute of "number" is 'real'. The type 'name' is defined in the global information as:

```
name = packed array [1..idlength] of char;
```

The input symbol "identifier" is represented by the integer value 2. Its attribute can be referenced in the semantic actions by :

```
@"identifier"
```

which denotes a variable of type 'name'.

5.1.2. The translation syntax modules

The formalism that is used in LILA to describe the syntax of the input language is the extended context-free (ECF) syntax. The ECF syntax underlying the translation syntax for UC is :

```
<program> =
  <statement>  ( "," <statement> )*

<statement> =
  <assignment> ¦ <question>

<assignment> =
  "identifier" "=" <expression>

<question> =
  "how" "many"  <expression>
        "in"  <expression> "?"

<expression> =
  <term>
    ( "+" <term>  ¦  "-" <term> )*

<term> =
  <factor>
    ( "*" <factor>  ¦  "/" <factor> )*

<factor> =
  <secondary>
    ( "^" <factor>   ¦  & )

<secondary> =
    "-" <primary>
  ¦ <primary>

<primary> =
    "identifier"
  ¦ "number"
  ¦ "kg"
  ¦ "m"
  ¦ "s"
  ¦ "(" <expression> ")"
```

The symbol '¦' indicates alternative choices, '*' means repetition zero or more times, '+' means repetition one or more times and '&' stands for the empty string of input symbols.

An attribute may also be associated with a nonterminal symbol. In UC, an attribute is associated with each expression, term, factor, secondary and primary. This attribute is of type 'unit' and describes the dimension of mass, the dimension of length, the dimension of time and the conversion factor. The type 'unit' is defined in the global information :

```
dimension = record mass,length,time:integer end;
unit = record dim:dimension; conversion:real end;
```

The calculation of the attribute of the nonterminal symbols <expression>, <term>, <factor>, <secondary> and <primary> is done in the corresponding translation syntax modules by the semantic actions.

A semantic action has access to the attribute of the input and nonterminal symbols that appear in the rule where the semantic action is defined. The attribute of a nonterminal symbol, e.g. <expression>, can be accessed by :

```
@<expression>
```

which denotes a variable of type 'unit'.

The semantic actions in the syntax-semantic analysis deal with three program-defined types of data structures. These three types of data structures together with the operations defined on them, are summarized below. The actual representation of the types and the implementation of the operations are defined in the global information.

1) The type for the units

```
type unit;
procedure init_unit (var un:unit; cv:real;
                     m,l,t: integer);
procedure add_unit (var un1:unit;
                    un2:unit);
procedure subtr_unit (var un1:unit;
                      un2:unit);
procedure negate_unit (var un:unit);
procedure mult_unit (var un1:unit;
                     un2:unit);
procedure divide_unit (var un1:unit;
                       un2:unit);
procedure exponentiate_unit (var un1:unit;
                             un2:unit);
function convert_unit (un1,un2:unit): real;
procedure print_unit (un:unit);
```

2) The symbol table

```
var symbtab;
procedure add_symbtab (nm:name; un:unit);
function in_symbtab (nm:name): boolean;
procedure obtain_symbtab (var un:unit;
                          nm:name);
procedure print_symbtab;
```

3) The error messages

```
type message;
procedure error (m:message);
```

All the translation syntax modules will now be described.

```
##rule;
  <program> =
    init
      <statement>  ( "," <statement> )*
    final

  ##action;
    #init;
```

```
      symbtabp := 0;
      writeln(output,'ANSWERS TO THE QUESTIONS');
      writeln(output,'************************');
      writeln(output)

    #final;
      print_symbtab
```

The syntax-semantic analysis of a program is as follows. First, the semantic action 'init' is activated, then the first statement is processed, followed by zero or more times the processing of a comma symbol followed by a statement. Finally, the semantic action 'final' is activated. The semantic action 'init' initializes a table, called 'symbtab'. The semantic action 'final' prints the contents of 'symbtab' for debugging purposes.

```
##rule;
  <statement> =
    <assignment> ¦ <question>


##rule;
  <assignment> =
    "identifier" "=" <expression> assign

  ##action;
    #assign;
      if  in_symbtab(@"identifier")
        then error(re_assignment)
        else add_symbtab (@"identifier",
                          @<expression>)
```

The key thought here is that we assume that as a result of the syntax-semantic analysis of an expression, the attribute value of that expression has been calculated and is associated with the nonterminal <expression>. In the definition of the translation syntax module for expression, we will see that we can always make this assumption.

The semantic action 'assign' has access to the attribute of the terminal symbol "identifier" and of the nonterminal symbol <expression>. The semantic action 'assign' will take the attribute value of expression and store it at the appropriate entry in 'symbtab' for later use. This entry in 'symbtab' is calculated by means of the attribute value of "identifier". If the identifier is defined for the first time, a new entry in 'symbtab' is created, otherwise an error message is produced. The calculation of the entry in 'symbtab' is performed by the routine 'add_symbt'.

```
##rule;
  <question> =
    "how" "many"  <expression>
    "in"  <expression> "?"  print_result

  ##action;
    #print_result;
      writeln(output,
      convert_unit(@<expression>1,
                   @<expression>2):9)
```

Again, the key thought here is that each time an expression has been syntax-semantically analysed, its attribute value is available.

The semantic action 'print_result' checks for consistency of the dimensions of the units described by @<expression>1 and @<expression>2 and calculates the answer.

Here, @<expression>i denotes the attribute of the ith occurrence of the nonterminal symbol <expression>, where i stands for any positive integer. Different occurrences of the same nonterminal symbol in a syntax rule are numbered from left to right, starting from one.

```
##rule;
  <expression> =
    <term>  trans_et
      ( "+" <term> add
      ¦  "-" <term> subtract )*

  ##attribute;
    unit

  ##action;
    #trans_et;
      @<expression>  := @<term>1;

    #add;
      add_unit( @<expression>, @<term>2)

    #subtract;
      subtr_unit( @<expression>, @<term>3)
```

First, the syntax-semantic analysis of a term is activated, followed by the activation of the semantic action 'trans_et'; this action has access to the attribute associated with <term>1 and <expression>. Then, each time the operator '+' is processed the syntax-semantic analysis of a term is activated, followed by the activation of the semantic action 'add'. The semantic action 'add' has access to the attribute of <expression>, <term>1 and <term>2.

Each time, the operator '-' is processed, the syntax-semantic analysis of a term is activated, followed by the activation of the semantic action 'subtract'. The semantic action 'subtract' has access to the attribute of <expression>, <term>1 and <term>3.
The attribute of an expression is of type 'unit'.

In the calculation of the attribute value in the syntax rule for an expression, there is a loop invariant assertion : each time the semantic action 'add' ('subtract') is activated, the attribute value of the left operand of the adding (subtraction) operator will always be @<expression>, whereas the attribute value of the right operand will always be @<term>2 (respectively @<term>3). Therefore, the semantic action 'trans_et' will simply transfer

@<term>1 to @<expression>.

```
##rule;
  <term> =
    <factor>  trans_tf
      ( "*" <factor> multiply
      | "/" <factor> divide )*

  ##attribute;
    unit

  ##action;
    #trans_tf;
      @<term>  := @<factor>1;

    #multiply;
      mult_unit( @<term>, @<factor>2)

    #divide;
      divide_unit( @<term>, @<factor>3)
```

This case is similar to the syntax-semantic analysis of an expression.

```
##rule;
  <factor> =
    <secondary>  trans_fs
      ( "^" <factor> exponentiate   |  & )

  ##attribute;
    unit

  ##action;
    #trans_fs;
      @<factor>1 := @<secondary>

    #exponentiate;
      exponentiate_unit(@<factor>1, @<factor>2)
```

The syntax rule for factor is recursively defined in terms of factor, in order to implement the association of exponent operators and their operands from right to left. This implementation would be more complex using an iterative definition of the syntax rule for factor.

```
##rule;
  <secondary> =
      "-" <primary>  negate
    | <primary>      trans_sp

  ##attribute;
    unit

  ##action;
    #negate;
      negate_unit(@<primary>1);
      @<secondary> := @<primary>1

    #trans_sp;
      @<secondary> := @<primary>2


##rule;
  <primary> =
      "identifier" identifier
    | "number"      number
    | "kg"          mass_unit
    | "m"           length_unit
    | "s"           time_unit
    | "(" <expression> ")" trans_pe

  ##attribute;
    unit


  ##action;
    #identifier;
      if  in_symbtab(@"identifier")
        then obtain_symbtab (@<primary>,
                             @"identifier")
        else error(undef_unit)

    #number;
      init_unit(@<primary>, @"number", 0, 0, 0)

    #mass_unit;
      init_unit(@<primary>, 1.0,       1, 0, 0)

    #length_unit;
      init_unit(@<primary>, 1.0,       0, 1, 0)

    #time_unit;
      init_unit(@<primary>, 1.0,       0, 0, 1)

    #trans_pe;
      @<primary> := @<expression>
```

The semantic action 'identifier' checks if the identifier has already been defined in symbtab. If it is, the attribute value is simply transmitted from the symbtab entry to the nonterminal <primary>. If the answer is no, an error message is produced.
The semantic action 'number' simply calculates @<primary> by means of @"number".
The semantic actions 'mass_unit', 'length_unit' and 'time_unit' initialize @<primary> to the unit of mass, the unit of length and the unit of time, respectively.
The semantic action 'trans_pe' transmits @<expression> to @<primary>.

5.1.3. The global information

The global information defines in Pascal the global constants, types, variables and routines (procedures and functions) that may be used in the semantic actions. It defines also the parameters of the generated Pascal program or procedure.
The elements that have to be defined for UC have already been mentioned when they were used in the semantic actions. Because of space limitations, their definitions will not be given.

5.2. Lexical analysis

The translation syntax for the lexical analysis of UC consists of:
1) an input vocabulary,

2) an output vocabulary,
3) translation syntax modules,
4) the global information.

The same kind of translation syntax as for the syntax-semantic analysis is used for the lexical analysis.

5.2.1. The input vocabulary

The input of the lexical analyser for UC is a sequence of characters. The input vocabulary is :

```
###inputvocabulary  rep(char), file(input);

  "bl"= 32    "(" = 40    ")" = 41
  "*" = 42    "+" = 43    "," = 44
  "-" = 45    "." = 46    "/" = 47
  "0" = 48    "1" = 49    "2" = 50
  "3" = 51    "4" = 52    "5" = 53
  "6" = 54    "7" = 55    "8" = 56
  "9" = 57    "=" = 61    "?" = 63
  "^" = 94    "a" = 97    "b" = 98
  "c" = 99    "d" =100    "e" =101
  "f" =102    "g" =103    "h" =104
  "i" =105    "j" =106    "k" =107
  "l" =108    "m" =109    "n" =110
  "o" =111    "p" =112    "q" =113
  "r" =114    "s" =115    "t" =116
  "u" =117    "v" =118    "w" =119
  "x" =120    "y" =121    "z" =122
```

The input symbols are represented by characters as defined above. The representation that has been chosen for UC is the ASCII code.

5.2.2. The output vocabulary

The output vocabulary describes the attributed output symbols to be produced by the lexical analyser of UC.

```
###outputvocabulary rep(integer);

  [identifier] = 2 : name

  [number] = 3 : real

  [how]  = 4     [many] = 5     [in] = 6
  [kg]   = 7     [m]    = 8     [s]  = 9

  [(] = 10   [)] = 11   [*] = 12   [+] = 13
  [,] = 14   [-] = 15   [/] = 16   [=] = 17
  [?] = 18   [^] = 19
```

Clearly, the output vocabulary of the lexical analyser must be identical to the input vocabulary of the syntax-semantic analyser.

5.2.3. The translation syntax modules

The underlying ECF syntax for the lexical analysis of UC is :

```
   <program> =
     ( ( <identifier keyword> | <number> | & )
         <delimiter> )*

   <identifier keyword> =
     <letter> ( <letter> | <digit> )*

   <number> =
     <digit>+
       ( "."  <digit>+
       | &
       )

   <delimiter> =
         "," | "=" | "?" | "-" | "+" | "*"
       | "/" | "^" | "(" | ")" | "bl"

   <letter> =
         "a" | "b" | "c" | "d" | "e" | "f" | "g"
       | "h" | "i" | "j" | "k" | "l" | "m" | "n"
       | "o" | "p" | "q" | "r" | "s" | "t" | "u"
       | "v" | "w" | "x" | "y" | "z"

   <digit> =
         "0" | "1" | "2" | "3" | "4"
       | "5" | "6" | "7" | "8" | "9"
```

Only the translation syntax module for <number> will be illustrated :

```
##rule;
  <number> =
    init_value
      ( <digit> whole_value  )+
        ( "."  ( <digit> fract_value   )+
        | &
        )
    out_number

  ##var;
    scale : real

  ##action;
    #init_value;
      @[number] := 0.0;
      scale     := 0.1

    #whole_value;
      @[number] := @[number]*10
                 + (ord(@<digit>1) - ord('0'))

    #fract_value;

      @[number] := @[number]
                 + (ord(@<digit>2) - ord('0'))
                 * scale;
      scale := scale/10

    #out_number;
      out(%[number])
```

The lexical analysis of a number activates the semantic action 'init_value', which initializes the attribute variable @[number] and the scale factor.

For each digit of the integer part, the attribute @[number] is calculated in terms of its previous value and the value of

@<digit>1.

For each digit of the fractional part, the attribute @[number] is calculated in terms of its previous value, the attribute @<digit>2 and the scale factor.

Finally, the semantic action 'out_number' is activated producing an output symbol [number]. The production of this output symbol is performed by the standard procedure call

out(%[number])

%[number] is a LILA defined notation for the representation of [number] and the attribute value is @[number]. This attribute value must have been calculated prior to the activation of out. Notice that @[number] is local to the syntax rule and is commonly accessible by any semantic action involved in that syntax rule. The global information will not be given because of space limitations.

6. Error recovery

A serious problem in the development of compiler writing systems is the production of compilers with error recovery. Insertion of error recovery by hand in the generated compiler is impractical and in most cases impossible; it destroys the modular structure of the generated compiler. Each time a new version of the compiler is generated, the entire insertion process has to be redone. LILA offers an elegant solution for this error recovery problem. The error recovery in compilers generated by LILA is mechanically produced from the error recovery information in the LILA input.

An adequate error recovery strategy incorporated in a translator writing system must satisfy the following design objectives:

1) The error recovery strategy must be powerful. The generated compilers should detect as much errors as possible in the input and should produce as few error messages as possible due to incorrect error recovery.

2) The error recovery strategy must be conceptually simple and the generation scheme of parsers with error recovery must be manageable.

3) The compiler writing system must offer some control over the error recovery to be performed in the compilers it generates. In a translator writing system, a number of important decisions must be the user's responsibility. This is conform with our general philosophy on software tools.

4) The overhead in the parser due to the error recovery must be within reasonable limits.

The general principles of the error recovery strategy imposed by LILA can be roughly explained as follows. The parser of a compiler operates in two modes : the parsing mode and the error mode.

1) The parser starts in the parsing mode. This corresponds to the activation of the parsing routine for the start symbol A_0 of the ECF syntax. This parsing routine activates other parsing routines.

2) In the parsing mode, the error routine is activated as soon as a syntactic error is detected and the error mode is entered for that error.

3) In the error mode, input symbols are skipped until an endmarker is found, terminating an activation of a given parsing routine. From this moment, the parser is able to react as if no syntactic error has occurred. This process is called synchronization based on endmarkers.

4) In the error mode, input symbols are skipped until a beginmarker is found, characterizing the start of a given parsing routine. Then the error mode is left and the parsing routine is activated. When the parser returns from this parsing routine, the error mode is entered again. This process is called recognition based on beginmarkers.
The beginmarkers as well as the endmarkers are derived from the error recovery information in the LILA input.

The error recovery mechanism has a recursive aspect. More information can be found in [5] and [6].

7. Design of LILA

LILA is a tool that helps to develop programs. Since this tool is itself a program, one needs a methodology and a tool to develop that program. The methodology described in this paper is used in the design of LILA. Therefore, LILA meets exactly the same software engineering requirements as the transducers produced by it. Indeed, the tool is also simple, reliable, adaptable, portable and efficient.

An original approach in the design of LILA is the use of a high-level description of LILA as a 17-pass compiler, each pass being described in a syntax-oriented way ([5]). This high-level documentation turned out to be a very efficient tool to adapt and maintain the system LILA. As an example, the modification of LILA to produce compilers in PL/1 instead of Pascal has become an easy job.

An important design decision was to use the top-down ELL(1) parsing method. This made it possible to generate transducers as Pascal programs that perform syntax and semantic analysis in one single pass.

The LILA methodology promotes the writing of compilers that are not only simple, reliable and adaptable, but also portable at a low cost, and efficient at compile-time as well as at run-time. As for compile-time efficiency, a great part of the LILA project was devoted to a systematic study of optimization, allowing the production of compilers which are optimized in time and space. The run-time efficiency of the generated compilers is dealt with by the semantic actions. Since the semantic actions are entirely written by the LILA user, there is no loss of run-time efficiency with respect to hand-coded compilers. Portability of compilers produced by LILA has two aspects.

1) LILA offers the user an excellent infrastructure to localize the machine-dependent run-time features within the compiler design.
2) The compiler produced by LILA is generated in standard Pascal, which turned out to be a very portable language.

8. Conclusion

The design of LILA was characterized by a trade-off between the degree of automation and the degree of generality and flexibility. If the degree of automation is too high, the system becomes inflexible for many applications. This trade-off is strongly related to the aspect of human engineering of software tools. The authors believe in the usefulness and the need of a compiler writing system that offers the appropriate infrastructure supporting a sound methodology in the construction of compilers, based on mathematical concepts.

LILA is also a didactic tool to support a course on compiler construction, where the students experiment in both language and compiler design. With the help of LILA, student projects with a degree of complexity sufficiently high to illustrate compiler design in a realistic way, can be worked out.

The LILA system is also distributed by a company and is as such used succesfully in several industrial environments. The LILA system is entirely written in standard Pascal and is thus available on a large variety of machines.

A number of extensions of the current LILA system are envisaged. Among these are a version for generating interactive language processors with an adapted error recovery mechanism, and a LILA version with ADA instead of Pascal as metalanguage.

REFERENCES

[1] ADDYMAN, A.M. [1980]. A Draft Proposal for Pascal. SIGPLAN Notices, Volume 15, number 4, april, pp. 1-66.
[2] COHEN, J. [1973]. Syntax-directed unit conversion. Information Processing Letters 2, North-Holland Publishing Co., Amsterdam, pp. 100-102.
[3] JENSEN, K., WIRTH, N. [1974]. Pascal user manual and report. Lecture Notes in Computer Science 18, Springer-Verlag, New York.
[4] LEWI, J., DE VLAMINCK, K., HUENS, J., HUYBRECHTS, M. [1979]. A Programming Methodology in Compiler Construction. Part 1 : Concepts. North-Holland Publishing Company, Amsterdam.
[5] LEWI, J., DE VLAMINCK, K., HUENS, J., STEEGMANS, E. [1982]. A Programming Methodology in Compiler Construction. Part 2 : Implementation. North-Holland Publishing Company, Amsterdam.
[6] LEWI, J., DE VLAMINCK, K., HUENS, J., STEEGMANS, E. [1983]. Error recovery in batch ELL(1) parsers: automatic generation. Report CW30, K.U.Leuven, Department of Computer Science.

MICROCOMPUTERS: Developments in Industry, Business and Education
D.R. Wilson and C.J. van Spronsen (eds.) /© EUROMICRO, 1983
Elsevier Science Publishers B.V. (North-Holland)

IMPLEMENTATION OF A COMPILER FOR CHILL

J. De Man, M. Peerlinck, D. Genin, V. Goovaerts
Bell Telephone Manufacturing Company
Francis Wellesplein 1
B-2000 Antwerp, Belgium

This article describes the development of a compiler for CHILL (the CCITT High Level programming Language). Although this language is at least as complex as Ada, a compiler for the complete language with intermediate code generation could be produced within 1.5 year by a group of 3-4 people. Factors contributing to this reduced effort are the use of advanced methods and automated tools and the efficient cooperation in a small team of motivated designers.

1. THE PROGRAMMING LANGUAGE CHILL

CHILL stands for the "CCITT High Level programming Language". It is a language designed by a working group of the CCITT (International Consulting Committee on Telecommunications). This language has been designed primarily for programming SPC ("Stored Program Control") telephone exchanges, but is considered to be general enough for other applications (Chil80). A full length description of CHILL is beyond the scope of this article. A brief overview is given below.

- CHILL offers a wide range of sequential flow control constructs : the well-known if-then-else, case, do-while and do-for constructs, but also more sophisticated ones. Do-for loops can be specified to range over enumerations (and their subranges), arrays and powersets. The case statement is not limited to one control variable (very practical for the implementation of finite-state machines).

- The "module" construct is provided to limit the scope of names in a program. Names can be made visible outside a module with a "grant" statement and names can be made visible inside a module with the "seize" statement. There is however no "module mode" (the CHILL description uses Algol68 (Wijn75) terminology for types) nor is there a separation between the interface specification and the implementation like in Ada (Ichb82). Modules can't be passed as parameters to procedures.

- The limitation, found in many programming languages, that a name must be defined before it is used, is not imposed in CHILL. This seemingly unimportant fact has severe consequences for the structure and the complexity of the compiler.

- A distinction is made between static semantic conditions (which can be verified at compile time) and dynamic semantic conditions (which can only be verified at run time). Extensive run-time checks, including dynamic mode checks and life-time checks, are specified but not made imperative.

- CHILL adopts "structural equivalence" between modes as opposed to "name equivalence" in e.g. Ada. The relations between modes are defined by a collection of recursive procedures. The following modes are e.g. equivalent in CHILL :

```
SYNMODE A = ARRAY (BOOL) OF INT;
SYNMODE B = ARRAY (0:1) OF INT;
```

  Modes are equivalent if they have the same structure and not only if they have the same name. This is certainly a more "natural" approach, but it is also more difficult to implement. The main disadvantage is however the considerable overhead for dynamic (at run-time) mode checks.

  With a "newmode" definition, modes can be "trademarked" (Morr73) and are only equivalent if they are also textually equal. This implies that the "name equivalence" of Ada is included as a special case in CHILL.

- Exception handling is similar to the mechanism provided in Ada and based on (Bron76).

- Concurrent processes can be created dynamically. The number of processes is not determined at compile time. CHILL offers a wide variety of communication and synchronisation primitives.

  1. Regions and events

     Regions are similar to monitors in Concurrent Pascal (Brin75). Activation of "critical" procedures in a region is mutually exclusive. A "continue" action on an event location allows a process that is delayed on that event location to be activated. If there is no process delayed, the operation has no further effect. A process executing a "continue" action cannot be delayed. Events are not persistent.

  2. Buffers

     Processes can send messages to buffers and receive messages from buffers. There is also a "receive case" statement which allows a process to wait for messages from several buffers in parallel. Messages in buffers are persistent. If a buffer is full, the sending process is delayed. This mechanism alone is almost as powerful as the Ada "rendez-vous" mechanism (it is not possible to define "guarding conditions" in CHILL).

3. Signals

Signals declare modes of messages that can be exchanged between processes. Here again it is possible for a process to wait for several signals in parallel.

2. THE COMPILER PROJECT

CHILL exceeds Ada in complexity and the design of a compiler for this language was expected to involve a considerable amount of effort. The undertaking of a CHILL compiler project could therefore only be justified, if our objectives couldn't be satisfied by an existing and available compiler. The objectives of our project were the following :

1. The compiler should implement the complete CHILL language with as little concessions as possible.

2. The compiler front-end should be general enough to allow code generators for several target processors to be plugged into it.

3. The first target machine would be a "CHILL processor", developed in cooperation with the University of Ghent. This processor provides support for the verification of dynamic semantic conditions and has a CHILL-oriented machine language.

4. The compiler should be designed as the first part of a programming support environment and it should be possible to add facilities like high level debugging and piece-wise compilation.

Besides the actual CHILL compiler, the project would also produce other benefits. It would be possible to evaluate the effect of advanced methods and tools on product quality and development time. We would also gain valuable experience in the management of a relatively large software project.

2.1. Automated tools

The key to a timely implementation of a CHILL compiler has been the use of the powerful compiler generator LILA (Language Implementation Laboratory) (Lewi79,82), which promotes the modular design of syntax-directed compilers. The input of LILA is an attributed LL(1) context-free grammar (Knut68,71). Semantic actions, attribute handling and information for error recovery can be specified local to each syntax rule. The system works highly interactive and default options can be overridden by the user. LILA produces a compiler expressed in Pascal (Jens74) (semantic actions and attribute handling must be written in PASCAL by the user).

Our PASCAL compiler offers limited facilities for separate compilation. Besides the main program, sets of procedures and functions can be collected in "modules" (not to be confused with the CHILL modules) and compiled seperately. These modules can't have their own permanent data. No type checking is performed when these modules are linked together. This primitive and dangerous facility for separate compilation has nevertheless proven to be very helpful to manage a program of this size, and keep recompilation times within reasonable limits.

For the debugging of the compiler, only explicitly written logging and error routines embedded in the source text have been used. The (available) debugging package was never linked with the compiler. This strategy encourages defensive programming, which is especially useful in a compiler where only few assumptions can be made about the input. The compiler must stay alive, even if the input text contains many syntatic and semantic errors.

Automatic version control has also proven to be very helpful in a project involving many program modules. Before this was adopted, people had to track manually of who was in the process of modifying which modules. As a result files had to be merged manually and modifications were often lost. A history of modifications is now maintained automatically. The modular structure of the source text for the compiler generator allows several people to work in parallel, without inexpected interactions. Several people can "reserve" the same source file. The two modified files can be merged automatically.

As an exercise to become familiar with LILA, one of the people who came on board, implemented a PASCAL formatter. This program was later used to produce compiler source texts with a uniform format.

2.2. The language specification

Initially the implementation was based on the CCITT Recommendation Z.200 (Chil80) and also on a formal description (Haff80) using VDM (based on denotational semantics) (Bjor78). The latter description is based on an abstract syntax, which mirrors the Z.200 concrete syntax. Static semantic conditions are expressed as "well-formedness" predicates on this abstract syntax. This syntax is transformed in two steps to the AS2 syntax of the dynamic semantics part. The AS2 syntax only contains information, required at run time (e.g. only information about the life-time of names, and not about their scope, is maintained).

The meaning of the CHILL constructs is given in terms of mathematical functions on the state of an abstract machine. Concurrency is described by means of an abstract model for an interpreter, which is based on CSP (Hoar78). At a later stage a less formal description using a notation inspired on attributed grammars (Bran82) was studied as well. Unfortunately, the more formal specifications couldn't resolve all the ambiguities in the Z.200 language description. The absence of automated verification tools and the size and complexity of the description make also the formal language specifications error-prone.

The study, but even more the development of a formal specification, gives the compiler implementer a good understanding of a language. But it isn't always a good idea, to use this specification, even if it is "constructive" as a basis for the compiler implementation.

A small example illustrates the problems that can be encountered. According to Z.200 one of the dynamic conditions is that the mode name in a dereferenced free reference (pointer) must be read compatible with the mode of the referenced location. In Z.200 (Chil80) was specified that a MODEFALL exception should occur if this check failed. In a later corrigendum (Chil82) this exception has been removed, leaving it to the implementer to decide whether this error is to be handled at run-time. In the VDM description properties like read-onlyness and novelty are not included in the run-time description. These properties are however needed, if it is decided to perform a run-time check for read compatibility. One must therefore be cautious to use this specification as a basis for the compiler implementation. Some implementation decisions may already be implied by the specification.

2.3. The designer team

The compiler was designed and implemented by a small group (3-4 people) having permanent access to an interactive programming support environment (in our case VAX/VMS). Except for the group leader, all members of the group had little or no experience in compiler design. In such a small group information exchange is verbal and informal. Strong discipline is required to maintain a good documentation. The version control system automatically keeps a history of modifications to source files and documentation files.

We have followed a strategy of incremental design and implementation. A syntax analyser and associated lexical analyser was up and running in a very short time. Semantic actions could than be added in successive steps, making the compiler more and more powerful. Such a strategy is encouraged by the LILA compiler generator. It is also stimulating for the compiler implementers to see working results of their efforts within a short time. To increase confidence in the correct functioning of the compiler, each member of the group was encouraged to write test programs for parts, developed by others. A "debugging assistant" (Chap82) to collect and control these test routines and execute and verify them automatically, would have been helpful. The manual classification of these routines requires a discipline, which was difficult to enforce.

A CHILL compiler including code generation for the above mentioned CHILL processor was completed in less than 1.5 year with 4 people the first year and 3 afterwards. This includes time to learn the LILA notation and methodology as well as the notations used in the Z.200 Recommendation and the two formal specifications. The object size of the compiler is about 0.5 Mbytes.

3. STUCTURE OF THE COMPILER

Most programming languages require that "applied" occurences of a name must be preceded in the program text by a "defining" occurence. In this case the "syntatic-semantic" analysis of the compiler can be implemented in a single pass.

The absence of this rule in CHILL complicates the design of a compiler considerably and makes it impossible to perform semantic analysis of CHILL programs in one or even a limited number of sequential passes over the lexical representation of the program. At least two compiler passes are required (Dema82). In the first pass all name declarations are resolved and a symbol table is built. In a second pass the semantic conditions in the action statements are verified and intermediate code is generated. But even declarations can be written in a random order, so that a symbol table with information about all the declared names can't be constructed in a single pass.

The following example illustrates some of the difficulties to be overcome.

```
SYNMODE TINY_INT       = SHORT_INT(A+B:C);
NEWMODE SHORT_INT      = RANGE(0:255);
SYN     A SHORT_INT    = 1,
        B SHORT_INT    = 10,
        C SHORT_INT    = 20;
```

The mode SHORT_INT can be resolved first. Next, the synonyms A, B, C can be evaluated and the range expression A+B can be evaluated. Finally the mode TINY_INT can be resolved. Unlike e.g. in PASCAL, it isn't possible to resolve all synonyms and constant expressions before the mode definitions. The only solution here is to evaluate expressions first without mode checking, resolve the mode definitions, and return once again to the expressions to check for mode incompatibilities. Matters become even more complicated when e.g. SHORT_INT is declared in another module and made visible with a "grant" statement.

Such problems can be solved by first constructing an abstract syntax tree (or more precisely a syntax graph) and to perform semantic analysis in a number of tree (graph) traversals. We have applied this method only partially. The abstract syntax graph is limited to the declarations and definitions. Verification of the static semantic conditions for these statements is performed on this abstract representation. For the semantic analysis of the action statements, a syntax-directed approach was preferred. This has two advantages : the abstract syntax graph is much smaller and this pass can be constructed with a compiler generator. It has the disadvantage that it isn't straightforward to generate code in another than lexical order. This is e.g. required for some initialisation code which must be performed at the beginning of the block inclosing the declaration of the locations to be initialized. In such cases, the required information can be collected during the first compiler pass and stored in the abstract syntax tree, for later use by the second pass.

The compiler thus has the following structure :

1. The lexical analysis.

2. The syntax analysis decorated with semantic actions to construct the abstract syntax graph for definitions and declarations (the symbol table).

3. A number of procedures to resolve the symbol table and perform semantic analysis on the definition and declaration statements.

4. A second syntax-directed pass to perform semantic analysis of the action statements and to produce the intermediate code.

The compiler produces a list of syntactic and semantic error messages with their line numbers. A separate program is used to generate a program listing with error messages from this file and the source file. The format of the listing can be tailored to particular needs, without affecting the compiler proper.

We now give a more detailed description of each of these parts.

3.1. The lexical analyser.

The lexical analyser scans the source text and produces a stream of lexical tokens to be parsed by the syntax analyser. It screens formatting characters, comments and compiler directives, and keeps track of line numbers (for the error messages). The lexical analyser is implemented as a procedure, called from the syntax analyser.

3.2. The syntax analysis and construction of the symbol table.

This pass is generated with LILA and is based on an LL(1) syntax for CHILL. LILA will however only generate a syntax analyser if the submitted syntax is unambiguous and satisfies the LL(1) conditions. This means that the Z.200 syntax cannot be copied literally. We have several options to solve this problem. Each of these methods has been applied in this parser.

3.2.1. Syntax modification.

The syntax description can be modified without changing the syntax, in order to make it satisfy the LL(1) conditions. A typical example is the factorisation of common lexical symbols. E.g. all modes starting with "char" are combined in one syntax rule :

```
"char"                          character
"char" "(" <exp> ")"            character string
"char" "(" <exp> ":" <exp> ")"  character
                                range
```

This method has the disadvantage that the syntax description becomes less readable.

3.2.2. Introduce distinguishing lexical tokens.

Some LL(1) problems can be eliminated by pushing some complexity into the lexical analyser. In this way we can keep the structure on which the semantic analyser will be built as simple as possible. By building a look-ahead facility into it, the lexical analyser can distinguish between classes of program constructs and pass this information to the syntax analyser by means of "distinguishing" lexical tokens. These tokens don't correspond with a sequence of characters in the source text. They are inserted at the beginning of some constructs, to enable the selection of alternatives in a syntax rule by the syntax analyser. In this compiler, the lexical analyser makes a distinction between labels of definition statements and labels of action statements. A "distinguishing symbol" is inserted if a definition statement is seen. In this way, separate syntax rules can be used for definition and action statements.

3.2.3. Impose restrictions on the syntax.

In some cases the syntax description cannot be modified without cluttering the description so much that it severely complicates the later addition of semantic actions. Only a few restrictions have been introduced to keep the syntax description well structured.

1. Predefined words cannot be redefined and reserved words cannot be made reusable by means of the FREE-directive.

It is considered a bad programming practice to use these words for other purposes than those for which they are normally intended.

2. The keyword ARRAY is not optional.

3. If layout information is specified for more-dimensional arrays, the derived syntax mustn't be used.

ARRAY (1:9,1:9) BOOLEAN NOPACK PACK

is not allowed, but must be written as

ARRAY (1:9) ARRAY (1:9) BOOLEAN NOPACK PACK

4. Locations mustn't start with the "("-character. It is very hard to find examples of location expressions between parentheses, that can be used for other purposes than the confusion of the reader.

5. The level structure notation isn't implemented.

3.2.4. Use the LET option.

If the LET option is used, LILA will generate a parser, even if the LL(1) conditions aren't satisfied. It is left to the programmer to verify carefully that the parser generated by LILA is indeed conform to the language specification.

LILA supports a powerful syntactic error recovery mechanism. For each syntax rule, the recovery information can be specified in a very compact way. The compiler generator automatically inserts code for synchronisation after a syntax error. It is also possible to let the compiler perform partial syntax analysis during the synchronisation phase. At a negligible cost, an error recovery mechanism could be incorporated in the compiler which outperforms many commercial compilers.

To keep this pass as simple as possible no attempt is made to try and resolve the properties of names appearing at the right hand side of definitions and declarations, even if these names have already been parsed. With an incomplete symbol table, it is of course not possible to verify many static semantic conditions. The semantic checks are limited to syntactic conditions that couldn't be incorporated in the LL(1) syntax. A few semantic checks, which don't depend on mode information of defined names are also included.

The "backbone" of the symbol table is a tree, representing the nesting of "groups". Groups in CHILL delimit the scope defined names. Each of these group nodes has lists attached for the locally defined modes, variables, synonyms, etc. In this pass "empty" nodes with only a name are appended to these lists.

3.3. Semantic analysis of declarations and definitions.

The symbol table is checked and modified in consecutive steps by a number of procedures. These procedures aren't syntax-directed, but traverse the symbol table in an order most appropriate for the task to be performed. They are written as separately compiled PASCAL modules, called from the "epilogue" of the first syntax-directed parser.

First, the "loose ends" of the symbol table have to be resolved. This is accomplished by applying the following operations (in this order) :

- Resolution of granted and seized names. Granted names are moved upwards, seized names are moved downwards in the "group tree".

- Name binding and check for unsafe circular definitions.
  The names on the left hand side of declarations and definitions are bound to their defining node in the symbol table. Unsafe circularities, like infinite recursive mode definitions, are detected.

- Compile-time evaluation of literals and constants (without mode checking).
  In CHILL, a difference is made between literals, for which compile-time evaluation is required, and constants for which it is possible.

- Evaluation of all name attributes.
  Name attributes are e.g. the read-onlyness, novelty (used for mode equivalence), referencing property.

Eventually a completely resolved symbol table is produced. Verification of static semantic conditions in the definitions and declarations can now be performed in a final pass over the symbol table.

3.4. Semantic analysis of actions and code generation.

In a second syntax-directed pass (based on the same syntax as the first one), the static semantic conditions in the action statements are verified and intermediate code is generated. Instead of scanning the source text (using the lexical analyser), this pass scans a file of lexical tokens, produced during the first pass.

Many functions, defined in the first pass, e.g. mode equivalence functions, can also be used in the second pass. These functions are collected in a separate module and can be called from the two syntax-directed passes.

The compiler directly generates code for the CHILL processor, which has a high-level, CHILL-oriented machine language, based on the AS2 in the VDM description of CHILL. Only few optimisations can be performed by the compiler, the CHILL processor takes care of most optimisations at run-time. This intermediate code can be used as the input for code generators for more convential machines.

Care has been taken to make the compiler easily retargetable. The code generator is of course a separate module, but some of the static and dynamic semantic conditions are also target machine dependent. A few examples :

- Overflow in compile-time evaluation of literals depends on the representation of these literals (e.g. 16 or 32 bit integers).

- Built-in functions, e.g. to compute the size of a location or for explicit mode conversion also depend on the representation in the target machine.

To keep the compiler front-end independent of the target machine, values and functions like "maximum-integer" and "mode-size" are defined in a separate target dependent module.

4. CONCLUSIONS.

Some important results of this project are summarized below :

- Advanced programming support tools but also the efficient cooperation of a small group of motivated designers have contributed to the development of a high-quality CHILL compiler, within a short time.

- A formal specification of the language was helpful to understand the finesses of the language. During the implementation we were hampered by the large distance between the design methodology and the specification method.

- Testing and debugging (in this application, which isn't time critical) can be performed without the aid of a debugging package. However, the process remains largely un-automated. Support for the generation, classification and automatic verification of test programs would help to cut down on debugging time.

- Good support for modular program design is indispensable in a large project.

References.

(Bjor78) Bjorner, D, Jones, C.B. (ed) "The Vienna Development Method : The Metalanguage" Lect. Notes in Comp. Sc. 61, Springer Verlag Berlin (1978).

(Bran82) Branquart, P. et al. "An Analytical Description of CHILL, the CCITT High Level Language" Lect. Notes in Comp. Sc. 128 Springer-Verlag Berlin (1982).

(Brin75) Brinch Hansen, P. "The programming Language Concurrent Pascal" Data Transactions on Software Engineering. Vol SE-1, 2 (June 1975).

(Bron76) Bron, C., et al. "A proposal for dealing with abnormal termination of programs" Memo nr. 150. Technische Hogeschool Twente (Nov. 1976).

(Chap82) Chapman, D. "A program testing assistant" Comm. ACM vol 25, no 9 (Sep. 1982).

(Chil80) "The CCITT High Level Programming Language (CHILL)" (Recommendation Z.200), Geneva (Nov. 1980).

(Chil82) "Report of the sub-working party XI/3-2 (CHILL)" (June 1982).

(Dema82) De Man, J. et al. "A compiler for the CCITT High Level Language" BTM Lab Report JDM/300682.

(Haff80) Haff, P. and Bjorner D. "CHILL formal definition" Danish Datamatics Centre (Aug. 1980).

(Hoar78) Hoare, C.A.R. "Communicating Sequential Processes" Comm. ACM vol. 21, no. 8 (Aug. 1978).

(Ichb80) Ichbiah, J. et al. "Reference Manual for the Ada Programming Language" U.S. Department of Defense, (July 1980).

(Jens74) Jensen, K., Wirth, N. "Pascal user manual an report" 2nd ed. Lect. Notes in Comp. Sc. 18 Springer-Verlag Berlin (1974).

(Knut68) Knuth, D.E. "Semantics of context free languages" Math. Syst. Theory 2, pp. 127-145 (1968).

(Knut71) Knuth, D.E. "Semantics of context free languages : correction" Math. Syst. Theory 5, pp. 95-96 (1971).

(Lewi79) Lewi, J. et al. "A Programming Methodology in Compiler Construction. Part 1 : Concepts". North-Holland (1979).

(Lewi82) Lewi J. et al. "A Programming Methodology in Compiler Construction. Part 2 : Implementation". North-Holland (1982).

(Morr73) Morris, J.H. "Protection in programming languages", Comm. ACM vol. 21, no. 8 (Jan. 1973).

(Wijn75) Van Wijngaarden, A., et al. "Revised Report on the Algorithmic Language Algol68" Acta Informatica 5 fasc. 1-3 (1975).

MICROCOMPUTERS: Developments in Industry, Business and Education
D.R. Wilson and C.J. van Spronsen (eds.) /© EUROMICRO, 1983
Elsevier Science Publishers B.V. (North-Holland)

ANALIZADOR: AN LALR(1) PARSER GENERATOR FOR MICRO-COMPUTERS

Karmele Inchausti, Francisco J. Garijo

Facultad de Informatica
Universidad del Pais vasco
Apartado 649, S.Sebastian
Spain

ANALIZADOR is an LALR(1) parser generator actually running in an APPLE II micro computer. It accepts as input a context free grammar in BNF notation and outputs a LALR(1) parsing table. ANALIZADOR is made up of two modules. The first, VALID, validates the grammar (eliminating useless symbols); and the second, GENERADOR builds the parsing table. The system has been implemented in standard UCSD PASCAL.

1. INTRODUCTION

Due to their size and complexity, most software tools for writing translators (scanners and parsers generators program tree constructors, attribute evaluators, optimizators, intermediate code generators, etc.) have been implemented in large systems (PDP-11, VAX-11, CRAY, UNIVAC 1100, etc).

The need for language design and translators makes this software increasingly important in micro computer based systems. We must overcome the specific limits which characterise the micro computer in order to be able to implement these tools. This poses new and interesting problems to be solved.

The ANALIZADOR system has been implemented at the Pais Vasco University and is currently running in an APPLE-II plus 64K under UCDS-PASCAL operating system. ANALIZADOR accepts a description of grammar in BNF format as input and gives a syntactic analyser based on a LALR(1) parsing table as output.

The general system structure is as follows:

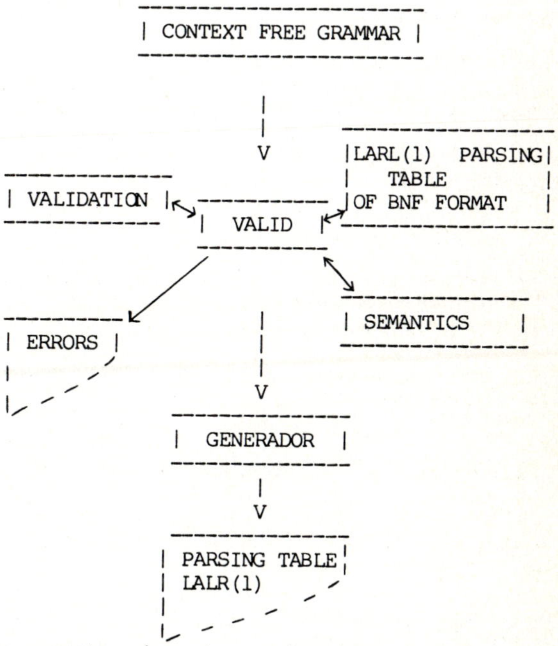

The system has two subsystems: VALID and GENERADOR

VALID tranlates the input (CFG grammar in BNF format) to an internal representation. The system will use this representation for grammar validation.

Among the tasks performed by VALID are the following:

- Detection of non reachable terminal and non terminal alphabet symbols.

- Detection of non terminal elements deriving chains not belonging to the terminal alphabet

GENERADOR takes as input validate grammar (a CFG grammar without useless symbols) and gives as output an LALR(1) parsing table for the input grammar.

The goal will be atempted in three steps:

1st step: Kernel construction: Find the kernels of a set of LR(Ø) items and compute the first element of non terminals.

2nd step: Set of LALR(1) items: From the set of LR(Ø) items, compute sets of LALR(1) items.

3rd step: LALR(1) parsing table construction.

In Parts II and III of this paper, we shall study the characteristics of the VALID and GENERADOR modules. The characteristics of system implementation will be summed up in the conclusion.

2. VALID SUBSYSTEM

2.1 Grammar specification

VALID input is made up of CFG grammars in BNF notation. The VALID specification of the usual grammar notation (V_N, V_T, P, s) is as follows:

Non terminal and terminal alphabet specification: V_N, V_T

The elements of V_N are specified by means of reserved words NONTERMINAL followed by the list of nonterminal between < >

e.g. Let V_N be {A,B,C,D}

we would express it as NONTERMINAL: <A>,<B>,<C>,<D>;

In a similar way, V_T elements are specified by TERMINAL:

followed by the list of terminals between ' '

e.g. Let V_T be {a,b,c,d}

we would express it as TERMINAL: 'a','b','c','d';

Rule specification: We use pure BNF syntax

e.g. Let P be {A -> A b C} where $A \in V_N$; $b \in V_T$

we would express it as <A> : = <A> 'b' <C>

Example: Let

G ({A,B,C,D,E,F,G,H},{;,<,>,:=,id,cte,/,'},P,A)

P={ A->A;B A->B B->CD C-><id>:= D->EF D->F

E->F/ F->G F->Ø G->GH G->H H-><id>

H->'cte' }

NOTERM:<A>,<B>,<C>,<D>,<E>,<F>,<G>,<H>;

TERM: ';','<','>',':=','id','cte','/',''';

<A>:=<A>';'<B>/<B>;

<B>:=<C><D>;

<C>:='<''id''>'':=';

<D>:=<E><F>/<F>;

<E>:=<F>'/';

<F>:=<G>/;

<G>:=<G><H>/<H>;

<H>:='<''id''>'/''''cte''''

This grammar generates the production rules of BNF format.

2.2 Grammar Validation

The main aim of VALID is to verify the input grammar coherenceby validating it. The validation process is made up of the following actions:

- Detection of duplicate productions.

- Detection of multiple declarations of terminals and non terminals of the grammar.

- Detection of unreachable symbols.

- Detection of non terminal symbols not deriving terminal elements.

The first two actions are performed directly from the internal representation of the grammar elements (terminal, non terminal and rules). The last two, however, require specific treatment. From the set of grammar productions, VALID constructs a direct graph whose vertices are terminals and non terminalsforming part of the production. For each non terminal to the left of the rules there is an edge connecting it with each element(terminal or non terminal) on the right.

Example:

<A>:=<B><C>;

<B>:=<C>/'b';

<C>:='d';

<D>:=<D>'d'/'e'

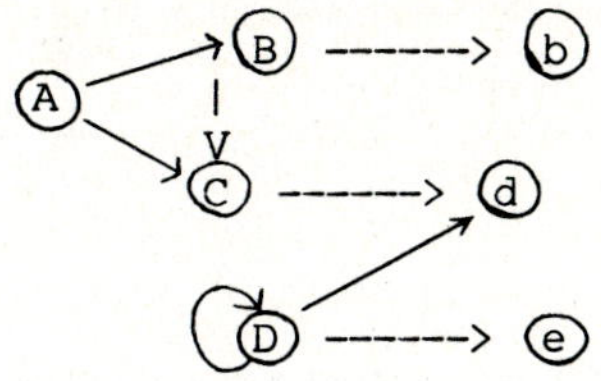

Validation actions:

Unreachable symbols: $X_i \in V$, $S \stackrel{*}{\not\Longrightarrow} X_i \alpha$
S - Start symbol
$\alpha \in V^*$

Symbols not deriving terminal elements:

$A_i \in V_N$, $A_i \stackrel{*}{\not\Longrightarrow} a_k \alpha$
$a_k \in V_T$

are reduced respectively to a path search on the graph: from the root to the vertices and from non terminal to terminal vertices. The algorithms implemented are quick and efficient.

2.3 Output

In parallel with the validation process, the system constructs an internal representation which will be used by GENERADOR to construct the syntactic analyser of the input grammar. If there are no errors in the validation process, VALID will generate the internal representation and pass the control to the GENERADOR module. When errors occur, the system advises the user. No representation is generated.

For each element of the grammar, the internal representation contains the following information:

- non terminal symbols: name, production rules in which the symbol appears on the left, empty rules and set of rules reachable from the symbol.
- terminal symbols:name.
- production rules: left part and right part.

Example of a representation:

NOTERM:<A>,<B>,<C>;

TERM:'la','lb','lc';

<A>:=<A><B>/<A><C>/<C>;

<B>:='la'<B>/'lb';

<C>:='lc'

NONTERMINALS STRUCTURE

SYMBOL	A	B	C	
FIRST RULE	↑	↑	↑	
RULE NUM.	3	2	1	
EMPTY DER.	false	false	false	
OTHERS				

TERMINALS STRUCTURE

SYMBOL	la	lb	lc	
OTHERS				

PRODUCTION RULES

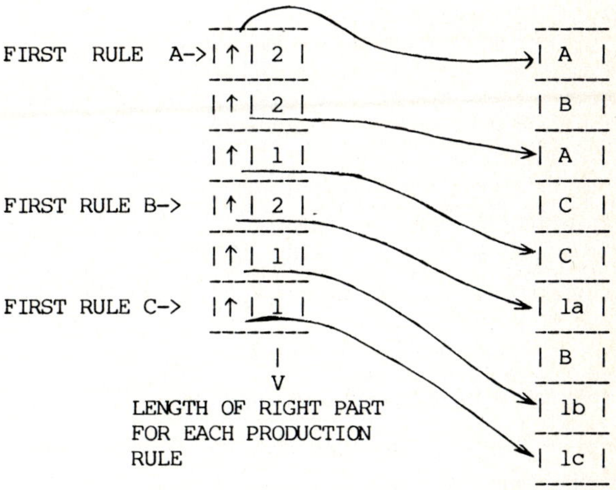

3. GENERADOR SUBSYSTEM

GENERADOR accepts as input the internal representation of the grammar validated by VALID. It varifies that the grammar is LALR(1) and outputs the parsing table corresponding to the input grammar.

The construction of the parsing table is carried out in the following steps:

1- construct the kernels of LR(Ø) items

2- obtain the LALR(1) set of items from the LR(Ø) collection

3- verify that there are no parsing action conflicts and construct the parsing table

To obtain the set of items LALR(1) from the collection LR(Ø), we follow the method of propogated and spontaneous lookaheads [Aho & Ullman, 77]. This method has been successfully employed in the construction of parser generators (YACC). Its implementation in a micro computer has led to a radical adaptation of algorithms using a representation more in accordance with the hardware requirements (memory space limitation).

3.1 Working example of GENERADOR

NOTERM:<S>,<A>,<B>;

TERM:'Ø','l','al','bl','c';

<S>:='Ø'<A><B>'bl'/'Ø'<A><B>'c';

<A>:='al'/;

<B>:=<B>'l'/'l'/

FIRST STEP.- Kernels of set of LR(Ø) items construction:.

$I_\emptyset$ ={[<S'>-->.<S>]}

I_1 =GOTO($I_\emptyset$,Ø)={[<S>-->'Ø'.<A><B>'bl']
[<S>-->'Ø'.<A><B>'c']
[<A>-->.]}

I_2 =GOTO($I_\emptyset$,S)={[<S'>--><S>.]}

I_3 =GOTO(I_1 ,al)={[<A>-->'al'.]}

I_4 =GOTO(I_1 ,A)={[<S>-->'Ø'<A>.<B>'bl']
[<S>-->'Ø'<A>.<B>'c']
[<B>-->.]}

I_5 =GOTO(I_4 ,l)={[<B>-->'l'.]}

I_6 =GOTO(I_4 ,B)={[<S>-->'Ø'<A><B>.'bl']
[<S>-->'Ø'<A><B>.'c']
[<B>--><B>.'l']}

I_7 =GOTO(I_6 ,bl)={[<S>-->'Ø'<A><B>'bl'.]}

I_8 =GOTO(I_6 ,c)={[<S>-->'Ø'<A><B>'c'.]}

I_9 =GOTO(I_6 ,l)={[<B>--><B>'l'.]}

The sets DERIVADO(I_i) and GENERA(X) X∈V are also created.

DERIVADO(I_k)={(I_j ,X)/I_j =GOTO(I_k ,X), X∈(V_N U V_T)}

It will be chained to each Kernel Ii and will be used in the parsing table construction.

GENERA(X)={I_k /I_k =GOTO(I_j ,X)}

It will be used to performe at quick access to the set of Kernels in order to verify if the kernel has already been created.

SECOND STEP.- Construction of LALR(1) set of items from LR(Ø) items collections.

$I_\emptyset$ ={[<S'>-->.<S> ,$]}

I_1 =GOTO($I_\emptyset$,Ø)={[<S>-->'Ø'.<A><B>'bl' ,$]
[<S>-->'Ø'.<A><B>'c' ,$]
[<A>-->. ,bl/l/c]}

I_2 =GOTO($I_\emptyset$,S)={[<S'>--><S>. ,$]}

I_3 =GOTO(I_1 ,al)={[<A>-->'al'. ,bl/c/l]}

I_4 =GOTO(I_1 ,A)={[<S>-->'Ø'<A>.<B>'bl' ,$]
[<S>-->'Ø'<A>.<B>'c' ,$]
[<B>-->. ,bl/c/l]}

I_5 =GOTO(I_4 ,l)={[<B>-->'l'. ,c/bl/l]}

I_6 =GOTO(I_4 ,B)={[<S>-->'Ø'<A><B>.'bl' ,$]
[<S>-->'Ø'<A><B>.'c' ,$]
[<B>--><B>.'l' ,bl/c/l]}

I_7 =GOTO(I_6 ,bl)={[<S>-->'Ø'<A><B>'bl'. ,$]}

I_8 =GOTO(I_6 ,c)={[<S>-->'Ø'<A><B>'c'. ,$]}

I_9 =GOTO(I_6 ,l)={[<B>--><B>'l'. ,c/bl/l]}

THIRD STEP.-Parsing table generation.

STATES	TERMINALS						NONTERMINALS		
	Ø	1	al	bl	c	$	S	A	B
Ø	S1						2		
1		R4	S3	R4	R4			4	
2						ACC			
3		R3		R3	R3				
4		S5/R7		R7	R7				6
5		R6		R6	R6				
6		S9		S7	S8				
7						R1			
8						R2			
9		R5		R5	R5				

We could seen there is a confilct in state 4 for input 1. The system would write the parsing table as above with an error message to the user indicating that a conflict occurs and the grammar is not LARL(1).

<S>-->'Ø'<A><B>'bl' Rule 1

<S>-->'Ø'<A><B>'c' Rule 2

<A>-->'al' Rule 3

<A>-->Ø Rule 4

<B>--><B>'1' Rule 5

<B>-->'1' Rule 6

<B>-->Ø Rule 7

4. CONCLUSIONS

ANALIZADOR has been implemented in an APPLE II plus with 64k memory bytes and two diskette units with a storing capacity of 14Øk bytes per diskette.

The structure of the system has been influenced by the memory limits imposed by the hardware. Two independent modules make up ANALIZADOR: the VALID and GENERADOR subsystems. VALID consist of a single routine the objective of which is the translation of an input grammar in BNF to an internal representation permitting grammar validation. GENERADOR's task is to construct an LALR(1) parsing table for the input grammar using an internal representation obtained from VALID. This job is carried out in three steps, each of which is implemented through a routine. The first routine constructs the kernels of the set of LR(Ø) items and obtains the first symbol list of each non terminal. The second routine calculates the set of LALR(1) items from the set of LR(Ø) items. Finally, the third constructs the parsing table.

The system has been implemented in PASCAL (UCSD). PASCAL is used instead of other languages more commmonly used in microcomputers because of the advantages it offers in structuring, portability, and ease of programming. On the other hand, the use of a standard PASCAL (UCSD) make it possible to run ANALIZADOR in a micro as well as in a large computer.

ANALIZADOR is actually running in the Faculty of Computer Science in San Sebastian. It has been used in different projects. For a grammar with about 2Ø production rules, the running time is approximately 5 minutes. This time, which increases proportionately according to the number of production rules and lookaheads of each rule, may be greatly reduced in a computer without the memory limitations of a micro computer.

In short, ANALIZADOR is a modular structured system easily portable, which can be used as a software tool as well as a teaching aid in compiler writing.

REFERENCES:

[1] Aho, Alfred V.; Ullman, Jeffrey D. The Theory of Parsing, Translation and Compiling (Prentice-Hall International Vol1 1972 Vol2 1973).

[2] Aho, Alfred V.; Ullman, Jeffrey D. Principles of Compiler Design (Addison-Wesley Publishing Company 1977).

[3] Backhouse, Roland C. Syntax of Programming Languages-Theory and Practice(Prentice-Hall International 1979).

[4] Kristensen B.,Madsen,O.,Methods for Computing LALR(k) Lookahead, ACM Trans. Program. Lang. Syst. 3, 1 (Jan, 1981)

[5] Ancona,M.,Dodero,G.,Gianuzzi,V.,Building Collections of LR(k) Items with Partial Expansion of Lookahead Strings, SIGPLAN Notices (ACM) 17, 5 (May, 1982).

[6] Park, J. A New LALR Formalism,SIGPLAN Notices (ACM) 17, 7 (July, 1982).

[7] Soisalon-Soininen,E.,Innessential Error Entries and Their Use in LR Parser Optimitation ACM, Trans. Program. Lang. Syst. 4, 2 (April, 1982)

[8] Tokuda,T.,Eliminating Unit Reductions from LR(k) Parser Using Minimum Contexts. Acta Informatica 15, 4 (August, 1981).

Session B2: INDUSTRIAL SYSTEMS

Chairman: Lionel R. Thompson
HSDE Ltd.
Welwyn Garden City (U.K.)

Industrial applications of microprocessors and allied devices are being seen everywhere. However, where replacement of existing designs is the purpose, the applications are not generally appearing as like-for-like equipment, since the unique advantages that are offered by stored program devices can only be used if the designer recognises what they are, and responds accordingly. The more successful new products have been those in which this recognition has been worked out completely and the equipment meets the objective in an optimum fashion for the method employed.

However, generally speaking, end-users are not interested in the technology employed within the products, or equipment, which they use. Their requirement is that the system does the job they require efficiently, economically and reliably. It is important that the designer should use all the advantages of the new technology which allow him to address these three features properly.

Efficiency requires a thorough understanding of the application by the designer and his meeting the goals and constraints for that job, and that job only. Economics embrace the total cost of ownership and use, including initial costs, running costs and maintenance. Reliability also effects costs, not only in terms of downtime, disruption and replacement, but also such factors as safety and confidence. All three papers being presented in this session have something to say about all of these factors.

The paper by Robach & Michel is an evaluation of a case study to do with the choice of a component to do a job in a difficult environment satisfactorily. Its overall reliability under these conditions has a considerably bearing on the maintenance that will be required. There is a balance between choosing a very high grade military type component which has been evaluated in a high temperature environment and the much lower cost commercial versions. In the industrial field it is not often viable to use the lower cost devices. The workers in this case are trying to determine whether a commercially oriented device can survive satisfactorily in the stringent condition of a bore hole.

The paper also discusses testing methods. Again, these are aimed at keeping costs down since obviously, high manufacturing and testing costs are reflected in the initial cost of the product to the user.

The paper by Capizzi, Cianci and Melgara deals with the special design of a chip for the specific application of speech synthesis. This is apparently to meet user requirements economically and again, the authors deal with testing methods in production.

The third paper by Ferrero describes various design philosophies which are very much aimed at keeping the costs of ownership of a system to the minimum. Control and protection of electrical distribution systems needs reliability. A traditional approach has been to ensure that the reliability and integrity of each component in the system is of the highest order, but experience has shown that this is often too costly. The alternative approach described in the paper, using system configurations, indicates ways in which economies can be obtained without reducing the efficiency of the system to the end user. A balance between costs and performance is achieved.

The theme of testability runs through all three papers of the session. Now, experience is showing us that products of modern design, which use LSI chips in the electronics, consume considerably less labour during construction that did their predecessors. This results from all the complexities being in the various chips that comprise the assembly. Testing can present a peculiar problem. It is generally assumed that in-circuit testing will quickly identify areas of short circuit on printed circuits, or the wrong insertion of components and that automatic test equipment will allow functional testing to be carried out quickly and cheaply. However, experience shows that fault-free equipment is quickly passed out, whereas equipment with in-built faults can cause considerable difficulties. In fact, time consumed in identifying what is wrong can easily exceed the valued of the product! The difficult problem for the designer is to ensure that he deals with the matter of diagnosis sensibly at the design stage so that the problems of reliability in production are minimised.

I would like to pose the following questions:-

"What methods can and should be used in order to diagnose faults in production testing, and what experience is there in the various methods?"

Self-testing capability should be an advantage in production testing, but it is presumably designed primarily for the improving of the integrity of the system in its application. The paper dealing with power systems lists four levels of reliability. My question following from this is

"Is self-diagnosis a useful feature in field applications in practice?"

There is an implication that test programmes can be held within the equipment or the system somewhere. Hence a further question is

"How far can such imbedded test programmes help in the critical areas of ecomomics and reliability?"

Is there documentary evidence that true economies have been achieved in systems which do have built in self-test or self-diagnosis programmes?

In considering these questions, we must ask ourselves whether those people involved in research and development ought to perhaps pay more attention to the problems arising from industrial application of their ideas. Are new tools needed to be developed for cutting down the cost of production testing and/or improving the reliability of equipment and systems in service.

In a meeting such as we are having here in this synposium, with its interactions between academia, research institutes and industrial appliers interchange of our ideas on these questions should stimulate new ways of thinking in these critical areas.

MICROCOMPUTERS: Developments in Industry, Business and Education
D.R. Wilson and C.J. van Spronsen (eds.) /© EUROMICRO, 1983
Elsevier Science Publishers B.V. (North-Holland)

A STEP TOWARDS FURTHER RELIABILITY IN POWER SYSTEMS CONTROL AND PROTECTION: MICRO AND MULTIMICRO STRUCTURES

Alessandro Ferrero

Landis & Gyr S.p.A. / Divisione Daco Systems
Peschiera Borromeo - Milano, Italy

As power systems increase in importance and complexity they need more efficient and reliable control and protective equipment. Starting from brief considerations on what reliability means when speaking of control and protective equipment, this paper will shortly consider the most significant methods presently employed to increase it. Then microprocessor and multimicro based devices will be taken into account, paying particular attention to all characteristics of such structures that are quite suitable in improving reliability. Self-test capabilities are examined, being the basic element that makes microprocessor-based devices intrinsically more reliable than other technology-based ones. Some examples are given on how to obtain self-monitoring equipment able to detect its faulty status and to prevent uncorrect operations or even to operate correctly when faulty. Finally a general purpose multimicro protective device is illustrated, in order to show how the general considerations reported can be applied.

1. INTRODUCTION

At present time power systems have become more and more important, thus requiring control and protective equipment able to perform high speed complex operations with a high degree of reliability.
This high reliability need is essentially due to the high cost of the power system to be protected, as well as to the high cost of any outage; in order to avoid damages to the power system or erroneous outages, control and protective devices are required that operate only if and when the system to be controlled needs it and that operate correctly when they do it.
In order to point out the basic problems concerned with high reliability control and protective equipment designing, this paper will briefly report the most significant methods presently employed to increase reliability; then it will consider micro and multimicro architectures, showing why these structures can be considered optimal as far as high reliability is concerned.

2. TRADITIONAL STRUCTURES

Nowaday power systems control and protectice equipment is to a great extent based on electromechanical or electronic technology, being digital programmable devices still object of theorical study or of in-field tests on prototypes.
Reliability of conventional devices strictly relates to the reliability of each component employed and is usually improved, when needed, by adding redundant components. However this redudancy, although useful in some cases, can sometimes result in a drawback, as basically represented by the diagrams of fig. 1 : in fact it is obvious to realize that the redundant circuit of fig. 1-a) is quite useful in preventing erroneous operations due to failures (i.e. short circuit) on one of the components, but can otherwise prevent the device to operate, and viceversa does the circuit of fig. 1-b).

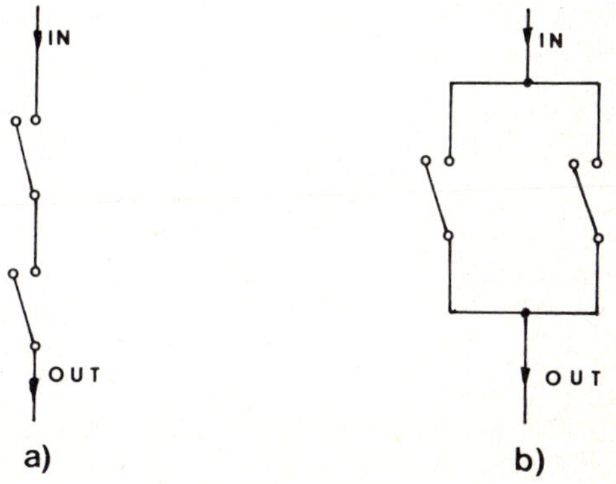

Fig. 1
Simple redundant structures when: a) no erroneous operations are allowed or b) high security is required in operating.

Anyway, more complex schemes with greater redundancy have a cost that is generally not justified by the actual structure of power systems, so that system redundancy (1) is now preferred. [3]
The maintenance of systems reliability is then assigned to functional tests operated on the whole control and protective equipment during periodical inspections, being fully self-monitoring devices not yet cost effective.
Moreover it is quite possible that, unless single components reliability increases, traditional devices reliability can't come to a further improvement at a reasonably low cost: next section will show, however, how microprocessor-ba-

sed devices can solve, in a cost effective way, most of the problems that arise with conventional structures.

3. MICROPROCESSOR STRUCTURES

Introducing microprocessor in control and protective systems turned into these systems all capabilities which are peculiar of any microprocessor based device.
In particular these systems, compared with other technology-based ones, present a higher versatility and consequently a higher reliability at a lower cost; in fact, taking advantage of the capability of any microprocessor-based hardware to perform different functions, they can be fitted to different situations simply by rewriting part of the software, thus minimizing hardware changes and intrinsically improving reliability.
Furthermore, the capability of such an hardware to perform different functions is one of the most interesting features of these systems, as it provides an effective tool to improve reliability; thanks to this capability it is possible to have systems executing both the operating procedures and other procedures, able to monitor them continuously : in other words, self-test capabilities can be added to microprocessor-based equipments simply by adding dedicated software and with very little changes in hardware.
There is no interest, in this paper, in examining what self-test procedures are and how they can be obtained [1] , [5] ; however it is quite interesting to see what they do, which information they can give and how they can improve system reliability.
As their peculiar feature, such procedures can exercise the components of a microprocessor-based system in the absolutely same way they are exercised by the operating procedures [2] , but self-test procedures can then test the result of the operation and decide whether or not it has been successfull.
If care is taken in hardware design and in self-test software design [1] , [5] , when a failure occurs, these procedures can detect the errors it caused and can determine which group of components (and in some case which component) is involved in the failure. This immediately results in the capability of the equipment to automatically monitor itself and so to know, at any moment, whether or not it can operate correctly, thus giving the control and protective systems' manufactures and users a powerful tool to increase reliability.
This last statement can be fully understood if the following considerations are taken into account:

- functions usually performed by analogical circuits can be performed by the microprocessor, by means of dedicated algorithm (i.e. input signal filtering can be digitally performed), thus reducing the global number of components and assigning these functions to more easily monitorable components;
- the state of the system - and in particular the state of the most critical components of the system - can be known at any moment;
- all information concerned with the state of the system can be obtained adding as few components as possible (in some cases even none) to the operating hardware, thus reducing the risk of decreasing reliability by adding new possible points of fault;
- since the self-test procedures exercise the system components just as operating procedures do, the information obtained through these procedures can be considered realiable at all; in fact if the system can't run the self-test procedures correctly, it will execute neither the operating procedures or viceversa : so if the self-test procedures indicate that the system failed, it can no more operate correctly without any doubt.

Besides all previously stated, at least one more condition must be satisfied to achieve as high reliability as possible : the system capability to output the result of self-test procedures and to perform some elementary operations must not be affected by any possible failure, otherwise all efforts would be vanished.
If this condition is satisfied, the system itself can detect error conditions quite in the same moment they occurs, can indicate the presence of an error condition and prevent uncorrect operations or allow the operator to prevent them.
However it can improbably prevent uncorrect operations that immediately follow a failure, since it has no time to detect the failure itself and to operate in order to prevent them. Though it is still possible to prevent these uncorrect operations by means of duplication of critical paths, nothing can be done if the failure does no longer let the microprocessor operate and signal the error condition.

4. MULTIMICRO STRUCTURES

4.1 General considerations

Since power systems continuosly evolve towards an ever increasing complexity, control and protective equipment too has to perform more and more complex operations in shorter and shorter times. In order to get these results, contemporary computations on the input signals can be useful, so that multimicro structures become optimal.
Moreover, such structures can be considered optimal also with regard to realiability, since, if all microprocessors employed in the multimicro structure feature self-test capabilities, they can solve most of the problems shown in the previous section.
In fact all microprocessors of the multimicro device can run their own self-test procedures, thus monitoring themselves; then they can periodically ask one another their status, so that if one failed in such a way that it cannot output any information concerned with its status or that it can no longer operate at all, the others

can realize this anomalous condition and operate in order to prevent uncorrect actions. In other words, a multimicro equipment can, in this way, practically detect all failures on its critical components.
If now this multimicro device is not required to operate continuously, but with long time intervals between two successive operations(3), and if the detected failure will prevent it to operate but will not cause any immediate uncorrect action, self-test capabilities can prevent any failure to operate either by calls for repairs or by switching its task to another similar device (back-up device). On the opposite side, if the multimicro device is required to operate with very short time intervals between two successive operations(4), or if the detected failure will cause an immediate erroneous operation, self-test procedures do no longer suffice to prevent it. These erroneous operations can however be avoided if all commands are issued by the device only if at least two signals, coming from two different microcomputers of the multimicro structure, are present for each command. In this way no erroneous commands can be issued by the whole system, even if one microcomputer failed and output an erroneous signal, since the others do not let any command to be issued.
As shown by these two examples, multimicro structures featuring self-test capabilities and signal conditioning, allowing the designer to assembly systems that do not operate erroneously when faulty, let it obtain more reliable devices in an easier and more cost effective way than other technology-based ones. Anyway, that is not enough whenever an equipment is required that must correctly operate even if some of its components are faulty.
When more traditional systems are employed, this very high reliability is usually achieved having two or more redundant devices, as shown in one of the previous sections. This full redundancy, however, can be avoided by a correct use of the multimicro structures' resources, both limiting the redundancy itself to some of the critical components of each microcomputer and carefully assigning their job to the different ones [2].
To fully understand what written above, suppose to have a multimicro structure, in which each microcomputer has 4 kbyte RAM, divided into 4 banks each one of 1 kbyte, and a fifth redundant 1 kbyte bank on stand-by, as shown in fig. 2.
Suppose then that one out of the four 1 k byte blocks of RAM failed: both self-test procedures and signal conditioning prevent the whole multimicro system to perform uncorrect operations; then self-test procedures locate the faulty block of RAM and appropriate fault recovery procedures assign the task of this block to the auxiliary one. If error detection circuitry and software too were provided, all data in the faulty RAM could be saved and the system can still operate correctly and, in the meanwhile, call for repairs.
Suppose now that in the same multimicro structure one of the microcomputer failed in such a way that it can no longer operate : as stated above, the self-test procedures of the whole system let the other ones to detect the faulty status of this one and to operate in order to prevent uncorrect actions and to call for repairs.
Although the whole system seems now to be unable to go on operating, a further step towards reliability can be made if each microcomputer has to execute tasks that do not fully busy it and if all microcomputers are interfaced with the system to be controlled : under these conditions, it is possible to share the tasks of the faulty one among the others, so that the whole system can continue to operate correctly. In this way a redundance is obtained by slightly overdimensioning each microcomputer and not by duplicating critical components : this means, after all, that the more are the microcomputers in the system, the slighter should they be overdimensioned, so reducing the global cost.

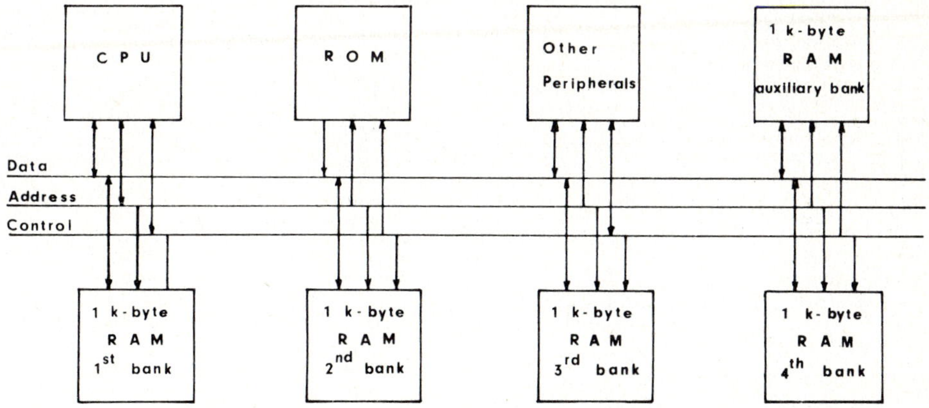

Fig. 2
Typical microcomputer structure, with four banks of 1 kbyte RAM active and one on stand-by

The general considerations reported, as well as the examples, clearly show the effectiveness of multimicro systems whenever high reliability is required; it is then worth while to point out how the general criteria always employed to improve reliability (redundance on signals, components and systems themselves) are still employed with microprocessor structures. In this case, however, a high degree of redundancy is not required, since these systems can detect most of the possible failures by themselves and, if needed, can go on operating, automatically assigning the task of the faulty part to the others, so improving reliability at a lower cost.

4.2 A multimicro-based control device

In order to verify how the general considerations written above can be applied, a general purpose multimicro control device was studied and a prototype is now at its final implementation. This device is based on a three microcomputers hardware, as shown in Fig. 3.

The tasks of each microcomputer are indicated in fig. 4 and can be explained as follows :

- the three microprocessors can communicate one another through a common memory (RAM); they all can access this memory, being forced in a wait state if another one is already accessing it;
- the first microcomputer (μP1) acquires the signals coming from the system to be controlled (both analogical and digital signals) and stores them in the common memory; the analogical signals are sampled at a programmable sampling frequency and then converted to digital by an ADC;
- the second microcomputer (μP2) continuously monitors the system processing the signals acquired by μP1, in order to detect any operating condition;
- if an operating condition is detected, the third microcomputer (μP3) determines the operation to perform; since this task requires high level mathematical capabilities, it can access a fast floating-point unit.

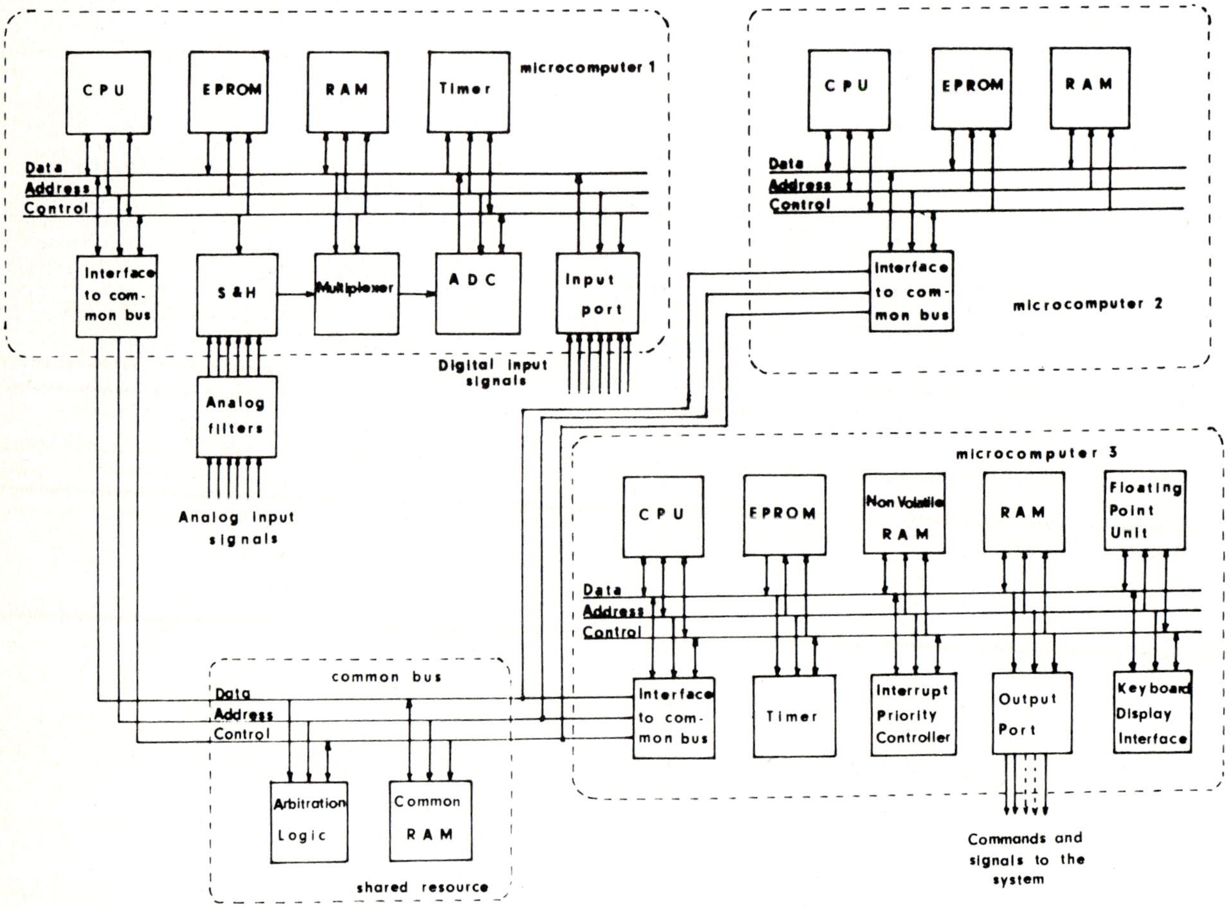

Fig. 3
Hardware architecture of a general purpose three-microcomputer-based control device

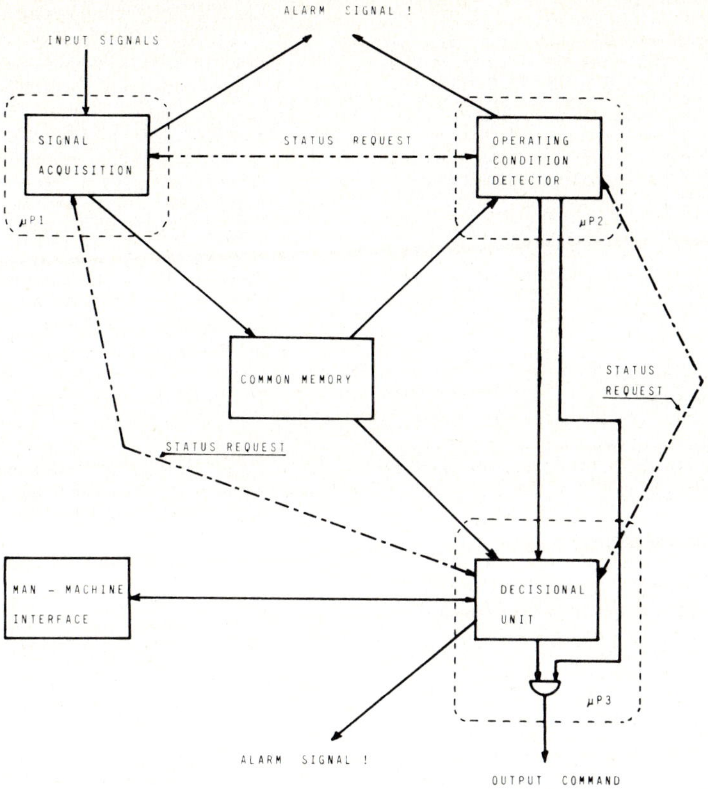

Fig. 4
Block diagram of the control device. The tasks of each microcomputer are indicated as well as the operating signals and the self-test signals

As far as reliability is concerned, most of the measures illustrated in the previous sections have been taken; all three microcomputers feature self-test capabilities, that let them monitor their most critical components [1], [5]. Moreover, they can ask one another their status, so that an alarm signal can be output by any of them, if the faulty one cannot output any signal by itself (as indicated in fig. 4).
The device can thus detect virtually any fault and can then signal it; since this device was supposed to carry out protective functions, so that it will stay in idle status for very long periods, it was assumed that the fault could be repaired before the equipment is required to operate. Anyway, in order to prevent any uncorrect tripping command, the command itself coming from μP3, cannot be issued if μP2 does not issue a command too when an operating condition is detected thus having an hardware redundancy of software operations.
Although not all measures indicated in the previous sections have been taken, the device was considered reliable enough with regard to its real functions, being not worth while the incremental cost of any further increment of reliability.

5. CONCLUSIONS

The paper showed how microprocessor structures, and particularly multimicro structures, are optimal when highly reliable systems are required.
Then indications were given about how to apply multimicro capabilities in control and protective systems : of course lots of possible combinations of the examples given are possible, in order to obtain, in the sense of increasing reliability :

- systems that can detect and signal their faulty status;
- systems that, when a failure occurs, stop operating;
- systems that, when a failure occurs, prevent uncorrect operations;
- systems that can go on operating correctly even if a failure occured (fault-tolerant systems).

The choice between these possible levels of reliability is anyway submitted by the correct evaluation of the needs of the system to be controlled or protected and, after all, by economical considerations.

REFERENCES

[1] D. Jones, Built in test capabilities could cure µP-based-system ills, E D N, April 15, 1981

[2] F.G. Snyder, Modular fault tolerance keeps computer systems reliable, Electronic Design, May 14, 1981

[3] A. Retus, P. Turri, Testing criteria and their influence on reliability and availability of protective relays, EUROCON 82, Copenhagen

[4] L. Benetazzo, Affidabilità ed autodiagnosi dei sistemi di misura a microprocessore, Convegno scientifico su il microprocessore nella misura delle grandezze elettriche. Stato dell'arte e prospettive di sviluppo, Milano, 15 - 16 ottobre 1982

[5] A. Ferrero, L'autodiagnosi come strumento per aumentare l'affidabilità dei sistemi di misura a microprocessore, Convegno scientifico su il microprocessore nella misura delle grandezze elettriche ...... Milano, 15 - 16 ottobre 1982

(1) Generally, in order to achieve a high reliability of the whole system, multiple control and protective devices are provided for the same function.

(2) A memory read or write operation stimulates all components interested (CPU, memory, bus) quite in the same way both if run by a self-test procedure or by an operating procedure.

(3) This is the typical case of protective relays on electrical power networks, that can stay in idle status even for months, but must operate correctly whenever a fault occurs on the protected section of the network.

(4) This is the typical case of any regulating-device (voltage, frequency, power, ... regulators) on electrical power networks, that have operating to idle status ratio shorter than that of protective devices.

MICROCOMPUTERS: Developments in Industry, Business and Education
D.R. Wilson and C.J. van Spronsen (eds.) /© EUROMICRO, 1983
Elsevier Science Publishers B.V. (North-Holland)

AN EASILY TESTABLE SPEECH SYNTHESIZER

Giuseppe CAPIZZI - Cesario CIANCI - Marcello MELGARA

CSELT - Centro Studi e Laboratori Telecomunicazioni
Via G.Reiss Romoli, 274 - 10148 Torino (ITALY)

This paper deals with the design of a functionally reconfigurable test-oriented LSI chip[1]. The device implements a high performance speech synthesizer, including internal microprograms for on-line non-concurrent functional self-testing.
After a brief presentation of chip performance, the paper describes the internal architecture in relation with system testability.
The control unit design uses Finite State Machine (FSM), implemented with PLAs and registers, and an internal microprogram ROM, the operative unit is implemented with functionally partitioned blocks communicating through buses.
The testing strategies adopted are different for the two parts and make use of two external test pins. The control unit test is achieved through a scan path of the PLAs and the microinstruction register.
The operative part is tested at functional level, isolating and verifying the different blocks one by one by means of internal microprograms.
The external microprocessor, which the speech synthesizer is connected to, can force the chip into test mode and then run internal microprograms, which functionally energize each block belonging to the operative part. The microprocessor can also monitor the test evolution either observing the external data bus or collecting bits from the serial output.
During normal operation, the microprocessor can observe chip state reading a status word which contains some significant internal information.

Keywords:
Speech synthesis, testing, functional reconfiguration, on chip firmware implemented functional test, scan path.

1. INTRODUCTION

In 1979 a prototype of an eight-channel digital speech synthesizer[2] [5, 6] called MUSA (MUltichannel Speaker Automata) was built by CSELT. It was employed in an automatic vocal response system for the Italian language.

In perspective of future applications, for instance telecommunications, office automation and computer aided instruction (CAI), a single-channel version of the synthesizer has been designed to be implemented on a monolithic chip.

The synthesizer exploits a speech production model composed of a 10th or 12th order digital lattice filter and two excitation generators for voiced and unvoiced sounds.

The Speech synthesis is based on LPC (Linear Predictive Code) technique. To recall the meaning of some parameters, the basic elements of an LPC voice synthesizer are illustrated in Figure 1. The filter modeling the vocal tract (which is normally characterized by the reflection coefficients ki of

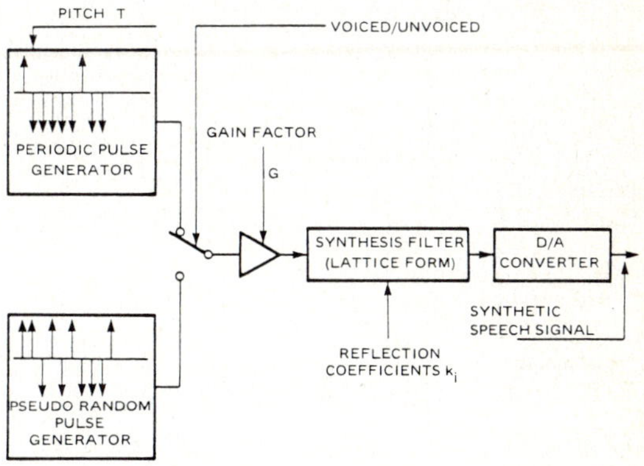

Fig. 1 - Model of human speech production; speech synthesizer based on LPC techniques; k_i coefficients, G and T are assumed to be constant in the time interval D

[1-2] *Patent pending*

an acoustic tube with stiff walls and variable cross-section) is excited by a periodic sequence of pulses of period T equal to the pitch or by a sequence of random pulses according to whether the sound is voiced or unvoiced. The intensity of the output sound is controlled by a gain factor G.

The filter parameters are held constant for a variable frame length identified by the coefficient D, which corresponds to the steady state of the filter. In the case of a pitch synchronous synthesis, the speech parameters are updated at the end of period T after the scheduled time interval D is elapsed, meanwhile the new D coefficient is loaded to take care of the next frame period.

The main features of the chip are:

- selectable sampling frequency (8 or 10 kHz);
- pitch synchronous synthesis;
- variable frame length;
- programmable de-emphasis capability;
- analog output (10 bit D/A converter);
- digital serial output (12 bit linear or 8 bit μ-law PCM samples).

These features raise from the need to obtain a device which covers a wide application field and produces a high quality speech synthesis [2].

Figure 2 shows a general structure for a vocal synthesis system, composed by the speech synthesizer, an eight-bit microprocessor, a memory (PROM) storing the parameter codes of the speech signal.

The goal was to design a chip implementing the aforementioned features and easy to test: the operative part is made up of functionally reconfigurable blocks controlled by a horizontal microinstruction. The internal memory also contains some microprograms capable of a functional test of the separate blocks.

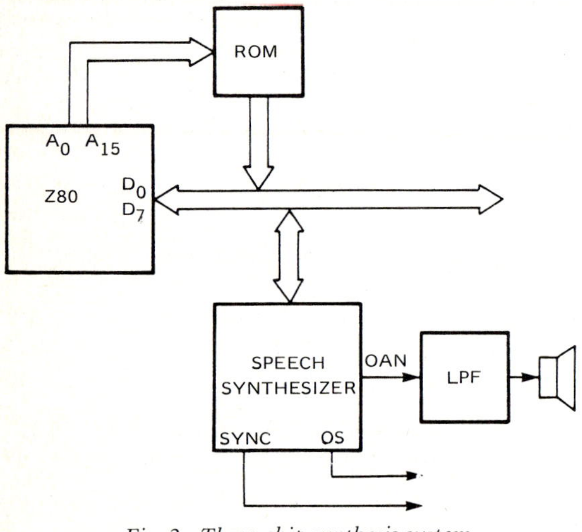

Fig. 2 - Three-chip synthesis system

The modes of operation are two: normal and test mode. The operation mode is selectable by an external pin. During the normal operation mode, the control unit is configured so as to execute the vocal signal synthesis microprogram; in test mode, the unit is arranged so as to address the test microprogram to be run, while some blocks belonging to the operative part are reconfigured to simplify test procedures.

The control unit is implemented as FSM, using multiple PLAs; the algorithmic state machine (ASM) [3] which describes each FSM includes different paths depending on the operation mode selected.

Since the operative part test is conditioned by correct working of the control unit, a scan path [4] is implemented for a statical test of PLAs, program counter and instruction register.

The external microprocessor, which the speech synthesizer is connected to, can force the chip into test mode and then run internal microprograms, which functionally excitate each block belonging to the operative part. The microprocessor can also monitor test evolution either observing the external data bus or collecting bits from the serial output.

During the normal operation mode, the microprocessor can observe the chip state reading a status word which contains some particular internal parameters.

2. CHIP ARCHITECTURE

The choice of the chip architecture has been suggested by the synthesis algorithm (pitch synchronous) and by the need to implement an easily testable device.

In the normal operation mode, the device has to execute real time computations, then the data processing system should be released, in a clever way, from the data exchange time with the microprocessor. In test mode, according to the test strategies used, as described in the next section, the different functional blocks should be usefully partitioned and excited independently.

Figure 3 shows the block scheme of the chip. The overall structure is hinged on three buses which the functional blocks of the speech synthesizer are connected to. The eight bit input/output bus is connected to the microprocessor and through it data are exchanged, according to the operation mode selected: vocal signal parameter codes, control words, interrupt vector, virtual address and loop number of the test microinstructions.

In test mode, this bus is directly connected to the internal bus BUSDAT; in such a way the system observability can be improved.

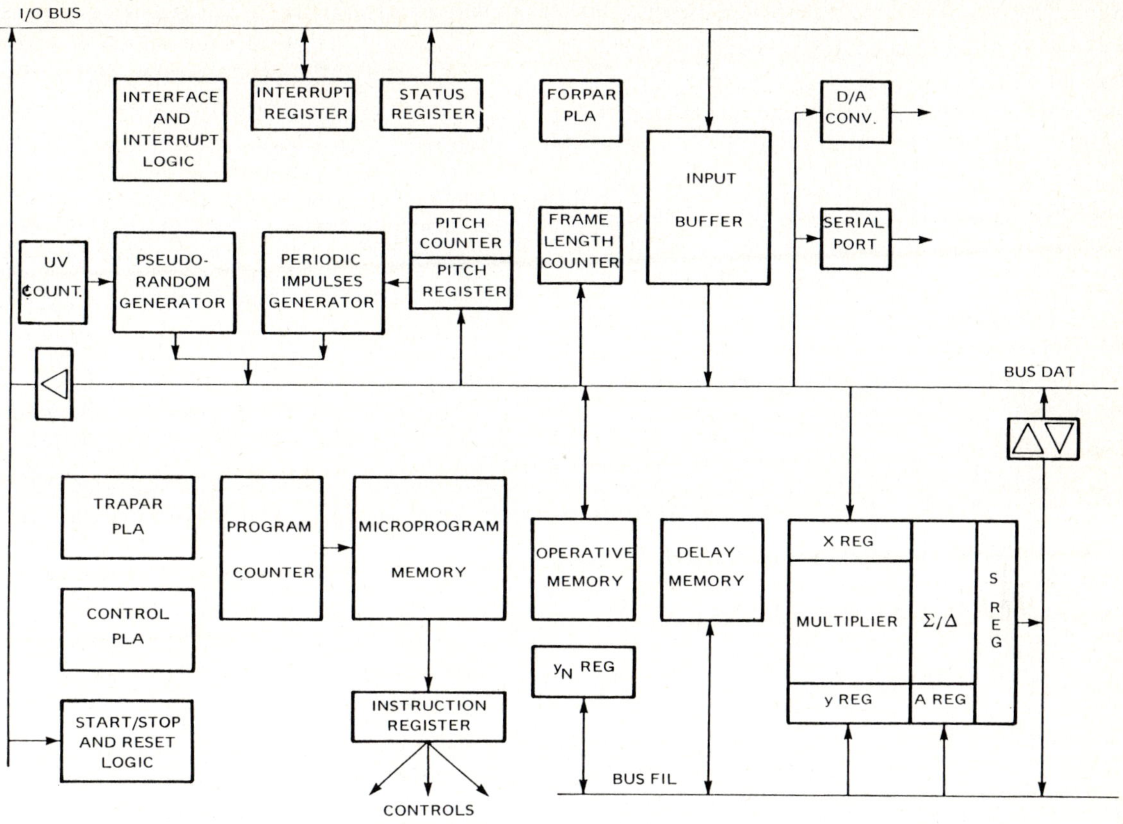

Fig. 3 - Block diagram of the speech synthesizer

On the last bus, eight up to twelve bits travel according to the specific function.

The sources for BUSDAT are represented by: LPC parameter input buffers, ROMs containing the excitation samples, operative memory which stores lattice filter coefficient, arithmetic unit whose internal bus is called BUSFIL. The data destinations for BUSDAT are represented by: pitch register, frame length counter, operative memory, X register of multiplier, DAC register, serial port.

The fourteen-bit bus BUSFIL connects: filter delay memory, YN register containing the present sample, Y register of the multiplier, input register of the algebraic adder, S register containing the result of the arithmetic computation.

The operative unit is controlled by a twentythree-bit microinstruction. The microprogram sequencing is handled by an FSM implemented with the PLA, called CONTROL. In normal mode, the jump address and the loop count of the microinstructions are mapped through two ROMs. The ROMs addressing is achieved by the concatenation of the contents of a two-bit counter and of a two-bit register. In test mode the register and the counter are externally loaded to address the test routine selected. The parameter transfer from the input buffers to the operative memory is monitored by an FSM implemented with the PLA TRAPAR. The data exchange process with the microprocessor and the data formatting are controlled by the PLA FORPAR and the interrupt logic network.

3. TEST STRATEGIES

The speech synthesizer has to produce a vocal signal sample every 100 or 125 microseconds depending on the sampling frequency selected. If a device is implemented according to those specifications without foreseeing some convenient mechanism to test it, the test itself and the diagnosis would become a jig-saw puzzle. As a consequence, the time consumed to produce test patterns would be longer than the chip design; besides production test time would not be acceptable.

The first aim was to find an architecture and a hardware implementation allowing test patterns to be run at clock frequency (2 MHz) rather than at vocal signal sampling frequency (8 or 10 kHz). The architecture described in the previous section allows this strategy and raises the total controllability and observability.

While the detailed test procedures for the control unit and the data path are analysed in the next sections, the general test strategies are here presented. An external pin (TEST1) forces the speech synthesizer running either in normal operation mode, giving a vocal signal sample every 100 or 125 microsec, or in test mode. Using simplified external procedures, the circuit can be reconfigured in different functional blocks, easier to test.

The design architecture shows immediately that the test strategies of the control unit and the operative part have to be different. When the control part is tested, the operative part is kept in an idle state, for not writing the internal buses; this state is achieved by a second pin (TEST2); the control part static test is performed with a simplified scan set technique, using the I/O bus to enter the control signals and to manage the data.

Once the control unit test is over, the device is externally reconfigured as simpler functional blocks which are tested one by one; the machine is split into the following parts: excitation sample ROMs, input buffer and operative memory containing the LPC filter parameters, filter delay memory, pitch and frame length counters, digital serial output register, YN register and arithmetic unit. Since the D/A converter is not functionally testable, dedicated test procedures are foreseen.

A trade off had to be reached among the number of functional blocks to be independently tested, the microprogram row count and the architecture complexity. The actual solution allows homogeneous functional blocks to be obtained whose test pattern generation is automatic or at least repetitive; the only block not splitted into simpler parts is the arithmetic unit composed by multiplier, adder/subtractor and overflow control logic; nevertheless, this part of logic is combinatorial and test pattern generation is quite fast and automatic.

An horizontal microinstruction without coding of functional block control field and without field overlay has been implemented for driving in parallel each single signal; on the other hand, the actual instruction length (23 bits) did not strictly require coding. This decision was also conditioned by the choice of using a unique ROM for running test programs without fundamental modifications of the control unit design.

Finally, for a partial but continuous on-line monitoring, an eight-bit status register has been added, which contains information about some basic internal signals.

4. CONTROL UNIT TEST

The control unit includes: three PLAs which synthesize FSMs and a microprogram ROM along with the sequencing logic associated. The PLA FORPAR controls the reception and the formatting of the data transmitted by the microprocessor; the PLA TRAPAR monitors the parameters transfer from the input buffers to the operative memory. The PLA CONTROL manages the microprogram sequencing, monitoring the virtual address register and the loop counter.

Figure 4 shows a detailed block diagram of the control unit concerning the microprogram sequencing logic, ROM and the pipeline register. The control unit architecture was dictated by both consideration about the algorithm to be implemented (neither jump on arithmetic flag condition nor jump to subroutines are foreseen), and the possibility of virutally addressing the test microprogram specifying the repetition number.

The sequencing operations of the control unit are:

a) continue;

b) jump to the entry point specified, until loop counter contents are not zero.

When the microinstruction signal BIR is active, the loop counter contents are examinated. if they are equal to zero, their contents are decreased and the jump address, derived mapping the virtual entry point through ROM ENTRY, is loaded into the program counter, otherwise different paths are foreseen depending on TEST1 logic value.

The part of ASM referred in Figure 5 shows how the control unit behaviour is conditioned by the actual functional mode selected by the pin TEST1; the meaning of the other signals appearing in the drawing are not important in this context.

In normal mode, the instructions implementing the vocal signal synthesis have to be executed. sequencing and iteration number are defined a priori. The less significant bits of the entry point register address both the entry point memory and the loop memory; the entry point register is increased every time the loop counter reaches its terminal count.

In test mode, the virtual address and the repetition number are derived from the control words written by the external microprocessor directly into the respective registers. Again, when the microinstruction signal BIR = 1, if TCLOOP (terminal count) = 0, the jump address is loaded and the

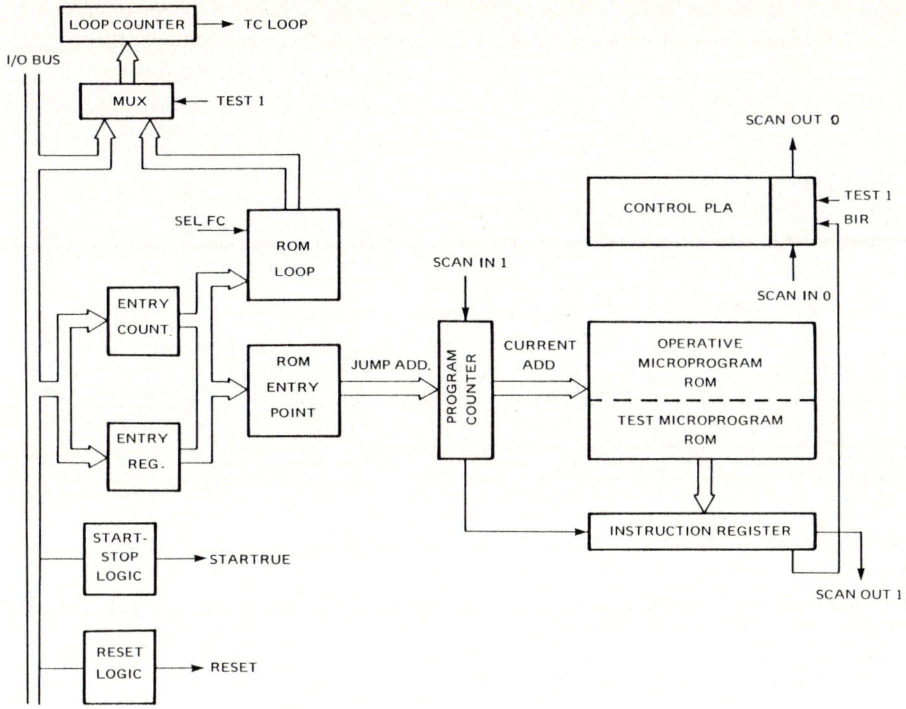

Fig. 4 - Functional block diagram of the control unit

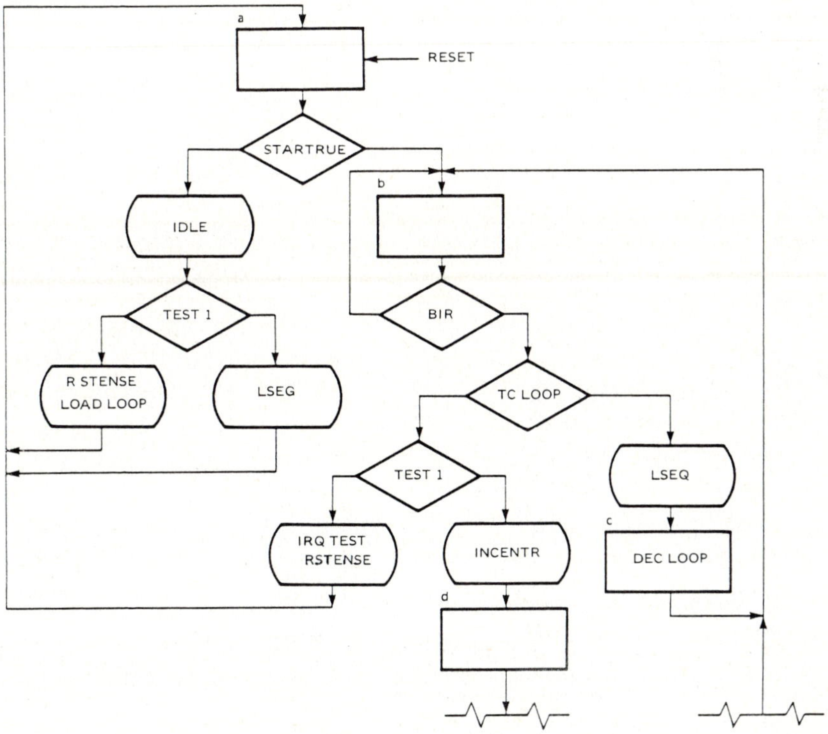

Fig. 5 - Part of control unit ASM

loop counter is decreased; on the other hand, if TCLOOP = 1, an interrupt is sent to inform the microprocessor that the test program is over.

The control unit represents the hard core for the operative part functional test, then an as exhaustively as possible verification of the correctness of its operation is convenient. Since the control unit has been designed using multiple PLAs and a microprogram ROM, a scan set technique is quite easy and unexpensive to connect the nerve-centers. Two shift register chains, with independent I/O, have been implemented: the first links PLA input and output all together, the second connects the program counter to the instruction register.

The Scan procedure is enabled by pin TEST2; the I/O bus is used to transfer both serial patterns and the control signals associated. Figure 6 shows the network implementing the scan register for the PLA inputs and outputs; the logic added to the standard PLA can be easily seen on the drawing. The input one-bit decoders have been modified adding two transfer gates to implement the register. The scan path allows the PLAs to be isolated from the other circuitry, injecting data into the inputs and observing the corresponding outputs. The data inputs sent to the PLAs can also be read by the other modules or the outputs for driving the downstream logic in a controlled way can be directly written, thus complete controllability and observability of FSMs is achieved.

The second scan register accesses the program counter and the instruction register. The decision was taken because the diagnosis of this part of the network is basic in the prototype debugging in fact a fault occurring in some operative block could not be distinguished from a fault due to a non correct functionality of the addressing logic and the microprogram ROM.

The executable procedures using this part of logic are:

- to test the network logic feeding the program counter and looking at their contents;
- to test microprogram ROM by loading a known address into the program counter and looking at instruction register contents;
- to program the instruction register for both controlling operative part functional blocks and producing a new microinstruction not written into ROM.

5. OPERATIVE PART TEST

As earlier mentioned, the operative part test consists of: isolating the different functional blocks, stimulating each of them with appropriate test patterns, observing the response via I/O bus or the serial port and verifying their correctness.

The operative part test is subsequent to the control part test, which is executed only if the first ran correctly. The funcitonal test steps for the operative part are listed below.

(1) The microprocessor loads the test patterns into the input buffer (Fig. 7a) via the I/O bus with the usual procedure as in normal mode.

(2) The device is put into test mode (by means of the pin TEST1).

(3) The microprocessor sends the circuit the virtual address of the first test microprogram; it allows the correct loading of the data into the input buffer to be verified observing, through the serial port, the signals transferred to the operative and delay memories (Fig. 7b).

(4) The next microprograms are addressed: they allow the operative memory and the delay memory opera-

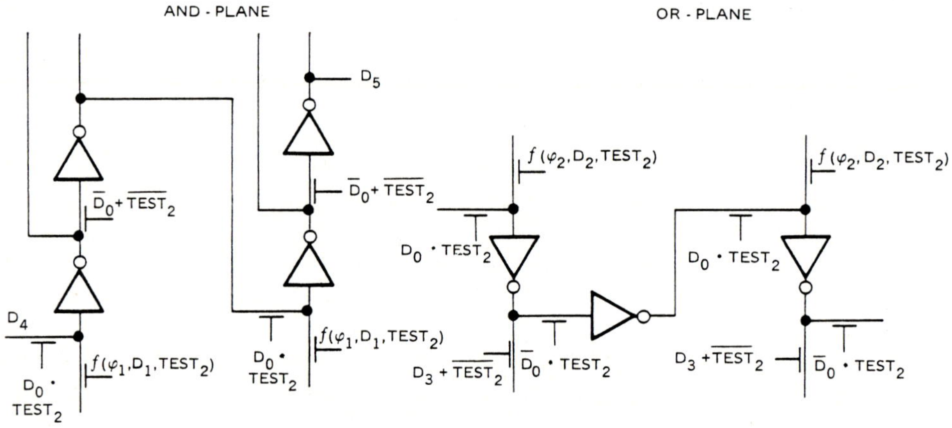

Fig. 6 - Scheme of scan register connected to PLAs

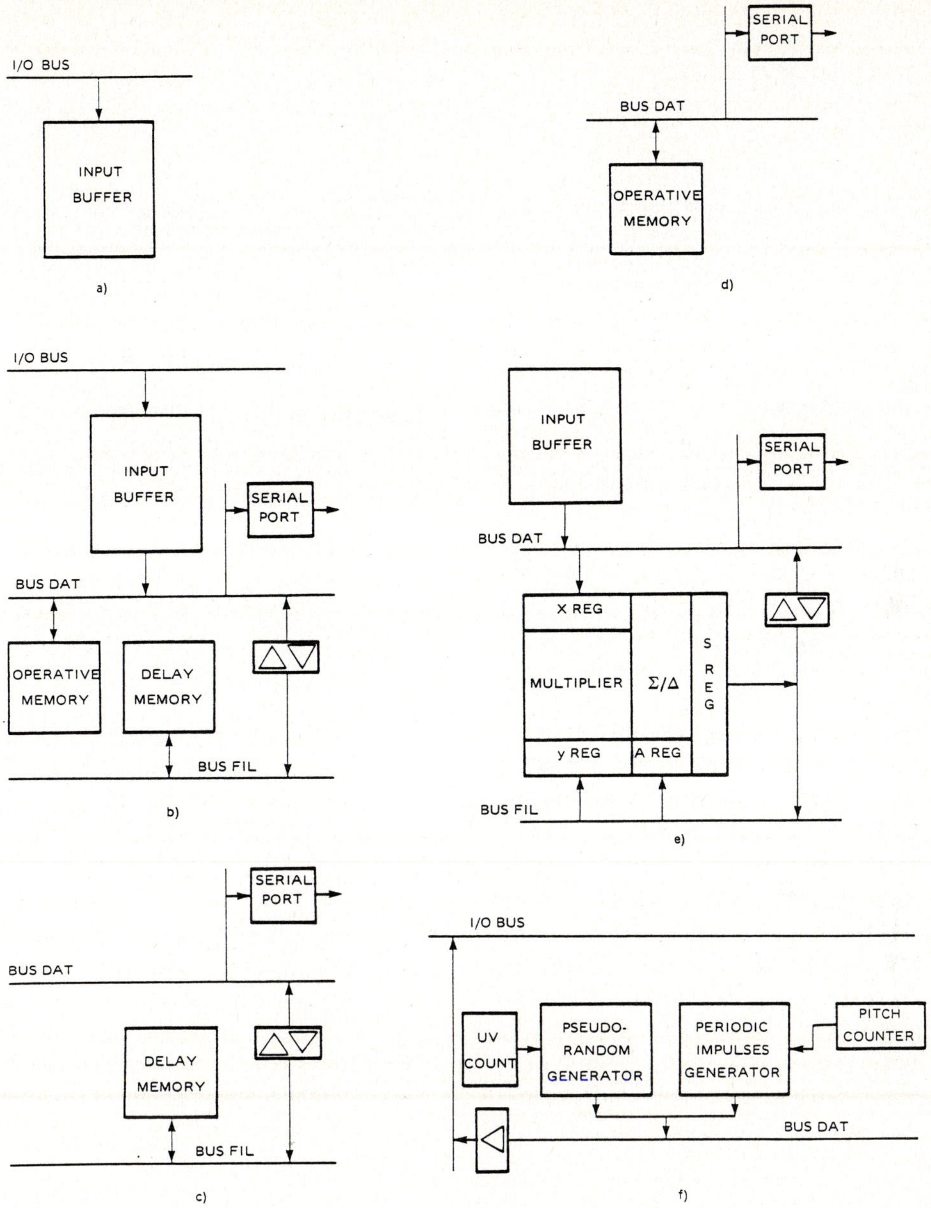

Fig. 7 - Partitioning of the operative part

tions to be verified observing through the serial port the data previously loaded (Figs. 7c, 7d).

The register YNREG is tested with a similar procedure and the drawings are leaved out for brevity. The multiplier and adder/subtractor test is achieved loading appropriate patterns from the input buffers into XREG, YREG and AREG; the contents of SREG are read through the serial output (Fig. 7e).

The contents of the ROMs, containing the excitation samples of the voiced and unvoiced sounds, are tested in the following way:

a) the device is put in test mode; the ROM (periodic pulse generators or pseudorandom generator) under test is selected by an appropriate control word sent by the microprocessor. The ROM addresses are taken from the pitch counter.

b) The loop counter and the microprogram virtual address are loaded using external control words.

c) The I/O bus is connected to BUSDAT.

d) The test microprogram increases step-by-step the contents of the pitch counter and transfers the addressed sample (ROM word) to the I/O bus.

It is worthwhile noting that the excitation samples written into ROMs are quantized or decoded with eight bits so they are efficiently read through the I/O bus.

CONCLUSION

The structured design and testability techniques adopted in implementing this high performance speech synthesizer led to a large use of regular structures and to a quite easy solution of test problems.

Only two external test pins are used within a standard 28 pin package, adopting for test purposes the idle pins and paths; as a matter of fact, for some test procedures up to 13 pins are employed to settle externally the device feeding different functional blocks and the control unit part through the various buses, enabling appropriate control signals. The most remarkable advantage results in test-cost saving, i.e. time for test pattern generation and pattern number, as a consequence time to run test on automatic test equipment (ATE) is drastically reduced.

The chip architecture implemented and the test strategies applied, on the other hand, led to a more involved control unit design in comparison with a trivial design solution, which could result to be hardly testable. Besides, the internal bus architecture and the control signal paths required an harder work in the chip planning and routing.

The area added to enhance device testability is about 10 to 15 percent, while some logical solutions implemented, such as parallel/parallel 10 by 14 bit not pipelined multiplier and the memories built with shift registers (instead of RAMs) were adopted for design simplification and circuit evaluation but they do not depend on test procedures.

A last remarkable feature of the chip concerns the capability of the architecture implemented to be tested by the microprocessor, either off-line or in idle time. The microprocessor, conveniently programmed, can force in test mode the circuit and then write and read test patterns. The tests performed and their cover obviously depend on the software development and the additional extra ROM, where the patterns are stored.

REFERENCES

[1] Bose P., Abraham J.A.. "Test generation for programmable logic arrays", Proc. 19th D.A.C. (June '82), 574-580.

[2] Capizzi G., Cianci C., Melgara M., Nebbia L., Ponte G., Babini G.. "Caratteristiche del circuito integrato progettato in CSELT per la sintesi della voce", CSELT internal report n. 82.07.239 (July 1982).

[3] Clare C.R.: "Designing logic systems using state machines" (Mc Graw Hill, New York, 1973).

[4] Eichelberger E.B., T.W.Williams. "A logic design structure for LSI testing", Proc. 14th D.A.C. (June '77), 462-486

[5] Lucchini P., Nebbia L., Ponte G., Panarotto G.: "Realizzazione di un prototipo di sintetizzatore vocale", CSELT internal report n. 78.06.291 (June 1978).

[6] Nebbia L., Lucchini P.: "Eight channels digital speech synthesizer based on LPC techniques", Proc. IEEE ICASSP, Washington D.C. (1979).

MICROCOMPUTERS: Developments in Industry, Business and Education
D.R. Wilson and C.J. van Spronsen (eds.) /© EUROMICRO, 1983
Elsevier Science Publishers B.V. (North-Holland)

TEST AND RELIABILITY EVALUATION OF MICROPROCESSORS : A CASE STUDY

Chantal ROBACH
IMAG Laboratory
BP 68 - 38402 SAINT-MARTIN D'HERES Cedex
FRANCE

Gilles MICHEL
E.P. SCHLUMBERGER
BP 202 - 92141 CLAMART Cedex
FRANCE

Introduction of microprocessors and their auxiliary circuits for downhole instrumentation used in oil and geothermal wells requires a high-level confidence in the failure rate of these circuits in a given environment : temperature ranging from -55°C uphole to +200°C downhole.
The main purpose of this study is to determine the mean life-time at 200°C for the N-MOS Zilog Z80 microprocessor and its family devices. This paper summarizes the results obtained on several samples of Z80 devices tested up to 210°C.

1. INTRODUCTION

The main purpose of this study is to determine the failure rate of the N-MOS Zilog Z80 microprocessor after 200 hours' heating.
In a first step we determine the number of CPUs which run at 200°C. This first heating eliminates the chips which present youth failures. In a second step we determine the failure rate λ at 200°C.
In order to perform this temperature ageing a special harware system has been designed. It allows to run a dedicated software on the devices under test. Every device is aged by using a dynamic life test circuit : it exercises the clock and executes a continuous series of RESET operations which activate much of the circuit. At previously defined intervals the test software is executed on each device.
This paper successively describes :

* the test method principles for the microprocessor,
* the hardware test system,
* the experiment outlines and the reliability evaluation results.

2. THE TEST PROGRAM FOR THE ZILOG Z80 MICROPROCESSOR

2.1. The test method [1]

The test method is based upon a normalized description of the microprocessor : this description is deduced from the symbolic operations of the microprocessor and it is obtained from two pieces of information :

- functional data, which is the set of particulars describing the microprocessor functions i.e the instruction set.
- hardware data, which is the set of particulars related to the microprocessor architecture i.e. the functional block diagram.

a) Microprocessor description
Every microprocessor is described by a set of graphs which feature all the possible functions of the microprocessor together with its architecture : so, an abstract execution graph is associated with every instruction of the microprocessor and it indicates the functions and hardware exercised during the instruction execution.
An abstract execution graph is a bipartite p-arborescence [2] such that :

- the memory elements which are used by the instruction are associated with the first type vertices
- the micro-operations performed during the instruction execution are associated with the second type vertices
- there is an arc between a memory element ME_i and a micro-operation if the micro-operation processes the data stored in ME_i ;
- there is an arc between a micro-operation and a memory element ME_j if the micro-operation issues its result towards ME_j

Example :instructions of the Zilog Z80 microprocessor

Load A, B

The contents of register B is moved to the accumulator A

Load (HL), A

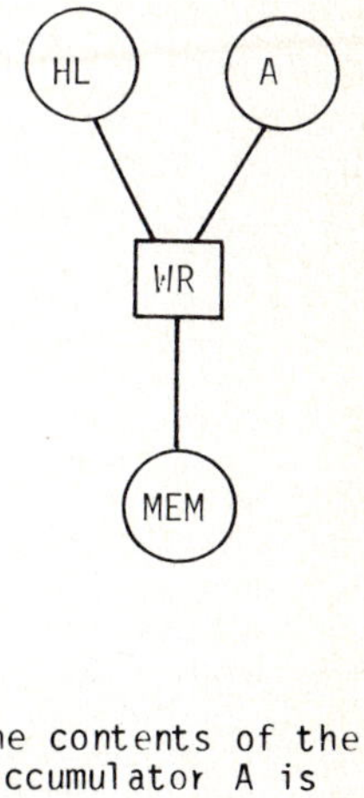

The contents of the accumulator A is moved to the memory location whose address is in registers H and L

Load A. (IX+d)

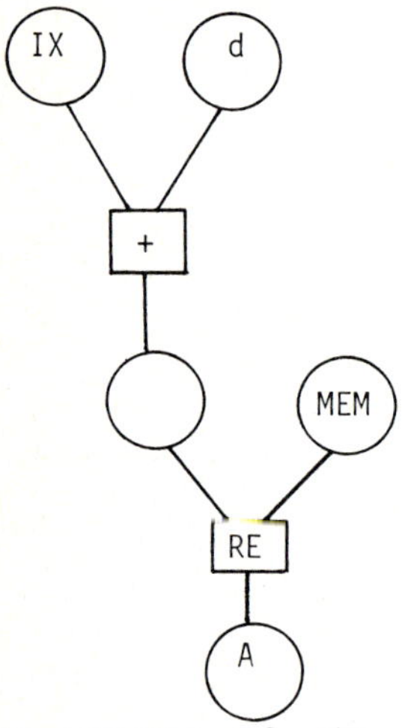

The contents of the memory location whose address is pointed to by IX with an offset of +d. is moved to the accumulator A.

CPI

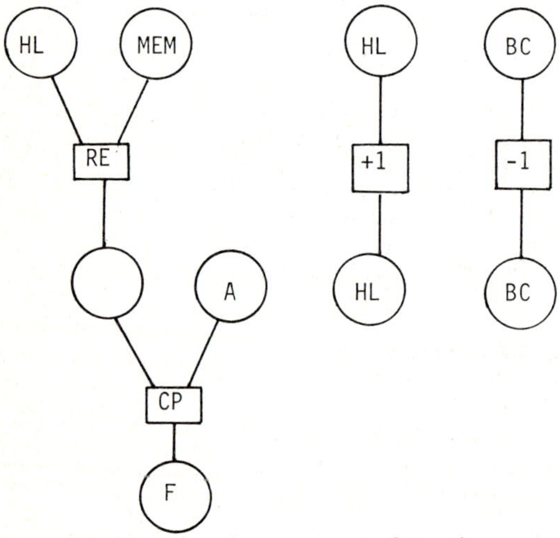

The contents of the memory location whose address is contained in the H and L registers is substracted from the accumulator. The accumulator remains unchanged The condition flag is set as a result of the substraction.

b) Analysis of the instructions

Every instruction being represented by its abstract execution graph. significant test properties for these graphs are looked for . The following criteria are considered :

- the complexity which is measured by the amount of hardware exercised by the instruction
- the accessibility which is measured by the ease of access for the test information while executing the instruction.

Two levels of analysis are considered

* **a structural analysis** whose aim is to analyze the complexity of the non-labelled graphs
We mainly define

- a relation of structural dominance : the graph of an instruction I1 is structurally dominated by the graph of an instruction I2 if the graph of I1 can be embedded into the graph of I2
- refining parameters such as the graph depth i e the number of layers of the deepest arborescence and the degree of multiplicity i e the number of strongly connected components of the graph.

* **a functional analysis** which is performed upon the labelled graphs and allows the instructions accessibility to be studied . This analysis is based upon :

- the commandability of the graph sources i.e. the ease of generating test data towards the sources
- the observability of the graph sinks i.e. the ease of observing a test result from these sinks.

The accessibility of an instruction is then defined as a pair (t.t') where
t is the greatest commandability value of the sources.
t' is the greatest observability value of the sinks.
A relation of functional dominance is then defined as follows
an instruction (t1 t'1)-accessible is functionally dominated by an instruction (t2 t'2)-accessible iff (t1 t'1) ⩽ (t2.t'2) (comparison of boolean vectors).
Refining functional parameters are defined : size of sources and sinks , type of micro-operations.

* **ordering the instructions for testing**
Those two levels of analysis induce a partition of the instruction set into ordered test groups. This partition depends upon the chosen test strategy (Start-Small Start-Big [3]).

c) The test algorithms

The aim is to check the possible errors (or malfunctionings) of the microprocessor by analyzing the logical behaviour of the abstract execution graphs.
Testing is done in two steps :

- verifying the identity of the abstract execution graph associated with the instruction.
- verifying the graph nodes.

* **the conformity test** aims at checking that the graph which is actually executed is the graph which is described
Three types of errors are considered :

- errors concerning source selection.
- errors concerning sink selection.
- errors concerning micro-operation activation.

The conformity test of the abstract execution

graph amounts to checking the sequencor of the microprocessor as well as the activation of internal and external signals

*** the test of the graph elements** aims at ensuring th correct functioning of the operative part
We distinguish :
- the memory elements for which classical memory test methods are applied [4 5]
- the computing units (arithmetic and logic unit shift unit counter .) which are not checked as hardware elements but indirectly through the correct functioning of their actions i.e the micro-operations.

This test is based upon an algebraic analysis · every function is represented by a system of simple equations which display the dependence between the ith component ot the result and the ith components of the operands

$$f_i = \sum_j (\tilde{x}_i \cdot \tilde{y}_i \cdot \quad) \cdot C_i^j$$

The analysis of these functions allows a set of test vectors to be determined for every operation [1]

*** the test program** is then modular : every test module consists in three phases
- initializing the sources with a test vector
- executing the instruction
- observing the sinks of the graph.

These procedures are identical for every graph and are parametered by :
- the graph sources
- the graph sinks.
- the graph micro operations
- the status of the tested elements

2.2. Test program implementation for the Z80 microprocessor

The test program is divided into nine modules as follows

module number	bytes number	number of result bytes
0	512	416
1	1792	176
2	1790	352
3	2591	3200
4	420	304
5	1103	2080
6	111	112
7	444	320
8	105	16

i e 8K bytes for the test program which is stored in PROM and 7K bytes for the expected test results.

3 - THE TEST SYSTEM

The test system has to fulfill two objectives
* testing a device with a verdict about its good or bad functioning · it is a Go/noGo automatic test :
* locating the defect at the level of the faulty instruction : when a fault is detected an error message is edited.

3.1. Hardware architecture

The test system is made up of two identical Z80 microcomputer boards (boards Z80 MCB from Zilog) with REPROM and RAM memories and input/output circuits.
The first board or "Master Board" is organized around a reference microprocessor and manages the test program · the second one or "Slave Board" uses the microprocessor under test as a central processing unit. The CPU of the Slave Board is heated in an oven while the board itself is working at 25°C.
Both boards are connected through the Z80 bus and an electronic switch. The Master Board may read the RAM or REPROM memories on the Slave Board through the switch. Every CPU to be tested executes the test program on the Slave Board
The test program is stored in a REPROM on the Slave Board the test results are saved in the slave RAM. A monitor on the Master Board allows the interaction between the user and the system. and the comparison of prestored reference test results with those given by the microprocessor under test.
The Master Board has a 8K bytes REPROM for the monitor and the reference test results and a 4K bytes RAM used as a general working space area. The Slave Board has a 16K bytes REPROM for the test program and a 4K bytes RAM for the obtained test results The address space is common to both memories : the bus switch is controlled by the Master Board
The test system architecture is given in Figure 1

3.2. Software analysis : the test monitor

The test monitor is constituted by
- a general purpose monitor considered as a supervisor.
- a master monitor
- a slave monitor

a) the general purpose monitor allows the verification of vital functions such as clock generation busses ... : it initializes all peripherals and manages the communications between the system and the operator. While testing is performed it acts as a relay towards the master monitor : otherwise it may be used for checking the test system memories.

b) the master monitor has two main functions
- to choose a test mode.
- to process and to send error messages to the operator.

Three test modes are defined
* an automatic mode in which all the modules of the test program are sequentially executed without any interv ntion from the operator ·

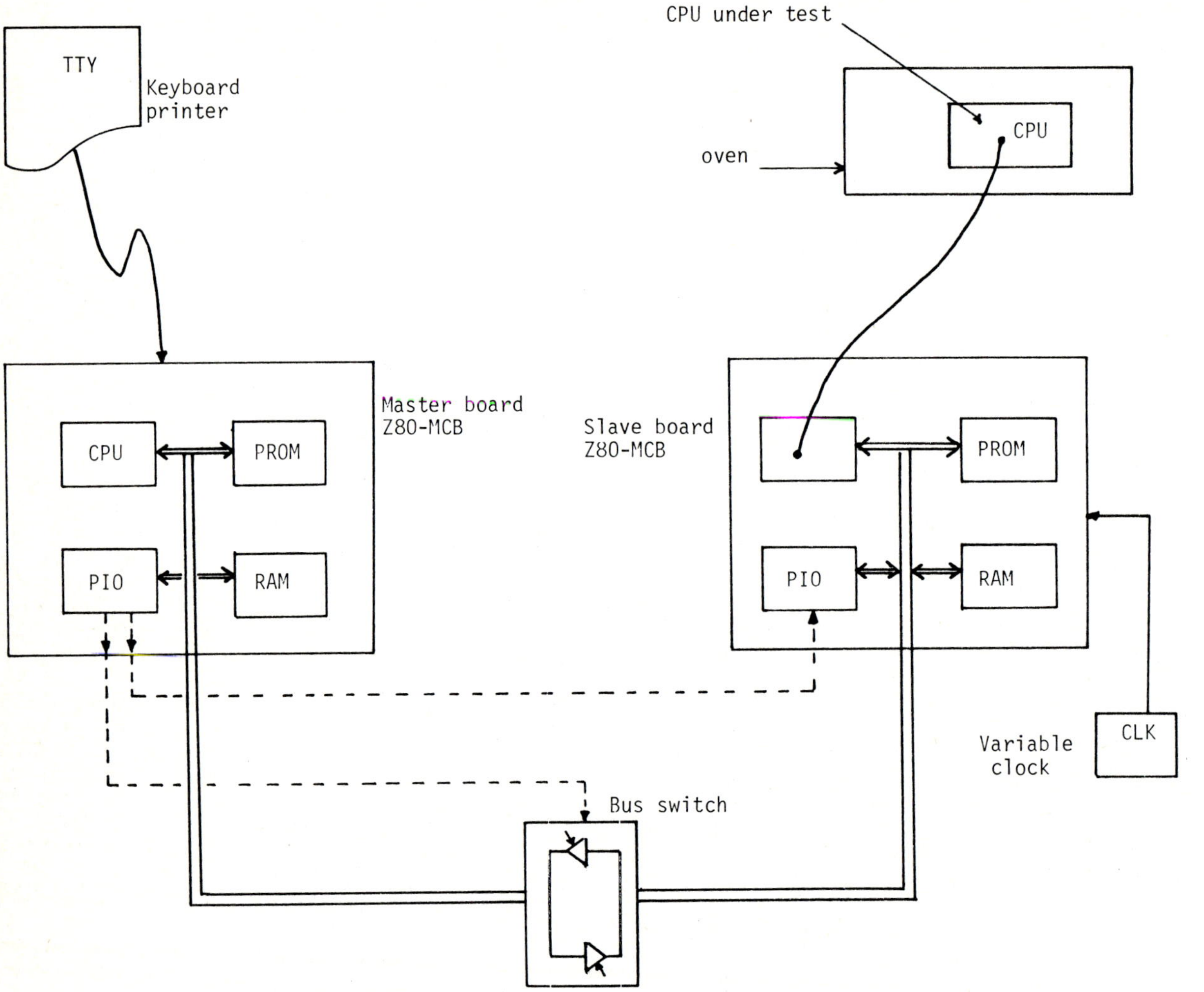

Figure 1: The test system architecture

* a location mode in which the operator selects one of the modules in the test program · the chosen module is executed and the test system waits for another module or another mode ·
* a loop mode in which the test program is entirely and indefinetly repeated unless a stop command is issued by the operator

In each of those modes whenever an error occurs an error message is edited The contents of the error message consists in the number of the test module which detected the fault. the correct and faulty results and the address of the computed result.

c) the slave monitor initializes the parallel interface of the Slave Board and waits for the interrupt which is sent by the master monitor when receiving the interrupt it reads the number of the test module to be executed. through the interface. and calls the test module At the end of the test it sends an interrupt to the master monitor and waits for another order.

3.3. Temporal analysis of the test system functions [7]

The test monitor size is 800 bytes in PROM. i.e 570 bytes for the master monitor and 230 bytes for the slave monitor

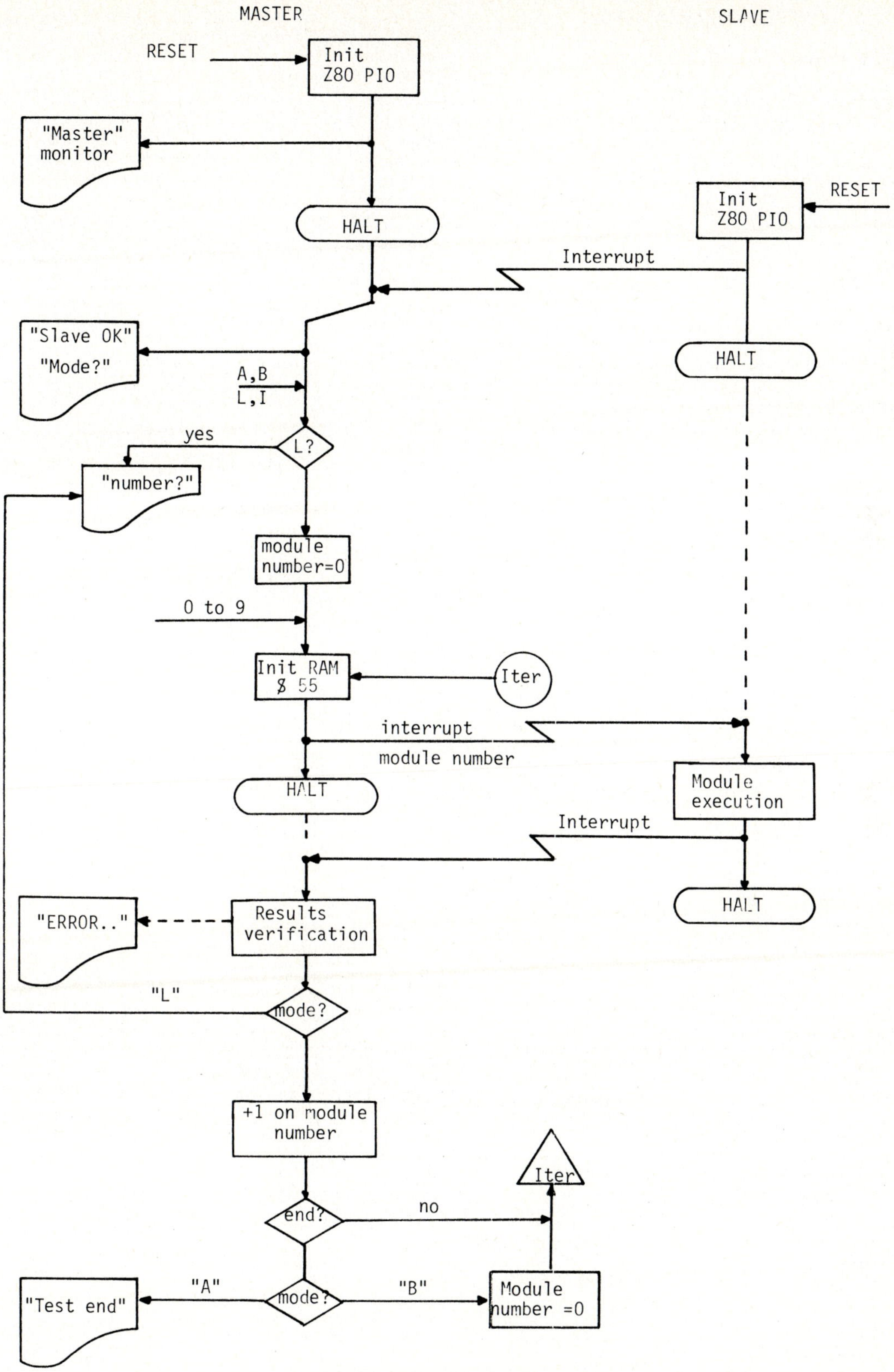
MASTER
SLAVE
RESET
Init Z80 PIO
"Master" monitor
HALT
RESET
Init Z80 PIO
Interrupt
"Slave OK" "Mode?"
HALT
A,B
L,I
yes
L?
"number?"
module number=0
0 to 9
Init RAM $ 55
Iter
interrupt
module number
HALT
Module execution
Interrupt
HALT
"ERROR.."
Results verification
"L"
mode?
+1 on module number
Iter
end?
no
"A"
mode?
"B"
"Test end"
Module number =0

4 - EXPERIMENT AND RELIABILITY EVALUATION

4.1. Experimental study

A series of experiments. derived from the field working conditions has been defined in order to :

- determine upon a batch of microprocessors. the percentage of these circuits which are still working correctly at 200°C
- define the failure rate or the mean life-time of these devices at 200°C.

Every microprocessor is aged during 200 hours at 200°C with a dynamic life test circuit it exercises the clock (1MHz) and executes a continuous series of RESET operations (which exercises much of the CPU) Three high temperature boards with four chips on it, are heated simultaneously The experiment concerned a set of 36 microprocessors (3 batches of 12 chips) They are aged according to the temperature cycle given in Figure 2.

The test program is executed at periodic intervals (marked with the sign Δ). After 100 hours on each batch tests were performed at 210°C for an hour.

4.2. Experimental results

The results of the temperature ageing on the three batches are summarized in Table 1. This table mainly shows that :

* Only 3 out of the 36 microprocessors gave errors at the first heating at 200°C
* 3 more had catastrophic failures during cycles at 200°C
* Two types of intermittent errors are detected; these errors are detected when the devices are heated at 200°C or more and do not occur otherwise These intermittent errors are :
  - either the SRAr instruction (Shift Right Arithmetic) is faulty (denoted *).
  - or both SRAr and RRC r (Rotate Right Circular) instructions are faulty (denoted **)
* Intermittent errors also appear for two undefined bits of the flag register the undefined value is X = 0 for temperatures inferior to 195°C and is changed into X=1 for higher temperatures (denoted X). This type of error does not affect the device correctness.

Table 1 gives the general results on the three batches.

Table 2 presents the evolution of the experiment for batch n°2 It can be seen that catastrophic failures do not appear at the beginning of the ageing.

Table 3 presents the results for the three different manufacturing series tested it appears that the third batch and the second ones are better than the first one resulting probably from changes in the manufacturing process and from improvements in the hardware test system

Figure 2: Temperature ageing cycle

	Devices working at 200°C	Devices working at 200°C after 200 hours	total number of of failures	Catastrophic failures
Batch n°1	12	6	6	0
Batch n°2	9	8	4	2
Batch n°3	12	11	1	1
Total	33	25	11	3

Table 1 General results on the three batches

24h cycles	T °C	13	14	15	16	17	18	19	20	21	22	23	24
		Microprocessor number											
C1	160	-		-	-		-	-	-		-	-	-
	170	-		-	-	-	-		-	-	-	-	**
	180	-	-	-	-	-	-	-	-		-		**
	190	-	-		-	-	-			-	-		**
	200	X	X	X	-	-	**	-	-	-	*		**
	25	-		-	-	-	-	-	-	-		-	-
C2	200	X	X	X	-	-	**	-		-	*	-	**
	25	-	-		-	-	-	-		-	-	-	-
C3	200	X	X	X	-	-	**	-	-	-	*	-	**
	25	-		-	-				-		-	-	
C4	200	X	X	X	-	-	**	-	-	-	*	-	
	25	-	-	-	-		-			-	-	-	
C5	200	X	X	X		-	**	-	-	-	*	-	
	210	X	X	X	X	X	**	-	*	*	**	-	
	200	X	X	X	-	-	**	-	-		*	-	
	25	-	-	-	-		-	-	-	-	-	-	
C6	200	X	X	X	-	-	**	-		-	*	-	
	210	X	X	X	X	X	**	-		*	**	-	
	200	X	X	X	-	-	**	-		-	*	-	
	25	-	-	-	-	-	-						
C7	200	X	X	X	-	-	**			-	*	-	
C8	210	X	X	X	X	X	**	-		*	**	-	
C9	200	X	X	X	-	-	**	-		-	*	-	
	25	-		-	-	-	-	-			-	-	
T=200h 200°C		G	G	G	G	G	**	G		G	*	G	

G = Good

Table 2 : Experiment results for batch n°2

SERIES 7727-14305: Microprocessor number [batch number]	200°C	7714 04501: Microprocessor number	200°C	7917-8400 WO/XO: Microprocessor number	200°C
1 [1]	**	5 [1]	G	25 [3]	G(X)
2 [1]	**	6 [1]	G	26 [3]	G(X)
3 [1]	G	10 [ ]	G	27 [3]	
4 [1]	**	11 [1]	G	28 [3]	G
7 [1]	**	13 [2]	G(X)	29 [3]	G
8 [1]	G	14 [2]	G(X)	30 [3]	G
9 [1]	*	15 [2]	G(X)	31 [3]	G
12 [1]	**	16 [2]	G	32 [3]	G
18 [2]	**	17 [2]	G	33 [3]	G
19 [2]	G			34 [3]	G(X)
20 [2]				35 [3]	G(X)
21 [2]	G			36 [3]	G(X)
22 [2]	*				
23 [2]	G				
24 [2]					

Table 3 : Results according to the manufacturing series

4.3. Reliability evaluation

According to the results per manufacturing series the failure rate is performed on two groups :

- group A composed of the 36 tested microprocessors
- group B composed of the 21 devices which have given homogeneous results (series 7714-04501 and 7917-8400 X0/W0)

* The first point consists in determining the ratio p of microprocessors which are working at 200°C.

group A : total number of devices : N = 36
number of devices working at 200°C : n = 33

$$\tilde{p} = N/n \quad 0\ 91$$

This estimation is completed by a 5% confidence interval :

$$0.779 \leqslant p \leqslant 0.972$$

group B: N = 21 , n = 21

$$\tilde{p} = 1 \qquad 0\ .84 \leqslant p \leqslant 1$$

* The second point is the evaluation of the failure rate which is estimated with the probability of correct functioning at T = 200 hours.

$$p(T) = e^{-\lambda T}$$

group A :
number of devices working at 200°C : N = 33
number of devices working at T=200 hours n = 25

$$\tilde{p}\ (T) = 0.757$$

which gives $\tilde{\lambda}$ = 0 0014 failures per hour.
So the mean life time $\tau = 1/\lambda$ is then 718 hours and with a 5% confidence interval :

$$370 \leqslant \tau \leqslant 1470 \text{ hours}$$

group B : out of the N = 21 microprocessors working at 200°C (T = 0), 20 are still working at T = 200 hours

$$\tilde{p}\ (T) = 0\ 952$$

which gives $\tilde{\lambda}$ = 0 00024 failures per hour and $\tilde{\tau}$ = 4166 hours
with the 5% confidence interval

$$750 \leqslant \tau \leqslant 24000 \text{ hours.}$$

These results may seem paradoxical since we estimate a mean life time above 700 hours with an experiment limited to 200 hours. This estimation lies upon an exponential law with a constant coefficient. which is not true during the first stage of life cycle So the most credible estimation is the reliability at T=200 hours i.e p(T) = 0.952.

4.4. Reliability evaluation for auxiliary devices

Similar experiments were done on some auxiliary circuits belonging to the Zilog Z80 family :

- the parallel input/output device : PIO
- the serial input/output device : SIO
- the counter timer circuit : CTC.

The results of the experiments are given below

type of device	PIO	SIO	CTC
number of tested devices	24	20	20
experiment time (hours)	72	72	72
temperature °C	180	180	180
mean life tim (hours)	577	480	480

5 - CONCLUSION

The obtained results are significant and homogeneous there is no random dispersion and a precise conclusion was derived : failures in given instructions and in manufacturing batches. The general conclusion is that the considered devices may be used at a high temperature no problem appears at 175°C and the reliability at 200°C is close to 0.95. Besides a chance temperature of 210°C does not generate catastrophic failures These results show that the N-MOS technology in Large Scale Integration presents a very good reliability in high temperature conditions.

REFERENCES

1 ROBACH C and SAUCIER, G , Microprocessor functional testing. 1980 Test Conference. Philadelphia (November 1980) 433-443.

2 ROBACH C. SAUCIER. G.. VELAZCO. R. Flexible test method for microprocessors EUROMICRO Symposium. London (September 1980) 31-37.

3 DENT, J.J. Diagnostic engineering requirements. Proc AFIPS, SJCC (1968) 503-507.

4 Special issue COMPUTER Fault-Tolerant Computing. IEEE Computer Society (March 1980).

5 Tutorial on LSI testing IEEE Catalog N° EH-0 122-2. IEEE Computer Society (1978).

6 ROBACH C. SAUCIER G. Test et fiabilité des microprocesseurs. Second International Conference on Reliability and Maintainability. Perros-Guirec / Tregastel (France) (September 1980) 13-18.

7 ROBACH C MICHEL, G Evaluation expérimentale de la fiabilité d un microprocesseur dans un environnement critique. Schlumberger internal report (November 1979).

MICROCOMPUTERS: Developments in Industry, Business and Education
D.R. Wilson and C.J. van Spronsen (eds.) /© EUROMICRO, 1983
Elsevier Science Publishers B.V. (North-Holland)

A RECONFIGURABLE MULTIPROCESSOR DEVELOPMENT SYSTEM: A POWERFUL TOOL IN COMPUTER SCIENCE EDUCATION

Y. Hoffner

Microprocessor Unit, University of Reading
Reading, United Kingdom

Uni-processor systems simulating multi-programming environments are often used for teaching concurrent programming. Such an approach can obscure the real issues and so confuse the understanding of the concepts involved in concurrent programming. A more desirable approach would be to use a multiprocessor development system. An inexpensive flexible multiprocessor development system, built by the author at the University of Reading is described. Its use in the teaching of the principles of concurrent programming is demonstrated by two examples dealing with the two major problems of concurrent programming:

i) mutual exclusion
ii) communication mechanisms.

1. INTRODUCTION

Uni-processor systems simulating a multi-programming environment are often used for teaching of concurrent programming [1]. It is felt that such an approach may obscure the real issues of the subject and may further confuse undergraduates struggling to understand the concepts involved with concurrent programming. To make a uni-processor appear to be executing processes in parallel, CPU time must be divided between processes. This is usually implemented using a wide range of mechanisms such as: interrupts, software interrupts, interrupt service routines, supervisor calls and schedulers. If these are 'hidden' from the student, there is a risk that he will not be able to fully understand what he is doing. If he is required to be aware of those mechanisms, on the other hand, he is likely to be distracted from the issues of concurrent programming. An alternative approach is to use a multiprocessor development system. Commercially available multiprocessor development systems are, however, beyond the means of most institutions.

This paper describes an inexpensive flexible multiprocessor development system, built by the author at the University of Reading [6,7,8], and its use in the teaching of problems and principles of concurrent programming. Examples of basic exercises are given. These deal with the two major problems of concurrent programming [1]:

i) mutual exclusion
ii) communication mechanisms.

2. THE IMPORTANCE OF TEACHING CONCURRENT PROGRAMMING PRINCIPLES

The concepts of concurrent programming are applicable to a wide range of systems and are therefore of utmost importance to computer science undergraduates. Systems in which such concepts are relevant include:
operating systems, real-time systems, distributed systems and multiprocessor systems:

i) operating systems - [1,4] in which processes interact and compete for shared resources such as printers and memory etc.

ii) real time systems - in which several processes must respond to external events in a specified interval of time.

iii) distributed systems - [2] in which independent units communicate and share resources over short or long distances, e.g. computer networks and distributed data bases.

iv) multiprocessor systems - in which a collection of closely-coupled processors [3,2] cooperate in the execution of an overall task.

The two most important concepts of concurrent programming are:

i) mutual exclusion: because .."it is the abstraction of many synchronisation problems." (Ben-Ari [1]). Mutual exclusion deals with excluding any process from using a resource in use until it has been released.

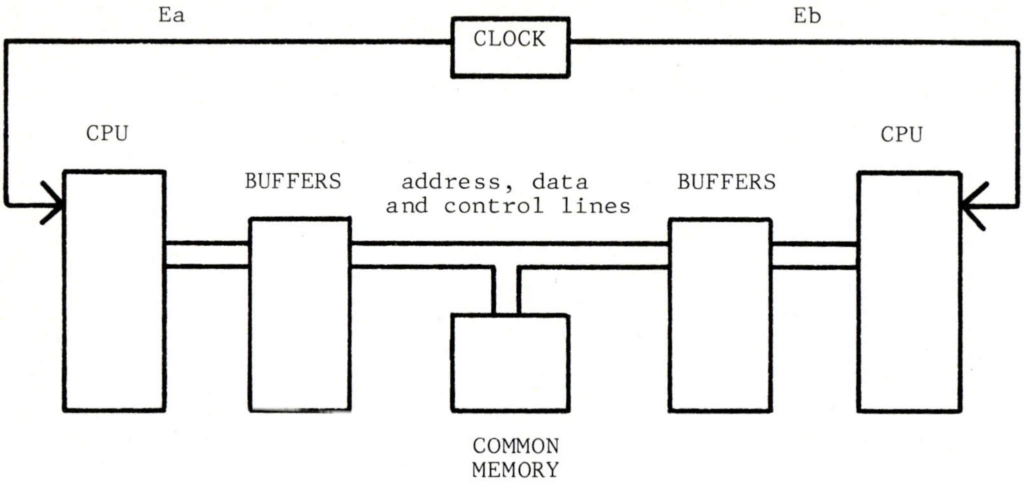

Figure 1. Dual processor system with buffers separating the CPUs from one another and from the common memory.

Figure 2. Diagrams of the non-overlapping synchronization signals used between two communicating systems. Each processor can only access memory on the "high" part of its own clock.

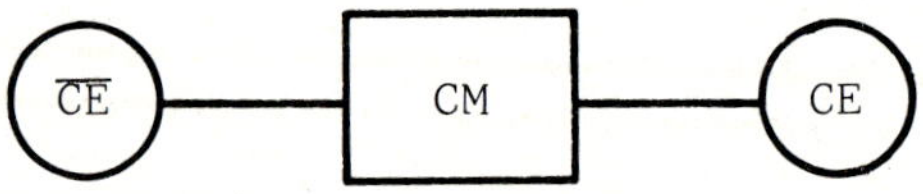

i)
CE = Computing Element

$\overline{CE}$ = Computing Element operating on the alternate phase of a clock
CM = Common Memory

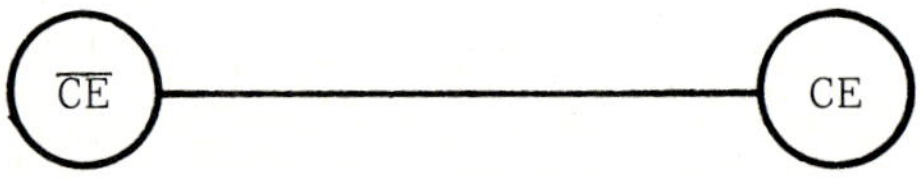

ii)
An equivalent representation in which a Common Memory module is assumed between any two CEs connected to each other.

Figure 3. A schematic representation of a dual processor system.

ii) communication between processes: the provision of data transfer mechanisms that allow, for example, computed results to be passed from one processor to another [1,3,12].

3. MULTIPROCESSOR DEVELOPMENT SYSTEMS

An important advantage of multiprocessor development systems is that they provide students with practical experience in hardware, software and their integration. A flexible and expandable multiprocessor development system also affords experimentation with different processor topologies. This is possible in two different ways:

i) testing all possible topologies with a given number of processors

ii) testing possible topologies with a varying number of processors.

In either case it would be beneficial to investigate the following:

i) the effect on the performance of the system when the number of processors is increased

ii) different topologies and their suitability for different tasks

iii) the relationship between algorithms and the topologies on which they may be executed.

4. INEXPENSIVE RE-CONFIGURABLE MULTIPROCESSOR DEVELOPMENT SYSTEM

The system consists of a collection of Computing Elements connected together through common memory modules. A Computing Element (CE) is an MC6809E based microcomputer capable of interfacing to a user VDU and a host computer; these together with a monitor program residing in ROM help develop, run and debug user software [13].

4.1 System Architecture

The interconnection method used to facilitate the communication between CEs is an extension of an earlier dual processor system which consisted of two microprocessors operating on opposite phases of a common clock [5,6]. Tri-state buffers are used between the processors and the common memory modules thus enabling two processors to share a common memory module which can be accessed on alternate phases of the common clock (Fig. 1,2). All the CEs are synchronized by clock signals through a common bus. The common bus feeds signals from a timing board to the rest of the CEs to ensure their synchronization with respect to each other. The Common Memory modules reside on a different board together with connectors that facilitate the connection of any CE to any other CE through the Common Memory module, provided they are out of phase. This makes the system reconfigurable by simply changing the connectors of the CEs to each other through the Common Memory board (Figs. 10,11). It is not, however, a run-time dynamically re-configurable system [9].

Such a distributed architecture imposes the following rules upon the organisation of the system:

1) Each common memory module can be shared by two CEs only

2) two communicating CEs (neighbours) share a common memory module

3) a CE can have more than one neighbour

4) any two neighbours must operate on alternate phases (Fig. 3).

As stated in the rules above, Computing Elements will not be able to share memory with other CEs unless they are out of phase. In spite of this restriction, most topologies can be implemented directly. Some topologies would, however, require additional CEs to facilitate communication between CEs of the same phase.

4.2 Re-Configurable System Organisation

The system currently used consists of four Computing Elements organised as a 2x2 Array/Ring of processors (Fig. 4).

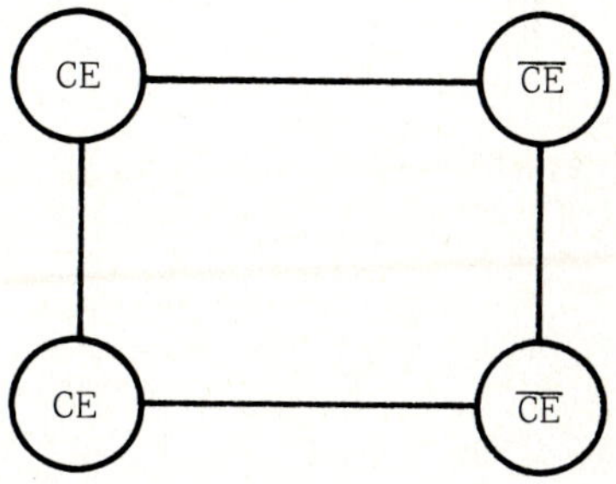

Figure 4. An Array/Ring topology of four CEs.

Other topologies can easily be configured with the same number of Computing Elements by changing the connections to the common memory modules; these are - the star topology and a pipeline topology (Fig. 5).

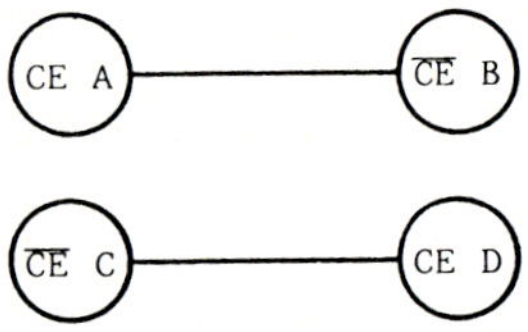

i) Two dual procesors

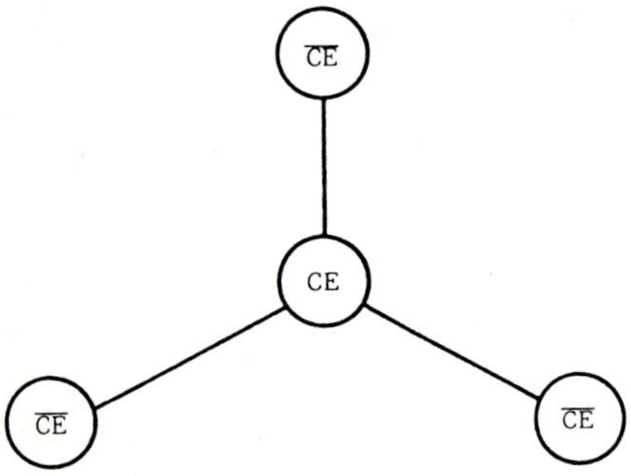

ii) Star topology

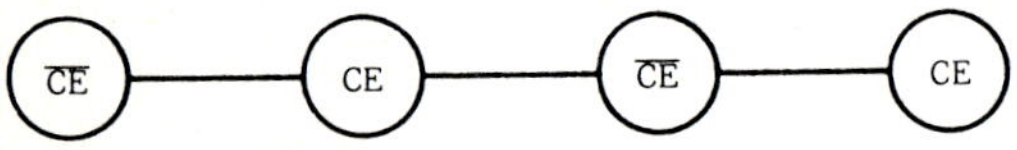

iii) Pipeline topology

Figure 5. Alternative topologies consisting of 4 CEs.

The shared memory technique caters for the expansion of any system by the addition of extra buffers and the addition of extra CEs (Fig. 6). For example:

i) tree (polynomial) topology
ii) an expandable Array (Mesh) topology
iii) a star topology
iv) other special topologies

4.3 System Hardware

The basic CE station consists of a bussed multi-board rack, power supply and a CPU board [13]. The CPU board has (Fig. 7):

i) MC6809E processor [10,11]
ii) Monitor RAM (2K) and ROM (6K)
iii) User RAM and ROM extendable to 48K
iv) MC6840 (PTM) Programmable Timer Counter for program tracing and baud rate generation for serial interfaces
v) MC6850 (ACIA) serial interface for the console terminal
vi) MC6850 (ACIA) serial interface for down-loading object code and communication between the host and console device.

The cost of a four CE system with the power supply and rack is less than £1000.

Any computer with a serial interface and a cross assembler for the MC6809 may be used as a software development system. The described system uses a PDP-11 as the software development host [14] (Fig. 8,9).

In addition to the Computing Element board, the timing board generates clock signals which are transmitted via the common bus to ensure synchronization of the CEs with respect to each other. The CEs communicate with each other through common memory modules which reside on the Common Memory board(s) (Figs. 10,11). These also contain connectors which enable any two CEs out of phase to be connected together.

4.4 Monitor Facilities

With the aid of the monitor [13] the user can:

i) communicate with the host development system and the console
ii) download software from the host via a serial link
iii) examine and change memory and registers
iv) run user programs
v) trace, single step and halt programs
vi) disassemble machine code to mnemonics
vii) obtain performance statistics on a given block of code
viii) re-define NMI, IRQ, SWI, FIRQ vectors
ix) create breakpoints with embedded SWI instructions.

4.5 System Software

Mutual exclusion for two processes can be achieved by the use of two binary semaphore operations. These are based on Dekker's algorithm [1] and are denoted as procedures WAIT and SIGNAL. They operate on a shared variable residing in the memory common to the CEs and are implemented with "busy waiting". All the student is required to know is that in the case where one process is in the critical section and the other wishes to enter it, it will be suspended by the continual testing of the shared variable. The operations are implemented on any two communicating CEs and can be called by the user as procedures.

5. SYSTEM RE-CONFIGURATION

The system is not a dynamically configurable system [9] since changes to the topology may not be done during run time. The system does allow the user, however, to reconfigure the physical topology of the system in accordance with the rules stated above. By altering the connections between the CEs and the Common Memory modules residing on the Common Memory board (Figs. 10,11), it is possible to configure different topologies (Fig. 4,5). The software required for the system will vary according to the topology although the communication primitives provided can be used with little or no change.

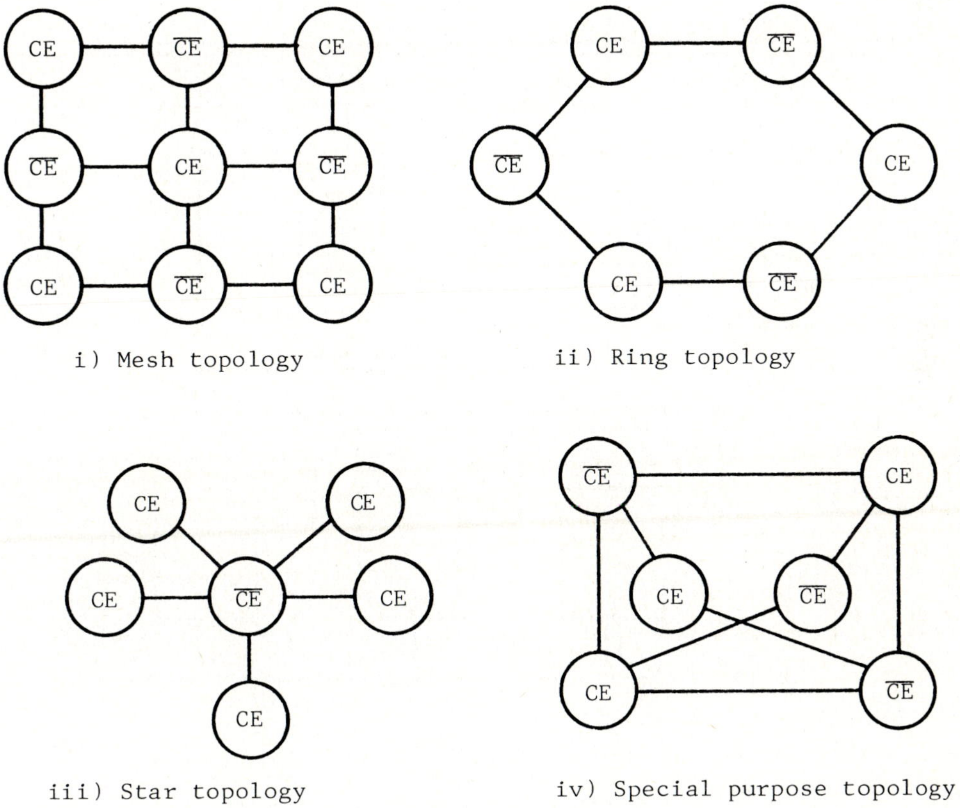

Figure 6. Possible extended systems consisting of 6 CEs.

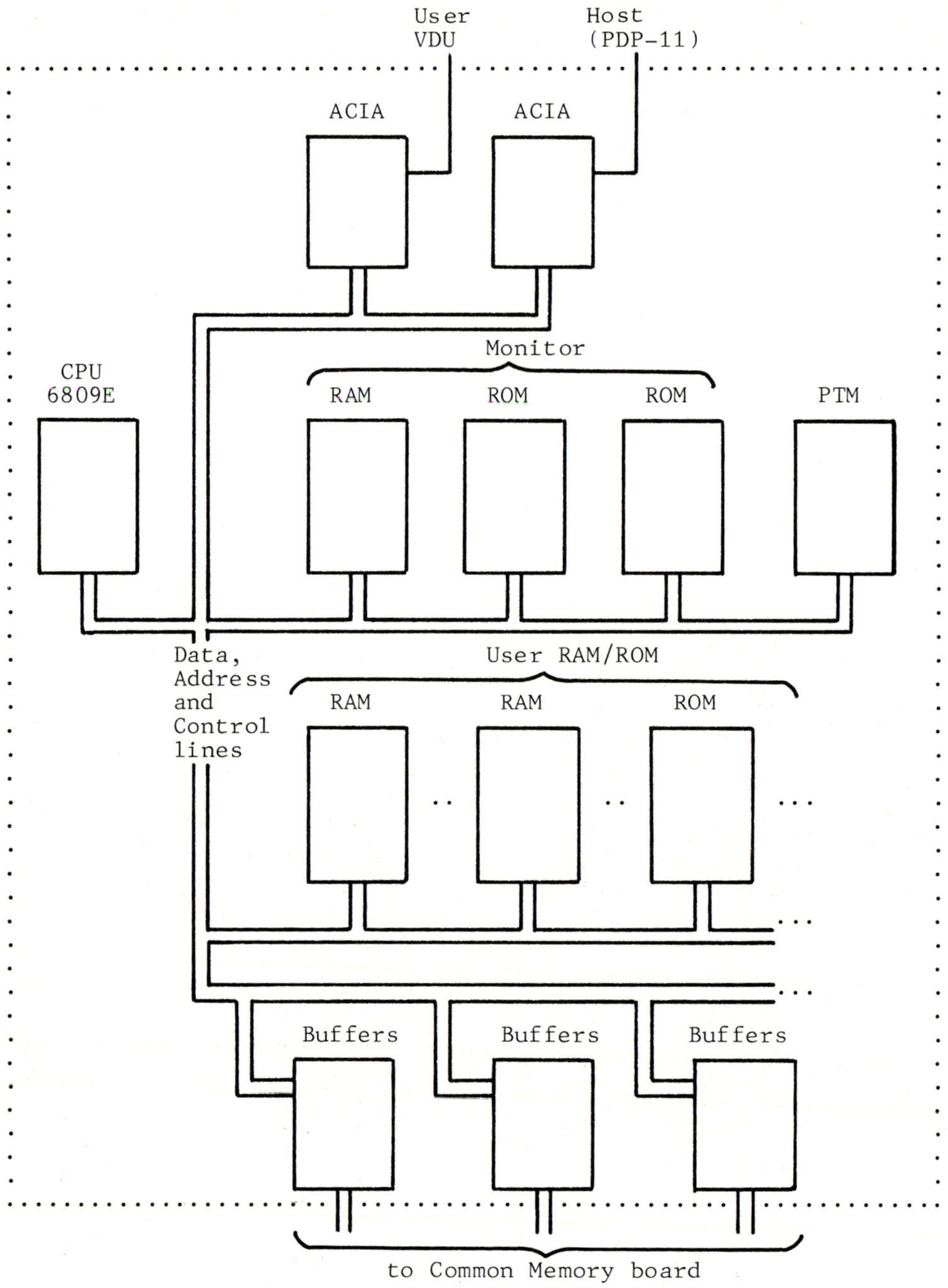

Figure 7. Hardware schematic of a one Computing Element development station with the buffers connecting the station to common memory.

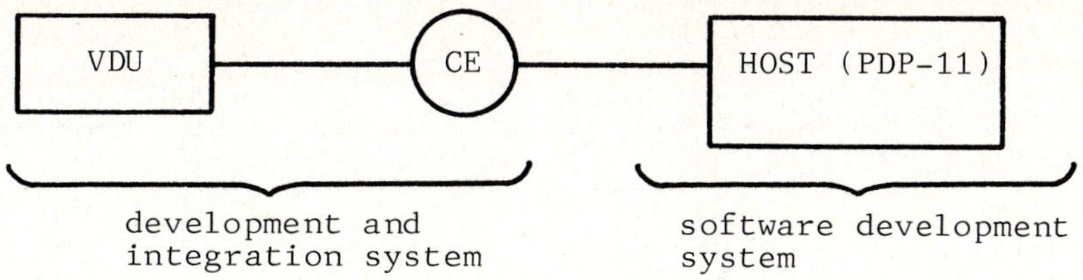

Figure 8. A single user single CE (Computing Element) development station with a link to a HOST (PDP-11) and a user VDU.

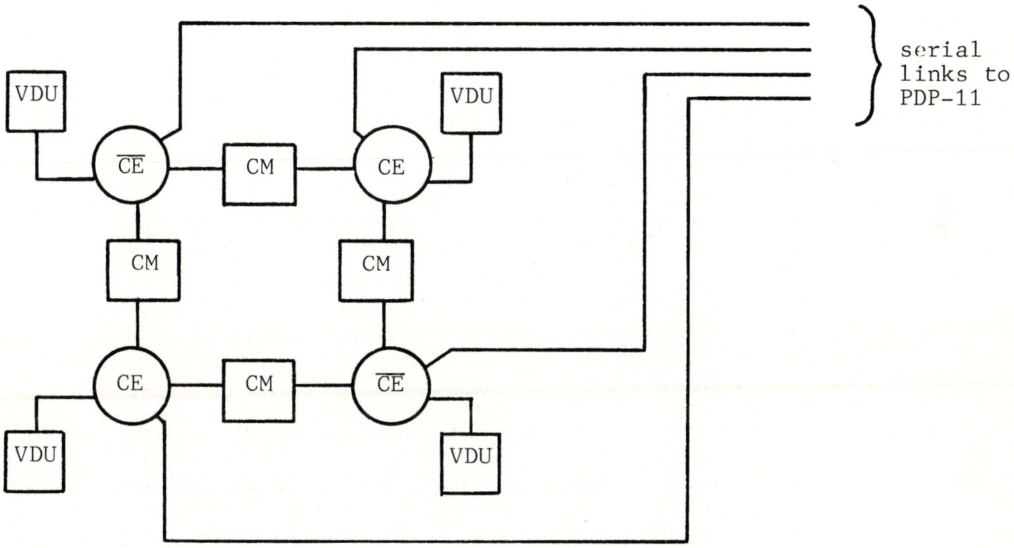

Figure 9. A multiprocessor development system configured as an Array/Ring with four CE stations and their connections to a Host-computer and user VDUs. The CEs and the Common Memory modules reside on seprate boards inside a single rack. Their inter-connections are shown in Fig. 10 and 11.

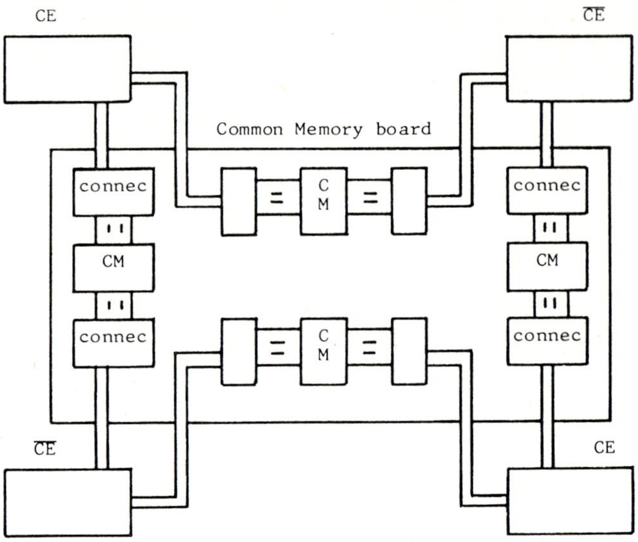

connec = connector socket
CM = Common Memory module

Figure 10. An array/ring topology of four CEs with their associated buffers connecting the CEs through Common Memory to each other.

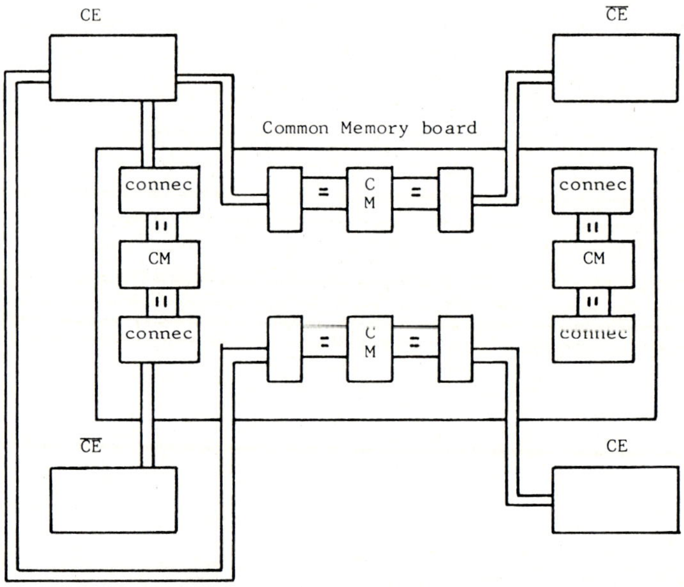

connec = connector socket
CM = Common Memory module

Figure 11. A star topology of four CEs and their corresponding buffers connecting the CEs through Common Memory to each other.

6. EXAMPLES OF CONCURRENT PROGRAMMING

These examples are implemented using the WAIT and SIGNAL operations provided by the system software. In the first example, the student is required to implement two concurrent programs each of which contains a critical section. These critical sections must not be executed simultaneously. The problem can be solved on a dual processor configuration (Fig. 5-i) in the following way (cf. Lister [12] (Example 1):

```
Process X (CE A):            Process Y (CE B):

      .                            .
      .                            .
Call proc WAIT               Call proc WAIT

CRITICAL SECTION             CRITICAL SECTION

Call proc SIGNAL             Call proc SIGNAL
      .                            .
      .                            .
```

Example 1: Providing mutual exclusion with the use of a binary semaphore.

The second example deals with a shared resource such as a cyclical buffer used for the transfer of data between two concurrently executing processes. To avoid data corruption, only one process is allowed access to the common buffer and its associated pointers (Producer-ptr and Consumer-ptr) at any time (cf. Lister [12] and Ben-Ari [1] (Example 2):

```
PRODUCER (CE A):

REPEAT
Start:
   Call procedure PRODUCE
   Call procedure WAIT
   IF Producer-ptr (+) 1 = Consumer-ptr
   THEN Call procedure SIGNAL
        GOTO Start
   ELSE
        Buffer[Producer-ptr]:=Data
        Producer-ptr:=Producer-ptr (+) 1
        Call procedure SIGNAL

   FI
FOREVER.
```

```
CONSUMER (CE B):

REPEAT
Start:

   Call procedure WAIT
   IF Consumer-ptr (+) 1 = Producer-ptr
   THEN Call procedure SIGNAL
        GOTO Start
   ELSE
        Data:=Buffer[Consumer-ptr]
        Consumer-ptr:=Consumer-ptr (+) 1
        Call procedure SIGNAL
        Call procedure CONSUME
   FI
FOREVER.
```

(The (+) operation means modulo buffer-length).

Example 2: A cyclical buffer implementation as a data transfer mechanism using the WAIT and SIGNAL binary semaphore operations. Initially the Consumer-ptr points to the beginning of the Buffer and Producer-ptr to the next cell. (A dummy item of data is put in Buffer[1]).

Other protection and synchronization mechanisms can be implemented in a similar fashion using the binary semaphores provided and there are a wide range of exercises that may be given to students to be solved on such a system. When the student becomes proficient with certain aspects of concurrent programming, additional levels of complexity may be introduced. These could include, for example, general semaphores capable of suspending and re-awakening processes. Such mechanisms can be used to construct distributed operating system kernels.

7. CONCLUSION

An inexpensive flexible multiprocessor development system, can be useful in teaching the principles of concurrent programming. Such a system enables the student to study the problems involved with such an intricate subject without being hindered by the problems uni-processor systems environments present.

Acknowledgements

The author would like to thank Dr J.D. Roberts, Dr M.F. Smith, Jim Bowen and James Wallace for many valuable discussions.

REFERENCES:

[1] Ben-Ari, M., Principles of Concurrent Programming (Prentice-Hall, Inc., Englewood Cliffs, N.J. 1982).

[2] Bochman, G.V., Architecture of Distributed Computer Systems, Lecture notes in computer science no 77, (Springer-Verlag 1979).

[3] Bowen, B.A., Buhr, R.J.A., The Logical Design of Multiple-Microprocessor Systems. (Prentice-Hall, Inc., Englewood Cliffs, N.J. 1980).

[4] Brinch Hansen P., Operating Systems Principles (Prentice-Hall, Inc., Englewood Cliffs, N.J. 1976).

[5] Farrel, J., Synchronizing two Motorola MC6802s on one bus. Application note AN-783, Motorola Semiconductor Products Inc.

[6] Hoffner, Y. and Smith, M.F., Communication between two microprocessors through common memory, Microprocessors and Microsystems, Vol 6, no 6, (1982) 303-308.

[7] Hoffner, Y., The implementation of an inexpensive flexible multiprocessor system, Microprocessors and Microsystems, Vol 7, no 3, (1983) 111-116.

[8] Hoffner, Y., An inexpensive implementation of a flexible multiprocessor system, In Microprocessor Workshop at the Liverpool University. (6/7 Sept. 1982).

[9] Kartashev, S.I., Kartashev, S.P., Dynamic architectures: problems and solutions. Computer, Vol 11, (1978) 6-40.

[10] MC6809 Preliminary Programming Manual, Motorola Inc. (1979).

[11] Microcomputer Components, Motorola Semiconductors, Motorola Inc. (1979).

[12] Lister, A.M., Fundamentals of Operating Systems, (The Macmillan Press Ltd., London 1975).

[13] Smith, M.F., A microprocessor teaching laboratory based on MC6809, Mini-Micro Software, Vol 7, no 4, (1982) 2-8.

[14] Smith, M.F., PDP-11/60-MC6800 microprocessor development system, Microprocessors and Microsystems, Vol 4, no 5, (1980) 175-180.

MICROCOMPUTERS: Developments in Industry, Business and Education
D.R. Wilson and C.J. van Spronsen (eds.) / © EUROMICRO, 1983
Elsevier Science Publishers B.V. (North-Holland)

High level Debugging aids for Real time software

Marnix Goossens(*), Jacques Tiberghien
(*) IWONL Researcher

Free University of Brussels (VUB)
Department of Informatics
Pleinlaan, 2 B1050 Brussels
BELGIUM

Real time software is characterised by a time relationship between program execution and independant external events. It is therefore essential that any debug technique used with such software should have no impact on the execution speed of the programs. Tracing the execution of programs by mean of logic state analysers fullfills the above requirement, but is unpractical, or almost impossible when the programs are of considerable size and/or written in a high level language. The storage capacity of traditional logic state analysers is indeed too limited to record all consecutive states of a program over a significant time span, and typical high level language techniques such as dynamic storage allocation make highly selective state recordings uninterpretable. The present paper describes additional circuitry to be included in logic state analysers, in order to make them suitable for "intelligent" tracing of programs written in a block structured high level language such as Pascal or Modula II. Although the circuitry is fairly complex, it seems feasible and worthwhile to include such devices in microprocessor development systems to facilitate the use of high level languages for real time software.

Keywords: - development system - logic state analyser
- Real time software - High level language
- Debugging

1. Testing and debugging

Although testing cannot prove that a program fullfills its requirements, it remains the most important technique available to discover programming errors, and to increase the confidence a user has in a given program.

Therefore much attention should be paid to the test environment. It should allow easy specification of tests, and equaly easy interpretation of the results. In particular testing should be possible at the level of abstraction chosen for the programming i.e. when a program is written in a high level language such as Pascal, no knowledge of object code features such as hexadecimal addresses, or opcodes, should be required in order to test the program. All tests should be specified in terms of Pascal statements or identifiers, and the results should be directly related to the text of the source program.

An environment with the above features will be called a "High level language debugging" environment, and will be illustrated in the following section by the specifications of such an environment for the Pascal or Modula II languages:

Two complementary approaches can be considered in order to acquire relevant information about the execution of a program:
- The activity of the program can be monitored and/or recorded (tracing)
- The execution can be interupted at a certain point, and the state of the program examined (checkpoint).

Obviously some benefits can result from the combination of both approaches for example, by monitoring the value of a given variable, an adequate moment for the interuption of the execution can be determined.

1.1. Source level tracing

An execution trace of a program describes the evolution of the control flow, the data flow, or both. This description should be made in terms of the source code, and contain no visible references to object code.

1.1.1. Control flow

The history of procedure activations, down to a specified level of nesting is a rough, but often sufficient image of the control flow. Which branches of control statements and how many times specified statements are executed, are other important aspects of control flow analysis. Procedure names and source line numbers are probably most adequate to specify the considered statements.

1.1.2. Data flow

A list of all consecutive values of a specified variable, and/or the list of all statements accessing such a variable can provide insight into the data flow of a program.

1.1.3. Range checking

The monitoring of the value of specified variables, such as array indexes, or branch addresses can provide early warnings for misbehaviour of programs, often before the error has corrupted so much data as to become untraceable.

1.2. State analysis

Means to stop the execution of a program when a specified line has been reached for the n th time, or when a specified variable is assigned an unacceptable value, or even simply accessed, should be available.

When the execution has been stopped, the programmer should be able to examine all variables by simply specifying their name, and the block they belong to. The ability to restart a program, after modification of the value of some variables, can be very usefull in debugging situation, although seldom applicable in true real time situations.

2. Symbolic debuggers

The abilities described in the above paragraph are typical for the so called symbolic debuggers, available in many programming environments. SDB under UNIX [1], and the "Pascal Debug" in the Tektronix package are typical examples [2].

Unfortunately these debuggers are not designed for real time situations. Basically they either add statements to the object code to acquire the relevant informations directly from the executing program (this is similar to the programmer who adds write statements at initial places in his program), or they execute the program step by step, and between each instruction, they filter out the relevant state information [3]. Both techniques obviously slow down very significantly the execution of the program, and therefore are not applicable in time critical environments. [4]

One class of instruments, the "logic state analysers" allow the observation of executing program, without slowing it down. One could imagine a logic state analyser, recording all buss states during a test run, and an analysis program, filtering a posteriori the recorded trace to display the relevant information. Unfortunately, memory technology does not yet allow the recording of hundreds of millions of consecutive buss states in real time, at reasonable cost. Therefore in order to allow real time debugging the logic state analyser must contain some real time filtering devices, allowing a highly selective recording of buss states.

Most logic state analysers contain such filters, but they are tailored to the needs of low level language debugging: selection is based on absolute address ranges, data values, control buss states, or combinations of the above. With such instruments control flow can be traced, but variables located in a stack or a heap cannot be monitored since their address is not known before the executive starts, and even worse, several different variables can share the same address or the same variable can exist several times.

Circuits to be added to logical state analysers in order to adapt them for the debugging of high level languages are described in the following paragraphs.

3. The logic state analysers:

The logic state analyser required for these complex tracing operations should be able to recognise several different events during program execution, and take appropriate action.

The events to be recognised are the execution of specified instructions, and the access to specified variables. The recognition can be performed by an associative memory, containing the addresses of all "interesting" memory locations, and, a code specifying the actions to be taken upon recognition.

Since the number of "interesting" addresses will probably be fairly large in a normal debugging session, the use of true associative memories seems to be economically unattractive.

Instead, a normal memory, with the same number of words as the memory of the system, under test can be used. This memory associates with each address a log specifying the action to be undertaken.

Figure 1 shows the principle of such a tag memory. The width of the tag field depends on the number of different actions that can be specified upon recognition of an event.

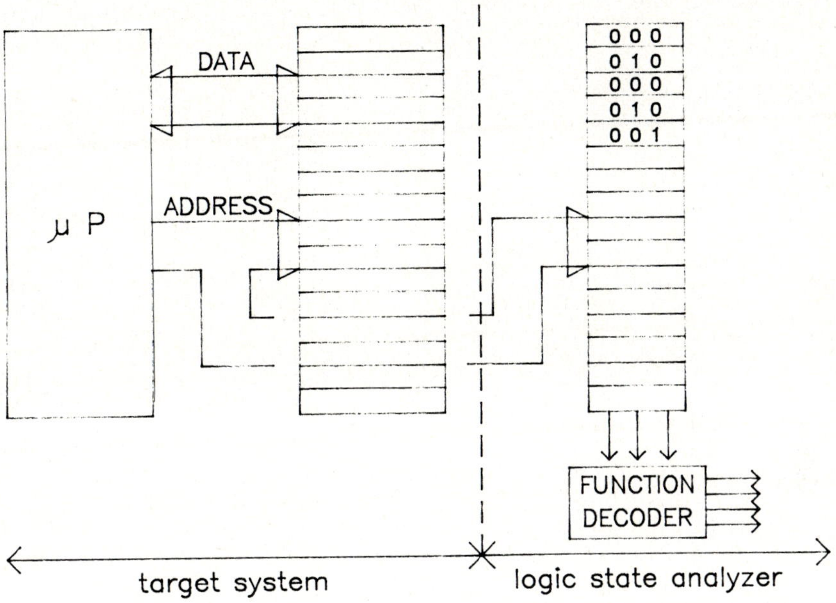

Fig.1 Tag memory as filter in a logic state analyzer

The recording in a trace buffer of the address of specified instruction when they are executed, is sufficient for all control flow tracing. To limit the amount of data in the trace buffer, the monitored instructions should be carefully selected in function of the static control structure of the program.

Figure 2 shows an example of such an optimal selection.

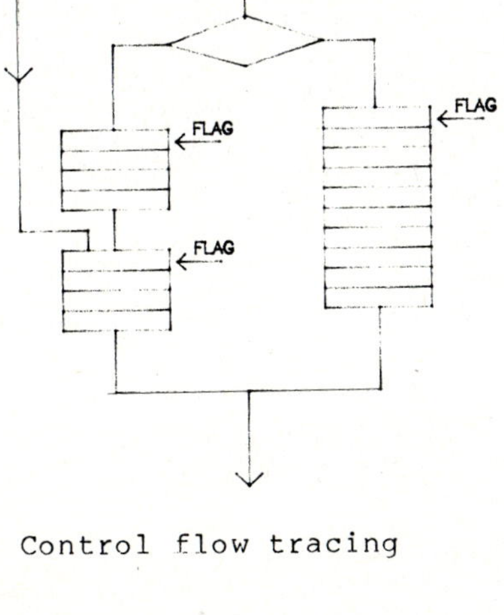

Fig.2 Control flow tracing

To trace the data flow additional hardware provisions must be made. They are described in the following sections.

4. Monitoring of stack variables

In a majority of the implementations of block structured languages, variables are stored on a stack. Such dynamic memory management scheme insures that variables local to a procedure only occupy storage when the procedure is being executed, and that in case of recursive procedure activations several copies of the local variables can be made. Variables on a stack have no longer one absolute address, but are characterized by the block they belong to, and an address within this block.

The proposed observation technique is based on the assumption that the static structure of the program (which defines the accessibility of variables) and the dynamic history of procedure activations is kept on the same stack as the variables, and that a base register B exists that contains the address of the begin of the current local block on the stack. The contents of B are modified at each call and return operation.

Figure 3 shows the considered stack structure, which is typical for a majority of Pascal and Modula II implementations. The left side of the figure shows the block structure of an illustrative program, and the right side shows the state of the stack after following sequence of procedure activations.

Program P activates procedure P1
Procedure P1 activates procedure P11
Procedure P11 activates procedure P2
Procedure P2 activates recursively itself
Register B points to the begin of the current local block

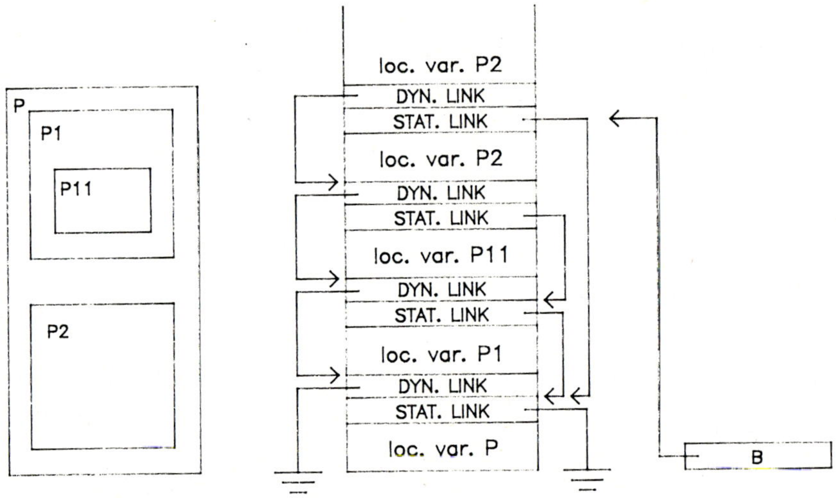

Fig.3 Typical stack organisation

In order to observe a variable, the logic state analyser must first of all check if the variable is activated, and, if so, find the corresponding base address.

Circuits performing these tasks are shown in figure 4.

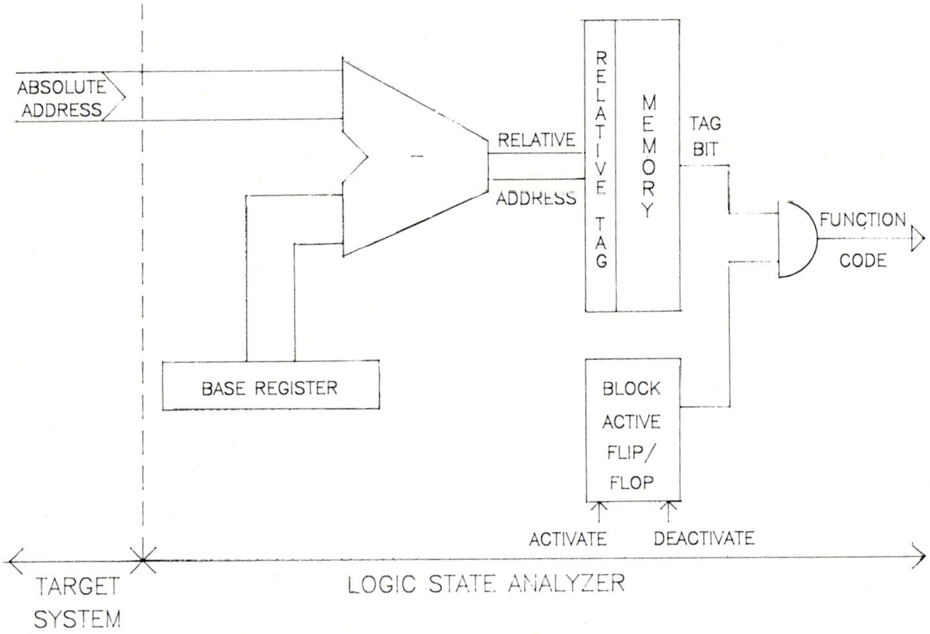

Fig.4 Simplified address translator for stack variables.

Adequate tag fields associated with the first and the last instruction belonging to the specified block set and reset the "BLOCK ACTIVE" flip flop.

Soon after entering a procedure, the processor must fill in the static and dynamic link fields on the stack. By watching these instructions, the logic state analyser can obtain the base address, and can load it in its base register. By substracting the contents of that base register from all addresses, stack addresses will be translated in local addresses within the specified block. These relative addresses are used to access a local tag memory, containing the code of the action to be undertaken when specified variables are accessed.

The circuits of figure 4 are adequate as long the observed procedure is not activated recursively. For each recursive activation a new set of local variables is created on the stack, only the upper one being accessible. It seems reasonable to monitor the accessible versions of the specified variables. This can be done by replacing the base register of figure 4 by a LIFO stack of base registers, and the "BLOCK ACTIVE" flip flop by an up-down counter that keeps track of the number of active versions of the procedure. This is shown in figure 5.

The circuitry of figure 5 allows the monitoring of any number of variables belonging to the same block. If, in one experiment, variables belonging to different blocks must be monitored. The circuitry of figure 5 should be replicated.

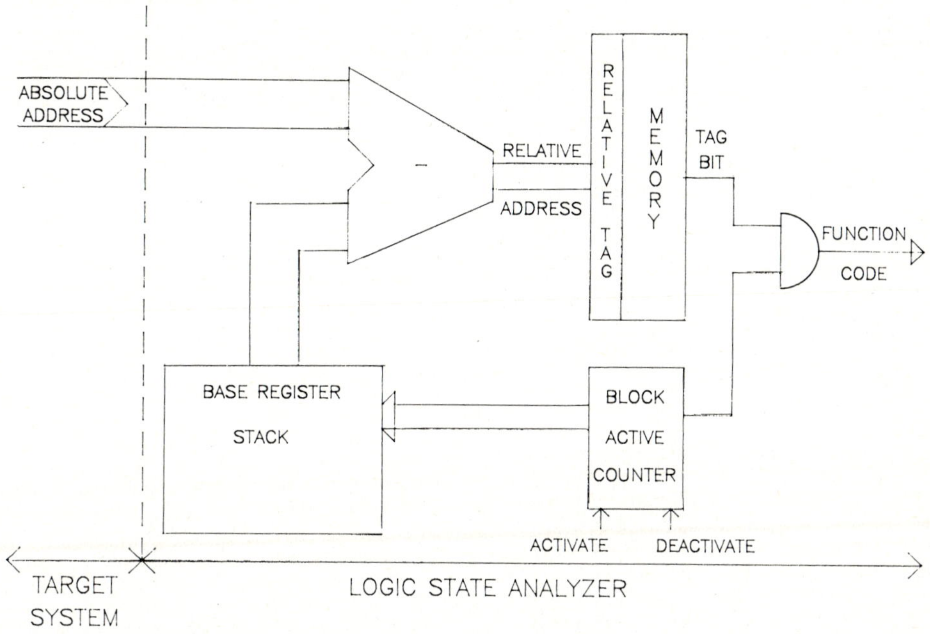

Fig.5 Complete address translator for stack variables.

5. Monitoring of heap variables.

Pascal and Modula II allow dynamic memory management through the use of so called dynamic variables. These variables have no name, they must be accessed indirectly by means of pointer variables. Dynamic variables are created at execution time by the procedure NEW, and storage reserved for such variables can be released by the procedure DISPOSE.

Tools to observe the evolution of dynamic data structures, and to monitor the value of some dynamic variables should be very helpfull to debug what often appears to be the least structured, and therefore the most delicate part of a Pascal or Modula II program.

Techniques similar to those described in section 4 can be used to build such tools. Figure 6 shows the proposed circuitry.

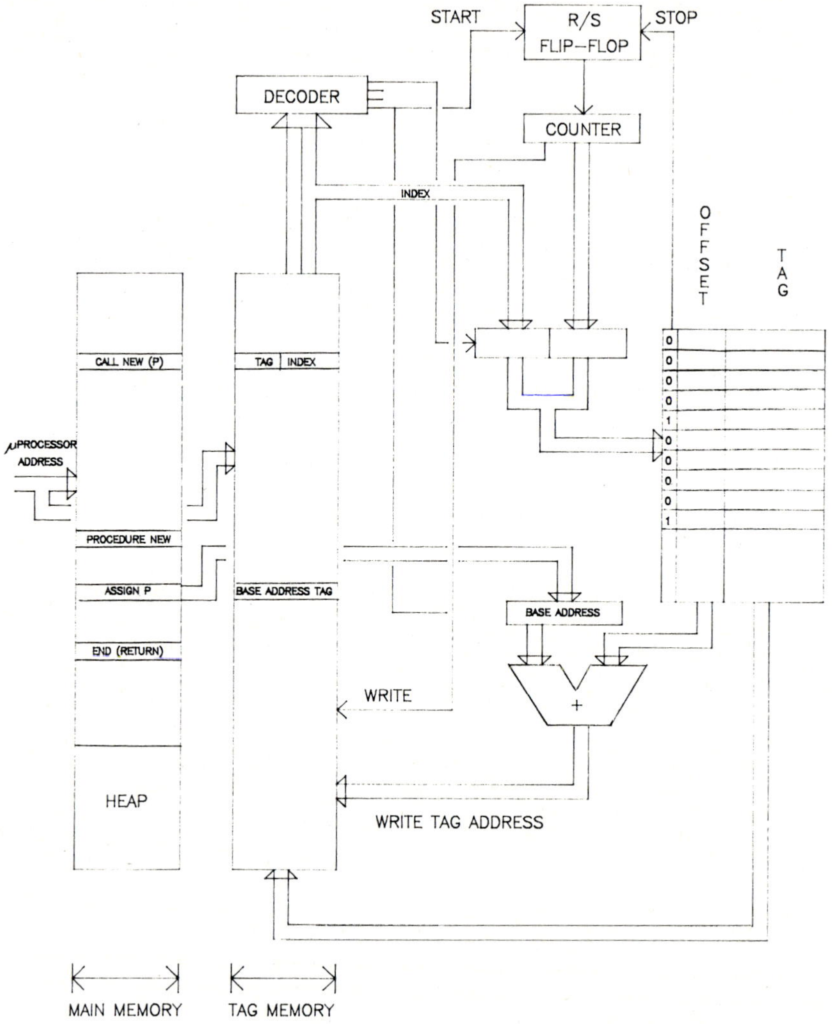

Fig.6 Circuitry to monitor dynamic variables

The creation of a new dynamic variable is detected by associating with the CALL NEW instruction, a specific tag. This tag contains an index that is used to find, in a special table a description of the type of the dynamic variable, to be created. This table contains for each dynamic variable, one entry per field that is to be monitored. Each entry contains the offset within the variable of the field, and the code of the actions to be taken when the field is accessed.

When NEW is called, storage is made available for a dynamic variable, and the address of that storage is assigned to the parameter of the procedure NEW. This assignement too is watched, so that the logic state analyser can note in its BASE REGISTER the address of the newly created dynamic variable.

As soon as this address is available, the logic state analyser should copy in the main tag memory, all the tags that correspond to the newly created variable. These tags, as well as their addresses can be obtained from the dynamic varibles descriptor table.

The inscription of the tag fields in the main tag memory cannot be done at once. Provided that the assignement of a value to the parameter of NEW is done as soon as possible within NEW, and that the number of fields to be tagged is reasonably small, the installation of tags can be done while control is still within NEW, so that the tags are present before they can possibly be needed. The ability of the logic state analyser to write in the tag memory during the execution implies some kind of dual access mechanism for the tag memory, but considering the normal access times of microcomputer memories, the realisation with normal address and data multiplexers should cause no major problems.

6. Range checking

In a debugging situation it is often usefull to check if the values assigned to a specified variable are within preassigned bounds. The technique of memory tags, containing an index field can be used to perform such tests.

Figure 7 shows the specific circuitry to be included in the logic state analyser.

An interesting problem occurs when scalers are stored as consecutive data words in memory. Simple situations can be handled by planning specific tags for the different parts of the variable, and keeping partial composition results in a flip flop. Clearly this technique is unable to solve all problems resulting from crazy data formats, but a reasonable compromise between usefull-ness and complexity is not difficult to reach in a particular high level environment.

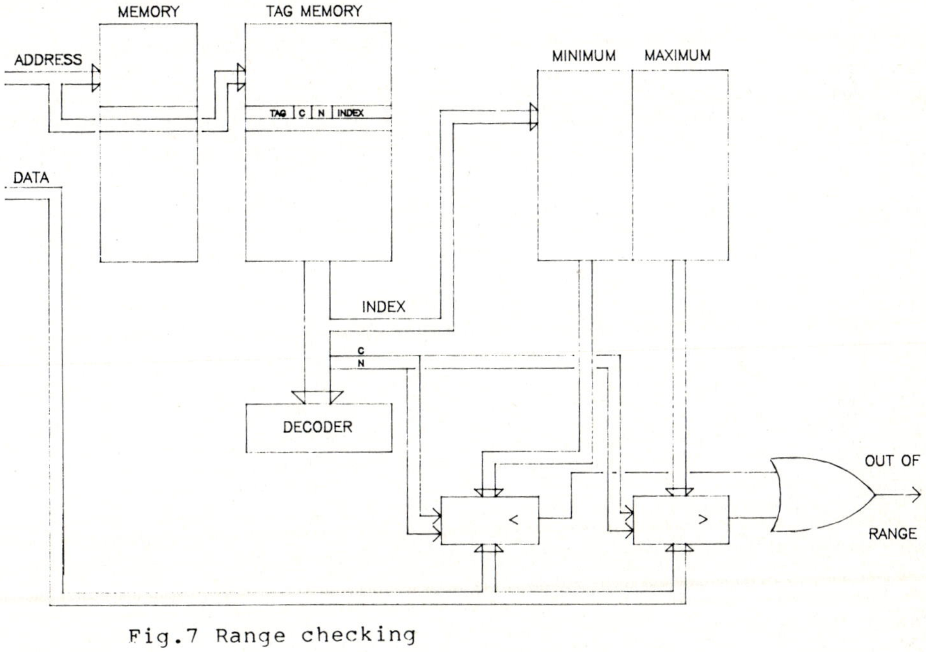

Fig.7 Range checking

7. Supporting software

It is clear that the number and the complexity of tag fields to be installed before a real time program can be monitored is such that the operator should be assisted by a computer program in doing this. Figure 8 shows a block diagram of the support software required to use the logic state analyser introduced here.

An interactive test setup program loads the hardware registers of the logic state analyser by translating the operator wishes in hardware addresses and tags. This translation is done with the help of the different tables.

After data has been accumulated in the trace buffer of the analyser a second interactive program can analyse these data, to present a synthetic, high level overview of the program execution to the operator.

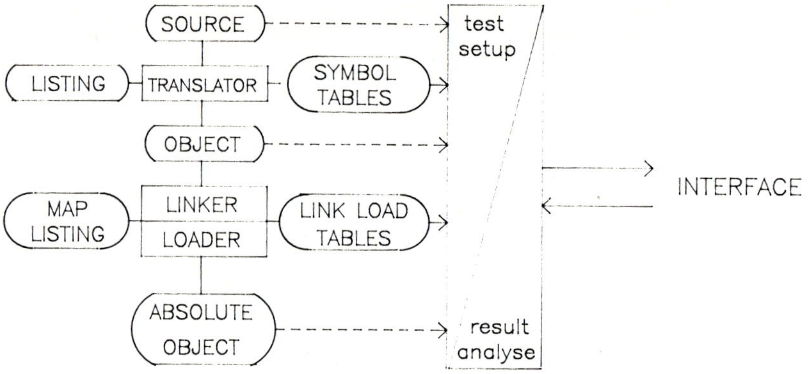

Fig.8 Support software

The same conversational program can be used to access the state variables of a halted process under test.

8. Conclusions

The principles underlying electronic circuits to analyse effectively the behaviour of real time programs written in high level languages have been described. The different devices have all been integrated in one coherent design, and a prototype system, intended to demonstrate the feasibility of such high level debugging is being constructed in the authors laboratory. It is scheduled to be operational in the fall of 1983.

The authors have the hope that such studies could inspire the manufacturers of development systems in their search for more performant tools.

9. Acknowledgements:

Part of the research described in this paper has been supported by grants of the IWONL and the FKFO. The authors wish to express here their grattitude for this support.

10. References

[1] Howard P. Katseff
Sdb: A symbolic debugger
Bell Labs '79

[2] C.C.SMITH & P. VERSTEEG
Software Project management with the 8560 multi-user software development system.
Preprints of the international meeting on development aid for microprocessor systems
Liege, october 25-26, 1982.

[3] M.F.SMITH
Debugging with filtered traces
Computer Design, April 1982.

[4] R.L.GLASS
Real-time: The "lost world" of software debugging and testing
CACM 23, May 1980, N 5.

Session C2:

SOFTWARE QUALITY ASSURANCE

Chairman: Torstein Skard
Tandberg Data A/S
Oslo (Norway)

INTRODUCTION

Quality Assurance (QA) has a long tradition in engineering disciplines. QA in connection with computer systems started out on the hardware side of the systems. Software Quality Assurance (SQA) did emerge at a later stage. It is not surprising that SQA has only been able to develop in step with software as an engineering discipline.

With the increasing importance of software in micro computer systems, it is likely that the micro computer community will see an increased attention being paid to software engineering in general and software quality assurance in particular.

The reasons for doing software quality assurance may for instance be:

- customer requirements (e.g. (1))
- legal liability
- cost-effectiveness

DEFINITIONS

There are at least two quite different definitions of "quality":

- (2) defines quality as: "The totality of features and characteristics of a product or service that bears on its ability to satisfy given needs".

- (3) defines quality as: "conformance to requirements".

(2) defines quality assurance as "A planned and systematic pattern of all actions necessary to provide adequate confidence that the item or product conforms to established technical requirements".

Please note that "software" in this connection means much more than just computer programs, it includes all associated documentation, (test-)data, rules, and procedures, pertaining to the operation of a computer system. See (1).

WHAT IS SOFTWARE QUALITY ASSURANCE?

To get an impression of what SQA does encompass, it may be illustrative to look at an extract from the table of contents of (1):

- Management
- Documentation
- Standards, Practices, and Conventions
- Reviews and Audits
- Configuration Management
- Problem Reporting and Corrective Action
- Tools, Techniques, and Methodologies
- Supplier Control

Note that SQA is much more than evaluation of software quality. Actually most of the above points are of a preventive nature. Quality must be "built-in" at every step in the software life cycle.

Advise on how to get started on SQA may for instance be found in (4) and (5).

ABOUT THIS SESSION

This session will start out with a short introduction by the chairman. The introduction will treat SQA in general and expand on some of the topics mentioned above.

The paper by J.L. Darlington on software validation covers a very important aspect of SQA. In this context "validate" means "determine the correctness and reliability". Because of the size and excellence of this paper, the program committee has decided to devote an entire session exclusively to the paper.

Actually, the paper consists of two large and fairly independent parts which will be presented separately. One part gives a general tutorial style introduction to software validation. The other part is a more technical presentation of one tool (SPECINT) for validation of program specifications by direct execution of program specifications.

REFERENCES

(1) ANSI/IEEE Std 730-1981, Standard For Software Quality Assurance Plans (IEEE Service Center, 445 Hoes Lane, Piscataway, NJ 08854).

(2) IEEE Std 729-1982, Standard Glossary of Software Engineering Terminology (IEEE Service Center, 445 Hoes Lane, Piscataway, NJ 08854).

(3) Crosby, P.B., Quality is Free (McGraw-Hill, 1979)

(4) Perry, W.E., Effective Methods of EDP Quality Assurance (Q.E.D. Information Sciences, 1981)

(5) Dunn, R. and Ullman, R., Quality Assurance for Computer Software (McGraw-Hill, 1982).

MICROCOMPUTERS: Developments in Industry, Business and Education
D.R. Wilson and C.J. van Spronsen (eds.) /© EUROMICRO, 1983
Elsevier Science Publishers B.V. (North-Holland)

THE ROLE OF VERIFICATION AND TESTING IN SOFTWARE DEVELOPMENT

J. L. Darlington

Gesellschaft fuer Mathematik und Datenverarbeitung m.b.H, Bonn
P. O. Box 1240, St. Augustin 1, Germany

The state of the art of software validation, as it pertains to the verification and testing of sequential and concurrent programs, is reviewed. Among the topics covered under the validation of fully-coded programs are the main types of theorem provers employed in verification, some commonly made criticisms of the verification enterprise, ideal tests, symbolic execution, interaction between testing and verification and the interactive construction of test cases. The investigation supports the view that the principal automated or semi-automated validation methods of verification and testing, and the increasingly important manual techniques such as inspections and walk-throughs, are more effective when constructively applied during the software development process than when applied just to the end product. Such constructive or developmental approaches include verification-oriented programming, deductive program synthesis and example-based programming.

1. INTRODUCTION

The first steps toward a science of program validation, which would establish a sound, rigorous and formal basis for determining the correctness and reliability of computer software, were taken by Floyd [18], who laid the foundations of the "inductive assertion" method of program verification, and by Hoare [27], who developed this method into a logic of programs, i.e. a system of axioms and rules for proving program correctness. It was perhaps not sufficiently emphasised at the outset that such correctness, whether "partial" or "total", is not an intrinsic property of a program but is defined in terms of its fulfilling a <u>specification</u> stating, in a formal language such as first-order functional logic, what the program is expected to do. The specification is part of a program's "documentation" which must be supplied to the verifier, and includes an entry assertion or input condition, which places constraints on the values of the input variables, and an exit assertion or output condition, which states the intended relation between the values of the input and output variables. The rest of the documentation required by the verifier includes at least one inductive assertion or predicate for each loop of the program, stating properties of the variables that are presumed to be invariant with respect to the number of executions of the loop to which it is attached. Though considerable research effort has been expended on their automatic generation [21,32,57], it is still the case that these loop predicates must be devised primarily by the ingenuity of human programmers on the basis of their "understanding" of how the program is supposed to perform.

The main alternative to verifying a program formally has usually been simply to try it out on different input values or "test cases" and see if it "works", i.e. gives the correct output values, where correctness is again understood in terms of conformity with specifications. This procedure has been systematised and refined [8,28], and tools have been devised to aid the programmer in the definition and execution of test cases [9]. In terms of the logical rigour and completeness of the validation provided, formal proofs of partial or total correctness are undoubtedly better guarantees of the quality of software than the more empirical procedures of program testing which, no matter how carefully the test cases are selected, at best prove program correctness just for the input values tested, or, in the case of "symbolic execution" [34], for the classes of values tested. Testing of concurrent programs is even less conclusive, and verification therefore all the more important, because of the lack of implementation of most concurrent programming languages, and the nonreproducibility of most test results due to the arbitrary order of execution of concurrent statements, though some concrete results in this connection have been obtained [7]. But whatever their theoretical virtues, the difficulties in finding or generating the required inductive assertions, and the current state of the art of mechanical theorem proving, have until recently confined the effectiveness of verification methods to a limited range of mainly algorithmic programs that perform such tasks as sorting linear arrays or computing simple mathematical functions. Fully automatic verification has not therefore been regarded as a computationally feasible way of establishing the reliability of most programs or "packages" on the scale required by current software production systems or "environments" [26,29], for which the various program testing techniques, unsatisfactory though they may be from a theoretical standpoint, remain the predominant means of validation, or at least of automatic or computer-aided validation.

The practical difficulties connected with automatic verification, and the logical incompleteness of program testing, have led various authors [1,17] to advocate "disciplined manual techniques" as the most effective procedures currently available for assuring the quality of software. These are understood as including such "pencil and paper" or "desktop" validation methods as walk-throughs, reviews and inspections. On the face of it, such techniques seem to be a reversion to the bad old days before the discovery of automated tools for verification and testing. This has some justification if one is concerned merely with the validation of code, i.e. completed programs. But the advocacy of manual techniques often goes hand in hand with emphasis on their applicability to all phases of the software development process, including the "requirements" and "design" phases which have not yet attained the degree of formalism necessary for automation, and with increasing awareness of the importance for software production of these earlier phases. There is a growing feeling, backed up by evidence, among those concerned with the quality assurance of software that any effort expended on the validation of requirements and design more than pays for itself in decreasing the work of finding and correcting errors "downstream" [2].

Together with the application of validation techniques to the earlier phases of software development, there is increasing emphasis on their "constructive" use, whereby program designs or specifications are progressively converted into executable code by means of "correctness-preserving" transformations. This critical review of software validation techniques will therefore discuss the constructive or transformational use of verification and testing methods as well as their application to completed program code, while the validation of software specifications is the subject of another paper in this volume.

2. VALIDATION OF PROGRAM CODE

The importance for the orderly and precise development of software of the distinction between formally specifying what a program does and writing the code describing how it does it [31,50] is by now well established. In the area of software validation, this distinction manifests itself in the difference between design proofs, or formal proofs that software specifications possess certain desirable properties, and implementation proofs, or formal proofs that program implementations conform to their specifications [55]; in the devising of methods for the testing or execution of software specifications as well as of program code, and in the development of different inspection techniques for the design and implementation phases. The increasing importance given to the validation of software design results at least in part from the current unsatisfactory state of the art of the verification and testing of completed code, which makes it costly to detect and remove errors in the later stages of implementation. It is thus desirable to eliminate as far as possible in advance at least those programming errors resulting from mistakes in design or specifications. But before discussing in detail the validation of software design, we shall here outline some of the problems with current methods of validating program code and possible ways of overcoming them.

2.1 Formal verification of code

A program verifier based on the previously mentioned approach of Floyd and Hoare, such as the Stanford PASCAL verifier [20] or the Boyer-Moore verifier used in HDM of SRI-INTERNATIONAL [55], is given as input a program together with its "documentation", i.e. entry and exit assertions and loop predicates, which are usually stated in the terminology of first-order predicate calculus. It then generates, and attempts to prove, a first-order logical "verification condition" (VC) for each "path" of the program, i.e. for each section of the program's flowchart beginning at a "cutpoint" (point to which an assertion is attached), ending at a cutpoint and containing no intermediate cutpoint. Given a path whose assertions at the beginning and end cutpoints are P and Q respectively, the corresponding VC is a statement [42] that the truth of P for the current values of the program's variables, together with the truth value of any branch test condition lying on the path, implies the truth of Q for the new values of the program's variables after the path is traversed, i.e. after the intermediate code S is executed.

The Hoare logic of programs provides a formal set of axioms (of assignment) and rules (of consequence, composition and iteration) for computing the instantiations of these assertions Q from the initial assertions P and the execution of sections of code S. In Floyd-type systems that do not use the Hoare logic (e.g. [32]), the VCs are generated directly from the analysis or inspection of the annotated flowchart, while systems that are based on Hoare's logic [30,48] generate the VCs automatically as unproven premises, or "lemmas", in the course of attempting to construct correctness proofs in this logic, though the VCs generated as lemmas in this way are not always identical with those resulting from direct analysis of the flowchart.

The generation of VCs, whether or not it is done by Hoare logic, must in any case be supplemented by a logical system capable of proving the VCs. Proof that all VCs are theorems in the underlying logic demonstrates a program's partial correctness in terms of a theorem which states that, for all values of the program variables, if the entry assertion P is true before initiation of a program S, then the exit assertion Q is true upon its termination, or in Hoare's notation, $_n$-P{S}Q. For total correctness, the property of termination for all input values must also be proved. Once the VCs have been generated, the task of verifying a program thus becomes a problem in theorem proving, and the efficiency of a verification program is therefore linked intimately to that of its associated theorem prover and to the relevance and completeness of the information in the form of axioms, lemmas and simplification rules, that the prover is provided with.

2.1.1 Types of theorem provers employed in verification

The theorem provers that have been applied to or adapted for program verification include general-purpose provers, operating either interactively [5] or in batch mode [45] and designed for proving any logical or mathematical theorems that can be stated in first-order predicate calculus, and special-purpose provers [6] designed to exploit heuristics for efficient theorem proving in such areas of software reliability as program correctness and the multilevel security of operating systems. The "generality" of a theorem prover has two aspects, namely (i) the logical completeness of its deductive mechanism, which is usually defined as its ability to generate a refutation from any unsatisfiable set of clauses, and (ii) the completeness relative to a particular problem domain of the "knowledge", or lemmas and special rules of inference, that it is provided with -- in other words, to what extent the theorem prover constitutes an "expert system" of the problem domain. Experiments with a wide range of theorem provers [41] in the context of program verification indicate that the more general a prover is in either sense the more VCs (verification conditions) it can prove unaided but the longer it takes to get the proofs, while the more specialised a prover is the fewer VCs it can establish on its own but the faster it can prove those it does get, particularly if the user gives it the relevant lemmas.

The last point indicates that efficient program verification, like efficient theorem proving in general, seems to require a certain degree of user assistance or direction, whether it be providing the theorem prover with factual information in addition to the axioms of the system, in the form of relevant lemmas, atomic facts or even steps of the proof as in a proof checker, or with control information in addition to its built-in logic (or "autologic"), thereby intervening in the actual inferences or choices the prover makes. Both of these types of supplementary input may be provided interactively [22], in batch mode, or by means of a combination of the two as in a system like STP [54], in which the axioms and relevant lemmas are supplied by the user at the start of the proof but the system queries the user interactively whenever it needs a value of an existentially quantified variable occurring in the theorem to be proved or in an axiom or lemma required by the proof.

2.1.2 Verification of parallel programs

The program verifiers currently in existence have been designed primarily for proving the correctness of sequential programs, though efforts are now underway toward the verification of parallel programs. The current status of the verification of "concurrent algorithms" is thoroughly discussed by Lengauer [38], who distinguishes between two main approaches to this problem. According to the first, the sequential units (or "modules" [25]) of the parallel program are verified by the techniques for sequential programs described above, and the assertions employed by these proofs are then shown to remain true under every possible concurrent execution of these processes, a property termed "noninterference" [4,38,49]. A noninterference argument is not required by the second approach [33], according to which assertions are formulated that pertain directly to nodes of the graph representing the parallel program. Both approaches formulate the program specifications in terms of entry and exit assertions as in sequential program verification, regardless of what sort of assertions they attach to the other states of program execution. A logical framework that appears general enough to encompass both approaches has been provided by Lamport's [37] "Hoare logic" of concurrent programs.

The state of implementation of parallel verification methods naturally lags far behind that of sequential methods, so little practical experience can be adduced in support of either general approach as opposed to the other. On the face of it, the first approach promises quicker short-term results, since it permits the by now considerable technology of sequential verification (pace De Millo et al. [13]) to be brought to bear on the parallel verification problem, and appears moreover to reduce the problem to smaller units than does the second approach, though there may be a trade-off here depending on the difficulty of the noninterference proof. The second approach is more satisfying theoretically, in that it calls for designing new verification tools specifically for parallel programs instead of trying to adapt old ones, and may therefore offer better hope for the efficient verification of parallel programs in the long run.

2.1.3 Criticisms of the formal approach

The scenario for program verification implicit in the above methods is that a program is (a) written, then (b) documented or annotated with the appropriate assertions, and finally (c) given to a theorem prover that attempts to prove its correctness. Among the more serious criticisms that have been levelled against this general procedure are that it has thus far succeeded in verifying only a limited range of relatively simple programs which can be specified formally, such as programs embodying sorting or searching algorithms, and that it is inappropriate or irrelevant to the validation of many other types of program since, as pointed out by Winograd [61], "computers are not primarily used for solving well-structured mathematical problems". For example, programs for parsing or translating natural language text succeed approximately at best, and can be "validated" only by having human proofreaders check their output. Most such programs furthermore, however "clean" their original formulations may be, go through several versions written by or contributed to by different people and thus come to contain so many special rules or error fixes that they are difficult or impossible to document. If tasks (a) and (b) above are performed by different people, then those doing the assertions, which is a hard enough job in itself, have the additional problem of guessing what the original programmers intended. Furthermore, task (c) is necessarily dependent on the state of the art of mechanical theorem proving which, as already indicated, is not sufficiently advanced to permit efficient and fully automatic proofs of all VCs. A more radical criticism is that even if such proofs could always be produced they would not necessarily "increase dramatically one's confidence in the correct functioning of a piece of software" [13], since mathematical proofs themselves are always subject to reasonable doubt, and if generated by computer, depend on the "correctness" of the theorem prover itself.

Despite the force of the objections stated above, it does not follow that the verification enterprise should simply be abandoned for, as pointed out by Lamport, this would mean returning to a situation analogous to the days of geometry before the techniques of axiomatic proof were developed, primarily by Euclid: "To see if a theorem was true, all they [the geometers] could do was to test it on some diagrams." [36] The critics of verification have undoubtedly had a positive effect, in that they have stimulated researchers to look beyond the solution of "toy" problems and to tackle the verification of large-scale "real" systems, such as a PASCAL compiler [51] and the SIFT operating system for aircraft flight control [54]. The efficient proving of desirable properties of such large systems depends not only on improvements in interactive theorem proving techniques but also on the development of methods of incremental verification [14,46,47], which make it unnecessary to reverify a program or system completely whenever a change is made. Furthermore, there is a growing feeling that the difficulties inherent in the *ex post facto* verification of previously written programs might be partly avoided by incorporating the techniques of verification and predicate calculus theorem proving into the programming or software design process itself, in such a way as to ensure that no incorrect programs, functions or procedures are ever written. These methods will be discussed in more detail in Section 3, as will the application of testing techniques as aids to program development.

2.2 Testing of code

The most commonly employed type of code validation is that of program testing, not only because it is easier to carry out than formal verification, but also because it is a more direct type of validation than either verification or inspection, since a program P is tested by running P itself on a machine rather than running a different and frequently more complex verification program V or confirming by manual techniques that P looks all right on paper. But the testing of a program has, at least until recently, been a mainly random and haphazard process, consisting primarily of running it on some standard or benchmark examples. This is usually done more with the idea of seeing how fast or efficient the program is, particularly in comparison with rival programs or with previous versions of the same program, than for the purpose of discovering bugs or errors (the occurrence of which often comes as a surprise), and does not therefore constitute rigorous testing. Accordingly, considerable effort is now underway toward the definition, formalisation and refinement of techniques for testing program code [1,8,28].

A distinction is frequently made between "structural" and "functional" testing procedures, where the former (also called "white box analysis") derives test data from the internal structure of a program, and the latter (also called "black box analysis") derives test data from the functional specification of a program apart from its implementation. This is strictly speaking a distinction not so much between different testing procedures as between ways of generating test data, since sets of test data generated by both procedures could contain elements in common.

As is well known, it is impractical to test any but the most elementary programs for all possible inputs. Efforts to devise comprehensive testing procedures concentrate therefore on generating sets of test data that are in some way representative, in that they "exercise" all parts or aspects of a program. In structural testing, these parts or aspects might be the statements that the program contains or the paths through its flowchart, while in functional testing, a representative set should include test data from every variable domain. The failure of such "comprehensive" tests to discover errors in a program increases its chances of correctness or at least of "acceptance", though it does not amount to actual verification, since a clever programmer can always implant errors that will fool any given test.

2.2.1 Ideal tests

The above considerations have led to the notion of an "ideal" test [23], whose successful outcome would guarantee that a program is error-free. Specifically, an ideal test for a given program P would consist of testing P on a (finite) set T of test data such that: there exist some data d that meet P's input conditions and for which P produces incorrect output, if and only if T contains some data t that meet P's input conditions and for which P produces incorrect output. Unfortunately, the construction of such a set T, and the proof that it has the required character, would seem to involve as many complications of a logical or theorem-proving nature as formal verification. The actual development of the notion of an ideal test, therefore, concerns various attempts to explicate it as a yardstick for comparing the relative adequacy of more easily constructible sets of test data.

2.2.2 Symbolic execution

Closely related to the notion of an ideal test, but less ambitious in conception and therefore more readily implementable, is that of symbolic execution, which is regarded by one of its advocates [34] as a halfway house between the two "extremes" of verification and testing. The basic idea is the testing of programs by means of symbolic or algebraic inputs that stand for whole (perhaps infinite) classes of actual, e.g. integer, inputs. The specification of test cases, as required by testing by means of direct execution, is not necessary in symbolic execution [4]. To take an elementary example: in order to test a program that adds three integers, one need not provide it with the denumerable infinity of integer triples as input but merely with the "symbolic" input triple $\langle\beta_1,\beta_2,\beta_3\rangle$, which produces the symbolic or algebraic output $\beta_1+\beta_2+\beta_3$ if and only if the program is correct. Knottier problems arise with more complicated programs having many conditional branches, whose symbolic evaluation frequently requires a nontrivial case analysis. As with ideal tests, the amount of work involved in symbolic execution can therefore approach that of actual verification. Some experimental systems for symbolic evaluation and testing of programs have been implemented by Clarke [11], King [34] and Cheatham [10].

2.2.3 Interaction between testing and verification

As already indicated, a principal dilemma inherent in the problem of software validation is that formal verification is theoretically complete but difficult to carry out in many cases, while testing is simpler in practice but insufficient to prove correctness (cf. Dijkstra's widely quoted aphorism: "Program testing can be used to show the presence of bugs, but never to show their absence" [16]). A way of drawing more positive conclusions from program testing indicated by Geller [19] uses information gained from testing to help prove program correctness. The basic idea in this approach is for data as to the program's behavior on certain key examples or at certain critical points to be incorporated into the specifications themselves. To this end, the programmer is required to attach three assertions (instead of just one as in the Floyd-Hoare procedure) to each arc of the program, namely, (1) a "synthesised" (or Floyd-type) assertion, (2) a "test data" assertion, and (3) a "generalisation" assertion, where (2) and (3) must be satisfied and shown to imply (1). The most significant difference between this approach and the Floyd-Hoare verification techniques is that one type of assertion, namely the "test data" assertion, is verified not by formal proof techniques but by a small number of test runs, thereby providing a link between testing and verification.

2.2.4 Interactive construction of test cases

The idea, mentioned in Section 2.1.3, of using verification methods as tools in interactive incremental program development instead of trying to verify already written programs, has its analogue in the area of program testing. As Geller puts it: "We wish to execute sections of a program as they are being developed rather than attempt to find test data that will prove the correctness of a program that has already been written." [19] The process of constructing or defining test cases for sections of a program under development may be aided and abetted by a program testing assistant such as that of Chapman that "makes it easy for the programmer to define test cases; automatically runs test cases when appropriate; automatically modifies test cases to preserve their usefulness when the program they test undergoes certain types of design changes, and generates test cases at the programmer's command from a library of common forms" [9]. A related approach is that of Lieberman [40], whose TINKER system (cf. Section 3.3) attempts to synthesise programs from examples, which are not input/output pairs as in most systems for programming by example but fragments of code which also serve as test cases for the program being developed. The work of Geller, Chapman and Lieberman attempts in various ways to incorporate the construction of test data and the running of examples more intimately into the program design process, and in some cases into the actual program specifications.

3. VALIDATION TECHNIQUES AS AIDS TO PROGRAM DEVELOPMENT

As indicated in the previous sections, the primary validation techniques of verification, testing and inspection are being increasingly applied to all stages of the software development process, rather than just to the final product. Such techniques are used not only to check the correctness of requirements and specifications in the earlier stages, but are also finding increasing application as tools for transforming certain program forms or descriptions such as models, specifications or inefficient programs into more complete or more efficient versions [39].

The transformational or "constructive" use of verification methods has been more extensively investigated than the constructive use of testing or inspection procedures, perhaps because verification is more costly to apply to completed programs than testing or inspection procedures. The basic idea is to "interweave program development and proof of correctness" [4] in such a way as to ensure that no incorrect programs, functions or procedures are ever written. There are many variants of this approach, but they may be classified roughly, according to the way in which they incorporate the principles of verification and theorem proving into the programming process, into three main but not necessarily exclusive categories, namely, verification oriented programming [41], wherein the principles of verification are applied primarily by human programmers or designers; deductive program synthesis [44], wherein these principles are applied automatically in program generation, and logic programming methods [35], wherein programs are written in such a way that they may be interpreted or executed directly by a theorem prover.

Of these three main ways of applying deductive methods in programming, only the first two are strictly speaking transformational or developmental techniques, in that they are tools for transforming requirements or specifications into programs, while logic programming directly executes logical specifications without transforming them, except of course in the sense of compilation or interpretation. This approach is considered in a related paper on the validation of specifications, and will not be further discussed here. In addition to these three main ways of applying verification and theorem-proving techniques to the programming process, the example-based programming approach [40] is assuming increasing importance as a development technique, although it makes relatively less use of theorem proving methods than the others.

3.1 Verification oriented programming

The basic idea of "verification oriented programming" as described by Luckham [41] is that the documentation of the code, i.e. the entry/exit assertions or input/output conditions and the inductive assertions or loop predicates, are written at the same time as the code itself, thereby saving the programmer and other would-be verifiers the trouble of trying to document the code later on. More important, it is intended to have a salutary effect on the programming process itself, by inducing programmers to write programs from the point of view of their eventual verification.

Verification oriented programming as thus conceived often goes hand in hand with the structured programming approach, which has been described as "the philosophy of structuring programs in such a way as to make them more intellectually manageable and hence more amenable to a convincing proof of correctness" [3]. Both approaches thus call for the programmer to assist the verifier as much as possible, by writing programs in a prescribed or recommended way. It is coming to be recognised that this endeavour is a two-way street, wherein the system or "environment" must also "support" the user or programmer as much as possible in the writing of assertions, in the quick automatic synthesis or verification of small bits of code, and in various other ways provided by programming "assistants" or "apprentices" [59] currently being developed.

The term "structured programming" may refer either to the writing of structured programs, or to the writing of programs in a structured way, whether it be the construction of programs in a "bottom-up" way from smaller (and preferably completely verified) "modules", or in a "top-down" manner, also called "stepwise refinement", whereby each "level" of the program may be verified before the next is coded. As pointed out by Lamport [37], the Hoare logic of programs is particularly well suited to this sort of procedure, since it allows one to specify a statement P{S}Q in terms of its input and output predicates P and Q, and to prove the correctness of a program containing that statement, without having to describe how the statement is implemented, i.e., without having to fill in the S. If a program containing incomplete statements of this sort cannot be verified, then it is a waste of time to try to complete these functions, since at least some of their specifications must be wrong.

The verification oriented programming approach has been further developed in such a way that it has certain features in common with partly or fully automatic program synthesis. In Wegbreit's [60] method, for example, the programmer is required not only to attach assertions to the program he is writing but also to supply for each assertion an accompanying "proof justification", the reasoning of which is similar to that employed in writing the actual section of code to which the assertion is attached, while in Dijkstra's [15] method, the programmer in effect starts with assertions to which he then attaches code that will guarantee their truth. Wegbreit's method has therefore been termed "partially synthetic", and that of Dijkstra "fully synthetic" [4]. But once the programmer has supplied all the relevant assertions together with information sufficient to justify them, an obvious next step is for the code itself to be written by machine, as in the approach described in the next section.

3.2 Deductive program synthesis

The generation of correct programs from their specifications by means of constructively proving the existence of such programs is the basis of deductive program synthesis. This approach has most recently been advocated by Manna and Waldinger [43,44] as follows:

> "Once we have techniques for proving program correctness, why should we wait to apply them until after the program is complete? Instead, why not ensure the correctness of the program while it is being constructed, thereby developing the program and its correctness proof 'hand in hand'?" [43]

This could so far serve as an argument for verification oriented programming just as well as for automatic program synthesis, but the authors go on to say:

> "The point is particularly well-taken when we consider that program verification relies on automatic theorem-proving techniques. These techniques embody principles of deductive reasoning, the same principles that are applied by a programmer in constructing the proof in the first place. Why not apply these principles in an <u>automatic synthesis system</u>, which would construct the program instead of merely proving its correctness?" [ibid.]

The authors have illustrated their method by applying it to several "toy" examples, in addition to at least one "hard" problem, the deductive synthesis of the unification algorithm of resolution theorem proving. In addition, there have been several other experimental program-synthesis systems or programs [12,24,58], but the difficulties inherent in fully automatic program verification as outlined in Section 2.1.3 seem to exist in even greater degree in fully automatic program synthesis. Accordingly, the most promising future for program synthesis would seem to lie in its incorporation into an interactive programming system or "environment".

3.3 Example-based programming

Example-based programming was originally studied within the context of computer learning theory [56], where the paradigm is that the machine is presented with a set of (usually) incomplete input-output pairs, from which it generalises or generates, by means of <u>inductive</u> learning, a complete program. The program is then tested on further samples of input, for which the programmer or user indicates any incorrect output and what the the correct output should be. <u>Adaptive</u> learning is then applied to make the indicated changes in the generated program, so that it improves its performance on subsequent examples. This paradigm of computer learning has been investigated in the context of developing programs for game playing, robot problem solving and inference of formal grammars, among other areas, and is attracting renewed interest as a means of acquisition of specialised knowledge, in the form of sets of inference rules, in the context of research on expert systems [52,53]. The motivation of the research in all these areas is that specialists in given domains are almost invariably better at applying their knowledge or ability in specific cases than at providing general descriptions or sets of rules formulating their expertise. A similar point is made by Lieberman:

> "It is often said that people learn best by example. I would go further, to say that people <u>teach</u> best by example as well ... Since programming is the activity of teaching procedures to a computer, it may well turn out that presenting examples will provide a more natural, convenient, and reliable means of specifying procedures than conventional programming does today." [40]

Lieberman's own TINKER system, which synthesises LISP programs from sample fragments of code instead of from input-output pairs, has already been mentioned in Section 2.2.4. In the interactive synthesis of a list editor, for example, the user introduces new commands, such as <u>insert</u> and <u>delete</u>, by showing the system how to insert or delete a specific item in a specific list. Example-based programming may thus be regarded as a program transformation technique, in which the input-output pairs, or the fragments of code, that are given to the system as input, play the role of specifications from which executable code is generated. The more general or representative the examples are, the better are they able to serve as criteria for determining the correctness of the resulting code.

4. CONCLUSIONS

The current status of software verification and testing methods, as they are applied to the validation of completed program code, and as they serve as tools for the development of completed code from specifications or other descriptions, has been reviewed. The increasingly important manual validation techniques, such as inspections and walk-throughs, have been mentioned without being discussed in detail, while the verification and testing of software specifications are discussed in a related paper. The current paper is a "critical" review, not only in attempting to point out advantages and drawbacks of the individual validation methods, but also in judging them from the point of view that program verification, and to some extent testing also, is more effective when employed as a transformational or developmental tool than when applied merely to check the final result.

Acknowledgements: the author is grateful to J. Abbott of NCC and to H. L. Hausen of GMD for useful suggestions concerning earlier versions of this manuscript.

REFERENCES

[1] Adrion, W. R., Branstad, M. A. and Cherniavsky, J. C., Validation, verification, and testing of computer software, Computing Surveys 14 (1982) 159-192.

[2] Alford, M. W., A requirement engineering methodology for real-time processing requirements, IEEE Trans. Softw. Eng. SE-2 (1977) 60-69.

[3] Bates, D. (ed.), Structured Programming: Infotech State of the Art Report, (Infotech Ltd., Maidenhead, Berks., 1976).

[4] Berg, H. K., Boebert, W. E., Franta, W. R, and Moher, T. G., Formal Methods of Program Verification and Specification, (Prentice-Hall, Inc., Englewood Cliffs, New Jersey, 1982).

[5] Bledsoe, W. W. and Bruell, P., A man-machine theorem-proving system, Artificial Intelligence 5 (1974) 51-72.

[6] Boyer, R. S. and Moore, J. S., A Computational Logic, (Academic Press, New York, San Francisco, London, 1979).

[7] Brinch Hansen, P., Reproducible testing of monitors, Software-Practice and Experience 8 (1978) 721-29.

[8] Chandrasekaran, B., Special collection from workshop on software testing and test documentation, IEEE Trans. Softw. Eng. SE-6 (1980).

[9] Chapman, D., A program testing assistant, Comm. ACM 25 (1982) 625-634.

[10] Cheatham, T. E. Jr., Holloway, G. H. and Townley, J. A., Symbolic evaluation and the analysis of programs, IEEE Trans. Softw. Eng. SE-5 (1979) 402-417.

[11] Clarke, A., A system to generate test data and symbolically execute programs, IEEE Trans. Softw. Eng. SE-2 (1977) 215-222.

[12] Darlington, J. L., Automatic synthesis of SNOBOL programs, in Simon, J. C. (ed.), Computer Oriented Learning Processes (Noordhoff-Leyden, 1976) 443-453.

[13] De Millo, R. A., Lipton, R. J. and Perlis, A. J., Social processes and proofs of theorems and programs, Comm. ACM 22 (1979) 271-280.

[14] Deutsch, L. P., An Interactive Program Verifier, Xerox Palo Alto Research Center Report CSL-73-1 (1973).

[15] Dijkstra, E. W., A Discipline of Programming, (Prentice-Hall, Inc., Englewood Cliffs, New Jersey, 1976).

[16] Dijkstra, E. W., Notes on structured programming, in Dahl, O. J., Dijkstra, E. W. and Hoare, C. A. R., Structured Programming (Academic Press, New York, 1976).

[17] Fagan, M. E., Design and code inspections to reduce errors in program development, IBM Syst. J. 15 (1976) 182-211.

[18] Floyd, R. W., Assigning meanings to programs, Proc. Symp. Appl. Math. 19, Amer. Math. Soc. (1967) 19-32.

[19] Geller, M., Test data as an aid in proving program correctness, Comm. ACM 21 (1978) 368-375.

[20] German, S., v. Henke, F., Luckham, D., Oppen, D. and Polak, W., Program verification at Stanford, ACM Softw. Eng. Notes 5, No. 3 (1980) 13-16.

[21] German, S. and Wegbreit. B., A synthesizer of inductive assertions, IEEE Trans. Softw. Eng. SE-1 (1975) 68-75.

[22] Good, D. I., London, R. L. and Bledsoe, W. W., An interactive program verification system, IEEE Trans. Softw. Eng. SE-I (1975) 59-67.

[23] Goodenough, J. B. and Gerhart, S. L., Toward a theory of testing: data selection criteria, in Yeh, R. (ed.), Current Trends in Programming Methodology, Vol. 2. (Prentice-Hall, Englewood Cliffs, New Jersey, 1977) 44-79.

[24] Green, C. C., Application of theorem proving to problem solving, Proc. First Int'l. Joint Conf. on Artificial Intelligence, Washington, D. C. (1969) 219-239.

[25] Hailpern, B. and Owicki, S., Modular verification of concurrent programs, Report RC9130, IBM T. J. Watson Research Center, Yorktown Heights, New York (1982).

[26] Hausen, H. L. and Muellerburg, M., Software engineering environments: state of the art, problems and perspectives, Proc. COMPSAC '82, Sixth Int'l. Conf. on Computer Softw. and Appl. IEEE (1982) 326-335.

[27] Hoare, C. A. R., An axiomatic basis for computer programming, Comm. ACM 12 (1969) 576-580, 583.

[28] Huang, J. C., An approach to program testing, Computing Surveys 7 (1975) 113-128.

[29] Huenke, H. (ed.), Software Engineering Environments, (North-Holland, Amsterdam, New York, 1981).

[30] Igarashi, S., London, R. L. and Luckham, D. C., Automatic program verification I: logical basis and its implementation, Acta Informatica 4 (1975) 145-182.

[31] Jones, C. B., The role of formal specifications in software development, in Life-

Cycle Management: Infotech State of the Art Report, Series 8, No. 7 (Infotech Ltd., Maidenhead, Berks., 1980).

[32] Katz, S. M. and Manna. Z., A heuristic approach to program verification, Proc. Third Int'l. Joint Conf. on Artificial Intelligence, Stanford, California (1973) 500-512.

[33] Keller, R. M., Formal verification of parallel programs, Comm. ACM 19 (1976) 371-384.

[34] King, J. C., Symbolic execution and program testing, Comm. ACM 19 (1976) 385-394.

[35] Kowalski, R., Logic for Problem Solving, (Elsevier North Holland, Inc., New York, 1979).

[36] Lamport, L., Reply to De Millo et al., Comm. ACM 22 (1979) 624.

[37] Lamport, L., The 'Hoare logic' of concurrent programs, Acta Informatica 14 (1980) 21-37.

[38] Lengauer, C., On the axiomatic verification of concurrent algorithms, Tech. Report CSRG-94, Computer Systems Research Group, University of Toronto (1978).

[39] Levitt, K, N., Program manipulation systems: survey of available techniques, outstanding research problems, and a proposed system concept, GMD-IST Technical Report (1983).

[40] Lieberman, H., Designing interactive systems from the user's viewpoint, in Degano, P. and Sandewall, E. (eds.), Integrated Interactive Computing Systems (North-Holland, Amsterdam, New York, Oxford, 1983) 45-59.

[41] Luckham, D. C., Program verification and verification-oriented programming, in Gilchrist, B. (ed.), Information Processing 77 (North-Holland, Amsterdam, New York, Oxford, 1977) 783-793.

[42] Manna, Z., Mathematical Theory of Computation, (McGraw-Hill, New York, 1974).

[43] Manna, Z. and Waldinger, R., Synthesis: Dreams ==> Programs, IEEE Trans. Softw. Eng. SE-5 (1979) 387-401.

[44] Manna, Z. and Waldinger, R., Deductive synthesis of the unification algorithm, Science of Computer Programming 1 (1981) 5-48.

[45] McCharen, J. D., Overbeek, R. A. and Wos, L. A., Problems and experiments for and with automatic theorem-proving programs, IEEE Trans. on Computers c-25 (1976) 773-782.

[46] Moriconi, M. S., A designer/verifier's assistant, IEEE Trans. Softw. Eng. SE-5 (1979) 387-401.

[47] Moriconi, M. S., Reports on incremental verification, GMD-IST Technical Report (1982).

[48] Moriconi, M. S. and Schwartz, R., Automatic construction of verification condition generators from Hoare logics, Proc. 8th Int'l. Colloquium on Automata, Languages and Programming, Haifa, Springer-Verlag Lectures Notes in Computer Science (1981).

[49] Owicki, S. S. and Gries, D., Verifying properties of parallel programs: an axiomatic approach, Comm. ACM 19 (1976) 279-285.

[50] Parnas, D. L., Use of precise specifications in the development of software, in Gilchrist, B. (ed.), Information Processing 77 (North-Holland, Amsterdam, New York, Oxford, 1977) 861-867.

[51] Polak, W., Compiler specification and verification, Springer-Verlag Lectures Notes in Computer Science 124 (1981).

[52] Quinlan, J. R., Discovering rules by induction from large collections of examples, in Michie, D. (ed.), Expert Systems in the Micro Electronic Age (Edinburgh University Press, 1979) 168-201.

[53] Quinlan, J. R., Semi-autonomous acquisition of pattern-based knowledge, in Hayes, J. E., Michie, D. and Pao, Y-H (eds.), Machine Intelligence 10 (Ellis Horwood Ltd., Chichester, 1982) 159-172.

[54] Shostak, R. E., Schwartz, R. and Melliar-Smith, P. M., STP: a mechanized logic for specification and verification, Proc. 6th Conf. on Automated Deduction (Springer-Verlag, Berlin, Heidelberg, New York, 1982).

[55] Silverberg, B. A., An overview of the SRI hierarchical development methodology, in Huenke, H. (ed.), Software Engineering Environments (North-Holland, Amsterdam, New York, 1981) 235-252.

[56] Simon, J. C. (ed.), Computer Oriented Learning Processes (Noordhoff-Leyden, 1976).

[57] Tamir, M., ADI: automatic derivation of invariants, IEEE Trans. Softw. Eng. SE-6 (1979) 40-48.

[58] Waldinger, R. and Lee, R., PROW: a step toward automatic program writing, Proc. First Int'l. Joint Conf. on Artificial Intelligence, Washington, D. C. (1969) 241-252.

[59] Waters, R. C., The programmer's apprentice: Knowledge based program editing, IEEE Trans. Softw. Eng. SE-8 (1982) 1-12.

[60] Wegbreit, B., Constructive methods in program verification, IEEE Trans. Softw. Eng. SE-3 (1977) 193-209.

[61] Winograd, T., Beyond programming languages, Comm. ACM 22 (1979) 391-401.

MICROCOMPUTERS: Developments in Industry, Business and Education
D.R. Wilson and C.J. van Spronsen (eds.) / © EUROMICRO, 1983
Elsevier Science Publishers B.V. (North-Holland)

VALIDATION TECHNIQUES FOR SOFTWARE SPECIFICATIONS

J. L. Darlington

Gesellschaft fuer Mathematik und Datenverarbeitung m.b.H, Bonn
P. O. Box 1240, St. Augustin 1, Germany

The increasing emphasis on applying validation techniques at all stages of the software development process, rather than just to the end product, has led to the development of techniques for validating software specifications, such as verification, inspection, and the direct execution and testing of such specifications. The discussion is focussed on three executable specification languages, namely PROLOG, OBJ and SPECINT. PROLOG is the main existing implementation of the idea of logic programming, and is not merely a language for executing program specifications but is gaining in importance as a general purpose programming language, particularly in the domain of expert systems. OBJ exploits the use of equations as rewrite rules, as in complete sets of reductions, thereby implementing the idea of executable algebraic specifications. SPECINT supports the interactive and incremental development of functional specifications. By experimentally executing sets of specifications for certain test data, it is able to detect inconsistencies between the specifications and the designer's intentions. Executable specification languages not only provide help in validating software specifications, thereby reducing the frequency of errors in subsequent implementations, but as they become more efficient they are increasingly used as programming languages in their own right.

1. INTRODUCTION

The three main techniques of verification, testing and inspection all attempt in one way or another to validate a coded program by showing it to be consistent with its specifications. When it comes to the validation of these specifications themselves, that is to say, of the program's design as opposed to the implementation of that design [22], the same basic validation techniques are used but with essential differences in application. It is perhaps unnecessary to dwell on the importance of validating specifications as well as code. Suffice it to say that if the design is wrong, then not only is the effort of implementing it and proving the coded implementation consistent with the specifications wasted, but the software may deliver undesirable or even harmful results if it is prematurely pressed into service in the belief that it has been fully verified.

Obvious though these points may appear to be, relatively little attention has until recently been paid to the validation of software design in comparison with the effort expended on the validation of code. That this situation is starting to change is shown by the increasing application of formal verification techniques to prove desirable properties of specifications, and by the development of executable specification languages for the purpose of obtaining test results. Three such languages, namely PROLOG, OBJ and SPECINT, will be discussed in detail in this paper.

2. FORMAL VERIFICATION OF PROGRAM DESIGN

The formal verification of program design resembles that of program code, in that theorem proving techniques are used to show the presence of certain desirable properties. In implementation proofs, these include such properties as correctness and termination, while in design proofs, as in the "specification checking" done in HDM [22], they may include such properties as internal consistency or multi-level security (the requirement that the security level of any entity receiving information is at least as high as that of the sender).

The verification of partially coded programs, during the stepwise development of programs from their specifications in "verification oriented programming" [16], includes aspects of both implementation proofs and design proofs. A partially coded program contains certain procedures, functions or inner loops that are not coded in full but are merely specified. The formal verification of such a program proves that the program is correct insofar as it is coded, and is therefore a step toward fulfilling or "implementing" the main program specifications. But such a proof also verifies the "design" of the uncoded parts, to the extent of showing that their (lower-level) specifications are adequate to the task defined by the main (higher-level) program specifications. The top-level specifications cannot of course be verified in this way but must be validated separately, either by means of the various manual inspection methods that have recently been proposed [1,5] or by means of the techniques for direct execution and testing of specifications that are discussed in detail in the following.

3. TESTING OF PROGRAM DESIGN

In the validation of software design, it is more difficult to apply testing techniques than verification methods to program specifications, since only fully-coded programs can normally be tested. But a designer who has written and perhaps verified a set of specifications, or even implemented them to a certain level short of completion, might nevertheless find it extremely useful to be able to "look ahead" to the eventual completion of the program and generate sample output from the specifications in some more direct way than by the generation and testing of actual program code, thereby testing whether or not the results of implementing the specifications would conform to the designer's requirements or the user's specifications. The validation of specifications with respect to such imprecise or informal standards as "requirements" or "expectations" cannot be satisfactorily performed by verification techniques, which by their nature are able to test only for the presence or absence of formal properties.

The generation of sample output from specifications may be done either by constructing a cheap initial version, or "prototype", of the finished program, or by executing the specifications in some more direct way, such as by means of a "specification interpreter" [22], or even by programming directly in terms of specifications, as is done for example in logic programming [14] and specifically in PROLOG [2]. The use of a specification interpreter in a program development system may be regarded as a type of "excursion" [4] that provides information helpful to the user in performing his task, which in this case is the writing of a program, but without changing the state of his data, which in this case is the previously coded part of the program. In particular, the interpretation or execution of specifications is a type of <u>look-ahead</u> excursion that informs the user of the effects of certain actions not yet performed, which amount in this case to completing the implementation of the specifications.

3.1 Rapid prototyping

The term 'prototyping', or more commonly 'rapid prototyping', has just recently come into vogue in the world of software development and its usage has therefore not yet been definitely fixed, but it usually carries the connotation of an early implementation of specifications or requirements that is both quick and cheap, and without too much regard for considerations of elegance or efficiency. The idea is to observe the functional behaviour of systems and thereby to get user feedback as soon as possible in the software "life-cycle", in order to assist in the development and modification of the design of the "product" before too much effort is expended on implementing a particular design. An essential ingredient of any prototyping system is a high-level executable "prototype language", which allows for quick and easy writing of programs that serve as prototypes of programs in another presumably lower-level "implementation language". Examples are CASTOR [23], designed as a prototype language for ADA, and OBJ [6], which serves as a prototype interpreter for any implementation language that can be defined in it. Prototype languages are more commonly referred to as "specification languages" or "executable specification languages", particularly if, as in the case of OBJ, they are not designed to facilitate rapid prototyping for any specific implementation language. The role played by such languages in software validation is discussed in more detail in the following section.

3.2 Direct execution of program specifications

The motivation for direct execution of program specifications is much the same as that for rapid prototyping, namely, the validation of software design as early in the development process as possible. Insofar as there is any difference between the two concepts, it is that prototyping sometimes has the meaning of a kind of "pre-programming" for a specific implementation language. The prototype language must therefore contain some elements of its implementation language, and is therefore not a pure specification language in the sense of a language that expresses in a formal way what is to be done as opposed to how to do it [11]. The direct execution of specifications expressed in an algebraic or functional way may, on the other hand, be presumed to be carried out without reference to a specific implementation language, but rather through the medium of an "interpreter" that is able to take input, check whether it fulfils the "input conditions" stated in the specifications, and if so, generate output that satisfies the "output conditions". This is presumably less efficient in terms of computer time than actually implementing and testing the specifications, but more efficient in terms of programming and overall development time.

Although the original idea behind the development of specification interpreters was the rapid testing and debugging of specifications in order to avoid waste of programming time at later stages in the software development process, specification languages are increasingly being used as programming languages, as in logic programming. This has the obvious advantage of avoiding the "implementation" development phase altogether, with the necessity of subsequently verifying the correspondence between specifications and code, but the obvious disadvantage that the interpreted specifications may not run as efficiently as their implemented versions. It is therefore more suited to the sort of "experimental" or "throwaway" programming that is done in connection with doctoral theses or other university research work, where the main idea is to test or demonstrate the feasibility of some new concepts or algorithms, than to the development of software "packages" or "products" designed for repetitive use.

3.2.1 Logic programming

Logic programming, as it is currently understood and partially embodied in PROLOG, has its roots in the PLANNER [8] programming language, whose original purposes included the construction of a more efficient theorem prover or "deductive system" -- especially insofar as proving theorems in robots was concerned -- than the resolution-based [19] models then prevalent, by incorporating some of the key features of these methods into the programming language itself. Such features included (i) clause form, used declaratively in resolution as the standard form for logical formulae, and (when restricted to "Horn clauses", containing at most one "positive literal") as the standard representation for procedures in PLANNER and its successor PROLOG; (ii) unification-type pattern matching, used in resolution to determine whether an inference is possible from two or more clauses, and in PLANNER and PROLOG as the basis for procedure invocation, and (iii) a particular search strategy, which in resolution may be any of a wide variety of logically complete or incomplete strategies, and which in PLANNER and in non-parallel versions of PROLOG is the logically incomplete depth-first search with backtracking. PLANNER failed to win wide acceptance, partly because of the strident anti-theorem-proving (i.e. anti-resolution) rhetoric of some of its supporters, but mainly perhaps because automatic deduction research was then concentrated more on the development of strategies that it was hoped, rightly or wrongly, would be both efficient and logically complete, without special-purpose or "knowledge-based" heuristics and without the aid of interactive user intervention.

The success of PROLOG, based on the ideas of Colmerauer and Kowalski [13] and detailed by McDermott [18], is due not so much to its power as a problem solver or theorem prover, which seems to be confined mainly to the sort of "question-answering" problems that arise in "expert systems", as to its usefulness as a general-purpose "workhorse programming language serving a busy user community" [20] that "may become the FORTRAN of logic-based programming languages" [18]. At the same time, PROLOG is the next thing to being a specification language fulfilling the ideals of "logic programming", i.e., that a programmer need only describe what he intends his program to do in terms of a set of (first-order) logical formulae in any arbitrary order, and the system does the rest.

Supporters and critics alike have pointed out that PROLOG formulations fall short of, or at least differ from, the goal of programming in logic. For one thing, PROLOG does not provide for programming in fully quantified first-order logic, but only in the subset of first-order logic encompassed by Horn clauses. A set of formulae in full first-order logic is taken rather as a specification, from which a Horn-clause program may be deduced [14]. PROLOG differs further from logic programming, in use if not in design, in that theorem-proving examples are frequently formulated in prolog more nearly in the way in which they would be stated in LISP than in the way in which they would normally be posed to a theorem prover. This practice reflects both the continuing preoccupation of artificial intelligence researchers with list processing and the desire of PROLOG designers that their product compete with LISP on its own terms if not supplant it as the principal AI programming language.

A more serious limitation is that PROLOG procedures include various types of implicit and explicit constructs that count as imperative or control information rather than pure logic. In particular, the execution sequence whereby PROLOG attempts to satisfy "goals", is determined implicitly by the order of literals within clauses and of clauses within procedures, and explicitly by the inclusion within clauses of special operators such as CUT and FAIL. In programs without such operators, the order of literals and clauses usually affects just efficiency of execution, sometimes to the extent of determining whether or not the program gets into infinite loops. The arbitrary effects of such ordering could be reduced or eliminated altogether by the various software and hardware systems for concurrent execution of PROLOG literals (i.e., "AND-parallelism") and clauses (i.e., "OR-parallelism") currently under development [15]. But the actual meaning, and not just the efficiency, of procedures that employ CUT and FAIL is affected by the placement of these operators between the literals, and by the ordering of literals and clauses, within such procedures. A good example of this phenomenon is the standard way of expressing "if-then-else" in PROLOG [18]:

```
foo(...) := test, CUT, arm1
foo(...) := arm2.
```

When the procedure 'foo' is called (by unifying its arguments with those of some goal), the success of 'test' causes evaluation of CUT (which always succeeds) and thence 'arm1', and the failure of 'test' results in the evaluation of 'arm2', but the placement of CUT prevents the evaluation of 'arm2' in the event of failure of 'arm1' or of any subsequent goal. This is because the CUT literal (which strongly resembles FENCE in SNOBOL pattern matching) removes the "place-markers" from the literals preceding it in the clause so as to eliminate these literals as possible backtrack points in the event of failure of any goals following CUT.

A particular application of this construct is the usual PROLOG definition of "negation as failure" [2,20]:

```
not(P) := P, CUT, FAIL
not(P)
```

where FAIL is a literal that is always false. In order for not(P) to succeed if and only if P fails, the two defining clauses must appear in the above order -- if this order were reversed, then not(P) would succeed for any goal P. The order-dependence of procedures such as the above is a feature of PROLOG which designers of alternative logic programming languages such as LOGLISP [20] have tried to avoid. The inclusion of such procedures could also cause programs written in the various parallel PROLOGS currently under development [15] to deliver different results when run more than once with the same input.

3.2.2 Execution of algebraic specifications

In the algebraic approach to abstract data types, the definition of an "object" such as gcd (greatest common divisor) is stated in terms of algebraic equations, certain of which may be "conditional", i.e. containing an if-clause restricting their application [6]. Sets of equations may be taken as specifying a program for computing such an "object". They may, furthermore, be directly executed by interpreting each equation as a rule for rewriting terms and applying the set of equations to the term to be evaluated, as in [12]. The two general conditions for such a procedure to work properly are that there must be no infinite rewriting sequences (finite termination), and that all sequences of rewrites must give the same final result (Church-Rosser property). For example, the set of equations given by Goguen and Meseguer [6] for the algebraic specification of greatest common divisor is:

```
OK-EQNS
      gcd(i,i) = i
      gcd(i,0) = i
      gcd(0,i) = i
      gcd(i,j) = gcd(i - j,j) if i > j
      gcd(i,j) = gcd(i,j - i) if i < j
ERR-EQNS
      gcd(i,j) = neg-arg if i < 0 + j < 0
```

where '+' = 'or'. Given a term to be evaluated, e.g. gcd(1308,156), OBJ proceeds by scanning through the left halves of the above rules in sequence, attempting to find a pattern match. If successful, the term is rewritten as specified in the right half of the rule, provided all 'if' conditions of the rule are satisfied. The process is repeated until it terminates, in this case with the answer 12.

The sort of pattern matching employed by an algebraic specification language such as OBJ is just "one way", i.e. the substitutions are made just in the variables in the left halves of the rules and not in any of the variables that may appear in the input or "goal" terms, as in the sort of "two way" pattern matching or unification that is an essential feature of PROLOG. By way of comparison, a PROLOG program for the above example is given below, in which gcd is written as a predicate with three arguments, where 'gcd(x,y,z)' means 'greatest common divisor of x and y equals z', rather than as a function of two arguments as in OBJ.

```
gcd(i,i,i)
gcd(i,0,i)
gcd(0,i,i)
gcd(i,j,y) := i > j, j ≥ 0, gcd(i - j,j,y)
gcd(i,j,y) := j > i, i ≥ 0, gcd(i,j - i,y).
```

The input to this program is a literal, e.g. gcd(1308,156,z), where 'z' is in effect an output variable that is filled in by unification. (In both gcd-programs, information as to the data types of the variables, i.e. 'integer', has been omitted for the sake of brevity.)

Comparison between the foregoing OBJ and PROLOG programs illustrates the point that any rewrite rules can be expressed in terms of Horn clauses, a feature of PROLOG that is widely exploited in its applications to the design of "expert systems", which are essentially ordered sets of rewrite rules purporting to embody human "expertise" in various technical and scientific areas. The equations in OBJ, and the Horn clauses in PROLOG, thus admit of procedural as well as declarative interpretations, a feature that makes them particularly well-suited to serve as prototyping or executable specification languages.

3.2.3 Interactive development of specifications

The current implementations of OBJ and PROLOG are reasonably efficient in executing program specifications that are given in the appropriate declarative format, whether it be equations or Horn clauses, but they do not for the most part provide much help or guidance to the user in the event that these specifications are incomplete or incorrect in any way. That is to say, they just execute specifications that are executable, and fail to execute those that are not executable for any reason. But in fact the writing of program specifications, like any other programming activity with a human element, admits of errors. Most of the programming "environments" that are currently being developed are designed to provide users with "tools" to aid in the process of interactive and incremental program construction, but few if any are designed to provide help in interactive and incremental writing of program specifications.

The experimental specification interpreter SPECINT [3] is based on the premise that sets of specifications written by a user may fail to fulfil his requirements in various ways. In particular, they may be incomplete, in the sense that important conditions, such as 'x greater than y' or 'integer(z)', may have been omitted; they may be inconsistent, and therefore impossible to satisfy; they may contain undefined predicates, which may or may not be essential to the computation of output for a particular set of input data, or they may be just plain wrong, in the sense that they specify some program other than what the user had in mind.

SPECINT has been implemented in STRUBOL, i.e. structured SNOBOL [10], and (partially) in REDUMA [9,21], which simulates the operation of K. J. Berkling's "reduction machine". It is designed to execute specifications stated in the form used by Manna and Waldinger [17] in the context of deductive program synthesis, i.e.

```
f(a) <= find z such that Outputconds(a,z)
  where Inputconds(a)
```

where 'a' and 'z' each consist of one or more variables, and denote respectively the input and output of the desired program 'f(a)', as in the following specification of an integer square root program, given in the actual format used by SPECINT:

```
sqrt(n) = "find z integer(z); le(z ** 2,n);
           lt(n,(z + 1) ** 2);
      where  integer(n); le(0,n)" .
```

(The expression on the right of the '=' is placed in quotes in order to indicate that it is a <u>string</u>, that is assigned as value to the functional prototype 'sqrt(n)' on the left of the '='.)

But whereas Manna and Waldinger apply resolution-based theorem proving methods to specifications of this sort in order to transform them into structured programs in a simplified functional language, SPECINT attempts to execute them directly. Given a sample value, e.g. 37, of the input variable n, it first evaluates the input conditions, i.e. 'integer(37)' and 'le(0,37)'. If any input condition is false, it returns failure with an appropriate comment, but if, as in the example, they are all true, it proceeds to evaluate the output conditions, starting with the current value of the output variable z (in the SNOBOL4 languages, any variable not otherwise assigned is automatically initialised to 0). Whenever it encounters an output condition that evaluates to 'false', it (a) assigns the false output condition to the variable 'fcond'; (b) determines the predicate or function <u>fun</u> on which fcond fails, and (c) applies a corrective function or procedure <u>ffun</u> to the arguments of <u>fun</u>, in an effort to reduce the difference between the current values of the output variables occurring in fcond and values that would make fcond true. For integer predicates such as 'le' and '=', these corrective functions <u>ffun</u> are predefined, but in other cases the system may ask the user to define them as necessary.

In the integer square root example, with n=37 and z=0, the first output condition that evaluates to 'false' is

```
fcond = "lt(n,(z + 1) ** 2)"
```

whose predicate is 'lt', so the call

```
flt(n,(z + 1) ** 2)
```

is made to the corrective function 'flt', with the same values n=37 and z=0. This in turn calls a procedure

```
change(fcond,outputvars)
```

(i.e., "change the output variables with respect to the false output condition") whose arguments are instantiated respectively with the expressions 'lt(n,(z + 1) ** 2)' and 'z'. This procedure, which is in fact called by the corrective functions of all the integer predicates, first computes the difference in the values of the two arguments of the integer predicate 'lt'. It then tests whether increasing the value of the output variable z by 1 reduces this difference. Since it does, this change is made in z, and the output conditions are re-evaluated starting at the left in order to verify that they remain true under the new value of z. But if increasing the value of z by 1 were in fact to <u>increase</u> this difference instead of reducing it, then <u>change</u> would try <u>decreasing</u> the value of z by 1 and re-evaluating the output conditions. If neither increasing nor decreasing z reduces the difference between the expressions on the left and right of the integer predicate, then evaluation stops with the comment that the output condition fcond is unsatisfiable. This way of changing the values of the output variables by attempting to correct the false output conditions one at a time is of course a bit naive and <u>ad hoc</u>, and it should be easy to invent output conditions for which it will not work, but it is not <u>incorrect</u>, since by definition it cannot terminate successfully unless all the conditions in the specification are satisfied.

The SPECINT procedure for changing the values of the output variables differs from the way in which bindings are changed in PROLOG. In SPECINT, the value of an output variable z may be changed whenever a false output condition 'fcond' that contains z is encountered -- in PROLOG terms, whenever a "goal" containing z fails. The new value of z is determined by analysis of the goal fcond that fails, and is then applied to all of the output conditions in the specification (i.e. to all of the "literals" in the "clause"), including any that precede fcond. In PROLOG, on the other hand, a variable z may be unbound and reset to another value only by backtracking to the literal where the binding was made and finding another match. If this is a different literal from fcond, then the new value of z will normally not depend on examination of fcond as it does in SPECINT.

An input or output condition in SPECINT may consist of the equivalent of a single "literal" in PROLOG, as in the specification of sqrt(n), or it may be logically complex, since the disjunction operator '|' may be used within input and output conditions, as in the following SPECINT version of the gcd-program whose OBJ and PROLOG versions have already been given:

```
gcd(i,j) = "find z eq(i,j) bind('z',i)    |
                   eq(j,0) bind('z',i)    |
                   eq(i,0) bind('z',j)    |
      gt(i,j) ge(j,0) bind('z',gcd(i - j,j))  |
      gt(j,i) ge(i,0) bind('z',gcd(i,j - i))"
```

where the programmer-defined function 'bind(x,y)' assigns the contents of y to the variable denoted by x. The entire specification of gcd(i,j) thus contains just one disjunctive output condition, whose disjuncts are evaluated by SPECINT from left to right, and where the integer predicates 'eq', 'gt' and 'ge' denote what are in effect input conditions for each of the disjuncts. As soon as SPECINT encounters a disjunct that evaluates to 'true', the value of 'z' determined by that disjunct is the output of gcd(i,j).

SPECINT provides several types of error messages, or requests for further information, in the event that the set of specifications or the input to them are incorrect or incomplete, namely:

(1) If an input condition that evaluates to 'false' is encountered, the user is invited to correct the input.
(2) If a corrective function is required in order to satisfy an output condition, the user is invited to provide it.
(3) If an undefined function or predicate in either the input or output conditions is called, the user is invited to define or specify it, or merely to supply the particular value required in order that computation may proceed.
(4) If a predefined or programmer defined corrective function is unable to "correct" an output condition, then evaluation stops with the comment that the output condition is unsatisfiable.
(5) The comment "timelimit exceeded in <outputcond>" may sometimes indicate merely that the user should increase the time parameter (whose default value is one second), but more often indicates a defect of the specifications, such as the failure to define the terminating case of a recursive function, or an inconsistency within the set of conditions, either of which will cause SPECINT to run out the clock for however much time it is set.

A useful diagnostic in cases such as (5) is simply to include a 'print' command as the first output condition, as in:

```
foo(x) = "find z print(z); gt(z,x); ge(x,z)"
```

which for 'foo(57)', for example, will display the sequence 0,1,2,...,57,58,57,58,... until stopped by the clock. The occurrence of such repeating sequences of values of output variables usually indicates inconsistencies in the specifications.

The programming effort of the user of SPECINT is limited to supplying the functions that comprise the specifications, and the corrective functions requested by the system if and when any of the output conditions in the specifications are not fulfilled. Some of these corrective functions have been predefined, as in the case of the integer predicates. It is hoped that the definition of the others will usually be simple or obvious, as in the case of a function 'precede(x,y)', whose failure requires a corrective function fprecede that reverses the order of x and y, or of a function 'delete(x,y)', whose failure requires a corrective function fdelete that inserts x in y. This is a kind of "example-based programming", in which the system displays a value or set of values on which a given function in the specification fails and invites the user to supply a simple function, based on this example, for replacing the incorrect sequence of values with the correct one.

4. Conclusions

The validation of software specifications by means of their functional testing through direct execution has been discussed with reference to three executable specification languages, namely PROLOG, which implements many of the goals of logic programming; OBJ, which provides for the execution of algebraic specifications, and SPECINT, which employs heuristic methods in attempting to satisfy sets of output conditions and which supports the interactive development of functional specifications. Such languages are seen to resemble rapid prototyping languages in that they are designed to produce test results quickly and cheaply from specifications, but they differ from prototyping in that they are not intended to support programming in a specific implementation language. Executable specification languages are in fact increasingly being used as programming languages in their own right, and have much in common with functional programming languages.

Acknowledgements: the author is grateful to J. Abbott of NCC and to H. L. Hausen of GMD for useful suggestions concerning earlier versions of this manuscript.

REFERENCES

[1] Adrion, W. R., Branstad, M. A. and Cherniavsky, J. C., Validation, verification, and testing of computer software, Computing Surveys 14 (1982) 159-192.

[2] Clocksin, W. F. and Mellish, C. S., Programming in Prolog, (Springer-Verlag, Berlin, Heidelberg, 1981).

[3] Darlington, J. L., Interactive validation of program specifications, in Trappl, R. (ed.), Cybernetics and Systems Research (North-Holland, Amsterdam, 1982) 903-908.

[4] Darlington, J. L., Dzida, W., and Herda, S., The role of excursions in interactive systems, Int. J. Man-Machine Studies 18 (1983) 101-112.

[5] Fagan, M. E., Design and code inspections to reduce errors in program development, IBM Syst. J. 15 (1976) 182-211.

[6] Goguen, J. A. and Meseguer, J., Rapid prototyping in the OBJ executable specification language, ACM Softw. Eng. Notes 7, No. 5 (1982) 75-84.

[7] Griswold, R. E., String and List Processing in Snobol4: Techniques and Applications, (Prentice-Hall, Inc., Englewood Cliffs, New Jersey, 1975).

[8] Hewitt, C., PLANNER: a language for proving theorems in robots, Proc. First Int'l. Joint Conf. on Artificial Intelligence, Washington, D. C. (1969) 295-301.

[9] Hommes, F., Reduction Machine Simulator Reference Manual, GMD-ISF Technical Report (1982).

[10] Ingenbleek, B., STRUBOL, GMD-RZ Technical Report (1980).

[11] Jones, C. B., The role of formal specifications in software development, in Life-Cycle Management: Infotech State of the Art Report, Series 8, No. 7 (Infotech Ltd., Maidenhead, Berks., 1980).

[12] Knuth, D. E. and Bendix, P. B., Simple word problems in universal algebras, in Leech, J. (ed.), Computational Problems in Abstract Algebra (Pergamon Press, Oxford, 1970) 263-297.

[13] Kowalski, R., Predicate logic as programming language, in Information Processing 74 (North-Holland, Amsterdam, 1974) 569-574.

[14] Kowalski, R., Logic for Problem Solving, (Elsevier North Holland, Inc., New York, 1979).

[15] Kowalski, R., Logic programming in the fifth generation, Proc. Fifth Gen. Conf., (SPL International, London, 1982).

[16] Luckham, D. C., Program verification and verification-oriented programming, in Gilchrist, B. (ed.), Information Processing 77 (North-Holland, Amsterdam, New York, Oxford, 1977) 783-793.

[17] Manna, Z. and Waldinger, R., Deductive synthesis of the unification algorithm, Science of Computer Programming 1 (1981) 5-48.

[18] McDermott, D., The PROLOG phenomenon, SIGART Newsletter 72 (1980) 16-20.

[19] Robinson, J. A., A machine-oriented logic based on the resolution principle, JACM 12 (1965) 23-41.

[20] Robinson, J. A. and Sibert, E. E., LOGLISP: an alternative to PROLOG, in Hayes, J. E., Michie, D. and Pao, Y-H (eds.), Machine Intelligence 10 (Ellis Horwood Ltd., Chichester, 1982) 399-419.

[21] Schluetter. H., Introduction to the Reduction Machine Simulator, GMD-ISF Technical Report (1982).

[22] Silverberg, B. A., An overview of the SRI hierarchical development methodology, in Huenke, H. (ed.), Software Engineering Environments (North-Holland, Amsterdam, New York, 1981) 235-252.

[23] Smith, D. A., Rapid Software Prototyping, Technical Report No. 187, University of California at Irvine, Computer Science Department (1982).

MICROCOMPUTERS: Developments in Industry, Business and Education
D.R. Wilson and C.J. van Spronsen (eds.) / © EUROMICRO, 1983
Elsevier Science Publishers B.V. (North-Holland)

AN INTEGRATED SELF-SELECTION ARBITER

Pierluigi Civera, Gianni Conte, Dante Del Corso
Francesco Gregoretti and Franco Maddaleno

Dipartimento di Elettronica - Politecnico di Torino
Turin, Italy

This work will describe the implementation as an integrated circuit of a modular distributed arbiter that uses a self-selection arbitration mechanism. This technique allows us to set up a fully distributed system which uses N priority lines to arbitrate among 2**N users. The algorithm here described is an improvement of the usual one. The unnecessary arbitration cycles are eliminated, and the low priority modules are allowed to obtain the resource within a time shorter than a predefined maximum.
The integrated circuit has been designed following the well known Mead-Conway rules, and it includes the self-selection network, the control unit and the clock generator. The self-selection network is obtained by replication of a basic element, and the control unit is a PLA based finite state machine.

1. INTRODUCTION

An arbiter is a basic building block used in complex digital systems whenever a resource can be used by many elements. Examples of application are arbitration structures used in a system where more than one element can interrupt the central processor, or the mechanisms to identify the master in single bus multiprocessor architecture.

The paper describes the implementation of an integrated self-selection arbiter for multiprocessor systems based on M3BUS [1].

Section 2 will introduce and compare the different arbitration techniques focusing on the advantages of different solutions. Section 3 points out the characteristics of the self-selection arbiter and the arbitration policies used in this case. Section 4 describes the implementation and how the I.C. can be used to obtain the complete arbitration structure of a multiprocessor system.

2. ARBITRATION TECHNIQUES

The logical organization of an arbiter is shown in figure 1. The arbiter receives the resource requests from the would-be users and assigns the resource to one of them according to some predefined policy. The logical structure shown in figure 1 can actually be implemented in many different ways [2] [3] . It can be concentrated in a single unit or distributed through the system; different topologies and techniques support the users-arbiter-resource connections.

Even if one usually distinguishes between centralized and distributed implementations, it must be pointed out that the arbiter is a single logical unit associated with the resource to be arbitrated. When the arbiter is also implemented by a single physical unit, it is referred to as centralized. The structure of a centralized arbiter is shown in figure 2a. The simplest centralized arbiter is a priority encoder which activates only the output (GRANT) corresponding to the highest priority input (REQUEST). The arbiter however can also consists of a set of physically separated units, which are part of each requester. In this case the arbiter has a decentralized organization (figure 2b). If the complete arbitration system is composed of a set of identical units, it is also fully modular.

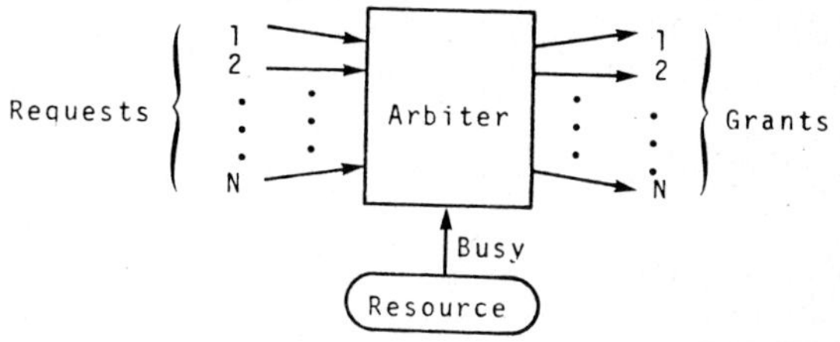

Fig. 1 - Typical arbiter organization.

Different techniques are used to carry the request and the acknowledge information. With a centralized arbiter, 2*N lines are required to arbitrate and select N users. This technique is not the most convenient for modular systems, because the request/grant lines are point to point connections, organized with a star topology. With this structure, to add a new requester, it is also necessary to add a couple of lines. For these reasons centralized arbiters are selected only when the users are very few, or the number is fixed. Distributed arbiters on the other hand use modular connection topologies, such as a bus. Distributed arbitration systems are becoming more widely used, since they can be designed in such a way as to have no single failure point.

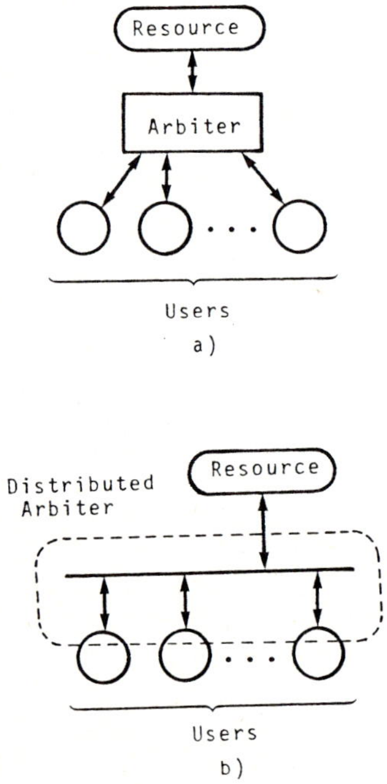

Fig. 2 - a) Centralized arbiter
b) Distributed arbiter.

A further degree of freedom, which identifies different arbitration structures is the priority algorithm. The priority level assigned to any request can be fixed or variable, according to different rules. When it is fixed, the arbiter can starve the users: if many high priority requests are continuously coming in, they cut off the service of low priority users. Some techniques have been developed to avoid starvation and to make the arbiter "FAIR": these methods are based on dynamic change of priority levels, or on "forced" fairness. Using these techniques, one can define the maximum delay which can elapse for any user from the request to the grant. The change of priority levels is dangerous; one must take care to have unique codes on each module, and so it can be used only with centralized controllers. Arbiter and resource activity must be synchronized to avoid "resource stealing" by higher priority requests. An example of synchronization is shown in figure 3.

A widely used technique for distributed arbitration is the DAISY CHAIN. In a daisy chain, as shown in figure 4, a generalized grant (GGR) ripples through the arbitration units of

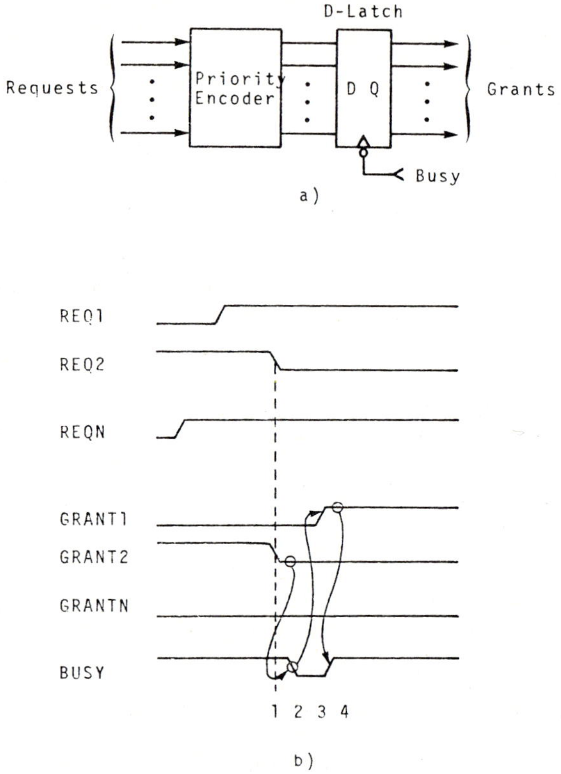

Fig. 3 - Centralized arbiter operation.
a) typical hardware implementation;
b) timing relations, asynchronous version:
1) user2 releases the resource;
2) the resource is now available, arbitration starts;
3) user1 wins the contention;
4) and uses the resource.

each user. When a request is active, the generalized grant is stopped and the local grant (LGR) is activated.

The daisy chain uses only two bus lines (three or four with synchronization signals); the number of users can be increased at will, with only the penalty of an increased arbitration time. The simple chain of figure 4 can cause starvation because the priority of each user is fixed. With additional hardware, a round robin scheduling of requests can be implemented [4]. The advantage of round-robin versus fixed priority is to avoid starvation and to guarantee an upper limit to the service time. The main weak point of the daisy chain is that the priority level of a module depends on the physical position in the backplane. Modules must have fixed slots, and there is no possibility of changing the priority levels at run time. Moreover, a single fault or a missing module can lock the coomplete chain or cause errors.

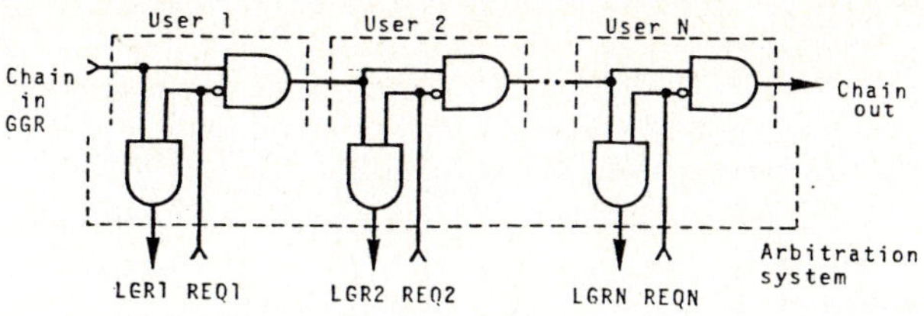

Fig. 4 - Simple daisy chain arbiter.

Another solution well suited for modular bus-based systems is the distributed arbiter with self-selection priority networks. A self-selection distributed arbiter consists of one unit on each master, connected by a set of priority lines and some control lines. Each control block receives a REQUEST from the user circuitry and handles the arbitration procedure by sending appropriate commands to the priority network and to the control lines of the arbitration bus. The self-selection networks identify the highest priority module by means of a "contention" process. One unit wins the arbitration and grants the resource to its requester.

3. THE DISTRIBUTED SELF-SELECTION ARBITER

The arbitration technique based on self-selection networks was first introduced to manage multiple interrupts in bus based single processor systems [5]. It has been used, with minor changes, as a tool to select among multiple bus access requests in single bus multimaster systems [1], [6], [7], [8]. The main advantages of this kind of arbiter are:

- it can be fully distributed; each master has its own circuit connected to a common priority bus, without any chain or centralized star connection. With N lines up to 2**N requests can be managed with an arbitration delay proportional to N.

- the resolution of the contention is obtained by the cooperation of all the arbiters; moreover the introduction of a new master simply involves adding the proper arbitration module.

- it can have a high degree of flexibility on the policy of priority assignement. The priority depends on a code written into a programmable register on each module.

3.1. Architecture of the arbitration system

A distributed arbiter with a self-selection network consists of a set of modules, one for each master, linked together by the priority bus and by some control lines. As shown in figure 5, the elementary arbitration units are divided into:

- self-selection priority network;

- control logic.

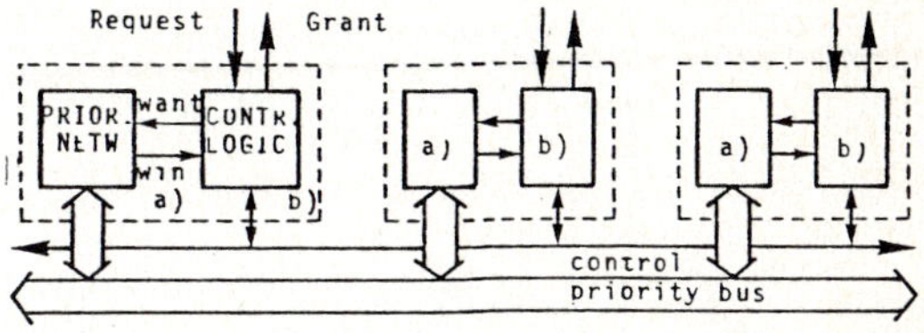

Fig. 5 - Distributed self-selection arbiter.
a) self-selection priority network
b) control logic.

Each unit which partecipates in the arbitration process puts its priority code onto the priority lines using open collector (O.C.) buffers. The self-selection networks carry out the contention process and, after a predictable time [9], the priority lines carry a steady code corresponding to the highest priority among the requests. The module that recognizes its own code becomes WINNER of the arbitration, while the others wait for the next contention cycle. This operation sequence is shown in figure 6.

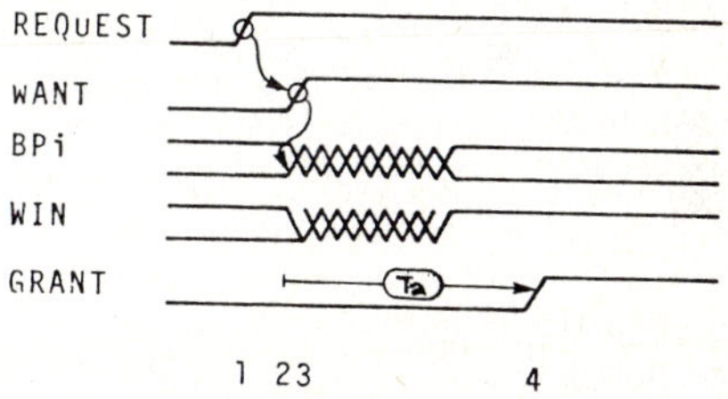

Fig. 6 - Arbitration cycle.
1) a unit activates REQUEST
2) as soon as the start condition for a new arbitration cycle is met, the control logic activates WANT. This happens for all modules with pending requests;
3) the priority networks with WANT=1 start the self-selection process. After this step no other module can activate WANT or interfere in the self-selection process
4) After a delay Ta (greater than the contention time), the WIN line of each network is sampled. If true, the GRANT signal goes active and the unit grants the requested resource. If false, GRANT remains not active and the unit waits. REQUEST stays active and the unit will participate in the next arbitration cycle.

3.2. Self-selection networks

The block diagram of a self-selection network is shown in figure 7. Two sections can be identified:

- a set of O.C. inverting buffers. They transfer, when enabled, the priority vector (IP) of the module to the priority bus (BP*);
- a set of two-input comparators. They verify if each bit of the code standing on the priority bus matches the corresponding bit of the module priority vector.

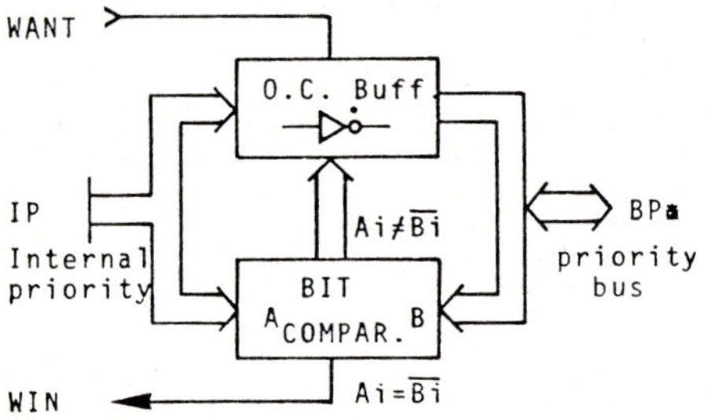

Fig. 7 - Block diagram of a self-selection network.

The elementary cell of this arbiter can be implemented with two different techniques, as shown in figure 8. The contention process begins when the WANT signal becomes active. The O.C. buffers are enabled on networks with WANT=1 and on the priority bus the logical NOR of the priority vectors (IP) will be present. Since on O.C. lines the low level wins over the high level, the following conditions apply:

IPi local code	BPi* priority bus	
0	0	BPi* is set to 0 by another module with IPi=1
0	1	IPi = 0 or BPi* driver disabled in every network network
1	0	IPi = 1 on the network; the value of IPi in the other priority networks is not relevant
1	1	Can occur only if the driver is disabled (otherwise with IPi = 1 BP*i must go to 0)

A detailed analysis of the self-selection process is given in [9].

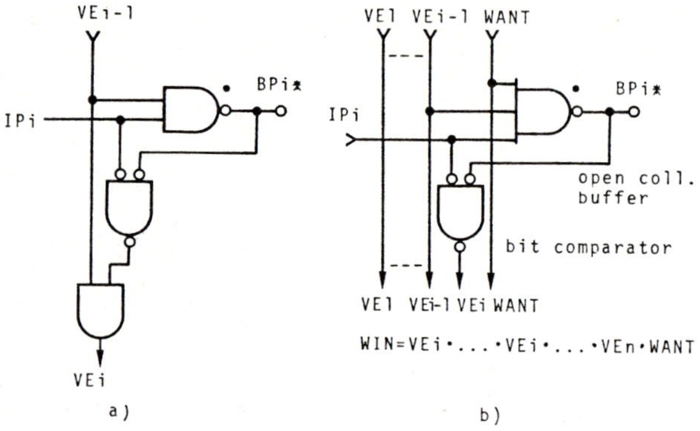

Fig. 8 - Self-selection basic cell.
a) carry logic
b) look ahead logic.

3.3. Contention time

The contention process causes logical transitions to propagate through the self selection networks and on the bus lines. The process begins when the WANT signal goes high and it ends when the WIN signal is settled; that is when it is definitively active for the winner module and not active for all the others.

The time needed to complete the operation is therefore a function of many variables: the delay introduced by the logic elements, the number of bits involved in the contention process, the set up and propagation times on the bus.

Figure 9 shows a model of the priority network and the delay associated with each element. The bus drivers and receivers are intentionally separated, because, for electrical reasons, they must be implemented using bipolar technology. If the arbitration circuit is implemented using NMOS technology, they must be external devices.

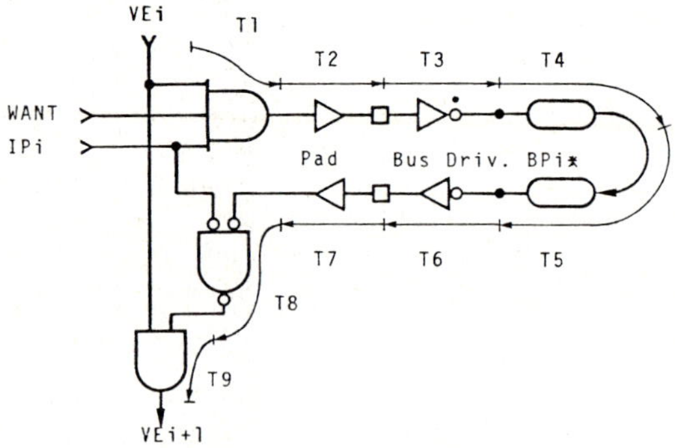

Fig. 9 - Delay model of self-selection cell.

It can be shown [9] that the maximum time needed to resolve the contention in a N bit system is equal to :

$$Tam = N*(T1+T2+T3+T4+T6+T7+T8+T9)+4*T5$$

Note that T5, the propagation time on the bus, must be multiplied only by 4 even in an N bit system [4]. The value of Tam becomes consequently a design parameter for the control network.

3.4. Control circuit

In M3BUS [1], the arbitration process can occur only during well defined time slots, so the lines involved in bus arbitration can be used also for other purposes. A bus signal (ADDREN*) identifies the cycle that is being carried on, and is used also to enable the contention process. The sequence of elementary operations needed to perform an arbitration as shown in figure 10 is the following:

1) The master needing the bus informs its own arbiter of the request setting LOCREQ to 1.

2) The arbiter then sets active the bus signal BUSREQ*, to warn the system of the pending request.

3) As soon as ADDREN*=1, that is when the time slot devoted to arbitration starts, the contention process on the priority bus begins. The only modules involved in the contention process are those with a pending request.

4) The contention process must be completed within a period of the clock signal; at the end of the contention process only the module with highest priority will find the WIN signal active. Only this module will be allowed to use the bus (LOCGRANT=1).

The control logic supervising these operations can be implemented in two different ways: synchronous and asynchronous. In both cases, a clock signal can be obtained by a centralized generator, or using a distributed technique. In the first case the clock is generated by one module and the period must be defined according to the requirements of the slowest arbitration unit. In order to obtain a fully distributed arbitration system, a self synchronized clock system can be distributed among the different modules. In this latter case, every module generates a clock signal.

3.5. Arbitration algorithm

In a priority arbiter, when the higher priority modules request the common resource too frequently, the modules with lower priority must

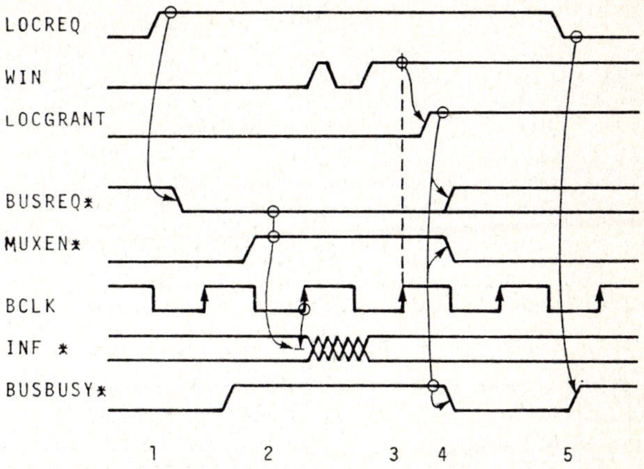

Fig. 10 - Arbitration cycle in M3BUS protocol:
1) a master issues a bus request;
2) when MUXEN* = 1 contention can start;
3) after a clock period the contention is stopped WIN signal is sampled;
4) if the bus is free the master with WIN active gains it and removes the request, otherwise it waits for BUSBUSY false. If other masters are waiting for the bus, the BUSREQ stays active;
5) the granted master removes the LOCREQ and releases the bus.

wait for an indefinite time (not a priori limited). This phenomenon, called "starvation", cannot be allowed in systems for real time applications.

In order to overcome this problem, two solutions can be chosen: to lower the priority of the modules as they are served, or to increase the priority of modules, which are waiting for the resource.

The priority assignement in a self-selection distributed arbiter can be dynamically changed during the operation. This gives great flexibility but can also cause problems. It may happen, for instance, that two modules involved in a contention process have the same priority. This event is very dangerous, particularly because it cannot be detected.

We shall here call "FAIRNESS" the algorithm that guarantees that the service time is less than a defined maximum. It works as follows:

- A flag (FAIR) in each requester is set to one when the module gets access to the bus.

- Until FAIR is equal to 1, the module does not make any bus request (BUSREQ* or WANT are not set active).

- FAIR is set to 0 only when no more requests are present on the bus (BUSREQ*=1).

So, after a first access, a module can access the bus again only when all the other requests, pending when the module is using the bus, have been served. This policy guarantees an upper bound to the waiting time. This bound is independent from the priority of the module; it simulates actually a "round-robin" policy.

A further improvement of the arbitration control logic has been introduced in order to eliminate arbitration cycles when they are not needed. When a module has accessed the bus and needs it again for the next cycle, if no other request is pending (i.e. no contention exists), the arbitration process is not activated. We shall call this algorithm "DEFAULT".

4. DESIGN OF THE INTEGRATED ARBITER

The implementation of one unit of a self-selection distributed arbiter using standard logic can require from 5 to 10 packages. This number is at least doubled if fairness and default options must be included.

Our main interest was in the bus arbitration of M3BUS; therefore the chip has been designed around this protocol. However the implementation is more general and can replace some random logic in any system with distributed self-selection arbitration.

4.1 System partitioning and chip planning

The block diagram of the integrated arbitration circuit is shown in figure 11. The arbitration unit has been divided into three independent blocks:

- contention unit:
  it consists of the contention resolving circuit, that is the self selection priority networks.

- control unit:
  handles the interfacing between the requesters and the processing units. It synchronizes the operations of all units which must participate in a contention.

- oscillator:
  produces a clock signal used by the control unit.

This partitioning simplifies the device testing because it allows to check each part independently. The drawback is that since some internal signal must leave the chip and then come back into it again, additional delays are introduced, and more I/O pads are required. Since the MPC uses in any case a 40-pin DIL

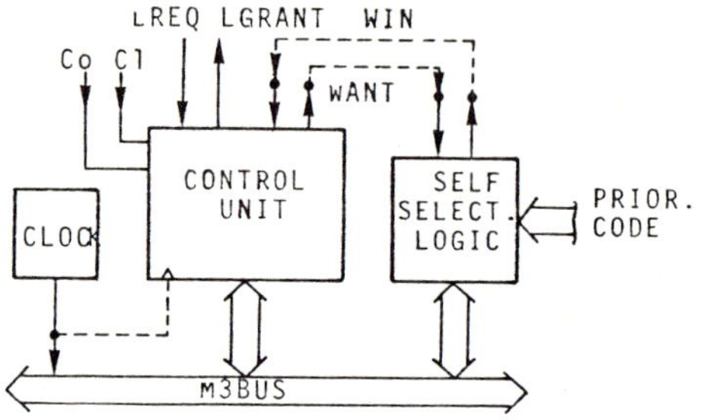

Fig. 11 - Block description of the integrated circuit.

package, the number of pads affects only the chip size. The area increase is caused by the fact that all pads must be placed on the periphery of the chip. This may leave large "empty" areas of silicon, and is acceptable only in an experimental device.

A final implementation, without test points, could use less than half of the pins for the same functions.

4.2 Electrical interfacing

The arbitration unit must be connected to a backplane with a length of about 50 cm and a characteristic impedance of about 120 ohms. The line drivers must supply the current required to drive the bussed lines to the proper logic levels. For instance, with TTL thresholds, the driver must sink at least 15 mA at the "low" output level. A set of TTL-compatible output pads is already available within any VLSI-CAD system, but the maximum current supplied by these drivers is limited to a few milliamps. To get higher currents using MOS transistors, one would increase the delay of the output buffer to unacceptable values. With current technology the only solution is to use TTL line drivers external to the chip towards the bus lines.

Since a "direction" signal is not available for all bidirectional lines, and some of them must be driven and sensed at the same time, all bidirectional signals are split into separate input and output pads. Using external buffers the logic part of the arbiter is completely separate from the electrical interface, and the same control chip could be used on busses with different electrical specifications. The drawback of this is once again an increase in the number of pins; in this case it could be avoided only by moving the electrical specification of the bus itself into the integrated circuit.

4.3 The contention unit

This unit consists basically of the self-selection contention network. To allow a fully modular design, we selected the ripple network shown in figure 8a. The complete contention logic is built by N-plicating this elementary structure. In this case N=4, and the system can arbitrate 2**4 = 16 requests. The ripple network has a higher settling time than the look-ahead logic of figure 8b. This however is completely masked by external delays; each level of internal logic adds about 5 ns, while the settling time on the bus lines lies in the range 50-80 ns.

This logic is fully combinational; the operations are activated by the WANT signal which enables the contention on MSB. The contention ripples on LSBs until it is blocked by a bit comparator. The priority code (IP in figure 7) is preset from outside. After the contention time the results of bit comparison on LSB gives the result of the process (WIN signal).

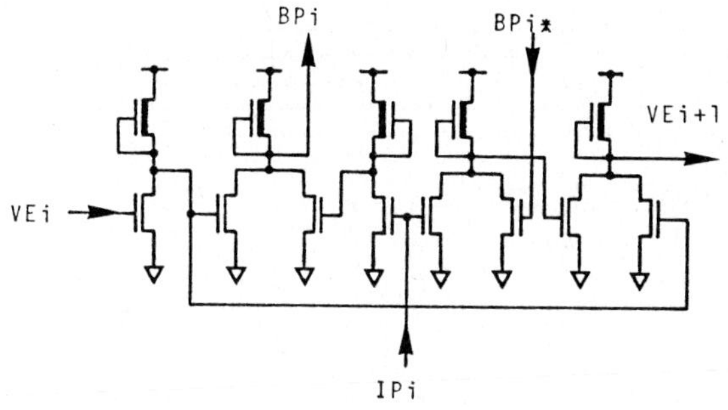

Fig. 12 - Circuit diagram of self-selection cell.

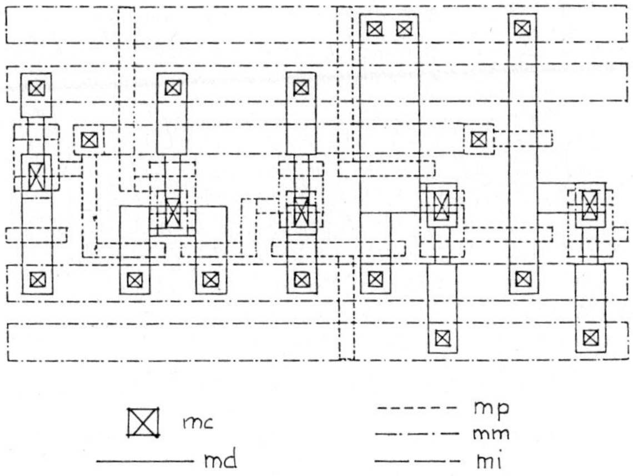

Fig. 13 - Layout of self-selection cell.

The transistor-level scheme of a cell of the priority network is given in figure 12; the layout of the cell is shown in figure 13.

4.4 Control unit

The control unit consists of a finite state synchronous sequential machine, which uses a PLA and two registers, as shown in figure 14. The registers are made using pass transistors clocked by a two-phase clock signal [10].

The state diagram of the control unit is shown in figure 15. The two mode flags C0 and C1 makes it possible to select four different priority policies:

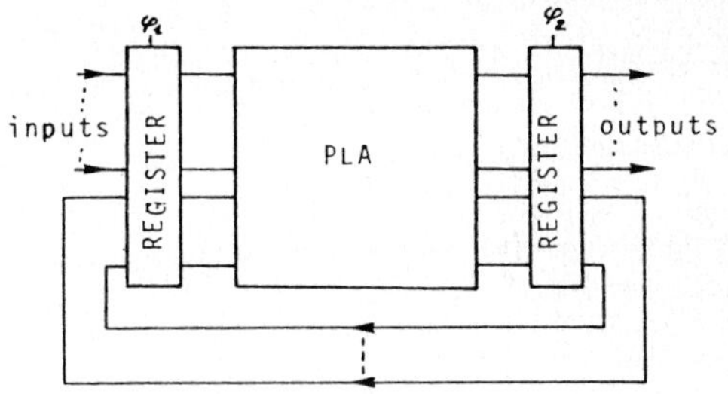

Fig. 14 - Block diagram of the control unit.

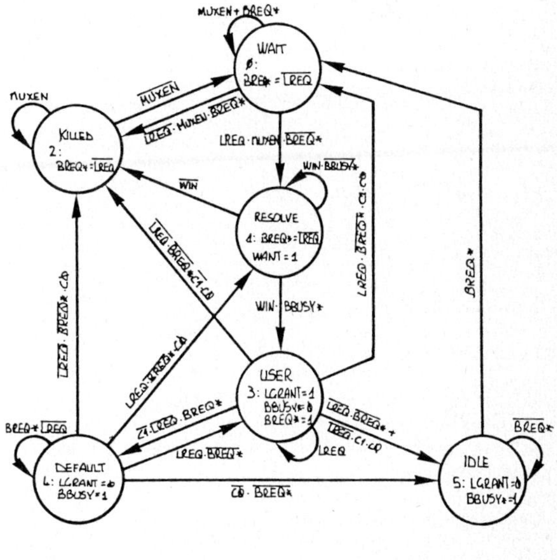

Fig. 15 - State diagram of the control unit.

mode 1: STANDARD
Only the basic algorithm is followed: the flag FAIR is ignored and a new arbitration cycle starts on any request.

mode 2: FAIR
The FAIR flag is used to obtain a round-robin priority and to avoid starvation.

mode 3: DEFAULT
The last module which accessed the resource can continue to use it without going through an arbitration, as long as no other request is raised.

mode 4: FAIR&DEFAULT
Both mode 2 and mode 3 are active.

The state diagram of figure 15 includes all these cases. The logic description of the PLA derived from this diagram has been used as input both in simulation programs for verifying the design's formal correctness, and in an automatic PLA synthetizer which generates directly the final layout. As shown in figure 16, the PLA uses two NOR planes; in the first one a transistor introduces a product term, in the second the sum terms are defined.

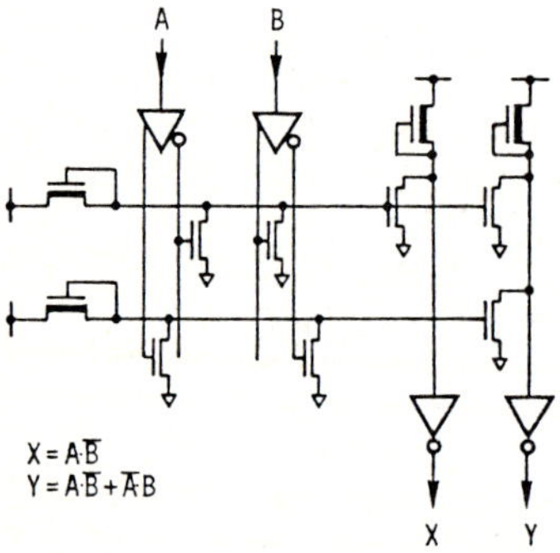

Fig. 16 - Simple PLA example.

4.5 Oscillator

This unit generates a square wave which can be synchronized with an external signal. The oscillator consists of a closed loop of an odd number of inverters, as shown in figure 17. The free run frequency depends on the delay of each elementary cell. This unit can also be used to check the performance of the technology by measuring the delay of a single gate. All clock generators can be tied to the same bus line, to act as a "distributed" oscillator using the technique described in [10]. The actual period depends on the slowest oscillator.

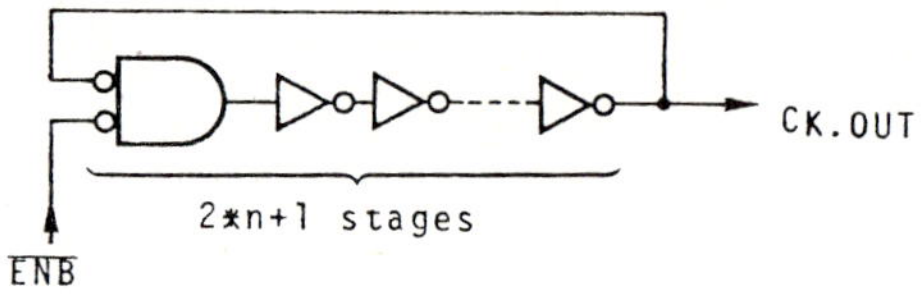

Fig. 17 - Oscillator synchronization principle.

4.6 Complete structure

In this case the chip area is imposed by the number of pads (33). The dimensions are 1080 X 1120 lambda; with lambda=3 µm this corresponds to about 3 x 3 mm.

The interconnection of the circuits to form a complete arbitration system is shown in figure 18.

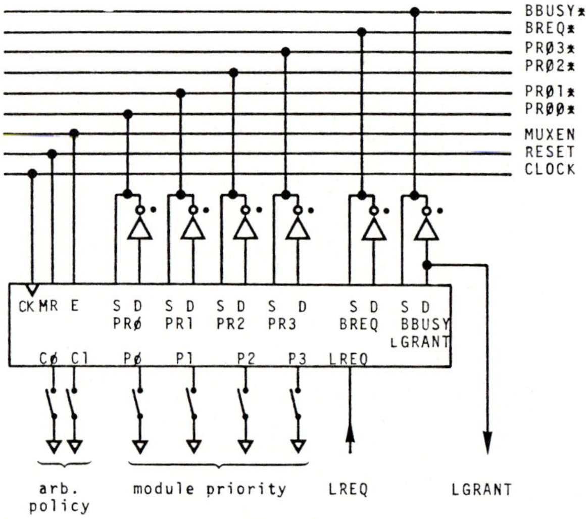

Fig. 18 - Typical application scheme of arbiter chip.

5. CONCLUSIONS

The design of a self-selection arbiter using NMOS technology has been described. An improvement on the usual arbitration policy is proposed: this new technique allows the arbiter to avoid useless arbitration cycles (DEFAULT option) and permits the low priority modules to be served in a finite and bounded time, thus avoiding starvation (FAIRNESS option). Using Mead Conway methodology, the circuit was designed very quickly, exploiting CAD tools developed at IMAG in Grenoble. The circuit is being built in the frame of the MPC supported by CNRS and organized by IMAG in Grenoble.

6. ACKNOWLEDGEMENTS

This work has been possible thanks to the collaboration of professor Antognetti (Istituto di Elettrotecnica of the University of Genova) and of professor Nicoud (Laboratoire de Microinformatique of the Ecole Politechnique Federale de Lausanne).

Particular thanks are due to professor Anceau, of IMAG (Grenoble University) for allowing us to participate in MPC and to professor Guyot for his help.

7. REFERENCES

[1] --- M3BUS - Modular MultiMicro BUS - Preliminary specification, PFI-MUMICRO report, December 1981

[2] K.I. Thurber et al.: A systematic approach to the design of digital bussing structures, APFIS Conference Proceedings, vol. 41, 1972.

[3] P. Civera et al.: Integrazione del sistema di arbitraggio per M3BUS, February 1983, to be published

[4] P. Civera et al.: The μ* project: An experience with a Multimicroprocessor System, Micro, May 1982

[5] D.M. Taub: Contention resolving circuits for computer interrupt systems, Proc IEE, n. 9, September 1976.

[6] --- Standard specification for S100 bus interfaces devices, IEEE task 696.1, Computer, July 1979

[7] --- FASTBUS - Tentative specifications, U.S. NIM Committee, August 1981

[8] --- P896 proposed standard specification, D 4.1, IEEE Committee 896 Backplane bus, February 1982

[9] D. Del Corso, L. Verrua: Contention delay in distributed priority network, Internal report, Dipartimento di Elettronica, Politecnico di Torino, Italy, February 1983

[10] C.Mead L. Conway: Introduction to VLSI systems - Addison Wesley 1980

MICROCOMPUTERS: Developments in Industry, Business and Education
D.R. Wilson and C.J. van Spronsen (eds.) /© EUROMICRO, 1983
Elsevier Science Publishers B.V. (North-Holland)

INNOVATION AND TECHNOLOGY IN THE CLASSROOM

Richard Fothergill

Director, Microelectronics Education Programme
Newcastle upon Tyne, England

The Microelectronics Education Programme for England, Wales and Northern Ireland started in 1980 and this has produced a major innovation strategy for the introduction of microelectronics into the curriculum of all schools. The paper describes that strategy and indicates the progress so far. It emphasises the way in which the most appropriate elements for success for a major innovation like this can be implemented.

Near where I live is an area which was once devoted to sheepfarming up to the middle of the last century. With the growth of the industrial revolution, there was demand for energy, and coal was the obvious resource. These same fields that once fed sheep were dug up for underneath was a rich source of this fuel. Some twenty years ago, the coal extracted, the area was reclaimed, and now there is a factory producing chemicals by highly automated means and an estate of houses, many with small businesses operating from them. I tell this story to illustrate the changes that have and are occuring in our society, changes to which education has to respond. In facing the information age, we must not just think of preparing children in an understanding of computers and skills in operating them, important as that is. Equally essential is the need to help them prepare themselves for working and living in our changed society and relating to each other under circumstances that incidentally are changing very rapidly. Thus, the other concern is the total school curriculum and how that has to be amended to suit the needs of our children.

The revolution caused by the new technologies has hit Britain fast and the changes we are seeing in home and work environments, although rooted in developments of the last thirty years, have really accelerated during the last four years. With the forecasts of technological developments that we have already heard, the prognosis is for greater and faster changes, and in education we have to learn to adjust and absorb them, to make use of them where appropriate for the benefit of our teaching methods and help our children to understand them so that they can cope with society when they leave school. In this paper, I want to outline some of the approaches that we have been making in Britain in response to this situation, a response which is clearly different from that in any other country and which so far has been very successful in meeting its aims.

It was in 1980 that the government announced a project for education to meet the challenge of the technology, and I was appointed to lead what has become known as the Microelectronics Education Programme or MEP. While initiated by the government through the Department of Education and Science and receiving its funds from it, the Programme has been given a relatively free hand to approach the problems in its own way, and that sense of independence continues to be very important in encouraging teachers to work closely with us. MEP formulated two main aims to guide our decision-making for the activities we were to initiate:

(a) to help children understand the technology and its effects on society

(b) to encourage teachers to use the technology in improving the effectiveness of their teaching.

It will quickly be obvious to you that this means that all curriculum subjects will be affected by our activities, science and maths of course but also history, geography, music and english. I am sure you will notice as well that children of all ages will be involved, from five years old to 18. Indeed the five to eleven year olds are some of the most responsive of all. So quick are they at acquiring the simple skills of controlling the machine and so fearless are they of the equipment that they also help to give their more reluctant teachers the necessary confidence.

Therefore you will have appreciated that the Programme is concerned with meeting its aims in all subjects of the curriculum and with children of all ages. In addition, it must be emphasised that it is also concerned with children of all abilities. As we are not concerned solely with turning children into bright computer scientists - more of which later - we are not targetting our work on the clever children alone. Rather, this is for all children, for all are going to live in a world dominated by this new technology and they all need to adjust to it. It is also true to say that this technology can bring out abilities, interests and enthusiasms which have been ignored by other areas of study, particularly in work with the technology itself.

There are over 400,000 teachers in Britain, and the question we faced was how to reach them all and make them relate to the work of the Programme. You may be aware that while there is a government department which gives guidance on education, the actual schools and teachers are organised by 109 local authorities, each with an independent viewpoint. With their co-operation, a word you will hear many times in this paper, we have organised them into 14 regions for the purposes of the Programme. This has given us the opportunity to get closer to the teachers in every part of the country for there are MEP activities scattered around in every one of these regions. Thus, the innovation strategy that we have adopted is based on encouraging teachers all over the country to join in a campaign of action. Many are working directly for the Programme, while others are meeting its materials and training. All have a national direction, amended locally to meet the particular needs of the area in which the teachers live.

More of this in a moment. Thus the strategy is based on an almost even split between activities that are initiated and controlled nationally by the directorate of the Programme and those that are operating in the regions to a nationally set list of aims, and monitored and co-ordinated by the same national leadership. To make this succeed, it requires a coherent plan and a co-operative approach.

The regional activities are divided into three parts. First, there is the Information Centre with staff to issue newsletters, show visiting teachers equipment and a wide variety of teaching materials in many media, help them over their problems and give them instruction, but above all keep them well-informed about curriculum developments and new software and devices in their subject areas.

Secondly there is an in-service training programme for teachers in all subjects and at all levels. This Programme is divided into four domains which I shall describe later, and in the first full year of operation, over 24,000 teachers have been on the courses offered. These range from two to ten day courses. Each is run in the region by regional staff so that local needs and interests are covered but the main elements of the courses are planned and developed by national co-ordinators. The aim is to concentrate on teachers in the regions who will then go on to train their colleagues so that the whole approach cascades down from the national initiative to the classroom itself. We are not in control of this last layer, but a rough estimate suggests that over 70,000 teachers will now have met some training from this approach. As for those regional staff, they too go on regular updating courses to keep them abreast of the latest developments and new materials.

The third of these regional activities is curriculum development, the preparation of new computer programs and other teaching materials, again arranged to a clear national plan of needs. This builds on the natural skills of the teachers and advisers in the regions who know what they want in the classroom, and thus here are more small groups of people involved in MEP work and generally supporting and spreading its message around the country. This increases widely the number of educationists who are co-operating with us to ensure the work succeeds.

Each of these three areas of activity are mirrored in national projects as well. Thus we provide central information in newsletters and on electronic systems like our Diamond discs which go out for our word processor network. Each of our regional centres has a Diamond word processor which can link through the telephone system to the others. This standardisation means that all the centres can share information, exchange discs of databases and make use of regionally produced information sheets, which they can personalise and print without major retyping. In addition, MEP has many pages on Prestel, the national viewdata system which schools are increasingly able to access through their computers.

For in-service training, we have a considerable project being prepared by the Open University. This will generally reflect much of the in-service programme and will be particularly valuable for those who find it difficult to attend courses or who are not very happy about attending them. The national software development units are now well established, and more are being created. They produce large numbers of computer programs, again to a national plan of work, and they reach very high standards of quality and classroom value. The important point about all these programs is that they are carefully planned with teachers much involved so that they fit the actual classroom needs.

Let me turn now to the coverage of the Programme and also its products to date. I am going to do this by talking about each of the domains in turn, but before doing so, let me re-emphasise the importance of the teacher training aspects. These materials and devices do not work to their maximum effect unless the teachers using them are trained in their value within the classroom situation. This is the conclusion from all our experience, and it is the reason behind all our emphasis on careful teacher training. One further point - all these domains do have overlaps with each other; but that is not a difficulty. It shows clearly the full curriculum pervasiveness of the technology and reflects also the well-established truism that one can approach a given piece of knowledge from several directions.

The first domain is electronics and control technology. In our view, all children must have some experience and understanding of this new technology so that they can deal with it in their future lives. This can begin effectively at 9 and 10 years of age, so that children begin to appreciate simple devices, the logic which arranges elements to perform specific jobs, and create them for themselves. This 'microelectronics for all' approach has led to some very exciting classroom work. Some is theoretical through filmstrips, simple kits and videotapes, but children really get involved and reach understanding when they start making items. Some approach this through breadboarding with children knitting together circuits that work. Others start from carefully planned boards with inputs and outputs that the children can work on experimentally. Each leads to further understanding of the different ways in which the various elements can be linked to achieve different results, all in the process of using programmable devices to achieve particular controlled results. The end product may be traffic lights or it may be a robot arm, but the process is the same in both. From the skill point of view, the children learn the fundamentals of problem solving.

With this as a basis, children may choose to develop further knowledge of electronics and control, and further devices and teaching materials have been developed to enhance that work. On the other hand, they may wish to concentrate on other science and technology subjects. Is it engineering and design? A computer program through which the children can design a shape, and then the computer can control a simple lathe and cut that same shape out of polystyrene. Is it physics or chemistry? A new laboratory instrument which merges many separate measuring, monitoring and controlling devices in one to record and replay many experiments in a modern way and help the children draw real scientific conclusions. Is it biology? Devices to monitor and measure temperature, humidity, movement and chemical change to reveal insights in the science of life, and display them in new ways. All the devices are microprocessor based; all help children develop understanding of scientific truths at the same time as absorbing the concept of control.

Our second domain is computer studies. For all children some understanding of how the computer works as a system, and the various elements of language and operation, are essential. There is nothing quite like using control to help children overcome initial anxieties and develop confidence. That is why we developed the buggy with its range of software to get children excited, but also through the range of programs to develop understanding of the elements of control and what the computer itself is doing. From this general background, some children will move on to more detailed studies. A range of texts have been prepared to help them grapple with the computer as a system, simple programming and most important its range of applications in society and in industry. Videotapes, books and case studies have been created to illustrate and deepen their knowledge of this all pervading device, above all giving them confidence and understanding of its use. As they get more experienced, more complex control options are opened up to them through kits and they begin to explore examples of database management as well. All provide a basis for stimulating interest in a career of computer science, but this degree of detail is only for a few. We do not believe that children should be trained as skilled programmers at this age. That seems unnecessary when languages themselves are changing as the power of the technology develops. It is helpful if they understand the principles of computer languages, but not to be tied down to the rigours of a particular one. Of course, some children will get carried away by the excitement and challenge of programming, and we do not wish to inhibit this. However, in terms of the curriculum itself, such activities are not an essential element.

I must add that the same comments can be made about teacher training. Our courses help teachers use programs, examine them to alter data statements, but we do not want them to become programmers. The best we look for is that they will be able to specify the content and approach of a program to meet a particular curriculum need.

In the electronics domain, we have been largely creating a curriculum and devices to help to teach it, whereas in this domain, computer studies, the general curriculum was established, and we have set out to prepare materials and approaches to help children learn in an interesting and practical way.

Our third domain, computer based learning, is different again. Here we are concerned with computer programs that the teacher can use to help children learn any subject in the curriculum at any age. We have programs for 3, 4, and 5 year olds and programs for 16, 17 and 18 year olds. They fit any subject too, languages or science, music and art or technology. Before looking at the types of program, let me just say how important we feel the packaging and presentation is to the teacher. The program must be capable of secure and safe storage under normal classroom conditions. It must also, and I want to stress this, have good, detailed documentation, not in the technical sense, but in the educational information it gives, for example objectives, age range, what the children must know before they use it, what they can go and do afterwards to consolidate and expand the learning that has taken place.

The easy and natural response that teachers make towards the computer is that the programs can question and test knowledge, so-called drill and practice. Now, in our opinion, there is no reason why these should not be developed by a teacher for his own use, and various content free programs have been prepared to help them. That is material for the teacher to develop for the children in his particular classroom, not for a national Programme. These programs do not begin to exploit the exciting learning opportunities of the computer. Instead our emphases are on simulations, models and conjectural programs, encouraging children to explore topics and how they work, and learn as a result. Children must be able to alter parameters or feed in their own ideas and react to the results by trying other approaches. They must draw conclusions and deduce concepts from these experiences. Exercises they undertake must bring out deductive thinking, exploit and manipulate the knowledge they have and force them in to decision-making routines. We want to encourage children to adventure in the programs to different degrees and discover meanings. For the teacher, these cause more challenging thinking and pedagogic problems, for they mean that they have to help the children work and deduce through careful leading and judicious questioning, but the rewards at all ages are more excited and stimulated minds. The inarticulate learn to express themselves; the unaware find insights.

You will appreciate my enthusiasm. Screen design is obviously very important too as is the way the simulation works, but most important of all is that the learning psychology and the suitability for the prepared teacher and the curriculum is right, and it is that with which we have taken care. While many of the programs are totally self-standing, it is interesting to see how teachers feel that a program is just one resource among others, and thus there is a great deal of associated learning going on away from the computers in other parts of the classroom, often with the children working in groups. The program is just one part of a total learning experience. MEP is much involved in developing these extra resources as well as the program itself.

Our fourth domain is communication and information studies. One half of its work is very obvious and clearly relevant, the understanding and use of word processing and other business studies work. We have developed materials which are specially designed for teaching purposes which can be used at any age. For it is already clear that teachers of many subjects find word processing for themselves, and for the children they teach, can be very useful. Not only are we interested in the full keyboard as an input system for word processing, but we also want children to experience and use other methods of manipulating text, one hand keyboards for example. It is clear that the standard typewriter layout will be only one among many input systems in the future, and children must be prepared to accept these changes without any qualms or hesitation. Together with all other aspects of electronic communication systems which children will find a major feature of their future, this forms one part of the work of this domain.

The other part, and in many ways some of the most significant aspects of the whole approach of MEP, is the area of information studies. You will all be familiar with information retrieval systems, and the Programme has fostered several approaches. These range from a system for young children to more sophisticated work for the older ones. Much early learning is spent on the collection, organisation and presentation of factual information, and information retrieval systems are colourful and exciting ways in which children can get their facts together, overcome the boring bits of sorting and come rapidly to groupings which can lead to deductions, planning and thinking. In our opinion, this introduction can start at even four and five years, particularly with pictorial presentations of the results. When they get older, the systems have to be more complex, but then they are dealing with larger and more sophisticated bodies of information and looking for deeper insights and understanding. A database of a census can be very large, but the information that children can deduce from its rapid sorting can reveal very interesting and educationally useful knowledge.

This is still only the beginning. Large databases are increasingly on tap at the end of a telephone line. While each might have its own protocols, the principles of access and search are the same and these are what children need to appreciate so that they can cope with developments in the future. Their microcomputer is the terminal from which very large quantities of data can be accessed and explored as necessary. But the core of this work is the nature of information itself. What is it? How does it arrive? How is it created? What questions do we ask in order to get what we really need? Most important of all, what do we do with it when we have the information? These are the fundamental educational issues and we are now working hard on materials that help children work towards the answers. As will be clear to you, these are issues that affect every subject in the curriculum, and so the work we do must help in each and every discipline. In the classroom itself, the changes will be profound, for it is not the information-giving role that will be the main purpose of the teacher but rather the information-using aspects. This is a change to the core of our understanding of the purposes of education.

Those then are the main domains of the Programme, each approached broadly and affecting all aspects of the learning environment and all parts of the curriculum. One further sector is receiving much attention, and that is special education. I had better explain what is meant by that. A number of children are slow learners or may even be mentally backward, and a small number suffer from physical handicaps, blindness, deafness or muscular problems. All these collectively are educated through special education schools or units. Programs for them work at a more patient and lower level of sophistication, helping them to practise skills and re-inforce knowledge that they have gained. A number of programs have been developed for these children, and some of those aimed at younger children can be specially adapted. MEP is also working with some simple devices to try and help these children manipulate and work in their environment. This is important if they are going to be able to fit into normal society and communicate comfortably and naturally with other people. The power of the products of the technology can be very helpful indeed in this area.

The approach to special education is the same as the rest of the Programme. We have information centres called SEMERCs that keep teachers informed and provide exhibitions of ranges of appropriate materials. They are also involved in stimulating co-operative work between the teachers. There are also teacher training activities which help to brief the teachers and keep them up to date with the latest developments, and also there are projects throughout the country where materials and devices are being conceived, created and tested in the classroom. The number of children who need this help is not very large, but the affect on them, their ability to communicate, work and join in with the rest of society is profound.

I am sure you will have noticed that up to now I have hardly mentioned equipment. Only in the electronics domain has it figured significantly. The theme of the Programme has been to answer the questions that have been posed by educational needs, the requirements of teachers and the curriculum initiatives that have underwritten them. However MEP has not ignored the equipment side, and by working in co-operation with another part of the government, the Department of Industry, it has encouraged the distribution and use of computers.

Three major schemes are now complete or under way to help schools purchase equipment, all of them involving government funding of half the price while schools have paid the other half. Only one computer or peripheral system has been on offer to each school in this way and they have been able to choose from two or three British machines, Research Machines, Acorn BBC and Sinclair, all of which are available throughout the world. The programs we have written work on these machines, but many are also available on Apples and Pets. Our ethos has been to write for one machine and rewrite for the others so that the programs take advantage of the particular specifications that each offers. In school use each of these computers has proved very successful and now networks are being established between groups of them. While the government offer only referred to one machine, the impact has been very considerable. Schools for the 11-18 year olds have at least five now and several have 20 to 30 computers, while the smaller schools for the seven to 11 year olds have one to two. Considering that resources for schools are limited, this is a very rapid uptake in a period of about only two years. Teachers must feel they are important and useful to have put such a priority on obtaining the equipment.

In supporting the issue of this equipment, MEP also produced in-service training packages to go with them. Teachers not only made use of these materials to help them understand the equipment but they also went on courses of two to four days to discuss and work with them. They have already reached some 15,000 teachers and the younger children's schools scheme has only just started. You will notice the wide range of materials in these packages, books, machine guides, audiotapes, overhead transparencies, tape slides and of course computer programs. The tutors who take the courses that the teachers attend also have carefully prepared kits of materials to use in their own personal way but based on a carefully designed national scheme.

Thus the Programme has been developing approaches, teaching and learning materials, and equipment. The final element in the complete impact on the school is the classroom itself, and we have been working here as well. A computer classroom is not just a place where children learn computer studies and are taught by a teacher dictating knowledge. It is a place where children can come and explore all the many ways in which this equipment can support learning in very many subjects, and thus such a classroom should be completely re-arrangeable, open-ended and exploratory. The design we have established meets all these requirements and provides a pleasant and exciting atmosphere in which to learn.

In a paper of this length, it is not possible to give more than a hint of the philosophies behind the MEP operation. We are obviously producing great quantities of tried and tested materials in a wide range of subjects and media, and in doing so, we have set a large number of wheels in motion for more and more such projects. In what I have discussed, and in the pictures I have shown, you have been given a small taster of the operation. I hope you have gained the impression also that all this work, although funded and sponsored from government funds, is firmly based in the curriculum and teachers needs in meeting the learning requirements of children. There is a carefully plotted and coherent set of plans for the development and production of these materials which fit certain curriculum aims and these are nationally developed. The important issue for the teachers is that they can add to this approach and interpret it in a style which fits the particular group of children with whom they are working.

You will have noticed also that the Programme is comprehensive. We came to the conclusion, early on, that it was not sensible to concentrate on only one aspect, computer studies for example, for the impact of this technology was pervasive throughout the curriculum just as it is throughout society. It was also producing major changes in the way in which subjects could be approached and learnt, and in the attitudes of the children. So you will have seen that we have covered all ages and all subjects. We have also interested ourselves in the teachers, the curriculum, the materials, the equipment and even the classroom. Affecting one without involving another aspect again means that you omit areas that could well prove to be the final constraint in preventing a teacher taking the value of the technology into his work.

At the beginning of this paper, I mentioned the word co-operation and I want to return to it now. While the Programme itself is a nationally directed operation, you will have gathered that the work is a joint participation between the teachers, our regional staff, many small working groups and the national directorate. It is not just focussed around the capital London - indeed the directorate is based in the North of England in Newcastle - but involves the whole country. Nor are the projects themselves only funded and supported by the education system. We have many joint activities with large and small companies in all parts of our work, another example of co-operation. To distribute and market our products, we have worked with many other commercial concerns, both large and small, publishers, manufacturers and software houses. They are co-operating with us in taking the materials, packaging them in our styles and distributing them all round the world. We too are working with other companies who have developed their own products, and where we think them of value, we are putting them in our information centres and on our courses and discussing how effectively they can be used.

This sense of co-operation has transformed the efforts of the Programme and made it possible to penetrate deeply into the heart of the education system. By involving many different enterprises and people, interest in the work of the Programme, and more especially committment to its aims and objectives are promoted throughout the country. This is a very useful and successful method of ensuring the propagation of an innovation. The more widespread the network of people the more likely that the effort is diluted and this means more careful control and monitoring, but, at the same time, the more people feel they relate to the work being done and therefore take it into their teaching. We also have to be realistic in our targets. A good supportive approach of co-operation with teachers and educationists does provoke a groundswell of spreading interest, but only those who are willing to allow themselves to be involved will take notice of it. Others will ignore the signs and continue in the same way that they have done for years, and they will not change, just as many other people in society. A classroom innovation is not a failure if it does not convert these as well, for it can only be successful with those who can mentally accept and attune themselves to the change. For many this is not possible.

Any innovation must be evaluated, but just how far should this go? The Programme itself is innovatory in strategy, and it could be evaluated as a whole. On the other hand, it is designed to meet one particular problem, and others that arise are likely to require different approaches. I would argue therefore for continual monitoring during the lifetime of the Programme, but no full evaluation as no-one will benefit from this except for historians. At the other end, there is evaluation of materials. Traditionally, this is often conceived as a lengthy process, but if one takes more than two or three months to check out a piece of software, either someone else has published the idea or the technology itself has changed. There is a curious belief among those who evaluate materials that they have to meet universal approval, but just as books are only wholly acceptable to a particular group of people, so it is with other materials. Thus, I would urge restraint on those who demand too much or purposeless evaluation.

In concluding this paper, I want to return to where I started. Change is accelerating as we move into the Information Age. Many parts of society will be different, and in response the school curriculum and the pedagogic approach itself has to alter to fit the new needs that we have to meet. MEP is also a source of papers and booklets to foster the debate that is needed to drive forward changes in the curriculum, for only through the arguments will the rigidities of the tradition be weakened and innovations prosper. This is not only a debate for Britain, but one for the whole of Europe, indeed the whole world. Just as the Programme thrives on national co-operation, let us hope that this spirit can be carried abroad to continue the curriculum debate.

Session E1: LOCAL AREA NETWORKS IN INDUSTRY

Chairman: A. C. G. van Strien
KMC - PTT
The Hague (The Netherlands)

Local Area Networks; many talk about them but few deliver. Much attention is paid to Local Area Networks lately, especially in the field of office automation. Some years ago manufacturers started the discussion about the office of the future in which Local Networks took a major part and many expectations were created. At this moment the situation still exists that most manufacturers announce more than they can deliver and only some (merely simple) implementations of LAN's are installed in the office.

In contrast with these developments few attention is given to the use of LAN's in the laboratory or factory. Although some applications in this field require much higher performance, for instance faster response for real-time purposes and high reliability, many LAN-like networks are already available and installed in factory environments. Only many times they are not called LAN but just "Industrial network".

In this session at first an overview is given of history and technical principles of LAN's by the session chairman. This overview includes topologies, media, control mechanisms and standardisation. Especially the last topic is very important concerning the great number of manufacturers that already deliver or have announced LAN's.

After this introduction a paper is presented describing a LAN with a bus type topology, designed to perform fast and accurate data collection in a manufacturing plant from widely distributed data aquisition oriented terminals.

MICROCOMPUTERS: Developments in Industry, Business and Education
D.R. Wilson and C.J. van Spronsen (eds.) / © EUROMICRO, 1983
Elsevier Science Publishers B.V. (North-Holland)

IMPLEMENTATION OF A DATA ACQUISITION ORIENTED LOCAL AREA NETWORK IN A MANUFACTURING PLANT

Xabier Ruiz del Portal, Carlos Lazaro, Gotzon Arregui

IKERLAN, Centro de Investigaciones Tecnológicas
Apartado 146, MONDRAGON (Guipuzcoa) Spain

Companies using Batch Production Methods have found out that the Product-Market relationship requires important reductions in decision times and a better cost benefit analysis.
To perform fast and accurate data collection in a manufacturing Plant from widely distributed data acquisition oriented terminals, a System based upon a Local Area Network has been developped.
This paper presents a description of this System, taking into account the following points: description of the terminals, topology of the network, communications protocol selected, network interface to the Production Control Computer, software structure and operation of the Network.

Keywords: Production control, local area network, data capture terminals, real-time control, hierarchical structure, process synchronization.

1. INTRODUCTION

The Production Control Methods at the Batch Production factories (more than 80% of the manufacturing world), are being modified due to the increasing demands of the Market and to the new technologies which low cost and high performance have made feasible.

The Product-Market relationship requires an important reduction in decision times and a better cost benefit analysis to all those Companies who are struggling to be competitive in the presente situation.

Solutions such as Flexible Manufacturing Systems and stock reduction policies are utilized daily as a means to solve these problems and a good combination of all these solutions is tending to convert production processes into flowline production processes. Therefore the Production Management System may be represented as the following figure shows:

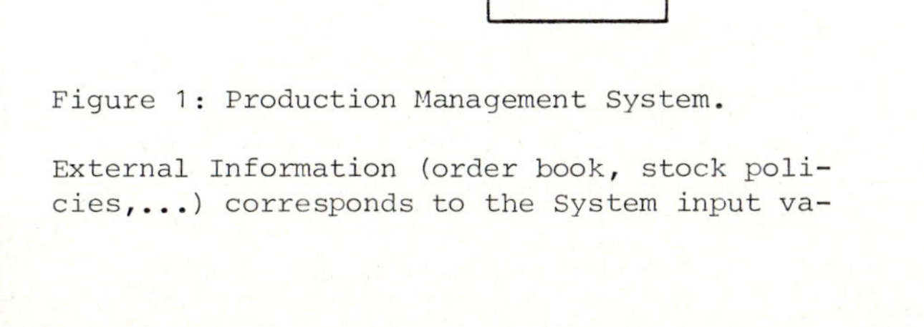

Figure 1: Production Management System.

External Information (order book, stock policies,...) corresponds to the System input variables. From these variables and Internal Information (state of production, medium term stocks) the Decision System elaborates appropiate orders to trigger the different operations that would enable End Products to be obtained which meet selected criteria.

The accuracy and reliability of the Global Production Control depends to a large extent on the quantity, quality and sampling time of the different data related to the Production System. Therefore the automation of the system of measuring these variables constitutes an important step towards collecting the decisions concerning the production system in a brief time and sumultaneously it permits a more rigorous analysis of the resulting costs and productivity losts.

Important contributions in the implementation of the production process Information Acquisition System which is presented in this paper are the advances in the microprocessor systems price/integration relationship, the better languages and Operating Systems that are available and also the large number of reports that are being made in the local area network arena. {BH73}, {DDH72}, {TAN81}, {VAL 80}.

2. CHARACTERISTICS OF AUTOMATED DATA ACQUISITION.

The purpose of this project is to facilitate the data collection and acquisition in industrial plants. Data can be of different kinds:

- Manufacturing orders for different machines.
- Complementary information to the employees who are in charge of them.

- Automatic reception of the state of the machines and of the manufacturing process: number of parts, machine breakdowns,...
- Manually introduced data.

The managers of the company's different sections would be abble to obtain a reliable status of different aspects of the production process based on accurate real time data.

The result is that the company's management team is provided with tools to permit an overview of the ongoing of each action and operation which is taking place in the factory and to facilitate desicions such as making readjustments in the programs or planning to meet delivery commitments as scheduled.

A good means of having the information at one's disposal and getting it ready to be used in short term decisions (tasks, activities, faulty parts, breakdowns, current stock situation, etc) is by collecting data right where they are generated: on the shop floor.

An Automated Data Acquisition System offers several benefits {BEN 78}:

. Simplicity

In seconds, from a work station the computer can be told the identity of the worker and the department, the job being done, the machines being used, the location of the work station and the time the job was started and stopped.

. Accuracy

Because the data collected are almost all generated by the system, the chance of human data-entry error has been all but eliminated.

. Speed

Data-input labour such as filling out time-sheets and job-sheets has been reduced.

. Enhancement of control of specific jobs and plant operation

Reliable information is quickly available to managers. Adjustement to schedules can be made sooner. Inventory status is more up to date. Labour distribution can be determined more readily. Efficiency can be improved because feedback can be given to supervisors more quickly.

3. INFORMATION SYSTEM

3.1. Global Features

A necessary feature of a good quality Production Control System is the reduction of the amount of decision times in order to fulfil market demands. Therefore the Decision System requires getting hold of the necessary information fairly in advance in order to assimilate the production process to a flow-line Process.

Furthermore, it is important that the internal information be acquired at the source, i.e. on the shop floor, and data transferred to the Decision System. These requirements pose several problems:

- The large number of variables to examine, a function of the company's size, its characteristics and the precission that the global control requires. These variables will correspond to those collected directly (number of parts, machines downtime, temperature measurements, and other physical magnitudes) and to those collected by specialized controllers (programmable logic controller, numerical controller, machining centers,...).

- The set up of a link between sensors and the Production Computer implies high costs and susceptibility to interferences due to the fact that distances between both could be considerable.

- In the case of point-to-point connection between each sensor and the Production Computer, CPU and interface costs would be very high.

After the exam of the above points an autonomous, low cost, easily interconnectable network with minimized wiring has been selected as described in the following.

3.2. Selected topology

Since the information is located in a physically distributed way, the selected network implements the interface between the different information collecting points and the Production Control Computer.

A bus-type topology has been chosen because it does not need much wiring (serial bus) and allows easy interconnection between work stations and itself.

Therefore the data acquisition system is supported by a hierarchy of stations (terminals) equipped with different "intelligence" as shown in Fig. 2.

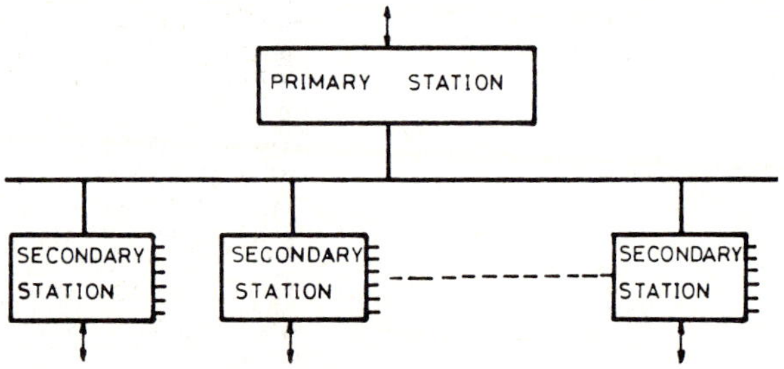

Fig. 2: Network Architecture.

Secondary stations constitute, in general, the true interface with the Production System. Their function consist in carrying out the collection of local data and transmitting them towards higher levels whenever they are asked for. Every secondary station has at its disposal a network interface (the same for all) and another interface to the process, depending on the particular characteristics of each secondary application.

The Production Control Computer is not directly linked to the Network but the link should be established through the Primary Station in the following way: the computer sends the necessary information related to a specific shop floor to its Primary station and it undertakes the task of monitoring the network, to implement a preprocessing of the collected data and to store them locally or send them to the computer.

Hence, the selected topology permits a simple and inexpensive interface between the different sensors responsible for the collection of data relevant to the production process and the computer that effects the production control.

3.3. Communications Protocol

The information exchange between Primary and Secondary station has been implemented with the aid of the synchronous line HDLC protocol (High level Data link Control) working in an unbalanced configuration {standards ECMA-4Ø, 49, 6Ø, 71}.

An unbalanced configuration has one Primary and one or more Secondaries. The configurations may be point-to-point or multipoint. The transfer may be two-way alternate or two-way simultaneous. The service may be switched or non-suitched. The Primary is responsible for setting each Secondary in an operational mode as appropriate.

Secondaries are addressed and identified by unique addresses in the related commands and responses. In this sense, the election that has been made is multipoint configuration, two way simultaneous data transfer, non-switched service, and Normal response Mode with non-extended addresses.

The Normal Response Mode (NRM) is a data link operational mode in an unbalanced configuration in which the Secondary may initiate transmission only as the result of receiving explicit permission to do so from the Primary. After receiving permission, the Secondary shall initiate a reply transmission. This is the Secondary opportunity to respond.

The reply transmission may consist of one or more frames while mantaining the active data channel state. The last frame of the reply transmission will be explicitly indicated by the Secondary. Following the indication of the last frame, the Secondary will stop transmitting until explicit permission is again received from the Primary.

In a similar way the Normal Disconnected Mode, is a unbalanced data link non-operational mode in which the Secondary is logically disconnected from the data link and is therefore not permitted to transmit or accept information. The Secondary has some limited capability to respond but only as a result of receiving an explicit permission to do so.

Henceforth the protocol selected will be the UNBALANCED NORMAL RESPONSE MODE (UNR) which is defined as HDLC-Procedure 2 from now on.

3.4. Access to the network

The shop floor based acquisition and data management system is formed of a hierarchy of different layers. On the top of the hierarchy is placed the Production Control Computer which receives internal information coming from the manufacturing process and external information (work order schedules, purchase orders) and elaborates the manufacturing strategy.

The Production Control Computer communicates with lower layers through the Primary Station. This is implemented by means of an asynchronous serial channel, available in all kinds of computers.

Secondary stations are placed at a lower layer. Their function is to implement the manufacturing system interface through the following features:

- Human operator interface, implemented through a terminal and/or a line printer.
- Machine interface. A serial line and several parallel I/O lines are available.

Tertiary stations constitute the last link of the data acquisition system. They are connected through an asynchronous serial bus to a Secondary station and this is suitable as a low cost solution. Their hardware is minimum, being build up around a microcontroller (i.e. i8Ø51) and specific drivers.

The complete architecture of the Data Acquisition System is shown in Fig.3.

4. SECONDARY STATION

4.1. Global features

Secondary stations fulfil a double function: interface function between the data sources and the Local Area Network and also a data acquisition function in an autonomous operation.

4.1.1. Interface Function

Considering secondary stations as communications devices, two Kind of links are set up:

* Local Area Network Link

  Concerned with a communications network interface to the primary station via serial line according to the HDLC Protocol.

* Application Interface

  Configured according to every particular application with which secondary stations are provided. It consists of two different interfaces:

  - Serial Line: a second serial line which is generally utilized as an asynchronous

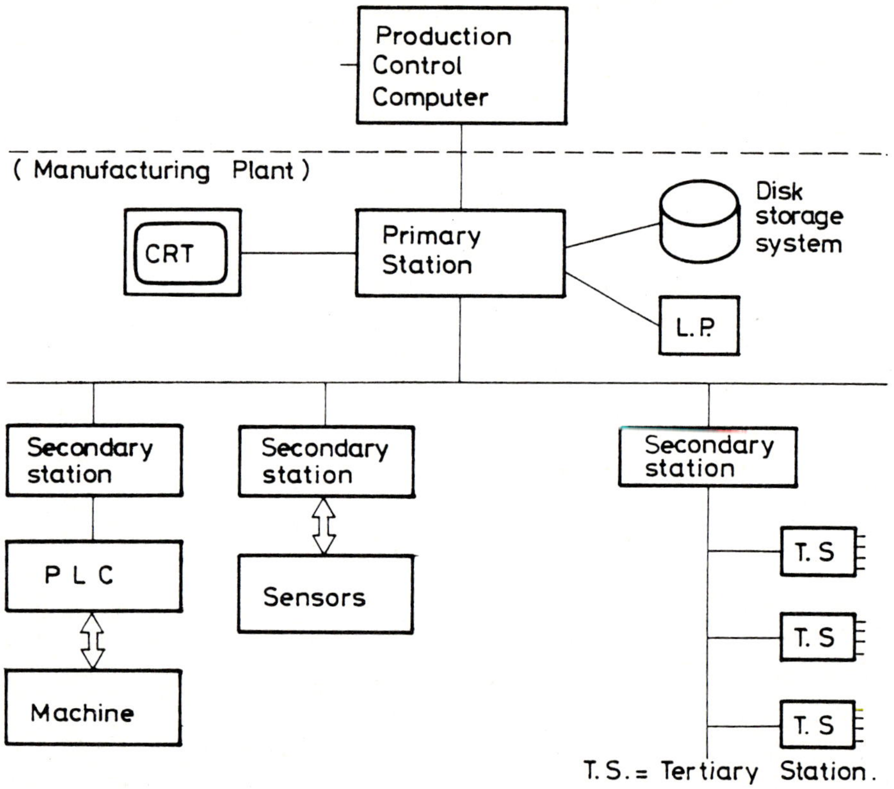

Fig. 3: Acquisition System Architecture.

line (connection to a terminal, programmable logic controller, etc.) but that could be considered also as a second HDLC channel or as a second serial bus channel to permit a subsidiary network implementation.

.. Parallel Interface: Constituted by 48 I/O lines allowing different configurations depending on the application but that will be used in general for data acquisition. As an example, it could be said that these lines can control a keyboard, several converters, LEDs, machine cycles and other sensors.

4.1.2. Data Acquisition Function

Secondary stations should be capable of working autonomously, acquiring data without the intervention of the Primary station, since they will be provided with enough information storage capability to permit this function.

In every application the appropriate elements (software and hardware) should exist to perform the function of data-acquisition and processing in such a way that they could be transmitted towards higher Information System hierarchies.

4.2. Secondary Station Hardware description

Secondary stations are built up around a microprocessor i8Ø85AH-2 which is responsible for the coordination of the rest of the components. As shown in Fig.4 the main circuits are the following {INT 82}:

* Multiprotocol Serial Controller (MPSC8274)

  A two channel serial line controller. Both channels are equivalent and can be programmed in several ways. In this case one of the channels (Channel A) has been programmed to control the synchronous line, using HDLC format, working at a transfer speed of 880 Kbit/sec. and the other channel (Channel B) to control the asynchronous line working at a lower transfer speed (9600bits /sec typical).

* Direct Memory Access Controller (DMAC8237A)

  A four channel controller that is used in conjunction with the MPSC described above, for data transfer through the two serial lines. In its operation it will make a CPU request for the control of the System Bus and once the transfer has been made, the DMAC will release the bus for use by the System. Its utilization permits higher serial line transfer rates and relieves the CPU of a large amount of work.

* Programmable Interval Timer (PIT8254)

  Which contain three independent counters that are employed to generate serial line baud-rate signals and as delay unit for

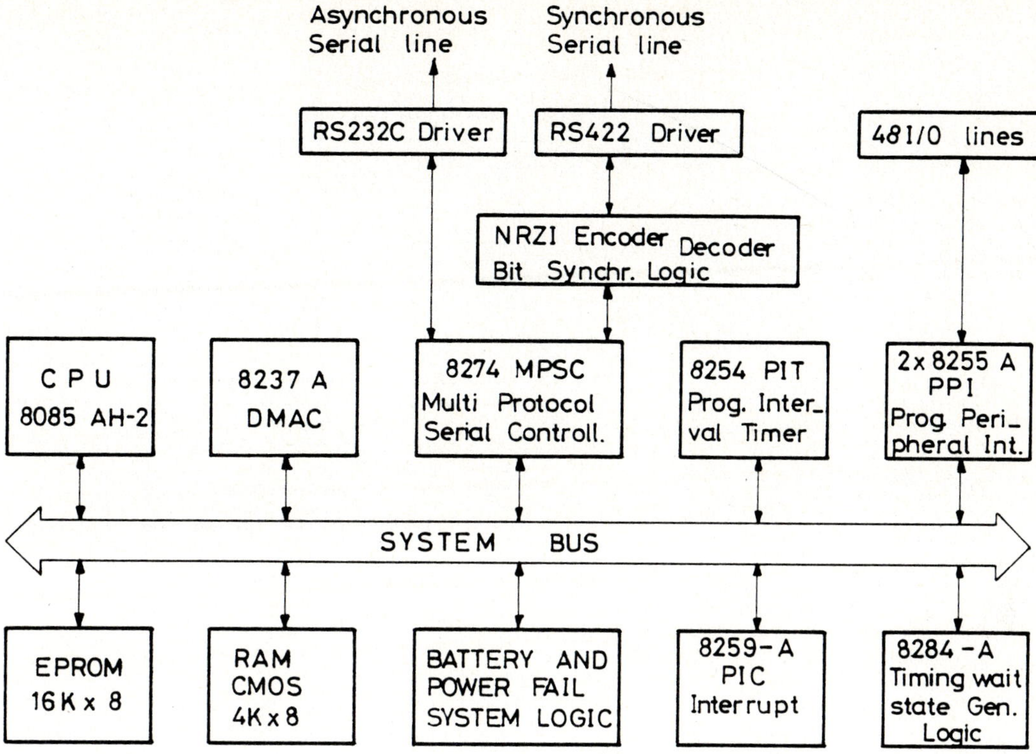

Fig. 4: Secondary Station Hardware Structure

real time control.

* Programmable Interrupt Controller (Pic - 8259A) with up to eight prioritized interrupt levels.

* Programmable peripheral Controller (PPI- 8255A).
  Two PPI's are utilized as control interface with the 48I/O parallel lines with which secondary stations are provided.

* Timing Signals Circuit and Wait State Generator Logic.
  Built around an 8284A chip, it is a circuit that permits synchronization among different peripherals.

* Battery Circuit and Power Fail Logic.
  Its aim is to preven the loss of the information stored in the RAM-CMOS memories in the event of a power failure.

* NRZI Encoder/Decoder Logic.
  NRZI code has been chosen for the data transfer through the synchronous line in order to achieve more secure control and to facilitate the possibility of performing a received bit synchronization logic that permits automatic correction of phase lags between clock signals coming from different stations; otherwise it would be necessary to send the clock signal along with the data.

* Serial Lines Interface Drivers.
  Data transfer through the synchronous line is made following the EIA-RS422 standard, using tri-state drivers to keep the line floating when no secondary intends to use it. Data transfer through the asynchronous line is effected following the EIA-RS232C standard {EIA}.

* Memory.
  Secondary boards are provided with two 28 pin sockets to allocate EPROM memory and another two 28-pin sockets to allocate RAM memory. Memory sockets are configured in such a way that would permit the utilization of different chips on the market. Until now the memory capacity of the secondary is of 16Kx8 of EPROM and 4Kx8 of RAM-CMOS.

4.3. Secondary Station Operation

In outline the secondary station fulfils two main functions, these are communication with the Local Network and survey of its concrete application. According to this, inmediately after power up, a standard secondary station would make an initialization of all its functions and enter into a situation in which it:

* Remains in NORMAL DISCONNECTED MODE until the Primary sets the data link forcing the secondary to enter into the operational mode (NRM).
* Starts its data acquisition tasks (scanning of I/O lines and of the asynchronous serial line, acquired data storage, temporizations)

Whenever the Primary station sends commands, the Secondary station will execute the actions derived from these commands, such as sending information frames, execution of secondary library resident routines, display of messages, acquisition of new data, etc... The Primary will also be capable of loading programs to be executed by secondaries.

Secondary stations will function in an autonomous way even if the data links are interrupted (i.e. the Primary sends a DISC command to force the secondary to enter the NDM).

In the event of a power failure detection, the secondary station will protect data stored in memories in order to keep information safe for once the power sets up again. In this case, the secondary will reinitialize all the functions and will remain in NORMAL DISCONNECTED MODE waiting for the Primary to set the operational mode again and on the other hand it will restart the normal data acquisition operation.

4.4. Secondary Station Software Description

The hardware implementation of the primary and secondary boards has been made in such a way as to make them compatible with the Real time Multitasking Operating System RMX8ØTM which serves as nucleus to our software. RMX8ØTM being a commercial product, it will not be described here {RMX80}.

The RMX8ØTM nucleus provides the basic primitive operations which take care of synchronization, concurrency, priority and communication among tasks. The basic communication mechanism among tasks is message passing.

The software structure is described as a "multilevel" system in which the modules allocated in the same level constitute a "layer" and utilize the services provided by lower layers and they themselves provide services to the higher layers. At the bottom of the structure is situated the real machine and at the top is the application module.

The software structure of the secondary station has been designed as a multilevel system composed of five layers, of which the three lowest ones constitute what is called "COMMUNICATIONS MODULE", the fourth layer is the "PROTOCOL MODULE" and the fifth the "APPLICATION MODULE", Fig. 5 shows the software structure of the secondary station which is described in the following.

4.4.1. Communications Module

This module provides functions that implement basic operation apart from that which make possible data transfer through parallel and serial interfaces. This module is composed of three layers whose description is presented as follows:

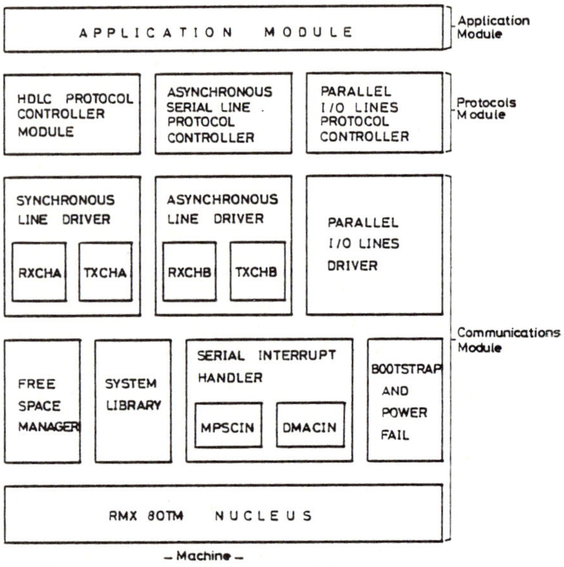

Fig. 5: Secondary station software structure.

* Layer 1.
  This layer is the core of the system and as has been mentioned earlier is occupied by the RMX8ØTM nucleus.
* Layer 2.
  This layer is formed by the conjunction of the tasks that make the interface with the hardware, such as:
  - Free space manager
    One of the modules of the RMX8ØTM package. It mantains a pool of free RAM and allocates memory from that pool upon request from a task. The Free Space Manager also allows memory to be returned to the pool when it is no longer needed.{RMX8ØTM}.
  - Serial Interrupt Handler
    This module is in charge of the management of the interrupts related to the serial lines. It is formed by two tasks: MPSCIN (Interrupts coming from the serial line controller) and DMACIN (Interrupts coming from the direct memory access controller).
  - System Library
    That contains the common system routines, such as those of different peripheral chip management.
* Layer 3. This layer is formed by the three

drivers that permit data transfers through parallel and serial interfaces:

.. Synchronous Serial Line Driver.
This module is composed of two tasks to control reception {RXCHA} and transmission {TXCHA} of frames through the synchronous line in HDLC format. These tasks in conjunction with lower layer functions allow HDLC frame transfers among stations.

.. Asynchronous Serial Line Driver.
This module is composed of two tasks to control reception {RXCHB} and transmission {TXCHB} of messages through the asynchronous line. These tasks in conjunction with lower layer functions allow message transfers between a secondary station and devices connected to the RS232C line.

.. Parallel I/O Lines Driver.
Module oriented to the I/O lines management, independently from the configuration that has been chosen for the station data acquisition system.

4.4.2. Protocols Module

It contains three modules forming layer 3 that controls the communication between secondary stations and the devices connected to the serial/ parallel interfaces.

* HDLC Protocol Controller Module.
It has been designed as a RMX8Ø task (HDLCON) and constitutes a HDLC Secondary, that is, that part of a station that executes data link control functions as instructed by the Primary. A secondary interprets commands and generates responses for transmission {ECMA-49; 3.4}.

* Asynchronous Serial Line Protocol Controller.
This module is application dependent, that is, dependent on the devices connected to the asynchronous serial line. Some exemples of this module may be those that make a CRT interface, a Programmable Logic Controller protocol interface, a mini-network of tertiary terminals configured as a serial bus, etc... In any case the functions provided by the ASYNCHRONOUS SERIAL LINE DRIVER would always be used.

* Parallel I/O Lines Protocol Controller.
Similarly, this module is also application dependent. In general, this module will manage the data acquisition operation from different machine oriented sensors or MDI (Manual data introduction) devices and produce a display for machine operator information.

4.4.3. Application Module

Corresponds to the fifth layer that is the top of secondary station software hierarchy. Its main role is to coordinate the secondary station operation using all the services provided by lower layers. Some functions of this layer would be,

. EXECUTION of commands coming from the Primary Station,

. COORDINATION of the execution of those commands,

. ELABORATION of reponses to be sent to the Primary station.

Is this way the primary station will be able to instruct a Secondary station to send the information it has acquired, or order the secondary station to start program execution or even to send the program itself to the secondary before executed.

5. PRIMARY STATION

5.1. Global Features

The Primary Station fulfils a triple function: communications function, network management function an a function of management and storage of data collected by the Information System lower hierarchies and at the same time it many offer an autonomous operation with regard to higher hierarchies of the Information System.

5.1.1. Communications function

The Primary station sets up several types of communications that can be defined by three kinds of link.

* Local Area Network Link.
Permits the Primary Station to be connected to the rest of the network via serial line according to the HDLC Protocol.

* Production Control Computer Link.
To permit the Primary station set up a link to the highest hierarchy of the Information System via an asynchronous serial line.

* Primary Station Operator Interface.
The primary station has a work station (CRT -keyboard) attached to it in order to allow the plant manager to survey the global operation of the manufacturing processes, and collect some information from it.

5.1.2. Network Management function

The primary station is responsable for the operation of the whole network. It must be capable of coordinating the whole data acquisition process in an autonomous way with regard to the PRODUCTION CONTROL COMPUTER to which the information will be transferred, periodically, once elaborated. According to this the Primary station should have a mechanism to ascertain the configuration of the network it is controlling and thus be able to set up a station polling policy.

The way the network has been designed, it surrenders communication initiatives to the primary station and consequently the responsibility of getting the information transferred towards the upper hierarchies is also a primary station task.

5.1.3. Data Storage and Management function

The Primary Station is equipped with a flexible disk unit in order to keep a local storage of data being collected by the Information System.

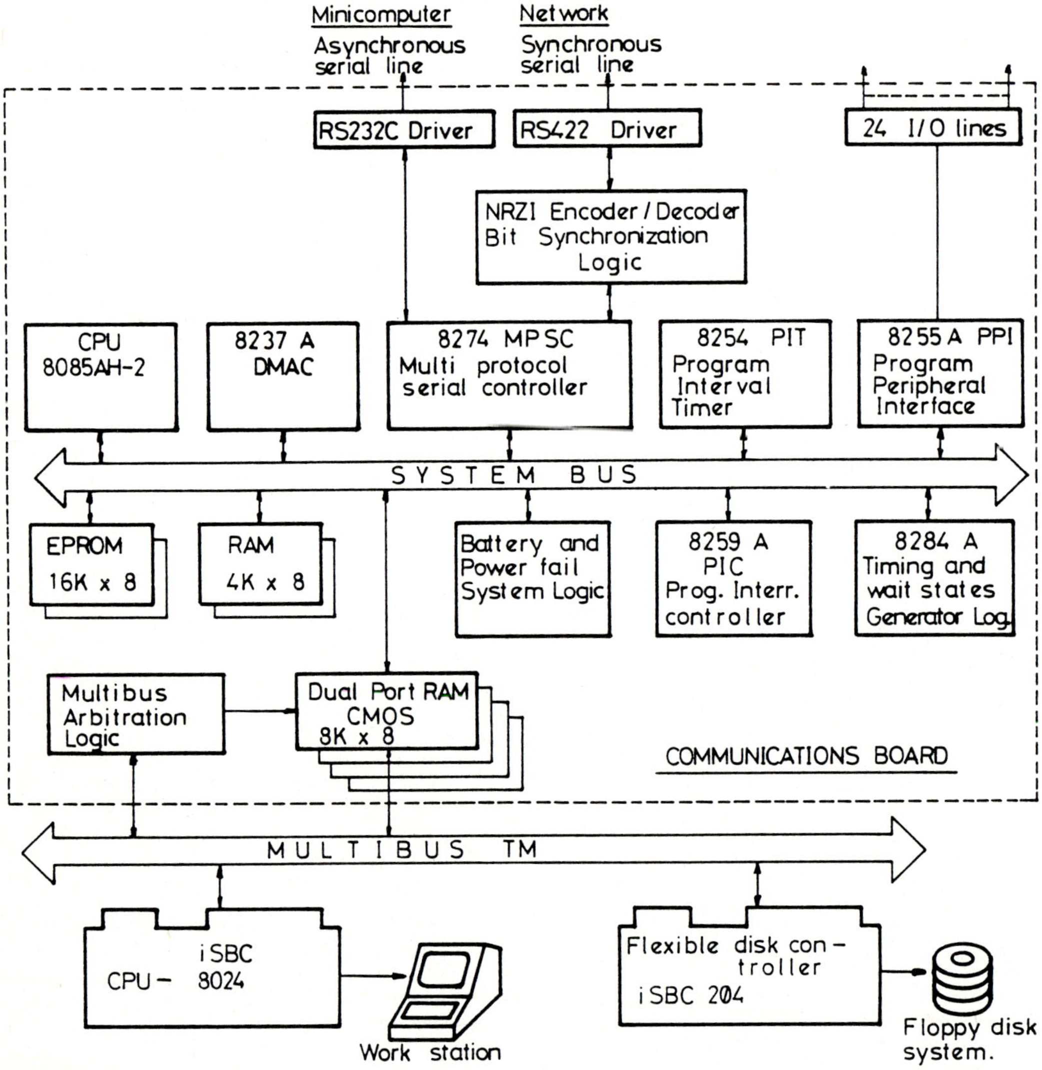

Fig. 6: Primary Station hardware structure.

The purpose of this unit is to give the Primary Station a certain autonomy so it can manage a bigger amount of information and to depend less on the PRODUCTION CONTROL COMPUTER to which the primary will pass more fully elaborated information.

5.2. Primary Station Hardware Description

The Primary Station is composed of three boards which communicate themselves through the MULTIBUS^{TM}{MULTIBUS}, as shown in Fig. 6. These three boards are {SBC81};

. COMMUNICATIONS BOARD
. CPU
. DATA STORAGE SYSTEM.

5.2.1. Communications Board

The communications board is basically a secondary board to which some features have been added. The rest follows what has been described in (4.2.). The particular features of the communications board are the following,

* Parallel Link.
The Primary Station is equipped with just one PROGRAMMABLE PERIPHERAL CONTROLLER (PPI 8255A) which allows the Primary to access 24 I/O lines.

* Memory Expansion.
The EPROM memory is kept the same as described in (4.2.) but the RAM configuration is changed. The primary station has one 28 pin

socket to allocate RAM memory for program variables, but the memory intended to allocate memory buffers controlled by the Information System has been organized as a dual port RAM-CMOS that could be accessed from the communications board local bus or else from external board through the MULTIBUS™ implementation. This memory expansion is composed of four 28 pin sockets that could be adapted to the different types of commercial chips. The present RAM-CMOS capacity of this dual port memory is of 8Kx8.

5.2.2. C P U

A commercial central Processing Unit board has been utilized (iSBC 8Ø24) to control Primary Station operation and to serve al the same time as a work station (it has a CRT terminal conexion) and as a management center for the data acquired throughout the network.

5.2.3. Data Storage System

A commercial flexible disk controller board has been utilized (iSBC 2Ø4).

In order to increase the performance of the Primary Station, some changes have been foreseen, such as a new CPU based upon a 16 bit Microprocessor and a hard disk storage system for the Primary Station. These changes do not alter the rest of the network due to the fact that the communications board has been designed taking into this contingency.

5.3. Primary Station Operation

5.3.1. Initialization

After power up the primary station executes the following operations,

* System Bootstrap
  In this period the primary station executes the initialization of the communication tasks related to the PRODUCTION COMPUTER, the DATA STORAGE SYSTEM, and the PRIMARY STATION OPERATOR WORK STATION, and gets ready to monitor these communications.
* Local Network Operation Bootstrap
  Before setting the data link in an operational mode, the primary station asks for the configuration of the network. After that a poll is started to confirm whether the secondaries are actually connected to the network or which ones are not linked, and in the first case set them into the operational mode (NRM). Once the data-link is set, and network configuration established, the primary station enters the fully operational mode.

5.3.2. Operational Mode

During the fully operational mode the primary station monitors four operations,

1/ Network Management:
Which implies the setting of sessions with the different secondaries that could be performed in the next two ways:

* Polling the Secondary Stations
  The Primary sets successive sessions with the different secondaries with the purpose of collecting the data they have stored and also to be informed of the incidents that might have occurred since the last communication. In particular this polling serves to concentrate in the Primary station all the data that have been acquired in the Network.
* Special Sessions
  The primary station can initiate a special session with a secondary to perform a non routine communication such as
  - Secondary station re-initilization; the station has lost the link due to some incident, or has been connected recently or its initial configuration has been changed. In all these cases the primary may decide to re-initialize the secondary station.
  - Program load on the secondaries with the aim of making them perform special operations not included in the secondary library modules.

2/ Communication with Different Peripherals
Under this heading are included the tasks of management of the data storage system (Floppy disk), the communications with the shop floor operator through the work station attached to the primary station and the communications with the production computer, the top level of the information system.

3/ Data Management
The Primary station will implement an operation of management and concentration of the information acquired all over the network, is such a way that the upper hierarchies of the information system receive more elaborated data than the ones which are transmitted by the data acquisition units.
It affects not only the data concentration and manipulation themselves but also the presentation and elaboration levels of the data management.

4/ Special Events
The primary station will be provided with a system which permit the restarting of the network operation in case of incidents such as power failure or station breakdown once the conditions that permit the normal operation have been re-established.

5.4. Primary Station Software Description

As in (4.4.), the software structure is presented as a multilevel system composed of five layers. The three lower layers constitute what has been called "COMMUNICATIONS MODULE" which need not be presented here, being identical to the

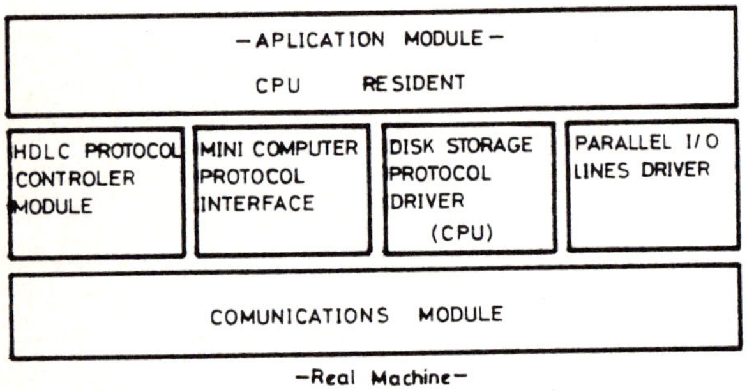

Fig. 7: Primary Station Software Structure.

one already described (4.4.1). This module is included among the software of the "communications board".

The two upper layers of the multi-level structure, the "PROTOCOLS MODULE" and the "APPLICATIONS MODULE" are presented in the following, as shown in Fig. 7.

5.4.1. Protocol Module

This module is "communications board" resident and is composed of four protocol controllers wihich permite communications with the network, the production computer and the different peripherals.

* HDLC Protocol Controller Module
  Has been designed as a RMX8Ø task (HDLCON) and constitutes what is called the Primary of the Network, that is, that part of a station that supports the primary control functions of the Data link. It is permanently responsible for the control of the data link. The Primary generates commands for transmission and interprets the responses which are received {STANDARD ECMA-49; 3.3}.

  Taking into account that the network which is being presented has a multipoint configuration, this means that the primary controls the data link being connected to several secondaries. This is performed through the setting of multiplexed sessions with each secondary. Some requirements that the HDLC PROTOCOL CONTROLLER MODULE must fulfil are derived from the following,

  1/ The HDLC Protocol Controller Module must be configured in each session so as to work with just one secondary station and to stay with it until ordered to end the session, or the information exchange has been exhausted.

  2/ It must be capable of ending a session in a controlled way, that is, making sure that the secondary will not send any more frames unless asked explicitly to do so. This is done in order to prevent the reception of frames coming from a secondary other than the one with which the session in being set and to make it seem, from the point of view of a secondary, as if the link were a point-to-point configuration, and the Primary were attending that secondary exclusively.

  3/ When ending a session the HDLC PROTOCOL CONTROLLER MODULE must inform the highest layer of the result of the session in order to be accepted or otherwise to proceed to an exception situation, should any anomalous incident have been detected in it. For example, the case in which a secondary declares that it has no free memory available to receive information or that it rejects the commands coming from the Primary or that it does not respond to the primary requests due to some breakdown.

* Production Computer Protocol Driver.
  This Module supports the protocols that govern the communications with the production computer, which are "communications board" resident, and also the interpretation of the computer commands and the generation of responses which are "CPU resident".

* Disk Storage Protocol Driver.
  Which supports the protocol of communications with the "data storage sytem" using the functions of the DISK FILE SYSTEM (RMX8Ø Module). This module is CPU resident {RMX8Ø}.

* Primary Station Operator Protocol Driver.
  This module is composed of different tasks which support the communication protocols with the peripheral associated with the primary station man-machine interface (a CRT terminal and a line printer). This module is composed of different tasks which are resident both in the "communications board" and in the "CPU".

5.4.2. Application Module

This module corresponds to layer 5 of the multilevel software structure, and is CPU board resident. It coordinates the Primary Station operation, utilizes all its resources and surrenders them to the Production Computer and to the Primary Station Operator.

6. CONCLUSIONS

The use the computer for data acquisition in production control has provided the management team with tools to determine "WHEN" (the right moment) "HOW" (which operations to be performed) and "HOW MUCH" (costs) to get end-products.

Microprocessors have improved the system permitting a faster collection of more parameters in the right location: the production plant. Factors involved in bringing about these improvements include: increase in sampling frecuency, the greater reliability of the data being collected, the real-time management of these parameters, the better adaptability to factory conditions and the facility for expansion by the addition of new stations.

As a result of the implementation of a system like the one which has been presented it is possible to obtain a better profit from human and material resources.

A reduction of machine downtime and a better specification of manufacturing costs, thus allowing better production control.

REFERENCES:

BEN78 Bentzen, S., Data Collection at work stations, American Machinist, November 1978.

BH 73 Brinch Hansen P., Operating System Principles, Prentice Hall, 1973.

CYP78 Cypser, R.J., Communications Architecture for Distributed Systems, Addison-Wesley, 1978.

DDH72 Dahl, O.J., Dijkstra E.W., Hoare C.A.R., Structured Programming, Academic Press, 1972.

ECMA European Computer Manufacturers Association.
HDLC Frame Structure -ECMA-40.
HDLC Elements of Procedure -ECMA-49.
HDLC Unbalanced Class of Procedure ECMA-60.
HDLC Selected Procedures -ECMA-71.

EIA Electronic Industries Association.
Application Notes for EIA Standard RS-232-C.
Electrical Characteristics of Balanced Voltage Digital Interface Circuits -RS-422.

INT82 Component Data Catalog, 1982. Intel Corporation.

RMX80 RMX/80 User's Guide, Intel Corporation.

SBC81 Systems Data Catalog, 1981. Intel Corporation.

TAN81 Tanenbaum, A.S., Computer Networks, Prentice-Hall, 1981.

VAL80 Valero, M., Contribución al diseño de redes locales de microcomputadores, Tesis Doctoral, Universidad Politécnica de Barcelona, 1980.

Session E2: OFFICE COMMUNICATION PANEL DISCUSSION

Chairman: Friedrich Winkelhage
G.M.D. mbH.
Bonn (F.R.G.)

Panelists: C. Garrigues
Agence de l'Informatique
Paris (France)

E. Howe
National Computing Centre
Manchester (U.K.)

F. Winkelhage

A. INFORMATION TECHNOLOGY AND THE NATIONAL AND INTERNATIONAL ECONOMY

The information- and communication-technology is of importance for the national and international economy in a threefold way:

1. As a selfstanding industry for hardware and software which in many cases is of strategic importance for the national economy.

2. As an infrastructure for and between organizations as companies, administrative offices, universities, last but not least the private households. The further development of this infrastructure will be of a decisive importance for the efficiency and effectiveness of administration, economy and science.

3. As part of many high-technology-products information technology plays a decisive role in the further development of the national economies and the international cooperation.

Office communication stands for the infrastructure part of the scenario. The current discussion of this special topic shows that the broad field of office communication is expected as one of the most growing markets in the technological field on one hand. On the other hand, it is one of the areas where especially regarding the organizational and behavioral implications we in the moment know more questions than answers.

B. TRENDS

Within organizations we have to be aware that we will have more information, more tools and instruments, and more intelligent power at the place of work. It is expected that the processing of text, data, speech and graphics in the long run will be integrated in the workstation. At the same time we notice rapid development in the field of computer conferencing and mailing, of local area networks, wide area networks and communication services. In this way the possibilities to communicate locally and in the wide area from the single workstation will grow.

Further we register very different possibilities to shift the work load within organizations or from organizations in a wider area. It will not always be necessary to be personally at the central place of work, as we have to see alternative work sites which we can establish with the help of the new information and communication techniques. In the United States under the item "Electronic Cottages" the possibilities are discussed to take for instance whole departments of an organization and bring it to another regional site so that at the new place the established infrastructure may be used also by employees of other companies. In this way the work load may come nearer to the home of the employee. On the other hand, there are also examples for instance in the field of programming where the programmers already work at home using the new technical communication facilities to cooperate with the central office.

So in many fields we see the trend towards the decentralization of the computing power supporting office work and a growing possibility to communicate within organizations and between organizations.

C. PROBLEMS

Besides the already available technical possibilities we have to see that there are still many technical problems unsolved. Besides these technical questions there is a wide-spread uncertainty about the best way of the organizational implementation of the new technical facilities and the question how the users will react on these new possibilities. Here we can see that the new information- and communication-techniques allow the horizontal concentration of tasks (job enlargement) as well as the vertical concentration of tasks (job enrichment). Tasks which have been separated until now will come together again. In this way we can see the tendency to more complex places of work and workstations.

Another area of implications are the management positions. It is expected that the management will have better means of control, have quicker and more complex information which can be gained by inhouse networks and information services. In this way maybe the extension of the span of control might be possible One of the most serious problems in this area is the question how we can control the information flood which we are expecting as a following-up of the new means of communication.

The third implication is regarding the regional structure and distribution of an organization. The new information and communication techniques allow a variety of decentralized organizations. The keywords are satelite work centers, electronic cottages or home-work in very different forms.

As mentioned, we have to notice that besides the open technical question as protocol, data formats, standards in a very broad sense, one of the weakest points is the question how we should implement an information- and communication-infrastructure in an organization without causing too much trouble for the daily performance of the company or the public administration.

D. ACTIVITIES

In the different countries we notice activities in at least two different areas. The industry is trying to solve the technical problems of the communication regarding networks and communication services and the integration of the different techniques at the workstation itself. On the other hand, many large companies and also the public administration are running experiments to find out how the whole organization in a learning process will react on the new facilities of office communication and office support. These experiments try to find out how the workstation itself, the presentation of information is developing and how the office work is really supported by these means. In many cases we can feel that the user interface still asks for a specialist coming from the data processing field to manage the workstation. The other field is the experimental use of computer conferencing and computer mailing systems which open new possibilities and forms of communication where we need more experiences to find the right way of integration of such means in the organization.

E. PANEL-DISCUSSION

The Panel will be opened by short presentations of the three panellists regarding the special situation in the three countries including some reflecting remarks about the trends, the special problems tackled by the activities in the respective country and results produced by studies and pilot projects. After the presentation the panellists will discuss the situation along the topics, trends, problems, activities and perspectives of the future development. They will try to point out the special European situation and maybe find some suggestions for a more intensive cooperation in Europe.

Panel Members:

Charlie GARRIGUES, President de l'Agence de l'Informatique, Paris, France

Eric HOWE, Deputy Director The National Computing Centre, Manchester, UK

Friedrich WINKELHAGE, Member of the Board, Gesellschaft für Mathematik und Datenverarbeitung mbH., Bonn, Germany

Session F1: DISTRIBUTED PROCESSING

Chairman: J. Billingsley
Electrical Engineering Department
Portsmouth Polytecnic (U.K.)

An entire generation of computers has been built on the philosophy of multi-tasking, in which a single processor performs a schizophrenic array of duties in order not to waste a moment of precious processor time. With the plummeting of processor and memory costs the pendulum has swung towards the use of many collaborating computers for the best achievement of the necessary task - a swing from the one-man-band to the orchestra. Early examples of multi-computer systems were a network of NORDIC 10's used at CERN for the control of the Super Proton Synchrotron[1], and the Cambridge University 'CLUMP' used for research in hierarchical control[2].

The trend away from multi-tasking was one which was not hard to foresee. The following is quoted from a synopsis submitted to an international conference more than 12 years ago.

> "As a computer peripheral, the human being is a waste of time. Inaccurate, inefficient, the user must be isolated from the machine behind offline or multi-access schemes if computer time is not to be lost. So we see the proliferation of monstrous machines, bristling with line-printers, disks, readers and terminals, together pursuing a caucus-race policy in which the peripherals must not hold up the processor, and the processor must not keep the peripherals waiting. These machines do much to enhance the prestige of the companies which own them, but little for their balance sheets. Clerks (grade 3) are replaced by an equal number of Computer Officers (grade 2), all striving to keep the monster busy. These dinosaurs must surely face extinction.
>
> For the past few years, it has become increasingly true that the cheapest commodity in a computing system is processor time. The cost of fast access store is tumbling too. When peripherals are chosen to interface directly with a single user, much processor time could be wasted - or could instead be used to advantage in enabling the simplest of controllers to be used. Once processor time ceases to be sacrosanct, a new philosophy is possible: that computer systems can be provided to assist people, rather than replace them."

In their paper published here Reijns van Spronsen, Bruins and Vree have taken a firm philosophical stand on "monoprocessing". They point out that interprocessor communication may itself constitute a multi-processing task and therefore propose a form of communication system into which all the complexities can be swept. The individual processors are left "pure" and able to pursue their tasks with undivided attention. The communication system has much in common with the Cambridge Ring, with the provision of additional memory to make a larger number of message time slots available. The authors have paid close attention to the protocol necessary to support their monoprocessing philosophy and have produced a thought provoking paper.

Karszt, Lausen and Salz addressed themselves to the problems of operating a database in a multi-machine environment. Although the database itself is held on a single central disk system, problems of concurrency arise unless the individual computers are to be unduly restricted in their operation. Unless locking is used, the data on which a processor has based a transaction may become obsolete by the time the result is available for writing back into the central file. By establishing a read-set and a write-set the data can be verified and if necessary the transaction can be abandoned and re-started. Only as a last resort need locking be used.

Columbo and his co-authors have considered a database which is geographically distributed over a network of computers. Through nodes on their SAD system files local to a host machine may be accessed by any other. The underlying philosophy is far from that of monoprocessing; families of concurrent processes are created whenever a user joins the system.

A hazard in the literature of computer networking is the temptation to use and mix metaphors (none of us is immune). In this session we will meet Post Offices with wagons, leaves on trees, bosses, butlers and families with roots - and finally partners which suicide.

References

1. M.C. Crowley-Milling, J.T. Hyman, G.C. Shering, "The multi-computer Control System for the CERN 400 GeV Accelerator". Proc. IEE Conference on Trends in On-line Computer Control Systems, April, 1975 pp 101-108.

2. J. Billingsley, D.R.S. Hedgeland, J.L. Moughton, "A Multiprocessor Research Facility for Simulation of Control Applications". Proc. IEE Conference on Trends in On-line Computer Control Systems, April, 1975, pp 109-115.

MICROCOMPUTERS: Developments in Industry, Business and Education
D.R. Wilson and C.J. van Spronsen (eds.) / ©EUROMICRO, 1983
Elsevier Science Publishers B.V. (North-Holland)

DISTRIBUTED PROCESSING: HARDWARE AND SOFTWARE STRUCTURES

G.L. Reijns, C.J. van Spronsen
Delft University of Technology, Electrical Department
Delft, The Netherlands

Th. Bruins, W.G. Vree
Applied Informatics Research
Department of Water Control and Public Works (RWS)
Rijswijk, The Netherlands

The application of distributed processing expands rapidly due to the increasing performance in micro-electronics, which have reduced the cost of processing power considerably. In this paper, a system of coupled microprocessors is presented, which behaves to the user as one abstract machine. Context switching is not allowed in this system, which means that a processor does not embark on another process before it has fully completed the processing of the current process.
A very useful aid in structuring the system was found in the philosophy presented in the ISO reference model for open systems interconnections.
The functions in the higher layers, such as the call of not locally available functions and the updating of directories are treated. Emphasis has been put on the descriptions of the interconnecting transport level, which incorporated storage and queueing functions. The system incorporates redundancy such that failure of a processor only degrades, but never stops the total service. A pilot system based on these principles is now operational.

1. SYSTEM REQUIREMENTS AND CONSIDERATIONS.

1.1 Hardware.

The architecture consists of a local area network, connecting a large number of identical microprocessors, each having its own local main memory.

1.2 Monoprocessing.

There is mono-processing in each processor which means that a single processor is not allowed to perform context switching. This decision breaks with the convention to share memory and CPU between different processes, a convention originally imposed by the high costs of CPU and memory. A considerable part of the overhead and of the complexity of a normal operating system vanishes when mono-processing is applied, of course at the expense of a less efficient use of CPU and main memory. We have taken the attitude that the drastical reduction in the cost of processing and memory electronics, justify to waste these electronics to a certain extent, provided the system becomes less complex. An operating system becomes simpler when context switching is avoided, reducing in that manner the overhead which counterbalances somewhat the waste of CPU power due to monoprocessing.

1.3 Decentralized control.

If a user wants to get certain processing functions executed, which are not available at his local computer, the operating system (O.S.) should assist to have the required functions executed elsewhere in the system. For that reason the O.S. needs to know the locations of the resources in the system. This O.S. knowledge is available in a table which we have called dictionary. Now there are two options, either the whole system contains only one dictionary or there are a number of identical dictionaries, one in each processor. Originally our system contained one central dictionary [4]. However the presence of only one copy makes the system vulnerable to break down when a failure occurs. For that reason and also in order to reduce the amount of traffic on the interconnecting network, it was decided to introduce a decentralized control by providing each processor in he system with a system dictionary. This system dictionary is rather simple and relates names of functions and files to the processor locations where they can be found. More detailed information about a file or function is provided at the side where the file or function is present. However, the introduction of more than one copy of the system dictionary, causes problems when this dictionary has to be updated, for instance when a function or file is added or deleted from the system. These problems are discussed in more detail in paragraph 4.

1.4 Message queueing.

Interrupts are not allowed since this is not consistent with monoprocessing. For that reason, a processor can only accept a message when it is idle. Suppose that a processor (source) is executing a user program which needs to send a message to a destination that is found to be occupied (for instance also executing a user program). Clearly, that message has to be stored somewhere temporarily, otherwise the source processor would not be able to continue the processing of the current process and would remain idle until the destination processor becomes free. The latter is in conflict with the aim of efficient parallel processing.
Message queueing is accomplished in our system in the transport layer. There are three possible places where messages can be queued:
at the source processor, at the destination processor or somewhere in between i.e. in the data-communications system.
Queueing in the data-com system means that a transmitted message is not immediately delivered, but is stored in the data-com system, freeing the source processor and allowing it to proceed with processing. In addition this central store and queueing system (which we have called post-office) provides a more efficient use of the queueing memory than the use of distributed local memories would do. The post-office enables also the implementation of a priority scheme in the message delivery, which is, as we will see in paragraph 4, an essential element in a system with distributed control.

1.5 Redundancy.

In the first place the proposed data-com system has to be designed in a redundant, fault tolerant fashion because it forms the one bottle-neck of the whole system. In the second place redundancy of all other system functions is achieved by creating groups of processors of which members of a group have identical hardware and software proporties. A group has been provided with a common group address. A source can direct a message to a group without having to know how many processors are actually present in that group. Clearly, only one processor in the group will actually receive the groupmessage tasking it out of a queue in the post office. The schema, as such, provides automatic load sharing between the processors of a group, allowing processors to go down or to be added to the group without any notification to the users. This group addressing scheme, where users are not aware of the members of a group, is easy to implement in a queueing system in the post office.
The data-com system provides a broadcast facility to update the replicated knowledge in a group. This broadcast facility is very similar to the group addressing allowing a user to send a message to a group without having to know how many members are actually present in the group. The updating system is thus compatible with the graceful degradation (and extension) of a function. It will be discussed in detail in paragraph 4.

1.6 Connection-less interprocess communication.

The interprocess communication is based on a connection-less function call. This facility means that any function can call any other local or remote function, merely by providing its name. How the total system is able to locate or load this function will be discussed in the next paragraph. The connection-less property means that the function-call will not be acknowledged to the originator. The calling processor always assumes that the call is successful and continues processing the remainder of its program. The central queueing data-com system allows the program to proceed in a real mono-processing fashion i.e. without starting up a pseudo parallel process to handle retransmission in case the destination is found to be occupied. If the result of a previously called function is required (by explicitly naming this result) the processor will wait for the data-com system to deliver the desired data. This waiting is consistent with mono-processing and necessary because the user obviously needs the result before being able to proceed.
Although we have not implemented any other acknowledgment in the system, this is not impossible, for instance in the transport layer, invisible to the upper layers and so without the processes being aware of it. In our system the result message constitutes however the only acknowledgement in the whole system.
The fact that a result is received acknowledges all previous transmissions on all levels. The waiting for a result as positive acknowledgement and the absence of any other acknowledgement implies that it is impossible to provide a negative result-acknowledgement. This problem is solved by running a watch-dog timer whenever a result is required. The time-out is then considered as a negative acknowledgement.

2. PRINCIPLE OPERATION OF THE SYSTEM.

The system consists of a number of microcomputers interconnected by a data communications system. The software in the processors is structured into several layers. At the top, we find the application level with higher level language programs. In the second layer runs an interpretator. The interpretation layer translates the high level statements into low level machine instructions. Execution attempts on not locally available functions will activate lower level communication functions.

When new functions or files are created the directories and routing tables contained in the presentation layer need to be updated at all processor locations. This updating is carried out by means of a broadcast message.

At the lowest level, one finds the storing and queueing of messages at the "post office". The transmission medium in our system consists of a high bandwidth ringnet [7].

Corresponding to the call to - and return from a function two message types have been introduced: the execute message and the result message.

The execute message contains the function name and the value of the input parameter, whereas the result message returns the function result value and the function name again, to identify the result. (fig. 1). Both input and result parameters can have an arbitrary complexity but transmission is always by value.

An execute message is always directed at a group of processors, but only one of them will receive the message because reception of a message implies its deletion in the transport layer. The result message, however, can only be sent to an individual member of a group because it has to be precisely directed to the one that initiated the call. (fig. 2).

In fig. 2 the function g is implemented in three processors, forming a group. When a user calls function g, it inserts an execute message in the transport layer, directed to the group address of g.

Processor g_3 is able to receive the message if it is free. It does not matter how many processors exist in the g-group. If there are more execute-g messages in the transport layer, load will be automatically shared in a true parallel fashion. It is assumed that faulty

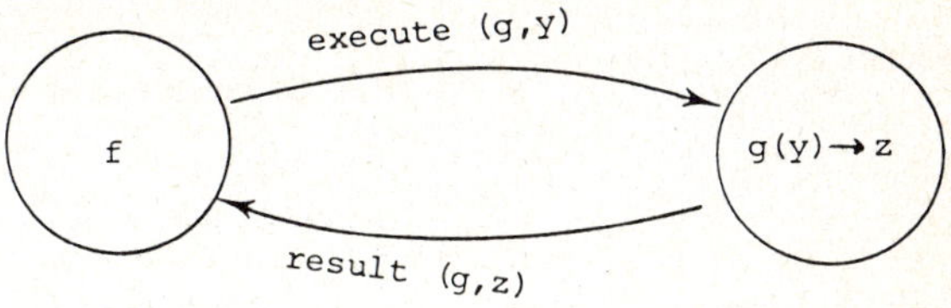

fig. 1

processors do not look for execute messages any longer and thus exclude themselves from the group.

In practice group addressing is implemented by assigning to each processor in a group a common address in addition to its individual address. Because messages are not delivered automatically, a processor has to look for a message itself and the selection criterion it applies consists of comparing the address field in a message with one of the two addresses it has been provided with. A free processor looks for messages directed at the group number, and will receive only execute messages.

When waiting for a result, messages are selected with the individual address and thus only result messages are received. This selective reception of results is necessary because a processor waiting for a result is already in the state of execution and not able to answer any execute message.

The selective result reception leaves all pending execute requests in the central queueing system.

To continue the example of fig. 2 let us assume that a processor in group g was free and has accepted the execute message. Before starting function g, the source address of the message is copied because it is needed after termination of g to return the result value. The source address is the individual address of the initiator of a function and the use of this address in the result message guarantees that all results are directed at individuals. (fig. 3).

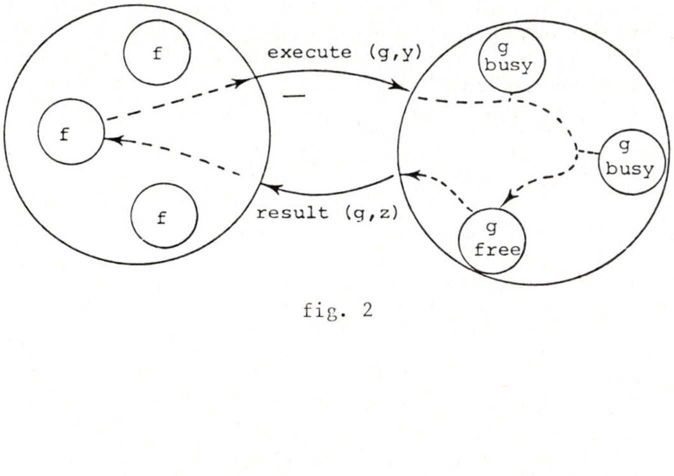

fig. 2

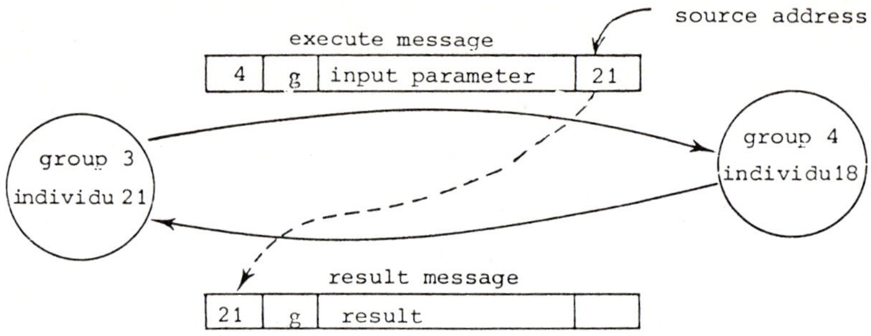

fig. 3

When the source address (21) and input parameters have been copied, processor 18 of group 4 starts the execution of function g. On termination, the result value of g is copied into the result message.
As soon as the data-com system has accepted this message, procesor 18 starts looking for subsequent execute requests.
Until now it has not yet been explained how a processor is able to find the appropriate group when it calls a function. This is accomplished by maintaining in each processor a table which registers the group address of each function present in the system. The problem is how to update such a table (which will be referred to a dictionary) without deadlock in a true monoprocessing fashion.
The data-com system offers a broadcast facility. When a function is loaded into a particular processor, (via the normal execute, result chain) this processor is responsible for updating all dictionaries. It broadcasts a normal execute message, activating the proper management function in all processors. This management function performs the update but does not send a result because then multiple result messages would appear and the broadcasting processor would have to know their number to properly absorb them. Moreover, the waiting for result messages would give rise to a potential deadlock when another processor also concurrently performs an update and waits for result messages. None of the two would then receive the proper number of result messages.
So, updating the dictionary does not cause any result message and thus the only acknowledgement in the calling sequence has disappeared and there is no more guarantee that the update has been applied in all processors. To reduce the impact of this problem, each processor always performs updates at regular time intervals. This algorithm, together with an alternative solution will be discussed in paragraph 4.

3. THE APPLICATION OF THE REFERENCE MODEL FOR OPEN SYSTEMS INTERCONNECTIONS IN OUR SYSTEM

Although the reference model for Open Systems Interconnections, mainly was intended as a guideline for facilitating and formalizing data communications standards, it offers however, significantly more. The hierarchical grouping of corresponding system entities in (N)-layers, providing horizontal abstraction boundaries, appears to be a very useful technique in the design of systems. Next to these horizontal abstractions, which allows a user of services to stay ignorant of the specific way this service is accomplished, the reference model allows certain process characteristics to be transformed, thus permitting processes with different characteristics to cooperate as if these differences were non-existent. So far the model has been specifically utilised for data communication procedures on public telecommunications media in a typical mainframe environment. The general concept of the layered architecture as described in chapter five of the ISO document however, appears to be applicable in the design of a distributed computer architecture. Although the general concept does not determine the number or position of the various layers, practical considerations gave rise to the well known seven layered reference model. In applying OSI methodology in a distributed architecture however, new entities have to be traced and localized appropriately. The basic principle applied has been illustrated in fig. 4 in a simplified way. It shows a cooperation between two peer entities Ei and Ej. This cooperation, however, requires tools, provided by hierarchical lower laying services (e.g. transformations or communications). Directories and routing tables, allow the entities Ei and Ej to determine the access point address to these services. The abreviated headers "P" on the horizontal data exchange stands for the coordination protocol information. The header "I" replaces the necessary interface control information. The occurrance of two Ej entities is supposed to illustrate the possible situation of two similar processes both able to cooperate with Ei.

together with the interface data to be interpreted. Next to the interface signals, two control signals called "Create and Delete" accompany the related functions or files.
Locally executable instructions, will of course not activate communication functions. Execution attempts on not locally available functions of course do. Similarly, control signals will activate communication oriented functions causing the update of directories and mapping tables.

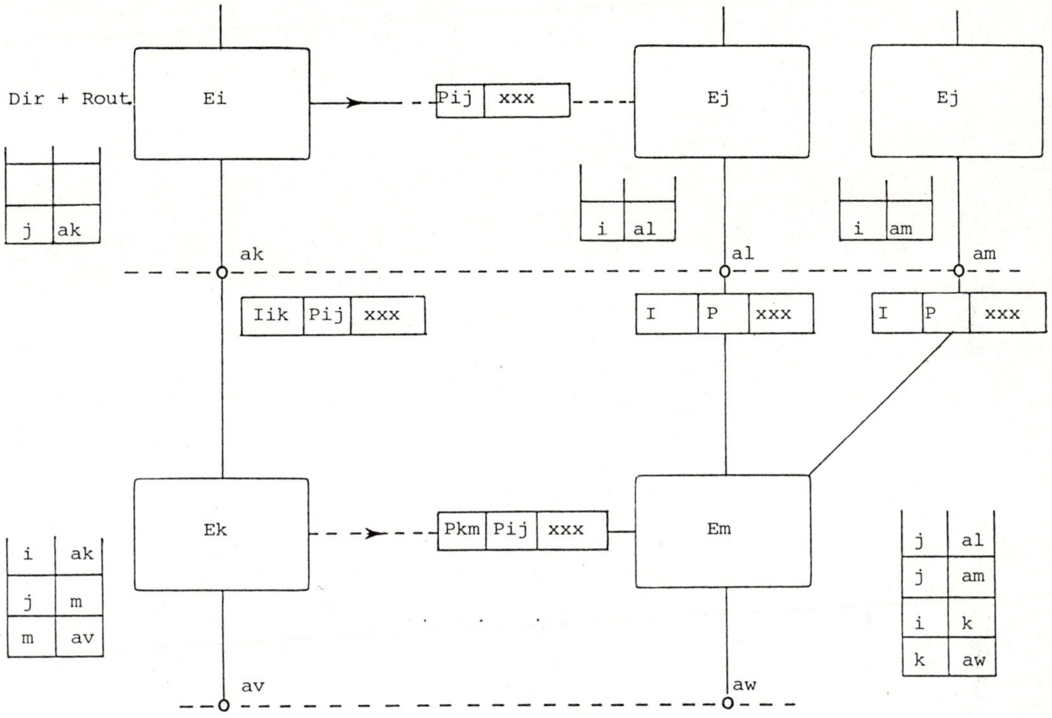

fig. 4

The conceptual aim to allow independant application processes, using each other, without the need to know their residence, particularly holds for the Applicaton layer. Up till now, this layer has been mainly used to reside the virtual terminals, files and jobs. It appeared to be appropriate to subdivide the aplication layer into two new layers (fig. 5). The highest of these layers, called Application layer, contains the actual processes. At this level, a user experiences the collection of multiprocessors as one high level machine. High level language programs may refer to non-locally available functions or files without a specific knowledge of their precise location, which knowledge is present at the lower layers.
The second layer has been called "The interpretation layer" due to its main task of interpreting the high level language statements into low level machine instructions. Application entities communicate with the lower interpretation entities in using the interface signal

The Interpretation layer directories contain the names of the programs able to execute (e.g. Read), Create or Delete the functions or files. The mechanism in which directories are updated has been described in paragraph 3.
The Presentation layer is supposed to provide the services, necessary for a proper collaboration and contains the directories and routing tables with the addresses of all the commonly available functions and files (dictionary). The dictionaries reside in every processor and are supposed to be identical.
The main task of the Session layer is to provide the synchronization of the cooperating presentation entities.
As it is, the layer pretends with its services to provide a message oriented point to point connection between a data source and a data sink which is supposed to be ready to receive. For this reason, the underlying Transport layer has been furnished with a large storage capacity. At the Sending end, the Synchronization of the

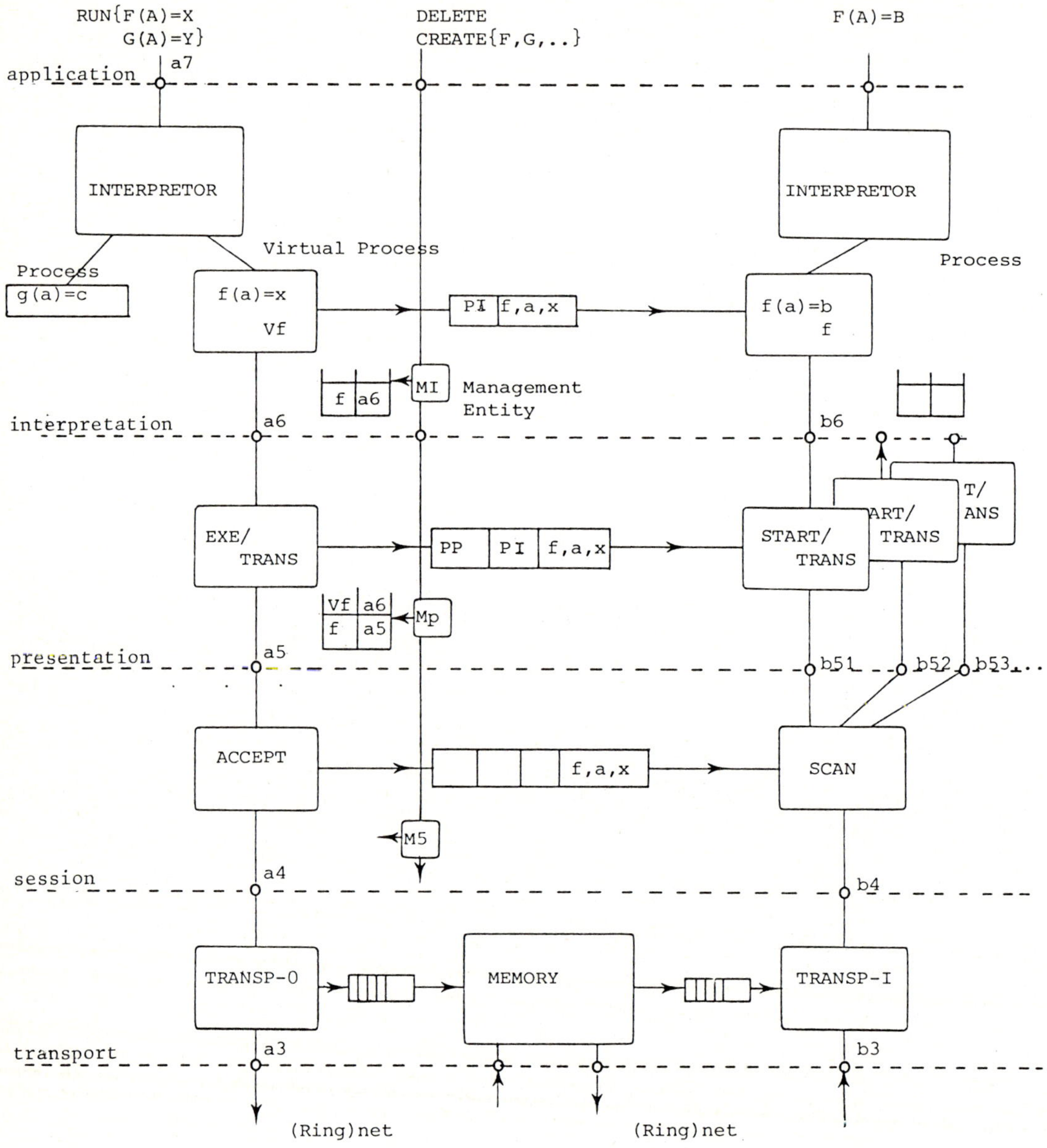
RUN{F(A)=X
G(A)=Y}
DELETE
CREATE{F,G,..}
F(A)=B
application
a7
INTERPRETOR
INTERPRETOR
Virtual Process
Process
Process
g(a)=c
f(a)=x
Vf
PI
f,a,x
f(a)=b
f
MI
Management
Entity
f
a6
interpretation
a6
b6
EXE/
TRANS
PP
PI
f,a,x
START/
TRANS
ART/
TRANS
T/
ANS
Vf
a6
f
a5
Mp
presentation
a5
b51
b52
b53
ACCEPT
f,a,x
SCAN
M5
session
a4
b4
TRANSP-O
MEMORY
TRANSP-I
transport
a3
b3
(Ring)net
(Ring)net

fig. 5

process could be called nearly perfect as messages are accepted almost without limitation. At the receiving end however, the Session layer has to keep track of the occupation status of the participating presentation entities. For this reason, all non occupied Presentation entities issue a "free" status thus allowing the Session layer to liberate the corresponding access point addresses in its special mapping tables. The entities responsible for these services have been called ACCEPT and SCAN.
The storage facility at transport level, called "Post Office" has been described in paragraph 5. In order to allow the Session layer to provide message oriented transports, sequency and ordering are one of the special services to be performed by the Post Office. Unfortunately, the present post office concept does not as yet enable it to be duplicated. From a reliability point of view the central Post Office is the weakest part of the system. The present activities of the project are directed to solve this problem.

4. MANAGEMENT OF DIRECTORIES.

In each layer of the OS model, actions are taken according to some layer specific knowledge. At the lower levels this knowledge is not likely to change but at higher levels the problem of managing distributed knowledge arises. In our system for instance, the Interpretation layer contains file directories and the presentation layer contains function distribution directories (= dictionary in paragraph 3) both of which are subject to changes during system operation.
As stated in the requirements, (paragraph 1) any knowledge in a group of processors has to be fully replicated in all members of the group and this applies to directories in particular. The management of both file directory and dictionary is identical except for the broadcast distribution. A file directory belongs to a group of processors implementing the file system whereas the dictionary belongs to all processors.
Corresponding to these two repartitions two broadcast services are offered by the transport system, one to a group and one to all processors.
The problem of updating fully replicated knowledge is a subject of current interest in the literature of distributed data bases. However, our system has three special aspects which obsolete all the algorithms proposed in this literature. And these aspects are

a) messages are not acknowledged and can fail.
b) the number of processors in a group may vary in time (requirement of redundancy and load sharing)
c) mono-processing per processor.

Let us consider the case when a processor from the file directory group creates a file and wants to update all other processors in its group. The creating processor is in the state of executing a create-file-request from a user and when terminating this action it should have updated the other processors. In our system, the only means to determine if an action has been correctly completed is to wait for its result message. The creating processor should wait for result messages from all updated processors and there, two difficulties arise. The first one is a deadlock; because one (or more) of the processors that should be updated might not accept an update request at all, but might be waiting itself for result messages (being a concurrent creating process). The deadlock problem might be solved by sequencing concurrent updates in time, using a central semaphore. The central semaphore might be implemented in the transport system, but this has not yet been done in our system.
The other difficulty arises from the fact that in the present system a processor does not know exactly how many other processors exist in its group and is therefore unable to determine if all update messages have arrived by interpreting the received result messages.
The knowledge how many processors are present in a group is however available at transport level in the Post office. Although not yet been implemented, we are working on a transport layer, which is able to communicate the exact number of active processors in each group. Both the deadlock and the confirmation problem should therefore be solved completely in future.

For the time being we have solved both problems by relying more or less on the fact that update broadcast messages will be executed correctly and do not need to be confirmed by result messages. The update requests will therefore not be answered by result messages, avoiding also deadlock, because processors will not wait for result messages after emitting an update.
However, in order to avoid the situation that one or more dictionaries would remain inconsistent with the others for a long time when an error has occurred, the present algorithm performs updates after a certain amount of time when a processor becomes free. Furthermore, each processor in the directory group maintains a private sequence number which is incremented after each update. Update requests are labeled with this sequence number and the combination of source address and sequence number is unique in the group.
Each processor in a group can now remember, for each received update request, the source address together with the last sequence number. Doing so each processor is able to check, after an update request has been received, if the sequence number of this update is indeed one higher than the previous update (from that particular source). This algorithm in general, enables a management service to assert the previous change when the next change is applied. In the period of time between two changes an omitted update remains unrevealed.
There are still two necessary constraints for the algorithm to work properly. The first one is that messages must arrive at the destination in

order of transmission. The second one is that all execute messages that originate from a broadcast are received with priority over the normal execute message. The priority of update requests is necessary to assure that the update has been applied in all processors of the group before any normal execute message is accepted. Both priority and preservation of transmission order are implemented in the present transport layer.
Now the problem remains what to do when an update is received and the sequence number appears to be out of order. The proposed algorithm implies that the sequence number in the message is the correct one and the receiver has apparently omitted one (ore more) update requests from this source. All it has to do is to direct an execute message to this source to obtain a copy of the full directory.

5. IMPLEMENTATION OF THE LOWER LEVEL FUNCTIONS

5.1 Introduction of storage facilities.

When we take a closer look at the transport layer, it proofs that a capacity problem arises, for several reasons.
There is no guarantee that messages, when put on the ring, will be removed, because the addressed processor can be busy. During times of dense traffic this would hardly leave any empty slots on the ring. For that reason a storage function had to be introduced on this level. A processor system with memory takes care of the storage function by removing messages from the ring and storing them in sequence and per destination. As stated in paragraph 1, this approach is the only one consistent with mono-processing and it gives less overhead than storing at the source or destination processor.
Because the functions that this storage medium performs, -accepting, storing, sorting and sending messages-, are similar to those of a post-office, we named this storage medium "Post-Office" (P.O.)
Once a P.O. is available, other functions can be allocated to it as well, like dealing with priority messages, detecting defective processors, etc.

5.2 Memory Organization of the P.O.

Memory of the P.O. can be organized in two ways:

-by train wagons as they appear on the ring or
-on a message basis.
When the memory is organized on wagon basis, it is enough to connect a FIFO (first in first out) buffer in series with the ring, as illustrated in figure 6
The total number of available wagons on the ring seems to be increased that way and if more are needed, the FIFO can be scaled up. Memory management is easy and more FIFO's can be added if necessary. Disadvantages are an increased transport time, large messages for a processor that is busy, can block the ring and transmission errors increase as a message stays longer on the ring.
Another possibility is a P.O. where each processor has its own FIFO. In that case, the P.O. inputs all wagons from the ring, assembles them to messages and queues the messages per processor into a FIFO. This architecture asks for a processor to control these functions and gives the following advantages: messages are on the ring no longer than needed, watchdog timers per processor indicate defective processors, insufficient RAM memory can be increased or a background memory can be added, statistics on the transport are possible and group addressing can be done by implementing a group queue.
We also encounter some disadvantages like a reduced speed, because the added administration and a certain send criterion are needed, indicating when a message can be sent to a processor.

5.3 When and how sending messages from the P.O. to the destination.

The P.O. has to determine somehow, when a message can be sent to the destination processor. This can be done

- on basis of statistics, available in the P.O..

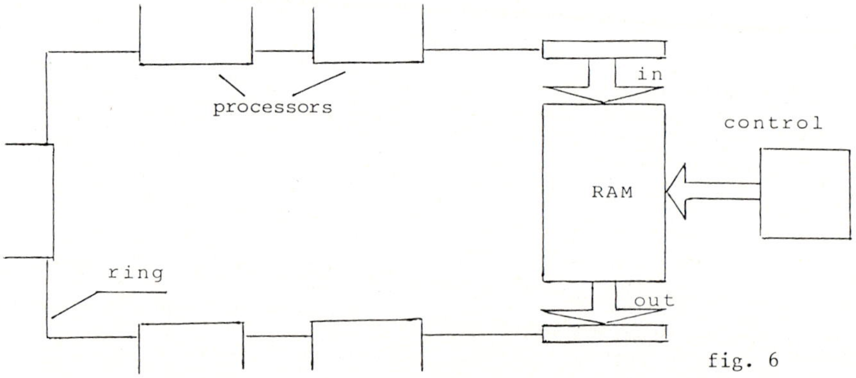

fig. 6

Additional software keeps track of the times that a processor is addressed and of the relation between messages sent and received from a processor. In that way an idea about the occupancy of each processor can be derived.

- by "polling". The P.O. sends regularly a special interrogation wagon to each processor. When the wagon returns, unaltered, it means that the processor was busy. This implies a special wagontype for polling-purpose.
- by " processor free " messages. A processor sends a special message to the P.O. when it is ready for accepting a new task. To the P.O. this means that the processor is free and still working.

One consideration in choosing the best of these three possibilities, is the influence that it will have on the traffic on the ring. This excludes the first mechanism because of the overhead it has on the ring-traffic and the speed requirements for operation of the P.O. That leaves polling or "processor free" messages.
The latter method results in less overhead on the ring than the first method. Also, when a processor is free, and it signals this to the P.O., the status is kept in the P.O.'s memory until a new message for the processor is received.
Keeping in mind the future extensions of the system, the choice was made for the use of "processor free" messages.

5.4 Structuring the data in the post office.

Messages, consisting of wagons, are stored in destination queues in the post-office. The transmission of a message to its destination is not started in the post-office until all wagons of a message have been collected.
Because messages have different lengths, the use of shiftregisters to implement FIFO's is not recommended. Instead, one large RAM is used in the P.O. to store all messages. The data is structured into queues. The wagons of a message are linked by pointers and a message descriptor indicates the beginning and the end of a chain of wagons by two pointers. Likewise, the message descriptors are linked (see fig. 7).
The messages are split into ones of which all wagons have arrived at the P.O. and into incomplete ones. The descriptors of incomplete messages are linked into a separate list.

Once all the wagons of a message have been received at the P.O. the related queue descriptor is taken out of the linked list of descriptors of incomplete messages and put into the linked descriptor list of complete messages. In reality this is accomplished by changing pointers in the message queue descriptor.
So, a wagon that is received, is added to a queue of an incomplete message. As soon as the first wagon of a message is transmitted from the P.O. to its final destination, the related queue descriptor is put into the list of incomplete messages again.

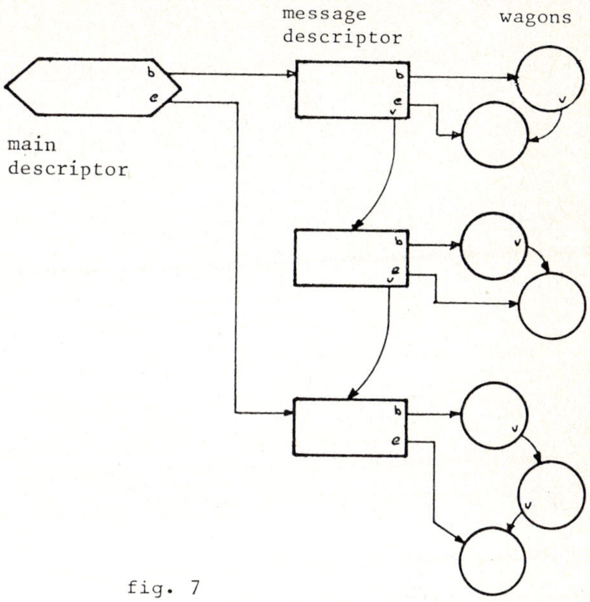

fig. 7

A new queue has to be defined when the first wagon of a message is received at the P.O. and likewise, when the last wagon of a message has left the P.O., the related queue must be deleted.
Transmission of a message from the P.O. to its destination can start, when there is a related "processor free" indication in the P.O. and a complete message is available for the processor. This can be either a message with a specific processor destination or a message addressed to a group, to which the available processor belongs.
The free space in the RAM memory is structured into a linked list consisting of "empty wagons". An object oriented programming technique manipulates the queues.

5.5 Ring interface of the Post Office.

Use is made of a previously developed ringnet as communication medium [1]. This ringnet is provided with shiftregisters to enable exchange of information between processors and the ring. Due to the restriction of mono-processing, a processor never simultaneously inputs and outputs data from and to the ring. Exchange of data between a processor and the ring, can therefore be implemented by the use of a single shiftregister. However, the Post Office needs to be provided with two shiftregisters; one for input and one for output (fig. 8).

This is due to the fact that the P.O. must be able to transmit and receive messages simultaneously, otherwise the message exchange between source and destination would not be efficient and/or the P.O. memory could overflow.

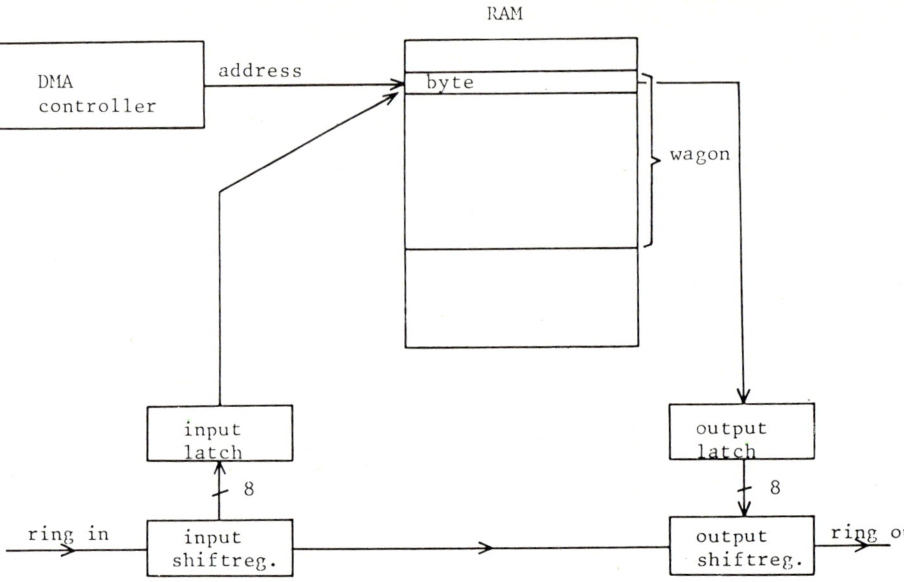

fig. 8

A message consists of a variable number of wagons and one wagon consists of a fixed number of bytes. The exchange of data between the ring interface and the RAM queueing memory is based on the transfer of single bytes under the control of direct memory access (DMA). When a wagon must be emitted from the P.O., the address register of the DMA is filled with the memoryaddress of the first byte of the wagon. Subsequently, the content of that byte is transferred to the output latch. The DMA-controller waits until the first byte of an incoming wagon is received in the input register.

Upon recognition of this event, the input byte will be written into the memory-address, which was just before read and emptied. The DMA- address register is then incremented. When the data in the ring has moved one byte, the output byte is transferred from the output latch to the shiftregister and simultaneously the next byte is moved from memory to the output latch, etc.. The input wagon does not need to contain meaningful data, it may be "empty". Similarly, the input wagon may contain meaningful data and the transmitted output wagon can be empty. After a complete wagon has been transmitted (and received), the DMA address register will be filled with another address under software control and a new wagon cycle can start.

6. STATUS OF THE PROJECT.

The system as described, has been built using five microcomputers, four of which are connected to the ring as executers and file dictionaries. Processor number five is used as a Post Office in the transport layer. The kernel software for the different processors has been written. Use is made of a previously developed ringnet as communication medium [1]. The correct functioning of the system has been demonstrated. The performance of the system in amount of data processing per second, is very dependent upon the inter processor communication means and, with the now applied ringnet and post-office, the performance is low. This is no problem for the application we have in mind: a large but slow, geographically distributed, system

A weak point in the present system is the Post Office, which does not allow for a redundant design. For that reason, the Post Office is being redesigned.

We are also investigating whether the outlined design can be used as a general purpose high speed multiprocessor system. In that case, the simple ringnet with Post Office must be abandoned or at least be supplemented by other means.

7. CONCLUSION.

This paper describes a multiprocessor architecture, particularly suitable as a framework for a modular, geographically distributed, system.
A small pilot system, consisting of four microcomputers connected to a ringnet and a "Post Office" processor in the transport layer, has become operational. The Post Office in the transport layer contains the central memory for queueing messages. Every processor in the system operates in the monoprocessing mode, e.g. there is no context switching allowed. Reliability is obtained by clustering processors with identical properties and data files, into a group with one group-address.
The system was designed, applying the principles outlined in the ISO reference model for Open Systems Interconnections. This reference model appeared to be particularly useful in distributed system design and has been a major guidance in structuring the kernel software.

8. REFERENCES.

[1] G.L. Reijns, Th. Bruins, W.G. Vree, A.C. Zwinkels
Simulation of a ringnet for a distributed processing system.
in "Microprocessor Systems", pp. 261-271
North-Holland Publishing Company, Amsterdam, 1980

[2] Draft International Standard IS/DIS 7498 182-04-22 (ISO/TC97)
Information processing systems - Open Systems Interconnection
Basic reference model.

[3] Liu, Ming, T.
Distributed loop computer networks:
Advances in Computer
M.C. Yovits (ed.)
Academic Press 1978, Vol. 17, pp. 164-216.

[4] G.L. Reijns, Th. Bruijns, W.G. Vree, C.J.van Spronsen
A distributed computer architecture
in "Implementing Functions", pp. 43-53
North-Holland Publishing Company, Amsterdam, 1981

[5] C. Delobel and W. Litwin (eds.)
Distributed Data Bases.
North-Holland Publishing compay, INRIA, 1980

[6] C.J. van Spronsen, D.A. Bearzatto
Data communication protocol processor
in "Microcomputer Architectures", pp. 193 - 199
North-Holland Publishing Company, Amsterdam, 1977

MICROCOMPUTERS: Developments in Industry, Business and Education
D.R. Wilson and C.J. van Spronsen (eds.) / ©EUROMICRO, 1983
Elsevier Science Publishers B.V. (North-Holland)

IMPLEMENTATION ASPECTS OF A DATABASE CONCURRENCY CONTROLLER IN A PERSONAL COMPUTER NETWORK

Jakob Karszt, Georg Lausen, Roland Salz

Institut für Angewandte Informatik
und Formale Beschreibungsverfahren
Universität Karlsruhe, West-Germany

In this paper, the implementation of the concurrency controller component in a database management system for microcomputers is described. The multi-user environment is realized connecting several single user personal computers to a global disc system via a network. First the concurrency controller is embedded into the framework of the underlying hardware and software configuration. Then we propose an integrated optimistic/ locking strategy as concurrency control scheme and discuss several implementation problems.

1. INTRODUCTION

In many application systems on microcomputers, a database management system (dbms) is an appropriate tool for fast and reliable software. Today, several dbms's on microcomputers are available [Ken82] or are discussed in the literature [SIG81]. Only e few support a multi-user environment. In this paper we describe a multi-user environment and especially a concurrency control scheme which is currently being implemented in the Datenbank-Pascal system [Kar83]. The Datenbank-Pascal system is an experimental dbms for personal computers with a language interface integrated in the programming language Pascal.

Multi-user dbms environments are realized either using a time-sharing operating system on a centralized machine or using a dedicated backend dbms server which is connected to several computers within a network [Mar80]. The approach discussed in the following is similar to the second type. A global disc system is connected via a network to several personal computers, each running a local dbms.

In [KKL82] we presented the transaction management including concurrency control and recovery in a disc-based configuration which was restricted to a star network around the central disc system. As concurrency control mechanism we adapted the optimistic method [KR81]. In this paper, we allow any network structure for the connection between personal computers and the global disc system. The concurrency control component is based on an integrated optimistic/ locking concurrency control scheme [Lau82].

In section 2 the hardware and software configuration is introduced and it is shown how the concurrency control module is embedded into the overall dbms software architecture of the Datenbank-Pascal system. In section 3 we describe the integrated concurrency control scheme in more detail and in section 4 we discuss some interesting implementation aspects.

This paper was partially supported by the Deutsche Forschungsgemeinschaft under Grant.No. Stu 98/2.

2. OVERALL ARCHITECTURE

The concurrency control of a dbms is based on the transaction concept. A transaction is a transformation of one database state into an other state. It has the properties of atomicity (either all results are visible or no results), durability (effects survive failures) and consistency (correct state transformation by a set of update operations).

A special dbms component, the Concurrency Controller (CC) is responsible for the correct execution of transactions. The CC is embedded into the framework of the underlying hardware and software configuration. The structure of this framework will now be described.

Hardware and Software Configuration

In the configuration proposed for the Datenbank-Pascal-system, there exists a collection of Personal Computers (PC), each running a user program together with a local dbms and an operating system. Each PC is called a host. Hosts are connected to a global disk system managed by an intelligent controller for physical access to the global storage. The global disc system contains the shared database on secondary storage. Local secondary storage devices are available on each PC to respond the demand for applications with high requirements to local data (see fig. 1).

The PCs can be connected via a star network or any other network structure around the global disc system. Since the concurrency control should be independent from the network structure, we design a CC which can be used in any structure. For communication the global disc is used. Therefore, the disc controller contains a shared synchronization area (SA) as part of the controller memory. The SA then is used as a global synchronisation area, which is needed for communication between the local CC's (see section 3).

To our knowledge, disc-based configurations applied for multi-user dbms environments as proposed throughout this paper have not been studied elsewhere. Compared to the dedicated (back-end) solution, we expect better performance. In dedicated solutions the main part of the dbms is running on a back-end machine which is sometimes called database server. Hence, the performance is restricted by the capacity of the back-end machine. In the disc-based configuration this bottleneck is substantially reduced, since only disc accesses and the maintenance of the SA are performed on the shared disc system. Other functions, as access path management, storage management or query optimization are performed by the local dbms's on each PC. Since a PC is a single-user machine, delegation of functions to a dedicated back-end computer without specialized hardware will not improve the performance of the PCs.

The concurrency controller as part of the DBMS

As mentioned above, on each host is running the whole dbms. The overall structure of the dbms is outlined in the following. It is based on the information hiding and data independence principles of the ANSI/SPARC architecture [Jar77], [Rob82].

Designing a dbms, we have to seperate the design decisions on three levels of abstraction: the external model, which represents the user views on the database as basis for application programs and dialog users, the conceptual model, which represents the overall structure of the database, and the internal model, which is responsible for access storage and transaction management. The machine level refers to the hardware itself, perhaps seen through a general purpose operating system for a PC (see fig. 2).

The Interface Manager is a collection of dbms-modules providing the external/conceptual mapping. The Record Manager is a collection of modules which realize the operations of the conceptual model and map these operations into operations of the internal model realized by the Memory Manager. In Datenbank-Pascal the objects of the conceptual model are data items (records/tuples) of the type RELATION. By the Record Manager the operations on data items ware mapped into operations on access and on storage objects. (We will later see in section 4 that this mapping is a critical point for the implementation of the CC.) The Memory Manager provides the mapping between the internal model and the machine level. It includes the CC, recovery, associative access and storage (buffer and secondary storage) management.

The objects supported at the internal level may be of various complexity. In the Datenbank-Pascal system, the organisation of associative access is realized by the Access Manager using well-known B*trees. The Access Manager maps the searchkeys into leaf-nodes of the tree, which contain references to the physical locations of the data items. The objects of physical access are PAGES. A page represents either a node of a B*tree or a set of data items of one relation. A set of pages is called an AREA. The whole database consists of a set of areas, which can be installed on different storage devices either on local discs or on the shared global disc system.

After the discussion of the overall system we now concentrate on concurrency control. The CC on each host is responsible for detecting and resolving conflicts, which may arise due to concurrent access of several hosts to the global disc. Of course, local discs are not critical for the CC since they contain only local data.

3. SELECTION AND IMPLEMENTATION OF A CONCURRENCY CONTROL SCHEME

A concurrency control synchronizes concurrent transactions such that no incorrect results due to concurrent operations on common data can occur. For a simple example consider the following situation: Two transactions T1, T2 running on different hosts increment a data item x stored on the global disc depending on the occurence of some real world events. Assume x = 5. The following concurrent execution of T1 and T2 is possible:

```
T1: read x from global disc
                    T2: read x from global disc
                        increment x by 1
                        write x to global disc
    increment x by 1
    write x to global disc
```

After termination x has the value 6, which of course is an incorrect result. The reason is the conflicting access of T1 and T2 to x. In general, two concurrent transactions are called conflicting, if both access a comon data item and at least one access is not a read access.

For the design of a concurrency control there exist several alternatives [Ull82]. Our solution can be characterized as follows:

(1) As part of the transaction manager (cp. fig. 2) each host has a local CC.

(2) Correct synchronization with recpect to the global data is achieved via a synchronization area SA, which is part of the disc controller of the global disc and is used as shared memory for communication between different CC.

(3) For each transaction correct synchronization either is achieved by the CC using the optimistic method (no locking),

(4) or using locking.

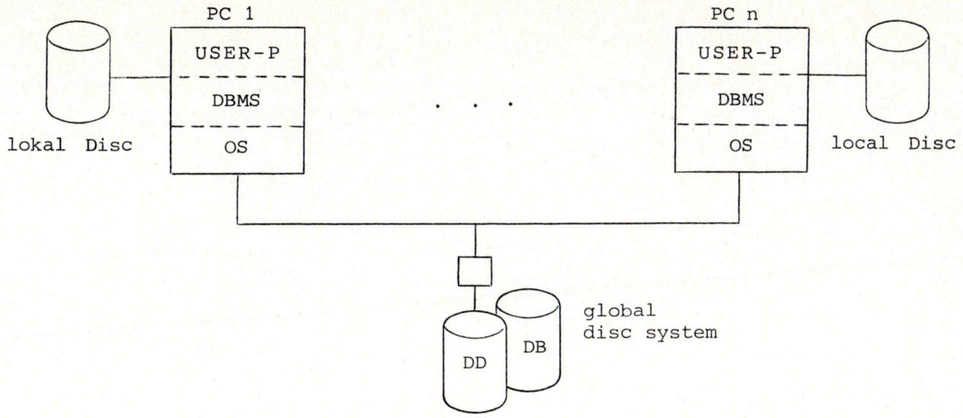

Fig.1: Disc-based personal computer network

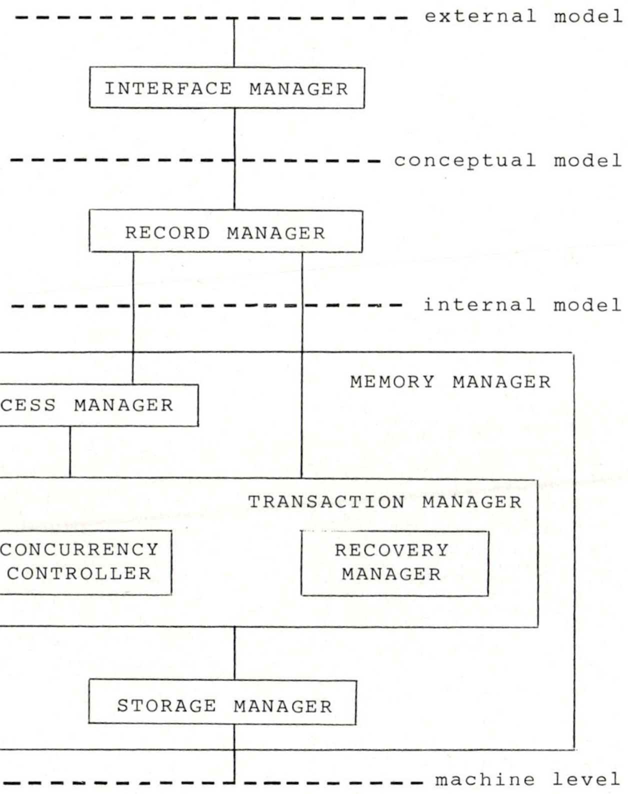

Fig.2: DBMS architecture

A detailed discussion of (1) - (3) can be found in [KKL82]. The integrated concurrency control scheme [Lau82] allowing either locking or no locking ((3),(4)) will be sketched in the folloing. We first give a high-level description of the concurrency control scheme, a more detailed description is presented later in this section.

The optimistic method can be described as follows:

(1) Each transaction consists of two or three phases: a read-phase, a validation phase and - if no conflict with another concurrent transaction has occured - a write phase.

(2) During the read-phase all read and write access are performed on local memory.

(3) If during the validation phase of a transaction T* its CC establishes by inspecting SA, that no conflicts occured with respect to T*, T*'s updates stored on local memory are made permanent on the global disc (write phase).

(4) If during the validation phase of T* conflicts are detected by its CC, the transaction T* is cancelled and may be restarted.

The validation and subsequent write phase have to be implemented as a global critical section. Within this critical section all accesses to SA are performed exclusively by the CC which obtaines the critical section. This can be implemented by a global semaphor of the global disc controller [Cor81].

One obvious drawback of the optimistic method is, that for long transactions the risk of being backed up is much higher than for short transactions, since the number of transactions which are to be tested for conflicts increases with the length of a transaction. For example, consider a balancing transaction executed concurrently with accounting transactions. If we assume that the rate of accounting transactions is rather high, the balancing transaction probably will never be executed to its end, since always an accounting transaction will update an account which has to be read to compute the balance. It is clear, that we need a mechanism to overcome this dilemma.

One solution is locking data items. When a transaction starts its execution (start of read phase) it locks the data items to be processed (preclaiming). The locks are recorded in SA. If a data item is already locked, the transaction has to wait. A transactions which has acquired its locks successfully will not be violated later by optimistic transactions. To guarantee this, whenever an optimistic transaction finishes, its CC tests during the validation phase by inspecting SA whether it has written a data item which currently is locked. If such a data item is found, the optimistic transaction is cancelled - the locking transaction is not disturbed. The algorithms for this procedure are presented in the following. (We further should mention that locking is not the only solution for the long-transaction-problem which is inherent to the optimistic method (cp. [PSU82]). A comparison and discussion of further design alternatives will be presented elsewhere.)

We distinguish between two types of transactions:

- 0-type: the transaction is executed under the optimistic method,
- 1-type: the transaction uses locking.

Conflicts between transactions of both types have to be detected by the CC's.

To detect conflicts with respect to an 0-type transactions, each local CC maintains during the execution of each transaction (1-type or 0-type) its so called readset (set of all data items read) and writeset (set of all data items inserted, updated or deleted). During the validation phase of an 0-type transaction T*, conflicts can be detected by intersecting the readset of T* with the writesets of all transactions which have performed their writephase concurrently. These writesets can be found in SA.

Conflicts between 1-type transactions are avoided via locking. The set of data items locked - the lockset - is stored in SA by the CC at the beginning of the readphase of a transaction of 1-type.

Further the CC of an 0-type transaction T* tests critical conflicts with respect to concurrent 1-type transactions by intersecting the writeset of T* with the corresponding locksets, which can be found in SA.

According to this, a CC is called by the following operations:

- tbegin:

A transaction starts its read phase. 1-type transactions acquire there locks (Preclaiming). The CC inspects SA and in case of already locked data items it forces the transaction to wait, or, if all locks can be accepted, it modifies SA accordingly and the transaction starts its execution.

- tread:, twrite:

A transaction reads / writes a data item. The CC maintains the readset and writeset accordingly, which are still stored on local memory.

- tend:

The validation phase starts. For 0-type transactions critical conflicts are tested by the CC. If no conflicts are found, the writeset is included in SA and the write phase is executed. Otherwise the transaction ic cancelled. For 1-type transactions the CC releases their locks by appropriate updating of SA and executes their write phase.

Concurrent access to SA by different CC must be implemented in a critical section to exclude synchronization errors of CC's. We describe this critical section using Hoare's well known monitor concept. Different to the original concept, if a process waiting to access the monitor is reactivated by a processed SIGNAL-operation, this process still waits until the signaling process has left the monitor.

Algorithms for tbegin, tend and the monitor

```
tbegin(T*):
begin
  if T* is of 1-type then
          CRITICAL-SECTION.SET-LOCKS;
end;

tend(T*):
begin
  CRITICAL-SECTION.VALWRITEPHASE;
  delete local copies of T*;
end;

CRITICAL-SECTION: monitor;

LOCKING-POSSIBLE: condition;

SET-LOCKS:
begin
  repeat
    begin
      get SA from disc controller;
      if lockset (T*) ∩ totallockset ≠ ∅ then
         WAIT(LOCKING-POSSIBLE);
         (* totallockset includes the currently
            locked data items *)
    end
  until (lockset (T*) ∩ totallockset = ∅ );
  totallockset := totallockset ∪ lockset (T*);
end;

VALWRITEPHASE:
begin
  valid := true;
  get SA from disc controller;
  if T* is of O-type then
     begin   (* validation *)
       for each transaction T having performed its
         writephase concurrently do
           if writeset(T) ∩ readset(T*) ≠ ∅
              then valid := false;
       if totallockset ∩ writeset(T*) ≠ ∅
          then valid := false;
     end
  else   (*  T*  is of 1-type *)
     begin
       totallockset := totallockset ∖ lockset(T*);
       while QUEUE(LOCKING-POSSIBLE) > 0 do
          SIGNAL(LOCKING-POSSIBLE);
     end;
  if valid then
     begin
       include writeset(T*) into SA;
       put SA to disc controller;
       writephase; (* globalize all actions done
                      locally by writing on
                      global disc *)
     end
end;
```

To summarize this section. As pointed out in [KKL82], the optimistic concurrency control method best fits into our configuration. But to overcome the indefinite restart problem, which especially may be crucial for long transactions, we introduce locking. Since locking only is introduced for the exceptional case, preclaiming seems to be sufficient as locking strategy. The critical point of preclaiming in comparison to incremental locking is, that large portions of the database have to be locked, since in general it is not known in advance what data items a transaction will process during its execution. The benefit is, that no deadlocks can occur, and that locks need only to be recorded in SA at the beginning of a transaction.

4. FURTHER IMPLEMENTATION ASPECTS

A general problem of concurrency control is the question whether objects of the conceptual level (also called logical objects) or objects of the physical (internal) level should be used for detecting conflicts.

We dediced, that the read- and writesets of O-type transactions are constituted by the objects on the physical level, namely the page numbers of the pages read/written by the respective transaction. The page is the physical granule of transportation throughout the whole system. Page numbers are determined by the Storage Manager. If a data item is read from a page and subsequently rewritten, it is guaranteed that the Storage Manager uses the same page.

Locking is performed at relation level. A relation is mapped by the Record Manager into a set of pages. Hence, the relation name identifies a set of pages. The names of the locked relations constitute the lockset of the respective transaction. Consequently, for detecting conflicts between a validating O-type and a still running 1-type-transaction we have to test whether the name of a relation modified by the O-type transaction is included in the totallockset.

Critical conflicts also can occur due to updates of the access path structures and other system information. Therefore, read and modified pages, which may result from the dynamic behaviour of the B*trees, are included into the read-/writesets as well. It is guaranteed, that the relation names included in the locksets cover the corresponding access path structures and system information. Hence, all possible conflicts can be detected by the CC. (This is true with respect to the phantom problem [EGLT76] which we will not further discuss here.)

Consequently, all updates of access paths and other system information are performed tentatively on local memory by the CC, too. This works, since each global access to a page requested by the Access Manager or Record Manager is performed by the Storage Manager via the CC (see Fig. 2).

Using the optimistic method a problem arises due to the repeated backup of a transaction. If an O-type transaction is backed up repeatedly, we can solve this problem changing the transaction to 1-type.

5. CONCLUSION

The main topic of this paper was the implementation of the concurrency control component in a disc-based multi-user dbms environment. Several interesting aspects of concurrency were discussed which result from the underlying disc-based system. An extension to several global discs (distributed database) in a network is possible. One solution for concurrency control is using one global critical section for all global discs. Further investigations for the improvement of this solution are necessery (also see [Schl81]).

ACKNOWLEDGEMENT

The authors wish to thank W. Stucky for advising and supporting this work.

REFERENCES

[Cor81] Corvus Systems (eds.): Corvus Disc and Network Handbook, 1981.

[EGLT76] K.P.Eswaran et al.: The notions of consistency and predicate locks in a database system, Comm. of the ACM, Vol.19, No.11, 1976, 624-633.

[Gray81] J.N.Gray: The Transaction Concept: Virtues and Limitations, Proc. VLDB 81, 144-154.

[Jar77] D.A.Jardine (ed.): The ANSI/SPARC DBMS Model. North Holland, Amsterdam, 1977.

[Kar83] J.Karszt: Datenbank-Pascal: User and System Manual, Institut für Angewandte Informatik und Formale Beschreibungsverfahren, Universität Karlsruhe, 1983.

[Ken82] P.Kenealy: Database software packages for micros, Mini-Micro Systems, Vol.XV, No.9, Sep.1982, 193-202.

[KKL82] J.Karszt, H.Kuss, G.Lausen: Transaction Management in a Multi Personal Computer System, Proc. of the EUROMICRO 82 Conference, North Holland, 203-210.

[KR81] H.T.Kung, J.T.Robinson: On Optimistic Methods for Concurrency Control, ACM Transactions on Database Systems, Vol.6, No.2, 1981.

[Lau82] G.Lausen: Concurrency control in database systems - Towards the integration of optimistic methods and locking, Proc. Annual Conference of the ACM, Dallas, 1982, 65-68.

[Mar80] F.Maryanski: Backend database systems, Computing Surveys, Vol.12, No.1, March 1980, 3-25.

[Rob82] J.T.Robinson: Design of Concurrency Controls for Transaction Processing Systems, Dissertation, Department of Computer Science, Carnegie-Mellon University, Pittsburgh, Pennsylvania,1982.

[PSU82] U.Prädel, G.Schlageter, R.Unland: Einige Verbesserungen optimistischer Synchronisationsverfahren, Proc. of the GI-Jahrestagung 1982, Informatik Fachberichte Nr.57, 684-698.

[SIG81] D.Lewis (ed.): Proc. of SIGMOD/SIGSMALL joint workshop on small database systems, SIGSMALL Newsletter, Vol.7, No.2, 1981.

[Ull82] J.D.Ullmann: Principles of Database Systems, second edition, Pitman Publ. Ltd., London, 1982.

[Schl81] G.Schlageter: Optimistic methods for Concurrency Control in a distributed database system, Proc. VLDB 1981, 125-130.

MICROCOMPUTERS: Developments in Industry, Business and Education
D.R. Wilson and C.J. van Spronsen (eds.) /© EUROMICRO, 1983
Elsevier Science Publishers B.V. (North-Holland)

DESIGN OF A DISTRIBUTED FILE SYSTEM FOR A GEOGRAPHIC NETWORK

P.Colombo (*), S.Copelli (*), G.Gottlob (*)(***)(****), L.Grossi (*), D.Mandrioli (*)(**), G.Oldano (*), P.Paolini (*)(***), A.Pellegrini (*)

(*) ARG srl, Via Strambio 11, 20133 MILANO (Italy)
(**) University of Udine, UDINE (Italy)
(***) Politecnico di Milano - MILANO (Italy)
(****) Technische Universität Wien, Wien - (Austria)

SAD is a distributed file system supported by a geographic network of heterogeneous minicomputers. Its design has been carried out within a research project (called "Progetto Finalizzato per l'Informatica") supported by the Italian National Research Council. SAD's main features are: 1) supporting file transfers between different nodes, avoiding transmission of useless data; 2) allowing a concurrent use of the network.
The main features of SAD architecture are described, enphasizing the purpose of achieving a high degree of portability.
A few notes on the prototype currently under development at ARG (*) are also given.

(*) ARG: Applied Research Group - Via Strambio 11 - 20133 MILANO (Italy)

1. INTRODUCTION

SAD is a system for handling files spread over a wide geographic area. It is being developed as a part of a research project supported by the National Research Council of Italy.
The ultimate goal of this project is to investigate and develop a prototype of a distributed data base on a geographic network, i.e. a distributed environment where the communication medium is generally low-bandwidth and error-prone.
SAD has been conceived both as an intermediate step in the data-base project, mainly as a support to distributed transactions, and as an independent application tool.
The design refers to the class of applications in which a set of cheap autonomous nodes (minicomputers), each one with its own local data repository, is involved in a common-based application requiring some form of loose interconnection through a low-cost communication media.
The nodes of the National Health Service are an example of such an application.
An important target of this project is that the nodes of the network may have different hardware and run different operating systems, each one with its own (and possibly different) conventions on data representation and storage.
This paper presents a short review of SAD functionalities (section 2) and the portable design which has been developed by the Applied Research Group during the first phase of the project (section 3). A short highlight on a prototype implementation on an Olivetti M40 minicomputer is also given in section 4.

2. OVERVIEW OF SAD FUNCTIONALITIES

As an independent application tool, SAD is addressed to the application programmers involved in the design of distributed applications and is made available as an extension of the native application language.
It enhances a programming technique in which all the required input data are first collected from remote node and, after a local processing, all results are sent to remote destination nodes. The goal is to optimize the network throughput which is indeed considered a bottleneck: the physical network is very often foreseen to be of the dial-up type with a low availability (switched telephone line). This is why a type of access based on the transfer of bursts of data bulks is highly recommended in order to achieve a reasonable throughput. The user may insert, through the SAD interface, any file from its own local file system into a global catalogue, by assigning to it a SAD name. This name is the tool by which a file belonging to a local file system is made visible to any remote SAD user on the network. These global files have hence two names: a local name according to the conventions of the host file system, and a global name (SAD name), which is structured as a couple (node name, local SAD name). This means that once a file has been inserted into the global catalogue it can be accessed either through the local file system interface (only by local users) and through the SAD interface. In order to gain access to any global file, the user must first connect, through a "CONNECT" command, to the SAD node (actually a subcatalogue of the global SAD file system) where the file resides. This will cause the underlying network handler to "open" a logical link with the host where the node actually resides. All read/write commands, called "executive" commands, have a whole file as an argument (a record-level access is not supported). In order to avoid the transferring of useless data through the network, the user may specify, as a parameter of the executive commands, a set of filters to select a subset of the records from the target file (horizontal filter) and a subset of the fields inside each single record (vertical filter).

Conflicts on the access to shared files may be regulated through the use of "lock" commands. Deadlock is easily avoided as it can occur only on the access to a single file.
The SAD interface provides to the user a set of commands for the direct control and optimization of the access to the communication network. (As mentioned above this is assumed to be a bottleneck in the system). These commands are termed "control" commands: COBEGIN-COEND and COEXECUTE. All the executive commands issued by the user inside a control section defined by a COBEGIN/COEND pair are not immediately executed: they are stored by the SAD subsystem until one or more COEXECUTE commands are issued. This causes the whole set of these "differred" commands, or a subset of them, to be sent for the actual execution to the destination nodes. This techcnique achieves two main advantages:

- A packet of requests addressed to a node may be sent through one single network session. (Sending one request at a time requires to establish a physical link each time a request is issued, thus resulting in long delays due to the low availability of the network).
- Packets of requests addressed to different nodes are sent for execution "virtually" in parallel. Physical parallelism can obviously be achieved in a natural way only if several physical links can be obtained by the host machine.

A complete description of SAD functionalities is given in the user manual /1/.

3. INTERNAL ARCHITECTURE

Since one major functional goal is to support SAD over a geographic network of heterogeneous machines with totally different operating systems, a few SAD implementations are being carried on in parallel by separate project groups on different host machines and, of course, all these SAD nodes are expected to interact in a coherent way.
From this requirement the need follows, in this project, for a first level of portable design, out of which any more detailed machine-oriented design and implementation should be derived.
The following ones are the main features of SAD internal architecture:

*** All the functionalities which are strictly dependent on the target host machine have been encapsulated into a few components. This has been done mainly for the interfaces to local File Systems, which are far from offering standard interfaces on different Operating Systems.

*** General mechanisms for data manipulation have been kept strictly separate from the policies which are followed in the control of the execution flow. In othe words we have tried to keep a clean separation between "what" can be done inside any SAD subsystem and "how" it can be done. This will make easier any future tuning and/or improvement of the "behaviour" of SAD.

*** Only a few general design decisions related to performance optimization have been taken at the current level of design. We believed that any further tuning of performance parameters should be done in the next level of design, which will be oriented to specific machines, and during the implementation phase.

3.1 Overview

A SAD system consists of several SAD nodes connected through a Network (fig. 1). A SAD node is the "owner", with respect to the SAD world, of a predefined collection of local files: any node includes all the components which handle accesses to these files both by local and remote users.
A SAD node resides on a unique physical machine, but in principle there could be more than one node on the same physical machine. For the sake of simplicity, in the following we assume that on each host (actually a small machine) there is only one SAD node.
A SAD user is always bound to one specific node but SAD applications may generally require the exchange of data to/from foreign nodes: in other words we say that any application implies that the user might be "connected" with a certain number of foreign SAD Nodes. For generality purposes we say that a user is also "connected" to his own node.
A node is composed of functional units. We do not make any assumption here whether they are implemented as processes, procedures, tasks, or other operating system objects.
From the point of view of their instances there are three classes of units:

a) units existing in a unique instance inside each node
b) units existing in as many instances as are the users active on the node (local users)
c) units existing in as many instances as are the local and remote users "connected" to the node.

In order to have a clear idea of the internal architecture of SAD environment we will look at it from these points of view:

- what are the units active inside any SAD Node to handle the connections with local and foreign users
- what are the units, spread through different Nodes, which are involved in a connection between a user and a foreign Node
- the interactions between the units when both (1) a connection with a remote node (CONNECT) and (2) the actual execution of a packet of file operations (COEXECUTE), are requested.

The interactions between units may be either synchronous or asynchronous. In the first case the control is given back to the invoking unit only after the completion of the requested operation (procedure-call or "synchronous" message exchange type of interactions). In the latter case the control is returned to the invoking unit after the request has been delivered either

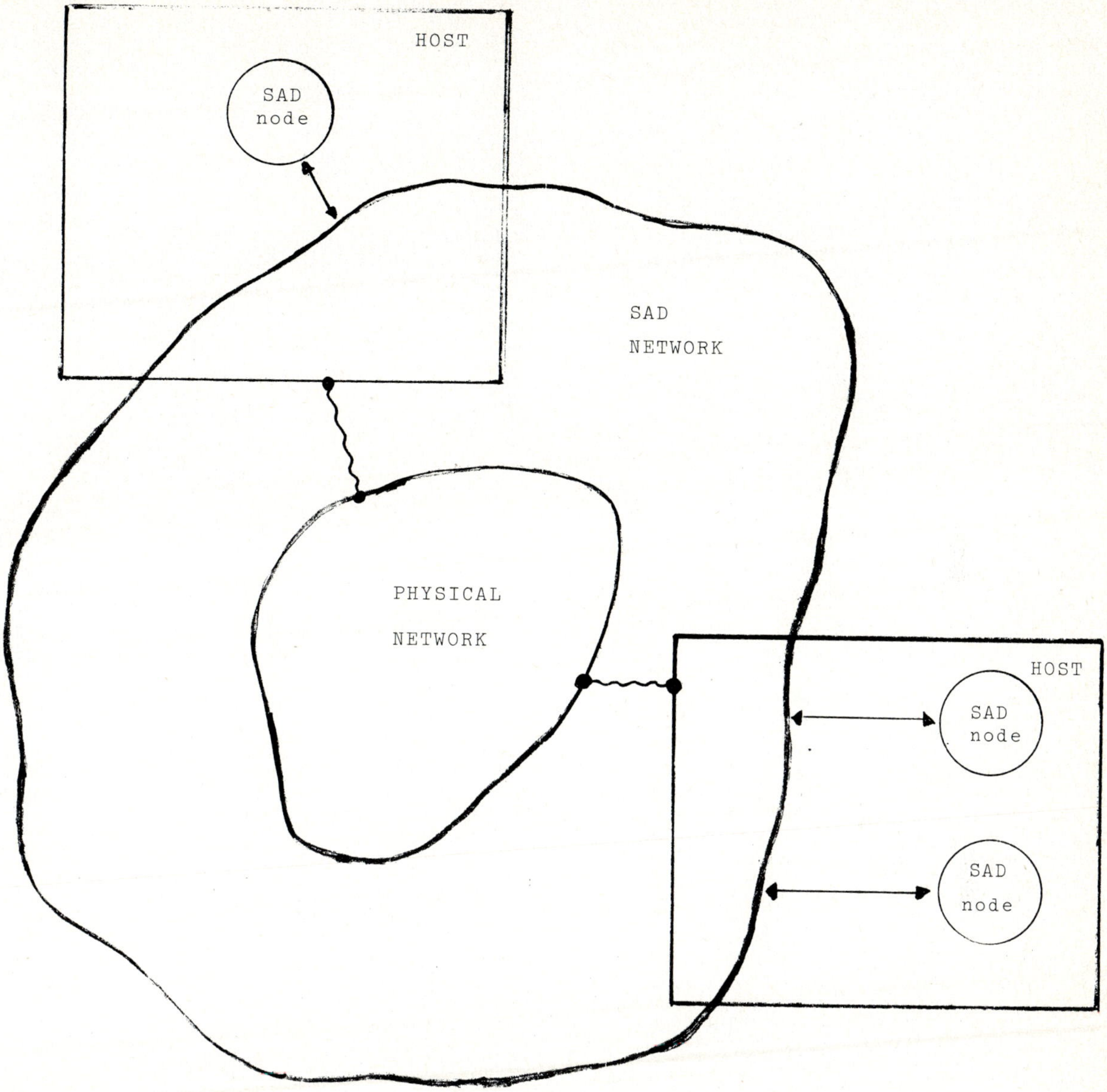

Fig. 1 - SAD Network

to the system or to the destination (server) unit ("no-wait" message-exchange type of interactions). Explicit synchronization mechanisms, such as WAIT and SIGNAL instructions, must be used to synchronize asynchronous units on specific events.

3.2 Units

The following types of units have been defined:

- Boss
- Butler (BT)
- Data Server (DS)
- Communication and Transmission Server (CTS)
- Network Server (NS)
- Network Handler (NH)
- Agencies: Boss Agency (BA) and Butler Agency (BTA)

The relations between different units are shown in figure 2.

3.2.1 Boss

The Boss is called directly by the user through SAD user interface. Its job is to receive and store these user requests. When it is asked by the user to execute them (COEXECUTE command), it assigns them, in packets, to the appropriate Butlers. The job of each Butler is to execute the requests related to one specific SAD Node. In a latter phase the Boss collects the replies from Butlers and returns all results to the user. Boss is a type b) unit: for any SAD node there is one Boss for each user active inside the node and it is dynamically created when a user enters the SAD environment.
Boss interacts synchronously with its own user, but asynchronously with Butlers: since it generally dispatches user requests to several Butlers, it is quite useful that such Butlers may operate in parallel.

3.2.2 Butlers

Butlers are encharged by Boss to "drive" the execution of user requests.
They are not concerned with the semantic of user requests but they are expected to handle a large class of failure by undertaking proper recovery actions (e.g. retry, undo, roll-back user requests).
There exists one pair of Butlers for each SAD node the user is connected with: a Local Butler (BTL) in the same node as the Boss and a Remote Butler (BTR) in the remote Node (fig. 2). BTR is the "agent" of BTL with respect to a remote SAD node the user is connected with: if the user is connected with his own local node there is only one Butler, called BTN. BTN performs, in an optimized way, the same functions as the two parties BTL-BTR.
BTL receives user requests (usually a "packet" of requests) from its Boss and sends them to BTR for their actual execution. Once they have been executed, BTR returns the results back to BTL. BTL will eventually reply to its Boss.
BTL-BTR interactions are supported by a Communication and Transmission Server (CTS). There is one CTS for each one of the two parties. No CTS is, of course, created for BTN.
BTR (BTN) interacts with the file system of its node through a Data Server (DS) in order to get the requests executed.
The interactions between any Boss and BTL's (BTN's) are of the asynchronous type, while the interactions between BTs and their servers (CTS, DS) are all of the synchronous type.

3.2.3 Data Server

The Data Server (DS) is the unit which is in charge of doing any local-data manipulation requested by its Boss. This component encapsulates all the calls to the host file system which are required in order to perform the operations on SAD files.
Inside any SAD node there are as many instances of DS as are the users "connected" to that node in the whole network, including the local users. The DS services are accessible only by BTR (BTN). The interactions between DS and BTR (BTN) are of "Synchronous Request" type.

3.2.4 Communication and Transmission Server

Communication and Transmission Servers (CTS) are the handlers of the communication channel between BTR and BTL. There are two CTS's for each connection: one in the Node of the user and one in the remote Node to which the user is connected.
CTS basic functions are to send/receive packets of requests/results and to transfer input/output data files associated to the requests. They are also encharged of format conversion when transmission occurs between nodes whose local file systems are not compatible.

3.2.5 Network Subsystem

The Network Subsystem is in charge of handling the physical connection of a host to the communication network.
This component is unique on a host: it is shared both by the SAD nodes residing on the same host and by the units inside a node.
The Network interface (/3/) allows the users (i.e. SAD units) to establish "logical" links with remote SAD nodes without being concerned with the details of the physical network.
In the SAD prototype which is currently being implemented, the physical network is the public telephone network (fig. 3). The physical connection of a host to the network is handled by a device, called MILC, by Italdata, which implements some automatic dial-up procedures and simple recovery actions.

3.2.6 Network Server

The Network Server (NS) is a type a) unit which is responsible of listening to asynchronous requests of connections coming from external Nodes. NS and CTS are the only SAD units which have a direct access to the interface of the underlying Network Subsystem.

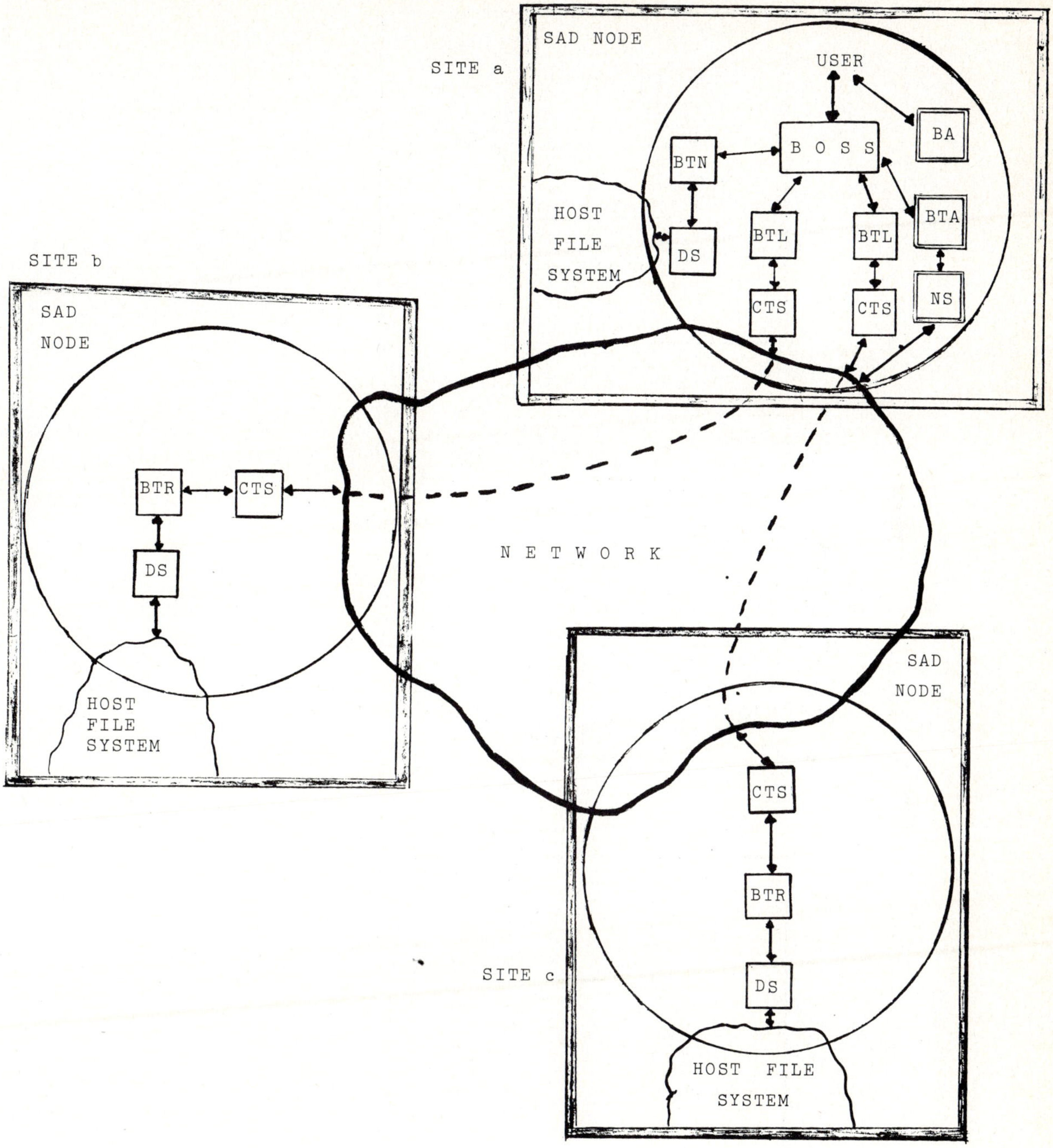

Fig. 2 - SAD Units

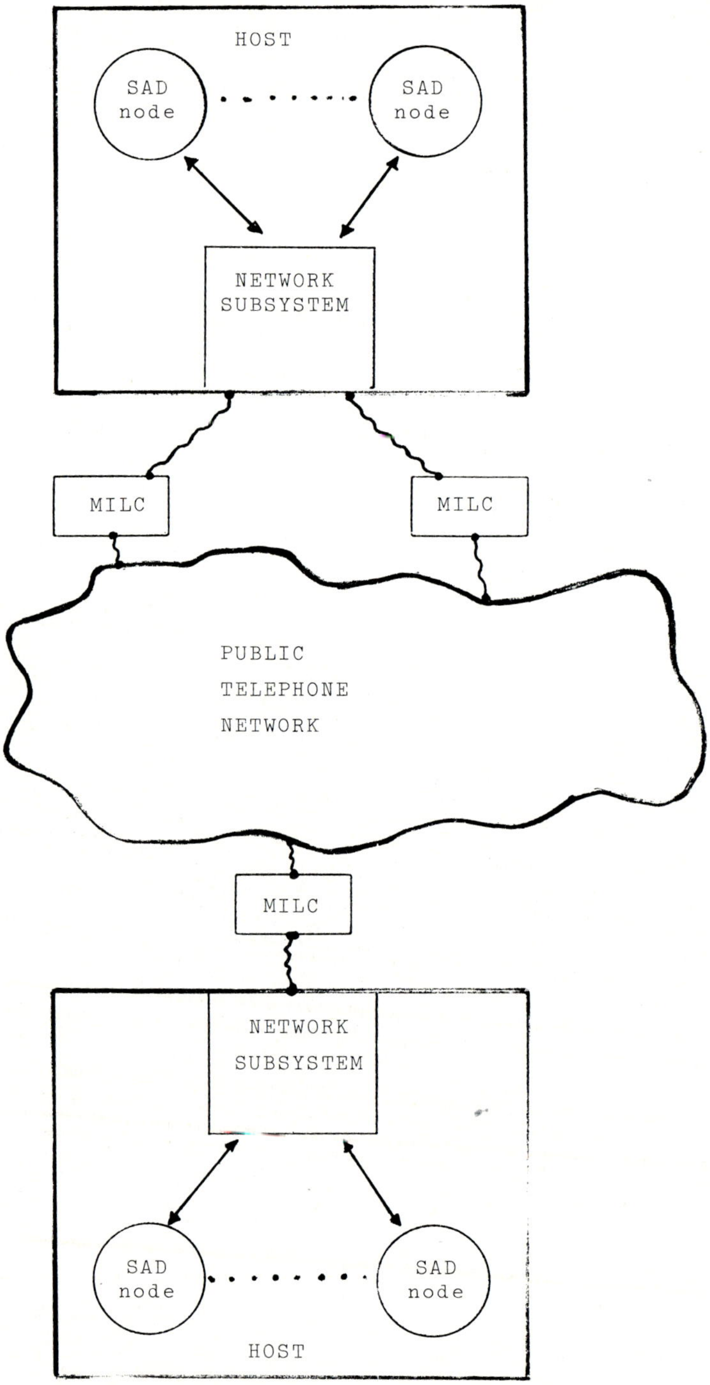

Fig. 3 - SAD prototype network

3.2.7 Agencies

Agencies are type a) units which are responsible of allocating dynamic objects.
Two agencies exist in each SAD Node:

1- Boss Agency (BA) which is responsible of creating a Boss component for each user entering the SAD environment.
2- Butler Agency (BTA) which is responsible of creating BTL, BTR, BTN, DS, CTS at CONNECT time.

3.3 Scenarios

A short overview is given here of the flow of interactions between SAD units when they are involved in the execution of a CONNECT and a CO-EXECUTE commands issued by the user.

3.3.1 CONNECT

1- The Boss receives the synchronous CONNECT request from its user and synchronously asks the Butler Agency of its Node to perform the connection with the requested Node.
2- The Butler Agency creates one BTL and CTS for each remote Node to be connected with and one BTN, if the connection with the local Node is also requested. All BTL's are asynchronously started and requested to get their corresponding BTR's.
3- Each BTL contacts, through a dialog local CTS - remote NS, the BTA of the corresponding remote Node.
4- The remote BTA creates one instance of BTR, CTS, DS in its own Node and asynchronously starts BTR. The identifier of BTR is then returned back to BTL.
5- When all the above operations are completed, their results are returned back to the local BTA which returns to the Boss and eventually to the user.

3.3.2 COEXECUTE

1- The Boss synchronously receives from the user the list of identifiers of requests to be executed (this is a parameter to the COEXECUTE command). Each sublist of requests to be executed on a single Node is passed to the BTL (BTN) associated to that Node through an asynchronous interaction.
2- Each BTL sends, through CTS's, to its BTR the list of commands to be executed. These may include: "write" requests of local files onto the remote Node, "read" requests of files from the remote Node onto the local Node, "lock" requests on files in the remote Node. All the data files associated to "write" requests are then transferred, through CTS onto the remote Node. The local requests are executed directly by BTN, through its DS.
3- BTR asks DS to perform the requests received from BTL, sets up the result files (from "read" requests) and sends back, through its CTS, to BTL the result of the execution.
4- At the end of the above protocol, BTL returns its results to the Boss.
5- The Boss collects all the results from BTL's (BTN) and returns to the user.

It is worth enphasizing that concurrent accesses to shared objects occur only

1. when requesting resource allocation (mainly at connect time),
2. when accessing the local file system, through DS,
3. when accessing the network.

4. SAD IMPLEMENTATION

The prototype version of SAD, currently under development at ARG, is being implemented on an Olivetti M40 minicomputer as a host.
M40 runs a new operating system, called COSMOS V, which implements a multi-user and multi-functional application environment. It provides a set of mechanisms for dynamically creating, destroying and controlling application processes. Application processes are structured into groups called "families", sharing the same address space. Communication between processes may happen through "monitor" based shared objects which are supported by the basic operating system.
A SAD node in the COSMOS V environment is divided into two sections: 1) a section which handles the requests coming from remote users; 2) a section handling the interactions of local users with the SAD network.
Section 1) is represented by a family of processes which is in charge of "serving" the requests coming from remote nodes. The "root" of this hierarchical family is a process which implements the Network Server functionalities: it is always listening for "connection" request coming from the network. Once a request is received a process is created (through a call to the operating system) to handle all the requests coming from that remote user. This process performs all the functionalities of the BTR and DS components associated to that connection. When the remote user issues a "disconnect" command, the server process suicides.
The number of server processes which may be active in parallel cannot exceed a fixed number, which is basically determined by the budget of system resources (mainly main memory) allocated to that family of processes. This is a configuration parameter. If the number of "connect" requests exceeds this number, these will be enqueued by the network subsystem until a server will be available.
As far as section 2) is concerned, each local user is represented in the system by a separate family of processes which has been previously created according to system policies (this is out of SAD concern): e.g. for interactive users a new family of processes is created when a user logs into a terminal. When a local user issues a connect to a subset of SAD nodes only some proper data areas are initialized. When the user issues a "COEXECUTE" a process is created for each remote node involved in the SAD command. Each process performs the job of CTS, as described in the previous section: it sends a packet of requests to its partner (BTR), waits for the re-

sults and after returning the results to the calling program, it suicides.
The Boss component is synchronous with the calling program and is implemented as a set of procedures.
All the above components share the network subsystem by calling the entry procedures of a monitor which handles the communication lines.

5. RELATED WORKS

A short overview of a few major data management systems on geographic networks is presented in this section. The National Software Works (/4/), the Digital DEC-NET (/6/) and the Olivetti ONE-V2 (/5/) have been examined from these points of view:

1- Types of Nodes: homogeneous and heterogeneous ones.
2- Program-Data locality: the traditional approach to program execution requires both program and data to have the same locality. In a network environment this is obtained either by moving programs to data sites (heavy in a heterogeneous network) or by moving data to program sites.
3- Data visibility: users may access data at the record level or at the file level.
4- User visibility: the user has the visibility either of a unique file system or of a multi file-system.

A summary of the main features of the systems mentioned above is given in the next table:

		NSW	ONE-V2	DEC-NET	SAD
Node type	Homog.			X	
	Heterog.	X	X		X
Prog.-Data Locality	Data migr.	X	X	X	X
	Progr. migr.			X	
Data visibility	Record		X	X	
	File	X	X	X	X
User visibility	Global FS	X			
	Multi FS's		X	X	X

6. CONCLUSION

As mentioned above, in the current implementation phase a few design aspects have purposely been kept as simple as possible. A relevant issue is here the handling of recovery actions mainly in the case of line failures. At present no more actions are undertaken to recover from a line failure, other than those automatically done by the automatic dial-up hardware device (MILC), which will make a few retries. If the failure is not recovered by the hardware, the SAD request for the packet of SAD requests) is considered as if it had totally aborted.
This design decision is proving quite satisfactory for the current requirements of the project (mainly "demonstration" requirements), where at least a file-transfer between two nodes is expected to be carried on with a high probability of success.
A better tuning of the recovery area is expected to be done in the next design phase, together with the development of automatic procedures for the management and control of the SAD network.

7. REFERENCES

/1/ ARG s.r.l. DATANET/SAD USER INTERFACE CNR-PFI/P2 documentation SAD/DS1, June 82.

/2/ ARG s.r.l. SAD INTERNAL ARCHITECTURE CNR-PFI/P2 documentation SAD/OV1, Sept. 82.

/3/ ARG s.r.l. SAD NETWORK INTERFACE CNR-PFI/P2 documentation SAD/NT1, Sept. 82.

/4/ E.Bayer ed. NOTES ON DISTRIBUTED OPERATING SYSTEMS: AN ADVANCED COURSE Springer Verlag, 1981.

/5/ ONE-V2 GENERAL INFORMATION MANUAL Ing. C.Olivetti & C., SpA, 1981.

/6/ DEC-NET GENERAL INFORMATION MANUAL Digital Equipment Corporation, 1980.

/7/ Bertino et al. DATANET/HERMES: UN SISTEMA PER LA GESTIONE DI BASI DI DATI DISTRIBUITI. Proceedings AICA 81

/8/ Tanenbaum NETWORK PROTOCOLS ACM Comp. Surveys, Dec. 81.

8. LIST OF ABBREVIATIONS

BA = Boss Agency
BTA = Butler Agency
BTL = Local Butler
BTN = Node Butler
BTR = Remote Butler
CTS = Communication and Transmission Server
DS = Data Server
NS = Network Server
SAD = "Sistema di Archivi Distribuiti"

Session F2:

EDUCATION

Chairman: Daniel Tabak
Ben Gurion University
Beersheva (Israel)

Introductory Comments

The issues of education, in conjunction with microcomputers, should be regarded as being composed of two basic aspects:

(a) education, whose goal is the acquisition of knowledge and skills in the theory, techniques and applications of modern microcomputer technology (as a part of the more general, computer science and engineering field)

(b) the implementation of microcomputers as effective tools of teaching in a variety of other fields, not necessarily related to computer science and technology.

These are some of the basic approaches to which the modern educational establishment should address itself. The papers offered in this session, represent very important steps towards the realization of the above.

The first paper by Aramberri, Garijo and Gurruchaga addresses itself to the problem of introducing a computer science curriculum in a specific geographical area. The third paper, by Barta, falls, in general, within the same category, stressing the medium scale educational environment.

The second paper, by Jameson, falls within the second category, describing the implementation of microcomputers in medical environment education.

MICROCOMPUTERS: Developments in Industry, Business and Education
D.R. Wilson and C.J. van Spronsen (eds.) /© EUROMICRO, 1983
Elsevier Science Publishers B.V. (North-Holland)

MODEL PLAN FOR THE INTRODUCTION OF COMPUTER STUDIES IN SECONDARY SCHOOLS IN THE PROVINCE OF GUIPUZCOA, THE BASQUE COUNTRY, SPAIN

J. Aramberri, F.J. Garijo, L. Gurruchaga and F. Verdejo

Facultad de Informática
Universidad del País Vasco
San Sebastián, Spain

This paper describes a model plan for the introduction of computer studies in the secondary schools (students aged 16-17) in the province of Guipuzcoa (Basque Country). The objectives, the content of the program and the equipment needed for the experiment are described. The syllabus is set out in some detail including a breakdown of the course hours, and some suggestions as to their specific content. Finally, the requirements for a Teacher Training Centre and the present status of the project are analysed. The plan has been requested for the Delegationn of Culture, Sport and Tourism of the Diputacion Foral de Guipuzcoa

1. INTRODUCTION

The present use of computers in a great number of areas of social activity, and especially its foreseeable extension to the majority of public and private sectors (production, politics, education, culture,etc.) has induced the education authorities of several countries to include computer studies in their secondary school curricula. The first effort to introduce youngsters aged 16 and 17 to computer science ocurred in the 70's, but the cost of the equipment made the spread of such experiments impossible. With the arrival of micro computers and the lowering of costs, it is finally possible to generalise the experiment in accordance with the initial hopes.

The paper we are presenting here resumes the content of a model plan for the introduction of data processing in the secondary schools.

The aim of the plan is to give the student a basic training in data processing which will help him to understand easily the functioning of computers, and, using them as a tool solve simple problems; to make him consider the social implications of the new technology which he is using; and, finally to awaken his curiosity sufficiently to make him want to know more about the computer and its applications.

Methodology is particularly stressed in this proposed plan. We believe that with the scientific study of data processing, a methodology is acquired wich makes it possible to solve problems using the computer as a tool. However, with the marketing of micro computers and their consumption by people unfamiliar with data processing, we are bound to see the same errors made with the program design of the first computers reappear. The design of the syllabus was determined by our belief that if the student is taught a proper methodology, he will acquire "good habits" in problem analysis and program construction.

We shall analyse the different aspects of the plan in the following sections.

In Part 2, we shall study the principal characteristics of the plan: duration of studies, general content of the program, equipment, etc.

Part 3 will be dedicated to the breakdown of the syllabus, analysing in detail the general objectives, programs and projects of each course.

Part 4 will deal with the characteristics of a training and coordinating centre for the plan, and finally, in Part 5 we shall explain the present status of the plan.

2. GENERAL CHARACTERISTICS

2.1 Training Period

The training period has been broken into two courses, each lasting a full school year (October - June). The first course is made up of a minimun of 90 hours: 3 hours weekly of class lecture and 2 hours of individual work in the laboratory for exercises.

The second year consists of a total 110 hours: 6 hours weekly (classes and individual work).

Both the first and second courses of data processing will be studied as part of the curricula along with the other subjects (math, physics, literature, etc.).

The program is designed to cover two years rather than one in part because of the novelty of the concepts and the material, but also because it is felt that the student needs the time to assimilate the subject matter. During the 2 year period, the student is given the theory and practice needen for the use of simple data processing equipment in solving real problems which may appear in this daily or professional life. Because we consider that a grasp of the concepts involved requires a certain baskground, we have suggested these subjects be studied in the 2nd and 3rd years of BUP and FP (16 and 17 years age).

2.2 General content of the programs

A. Syllabus

The general focus of the course is on techniques of problem solving and the construction of algorithms and programs, emphasing the various steps involved (specification, algorithm, program). This contradicts the classic method which taught a programming language to initiates of data processing as if that were data processing. This system was generally responsible for the student's inability to separate the problem to be solved from the tool to be used to solve it the programming language.

A modern and rigorously scientific teaching method may conflict with the older systems used in secondary education, but we believe that this conflict is inevitable and may result come to prove constructive.

B. Programming Language for Exerceses and Projects

One of the most controversial proposals of the plan es the choice of BASIC as the programming language. This appears to contradict the intentions stated above, especially if we consider that in choosing BASIC we exclude structured PASCAL language, more appropriate for a methodology of problem solving as proposed in the training program. Several factors have swayed us in our choice:

- no low-cost micro computer based equipment has PASCAL in ROM, whereas all have BASIC

- teaching material (texts, programs, exercises, etc) does exist with BASIC as a media, while there is almost none for PASCAL.

In any case, our choice is due to circumstance and is not absolute. It is not a question of institutionalising BASIC as the ideal language, but rather to solve a pressing problem with the tools we have at hand, especially with our financial limitations. The chapters dedicated to the teaching of BASIC have been written so that they may be easily substituted by equivalent syllabi designed to teach any other programming language.

C. Computers and Society

This subject is included for three reasons:

- to destroy the mystique surrounding data processing and computers

- to make the students reflect on the risks involved in an improper use of data processing by the powers that be (economic, social, political)

- to analyse the aspects of progress and social evolution inherent in a computerised society.

This subject matter is treated in debates, discussions, panels, and written papers in order to encourage the student's self-expression.

D. Projects

It is of the utmost importance to carry out a project of a practical nature (programming) to complement the teaching of theory. The realisation of a project according to the proposed methodology should assure the student's assimilation of the basic concepts of the program and his ability to put them to use in solving problems similar or even more complex than those studied.

2.3 Equipment

The equipment for the centers has been selected according to the following criteria:

a. a price/capacity and price/quality ratio

b. standardisation of the equipment

c. availability of educational software

d. possibility of software interchange

Each center will have a micro computer laboratory for 20 students arranged for use by a two-student team.

Each laboratory is to have two types of equipment:

a. Elementary equipment made up of the following:
   - one micro-processor with 16 kbytes RAM user-free, and BASIC in ROM
   - alphanumerical keyboard
   - black and white monitor
   - audio cassette

The elementary equipment, which is inexpensive, is adequate for the basic needs of the program (computer structure and alementary programming), but is insufficient for more advanced functions.

The realisation of certain projects of the program —among which are some of the most common applications— requires the enlargement of the system's memory (from 16 to 48 K) and the addition of E/S devices (printer, floppy-disc).

b. The complete basic equipment consists of the following elements:
- microcomputer with 48-kbytes, with BASIC in ROM
- Keyboard
- monitor
- printer
- 2 5-1/2 floppy disks
- operating system

3. SCHEME FOR COMPUTER STUDIES

3.1 Aims

Cultural: To inform the student as to what a computer is and its possibilities and limitations in order to demystify data processing

To familiarize the student with the computer and its applications in all aspects of private, social and professional life

To teach him how to use the computer

Educational: To stimulate the student's intellectual capacity for analysis, reasoning and problem solving, thus opening up for him new paths of interdisciplinary learning.

Training: To give a basic knowledge which will allow the student to continue to a higher level of computer studies or will help him in his specialized study.

3.2 First Year Course

3.2.1 Objectives

To achieve an understanding of the basic principles of a computer's architecture: functional organization, relation between functional blocks, input/output.

To gain a methodology for problem solving

To learn to formulate a specification, an algorithm and to construct a program to solve simple problems

To take an historic view of computers; to learn the principal applications of computers in today's society and their possibilities for the future

3.2.2 Syllabus

I. Introduction to the Computer

1. Computers Today ....2 hours (The concept of processes, processes of calculation, processes in offices, airlines, processes for washing machines, control processes)

2. History ....2 hours (Counting with fingers, first writing, the abacus, Arabic and Roman numerals, the machines of Pascal and Leibnizt, Napier's bones, Automatic machines (Babbage), the first computers)

3. Technological Evolution ....1 hour (The application of electronics to automatic adding machines, technological evolution: the vaccuum tube, the transistor, integrated circuit, generations of computers)

4. Vocabulary and basic terminology....2 hours (Hardware and software, processor, program, instruction).

OBSERVATIONS

The firts lecture should emphasize the concept of the computer as a processor of information: it receives information as input, processes it, and provides information as output. This concept should be reenforced with common examples of processors: the washing machine, office work, the calculator.

The introduction to history should begin with the most ancient and primitive systems of calculation and follow through to the present day. The way in which information was represented in each instance should be stressed, and the existence of certain rules which have been used on reflex, without thinking. This could be developed by a comparison of the abacus, Arabic and Roman numerals, Napier's bones, and the machines of Pascal, Leibnitz and Babbage.

This series ends with basic terms and vocabulary (hardware, software, processor, program, instruction). These concepts should be presented in their historical context as methoda of calculation.

II. Computer Architecture

1. Basic elements of the computer.......3 hours (Central memory, arithmetic unit, control unit, input and output devices, comparison of Babbage-Von Neumann, general functioning of the computer, comparison or likening to the work of an office worker, a deliveryman, a ccok, etc.)

2. Peripherals..........................2 hours (Problems of communication between man and machine, types of peripherals: input, output, secondary memory, punch cards and tapes, OCR characters, teletypes, consoles, printers, magnetic tapes and discs)

III.Problem Solving

PartI :Introduction to problem solving

1.- The world of the robot...............1 hour (Objects, basic actions)

2.- Basic instructions...................1 hour (Basic instructions and sequential composition, simple task solving)

3.- Aspects of design....................2 hours (Top-down design, abstraction, documentation)

4.- Alternative composition..............2 hours (Condition, nesting condition)

5.- Iterative composition................4 hours

OBSERVATIONS

This subject should be opened by an introduction to the basic concepts of action and processing with a simple example: a robot living in a simple environment where there are a type of objects he can manipulate. A problem is a task which the robot must perform. The solution of the problem involves the formulation of an algorithm in terms of the basic actions the robot must carry out.

This approach is attractive, first because there is always a simple visualisation of the problem, second because the application is not "numerical". This allows us to insist on the use of the computer as a processor of symbolic information and at the same time allows us to introduce simply and intuitively the vocabulary of structured programming.

Part II: A Method for Problem Specification and Top-down Construction of Algorithms (First part)

1.- Determination of steps...............1 hour

2.- From the problem to its specification...1 h (definition of the result, definition of data)

3.- From the specification to the algorithm.9 h (sequential definition, definition with conditions, definition with iteratives according to the termination condition)

4.- The one-dimensional array............2 hours (definition, treatment of all elements)

5.- The two-dimensional array............3 hours (definition treatment of all elements)

OBSERVATIONS

In this section, the universe of problems grows with the introduction of data types and different operations to be performed on them, and the appearance of a structured type of data with associated treatments.

IV. Introduction to Programming

1.- Introduction........................1 hour (programming languages, types of languages, an introduction to BASIC)

2.- Elements of BASIC....................5 hours (Types of data: Integer, real, strings, Literals and variables, conditions, arithmetical expressions)

3.- BASIC instructions (basic nucleus)..20 hours Assigment: LET; comments: REM; basic E/S: INPUT, PRINT, READ/DATA; termination: STOP; control statement:GO TO; conditional: IF; loop definition: FOR/NEXT; array definition: DIM.

OBSERVATIONS

An explanation of the different instructions of BASIC should be accompanied by simple examples which will ensure their assimilation by the student.

The problems to be solved should gain in complexity as new elements are brought forward, always calling for utilisation of the methods introduced in the previous lesson. When a theme has been covered, there should be several classes dedicated to the programming of "quasi-real" assumptions. To this end, it is vitally important that part III --Problem solving-- be well covered to allow the student to proceed systematically to the construction of programs.

Should the equipment available make it necessary, any other language other than BASIC may be taught, in which case it would be desireable to work towards a structured type of language such as PASCAL if this were possible.

V. The computer in daily life

Part I. Applications of the computer

1.- Applications of computers...........3 hours (Applications to management: bank accounts, reservations of tickets for transportation, payment of wages, warehouse inventory, registration in an educational center.
Applications in business: word processing, electronic mailing.
Industrial applications: process control, computer aid design and graphics applications, simulation, robotics.
Education and information retrieval: computer-assisted learning, electronic library, videotext, home computers.)

2.- Description of real applications by visiting a data processing center....4 hours (elemental explanation of the problem, complete visit of the installation showing the elements involved in problem solving, review in class of the visit).

3.- Organization of labor in a computer center...............................2 hours (reasons for the division of labor, categories and responsabilities of personnel, requisites for a career in data processing).

4.- Description of other applications using available equipment..................2 hours (word processing, mailing lists, computer-assisted learning, graphic applications, applications to the school's management).

OBSERVATIONS

The list of applications is meant as a guide and is by no means complete. It is wise to use those things related to the daily life of the students (for example rail or airline tickets, gas or electric bills, bank accounts cartoons or graphic effects of the television, etc.). It is also a good idea to touch on subjects which may awaken an interest in the effects of data processing on the future of society (robotics, process of images, automated offices, electronic mailing) and those which may open discussions (police control). The approach should be general and technical detail should be avoided as much as possible.

For the student's visit to a computer center it is suggested that an important installation be chosen --one which has large computers and a full department of classic personnel (coders, programmers, analysts, etc) in order to tie in with part 3 above.

The activities of subheading 4 above are proposed to give the student an opportunity to relate to the practical applications of data processing (word processing, CAI, mailing lists, graphics, etc). They depend, of course, on the means of the school's laboratory.

Part II. The Social Impact of Data Processing

I.- The society of the future ....2 hours (present applications which allow us to foresee the automated society of the future: access cards for bank accounts, shopping done from the home, industrial robots, disappearance of money, the importance of information).

2.- Problems of future society...........2 hours (unemployment due to automation; adaptation to new jobs generated by data processing; right to privacy; electronic delinquency).

3.- A written paper.................. 2 hours (a paper to be written on a subject suggested above)

OBSERVATIONS

The topics discussed in this part of the program will naturally elicit reflexion and discussion so they should be presented in way that will rouse the student's curiosity and provoke debate. The teacher should avoid an easy drift into the realm of science fiction and instead insist on real arguments of possible or probable developments.

The paper is proposed to make the student reflect. It would be a good idea for the teacher to organize a debate on the most common points appearing in the papers.

3.3 Second Year Course

3.3.1 Objectives

To gain a deeper knowledge of the computer's internal structure: representation of data and instructions, digital logic, machine language and assembler.

To improve the student's methodology in order to solve more complex problems.

To learn the programming techniques needed for manipulation of data structures.

To see the way a computer works, the tasks performed by an operating system and the usual software (editors, debugger, assembler, compiler, program library, environments).

To learn the basic defining principles of a programming language in their present levels, and their possible evolution.

To carry out a project thus putting the knowledge gained to work by tackling a real problem.

3.3.2 Syllabus

I. Computer Architecture

1.- Review of basic elements.............1 hour (Memory, ALU, CPU, input/output)

2.- Data coding and instructions........10 hours (Integers and real numbers, character coding (BCD, ASCII), machine language, types of instructions, description of a didactic machine language)

3.- Peripherals..........................3 hours (input and output, secondary memory, description of information media)

4.- Digital logic........................3 hours
(Basic functions, logic gates, flip-flop, tri-states, some complex circuits such as registers, adders, decoders)

OBSERVATIONS

This material is undertaken to widen the knowledge gained in the first course. The internal structure of each functional element of the computer is described in detail (CPU, M, I/o), and its job in the execution of a program's instructions.

At the end we take a look at logical circuits and their most important basic components. The idea is to give the student an elementary view of the design and organization of the computer's internal circuits. We do not want him to try to solve a problem of circuit design, but to give him a knowledge of the design of some complex circuits such as adders, half-adders, registers, counters, etc. Emphasis is on understanding circuit function and not on their design.

II Methodology and Structure of Information

Part I. Modular decomposition

1.- Procedures and functions.............3 hours
(procedure as an abstraction of a set of instructions, notion of a formal and actual parameter, local and global variables, environment of an object)

2.- Decomposition in subproblems.........3 hours
(solution analysis, modular decomposition, integration, reliability, maintenance)

3.- Program documentation................2 hours
(solution analysis, description of data and their domain, description of the result, modular decomposition, testing of each module and integration, comparative study of other solutions)

Part II. Structured types

1.- Arrays (definition, operations)......2 hours

2.- Records (definition, operations).....1 hour

3.- Tables.............................2 hours

4.- Sequences..........................2 hours

5.- Queue and stack....................2 hours

6.- Lists..............................2 hours

7.- Binary trees.......................2 hours

8.- Sequential and random access files...3 hours

Part III Order algorithms, search and fusion

1.- Sequential search...................2 hours

2.- Binary search.......................2 hours

3.- Insertion sort......................2 hours

4.- Bubble sort.........................3 hours

5.- External sort.......................6 hours

Part IV Databanks and data bases

1.- Definition and operations...........2 hours

2.- Security and privacy................1 hour

3.- Applications........................2 hours

III. Programming

1.- Subroutines and functions..........10 hours
Subroutines: GOSUB, RETURN
BASIC functions: types
Mathematic functions: ABS, INT, SIN...
String manipulation: VAL, ASC, CHRS..

2.- Files (1/O instructions)...........10 hours
Sequential files
Random acces files

3.- Implementation of structured types in BASIC
....................................10 hours
Cases

4.- Other instructions..................1 hour

OBSERVATIONS

Presentation of this theme should be eminently practical, returning to the methodology gained in the previous lessons. Problems proposed will be more real than in the first course.

IV. Function and Use of the Computer

1.- Software of the system: basic components...
....................................1 hour

2.- Operating systems...................2 hours
(basic structure and functions, modes of operation, user-operating system communication, system routines)

3.- Computer helps in the operating system......
....................................2 hours
(editors, compilers, assemblers, debuggers)

V. Programming Languages

Part I: Classes of programming languages

1.- Machine language....................1 hour

2.- Assembler and macroassembler language....... ....1 hour

3.- High Level languages (H.L.L.)........2 hours

4.- Translators and interpreters.........2 hours

Part II: Structure of high-level programming languages

1.- Basic structure of high-level language...... ....1 hour

2.- Types of objects and their statement.1 hour

3.- Types of instructions................2 hours

4.- Subprograms..........................1 hour

5.- Formal expresion of programming languages... ....2 hours

OBSERVATIONS

As in the preceding lesson, the idea is to give a general view of the characteristics of high-level languages. There is no point in going into detail on a given language, though it would be wise to explain the peculiarities of the most common languages (Fortran, Basic, Cobol, Pascal), using simple examples to clarify the format and the different structures studied.

3.4 Projects

3.4.1 Objectives

To have the student put to use what he has learned and so show the skills he has acquired:

in method: he will come to appreciate the importance of solving a complex problem by following a systematic procedure

in specific techniques: by analyzing the facets of a problem in depth, he will arrive at a choice of the most reasonable way to solve it.

To allow the student to get to know the hardware and software available in the school.

3.4.2 Recommendations

When considering a project, the following should be considered:

The type of project: it should be a problem of some substance involving specification from the text and requiring a real breakdown into subproblema which would not be simply an academic axercise.

The number of students: individual projects will be proposed; however, should students prefer to work together, they may do so in pairs in which case they will be given more complex problems.

The time: it is important that the student be given independence to work out the solution of his problem, though it is a good idea to fix some intermediary deadlines to provide him with help in the organization of the work.

3.4.3 Phase of development and control

In order to verify the work done by the students, the teacher should supervise each of the different stages.

- statment and analysis of the problem
- modular decomposition and modular specification
- development of each part
- modular integration and program reliability

If at any time the student comes to the teacher with a difficulty, it is the teacher's job to help him by reminding him of solutions previously studied and discussing which of them would best suit the problem in hand.

In order to stimulate the student to make an in-depth analysis, he will be required to present

- Specification of the problem
- decomposition and his reasons for choosing that particular solution
- the set of data used (input and output)
- The program, written legibly, with comments on the most delicate parts of the operation
- possible extensions or improvements; hardware or software requirements.

3.4.4 Suggested projects

A project may be applied to aby of several areas: business, simulation, control, scientific calculation, games, word-processing, CAI, organization of and search for information, etc.; always bearing in mind the student's level of knowledge, hard- and software required for the project and available resources.

When choosing a project, it is essential that the social context be taken into consideration. Because they form part of our specific environment, management, treatment and organization of information, scientific calculation, and control should be considered for the student's projects.

Projects involving control are particularly relevant since the applications to industry are numerous: control of assembly lines, machine tools, cutting machines, etc. Projects of this type will allow the student to develop real uses requiring an external control device such as train switches, etc.

The following is a list of suggested projects, classified according to type.

3.4.5 Suggested projects list

Management and word processing

- system of geographic information
- catalogue of books for a library

inventory for a shop

- editor for texts
- wages, bills, etc. (elementary)

Games

- tic-tac-toe
- chess

Scientific Calculation

- generator of two-dimensional statistical tables
- surface calculation by the Montecarlo method
- Calculation of matrices

Control

- keyboard based on commonly used coins
- simulation of a washing machine
- simple control of a robot
- music box
- simulation of a microwave oven
- simulation of traffic lights
- control system for an electric train
- monitor and control of temperatures in a miniature house

4. THE TRAINING CENTER

Both for the initial model plan and the later possible extension of Computer Science to all BUP schools, there is an urgent need for a training program and teacher counseling service. We can distinguish two separate stagest The first, the initial experiment and the second when the course is finally instituted as part of the Secondary Education Program.

4.1 Center for the Model Plan

In the first stage, due to the shortage of competent personnel for the Teacher Training Courses and the importance of maintaining a homogeneity in the material taugt, it is essential that there be only one Training Center. The organization of such a center would involve the following:

a. Resources

- a classroom prepared for lectures to groups of a maximum of 20 persons
- a laboratory of micro computers for the practice of programming work; for 20 teachers, a minimum of 10 units with floppy diskettes.
- a room for a library and reference section with the texts collected for the implementation of the model plan as well as other books and specialised magazines
- an office for the acting coordinator in charge of supervision and control of the model plan

b. Organization of the Center

Together with the student's curriculum, a curriculum has been prepared for teacher training. It consists of 120 hours of lectures covering the same subject matter prepared for the students. Due to the time shortage and the difficulty involved in bringing together teachers working in geographically distant centres, the course is to be intensive. However, there are minimum requirements which must be respected in order to allow assimilation of the subject matter: the lectures must last no more than 4 hours each day and the minimum length of the training period must be 3 months.

c. Personnel, Supervision and Control

The following openings must be filled for the Training Center by persons with extensive experience in Computer Sciences:

- one person to coordinate, supervise and control the Teacher's Training Course
- one or more teachers to cover the professorship pf the several independent modules which will make up the Training Course
- one person in charge of information, counselling, and the library, to start work in October of 1983. His job will be

to supervise and control the model plan and counsel the BUP and FP teachers once classes have started in the schools.

4.2 Future Training Centers

With the growth of the experiment and the inclusion of Computer Science in the normal BUP and FP courses new requirements are foreseen for the Training Centers:

- They should be institutionalised and publicly financed and fall under regular BUP and FP jurisdiction.

- The Teacher Training Courses will be official and institutional. A Diploma for Proficiency in Computer Science which would certify the teacher's training should be considered.

- The teachers of Computer Science in the future will be required to have a diploma in data processing, or to have obtained the proficiency diploma.

a. Human resources and materials

At least equivalent to those provided for the Centre for the model plan.

b. Organization of the centre

Although in the model training program, the teachers complete their training in three months, this is expedience, and in the institutionalised system, the length of the course will be considerably longer.

c. Information centre for the BUP and FP schools

A centre of this type can offer the following services:

- Training Course for the Proficiency Diploma
- Permanently on-going training courses
- Counseling services
- Preparation of text books
- Preparation of audiovisual material
- Informational pamphlets treating such subjects as:
  - Syllabi
  - Organisational norms for computer labs
  - Norms for the selection of material and equipment
  - Standards for the exchange of software

- Standards for the exchange of software

  - Documentation standards
  - Visits to computer centres
- A magazine publishing the different experiences of the BUP and FP centres, course projects, reviews of books, critiques of new soft- andhardware, etc.
- Possible plan of repair and maintenance of equipment
- Software exchange club

5. PRESENT STATUS

Certain conditions must be satisfied before the model plan may be implemented:

a. selection and acquisition of equipment for the Teacher Training Course

b. designation of the BUP and FP schools to participate in the project

c. teacher training

d. selection and acquisition of the equipment to be installed in the participating schools

e. implementation of the experiment in 10 secondary schools

Forty floppy-disk based micro computers have been acquired, sothat according to our proposed schedule phase (a) and part of phase (d) have been covered.

The designation of schools took place in February, and the training of teachers in June, July and September of 1983, so that the experiment may begin in October of 1983.

REFERENCES:

(1) ACM-SIGCSE, Symposium on Computer Science Education (ACM, 1982)

(2) Biondé, J. and Clavel, G., Introduction à la programmation (Masson, París, 1981)

(3) Bradbeer, R. De Bono, P. and Laurie, P., The Computer book. An Introduction to Computers and Computing (BBC, London, 1982)

(4) Coburn, P. and alters, Practical guide to Computers in Education (Addison-Wesley, Reading (Mass), 1976)

(5) Conway, Gries and Zimmerman, A primer on Pascal (Winthrop Publishers, Cambridge (Mass), 1976)

(6) Emery, G., Elements of Computer Science (Pitman, London, 1979)

(7) Fairley, T.H. Neil, C.M. and Folckhart, M.S., Computers in Action (Oliver & Boyd, London, 1980)

(8) French, C.S., Computer Science. An Instruction Manual (D.P. Publications, 1982)

(9) Goldschlager, L. and Lister, A., Computer Science. A modern introduction (Prentice Hall International, C.A.R. Hoare series editor, 1982)

(10) Grogono, P. and Sharon, H.N, Problem solving and Computer Programming (Addison-Wesley, Reading (Mass), 1982)

(11) Hunt, R. and Shelley, J., Computers and Common Sense (Prentice Hall, Englewood Cliffs (N.J), 1977)

(12) ICL, Computer Studies, Books 1,2,3 (ICL-CES, 1979)

(13) L'Informatique au Lycée (Ministère de L'Education Française, Paris, 1980)

(14) Meyer, B. and Baudoin, C., Méthodes de programmation (Eyrolles, Paris, 1978)

(15) Osborne, A., The Beginners Book (Osborne-Mc Graw Hill, New York,1977)

(16) Pattis, R.E., Karel the Robot (John Wiley & Sons, New York, 1981)

(17) Smith, J.C.H., Microcomputers in Education (Ellis Horwood, 1982)

(18) Wirth, N. Algoritms Data Structures= Programs (Prentice-Hall, Englewood Cliffs (N.J.), 1976)

MICROCOMPUTERS: Developments in Industry, Business and Education
D.R. Wilson and C.J. van Spronsen (eds.) /© EUROMICRO, 1983
Elsevier Science Publishers B.V. (North-Holland)

DEVELOPMENT OF MICRO-COMPUTER BASED LEARNING IN THE MEDICAL ENVIRONMENT

Computer-controlled Interactive Video

Dr. D. G. Jameson, Ph.D., M.A., M.Sc.

Head of Computer Services and Senior Lecturer
Department of Medical Physics and Institute of Nuclear Medicine,
The Middlesex Hospital Medical School, London, England

This paper traces the development of work with computer assisted learning techniques at the Middlesex Hospital to the present date when experiments are being carried out with computer controlled video methods particularly in the paramedical fields. Computer techniques have been applied in teaching in the lecture theatre, small groups and in programmed learning. The present day availability of video tape and video disc coupled with the availability of control interfaces for desk-top microcomputers has created a new dimension for this type of teaching aid. The CAVI 400 interface has been used in this project and a brief description is given of the facilities provided together with the level of documentation. This interface allows either VHS or Umatic equipment to be used. Video tape facilities have been used to produce a training lesson on the use of a defibrillator. The reasons for carrying out this exercise in the tape medium rather than video disc are discussed. The reaction of groups in the paramedical training field to computer based training is also reported and some ideas for the possible ways in which it might be of value are discussed.

Introduction

Work was started at the Middlesex Hospital Medical School some four to five years ago to investigate if micro-computers could be used successfully for teaching and training purposes(Jameson). At that time the choice was between a terminal connected to a mainframe computer or experimenting with micro-computers. The applications envisaged required graphical output and the only micro-computer providing graphics and colour was the Apple II. The recent availability of interfaces allowing the control of video cassette recorders by desktop micro-computers adds another dimension to computer based training methods. Our inquiries suggest that besides applications in undergraduate studies(Bender, Wood) there is a great potential in paramedical training. Because the Middlesex Hospital Medical School has close links with paramedical training schools in such fields as radiology, physiotherapy and pathology the potential exists to produce material for these areas, with the tutors playing an important part in organising the training material.

Early Projects

The objective of the first project was to convert a program written for a mainframe computer to a micro-computer. This program was the simulation of heart-lung function based on a model developed by St. Bartholomew's Hospital London and MacMaster University, Canada (Dickinson, Dickinson et al). The original version was written in Fortran IV and output was on a teletype. To implement this program with graphic output on the Apple required rewriting in the Basic language. This micro-computer version runs interactively with similar response times to the original program.

The success of this project encouraged us to investigate further possibilities of using the micro-computer in the teaching environment, and two more projects were implemented. One involved the use of the micro-computer in the lecture theatre, and the other as a programmed learning tool. The former project implemented a suite of computer programs, developed over a number of years, for teaching basic statistics to medical students; and the second used programmed learning methods to teach radiographers two mathematical principles - Similar Triangles and Inverse Square Law, because they are relevant to calculating beam sizes and radiation dose-rates.

There is no point in using a computer as a demonstration device in the lecture theatre unless it has a unique advantage of it's own. There was no point producing still computer frames which could just as easily be produced on 35 mm slides. The one feature that the micro-computer could provide is graphical presentation which is both dynamic and can be altered quickly and easily. Further the control of the program has to be simple and fool-proof. In this application various statistical graphs are shown, such as the Gaussian curve and this is drawn slowly on the screen and its various features shown dynamically, such as the proportion contained within a standard deviation. Each program itself only takes a few minutes to run, but incorporated into a lecture the overall time was much longer. There is considerable effort involved in providing several TV monitors in a lecture theatre so that everyone can read the screen, and no one will continue to do this year after year unless it is deemed to be worth-while. These programs have now been in their present form for 3-4 years and are considered established in that part of the curriculum.

The programmmed learning project was not so successful and possibly some responsibility must lie with the choice of subject - a mathematical task which is not generally considered very interesting. There were several problems with this project, the programming effort was large and there was difficulty in obtaining some of the graphic effects. The programming was in the Basic language and this has not proved the most suitable language for this type of application.

The Basic language necessitates a large amount of time being spent arranging tabulation values to position text on the screen and when one tries to move moderately complex diagrams around the screen smoothly and at a reasonable speed there are many problems. An attempt was made to incorporate self-corrections routines in the software so that if any mistakes were made by the student the system could recover. Since the student had to carry out calculations a special routine was written to handle the arithmetic operations such that an error in typing did not cause the program to break down. The effort to produce these programs was significant but they were not used enough to be worth-while. Any further effort in that field would require a major change in approach.

However certain information was gained from these projects. Three possible areas of application have been identified and experience gained on the use of programs. The applications areas are listed below:

1) Lecture theatre demonstraton
2) Simulation programs with interaction
3) Programmed learning.

Lecture theatre applications will be programs with little flexibility, applied in areas where dynamic graphics are powerful and the material presented in a manner suitable for large groups of people. There would be little or no interaction. The ability to display on the screen non standard character sizes would greatly facilitate the ease of viewing monitors in the lecture theatre.

The interactive simulation program is best directed at small groups of student, as a follow up to a lecture or tutorial on a specific subject. The Macman program has not found a place in the student curriculum, because of individual lecturers preferences, but nevertheless it has stimulated a large amount of interest as a powerful demonstration of what can be achieved on a desk-top micro-computer. It acts as a strong stimulus to argument and discusson amongst students and our experience has been borne out by other centres such as University College, Faculty of Medicine, London University and Newcastle University (DHSS Meeting on Computer Based Training).

The response times are critically important to the successful running of these programs and pilot studies have indicated that some of the larger simulation programs such as MacPuff would not be successful on an 8-bit microcomputer, because of the memory requirement for supporting graphics and the computation speed is not fast enough to give suitable response times. Perhaps this is where 16-bit micro-computers which have larger memory and more sophisticated instruction sets would give faster computation times and consequently shorter response times.

The programmed learning area requires an inordinate amount of programming effort if languages such as BASIC are used and there is a strong case for investigating whether the use of Pilot(Jameson) or Authoring Systems(Merrill and Bunderson) would make it easier to implement lessons. When small groups of students were exposed to this type of program, we have found the weakest student left all decision-making to other members of the group, so it is best used on a single person basis concentrating on remedial and revision applications.

Present Development

In the past year the situation has changed dramatically in the programmed learning fields, sufficiently to take a fresh look at the problem. Recently interfaces which allows the Apple II to control a video cassette recorder have become available thus allowing selected sequences of video tape to be played back under program control. Whilst there are many drawbacks to this method compared with video-disc it is at least a cheap medium which is well worth-while experimenting with before investing in the much more expensive video-disc technology.

The present project was undertaken as a pilot scheme to investigate the feasibility of using computer controlled video for teaching and training purposes. There is little doubt in many peoples minds that this is a good idea but relatively very few people have had any practical experience. The Middlesex Hospital Medical School was granted a sum of money to purchase a video-cassette recorder interface, and a video cassette recorder(VCR). The price of video interfaces vary considerably and we bought a CAVI 400 interface(BCD Associates Inc). This interface consisted of the physical interface card and cables, a floppy disks holding system software, and documentation.

The system was designed to operate with either a Sony VCR type 2631 or a Panasonic VCR type NV8200. The Sony machine operated with Umatic 3/4inch tape capable of high quality reproduction. If this technique is to be valuable the individual items must be portable. However the Sony machine is expensive and heavy requiring two people to carry it, and also the Fast Forward and Rewind speeds are such that the searching time on the tape is appreciably longer than with VHS machine. The Panasonic is a VHS 1/2inch tape machine and is more suitable in that it is lighter, cheaper and gives faster access, and although the reproduction quality is not as high as the Sony it is still fully acceptable for the purpose.

The choice of VCR is restricted to these two machines for the CAVI 400 system and the cables that come with the interface have end connections to suit those machines. Figure 1. shows the cable connections between computer,monitor and VCR.

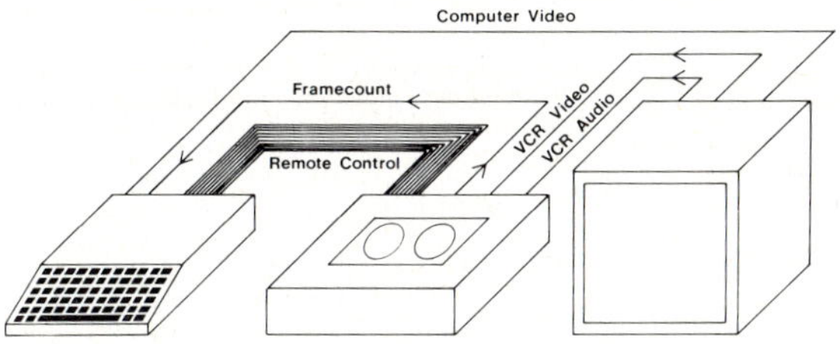

Fig. 1. Cable connections for computer, monitor and VCR

Whichever apparatus is used there are two basic requirements:-

1) Hard wired remote control.
2) Two audio channels.

The hard wired remote socket is connected by a cable to the computer interface and the various functions on the VCR are now controlled remotely by relays activated under computer control; ie. the buttons on the front panel of the VCR are now replaced by the computer and the program determines which relay is to be activated at any time.

The two audio channels are required, if a sound commentary is needed on the video tape. One audio channel will contain that commentary, whilst the second channel is known as the control channel. Each frame of the video is pulsed and numbered so that each frame can be identified in the absolute addressing mode and the computer program instructs the VCR to play from one absolute address frame number to another. When a specific frame sequence is to be played the computer software will select Fast Forward or Rewind to approach the initial frame number of the sequence. It will normally aim for a frame approximately 75 frames prior to the one required and then switch over to the normal playback mode. When the correct frame number is reached the computer switches from computer video to the normal video playback mode. The pre-run of 75 frames is chosen to allow the tape transport mechanism to switch from fast to normal mode and the system to stabilise. The system will now play back the video sequence, the computer monitoring the frames until the end frame of the sequence is reached when the computer will then switch back to computer video and the command is returned to the computer program.

From the above description it follows that facilities must be provided to place pulses on each frame of the video tape, and to have a numbering system for each frame. This is amongst a range of facilities provided in the software supplied on the CAVI 400 floppy disks. The disk software is divided into two main sections:-

1) Editing software
2) Authoring software and lessons

Editing System

The Editing system allows a number of operations to be carried out, and can be divided into two areas:

1) Emulation of controls of VCR
2) System manipulation.

The controls of VCR can all be emulated by pressing the appropiate key on the computer keyboard and these are listed below, in Figure 2.

Space Bar	– Stop	T	– Transport
P	– Playback	W	– Wait (Pause)
R	– Rewind	S	– Slow/Fast
F	– Fast Forward	X2	– Double Speed
V	– VCR Video	C	– Computer Video

Figure 2. VCR controls which can be emulated by computer

The second set of options are concerned with configuring and organising the system, and these functions are listed in Figure 3.

Goto	– goto a scene
In	– mark the beginning of a scene
Out	– mark the end of a scene
Display File	– manages the log-file
N	– initializes the video tape
Address/System status	– configures the system and sets status

Figure 3. Functions provided by the CAVI 400 system

Initialising simply clears the log-file and rewinds the tape to the beginning, setting the tape frame counter to zero. The log-file is a computer text file logging all tape sequences either by the beginning and end frame number or times. Since in playback there is a fixed rate of playing back frames per second, the frame numbers can be related to time. The CAVI 400 system can be obtained in a version modified to handle PAL rather than NTSC colour but the frame count is based on 30 frames/sec rather than 25 frames/sec which leads to some confusion.

The Display File command contains the facility to handle the log-file with sub-commands for loading and storing log-files on disk and also a sub-system for editing the frame sequence values. All the frame sequence values can be adjusted by the same amount, either to an earlier or later time. Alternatively individual frame numbers can be adjusted to control the exact beginning and end of a sequence. This is very important when tailoring the video sequences to a lesson. Also there is a facility to print-out the log-file and label each sequence.

The Address and System status command allows one to configure the system, allocating which channel is for audio commentary and which contains the frame counts. Also the subsystem allows the log-file to be named and given an identification code which is placed on the sound track used for control purposes. Another important facility is the dubbing of the video tape with the pulses to identify each frame. This is done by using a cable connection between the cassette output socket of the computer and the microphone input on the VCR and using the dubbing facility the sound pulses are placed on the appropriate sound track under program control.

The Authoring system exists to assist people who are not experienced in programming and this is really a program itself which guides the person building up a lesson, to answer questions deciding whether a particular computer frame should be informative, or interrogative and organising a branch or jump in the lesson sequence. This system also makes provision to play-back the lessons which have been developed in this way.

However there is an alternative approach which is made possible because the level of documentation, is good enough to understand how the system has been implemented. The memory locations of various machine code routines are provided and details of the BASIC language program controlling the system. This information was brought together in a program written in the BASIC language which initialised the system, contained calls to various control routines and loaded the log-file into memory. The program was then extended to contain the lesson with its text frames and instructions to control video sequences.

Video-disc v. video-tape

Why have we concentrated our effort, and experience to date on video-tape when all modern technology is direced at the video disc? (Bryce and Stewart). There are two principle reasons, firstly the video-disc technology is very expensive and for people who are investigating the feasibility or potential of the method it is better to experiment initially with the cheaper medium. Secondly the material that might eventually find its way onto a disc must be produced on tape originally. Technically the micro-computer controlled video disc will be superior to video cassette providing faster access time, and also the pause picture will be of superior quality and there will be no stabilisation problems when the head has homed in to a particular track. One must be very careful to determine whether one is using a CLV (constant linear velocity) or CAV (constant angular velocity) system. The latter has only one frame per track - and if the playback head is centered on that track a still picture of high quality can be obtained. Another advantage of the disc is that playback at variable speeds can be achieved far more easily and in the forward and reverse direction.

Our policy is to be aware of the potential of video-disc and at the same time build up material in the video-tape medium. If in the future we have built up sufficient good material and the video-disc technology becomes more readily accessible then the material is ready. Because of the expense and investment in disc production, the material which is to go on to a disc must be very carefully prepared so that more than one lesson can be developed from the material on the disc by using different track sequences.

Experience of Vide-tape Production for Computer Based Training

This medium has a great potential in the training of medical and paramedical personnel especially in its use for highlighting specific topics rather than its use to present a whole subjects (WICAT Report). In our pilot study we attempted to identify a topic which would have a reasonably high applicability and we decided to produce a short tape on 'The Use of a Defibrillator'. This equipment which is used in an attempt to re-start the heart beat of a patient who has suffered a cardiac arrest could be used by doctors, nurses or ambulance men. The intention was to divide the lesson into two sections, one which is instructional and the second which is interrogative. The instruction section was divided to teach these aspects of the defibrillator:-

1) The equipment controls
2) The safety aspects of its use
3) Clinical indications for its use.

The student is shown each section, interspersed with text frames which list the points that should have been noted and the student can decide to repeat that section if he wishes. In the interrogative phase the student is shown sequences of a defibrillation where there is a deliberate mistake in the procedure and has to spot the error. If incorrect then the student is returned to the instruction phase to go over that particular point. This is a simple lesson and test and its objective is to demonstrate the use of computer controlled video techniques rather than to explore and analyse different methods of computer based training. The effort to produce this film was not that great. Obviously the script preparation had to be done with great care, and whatever type of production is beng done, whether it is tape-slide presentation or CBT there must be very careful preparation and scripting before the video filming and programming is commenced. In our case the filming of video was carried out in one afternoon but a high degree of flexibility was required, because one cannot go to an Intensive Therapy Unit (ITU) by appointment - the filming had to be done at a time when the ITU was quiet and under no pressure. The staff of the ITU cooperated to make the film and one of the staff acted out the part of a patient. This avoided problems of copyright which would arise if a patient was involved. The editing of video film is necessarily a slow business and it is possible that the editing procedure can be made easier using the facilities of the CAVI 400 system. The tape is roughly edited together to form a continuous sequence which can be handled by the CAVI software to determine the exact frame sequence that will be used in the lesson. If then the selected sequences are produced from the original film without having to match sequences together, a higher quality of reproduction can be achieved. A lesson master tape is made up of a series of sequences with intervening blank tape. These blank sections are longer than the pre-roll numbered frames used in the searching procedure, thus time is not spent hunting for the correct frame. The computing phase of the production is not difficult and once a set of suitable subroutines have been written, the program writing is rapid.

There is room for considerable devlopment in the computer technology in this field particularly in the man-machine interface (Alvey). There can be improvements to the interface so that switching between computer video and VCR video are smoother and also the ability to mix computer video with VCR video would be very powerful tool. Interaction between the computer and student could also be developed from simplified keyboard input to touch screen techniques. Further there is ample scope to make use of existing software techniques as well as considering future developments. The computing language PILOT should be considered by people working in this field since it now includes commands for controlling video-tape and video-disc. Its implementation on Apple II has several advantages which make it easier for the person building up a lesson. It provides the ability to use upper and lower case characters, to use different fonts and different size characters and also several graphical tools are available within the package. The graphic capability of microcomputers presents a further extension of the technique because graphic material can come from the computer as well as from the video. The computer graphics can be in the form of stored graphic frames on floppy disk or real-time graphics. This whole process can be made more 'user friendly' by the use of Authoring systems whose object is to allow the computer to be accessible to more people who are not, and do not intend to be computer specialists. The general increase in computing power in the move from 8-bit to genuine 16-bit micro-computer will facilitate the development of more sophisticated systems as we have already seen with machines like the WICAT, and the recent release of the Apple LISA have indicated the power of the new software concepts which can be implemented on desk-top microcomputers. It may well prove that the sophistication that people require will mean that 16-bit microcomputer will have a significant part to play in CBT, but where economy is of paramount importance the system produced by 8-bit microcomputers will still be powerful and much sought after.

Reaction of people to Computer Based Training

The pilot project that we have conducted has been shown to groups from the various paramedical training schools associated with our Hospital

1. Radiology, Radiotherapy, and Nuclear Medicine
2. Physiotherapy
3. Intensive Therapy Unit
4. Pathology - Haematology and Chemical

In all cases an enthausiastic response was forthcoming and people could readily see the applicability of computer controlled video techniques to their areas of interest. Most people agree that computer-controlled video was a technique which could best handle specifically identified topics, rather than take on a large teaching program. It would be ideal for training in safety procedures and also a powerful tool in training how to handle personnel relationships. It was seen more as an extension of programmed learning methods - where it would be used by a person alone or in very small groups. It would be valuable as a means of making training material available to people who for reasons of time or geography would find it difficult to attend normal courses or seminars.

In summary computer control video

programs are an extension of existing techniques made possible by recent technological advances which will have its part to play in training and teaching fields. Successful implementation will as always depend on identifying the topics to which it is most suited. Because the technology is advancing very rapidly we can expect to see many developments in this technique of interacting with the machine.

Acknowledgments

I wish to acknowledge the assistance of two colleagues, Dr T Clutton-brock who planned the video sequences with the help of the staff of the Intensive Therapy Unit, and Mr L Roberts the video producer who produced the video tape. Also I would like to record my thanks to Dr Denis Hill, Regional Scientific Advisor of the North East Thames Regional Health Authority who provided the funds to buy equipment and my fellow members of the Regional Advisory Committee for Audio Visual Aids who sponsored the project.

REFERENCES

1. Alvey Report (1982). A program for Advanced Information Technology. HMSO, London, October, 1982.

2. BCD Associates Inc. 5809 S.W.5th Street, Oaklahoma City, OK, 73128, USA.

3. Bender, D.A. (1972). An Interactive Computer Program for Teaching the Use of Computers to Medical Students. Biochem J, Vol. 126, 25.

4. Bryce, C.F.A. and Stewart, A (1983). Videodisks in Medical Education. Medical Teacher, Vol. 5, No. 1.

5. Dickinson, C.J., Goldsmith, C.H. and Sackett, D.L. (1973). Macman - A Digital Computer Model for Teaching some Basic Principles of Haemodynamics. J. Clin. Comp. Vol. 2, 42-50.

6. Dickinson, C.J., Davies, M.A., Short, A.H., Lamb, J.F., Simmons, N.L., Weimer, W., Anders, W.H.., Lal, S., and Ingram, D. (1979). Novel Techniques in Teaching Physiology. The Physiology Teacher, Vol. 22, p. 25.

7. Jameson, D.G. (1983). Computer Graphics in Medical Education - Symposium on Computer Based Training in DHSS, St. Bartholomew's Hospital, 1983.

8. Merrill, P.F. and Bunderson, V.C. (1981). Preliminary Guidelines for Applying Graphics in Instruction. Journal of Instructional Development, Vol. IV, 2-8.

9. WICAT Report (1981) - Smith, Kline and French Pharmaceuticals - 'Diagnostic Challenges'. Continuing Medical Education Library.

10. Wood, A.W. (1978) - Computers in Undergraduate Physiology Teaching. Report to Board of Studies in Physiology, London University.

MICROCOMPUTERS: Developments in Industry, Business and Education
D.R. Wilson and C.J. van Spronsen (eds.) /© EUROMICRO, 1983
Elsevier Science Publishers B.V. (North-Holland)

ADAPTING MICRO-COMPUTERS TO MEDIUM-SCALE EDUCATIONAL USES

Ben Zion Barta
Ministry of Education and Culture, Jerusalem, Israel
Zehava Behar Mordehai Shorek
The Institute for Teaching Aids, Tel-Aviv, Israel
Chaim Schlesinger
The SML Project, Kiryat Shmonah Municipality, Israel

During the five years, 1977-1983, micro-computers were established in some 50% of our high schools and 10% of the elementary schools, in steadily increasing numbers. They are used for the teaching of Computer Sciences and Computer Literacy, as well as for a variety of Computer Aided Learning applications. Stand-alone micros were networked for educational uses, and some of the solutions of networking problems were developed locally by schools and local distributors.
The operations of tutorial and drill and practice CAL systems, on micros required solution of some special problems concerning manipulation of common files, package organization and courseware transfer. Several approaches to these problems are discussed.
Keywords: Micro-computers in Education; Computer Literacy; Teaching of Computer Sciences; Computer Aided Learning (CAL); Micro-computer Networks.

1. INTRODUCTION

From the early 70s, and even before, the teaching of informatics and educational uses of computers, was considered important, attractive and meaningful. With the widely expanded use of computers in industry, science, commerce and administration during the last decade, this trend became even stronger, to the point where computers are today an integral part of school activities in a developed educational system.

Almost all computer-related educational activities require access to computing resources. The great cost of early models was one of the obstacles to fast penetration into all schools (other obstacles being: lack of trained teachers and lack of suitable curricula and courseware).

As micro-computers became available, however, they were recognized as a possible solution of the computing resource problem for small and medium sized educational institutions - namely, schools requiring not more than 15-20 working stations (stand-alone micros or terminals) which would not need to perform the large data-processing tasks that usually require large memories, high speed processing, and large, fast secondary storage.

Micro-computers seemed attractive to the educational community for several reasons:

i) Low-price, compared to minis or terminals connected to main frames.

ii) Modularity, allowing a comparatively inexpensive start-up with elementary equipment and future expansion as applications develop and funds become available.

iii) Portability, for easy transfer to different rooms, buildings, or even use at home.

iv) Reliability, since there can be no main system crash to stop all possible activities.

v) Graphic and colour capabilities at relatively low price.

These advantages, but mainly (i) and (ii), caused a fast penetration of micro-computers into our educational system, despite some very clear disadvantages:

i) Capabilities are rather limited. This is especially true for the low-priced micros of the late 70s.

ii) Lack of cheap networking facilities for common usage of peripherals.

iii) Standards of manufacturing are, in many cases, low as compared to professional computer equipment.

iv) Distribution and maintenance service is not, in many cases, fast and reliable.

This paper intends to describe how the use of micro-computers developed in our country; what the main difficulties were in relation to the application of micros to educational uses; how several problems inherent in micros were solved; and how their uses are expected to develop.

2. MICRO-COMPUTER EQUIPMENT IN SCHOOLS

2.1 Penetration Into the School System

Computers first appeared in our schools in the late 60s, [1] and now, after some 15 years, are well established, but far from being universal.

The first micro-computers in our schools were purchased in 1978 - a set of five Commodore PETs with cassette recorders as back storage and no printer. They were installed at a school teaching "introduction to computing" at a rather remote location, whose pupils travelled about 1½ hours each way to a computer center for programming practice. The purchase was made with many doubts regarding its capabilities and the reliability of its equipment. However, despite the inconvenience of the system and the difficulties related to its operation, the system was considered a success, and proved useful, allowing acceptable programming practice. In any case, it was better and more convenient than the long distance travel needed previously.

Toward the end of 1979 the high school system had about 160 terminals, mostly mini-computers with 8 to 20 terminals each, installed at 17 sites and only 15 micros installed at three sites. Most of these installations were in the major towns. Pupils from the smaller townships still had to travel to reach a computer. Three years later, by the end of 1981, the number of high schools equipped with computer facilities had jumped to 110. Only 25 of these had minis, with some 300 terminals. The remaining 85 owned about 350 micros with only 4-5 pieces for each. Mechanically switched printers were available in most places but diskettes were scarce and only a few palces had networks.

During the 1982/83 school year the acquisition of micros increased even more dramatically. About 200 high schools (out of a total 450 in the school system) now have micro installations and another 30 use mini-computer systems. Most of the micro installations now have 6-8 pieces or more; a few have 16-20 pieces. Many of these are networked to a common printer and a common diskette drive.

About 150 primary schools (out of 1500) are using computers for CAL activities, mainly for drill and practice; 50 of them use micro computer installations. Most of these schools have 16 or more terminals or micros in one computer room, to allow whole classes access to the computer. Some of the schools have a few micros in some of their classrooms, geared to individualized learning.

Maintenance of the equipment is provided by the suppliers, usually at an acceptable level, but sometimes lack of adequate maintenance causes severe problems.

School teachers must be trained to use the equipment, mainly primary school teachers who have no computer knowledge. A training period of several days is enough for them to start using the system, but quite intensive on-going training and guidance, in technical aspects and teaching methodology, are required by the teachers during their first year of using CAL.

2.2 Requirements for School Usage

There are at least three different types of micro-computer usage in the schools:

i) Elementary programming for introductory courses of computer sciences and computer literacy.

ii) Advanced programming and data processing.

iii) Computer aided learning systems (CAL).

For elementary programming, the requirements are rather limited: simple operation (e.g. just one switch to turn on to have the computer "ready"); a good interpreter to help beginners with debugging; availability of printing; and some secondary storage. Elementary BASIC, 4-8 KB of RAM, may be enough for that purpose. Some graphic capability, perhaps colour, educational games, will make such a computer more attractive to pupils.

Such elementary micros are available at relatively low attractive prices. But schools should realize that elementary programming will not satisfy their needs. They must be prepared for CAL, to allow their pupils to advance to more sophisticated programming applications. If a school must start with lowest cost micros, it should select a modular type, which can grow to advanced applications, or prepare for the purchase of advanced micros within one or two years. In no case should a school expect to remain with only elementary equipment. The extra requirements from micros for advanced programming and for CAL are similar: RAM of at least 48-64 KB should be available; advanced BASIC including good file manipulation; availability of disks or diskettes; special input devices; interface to communication networks, perhaps to analogue devices. Several advanced languages (e.g. PASCAL) and ASSEMBLER must be available.

Networking of micros to a common printer (perhaps with spooling facilities) and to common back-storage are indispensable for school applications. When schools have a minimum of 6-8 micros, perhaps 16-20 or more, the lack of networking can render the printing and back-storage an almost impossible task. Also, effective use of a library of software and for management of common student files, indispensible for CAL, depend on networking. Back storage in the range of 0.5 - 1 MB, as provided by diskettes, may be sufficient for such a network, but obviously the 5-10 MB or more (with added on back-up facilities), as provided by hard disks are an advantage.

2.3 Networking of Micro-Computers

The need for networking was clear from the first stages of using micros in schools, but early models did not provide this facility. Networking was developed by cooperation between schools and the local distributor for one of the brands marketed in our country. Distributors of other brands waited for the manufacturers to develop networking. This approach slowed down the development of some of our educational applications, and perhaps of their marketing success.

A relatively cheap network of micros was built using the bus connecting the individual micro to its peripherals (e.g. the diskette drive), the processing power within the peripheral and special software. The development of the network required no special hardware, only a rather small software package. This approach allowed for local development at rather low cost. One of the 16 channels of the bus, namely the command channel, is used to control the performance of the network. One of the micros in the network is the "master" within the network and the others are "slaves." The master has the right of access to the peripheral for two-directional transfer of information (see Figure 1). A "slave" wanting access to the peripheral must be granted permission by the "master." If granted, the former slave becomes master in the network and the former master becomes one of the slaves. All micros within the network are identified by serial numbers; if several ask for access to a peripheral, the one with a number closest to the master will get access, without regard to the order of the demands or any other priority criteria.

The procedures for granting the peripheral, and releasing it, may be performed by the processor within the peripheral or by routines within the program executed by the micro. If the procedures are executed by the peripheral, then each individual program can freely use statements referring to the peripheral, and all accessing and releasing procedures are performed automatically. But in this case, the command channel must be dedicated to carry only network-control signals. If the procedures are performed within the program executed by the micro, the command-channel is used only while allocating/releasing the peripheral. In this case, the command channel can be used for signalling within the network (e.g. status or error signals), but the programmer must take care to include the network-control routines at adequate places within his program.

In fact, three modes of operation are used:

i) Automatic - access, release and sequencing are performed by the peripheral. This mode is the most convenient for the programmer who then does not deal with the peripheral at all.

ii) Half-Automatic - access and sequencing performed by the peripheral, release within the executed program. This mode allows the peripheral to keep busy until a series of statements is executed and prevents possible transfer of control between statements. In this mode, routines for release are the programmer's responsibility, within his program.

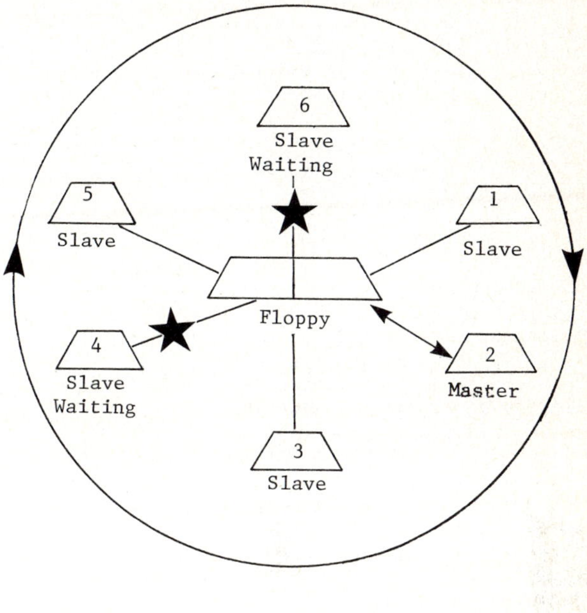

Figure 1: The Network

#2 is the master and has access to the diskette. #4 and #6 are waiting. #4 will be the next master, even if #6 asked for access before #4.

- - - - - - - - - - - - - - - - - - - -

iii) Non-Automatic - access and release routines within the executed program. Command-channel available for general usage.

3. EDUCATIONAL APPLICATIONS OF MICRO-COMPUTERS

Following is a short description of the main fields of micro-computer educational applications which are taking place in our school system at the elementary and secondary levels:

3.1 Programming Practice

Programming practice is required for teaching many aspects of computer sciences, programming languages and computer literacy. For the simplest aspects a primitive BASIC language interpreter is sufficient, without any peripherals, but for most school applications a more advanced BASIC is required, as well as a printer and some back-storage to save programs and perhaps data files. If several micros are available, one printer is sufficient when it is switchable. A simple mechanical switch performs this task but obviously automatic switching, perhaps with a spooling facility, is much more convenient. Back-storage is sometimes provided by relatively cheap cassette-recorders which allow each student to keep his own files on his personal cassette. Diskettes would provide much better back-storage but personal diskettes owned by each student, is not feasible on a large scale. A combination of diskette drives and cassette recorders provide processing facilities including file manipulations and cheap personal file storage. If software libraries are not used and common back-storage is not required, these simple programming practice applications perform quite well without networking of diskette drives. Also, the capacity of most diskettes, and their response-time, are sufficient for student use.

More advanced programming applications use advanced versions of BASIC, as well as the variety of programming languages available on micros: PASCAL, FORTRAN, COBOL, APL and, perhaps, ASSEMBLER.

For several applications, common back-storage is a great advantage and sometimes even indispensable. We obtain this by networking a common diskette or disk drive with several micros. Present day micro-computers have memory capacities of 64, 128 or more Kilobytes, executing advanced programming languages and addressing back-storage capacities which can reach the Megabyte range. We find that this capacity can satisfy almost any processing requirements that occur in high school teaching.

3.2 Computer Aided Learning (CAL)

CAL applications like drill and practice and tutorial programs must rely on common data bases as a source for teaching material and for the collection of the learning history of students. Such facilities were not available in the first generation of micros. The capacities of their diskettes were rather limited, no networking of the drive was available and access times were too long. As networks and special access methods were developed, CAL applications became feasible, as described in section 5. At present some 100 systems provide this kind of service at a variety of schools in our country, at the primary and secondary levels.

3.3 Simulation and Modelling

For educational applications simulation and modelling rely strongly on the graphic and color capabilities of micros. Most brands of micros can provide these usages and there are no difficult problems related to them. A common, networked diskette or disk drive facilitates this application by providing a convenient library of programs, but it is possible to do without it. Most micro-computer systems in schools can also be used to run educational simulation programs. The extent of the actual usage depends upon the availability of good programs and the efforts of teachers to integrate this usage into their teaching methods.

3.4 Games

Games for educational and learning purposes as well as for entertainment can easily be implemented on micro-computers. The resources for this kind of application are similar to those of simulation and modelling and the same remarks apply. There is probably no school that does not have a set of games in its micros.

3.5 LOGO

LOGO is available on several brands of micro-computers. For the last two years several projects have been active in trying to introduce regular large-scale usage of LOGO in primary schools. These projects are still experimental, relating to methods for training teachers, producing student materials and organizing school activities. The results to date have been satisfactory but not enough evidence is available to decide positively on large scale application within the whole school system.

3.6 Vocational Training

Vocational training in a variety of work areas must include computer applications specifically designed for different professions. Such applications often require computing capability greater than what is available from school owned micro-computers. Nevertheless, although professional packages may be too complex to be accessed by students in the first stages of learning, simplified training packages can be developed to illustrate basic principles which can easily be integrated into the teaching process. Such packages require more modest computing resources which are available at schools. This approach should, however, always include the usage, or at least the demonstration, of professional packages in the final stages of student training. Curricula based on this approach are in an experimental stage or under development for subjects such as computerized bookkeeping, office automation and word processing, computer aided design and manufacturing.

4. MICRO-COMPUTER BASED COMPUTER AIDED LEARNING SYSTEMS

Following are descriptions of two micro-computer based CAL systems:

MACAL, [2] originally developed on a mini-computer, was adapted to two other minis as well as to two types of micros. Courseware can be transferred among systems so that each implementation will deliver identical interactions.

SML [3] was developed on a micro system. Its transfer to other micros, as well as courseware transfer, is in process of development.

It should be mentioned that transferability is not simply a technical problem. There is also a question of property ownership. In this case both systems are in the public domain and, accordingly, there is no obstacle to transference.

4.1 The MACAL System

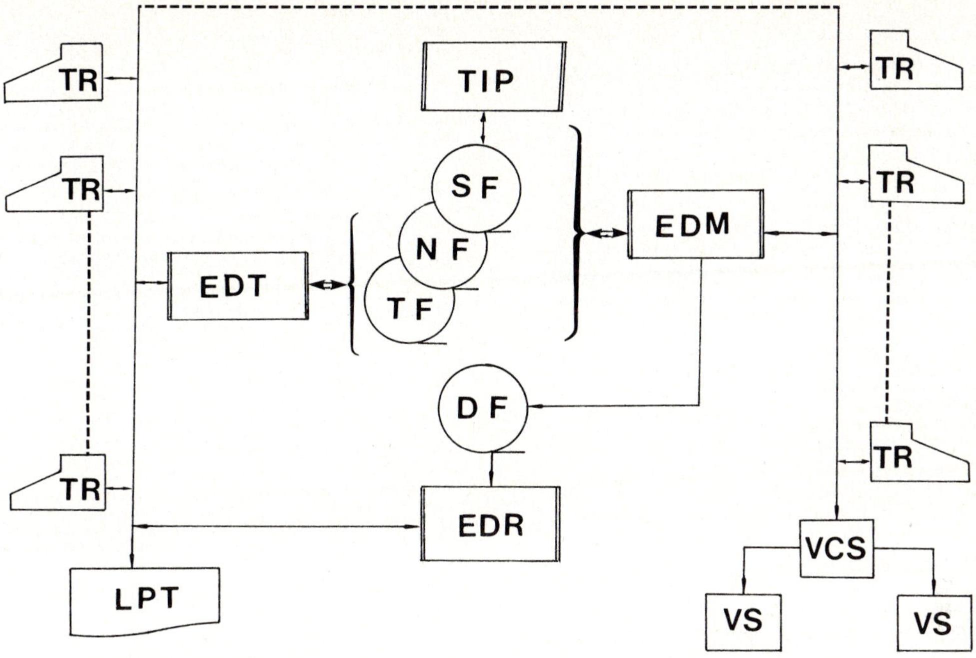

Figure 2: Graphic Description of MACAL's Computer Components

Hardware: TR: Terminal LPT: Line Printer VS: Video Source VCS: Video Channel Switch

Programs: EDT: Editor Course Generator EDM: Educational Message Transmitter
TIP: Teacher Intervention Program EDR: Educational and Didactical Report Generator

Files: SF: Student File NF: Network File TF: Text File DF: Data File

i) General Description

MACAL (Multimedia Approach to Computer Aided Learning) is a computer based teaching system intended to help the teacher improve the teaching and promote the individualized learning of pupils. It was developed by a joint effort of the Ministry of Education and Culture, the Ministry of Labor and Welfare, the Institute for Teaching Aids and BOSMAT, the Junior Technical College of the Technion. The learning process includes presentations by the teacher, use of books and booklets, interaction with the computer, use of a variety of media under computer-control or by assignment. All these are adjusted to the individual progress of each student. The interaction with the computer may provide tutorial material, drill, reinforcement with on-going evaluation of the student's progress, and adequate branching and short-cuts within the educational dialogue.

Individualized treatment of pupils is provided not only by the pupil-computer dialogue but also by progress reports from the computer to the teacher. These reports allow the teacher to work with small groups or with single pupils, according to their real needs.

The overall results of the usage of the MACAL System are, as expected, a clear increase of motivation and interest in learning, faster progress with the learning material and a more efficient use of pupils' time as well as a decrease of pupil failures.

Courses for MACAL are prepared by teams of teachers working together with specialists from the central team of the project. Before starting to produce courseware, teachers learn the principles of the computer system and curricula planning and development. Further, much practice is needed, with continuous advice and supervision by the more experienced members of the team. Preparing the computer dialogue and feeding it into the computer does not require knowledge of programming; an adequate editor package is used for this purpose. Courseware presently available covers High School Algebra, an Introduction to Computers, several chapters in English and experimental courseware integrating video playback into the pupil-computer dialogue.

ii) Technical Details

Figure 2 is a general description of the MACAL

System, as it was developed on a mini-computer system (originally an ECLIPSE, presently available also on PDP-11 and IBM 34). Following is a short description of the main components of the software package and the method of generating the pupil-computer interaction:

a) EDM (Educational Message Transmitter) deals with each student individually. It delivers texts to his terminal, accepts and evaluates his responses, makes decisions about his future learning path, updates the history of his learning activity and his personal record.

b) EDT (Editor) is a transparent course generator which generates, organizes and alters the course files without requiring that the course designer have any knowledge about computer programs or computer sciences.

c) EDR (Educational and Didactical Report Generator) processes the EDM collected histories of students' activities and generates reports as required for the teaching staff or the designers of the courseware.

d) TIP (Teacher Intervention Program) is used to generate the starting point of learning paths and to alter them upon the teacher's decision.

The process of student-computer interaction requires communication with several files. Since the starting point of each phase of a student's session depends upon his status (history-dependent), EDM communicates with a Student File (SF) containing this data. In this file each student is represented by a personal record, identified by his code number. Among other data, this record contains information about the learning phase to which the student is to be exposed next. EDM uses this information to communicate with the required course files to generate and transmit the correct messages to the student.

The course files contain two kinds of information: the description of the network of learning phases in the Network File (NF) and the contents of the messages in the Text File (TF). Once the learning phase is known from SF, EDM reads the respective record in NF and routes it to the appropriate message stored in TF.

NF has a record that represents each phase in the learning network, containing not only the link to the messages belonging to it but also the list of all its direct successors and the conditions for their choice, dependent upon the answer received from the student. Thus, the next phase in the student's learning path is determined by EDM.

At the completion of each phase, EDM updates the record of the student in SF and collects another bead of the student's learning history. For this purpose, one more file is used: Data File (DF).

iii) MACAL's Implementation on Micros

The transfer of MACAL to a variety of computers is based on:

a) Transferring the software packages to the new environment. The file structures, the main aspects of the interaction and the overall structure of programs must be maintained, but within these limitations, the programmers may adapt the program to the capabilities of the environment, even using different languages.

EDM, TIP, EDR (Figure 2) must be transferred to allow operation of existing courseware; EDT is required for authoring.

b) Linking between the different computers, so that existing courseware files (NF and TF) can be automatically transferred to the new environment.

When executing MACAL on a micro system, a copy of EDM is present in each micro. SF, NF, TF are kept on a common disk or diskette. As the files are accessed often, a conflict of access may occur, causing queuing and long waiting time.

The implementation on Commodore CBM machines uses a 2x0.5 MB diskette drive connected in a half-automatic network (Figure 1). Courseware files are on one of the diskettes (0.5 MB) so that the total available material must be divided among several diskettes. To save space, the information is very much compressed. Several fields of records are compressed and stored in a minimum number of bits, instead of using the original decimal format storage of the operating system.

When courseware files are transferred from the ECLIPSE, a special interface and communication software are used. After transfer, there is an information compression phase before the courseware diskette is ready.

When executing, EDM has special routines to decode the compressed information and reproduce it in its original format. The I/O routines for the diskette were written in ASSEMBLER; also, look-ahead transfer of data from the drive to the individual micros is executed.

By all these means, 8-10 micros can perform MACAL, using one common drive, with reasonable response time, scarcely more than two seconds. For larger systems, a hard disk must be considered to ensure acceptable worst-case response time.

The implementation on TRS Model III uses CORVUS system hard disks, working in a file-sharing mode. It is not available on diskettes. The file structure is similar to the original one, no compression of information is executed, only a reformatting procedure is required to have the files built up according to the new environment. The response time of the system is practically immediate and no down-grading was detected when up to 12 micros worked together. More stations will probably also perform well, but as of this time, larger systems have not been tested.

We expect similar results when the system will be transferred to other micro-computer systems.

4.2 The SML System

i) General Description

SML (Hebrew acronym for Computer Assistance to Teaching) was developed during the last four years by a team of teachers and computer professionals in the township of Kiryat Shmonah. This project was intended to provide computer assistance to individualized teaching methods already in use by these teachers.

It is presently implemented at some 25 schools all around the country. Available courseware cover several subjects, mainly at the elementary school level, namely: Arithmetic (grades 3-8), English (mainly grade 6) Hebrew Language and Comprehension, Enrichment Programs and Games. There is an ongoing process of courseware development. The existing courseware can provide for drill and practice, tutorials, remedial learning, simulations, educational games, etc.

One of the basic assumptions of SML is that the teacher has a central role in the process of computer assisted teaching. Without this involvement, the possible benefits of the introduction of advanced technologies into education may be severely damaged. The involvement of the teacher may occur at three levels:

a) The "user" level: the teacher-activated program delivers to the pupil a pre-programmed set of learning activities.

b) The "instructor" level: the teacher selects the type and the sequence of exercises from the existing set of learning activities in the system. This sequence can be used for groups of pupils or for individuals.

c) The "author" level: the teacher will feed the computer his/her own teaching materials, without necessarily having any programming knowledge.

Before installing SML in a school, its teachers must follow a training course of about ten days. Afterwards, they receive ongoing support, advice and training during the first year of use.

Regarding the results of using SML, the following picture emerges from reactions of teachers and pupils collected by the development team:

a) There was substantial progress in pupils' achievements.

b) An improvement in "text comprehension" by pupils was noted. Even learning arithmetic contributed to pupils' ability to read and follow instructions.

c) Teachers' involvement in courseware development intensified and improved the quality of their teaching.

d) The general methodology of teaching improved, not only in the areas of the subjects taught with computer assistance.

e) Pupils developed some understanding of computers.

f) In several cases, remarkable improvement of pupils' behaviour was observed.

ii) Technical Details

The computerized component of the SML program uses a micro-computer network, operating in non-automatic mode (see Section 2.3). Up to 16 micros can be connected to one diskette drive and a printer. Each micro has at least 16 KBs of memory free for the user; the diskette is a double drive with a total capacity of about 1 MB.

The software consists of four categories of programs:

a) Interaction Generators are each capable of generating a pupil-computer dialogue according to a fixed pattern but varying in content, according to parameters supplied to the generator. At present there are 35 types of generators, some of them completely programmed and ready for use, others providing alterable discourse by reference to data files. These files are built with the help of special editors available to teacher-authors.

b) Courseware Editors are used to build up the data files necessary for the Interaction Generators. There are now 20 editors, each one specific to one of the generators. They are user-oriented programs, ready to use without programming knowledge.

c) Report Generators produce and print reports such as individual or group achievements; courseware samples; etc.

d) Service Programs initiate or change pupil files, define learning sequences, back-up diskettes, etc.

The learning sequences, as defined by the author or teacher, are obviously general ones. Each pupil will follow his own path of study according to his progress and answers, at his own pace.

Data necessary for the operation of the system are kept in three types of files: pupil files, courseware files and service files, the last retaining general information about the system.

To generate the pupil-computer interaction, a general managing program is initiated to be responsible for loading the pupil's micro with the generator that contains the next lesson, as well as the necessary data from the courseware/pupil files. This loading may require a few seconds. When completed, the dialogue is very fast (in computer response time), with a further short pause, when files are updated and/or when reloading the micro is required.

5. SUMMARY

It is obvious that micro technology enables the large scale penetration of computers, and their applications, into the school systems.

At present it is an exciting aid to the teaching process and an attractive subject to teach. There is a steadily rising interest in all aspects of the influence of computers on the teaching/learning process in classes and school organizations. These aspects are often discussed by designers of schools and curricula. Nevertheless, school organization and activities are still basically the same as they were a few years ago.

There is no doubt that within a very few years most schools will own and use computers for a variety of educational purposes. The open question is whether computers will cause a profound change in the whole educational process, and if so, what kind of change it will be and how we can direct this change to ensure the improvement of education for the benefit of future generations.

6. REFERENCES

[1] Barta, B.Z., Computers in the Israeli educational systems, in Computers in Education (Proceedings of WCCE-81, North-Holland, Amsterdam, 1981) 617-623.

[2] Barta, B.Z., Javorsky, M., Millin, D., Artzi, A., and Berezansky, Y., A step towards low-cost CAI systems, in Proceedings, 3rd Jerusalem Conference on Information Technology, (North-Holland, Amsterdam, 1978) 151-156.

[3] Schlezingen, Ch., Teacher training for CAL in elementary schools, in Computers in Education (Proceedings of WCCE-81, North-Holland, Amsterdam, 1981) 815-816.

Session G1:

ASSOCIATIVE PROCESSORS

Chairman: Klaus Waldschmidt
J. W. Goethe Universität
Frankfurt (F.R.G.)

An associative processor is an architecture processing data according to their contents. It belongs to the group of single instruction multiple data stream (SIMD) computers and is able to apply particular commands on a set of data in parallel.

Bush delivered 1945 for the first time a paper on associative processing of data in form of search operations on a set of data /1/.

A hardware-realisation, however, was presented in 1956 by Slade and Mc Mahon in form of a Cryotron Associative Processor /2/.

The nucleus of an associative processor is its associative memory. Depending on the structure and the organisation of interrogation, various architectures are discernible:

- fully parallel associative processors
- bit-serial associative processors
- word-serial associative processors
- block-orientated associative processors

Parallel associative memory concepts could not be realised so far, but with very poor memory capacity, originating in the high number of pins required in the case of parallel associative operations. Serial concepts are representing an alternative, require however - in comparison - plenty of processing time.

Further, software-solutions were employed for reproducing an associative memory with the disadvantage of being very slow.

The contribution of D. Tavangarian "A General Purpose Associative Processor" describes a processor based on a new random associative memory. This concept is - as a fully parallel associative memory - VLSI integratable and modularly expandable with a high memory capacity. The processor not only performs arithmetic, but also non-arithmetic operations. It, therefore, can be used for associative, as well as universal applications. For arithmetic operations an ALU is employed and for the non-arithmetic ones the fully parallel search-capacity of the new associative memory. Further, the development and application of a flag-orientated data memory is described.

G. Goncalves and M. P. Lecouffe describe in their paper "An Associative Processor in a Dataflow Computer" an interesting range of application for an associative processor. This is especially suited for problems of coordination in dataflow-multiprocessor-systems, as shown also in previous papers by other authors.

In this contribution a dataflow architecture is briefly described, which is called MAUD. A set of processors are connected around a ring of circulating memory. A specialized processor, called the "updating processor", performs the management of waiting- and output-blocks of this architecture. For this purpose three associative memories are defined.

/1/ V. Bush "As we may think" Atlantic Monthly, Vol. 176 July 1945, pp 101-108

/2/ A.E. Slade, H.O. Mc Mahon "A Cryotron Catalog Memory System" Eastern Joint Computer Conference 1956, pp 115-120

MICROCOMPUTERS: Developments in Industry, Business and Education
D.R. Wilson and C.J. van Spronsen (eds.) / ©EUROMICRO, 1983
Elsevier Science Publishers B.V. (North-Holland)

A General Purpose Associative Processor

Djamshid Tavangarian

University of Dortmund
Postfach 50 05 00
D-4600 Dortmund 50

This is the description of a concept for a universally usable associative processor. Apart from a microprogram control unit the processor contains ALU, register and, as main memory, a newly designed associative memory. The processor can execute both arithmetical and non-arithmetical operations. The arithmetical operations are dealt with by the ALU. The non-arithmetical operations can be executed parallel either as simple search operations such as equal, greater-equal or less-equal operation respectively, or as complex search operations such as search between limits, search outside limits, search for maximum or minimum, etc. with the aid of the associative memory. Each word in the associative memory consists of a content addressable part and a data part. The content addressable part is only stored by way of a flag which is realized by a memory cell. The address of a cell is determined by the content addressable part of a memory word. The content of the cell as a match indicating flag (MIF) shows if the respective memory word is to be considered as stored. The relevant addresses of the MIFs for the respective search command are produced in the search operations.

The new concept of the modular associative memory makes it possible for simple circuits to be used for parallel search operations. The associative memory also fulfills the tasks of a conventional RAM, so that the processor can also be used for general tasks.

Keyword: Associative memory, Processor, CAM, RAM, Search, Association

1. INTRODUCTION

An associative processor (ASP) is a computer which processes the data according to their contents. The ASP belongs to the group of SIMD (single instruction stream multiple data stream) machines. This type of computer is in a position to apply certain instructions to a group of data parallel.

An associative memory (AS) forms a part of an ASP. The data contents and not their locations are decisive in ascertaining and processing the stored data in an AS. The data are determined with the aid of the comparison operations by the associations criterion.

Depending on construction and organization of the comparison operations of the associative memory, four forms of ASP architecture can be distinguished:

- Parallel ASP
- bitserial ASP
- wordserial ASP
- block oriented ASP

In the case of a parallel ASP, all memory cells of the associative memory can be used either simultaneously or in groups so that their contents can be compared with the data contained in the memory input.

For a bit-serial ASP the comparison is executed with a bit column of the associative memory in parallel form. This type of processor is also known as a bit serial word parallel ASP. The best-known ASPs of this kind are PEPE /1/ and STARAN /2/.

The word serial ASPs usually represent different forms of hardware realization of simple program loops which carry out a wordwise comparison for one part of the memory. The advantages of this method against a software implementation is that the comparison operations of a data group only need one command decoding cycle.

A block-oriented ASP represents a compromise between parallel ASPs which need high realization costs in spite of the development of integrated circuits and the slow but inexpensive word serial ASPs. To realize such an ASP mass storages are used as rotating storage units with additional hardware. The data are used blockwise for comparison operations /8, 9/. The ASPs which have been developed are usually installed as peripheral processors in normal universal computers to manipulate and manage the data. One of the reasons is that no one has been able to develop a cascadable parallel associative memory with sufficient storage capacity (i.e. approx. 4 MByte) within reasonable expenditure up to this time. Much of the time needed for data processing is needed in this form for the transport of data between both processors.

1.1 Associative processor with random access associative memory (ARAM)

The basic concept of the associative processor with ARAM includes an arithmetic/logic unit, an input/output unit, a unit for direct memory access (DMA), an associative memory unit and the control unit which is developed as a microprogram control unit (Fig. 1).

The most important part of this configuration is the associative memory unit which enables the realization of the processor as a universal associative processor by way of its new structure and organization. This improved memory (ARAM) has been planned so that it can be used both as a conventional random access memory (RAM) or as a parallel associative memory. At the same time no fixed limits are set, so that the division of the associative memory spaces and the write/read memory spaces can be varied as required. The splitting of the memory spaces can also be performed dynamically, i. e. varied, moved and/or omitted during a process run.

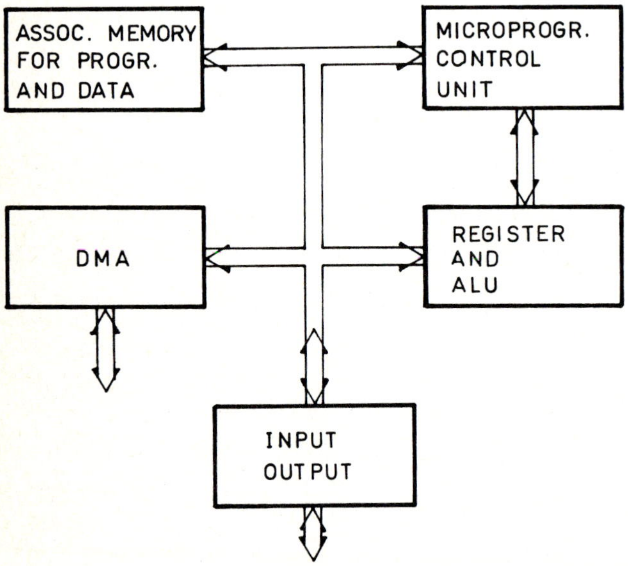

Figure 1: Blockdiagram of the associative processor

This attribute of the ARAM enables the use of this processor for implementing and realizing the problems which do not need an associative memory because the ARAM chips can be installed as main memory both for program and for data. The most important quality of a processor with ARAM chips is that it really does have an associative main memory and is in a position to carry out simple and complex search operations in parallel and with relatively small hardware expenditure in comparison to conventional parallel associative processors.

The parallel execution of complex search operations is enabled by the hardware extension of the ARAM basic concept /3/.

As the processor does not require a superior host computer it can carry out both simple and complex search tasks with minimum hardware and software expenditure. Further, the costs for a memory extension of the processor are kept to a minimum due to the modularity of the ARAM chips.

Here, we will consider in particular the non-arithmetic operations with a processor containing ARAM chips. Hardware concepts as an extension of an ARAM chip will be shown which enable parallel search operations in an ARAM.

2. RANDOM ACCESS ASSOCIATIVE MEMORY

A n-bit word-oriented associative memory (AM) has generally a n-bit search word and a n-bit mask word as inputs. The minimal outputs of an AM with a multiple match resolving circuit are an 1-bit match signal and a n-bit output word. The entire memory word can contain n+k-bit positions and is composed of a n-bit content addressable part plus a k-bit data part. The storing of information (write cycle), search for stored data (search cycle), and the read-out of data (read cycle) are the minimal different cycles which can exist in an AM /6, 7/. With the existing AM concepts integrated circuits can only be realized with limited memory capacities in comparison to the RAMs.

The concept of the associative random access memory (ARAM) is realized by using the search word of the AM together with the corresponding mask word to produce the address for an 1-bit organized RAM by an expanded address decoder circuit /3/. The 1-bit organized memory only serves for the storage of a "match indicating flag" (MIF). A MIF equal to 1 indicates that the required search word has already been stored into the memory.

For a search word to be stored and retrieved one memory cell is required for storing and retrieving a MIF. In the search cycle, the search word is used as a memory address. A "1" as the contents of the addressed memory cell shows that the word in question has already been stored. The contents of the memory cell indicates a possible match signal (MIF). If the search word is not masked, only one memory cell can deliver a match. Two memory cells must be addressed if one bit of the search word argument is masked. If one of the two cells contains a "1" there is a match. In general, for q masked bits of the search word 2^q cells must be addressed. No compare operation needs to be carried out.

Figure 2 shows the basic circuits of a 3 bit-ARAM example with the appropriate address decoder (ADR) and the corresponding memory cells. Each memory cell has an address line, a read-write signal input (WR), and the inputs TK for MIFs and D for corresponding data. During the write cycle the signals TK and D can change the content of the memory cells which have been addressed by the ADR. Setting M=0 and WR=1 only the memory word with the address S is activated to store MIF (indicating flag for content addressable part) and D (data part) into the corresponding memory cells. If a search word S is masked during the write cycle (M≠0 and WR=1), the input information will be stored into several memory words which are selected by the address decoder dependent on the mask word (multi write function). If all bits of the search word are masked, the input information (TK and D) will be stored into all memory words. This last case can also be used to clear the entire memory in one write cycle with TK=0 and D=0. This fully masked write function substitutes an extra clear input signal. The match output of the memory is realized by a wired OR connection of all memory match indicating flag cell outputs. The match output-signal shows a match as soon as one of the addressed memory cells shows a MIF=1. Search and read cycle of the memory are performed when WR=0. During the search cycle the match signal MS is ascertained dependent on the search word S and the mask word M by addressing the relevant memory words with the address decoder. When MS=1, there is at least one match in memory (Fig. 2).

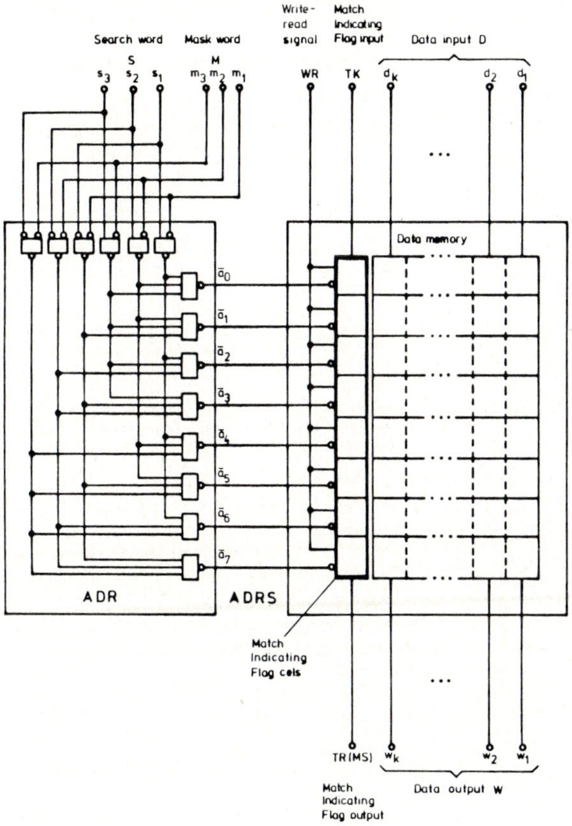

Figure 2: Basic circuit of the ARAM

A "masking counter" is installed as a multiple match resolver. The masking counter has the same word length as S. The circuit (Fig. 3), which serves as a dualcounter with a selection circuit, switches the same bit position of the search word S through for the not masked bit position of S. The bit positions of the search word which

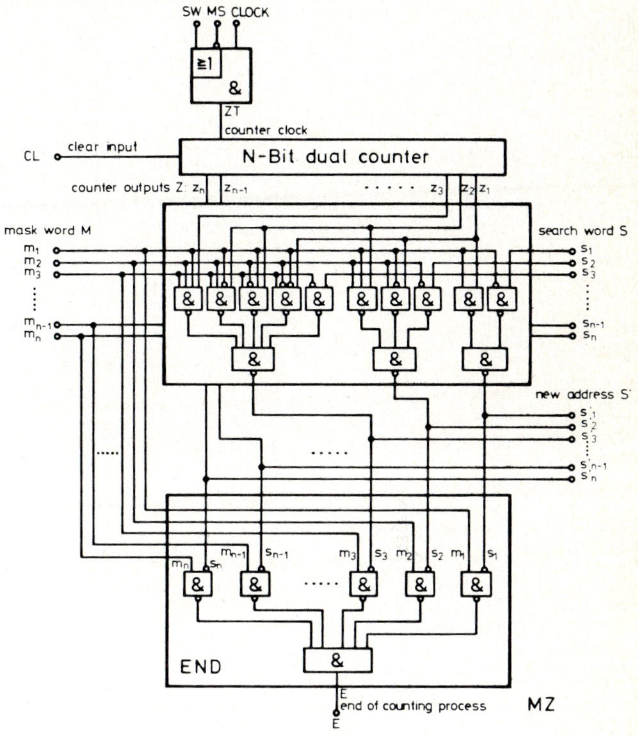

Figure 3: The circuit of the masking counter

are masked are replaced by the counter outputs Z starting with z_1. The counter output z_1 is fed through to the masked position of the search word with the lowest significant value. The counter z_2 is used for the position with the next highest significant value, and so on. In this way a counting process has been introduced in which only the masked bit positions are counted up and therefore only those memory words will be addressed which could possibly be a match.

The realization of large bus oriented memory arrays is enabled by combining the ARAM memory chips with the help of a special chip select circuit and a further search word remainder bit circuit /3/. Such a memory array can be used as random access memory or as associative memory at the same time. These arrays are then also cascadable themselves.

3. ORGANIZATION OF SEARCH OPERATIONS

The search operations can be divided into two categories which can be treated by way of simple and complex association criteria. The simple association criteria only require a search argument which sets the limit value for the search. The complex association criteria require two or more search arguments or limit values to carry

	Search operation	Operation	No. of search arguments	Command with corresponding arguments	
Simple search operations	Equality	$S = A_i$	1	E,S,M	Hardware implementation
	Greater/Equal	$S \geqq A_i$	1	GE,S,M	
	Less/Equal	$S \leqq A_i$	1	LE,S,M	
Complex search operations	Between limits	$S_1 \leqq A_i \leqq S_2$ $(S_1 \leqq S_2)$	2	BL,S_1,M_1,S_2,M_2	
	Outside limits	$S_1 \geqq A_i \geqq S_2$ $(S_1 \leqq S_2)$	2	OL,S_1,M_1,S_2,M_2	
	Maximum	S_{max}	(1), 2^n-1 +)	MAX, [S,M]	
	Minimum	S_{min}	(1), 2^n-1 +)	MIN, [S,M]	
	Next largest	S_n	1 , 2^n-1 +)	NG, S,M	Firmware implementation
	Next smallest	S_k	1 , 2^n-1 +)	NK, S,M	
	Similarity (next larger and/or next lower)	S_s	1 , 2^n-1 +)	SI, S,M	

+) maximum number of limiting values

Table 1: The most important search operations

out the search operations. The most important search operations are represented in Table 1. The search operations and their descriptions are shown in the first two columns of the table. The third column shows the number of search arguments. The search argument has to be interpreted as a search word of the associative memory. Two search arguments S_1 and S_2 are needed for the search operations BL and OL to fix the limits for the search. No search arguments are in principle necessary for the search for minimum or maximum of the data in the memory. However, it is possible to declare a search argument to set the limit for a search operation. This means that a maximum or minimum respectively up to this value would be of interest.

A limiting value cannot be shown for maximum and minimum searches and the following search operations, because the search result itself sets the limiting values. The result can, however, vary between search argument and the maximum possible value. The maximum possible value for a n-bit search argument is 2^n-1. In the third column the appropriate commands for the processor are shown. The search arguments in angular brackets can be declared if required.

The search arguments (S, S_1 or S_2) can also be masked with separate mask words (M, M_1 or M_2). It is still possible that masking will change a search argument. The reason for this is that several values arise for a search argument once it is masked. E.g. for a search word $S=s_n s_{n-1} \dots s_2 s_1$, which is masked with mask word $M = 00 \dots 01$ the values $S_0 = s_n s_{n-1} \dots s_2 0$ and $S_1 = s_n s_{n-1} \dots s_2 1$ are relevant. As exeample, all words are shown which are greater than S_1 for the search operation GE. In the case of search operation LE, however, all values are shown which are less than S_0 etc.

A search operation can be carried out in two steps with the help of the parallel associative memory. In the first step a match vector is determined which shows the positions which fulfill the appropriate association criteria together with the search arguments (search words) contained in the memory.

In the second step the words which have each been indicated as a match can be read out in sequence with the help of the masking counter in the associative memory.

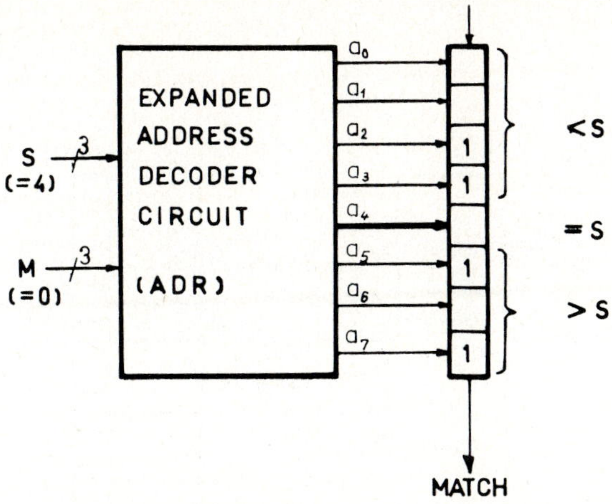

Figure 4: Display of the relevant parts for simple search operations in the ARAM

4. SIMPLE SEARCH OPERATIONS WITH THE ARAM

It is possible to use a n-bit ARAM as a vector in which the numbers 0 to (2^n-1) can be stored as contents addressable data by way of their respective MIF. It is sufficient in the case of greater-equal or less- equal search operations to address the relevant part for the search simultaneously. If an addressed MIF contains the value "1", then the result of the search will contain at least one match. Figure 4 is used as an aid in specifying and characterizing the addresses of a relevant part.

The figure shows the expanded ARAM address decoder and the cells for MIF of a 3-bit ARAM chip. By means of the appropriate MIF the 8 $(2^3=8)$ numbers 0 to 7 can be stored. The values 2, 3, 5 and 7 have been stored into the memory. Because no 1 is stored in the appropriate MIF, the remaining values are considered to be not stored.

To determine the values greter-equal to search arguments S=4 the MIFs 4 to 7 are simultaneously addressed as relevant part. The output lines of the MIFs are connected by a wired OR. If one of the addressed MIF cells contains a 1, a match signal exists. The match signal shows that at least one value is stored in the addressed part which is greater than the search argument S. To determine the values which are less than/equal to S, the MIFs 0 to 4 must be addressed. The problem is to develop a circuit which enables the simultaneous addressing of the relevant part. Table 2 is shown for the example of Figure 4 as a basis for the design of the circuit:

Search word S	Generated address from ADR (M=0) a_0	a_1	a_2	a_3	a_4	a_5	a_6	a_7	Addressable MIFs for GE operation 0	1	2	3	4	5	6	7	Addressable MIFs for LE operation 0	1	2	3	4	5	6	7
0	1								1	1	1	1	1	1	1	1	1							
1		1								1	1	1	1	1	1	1	1	1						
2			1								1	1	1	1	1	1	1	1	1					
3				1								1	1	1	1	1	1	1	1	1				
4					1								1	1	1	1	1	1	1	1	1			
5						1								1	1	1	1	1	1	1	1	1		
6							1								1	1	1	1	1	1	1	1	1	
7								1								1	1	1	1	1	1	1	1	1

Table 2: Determination of MIF addresses for GE- and LE-search operations

The search argument S is shown in the first column of the table. The search argument S only addresses a MIF cell if M=0 (second column). The cells which must be addressed by the appropriate search argument are specified in the third and fourth columns. This means that all MIFs which could represent a value which is greater-equal (column 3) or less-equal (column 4) will be addressed.

The relations for the new addressing of the MIF cells can be taken from the table and is summarized in the following equations:

Equations for LE :

$a'_0=a_0$

$a'_1=a_0 \vee a_1$

$a'_2=a_0 \vee a_1 \vee a_2$

$a'_3=a_0 \vee a_1 \vee a_2 \vee a_3$

$a'_4=a_0 \vee a_1 \vee a_2 \vee a_3 \vee a_4$

$a'_5=a_0 \vee a_1 \vee a_2 \vee a_3 \vee a_4 \vee a_5$

$a'_6=a_0 \vee a_1 \vee a_2 \vee a_3 \vee a_4 \vee a_5 \vee a_6$

$a'_7=a_0 \vee a_1 \vee a_2 \vee a_3 \vee a_4 \vee a_5 \vee a_6 \vee a_7$

Equations for GE :

$a''_0=a_0 \vee a_1 \vee a_2 \vee a_3 \vee a_4 \vee a_5 \vee a_6 \vee a_7$

$a''_1=a_1 \vee a_2 \vee a_3 \vee a_4 \vee a_5 \vee a_6 \vee a_7=\bar{a}_0$

$a''_2=a_2 \vee a_3 \vee a_4 \vee a_5 \vee a_6 \vee a_7=\bar{a}_0 \wedge \bar{a}_1$

$a''_3=a_3 \vee a_4 \vee a_5 \vee a_6 \vee a_7=\bar{a}_0 \wedge \bar{a}_1 \wedge \bar{a}_2$

$a''_4=a_4 \vee a_5 \vee a_6 \vee a_7=\bar{a}_0 \wedge \bar{a}_1 \wedge \bar{a}_2 \wedge \bar{a}_3$

$a''_5=a_5 \vee a_6 \vee a_7=\bar{a}_0 \wedge \bar{a}_1 \wedge \bar{a}_2 \wedge \bar{a}_3 \wedge \bar{a}_4$

$a''_6=a_6 \vee a_7=\bar{a}_0 \wedge \bar{a}_1 \wedge \bar{a}_2 \wedge \bar{a}_3 \wedge \bar{a}_4 \wedge \bar{a}_5$

$a''_7=a_7=\bar{a}_0 \wedge \bar{a}_1 \wedge \bar{a}_2 \wedge \bar{a}_3 \wedge \bar{a}_4 \wedge \bar{a}_5 \wedge \bar{a}_6$

In general:

$$a'_i = a_i \vee \bigvee_{j=0}^{i-1} a_j$$

with $i = 1,2,\ldots(2^n - 1)$ (1.1)

for less than/equal-operation and

$$a''_i = \bigvee_{j=i}^{2^n-1} a_j = \bigwedge_{j=0}^{i-1} \bar{a}_j$$

with $i = o,1,2,3,\ldots(2^n - 1)$ (1.2)

for greater than/equal-operation.

In these equations a_i is the address of the i-th MIF cell which results from the ADR. The new addresses a'_i and a''_i of the MIF cells are formed from the addresses a_i for the respective search operation (GE or LE). By comparing both equations for a'_i and a''_i it becomes evident that both relations complement each other partially. This means:

$$a'_i = a_i \vee \bigvee_{j=o}^{i-1} a_j = a_i \vee (\overline{\overline{\bigvee_{j=o}^{i-1} a_j}}) =$$

$$= a_i \vee (\overline{\bigwedge_{j=o}^{i-1} \bar{a}_j}) = a_i \vee \bar{a}''_i \qquad (1.3)$$

For specifying the type of a search operation two control variables GE and LE are inserted. With these variables the general relation to the addressing of the MIF cells can be shown:

$$a^+_i = a_i \vee [\,GE \wedge (\bigvee_{j=o}^{i-1} a_j)] \vee [\,LE \wedge (\overline{\bigvee_{j=o}^{i-1} a_j})] \quad (2)$$

The first part of the equation with a_i is put in without a control variable because the MIF cell i itself has to be addressed with a_i in all search operations. In this case, only the addressing of the cell i with a_i is relevant, even if neither the operation for GE nor LE is required. For the realization of the expanded ARAM circuit a new combinatorial circuit is installed. The combinatorial circuit contains the addresses a_i as well as the variables GE and LE as inputs. The outputs of the combinatorial network are the new addresses a^+_i. The expanded ARAM circuit is shown in Figure 5.

The combinatorial circuit represents the realization of equation 2. The figure shows the addressing of the relevant cells for greater/equal-operations (GE = 1) for the above shown example (S = 4).

To realize the internal circuit of the combinatorial network there is a choice between three forms of circuit:

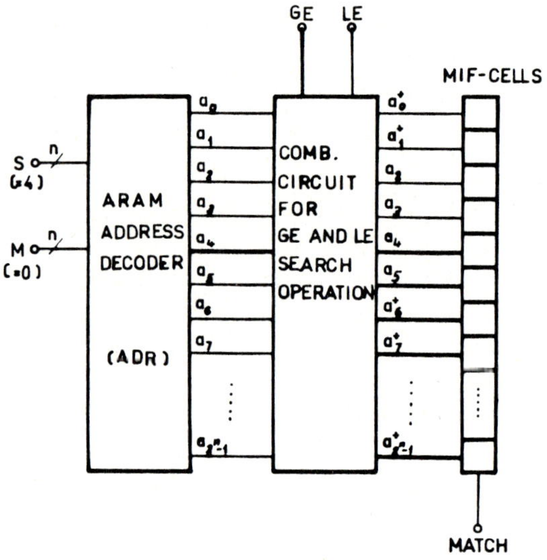

Figure 5: Expanded ARAM block diagram for parallel GE- and LE-search operations

- parallel circuit
- serial circuit
- parallel-serial circuit

4.1 Parallel circuit

The parallel working circuit makes it possible to shorten execution and response times. In this case the search operation is executed in one memory cycle. The circuit is, however, relatively expensive. The realization is performed directly from equation 2. The circuit for our example is shown in figure 6.

To make the chips cascadable, the output of the last OR-gate in the circuit (figure 6) is lead as CARRY-output to the CARRY-input of the next chip. The CARRY-output of the previous chip is connected to all OR-gates of the circuit because, as soon as a CARRY arises, all MIFs of the chip have to be addressed.

4.2 Serial circuit

The serial realization of the circuit is cheaper. The response time are, however, longer than the parallel version.

In order to define the circuit the equations (1,i) must be transformed so that the functional parts in the relations for a^+_i result from the previous ones (a^+_j, j=o, 1,... i-1)

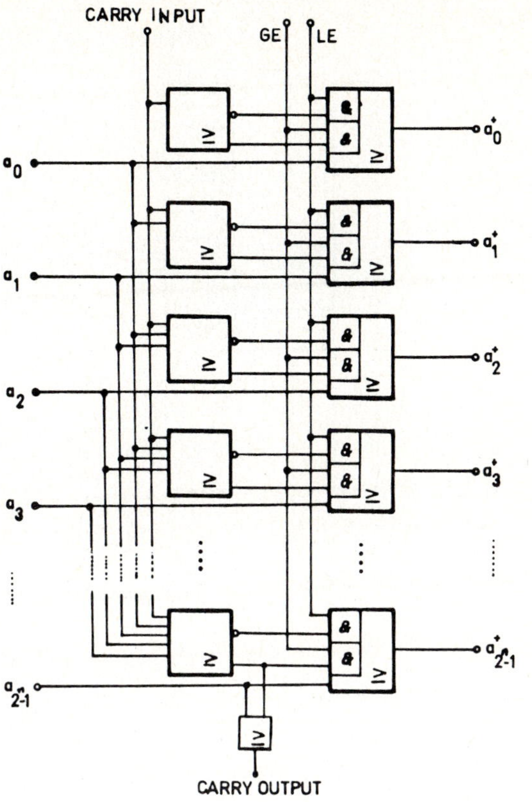

Figure 6: Hardware realization of the parallel GE and LE operation in an ARAM chip

$$a_0^+ = a_0 \vee (GE \wedge 0) \vee (LE \wedge 1) = a_0 \vee (GE \wedge CARRY) \vee (LE \wedge \overline{CARRY})$$
$$= a_0 \vee (GE \wedge X_0) \vee (LE \wedge \overline{X}_0)$$

$$a_1^+ = a_1 \vee (GE \wedge a_0) \vee (LE \wedge \overline{a}_0)$$
$$= a_1 \vee (GE \wedge (X_0 \vee a_0)) \vee (LE \wedge (\overline{X}_0 \vee a_0))$$
$$= a_1 \vee (GE \wedge X_1) \vee (LE \wedge \overline{X}_1)$$

$$a_2^+ = a_2 \vee (GE \wedge (a_0 \vee a_1)) \vee (LE \wedge (\overline{a_0 \vee a_1}))$$
$$= a_2 \vee (GE \wedge (X_1 \vee a_1)) \vee (LE \wedge (\overline{X_1 \vee a_1}))$$
$$= a_2 \vee (GE \wedge X_2) \vee (LE \wedge \overline{X}_2)$$

.
.
.

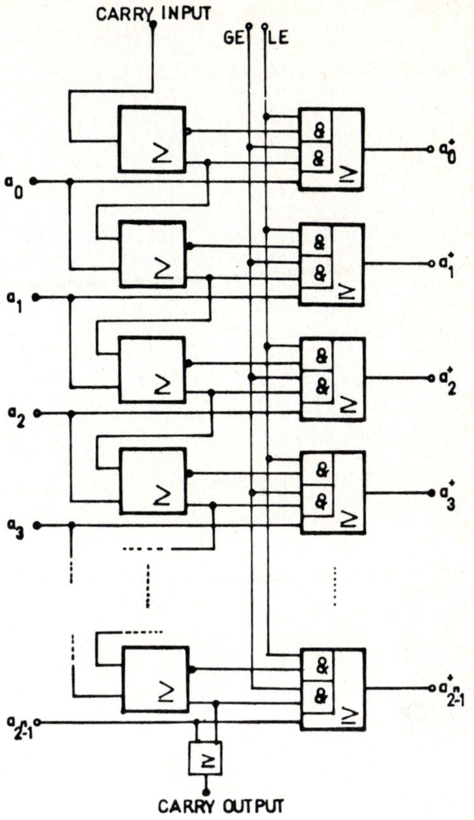

Figure 7: Hardware realization of the serial GE and LE search operations in an ARAM chip

$$a_i^+ = a_i \vee (GE \wedge (X_{i-1} \vee a_{i-1})) \vee (LE \wedge (\overline{X_{i-1} \vee a_{i-1}})) =$$
$$= a_i \vee (GE \wedge X_i) \vee (LE \wedge \overline{X_i}) \qquad (3)$$

with $X_i = (X_{i-1} \vee a_{i-1})$

The circuit solving these equations is shown in Figure 7.

The maximum response time needed to determine a match by this procedure amounts to:

$$T_{max} = t_g \cdot (2^n - 1) + 2tg = t_g (2^n + 1) \qquad (4)$$

The minimum response time would be:

$$T_{min} = 3t_g \qquad (5)$$

In this case t_g is the signal delay time of a gate level.

4.3 Parallel-serial circuit

A compromise between the two previously described methods would be a parallel-serial realization of the circuit. This method is favourable specially for cascading the ARAM chips. In this case the calculation is carried out in parallel inside the ARAM chip. In addition each chip contains a CARRY input and a CARRY output. The CARRY input (CIN_i) of a chip i in an ARAM array (Figure 8) will be connected with the CARRY output of the (i-1)-th chip ($COUT_{i-1}$). The CARRY output of the i-th chip $COUT_i$ will be connected to the CARRY input of the next chip CIN_{i+1}, etc. The first chip gets the value "0" as CARRY input. The connections of CARRY inputs and outputs for the i-th step of an ARAM array are shown in Figure 8.

Figure 8: The chip connections for CARRY inputs and CARRY outputs in an ARAM array

The CARRY inputs and CARRY outputs can also be used for the realization of an ARAM array which allows the parallel execution of the greater/equal and less/equal operations for the entire array. In this case, however, CARRY-LOOK-AHEAD chips (Figure 9) are necessary which can be designed using equation 2.

The CARRY outputs of the ARAM chips are connected to the CARRY-LOOK-AHEAD chip in the circuit. Here again parallel calculation of all CARRY inputs of the ARAM chips of the ARAM memory array is performed.

5. SEARCH OPERATIONS BL AND OL

In principle the complex search operations (compare Table 1) can also be carried out with the aid of the simple search operations. It is then necessary to take several search steps to carry out the complex search operations.

The ARAM concept permits the installation of simple but effective hardware to execute complex search operations. In the same manner as for simple search operations the hardware

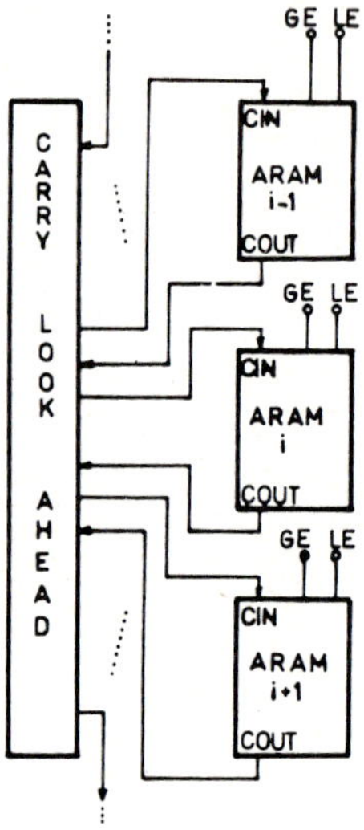

Figure 9: ARAM array with CARRY-LOOK-AHEAD chip for parallel search operations

solutions for the search operations "between limits" and "outside limits" can be defined. Each of these operations need two search arguments S_1 and S_2, whereby $S_1 \leq S_2$. It is necessary too, to address the relevant cells for each command to determine the match signal from the addressed MIF cells and solve the problem. For a search operation the solution should be carried out in one memory cycle, which means that both limiting values S_1 and S_2 are taken into account simultaneously. This requires two ARAM address decoders in the circuit for S_1 and S_2 respectively. These two address decoders (ADR 1 and ADR 2) are shown in Figure 10. The address decorders perform the masking of the search arguments S_1 and S_2 with regard to the mask words M_1 and M_2. The addresses which are derived from S_1 are called a_{1i} with i = 0,1,..,(2^n-1). The addresses which are generated with respect to S_2 are called a_{2i} with i = 0,1,...,(2^n-1).
The proper MIF addresses a_i with (i = 0,1,...,2^n-1) are formed by way of the pairwise OR gates of both addresses a_{1i} and a_{2i}. The MIF cells for S_1 and for S_2 must be addressed in this case by the appropriate address lines a_{1S1} for S_1 and a_{2S2} for S_2.
The combinatorial circuit (BLOL) generates the addresses of the relevant MIF cells from both addresses a_{1S1} and a_{2S2}. The relevant cells for the BL operation are those cells which lie between the two addresses a_{1S1} and a_{2S2}. In the case of an OL search operation it is necessary to address all MIF cells which are located outside the two MIF cells with addresses a_{1S1} and a_{2S2}.

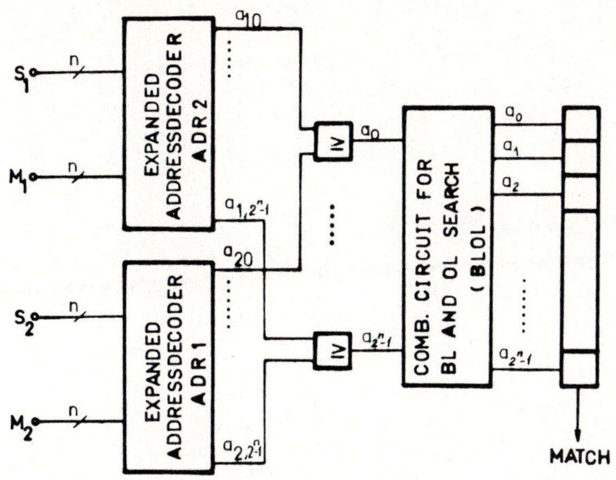

Figure 10: ARAM block diagram to execute BL and OL search operations

The calculation of the function of the combinatorial circuit for the BL search operation is based upon Table 3. The table has been developed as an exemple for the search arguments S_1 and S_2 each with a 3-bit length which are shown in the table as addresses a_{10} to a_{17} for S_1 and a_{20} to a_{27} for S_2. The addresses to be generated are inserted in the panels of the table. This table determines the equations for the MIF cells which are shown in their general form in equation 6.

$$a_i' = \left(\bigvee_{j=o}^{i} a_{1j}\right) \wedge \left(\bigvee_{j=i}^{2^n-1} a_{2j}\right);\ i=0,1,2...(2^n-1) \qquad (6)$$

The function in equation 6 represents the parallel solution of the search operation BL.

A solution for the realization of a serial combinatorial circuit can be determined from the equations 7.1 to 7.3:

$$a_o' = (a_{10}) \wedge \left(\bigvee_{j=o}^{2^n-1} a_{2j}\right) = Y_o \wedge X_{2^n-1} \qquad (7.1)$$

$\vdots$

$$a_i' = Y_i \wedge X_{(2^n-1)-i}\ ;\ i=1,2,3,...,2^n-2 \qquad (7.2)$$

with $Y_i = (Y_{i-1} \vee a_{1i})$

and $X_{(2^n-1)} = (a_{2i} \vee X_{(2^n-1)-i-1})$

$\vdots$

$$a_{2^n-1}' = \left(\bigvee_{j=o}^{2^n-1} a_{1j}\right) \wedge (a_{2,2^n-1}) = Y_{2^n-1} \wedge X_o \qquad (7.3)$$

The same principle lead to the determination of the equations for OL search operations. It must be taken into consideration in this case that the two search operations BL and OL are comple-

		Addresses for S_1							
	S_2 \ S_1	a_{10}	a_{11}	a_{12}	a_{13}	a_{14}	a_{15}	a_{16}	a_{17}
Addresses for S_2	a_{20}	a_0'							
	a_{21}	$a_0' - a_1'$	a_1'						
	a_{22}	$a_0' - a_2'$	$a_1' - a_2'$	a_2'					
	a_{23}	$a_0' - a_3'$	$a_1' - a_3'$	$a_2' - a_3'$	a_3'				
	a_{24}	$a_0' - a_4'$	$a_1' - a_4'$	$a_2' - a_4'$	$a_3' - a_4'$	a_4'			
	a_{25}	$a_0' - a_5'$	$a_1' - a_5'$	$a_2' - a_5'$	$a_3' - a_5'$	$a_4' - a_5'$	a_5'		
	a_{26}	$a_0' - a_6'$	$a_1' - a_6'$	$a_2' - a_6'$	$a_3' - a_6'$	$a_4' - a_6'$	$a_5' - a_6'$	a_6'	
	a_{27}	$a_0' - a_7'$	$a_1' - a_7'$	$a_2' - a_7'$	$a_3' - a_7'$	$a_4' - a_7'$	$a_5' - a_7'$	$a_6' - a_7'$	a_7'

Table 3: Table for the addressing of MIF cells of an ARAM chip for the BL-operation

mentary to one another. This means that for an OL search operation those MIF cells will be addressed which would not be addressed in the case of a BL search operation. Taking this into consideration the solution for a combinatorial circuit which will carry out the OL-search operation is:

$$a_i'' = a_i \vee \bar{a}_i' = a_i \vee \overline{\left(\bigvee_{j=o}^{i} a_{1j}\right) \wedge \left(\bigvee_{j=i}^{2^n-1} a_{2j}\right)} ; i=o,1,2...,2^n-1 \qquad (8)$$

In this equation a_i is the address of the i-th MIF cell because the MIF cell i has itself to be addressed with a_i in the OL search operation.

Equation 8 shows the parallel solution of an OL search operation. A serial generation of the addresses is also possible by the same means as for the simple search operations.

6. SEARCH OPERATIONS MAX AND MIN

The results for the hardware solution for the execution of search operations previously shown have only been determined from the addresses a_i of the MIF cells. For further search operations, as set out in Table 1, the contents of the MIF cells are needed as well as the addresses. In the cases of MAX and MIN search operations no addresses a_i are necessary if no search arguments exist. For the search operations MAX and MIN the corresponding limiting value of a search operation determines itself by means of the result. In the case of the search operation MIN this means that the MIF cell must be addressed which first contains a "1" in the MIF vector. In the case of a MAX search operation the MIF cell should be addressed which contains a "1" as last cell of the MIF vector. In other words, for the determination of the greatest or smallest value in the memory only the contents of the MIF cells for finding out the appropriate addresses are necessary. In the case of a MIN search operation the MIF cell i is addressed when it has a "1" as content and the cells up to it (i.e. from 0 to i-1) don't contain a "1".

$$a_{i_{min}} = MIF_i \wedge \left(\bigwedge_{j=0}^{i-1} \overline{MIF_j} \right) ; \ i=o,1,...2^n-1 \qquad (9)$$

Similar to this, the MIF cell i will be addressed for the MAX search operation if it contains "1" and the following MIF cells (i+1,...,2^n-1) each contain no "1".

$$a_{i_{max}} = MIF_i \wedge \left(\bigwedge_{j=i+1}^{2^n-1} \overline{MIF_j} \right) ; \ i=o,1,2,...2^n-1 \qquad (10)$$

The relations for the hardware realization of the further search operations e. g. search for next greater, search for next lower, search for similar words etc. can also be determined in the same way. But these search operations are realized by firmware with the help of simple searches. For the hardware realization of these search operations the parallel, serial or parallel-serial concepts can also be chosen. It is also possible to execute the search operations in parallel in an ARAM array by means of an appropriate CARRY-LOOK-AHEAD circuit.

7. CLOSING REMARKS

Modern standards of VLSI technology enable a circuit and system designer to use new means and new ideas to solve hardware problems. An attempt has been made in this paper to do justice to the main subject. The concept of an associative processor has been described which contains a newly developed associative memory. The memory can be installed either as an associative memory for the parallel execution of simple and complex search operations or as a conventional RAM chip. The memory chips can be cascaded as required. In this particular concept no pin-limitation problems arise. Memory arrays which also operate in parallel can be realized with the help of CARRY-LOOK-AHEAD circuits.

The hardware expenditure still remains small in comparison to other concepts developed up till now.

It is notable that several of the hardware solutions for complex search operations (MAX/MIN) shown in this paper could only be realized with great difficulty and more expenditure using conventional concepts.

The characteristics of the memory enable the use of the associative processor as a general purpose processor to solve various problems. In particular it is possible with the help of the ARAM chips to develop processors which can execute both arithmetical operations by means of the ALU and non-arithmetical operations by means of parallel searches.

The associative processor can be most effectively installed for example in the control circuit of a high speed mass storage. At the same time the empty spaces in the mass storage can be used to store new files, to do file manipulations, to generate indirect addresses, to calculate page addresses, etc., to name a few examples. The sequential search operations can be avoided with the associative processor and the software expenditure can be strongly reduced.

Acknowledgment

The author is thankful to Prof. Dr. K. Waldschmidt for helpful supports.

8. REFERENCES

/1/ Crane, B.A.; Gilmartin, M.J.; Huttenhoff, J.H.; Ruc, P.T.; Shiveley, R.R. "Pepe Computer Architecture" IEEE Compcon, 1972, pp 57-60

/2/ Rudolph, J.A. "A Production Implementation of an Associative Array Processor STARAN" Proc. AFIPS 1972, Vol. 41, N.J., pp 229-241

/3/ Tavangarian, D. "A Novel Modular Expandable Associative Memory" Microsystem, 8th Euromicro Symp. on Microprocessing and Microprogramming, Sept. 1982, pp 303-312

/4/ Wolf, G. "Associative Memories and Processors" Elektronische Rechenanlagen, 17, 1975, H. 6, pp 264-271

/5/ Yau, S.S.; Iung, H.S. "Associative Processor Architecture - A Survey" Computing Surveys, Vol. 9, No. 1, 1977

/6/ Kohonen, T. "Content-Addressable Memories" Springer Verlag, Berlin 1980

/7/ Leilich, H.-O. "Assoziative Speicher" Taschenbuch der Informatik, Bd. I Springer-Verlag 1974

/8/ Minsky, N. "Rotating Devices as Partially Associative Memories" Proc. AFIPS 1972, Montvale, N.J., pp 587-595

/9/ Parhami, B. "A Highly Parallel Computing System for Information Retrival" Proc. AFIPS 1972, Montvale, N.J., pp 681-690

MICROCOMPUTERS: Developments in Industry, Business and Education
D.R. Wilson and C.J. van Spronsen (eds.) / © EUROMICRO, 1983
Elsevier Science Publishers B.V. (North-Holland)

AN ASSOCIATIVE PROCESSOR IN A DATAFLOW COMPUTER

G. GONCALVES, M.P. LECOUFFE

Université de Lille I
LA 369
Bâtiment M3
59655 VILLENEUVE D'ASCQ CEDEX
FRANCE

This paper presents an implementation of the updating processor of a dataflow computer, MAUD. It is a conventional microprocessor using several levels of memory. These memories are conceptually associative memories. We give a functional description of this processor with associative memories, and an implementation with RAM memories.

KEY-WORDS : Data flow, associative memory, circulating memory.

I. INTRODUCTION

Data flow processing is a new way to the problems of expression and exploitation of parallelism. Conventional parallel machines, like pipeline machines or array computers, can exploit the parallelism explicitely described about the data of a program. On the contrary, data flow exploits the parallelism which flows naturally from the avaibility of data. In a general way, an operation (a primitive operation as well as a process composed of a number of operations), is executable as soon as its input data are calculated. That implies new control schemes for the execution of a program and new multiprocessor architectures [Den 79].

Generally, data flow processing is applied to the instruction level. We are investigating a dataflow multiprocessor where data flow processing is applied to the level of a set of instructions, grouped together with the data they used, in a module called a block. The problems are the same problems in data flow computers at the instruction level, except for updating the blocks and for searching the executable blocks, because of the size of the blocks and of the variable number of input data in a block.

In this paper, we briefly present that dataflow multiprocessor, called MAUD. Then, we described the UP processor whose function is to update the blocks and to find out the executable blocks. It is a conventional microprocessor using several levels of memory. These memories are conceptually associative memories. Consequently we give a functional description of UP processor with associative memories. Then we described a more realistic implementation with RAM memories.

II. FUNCTIONAL DESCRIPTION OF MAUD

MAUD is a data flow multiprocessor in which the data flow processing is performed at the level of a set of instructions grouped together into a block. A program for MAUD is a set of blocks. A block must also contain the objects used by the set of instructions, and a communication part allowing communication between the blocks of a program.

A block can be viewed as a generalized primitive applied to input objects (I-objects) which are calculated by other blocks, and providing output objects (O-objects) which will be used as I-objects by other blocks.

The communication part of a block is composed of two sets : an Input field (I-field) and an Output field (O-field). Let us note V the set of usable values in the system enlarged with a special value NYC, "not-yet-calculated". Then the I-field of a block is composed of a set of couples (NC_i, V_i) where the NC_i are communication names associated to the I-objects of the block, and V_i is a value element in V. The O-field is composed of couples (NC_i, V_i) where the NC_i are communication names associated with the O-objects of the block, and V_i is a value element in V.

A communication name is a name associated to I-objects and O-objects : it does not point out an explicit memory cell ; it is only used to point out values. The communication names are only known at the block level, and they are all different from each other. The Single-Assignment rule [TE 68] is applied to the communication names, allowing the natural expression of dependencies existing between the blocks of a program, and therefore the expression of parallelism at execution time.

Execution of a program

The execution of the blocks of a program is data-driven : a block is ready for execution when its I-field is full, i.e. when all its I-objects have received a value and when these values have been propagated to this block. Such a block is an executable block. If its I-field is not full, the block is called a waiting block.

The blocks are executed by execution processors whose function is the execution of a block. Executable blocks may be executable concurrently. The execution of a block produces an Output block (O-block) composed of the O-field of the block.

The important point in the execution of a program is the transmission of objects from the O-block, produced at the end of the execution of a block, to the I-fields of waiting blocks to find out new executable blocks. This work is performed by a special processor, the updating processor UP which will be detailed in Section III.

During block execution, two special operations may be used :

- Execblock operation, which allows the execution of another block, a model of this block existing in a library. It is similar to a procedure call and a FORK operation.

- Wait operation, which allows the calling block to wait O-objects calculated by the blocks called by execblock operations at the moment the calling block needs these O-objects.

These two operations give a dynamic behaviour to the system (for more details, see [Lec 80]). Execblock operation implies the existence of a BUILDER processor, whose function is to build a block using the execution requests produced by the execution processors when they perform execblock operations.

Finally, the multiprocessor is composed of :

- A set of execution processors, P_i.
- An updating processor, UP.
- A builder processor, BUILDER.

There is no direct communication path between those processors. They all communicate through shared memories (Fig. 1).

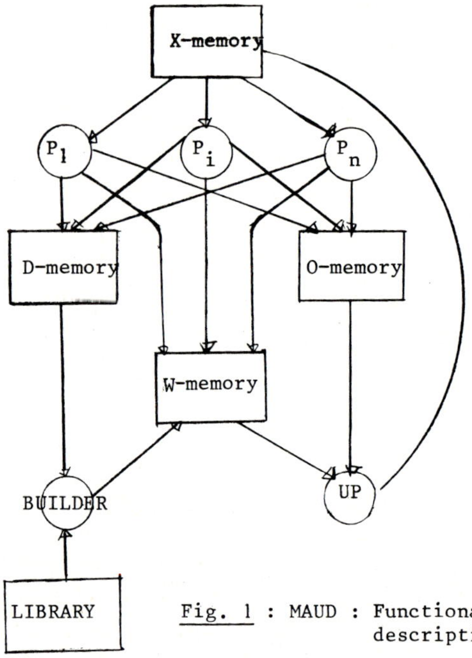

Fig. 1 : MAUD : Functional description.

An implementation of MAUD has been studied and realized using a ring of circulating memory which is both a mean of storage and a communication path. The processors are realized with conventional microprocessors ; they are distributed aroung the ring in front of the access points of the circulating memory (Fig. 2).

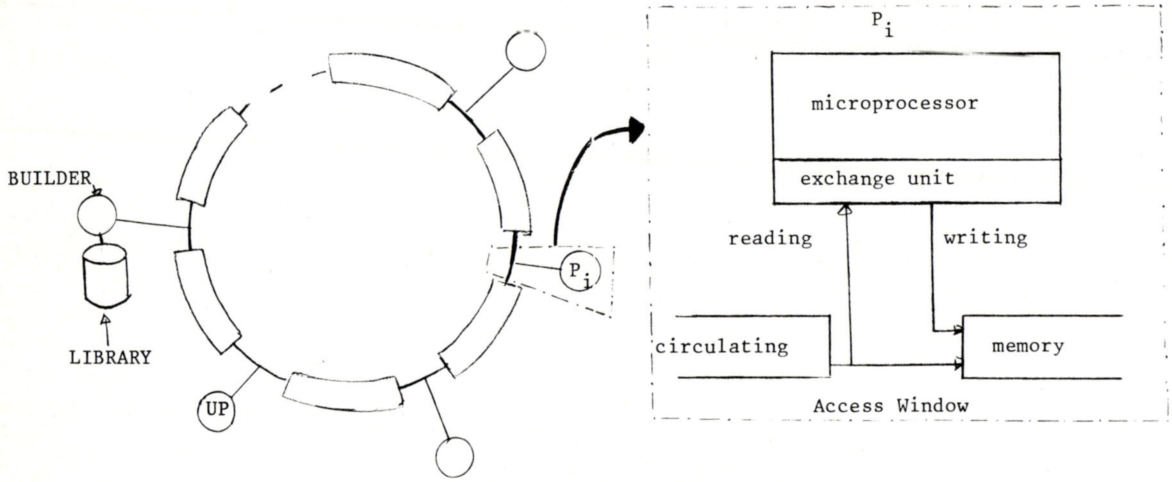

Fig. 2 : The implementation of MAUD.

III. THE UPDATING PROCESSOR

We have seen in the previous section that MAUD is a set of processors connected around a ring of circulating memory. Every processor can have simultaneous accesses to the circulating memory through an automatic exchange unit which has been described in [Gon 82]. In this section we shall look at the features of the specialized processor called "the Updating Processor" (U.P.) which must perform the management of the W and O memories.

III.1. The features of the Updating Processor (UP)

- Typically the U.P. must ensure two elementary fonctions with regard to our data flow model :

* The first one is the updating of Input fields of waiting blocks which are in the W - memory.

* The second one is to detect waiting blocks which have a full Input field, after each updating operation. In this case these blocks become executable blocks.

- In order not to slow down the different exchanges of the processors with the ring, we manage the circulating memory with an unburden policy. So all the blocks which cannot be used up by a processor are checked out of the ring. The output blocks and waiting blocks are stored in local memories of the U.P. processor named respectively W-Memory and O-Memory. Only executable blocks may be in the ring during several turns of the ring. The number of executable blocks in the ring is regulated by an other specialized processor called "Manager-Processor" which leaves in the ring a number of executable blocks equal or less than the number of free processors.

a) The updating of input fields

This operation consists to collect all the output blocks produced by processors which are terminating a block execution. For each couple (NC_i, VAL_i) present in this block, the U.P. processor must determinate if there is a waiting block in the W-memory which is waiting for it and then makes the transmission of VAL_i.

The following algorithm describes this operation :

Algorithm 1 : While Output block is not empty do
read (NC_i, VAL_i)
if* (NC_i, Nor Yet Calculated) $\in$ W-Memory
then • I-field$_j$:= I-field$_j$ – (NC_i, NYC)
• Detect if the input field$_j$ is full (see algorithme 2)
Else O-Memory = O-Memory + (NC_i, VAL_i)
endif
end while

* An associative W-Memory will fit very well for this searching operation.

The figure 3 shows the template of an output block and a waiting block. These blocks are fitted for slot size of the circulating memory which has been described in [Pet 80].

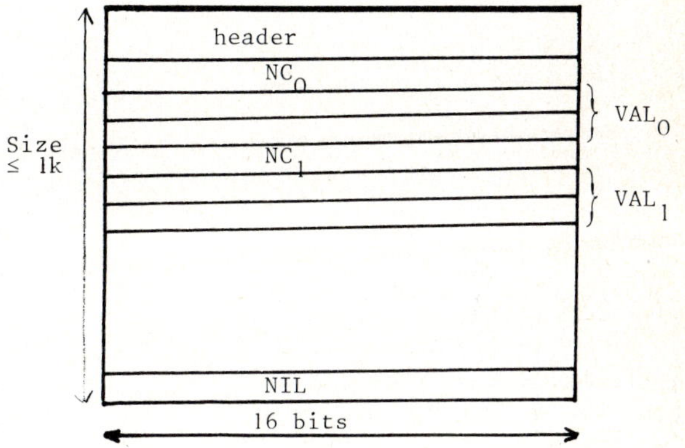

an output block

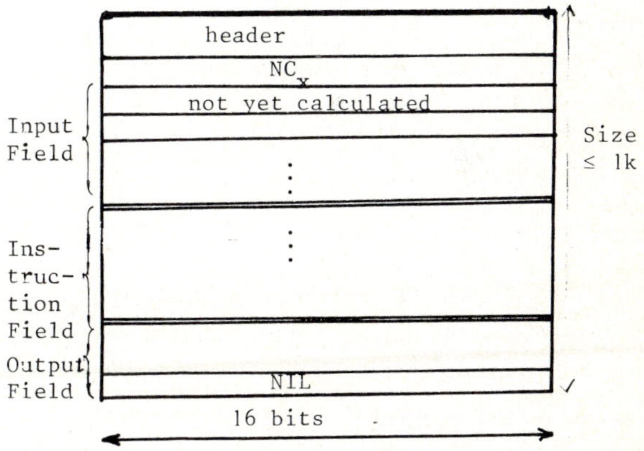

a waiting block

TYPE	NAME NB
slot number	

a block header

Fig. 3 : An output block and a waiting block.

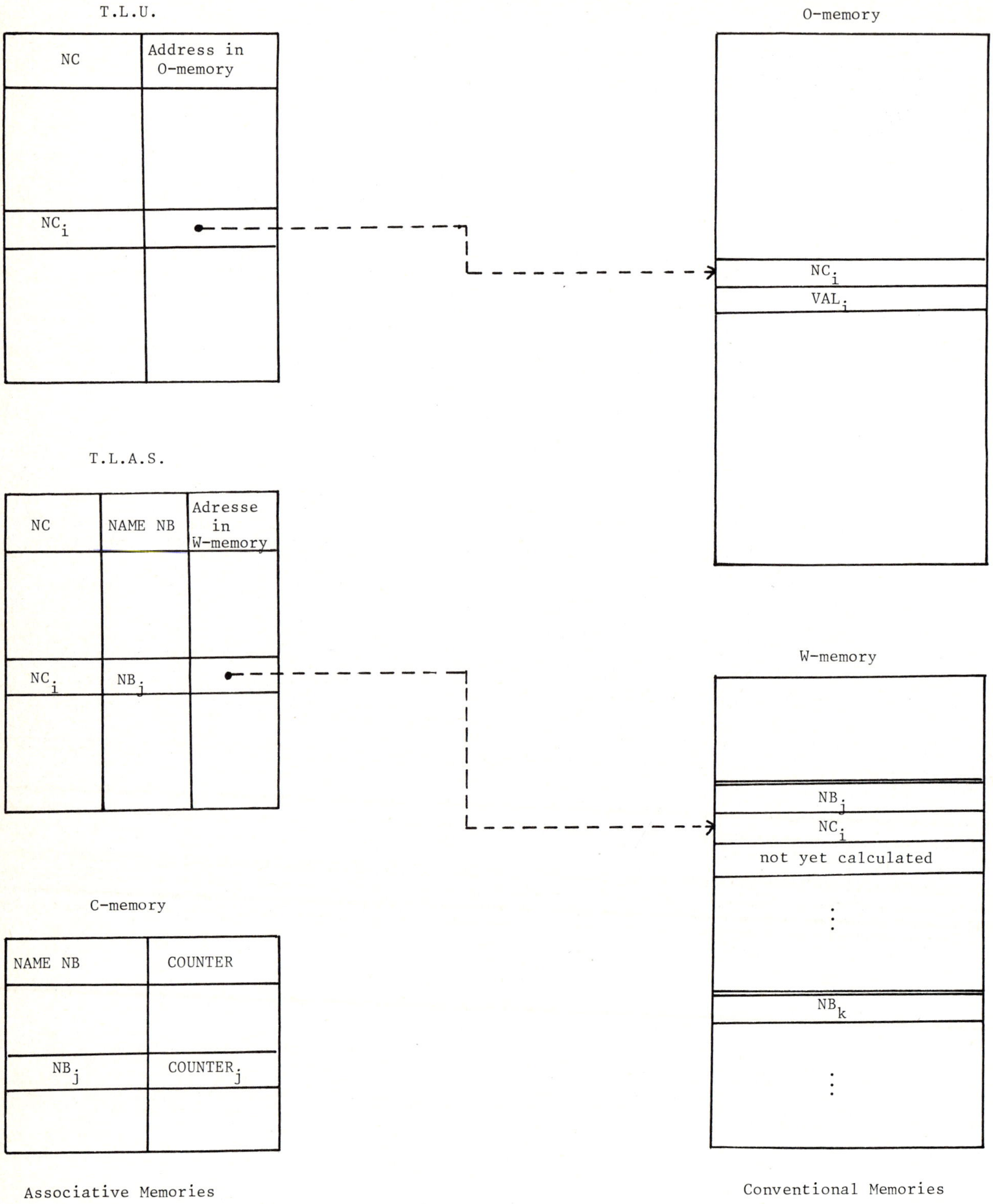

Fig. 4 : Memory Mapping.

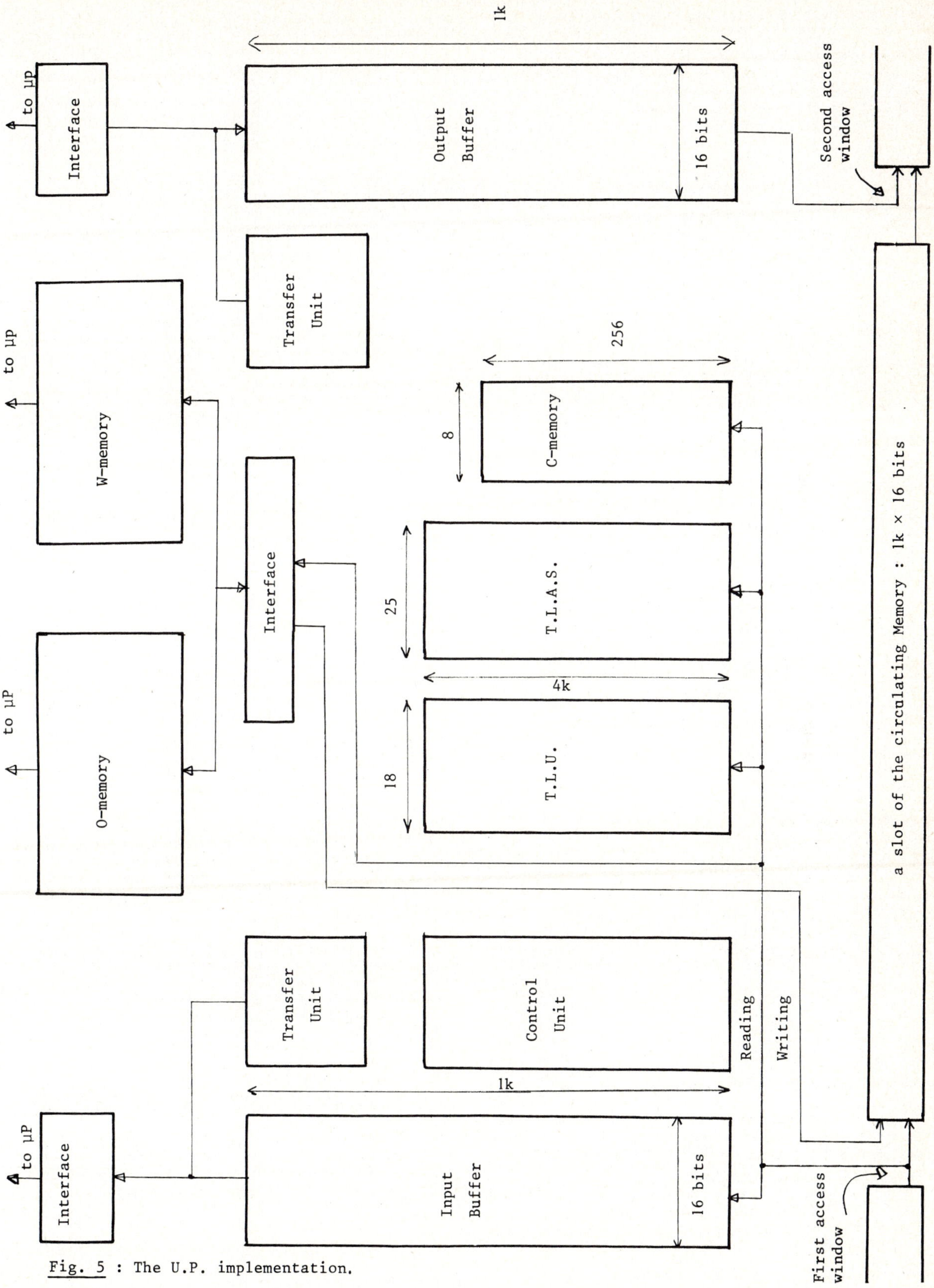

Fig. 5 : The U.P. implementation.

b) The detection of full input field

It may be possible that the last updating operation enables some waiting blocks to become executable blocks. The U.P. processor must perform the removing of these blocks from W-Memory to X-Memory. The algorithm 2 illustrates this operation :

Algorithm 2 : If Input field$_j$ is full
then W-Memory = W-Memory - waiting block j
X-Memory = X-Memory + executable block j
Endif

c) Conclusion

This section shows us that U.P. processor must perform associative accesses to do its job. The circulating memory used in our computer with its serial access allows easily associative accesses. This circulating memory has been designed to realize both :

- Communication tool between processors.
- Temporary storage mean for blocks.

In order to do the updating operation in real time, we shall use associative-memories to access the W-Memory and the O-Memory.

III.2. The architecture of the U.P. processor

This section describes the main characteristics of the U.P. architecture. We saw that the U.P. processor must collect both :

- Waiting blocks in W-Memory.
- Couples (NC_i, VAL_i) of output blocks which are stored in O-Memory.

These Memories are storage memories made of conventional memory. To make the updating operations easier for the U.P. processor we defined two associative memories (named T.L.U. and T.L.A.S.) in which the data NC_i are used to access the couples (NC_i, VAL_i) (or (NC_i, NYC)) which are stored in O-Memory (or W-Memory). The T.L.A.S. gives also the name NB_i of the corresponding waiting block. The third associative C-Memory uses as entries the names NB_i which are associated with a counter i. This counter is equal to the number of couples (NC_i, N.Y.C.) existing in the Input field of the waiting block whose name is NB_i. This counter allows us to know when an Input field of a waiting block is full. The figure 4 shows the architecture of these associative memories.

IV. THE IMPLEMENTATION OF THE U.P. PROCESSOR

Because the capacity of available associative memory does not exceed a few bits except for the ARAM described in [Tav 82] we must substitute them by high speed memories in which the data NC_i or NB_i acts for the address.

The figure 5 shows the implementation we have choosen for the U.P. This implementation is composed of 10 main units :

- a TLAS
- a TLU

} described above.

- an Output buffer
- an Input buffer

} which keeps temporarily information which are moved from the circulating Memory to the local Memory and vice-versa.

- A C-Memory which indicates the state of every waiting block present in the W-Memory.
- Two important storage memories, W-Memory and O-Memory.
- Two transfer Units which remove information.
- A control Unit which controls all the units.

a) The timing access of the Associative Memory

The Updating operations must be done in real time, i.e. the clock of the circulating Memory (1 Mhz) defines the Updating operation speed. In fact when a NC_i is detected in front of the access window of the U.P. processor, an associative access is made in either T.L.U. or T.L.A.S. depending on the type of the current block (either waiting block or output block). If the NC_i is present, then either a writing operation or a reading operation is made in the circulating memory during the next cycles. The figure 6 shows the timing access of the updating operation. The number of cycles needed in the second part depends on the length of the object associated to NC_i (Real, Integer, Single word, Double word, etc...).

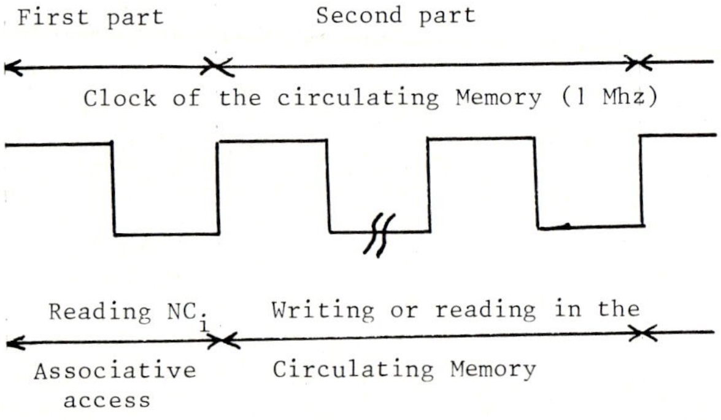

Fig. 6 : Timing of the updating operation.

b) Implementation of the T.L.U.

This memory gives us three types of information.

* The address in O-Memory where the (NC_i, VAL_i) has been stored (16 bits). This address is provided by the microprocessor of the U.P. which manages the free space of O-Memory and W-Memory.

* Two supplementary bits :
  - The first one is needed to indicate that a NC_i is present in O-Memory. This bit is also managed by the microprocessor.
  - The second one is set by an automaton when the NC_i is used during an Updating operation. This bit is useful to the microprocessor to make the free space management of the O-Memory.

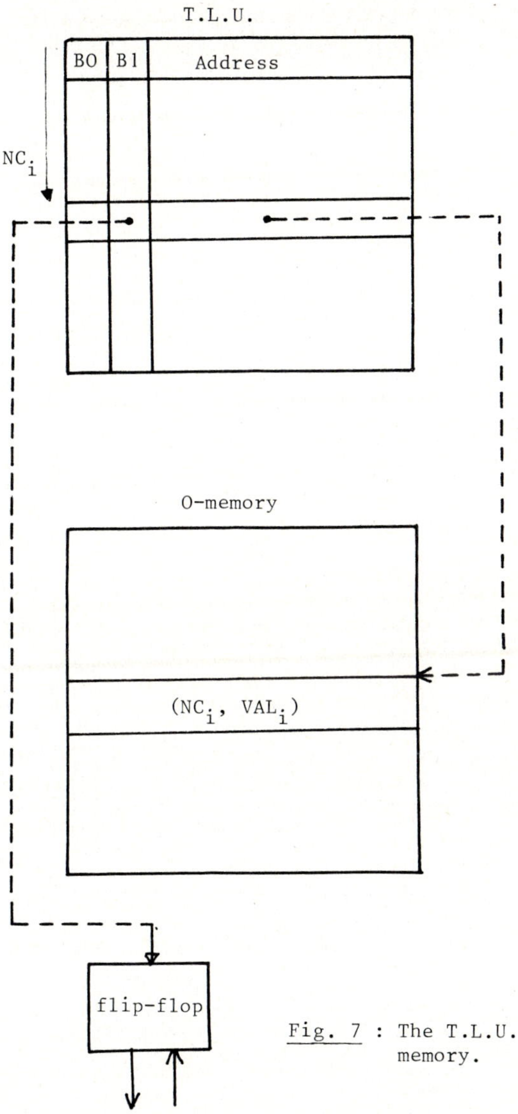

Fig. 7 : The T.L.U. memory.

Figure 7 shows the structure of T.L.U. in which the flip flop allows the control Unit to know if a NC_i exists in T.L.U. and so on to know if the current waiting block may become an executable block.

The table in Figure 8 summarises the part of the two supplementary bits.

Bit 0	Bit 1	Comments
0	0	The NC_i objet is present and available for an updating operation.
1	0	The NC_i objet is present in O-Memory but not available.
0	1	The NC_i objet is not yet present in the O-Memory.
1	1	

Figure 8

c) Implementation of the T.L.A.S.

- Three types of information must be stored in this memory (Figure 9).
  - The address of the couple (NC_i, NYC) in the W-Memory (16 bits).
  - The name of the waiting block in which NC_i stands (8 bits).
  - A bit which indicates if the NC_i object is or is not present in the W-Memory.

- The principle of this memory is described in the next :

  Each time a NC_i access is made, an output name NB_j is produced. This name selects one of the 256 counter values present in the C-Memory, which characterizes the state of the selected waiting block. An automaton loads this counter value in a physical counter and decrements by one its content.

As soon as the counter falls down to zero a flag is sent to the control unit which detects that the block is executable and may decide to insert it in the ring through the output buffer.

After this operation a writing operation updates the selected counter of the counter memory.

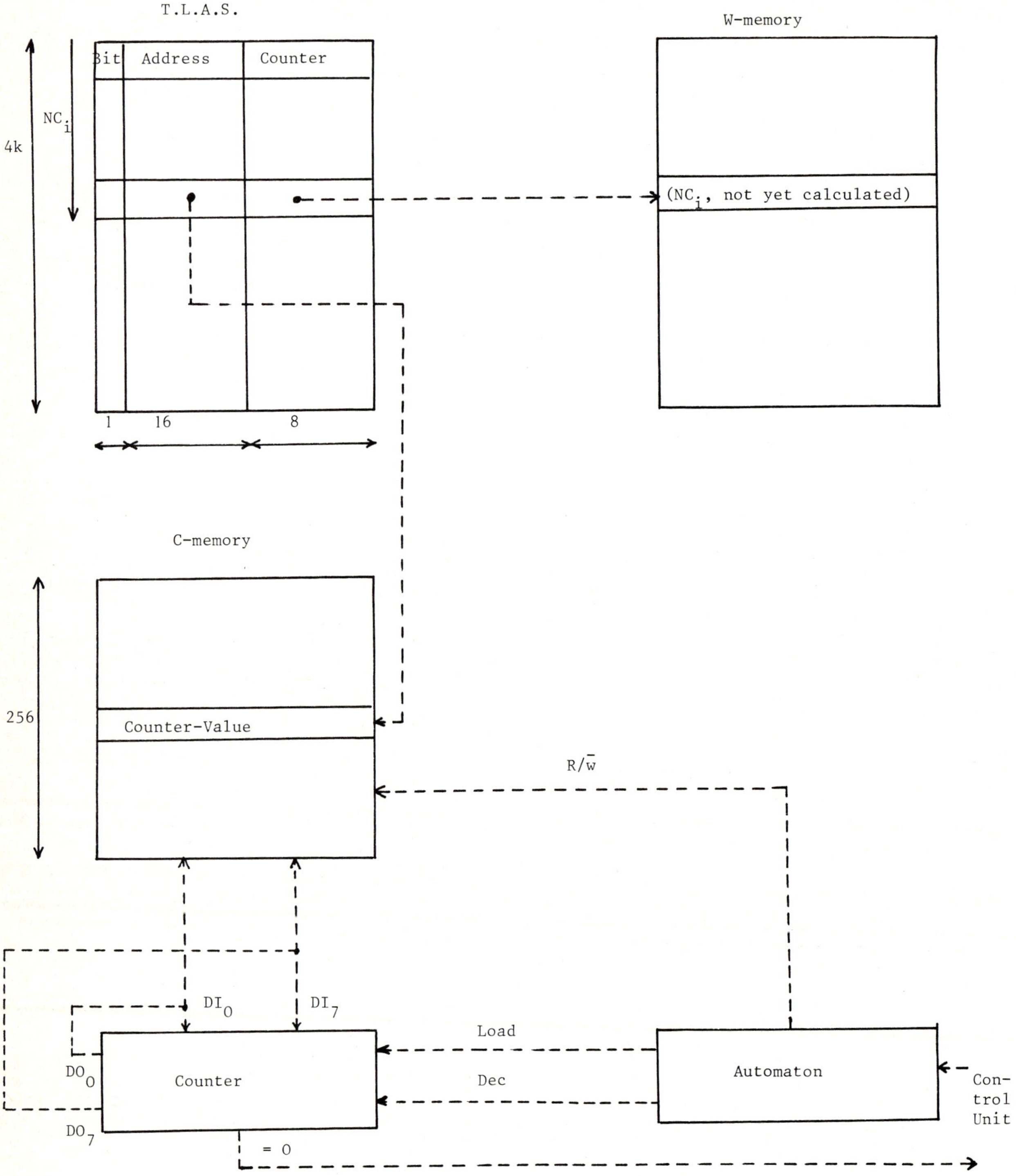

Fig. 9 : Implementation of T.L.A.S. memory.

CONCLUSION

In a data flow computer, the important problem is to check for ready operations : the unit which is responsible for that activity cannot slow down the activity of the execution operators.

In MAUD, the UP processor we described here performs updating operations at the circulating memory speed, i.e. in real time. So it cannot introduce delays in a program execution. Moreover, the chosen implementation easily allows modifications to implement other data flow models.

REFERENCES

[Den 79] DENNIS, J. *"The varieties of data flow computers"*. 1 st International Conference on distributed computing systems. Oct. 79.

[Gon 82] GONCALVES, G. *"An automatic exchange unit between a circulating memory and a microprocessor"* Euromicro Symposium, Haifa, Sept. 82.

[Lec 80] LECOUFFE, M.P. *"Traitement dynamique de programmes"*. Congrès AFCET Informatique, Nancy, Nov. 80.

[Lec 81] LECOUFFE, M.P. *"Architecture of a multiprocessor using data flow at a program block level"*. International Conference on parallel processing, Bellaire, Michigan, Aug. 81.

[Pet 80] PETITPREZ, B. *"A flexible circulating memory for communication in a multiprocessor"*. Euromicro Symposium, Londres, Sept. 80.

[Tav 82] TAVANGARIAN, D. *"A novel modular expandable associative memory"*. Euromicro Symposium, Haifa, Sept. 82.

[T.E. 68] TESLER, L.G. and ENEA, H.J. *"A language design for concurrent processes"*. Proceedings SJCC 1968.

Session G2:

OFFICE AUTOMATION

Chairman: P. de Bruyne
Bell Telephone Mfg. Co.
Antwerp (Belgium)

Office Automation is defined as the use of integrated electronic technology throughout the business office to improve the effectiveness, efficiency, and control of office operations. It is aimed at all levels of office workers, from chief executive to middle manager to secretary to clerk. It deals with information in all forms : words, numbers, voice and image.

In the past few years OA has graduated from "fancy word processors" serving secretaries and clerk-typists to full scale information systems. The professionals and managers using today's OA systems require a broad range of applications, only a few of which are addressed by WP.

OA had its roots in word processing, and today WP is still the functional core of any OA system, whether it is used by a secretary or manager.

Until recently, the only truly integrated OA systems were custom built by in-house groups using components from a variety of vendors. In 1983, we are seeing the integration of OA components from both a hardware and a software point of view. Several vendors now offer systems with multifunction workstations (offering WP, DP access, personal computing and graphics). And recent new product announcements herald the integration of OCR (optical character recognition), facsimile transmission, and laser printing. As a result, the OA components relating to text, data, and business graphics can be integrated successfully today with "off the shelf" systems.

Voice and pictorial image components are another matter. Several vendors offer digitized voice store and forward systems ("voice mail"), but they are not yet integrated with OA workstations, except in Bell Laboratory's experimental system, EPIC. Pictorial images can be captured digitally today on scanners (e.g., Xerox 1025 Graphic Input, IBM Scanmaster), and electronic "cut and paste" methods are available to combine pictures and text, but specialized equipment is required. And teleconferencing systems, be they freeze framer or full motion video, also require specialized equipment, although they can share cable with some local area networks.

Office automation evolution can be seen in two phases. First, the evolution of the separate components into truly integrated office systems, and then the emergence of new capabilities for those integrated systems.

The first paper in this session describes an office automation system, based on an object oriented model.

The second paper presents the concepts and a practical implementation of a system designed for supporting managerial planning, and decision processes.

MICROCOMPUTERS: Developments in Industry, Business and Education
D.R. Wilson and C.J. van Spronsen (eds.) / ©EUROMICRO, 1983
Elsevier Science Publishers B.V. (North-Holland)

Automated Office Procedures: an object-oriented system architecture

L. W. Bernhard InterFace Computer GmbH, Munich, FRG

Th. Kreifelts & G. Woetzel GMD, St. Augustin, FRG

The system consists of three major components:

1) INFIX, a standard workstation environment supporting multi-window, multi-process interaction with user/demon selected documents. The tools used to process the documents are syntax driven, using a "message" and "methods" approach similar to Smalltalk's. INFIX provides a uniform "message" oriented interface between user and document/tool, as well as to the surrounding system environment.

2) OFFICE, a file structuring system supporting tree-structured object files (= documents) in a sequential, byte-oriented file system.

3) OPL, a language system providing the means to describe office procedures which automatically coordinate individual workstation actvities into a single task. It supports concurrency and interactive process control in conjunction with the INFIX system.

The model described is implemented as a pilot version on a UNIX Operating System.

1. Introduction

With the exception of some experimental systems and such special application packages as VISICALC, office automation has almost exclusively focused its attention on word processing, i.e. typing tasks in the secretarial domain. A recent study indicates, however, that a major portion of the costs incurred in office activities falls upon groups other than the secretarial staff (see fig. 1). Nearly 60% is incurred by the specialized clerical, e.g. case workers, and customer service and staffs, followed by managerial staff with 25%. No more than 15% of the costs are ascribed to secretarial activities [11].

Why then are most systems aimed at the user group of least "significance" with respect to cost-benefit? One reason is that this group exhibits the least resistance to automation of their daily activities. This is not only a consequence of their familiarity with the keyboard. An oft overlooked study by the SRI determined that a major acceptance factor is the frequency with which the system can be usefully employed. Specifically, a 50% probability of acceptance requires an average usage of roughly 7 hours/week (see fig. 2). For secretarial work this proves to be no problem. As can be seen in fig. 1, however, the specialized clerk and manager requires support in a variety of organizational tasks, from data preparation, registration and interpretation, to decision making (appointments, production plans, etc) and communication, coordination and supervision of procedural tasks and responsibilities. This implies the need for broader, more complex systems, supporting a variety of specific tools and providing a means of coordinated communication among the individual tasks constituting the office procedures to be (semi-) automated.

A conservative estimate is that some 20 different applications must be supported to make such a system marketable. If such a workstation, including software, costs between $4000.- and $16,000.- (depending on the configuration), then each such software package must be sold (not rented!) for less than 200 dollars. In order to satisfy these market constraints, a practical and profitable system must be installed in the thousands and yet remain inexpensive with respect to distribution, modification and maintenance.

Fig. 1 Task distribution in a typical office environment

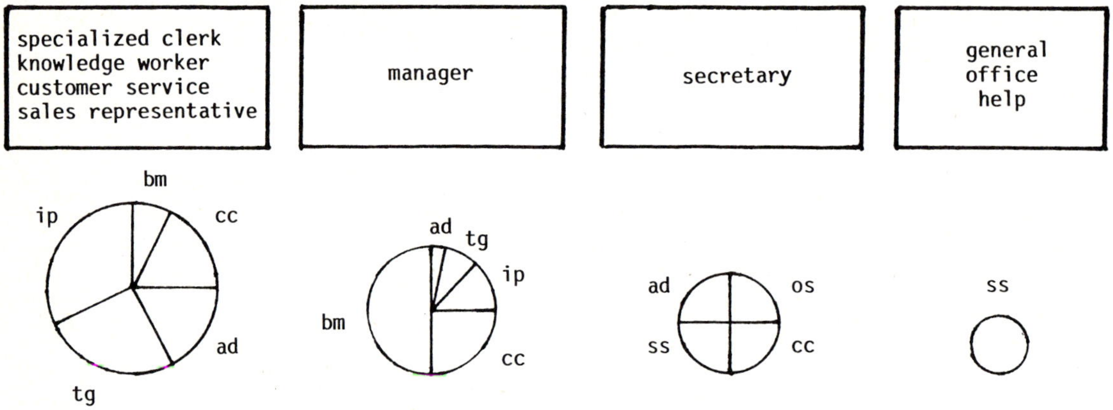

KEY

bm : business meetings & trips
cc : coordinating communications
tg : text, graphics, report generation
ad : administrative tasks & documentation
os : general office services (dictation, copymaking, etc.)
ip : information processing (data collection, statistical analysis, etc.)
ss : support services (mailings, collation, final drafting of graphics, etc.)

Fig. 2 Probability of acceptance of an office automation system in relation to frequency of use

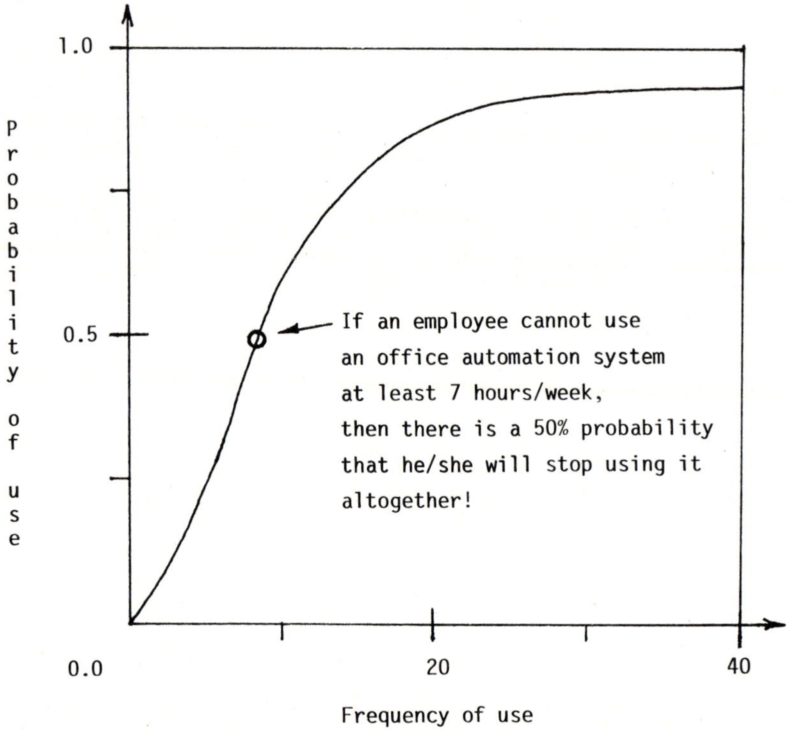

2. A software architecture for office automation

An office automation system for managers and special clerks must deliver support in the following areas:

- in user-system interaction (I= Interaction),
- in document management (F= Filing), and
- in inter/intra-office communications (C= Communications).

Now the average operating system does not satisfy the requirements in a manner suited to an office environment. What is needed is a software architecture which provides a user interface and system environment which can serve as basis for a wide variety of office applications of varying complexity and can run on a commonly avail- able operating system. It must provide a consistent data and functional model supporting

(I) interaction between the user and his task specific system tools via "virtual terminals",

(F) document management which preserves the syntactic structure of the objects typically produced and processed in an office environment (e.g. texts, forms, contracts, diagrammatic schedules and plans, etc.), and

(C) communications relating to entire "office procedures", which should be describable in a language suitable for procedure management.

The software architecture described here has been implemented as a pilot system named INFIX (Interactive Frontend for UNIX) in a joint effort by the Gesellschaft fuer Mathematik und Datenverarbeitung and InterFace GmbH. UNIX was selected as the underlying system environment for the following reasons:

1) its popularity and widespread availability for a variety of computers,

2) its support of multiple processes, and a pipe mechanism for interprocess communications,

3) its hierarchical, tree-structured file system, based on byte-stream "character" structured files,

4) its uniform, hardware independent system environment, making for relative ease of porting and ease of communication between remote applications via local and public networks.

3. The interaction model

The model underlying user interaction with the system is that of the display screen as "desktop". Just as a clerk might place several documents on his desk, the user fetches documents onto the screen. He fetches the documents into "windows" in the screen, whose size and position he may fix according to his needs/wishes. The INFIX system treats each such document and any of its associated "sub-windows" as a single "virtual terminal", dedicated to interacting with same. Via the virtual terminals the system can support independent processes to perform document processing. Typically the user selects a document of interest (by default the last one fetched) via explicit command [10]. The "active" document thus becomes the initial target for user commands. The actual processing of a document with respect to editing and the like is the task of specific tools. Normally, the user requests a particular tool to process a given document. As INFIX is an object-oriented system, such tools are usually of a syntax driven nature, and the documents are well structured (see 'The document model').

As may be seen in figs 3 and 4, INFIX performs two major functions related to coordination of communication between the user and the document/tool. On the input side, it assembles user input, i.e. requests for action, into "messages" (a la SMALLTALK [4]) which are placed in a "communications buffer" to be semantically interpreted by the document/tool. The interface to the tool itself is uniform, conforming to conventions of the UNIX system. On the output side, it transforms the (presumably modified) internal structure representation of the document into that of a so-called "terminal object" suitable for output in the window(s) of the "virtual terminal" on the real screen. The latter implies a multiplexing function on the part of INFIX.

It should be noted here that the user in fig. 4 is referred to as the "virtual user". This indicates that the interface may equally well communicate with a "demon" process [7]. Such a demon process interprets "dialogs" programmed in a language called PEN (Procedure Encoder [8]). The demon then mediates INFIX interaction with the user, automating portions of routine activities, such as filling out forms, prompting the user for input, positioning the cursor in predetermined fields, fetching necessary supplementary information for him, returning documents to the database, etc.

4. The document model

The document model upon which INFIX is based plays a vital role in the concept of information processing in the system. The term document generally refers to a tree-structured object, consisting typically of a well-defined collection of "sub"-objects. A given document is characterized by the class to which it belongs, e.g. a contract, a tax-form, a memo, a report, a chart, a net-diagram, etc.

For each such class of documents there exists a single document which defines the syntax of member documents of said class, i.e. the structure of their internal representation. It is noteworthy that such syntax documents themselves build a unique class, i.e. syntax documents! Furthermore, for alternative external representations of a given class of documents there also exist "format" documents, which define, for example, which objects of a given document class are "viewable" for given users, which are "modifiable", in what manner they are to be displayed, etc. (see fig. 5).

This model was selected for the following reasons. Firstly, as implemented, such tree-structured documents may be arbitrarily stored, as in UNIX, as a string of characters without any loss of structural information. Secondly, we feel that the best tools for non-programmer user communities are those which are syntax-driven and capable of intelligent interaction with the user [1]. Finally, as we shall later see, object-oriented tools are generally less complex and therefore easier to program, maintain and modify.

In traditional systems, where documents are essentially stored as minimally structured (scattered control characters and form markers at best) character strings, the tools must typi-

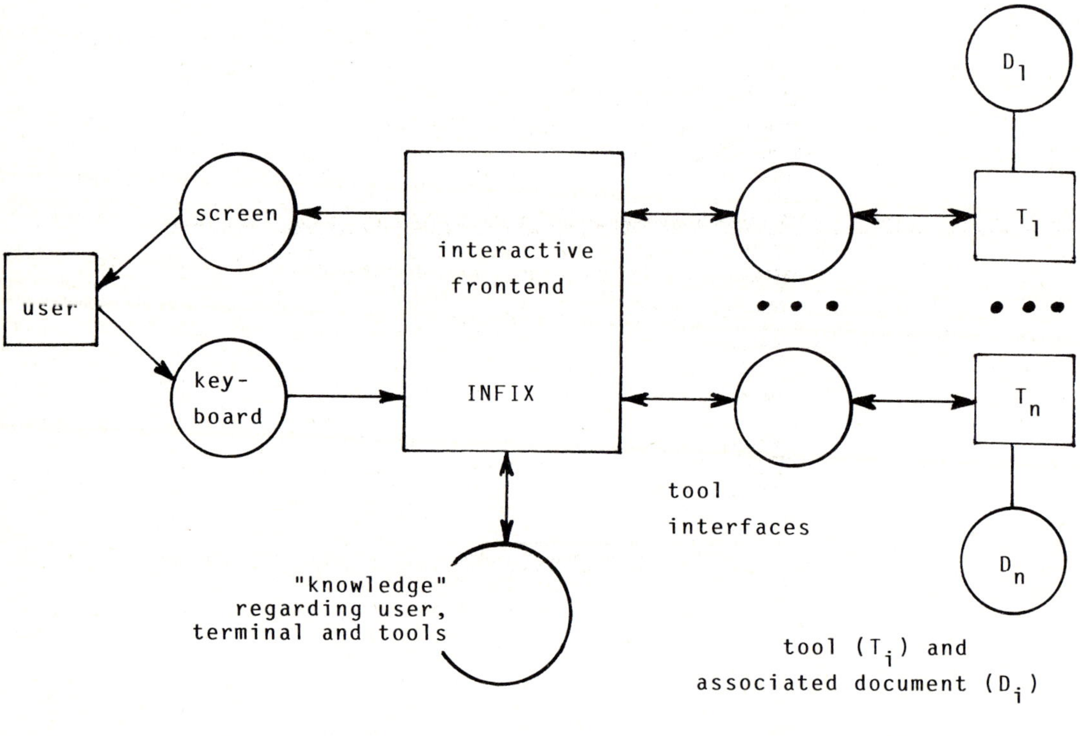

Fig. 3 INFIX: system diagram

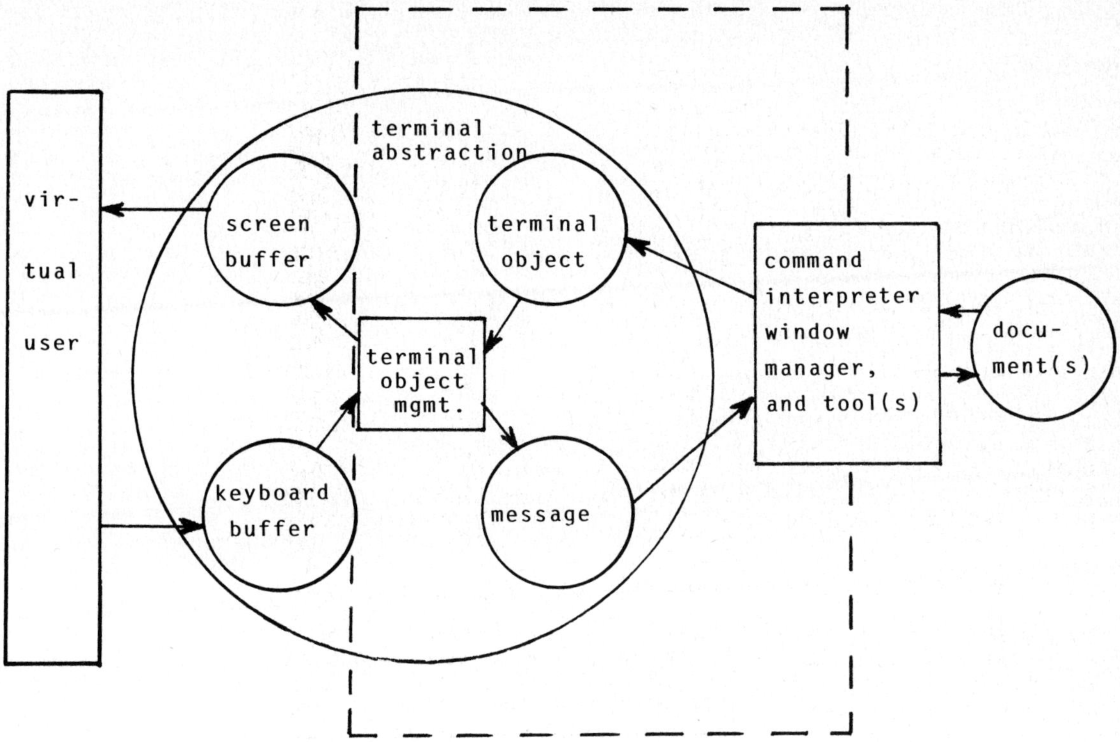

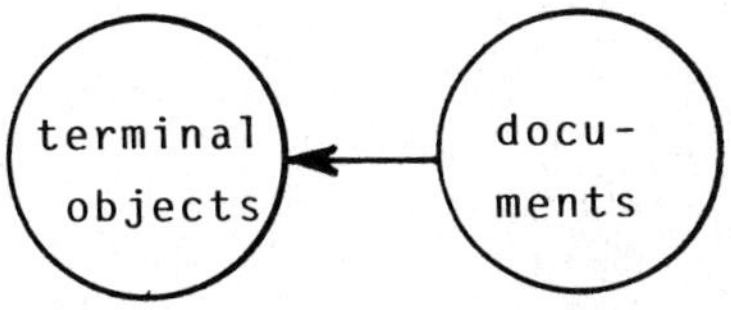

Resolution of "structure clash" [5]
(documents structure - line structure)

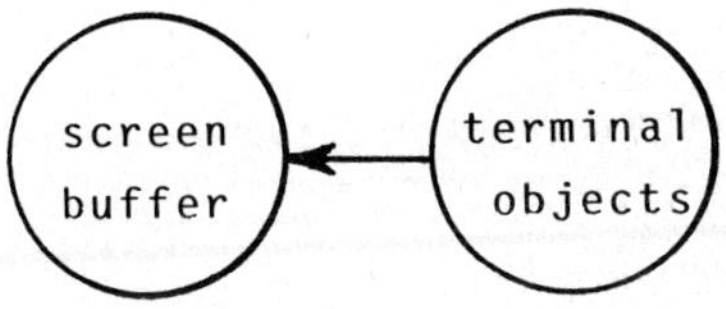

Multiplexing of the terminal objects in the windows

Fig. 4 Transformation of the data structures

cally resort to lexical and syntactic analysis prior to any semantic interpretation of user requests. This approach exhibits several weaknesses. Firstly, the required analyses make "tool making" a laborious and difficult task. Secondly, the required reconstruction of the underlying syntax of a document is a costly activity which is rewarded with a zero gain as soon as a document is returned to its essentially unstructured, stored state. Thirdly, in typical situations where a document is being repeatedly modified, the processing effort required to repeatedly redefine the syntax is prohibitive. Lastly, even the most sophisticated analyses founder when it comes to delivering meaningful error messages, and equally important, recovering syntactic integrity of a document when the user has made a, for the analyzer, grave error resulting in loss of context.

With the tree-structured document and its independent syntax description, tools may be constructed which require no interpreter whatsoever. The internal representation of the document is implicitly traversed (via cursor moves with respect to its external representation) and a given message (= user request) is "interpreted" by the well-defined object identified by the cursor in the document. Tools are thus reduced to a simple, canonical form. The constituent document object "active" upon reception of the message is identifiable via the predefined syntax.

The "toolmaker", given the knowledge of the syntax and the relationships defined therein, provides for the appropriate set of routines to respond to a well-defined class of potential messages for the given constituent objects of a given class of documents (= methods of the particular object class and type). The tool must merely branch according to the class and type of the "active" object to the appropriate set of methods. The semantics of the action to be taken are con-

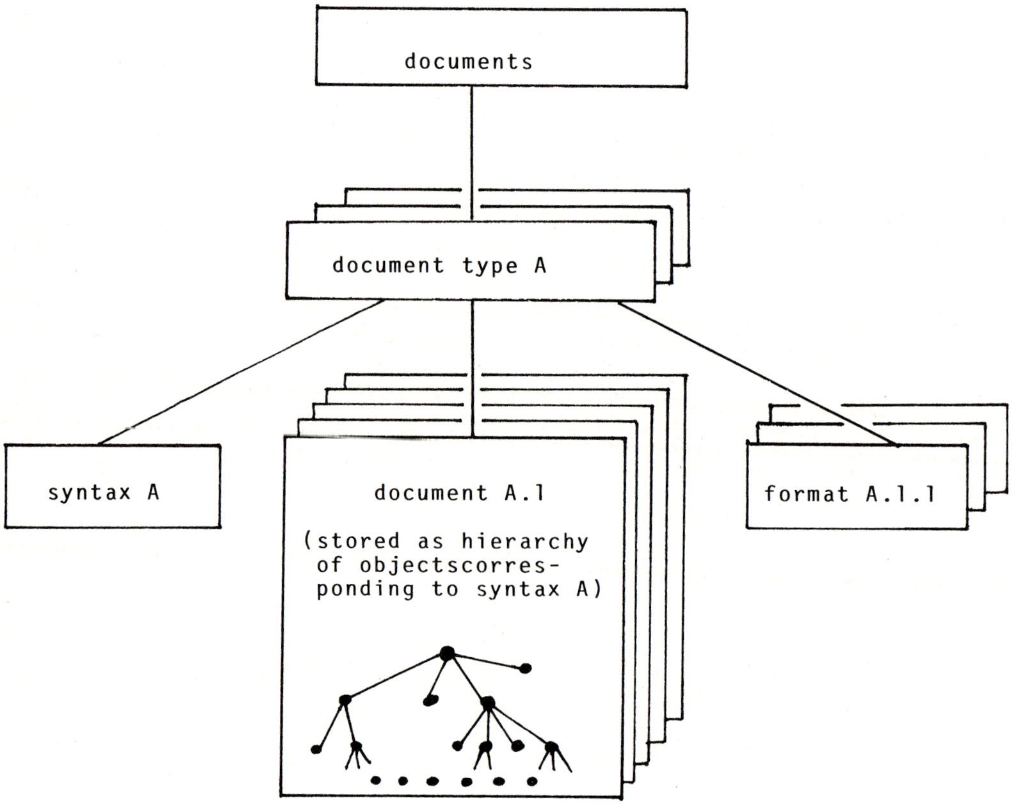

Fig. 5 Example of logical structure of the text document store

sistently well-defined. Moreover, the error messages can be tailored to the specific situation, as the context is always known. Thus TELEPHONE is a number, but it may not be multiplied! Recovery problems disappear, since errors are trapped prior to their being made. A bonus in this software architecture is the virtually automatic realization of data abstraction without the need for any artificial programming conventions.

There are some problems in implementing the tree-structured data model on systems like UNIX:

- The "featureless, randomly addressable sequence of bytes" [9] file structure is not inherently compatible with tree-structured documents.
- Conventional strategies for the external storage of tree-structured data is generally unsatisfactory for office systems, because frequent editing leads invariably to severe storage fragmentation and data delocalization. This can easily lead to "worst case" situations, where each action requires an external access, with the consequence that response time deteriorates to levels unacceptable for an interactive system.

On the other hand, a large portion of data processing in an office environment is sequential in nature, corresponding to a pre-order traversal of tree-structured documents. In order to optimize performance, the physical storage scheme for such trees should replicate the logical sequentiality of the traversal.

To resolve these seemingly contrary demands on the structure and storage of tree-structured documents we have developed OFFICE (Object Files For Interactive Computing Environments) file structures, to be superimposed on UNIX-like, sequential file structures. Fig. 6 illustrates a typical OFFICE file. OFFICE literally "flattens" a tree-structured file into a sequential form. The tree structure is preserved via internal, relative pointers. When the internal pointer of a document is moved through the tree, a stack maintains the pointer information of the nodes traversed. Thus even after repeated editing, the sequential characteristic of the pre-order storage (data locality) is retained. Insertions and deletions cause a minimum of text movement.

As can be seen in fig. 6, OFFICE currently recognizes the following classes of objects:

N = Nonterminals, i.e. subtrees consisting of Strings, Primitives and Nonterminals.

S = Strings, i.e. arrays of characters of unlimited length.

P = Primitives, i.e. "Words" whose contents depend upon their ultimately tool-defined interpretaion.

Every object has, in addition to its class, a type, which can be associated externally with a symbolic value and is coded internally as a numeric value (e.g. NAME, ADDRESS, ZIP). The class and type information is carried in the header of each object, as is the the relative pointer indicating the object's current length. As is shown in fig. 6, OFFICE files can be interpreted as regular expressions, helping to reinforce the formal specification and systematic testing of the tools designed to manipulate their contents. Furthermore, the functions used to implement the OFFICE files are the basic functions out of which the "tool maker" typically constructs the "methods" implementing the semantics of "messages" to given objects of a given document class.

It is interesting to note that the combined INFIX-OFFICE approach is virtually identical to the standard being suggested by the European Computer Manufacturers Association for future office information systems (see [2]).

5. The communications model

A major goal of office automation is not simply the automation of individual tasks, but rather the improved coordination of organizational productivity. The communications model developed in conjunction with the INFIX system is based on the observation that most tasks in a modern office environment are decomposable into a set of individual, often concurrent actions constituting an overall procedure. The establishment and coordination of these activities accounts for a significant portion of the costs attributed to "communication" in fig. 1. Typically communication between the participating parties involves an exchange of information either explicitly, in the form of verbal requests, memos, etc., or implicitly, as in a form delivered for approval, routine filling out, correction, etc.

Given a modern office, with workstations equipped with a number of specific software tools available to individual clerks and managers, the need is apparent for a flexible means to supervise and coordinate the development and dispatch of a variety of procedures [6]. The different "actors" or stations involved in a procedure must be provided with the necessary documents (no longer physical!) and signals, instructions, etc. to insure an orderly and logical carrying out of the actions dictated by a given task.

The following approach exploits the uniform interface to the UNIX system provided by the "shell" programming language. In our model a specific procedure is formally described in an OPL (Office Procedure Language). Such descriptions serve as standard procedures which may be incorporated in particular application packages. Insofar as the procedure is to be tailored to a specific organization, it might be "programmed" by a local specialist, or adapted from a general program for similar purposes. In general the OPL consists of two sublanguages:

1) a Coordination Procedure Language (CPL) to describe the data flow and the synchronization conditions between two actions, and

2) a Procedure Encoding language (PEN - see "demons" in section about interaction model) to describe the dialog between the user and his workstation tools to perform the necessary action. At the moment, the shell programming language serves as a less comfortable, tem-

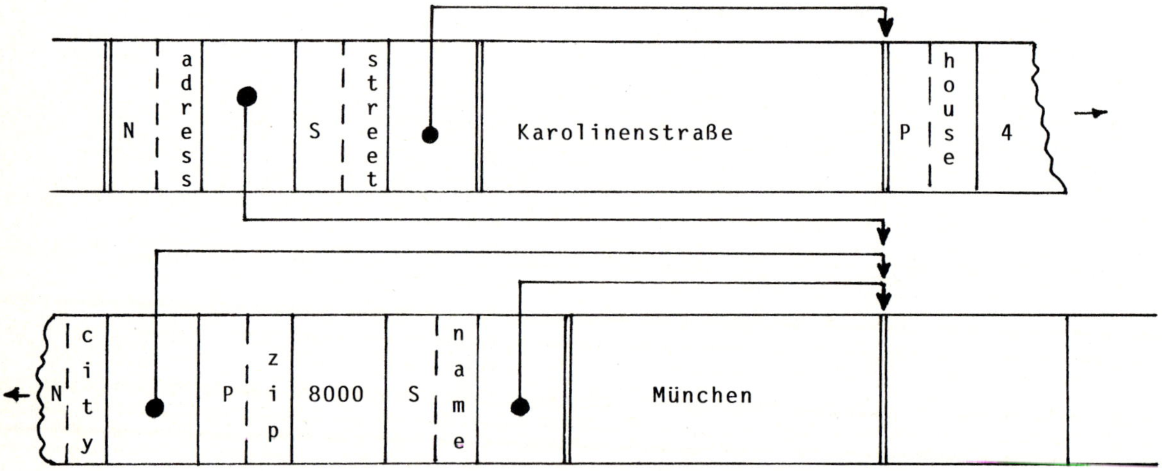


```
N (Address,
    S (Street, "Karolinenstraße"),
    P (House,   4),
    N (City,
       P (ZIP, 8000),
       S (Name, "München")))
```

Fig. 6 Internal structure of an object and its corresponding regular expression

porary substitute for PEN, which has been specified, but as yet not fully implemented.

In contrast to coordination procedures, PEN Procedures are user specific procedures. The PEN language is a means to locally automate the task of carrying out an action in a coordination procedure by partly (or fully) substituting a PEN programmed demon process for the user. In the following, we shall focus our attention on the CPL, as it defines the significant characteristics of the communications model, i.e. the descriptions of the actions, their causal dependencies represented by "procedure documents" needed and yielded by the various actions, and the workstations/persons ("roles" of a procedure) involved.

The model can be effectively represented by an acyclic graph with two sorts of nodes (boxes and circles), where the boxes correspond to the actions and the circles to "procedure channels", through which certain types of procedure documents are transferred from one action to another. Fig. 7 illustrates an example for the processing of orders received for merchandise. The action boxes are labelled with the "roles" to which they belong, the roles being essentially placeholders for persons responsible for the execution of the actions (in our example, clerks of the respective departments).

The procedure graph is to be interpreted in the following manner: Each action can be initiated after all its requisite documents have been produced, i.e. are available in the respective channels (incoming edges). The completion of a specific action yields one or more procedure documents to be deposited in the respective channels (outgoing edges) with like consequences for any actions dependent upon the foregoing. The procedure model may be formally based on a certain class of Petri-nets [6] (see also [3] for a different approach to modelling organiza-

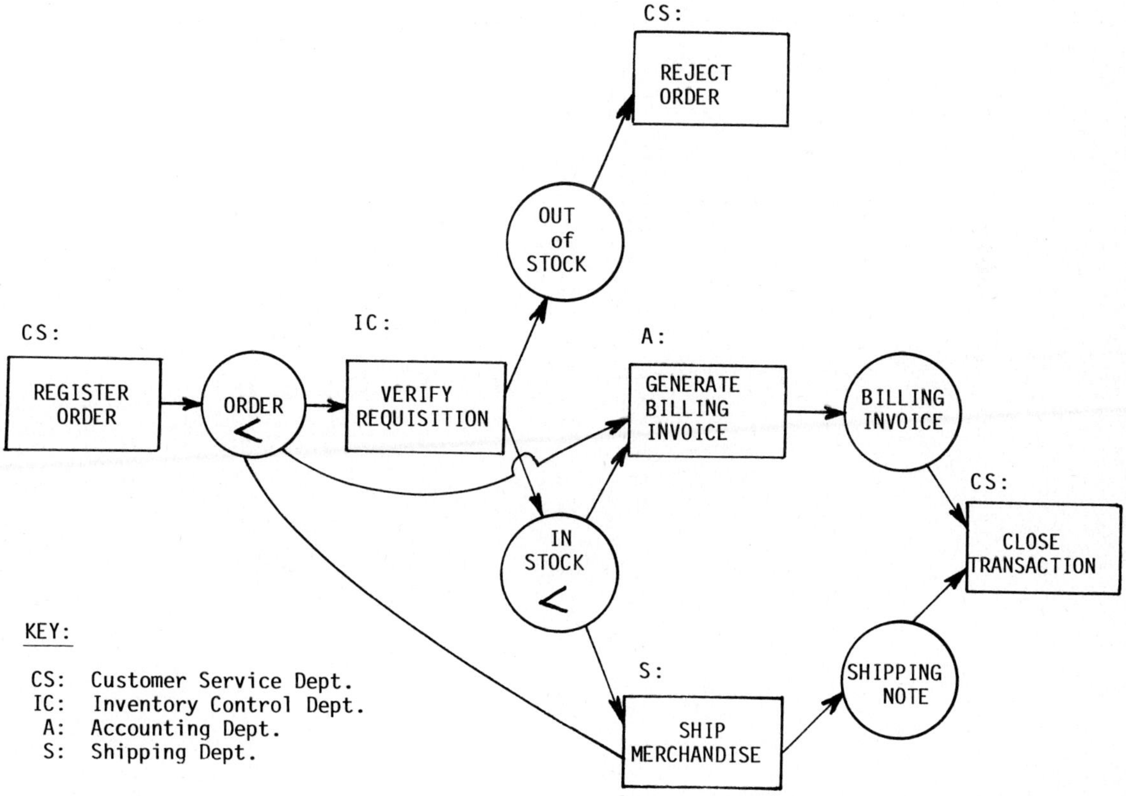

Fig. 7 Office procedure graph for merchandise order

Fig. 8 Processing a merchandise order

```
COORDINATION-PROC: merchandise order.

ACTIONS:            register_order, verify_requisition,
                    reject_order, generate_billing_invoice,
                    ship_merchandise, close_transaction;

ROLES:              customer_service, inventory_control,
                    accounting, shipping;

                    customer_service= register_order,
                                      reject_order,
                                      close_transaction;

                    inventory_control= verify_requisition;

                    accounting= generate_billing_invoice;

                    shipping= ship_merchandise;

DOCUMENTS:          order, in_stock, out_of_stock, billing_invoice,
                    shipping_note;

                    order= (customer, merchandise);

                           customer= (name, address);

                           name=     (first [string], last [string] );

                           address=  (no [int] , str [string] ,...);

                           merchandise= (item*);

                           item= (description [string] , quantity [int] );

                    . . .

PROCEDURE:          register_order          YIELDS order;

                    verify_requisition      NEEDS order
                                            YIELDS in_stock OR out_of_stock;

                    reject_order            NEEDS out_of_stock;

                    generate_billing_       NEEDS order, in_stock
                    invoice                 YIELDS billing_invoice;

                    ship_merchandise        NEEDS order, in_stock
                                            YIELDS shipping_note;

                    close_transaction       NEEDS billing_invoice,
                                                  shipping_note;
```

tions with Petri-nets).

The initiation of a coordination procedure is caused by some external stimulus, in our example the arrival of an order from a customer via mail or telephone. The procedure is started by assigning certain users to the roles of the procedure and by subsequently executing the initial action. The procedure ends with the successful completion of a final action. Decisions, i.e. actions which may yield alternative output documents, are graphically indicated by numbers on the outgoing edges. Procedure documents, which are needed by several actions, are supplied in sufficient numbers ("<" notation in the example of fig. 7). Note the concurrency of the actions "generate billing invoice" and "ship merchandise" in the example.

As can be seen in fig. 8, the CPL essentially describes such a procedure graph, along with the data structures of the procedure documents, in machine processible form. A CPL program consists of

1) the actions and document types constituting the overall procedure,

2) the causal dependencies of actions and document types (need/yield relation), and

3) the roles of the procedure representing the office workers participating in the procedure.

A computerized coordination procedure system will supply the following functions to the users of such a system. Firstly, users may specify coordination procedures and have them translated into an executable process structure. Secondly, users may initiate a given coordination procedure for a specific office task, keep track of its progress and receive its results along with a "history file". The system would then have to manage the control and data flow of the procedure. Thirdly, users need to be informed which actions are pending, they need methods to carry out those actions, and a way to use their own specific PEN procedures to this end.

In our implementation, there is a pseudo-user "coordinator" on every "system" of the workstation network, through which the users may access the coordination procedure system. The coordinator stores the coordination procedures thus far defined, and upon initiation of a procedure controls its performance. What constitutes a "system" of workstations with a separate coordinator depends on the network philosophy of the workstation network: It may be a single workstation, or a cluster of workstations with a special server for the coordinator. The relevant factors are sufficient security and availability of the coordinator machine.

Coordination procedures are types of cooperative processes (in a general sense), an initiated procedure is an instance of this type. Procedure instances are identified by the procedure name and a unique number. The coordinator has a working directory for every procedure in progress where the procedure deocuments of that procedure instance are stored along with the role assignment and the "history". The coordinator keeps a table of the pending actions for every user of his "system". An entry in such a table indicates that the user concerned has been assigned to the action identified in the entry and is therewith requested to carry it out. The coordinator supplies a basic tool for carrying out the action, which will in general present an actor (a user carrying out the action) with the input documents and receive (and typecheck) the output documents produced by the actor. The input and output documents of an action, together with this basic action tool constitute an abstract object "action document", which is to be manipulated during the execution of the action according to the action's rules.

Thus, there are basically four commands for interacting with the coordination procedure system:

1) defpro for defining a coordination procedure in the CPL language,

2) dopro for initiating a procedure,

3) lsjob for getting a list of pending actions, and

4) dojob for carrying out an action.

This set of commands will eventually be extended, e.g. by commands for getting a list of the procedures defined to date, for copying a procedure from one coordinator to another, or for inquiring about the state of a running procedure.

The connection of the coordination procedure system and the user specific PEN procedures is established by the following mechanism. Every time the coordinator makes a new action entry in a user's pending action table, a user defined procedure (currently a shell script) is executed, which may branch to the appropriate PEN procedure depending on the type of action requested. Note that these personal procedures may also use the commands of the coordination procedure system and, consequently, may even start a new coordination procedure as a "child process" of a requested action.

6. Conclusion

INFIX was originally implemented on a PCS Q68000 and then transported to a VAX and a PDP11/70. The ease with which we were able to port INFIX despite not only different hardware but different versions of UNIX itself, has deepened our conviction that the UNIX os is the ideal choice for commercial application systems. The pilot version of the INFIX/OFFICE system has been installed and the office system as described above is now being integrated into this environment. Although implementation problems have arisen, the fundamental models have remained unchanged and the system developers are confident that this approach will satisfy the demands described in the introduction. One feature which has clearly demonstrated great advantage is that of the canonical tools, i.e. the relationship between document structure and ease of tool construction. We have found that tool making can be conducted very much in the sense of "rapid prototyping", due to the modular nature of the individual tools.

7. Bibliography

[1] Burkhard, H., Nievergelt, J., "Structure-oriented Editors", in P.R. Wossidlo, ed., "Textverarbeitung und Informatik", Informatik-Fachbericht 30, (Springer, Heidelberg, 1980).

[2] European Computer Manufacturers Association: "Office Document Architecture: Second Working Draft for an ECMA Standard" ECMA/TC29/82/53 (October 1983).

[3] Holt, A.W., "Net models of organizational systems in theory and practice", in C.A. Petri (Ed.) Ansaetze zur Organisationstheorie rechnergestuetzter Informationssysteme (Oldenbourg, Muenchen, 1979).

[4] Ingalls, D.H., "Design Principles Behind Smalltalk", BYTE 6 (Aug. 1981) p. 286.

[5] Jackson, M.A., "Principles of Program Design", A.P.I.C.: Studies in Data Processing 12, (Academic Press, London, 1975).

[6] Kreifelts, Th., "Coordination Procedures: a model for Cooperative Office Processes", in Kommunikation in Verteilten Systemen - Anwendungen und Betrieb", S. Schindler, O. Spaniol, (Springer Verlag, 1983) p. 568

[7] Nagel, R., Schnupp, P., "Expected and Unexpected Acceptance Problems with an interactive Programming Tool", in "Pragmatic Programming and Sensible Software", (Online, Uxbridge, England, 1978), p. 321

[8] "PEN - Eine Dialog-Prozedursprache ('Procedure Encoder') fuer die Programmierung von rechnergestuetzten Dialog-Bearbeitungsablaeufen im Verwaltungsbereich", (Internal Specification, InterFace GmbH, Muenchen, 1982) p. 112.

[9] Ritchie, D.M., "UNIX Time-Sharing System: a Retrospective", Bell System Tech. Jrnl., V.57, No. 6 (July/Aug 1978) p. 1950.

[10] Schnupp, P.ET/X1150 - der Softwareentwickler am 'interaktiven Regietisch'", im 8. Jahrbuch der EDV (H. Heilmann, ed.), (Forkel Verlag, Stuttgart-Wiesbaden 1979), p. 204

[11] Sommerlatte, T., "Integration der Netze - Die Entwicklung verteilter multifunktionaler Systeme zum 'Office of the Future'", (CSMI, Muenchen, 1982).

MICROCOMPUTERS: Developments in Industry, Business and Education
D.R. Wilson and C.J. van Spronsen (eds.) / © EUROMICRO, 1983
Elsevier Science Publishers B.V. (North-Holland)

BUSYPLOT

Concepts and implementation of a microcomputer based generalized business data <-> business graphics interface

Ludwig Nastansky and
Hildegunde Peine
Business Data Processing Dep.
FB-5 Universitaet Paderborn
D-4790 Paderborn / W.Germany

Contents

Summary

In this paper we present concepts and practical implementation information about "BUSYPLOT", a system designed for supporting managerial planning and decision processes in computer based information systems. The BUSYPLOT model includes a microcomputer based software package for interactive manipulation of a varying set of multiple business graphics diagrams. The package is to be regarded as integrated tool. This within a concept where parts of remote data bases containing managerial data are loaded to locally available mass storage devices in a microcomputer workstation via data communication links. Information retrieval for the then locally available data base is technically supported using graphical diagram mapping of the data. This allows interactive visualization of implied patterns using a man-machine dialogue.

Host for BUSYPLOT can be a microcomputer with Pascal software development environment, and a Pascal run-time system capable of overlaying and chaining. This properties are given e.g. in the typical up to date CP/M-80 workstation, including 64 kB RAM, two diskette drives, and communication ports. A graphical display unit is used for visualization of the interactively produced and abandoned diagrams. The hardware specifications necessary for this display device can range from color graphic capabilities at low/high resolution to ordinary business environment CRTs with character based resolution allowing visual attributes like highlighting or reverse video.

Keywords

Business Graphics, CP/M Microcomputer, Visualization, Pattern Retrieval, Information Systems, Pascal, Man-machine Interaction

1. Introduction

The development of the business graphics package BUSYPLOT is motivated by the need of improving communication tools for users of computer based information systems in the business environment. It is basically designed for purposes where it is necessary to retrieve information patterns in data bases containing large quantities of detailed business oriented data. BUSYPLOT has been developed for using a microcomputer workstation for the information retrieval process as well as the graphical visualization of the retrieved data. Thus, the microcomputer has a dual task. It has to support the communication with the remote computer system resources where the data bases are kept. And, it has to perform local diagram processing, this process being basically man-machine interaction by its intended purpose. The graphs are interactively displayed on a locally available visual display unit.

Computer graphics provide visual communication channels between man and computer which are superior for pattern recognition processes performed upon numerous data underlying managerial decisions. This is especially true when compared with the character based presentation of tables of numbers or structural items. The visual perception quality can be considerably enhanced by additional use of color /ROBERTSON/.

In the last years, a variety of computer based graphic concepts has been developed to support the graphical visualization of business data. It is difficult, if not impossible, to characterize these approaches using a simple unifying classification scheme. This is because the structural properties of these different business graphics concepts are quite complex and made up of items as inhomogeneous as:

A (Virtual) Graphic concepts:
- + general structure of graphic model;
- + generated shapes;
- + visual attributes;
- + graphic primitives;

B Hardware implementation:
- + general system host: mainframe-, mini- and/or microcomputer environment;
- + implementation and distribution of graphic processing in hardware, firmware and/or software;
- + devices for graphics: display, printer, plotter, camera reproduction;
- + high, low vs. character based resolution;

C System interfaces:
- + stand-alone, set of general graphic driver routines, embedded graphic commands in higher level languages, interconnection through file communication;
- + all-purpose graphic concepts vs. specialized graphic enhancements in individual application environments;

D Application environment:
- + User interface: batch type vs. inter-active; for the latter: command-driven and/or menu-driven;
- + presentation graphics, decision preparation and/or (interactive) pattern retrieval.

These items, as seen primarily from a business application environment rather than computer graphics, still need to be specified in more detail to become operable. We have experience with such different concepts like the microcomputer based general interactice color graphic system IGS /IGS/, or the specifically business graphics oriented and CP/M based GrafTalk /GRAFTALK/, and the more mainframe implemented ISSCO system /VINBERG/.

2. Design Concepts

Summary. Using the above outlined scheme the basic properties of BUSYPLOT could be outlined as follows:

A The model is designed for interactive manipulation of a varying set of multiple business graphics diagrams, primarily in form of bar charts. The visual attributes which can be used are colors, gray shades, or character based graphic symbols, depending on the visual display unit hardware. Especially, the graphic processing allows selection of data to be visualized, ranging and scaling, assigning visual attributes, frame editing of charts, and arbitrary mapping of a changing set of diagrams onto the display. BUSYPLOT works with a virtual terminal concept allowing flexible simultaneous representation of diagrams on standard cursor-adressable CRTs.
B System host is a CP/M microcomputer environment with communication interfaces to remote data bases. Graphic processing is completely done within the BUSYPLOT software package. However, if firmware graphic primitives are available processing like e.g. vector-plot and rectangle-fill can be done outside of BUSYPLOT to increase speed. Due to the implemented virtual terminal concept images produced by BUSYPLOT can be mapped on a variety of displays with different characteristics. Terminal drivers are implemented for some standard B&W CRT-terminals with character resolution and an 8-color CRT-terminal with low resolution graphics.
C BUSYPLOT is principally designed for integrated use in a business environment where data bases produced in different application areas are available. In this context, BUSYPLOT provides a stand-alone tool to interactively retrieve structures and patterns out of these data using graphic mapping to diagrams. Communication is done by means of a data

file based concept for data transfer.
D BUSYPLOT is menu-driven. The interactive structure supports decision preparation by giving various possibilities to rearrange the process of mapping data to a set of charts.

<u>Workstation</u>. The typical environment for performing the data analyzing process by use of the concepts embedded in BUSYPLOT is an independent microcomputer workstation with data communication interfaces /NASTANSKY/. The data transfer process can be done e.g. via a local area network, or a point-to-point data communication link giving the microcomputer access to remote data bases. An analyzing session consists of loading necessary parts of the data base into mass storage devices available in the local microcomputer workstation. Thereafter, the pattern retrieval process will be performed locally using the available parts of the data base.

Within this perspective application environment we have already developped the characteristics and software for the visual interface and the underlying data model. We are working on an interactive scheme supporting the extraction process for a variety of data bases. There is no doubt that this appears to be a difficult problem in terms of finding a balance between such concurring aspects as e.g. generality for applications, user friendlieness, and performance. On the other hand, we do not realize a principally alternate and superior architecture for solving the intended interactive pattern retrieval process.
The data-interface problem has to be solved in any case in every computer-based information system where planning and decision tools are applied to support the managerial process. We have gained the impression that quite often in management application packages a rather inadequate balance is implemented concerning feature spaces like:

- general vs. special application,
- flexibility vs. "one-purpose" design,
- versatile vs. unchangeable interfaces between application packages and data bases,
- pre-formatted information supply using periodical batch processes vs. unpredictable information demands, concerning structure as well as time,
- management science related intelligence in the processing algorithms vs. intuitive straightforward heuristics,
- amount of information details vs. aggregate informations,
- company environment during the develop-ment period of the package vs. environment during the production period,
  or
- costs for bringing a package to work in the organization vs. gains by use of the package.

These problems are ubiquitous, and it appears naive to assume they are simply to solve. But we have the feeling that it is worth while to put more emphasis on developing application environments which provide flexible interactive means for users to retrieve data from data bases containing managerial informations. At the front end of this retrieval process simple graphical visualization of the data can help the user to gain insights for decision preparation which are otherwise not available. If the human perception ability of the people performing this pattern retrieval by structured viewing should not be sufficient intelligent software based tools can be added. But this seems to be a second step only possible when the first one of flexible retrieval is solved.

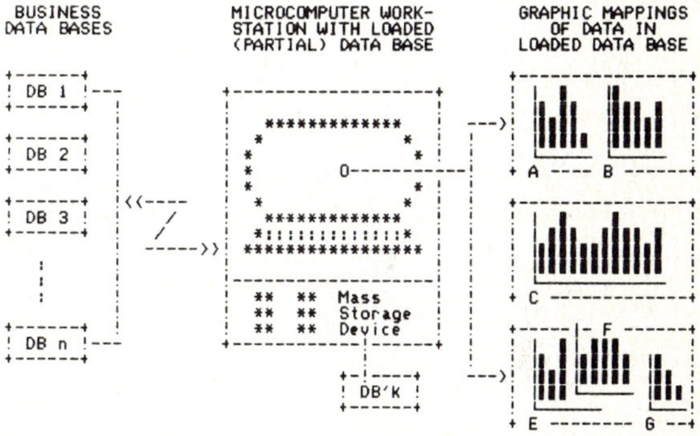

<u>Fig. 2-1</u>: Microcomputer workstation environment for BUSYPLOT

There are several developments in the microcomputer area which employ the kind of architecture intended with BUSYPLOT as well. It seems as if analogous schemes should come in widespread use in the next future. Recently designed microcomputer systems include approaches using generalized diagram visualization as important and integrated part of the user interface as well as underlying data models, e.g. the Grid-Compass workstation and the Apple-Lisa system /GRID; WILLIAMS/.

Fig. 2-1 shows the principal structure of the workstation environment used for BUSYPLOT. Given the remote data bases DB-1 through DB-n parts of DB-k are downloaded forming the active data base DB'-k for the microcomputer workstation.

Three mappings of the data included in DB'-k are shown as examples. Chart F is symbolized to be superimposed on top of chart G representing perhaps an enlarged part of chart G.

3. Graphic functions of BUSYPLOT

31. Structure of generated business graphics

BUSYPLOT allows business data to be graphically represented as two dimensional bar-, curve-, or symbol-charts, as usual the x-values (or independent variables) relating to the horizontal axis and the y-values (or dependent variables) relating to the vertical axis.

The actual representation of the desired graphical patterns diverted from the underlying data is mapped into a window called "plotting area" (Fig. 21-1). Scaling within the plotting area is defined in terms of a set of world-coordinates associated with the user data.

```
+--------------------------------------------+
! title of diagram      "EXPLANATION FRAME"  !
!                                            !
! title y-axis                               !
!                                            !
!   xxx   +----------------------+           !
!    :    !       "PLOTTING AREA" ! legends   !
!    :    !                      ! of        !
! y-scale !                      ! y-lists   !
!    :    !       add'nal legends            !
!    :    !                      !           !
!   xxx   !                      !           !
!         +----------------------+           !
!          xxx ... x-scale ... xxx           !
!                                            !
!         title x-axis                       !
!                                            !
+--------------------------------------------+
```

Fig. 31-1: BUSYPLOT diagram consisting of explanation frame and plotting area

The plotting area is surrounded by an "explanation frame" holding text information like the title of diagrams, the axes' labels, etc. in "text fields". For simplicity of use, the positions of these text fields are pre-assigned, with the exception of "additional legends" to be cursor-positioned arbitrarily within a diagram. The size of the explanation frame can be manipulated interactively. As a matter of fact, the user can shrink it to non-visibility, e.g. if multiple charts with repeating legends and homogeneous scales are to be shown simultaneously. The explanation frame holding the plotting area is defined in terms of a character based coordinate system.

Explanation frame with embedded plotting area form the graphical object BUSYPLOT-"diagram" which can be mapped onto arbitrary positions on the visual display unit hardware. The interleaving is performed using a 1:1 transformation between the character-based diagram outlay and a character-based normalized device coordinate system. If graphic mode is available on the visual display unit, allowing higher than character resolution, the plotting area can be be defined in terms of a pixel oriented coordinate system. If the device viewport is not sufficient to hold an entire diagram object the BUSYPLOT-software performs clipping at the physical edges of the visual display unit (Fig. 31-2). E.g., the dotted parts of projection B' of diagram B are non-visible and result of the clipping process. Thus, within BUSYPLOT a mechanism is provided to "pan" larger diagrams.

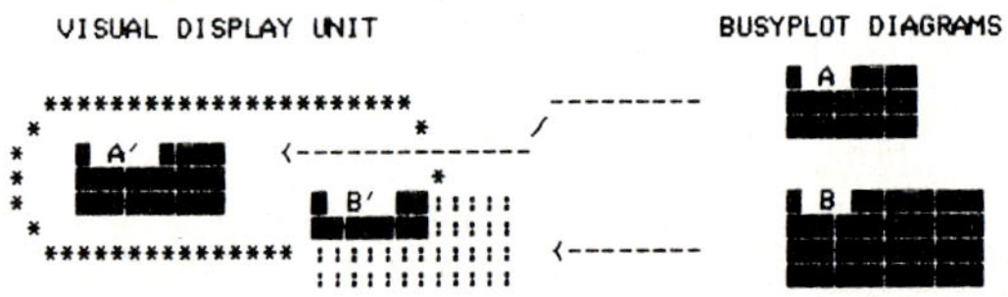

Fig. 31-2: Clipping mechanism for BUSYPLOT diagrams

Entities associated with the x-axis can be assigned quantitative as well as qualitative attributes. Quantitative x-values could be e.g. time periods, scales measuring production units, or money, qualitative x-values could include items like product names, the names of employees, plant identifications, or month names.
Entities associated with the y-axis are measured using a quantitative scaling scheme only. Choosing an appropriate range and restricting the feasable values to discrete ones various kinds of qualitative modelling are possible in the y-direction as well.

Up to five distinct phenomena related to the items associated with the x-axis can be represented within one diagram. Thus, a set consisting of up to five y-values can be attached to each of the x-values. Y-values describing one specific phenomenon (the turnover of a product measured over a sequence of years, e.g.) are called a "y-list". Formally speaking, it is possible to map up to five distinct y-lists onto one BUSYPLOT diagram.

The following examples are arranged to give an impression of the variety of different diagrams as they can be created with BUSYPLOT.

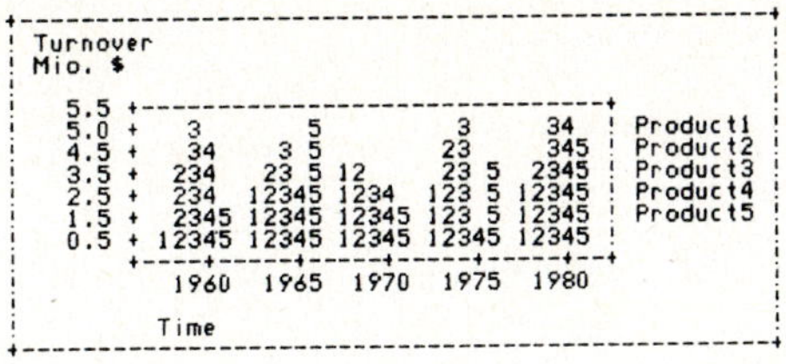

Fig. 31-3: Bar-chart with five y-lists

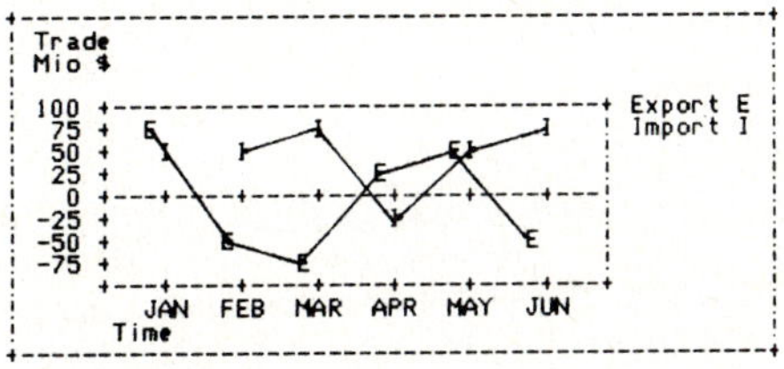

Fig. 31-4: Curve-diagram showing two distinct phenomena

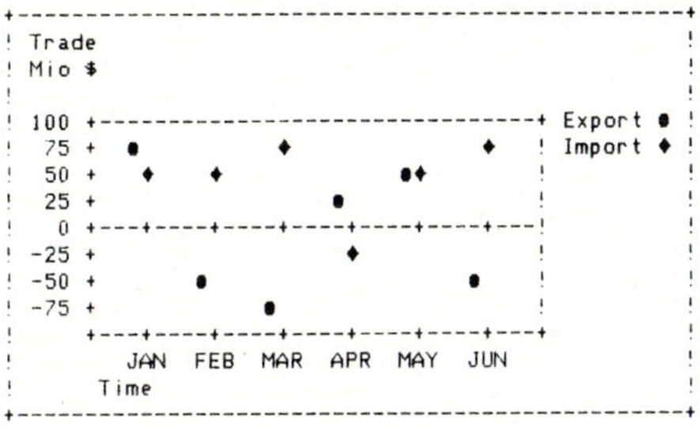

Fig. 31-5: Symbol-diagram

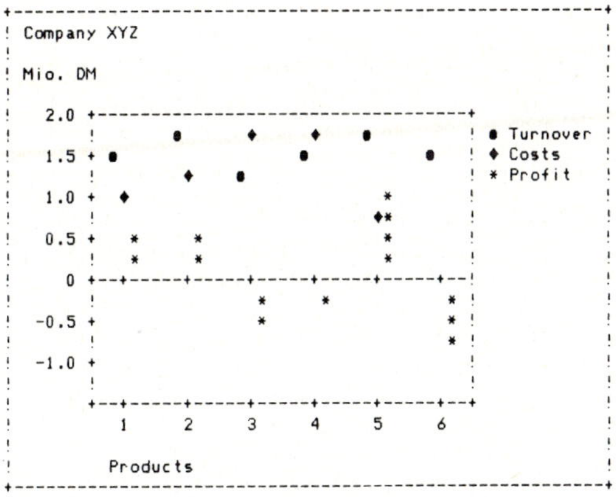

Fig. 31-6: Mixed diagram (for the underlying data structure see Fig. 44-2 and 44-4)

32. Supplied functions for generating business graphics

Concepts. In order to explain both, the manner how diagrams are created and the functions of BUSYPLOT, some terms and concepts should be outlined. Especially, it is worth while to explain the use of terms like "problem-data", "diagram-data", "input-program", and "output-program".

The user has to deal with two kinds of data to create a complete diagram. At first, there are the data base derived data which are to be presented graphically. Secondly, we have to cope with the parameters that describe the visual characteristics of a diagram. The first type is called "problem-data", the second "diagram-data". The files containing these informations are called "datafile" and "plotfile" respectively. BUSYPLOT offers functions to manipulate both types of data.

The available and implemented version of BUSYPLOT provides processing functions distributed over two distinct modules as seen from the user's point of view.
In one module, BUSYPLOT offers extensive menu-driven functions to enter, change, and/or delete problem-data as well as diagram-data. The unit containing the collection of these functions is called the "input-program". Especially, this module can be used for stand-alone graphical data manipulation purposes.
The second module supports the various functions within the BUSYPLOT concept to display locally available data on the visual display unit. Above all, the user can select different output options and manipulate the visual mapping process, or simply plot one diagram after another. All these functions are embedded in a unit called "output-program". Due to the aim of providing a means to interactively manipulate sets of y-value lists and sets of diagrams the menus for controlling these functions are designed to be very compact consuming little space on the visual display unit (if dialogue control is not performed using a separate console device; see 41. below).

Dialogue functions. Given the limited space in this paper we have chosen to outline the available functions showing the respective menu options within the BUSYPLOT input-program as they appear on the console screen.
The functions can be accessed using a selection-menu as anchor. Fig. 32-1 shows this menu giving an overall impression about the structure of the

graphical design process.

```
+---------------+
! DIALOG-MENUE  !         Explanation:
! ------------- !         --------------------------------------
!   Function:D  !   =>    Selected function
!               !
! -Plotfile---- !   =>    Functions concerning diagram-data
!  Design     D !    >    new diagram (creation of a plotfile)
!  Change     C !    >    change of an existing diagram (plotfile)
!  Erasure    E !    >    deletion of a plotfile
!               !
! -Datafile---- !   =>    Functions concerning problem-data
!  Input      1 !    >    creation of a datafile
!  Change     2 !    >    change of a datafile
!  Erasure    3 !    >    deletion of a datafile
!  Extension  4 !    >    insertion of records into a datafile
!               !
! -Program----- !
!  > Picture  P !   =>    program control transfer to output-program
!  > Quit     Q !   =>    termination of BUSYPLOT
+---------------+
```

Fig. 32-1: Selection menu for input-program functions

Designing a diagram. The user has complete control over the designing process of a diagram. He/she can specify diagram-data defining the size of the diagram, visual attributes for the plotting area and the explanation frame, text-fields, axis length, and the graduation of the axes. Furthermore, the relation between diagrams described this way and the associated problem-data has to be established.
The diagram-data the user has to input are subdivided into five blocks of data, each of which builds a logical unit. A block of data corresponds to an input mask. To give a survey on the kind of data the user can define to create a diagram the following five figures show the respective input masks. They are arranged in the same order as they appear on the console screen when a new diagram is designed. Additional explanation is given to point out some specific features.
These masks are embedded within a larger frame on the console device giving a variety of special and general user support functions during the dialogue process. Default values are suggested whenever possible.

Functions of input-program

Mask 1: Categories / ranges of values
Mask 2: Presentation / visual attributes of y-lists
Mask 3: Titles / Legends / Additional legends
Mask 4: Data selection / graduation
Mask 5: Axis attributes / text fields / screen position

```
+-----------------------------------------------------------+
! Categories / ranges of values                             !
! --------------------------------------------------------- !
!                                                           !
! x-axis (independent values)       Type of x-val:[D]       !
!                                                           !
! Xmin:[-5      ]          Xmax:[5       ]                  !
!                                                           !
!                                                           !
! y-axis (dependent values)         Type of y-val:[D]       !
!                                                           !
! Number of y-lists:[5 ]                                    !
!                                                           !
! Y1min:[-5        ]        Y1max:[5         ]              !
! Y2min:[-5        ]        Y2max:[5         ]              !
! Y3min:[-5        ]        Y3max:[5         ]              !
! Y4min:[-5        ]        Y4max:[5         ]              !
! Y5min:[-5        ]        Y5max:[5         ]              !
!                                                           !
! N =Next Menu  S =Stop  R =Repeat  Choice:[N]              !
+-----------------------------------------------------------+
```

Fig. 32-2: Mask 1

Mask 2 is shown referring to visual attributes as "colors". As mentioned above, the actual presentation depends on the characterisics of the visual display unit hardware. The user is supported by legends indicating a map for the actual visual representation and the color-ID to be chosen if the (logical) console device is assigned to the graphical display unit hardware.

```
+-----------------------------------------------------------+
! Presentation / visual attributes of y-lists               !
! --------------------------------------------------------- !
!                                                           !
! Colors of diagram            Colors of text               !
!                                                           !
! Background color:[1]         Text background:[5]          !
! Foreground color:[8]         Writing         :[8]         !
!                                                           !
!                                                           !
! Attributes of the y-lists                                 !
!                                                           !
! Form Y1:[B]   Color Y1:[2]   Symbol Y1:[*]                !
! Form Y2:[B]   Color Y2:[3]   Symbol Y2:[0]                !
! Form Y3:[B]   Color Y3:[4]   Symbol Y3:[.]                !
! Form Y4:[B]   Color Y4:[6]   Symbol Y4:[X]                !
! Form Y5:[B]   Color Y5:[7]   Symbol Y5:[+]                !
!                                                           !
!                                                           !
! N =Next Menu  S =Stop  R =Repeat  Choice:[N]              !
+-----------------------------------------------------------+
```

Fig. 32-3: Mask 2

```
+-----------------------------------------------------------+
! Titles / Legends / Additional legends                     !
! --------------------------------------------------------- !
!                                                           !
! Titles / Legends             Additional legends?[J]       !
!                                                           !
! Title      :[Title     ]     L1 :[*          ]            !
!                              L2 :[*          ]            !
! X - axis   :[x-axis    ]     L3 :[*          ]            !
! Y - axis   :[y-axis    ]     L4 :[*          ]            !
!                              L5 :[*          ]            !
! Legend Y1:[Legend1   ]       L6 :[*          ]            !
! Legend Y2:[Legend2   ]       L7 :[*          ]            !
! Legend Y3:[Legend3   ]       L8 :[*          ]            !
! Legend Y4:[Legend4   ]       L9 :[*          ]            !
! Legend Y5:[Legend5   ]       L10:[*          ]            !
!                                                           !
!                                                           !
! N =Next Menu  S =Stop  R =Repeat  Choice:[N]              !
+-----------------------------------------------------------+
```

Fig. 32-4: Mask 3

One mechanism BUSYPLOT provides to enable flexible mapping of stored data into diagrams is done by relative assignment of x-values. This relative reference scheme has to associate x-values representing the stored data in the data base and x-values defined by the valid range of the x-axis in the diagram. The diagram usually contains a sub-range of the x-values represented in the local data base. Matching is done by defining a "start-value" for the x-values which are assumed to be in a partial order (Mask 4).

```
+--------------------------------------------------------------+
! Data selection / graduation                                  !
! -------------------------------------------------------      !
!                                                              !
! Datafile                     Data selection                  !
!                                                              !
! Filename   :DEFAULT          No.of records:10                !
! Disk-drive:A                 Start-value  :-5                !
!                                                              !
!                                                              !
! Graduation x-axis            Graduation y-axis               !
!                                                              !
! Discrete values              Discrete values                 !
!                                                              !
! x-minimum :-5                y-minimum :-5                   !
! x-interval:1                 y-interval:1                    !
!                                                              !
! N =Next Menu  S =Stop  R =Repeat   Choice:N                  !
+--------------------------------------------------------------+
```

Fig. 32-5: Mask 4

```
+--------------------------------------------------------------+
! Scale attributes / text fields / screen position             !
! -------------------------------------------------------      !
!                                                              !
! x-axis                       y-axis                          !
!                                                              !
! x-tickmarks      :10         y-tickmarks      :10            !
! x-tick-distance:10           y-tick-distance:8               !
! Barwidth         :1                                          !
!                                                              !
! Text fields                  Screen position                 !
!                                                              !
! Textcolumns left :5          Horizontal origin:0             !
! Textcolumns right:10         Vertical   origin:0             !
! Textlines   below:3                                          !
! Textlines   above:3                                          !
!                                                              !
! N =Next Menu  S =Stop  R =Repeat   Choice:N                  !
+--------------------------------------------------------------+
```

Fig. 32-6: Mask 5

Manipulation of problem-data. BUSYPLOT offers a variety of functions necessary to manipulate problem-data. A new datafile can be created or an existing file can be completely erased. Furthermore, functions are implemented to alter datafiles. The user can change values, delete values from a datafile and insert additional problem-data into a datafile.

Mass storage functions. The diagram-data and the problem-data are stored on locally available mass storage devices, such as floppy disks or harddisks. The user has to independantly define filenames for datafiles containing problem-data and filenames for plotfiles containing diagram-data. By calling the names the user can always refer to the data. Using the matching scheme available for filenames under the CP/M operating system relation structures between datafiles and plotfiles can be embedded.

Diagram output. A diagram is completely defined and can be displayed on the graphical display unit using the data contained in both the associated plotfile and the datafile. The BUSYPLOT output-program allows to control the displaying process by offering output options. When no option is wanted to modify the graphical representation the diagram appears according to the data defined in the underlying datafile and plotfile.

The number of diagrams which can be displayed simultaneously is not limited by principles related with the design concepts of BUSYPLOT. Off course, practical limits are imposed especially by the resolution of the graphical display unit. In case of coordinate overlap diagrams invoked later are superimposed on top of diagrams invoked earlier (Fig. 32-7). As outlined earlier, parts of a diagram that do not fit into the assigned hardware coordinate space of the graphical device are clipped automatically.

Output options. One guideline for implementing output options was to give some means for possibly improving the pattern recognition process performed upon diagram data defined in a plotfile and the associated datafile.

One of these options allows to show only one single y-list in a diagram. This option is useful when more than one y-list is assigned to a diagram. In order to present the individual pattern underlying the values of a specific y-list more clearly only one single y-list of all assigned y-lists can be temporarily chosen for display in the plotting-area.

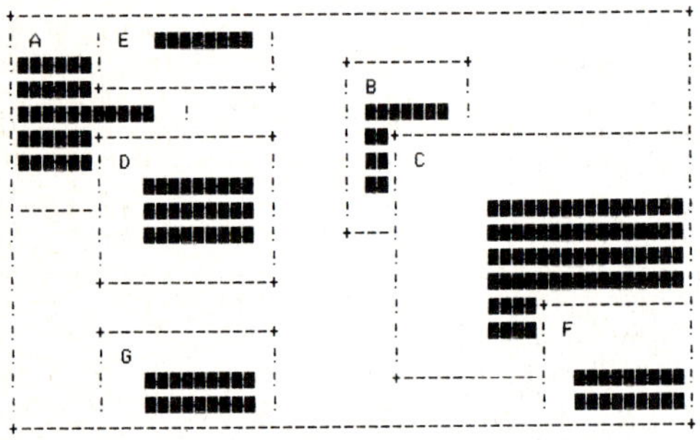

Fig. 32-7: Presentation of multiple diagrams with overlap and clipping

Another option is to draw horizontal and/or vertical grids in the diagram. The positions of the gridlines are determined by the tickmarks. This option can help to visually associate more precise coordinate values with the items shown in a graph.
A further option allows the inclusion of additional legends in the diagram. As indicated in mask 3, additional legend texts can be specified. By choosing this option these text-fields can be shown. When the diagram is displayed the text-fields are to be positioned interactively using cursor motion to the position where the text is to appear. The viewport associated to the diagram can not be overrun.

Variation of diagrams. There are many occasions where it appears necessary to change the graphical representation of one specific diagram or a set of diagrams. BUSYPLOT offers functions to alter diagram-data in a shortened dialogue within the output-program. The users don't have to return to the input-program but can input new values while the images of diagrams that are already outputted remain on the graphical display unit.

These alteration functions are especially helpful to perform the following kinds of modifications:

- selection of a different set of problem-data to be presented in the diagram,
- variations of the scale of the y-axis ("zooming"),
  or
- variation of the diagram position on the screen.

4. Implementation of BUSYPLOT

41. User interface

In designing the communication interface for BUSYPLOT we tried to implement many valuable features found in widely accepted microcomputer based interactive systems. As common in this context, a variety of concurring aspects has to be compromised upon. The system has to be easy to use, nevertheless offering flexible schemes to control the dialogue process and user interaction on problem data. Especially for systems using graphic concepts, requests for a rather high degree of portability impose many crucial design problems for the user interface. In case of the application environment BUSYPLOT is basically designed for interleaving with data base handling facilities demand further complex considerations.

All user input within BUSYPLOT is done using the keyboard, dialogue control information is given on the (logical) console display unit. It is assumed that the hardware device available for presentation of console information is usuallly identical with the graphical display unit hardware. Nevertheless, BUSYPLOT allows to re-direct console information to a separate console device. Dialogue control and user input is implemented using schemes like:

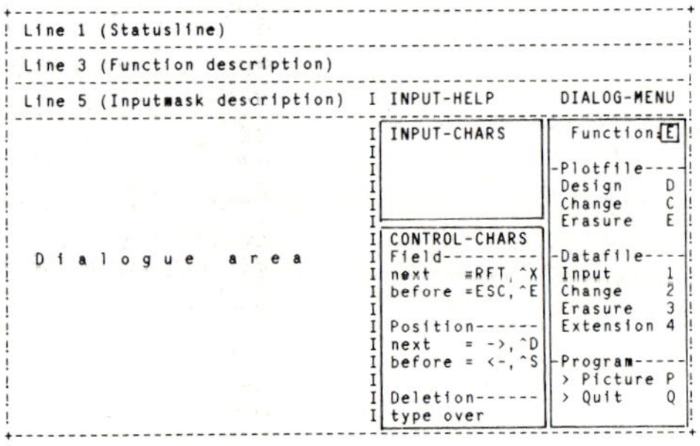

Fig. 41-1: Reserved sectors of dialogue console in input-program

- a unified screen outlay based upon certain reserved sectors,
- a unified approach for menu selection and data input in formatted input-fields and input-masks,
- error messages and provisions for error handling,
- information messages about system sta-

tus,
or

- a help system supporting especially data input.

Console outlay. For portability, the console uses a display area of 80 columns times 24 lines. It is divisioned in reserved sectors provided for: system and error messages, the dialogue-menu, input helps and the dialogue area (Fig. 41-1). We are using a scheme for dialogue control and user input applied in a similar way in various application packages for interactive microcomputer systems /NASTANSKY-BERNARTZ/.

Dialogue control for the output-program needs only space for three lines times 80 characters wide. Thus, there is no need to physically separate console device and graphical display unit in the highly interactive diagram processing phase.

Input technique. The user inputs data into formatted input-fields. Each input-field is defined according to the following principles:

- text description,
- fixed number of input positions,
- pre-defined set of permitted input characters,
  and
- editing, and control transfer using control characters.

The specific set of feasible alpha-numeric characters coding the input data depends on the context within BUSYPLOT and normally differs from field to field. The control characters are always the same. Control characters either cause movements within an input-field or the transfer to a preceding or following field.

```
Editing of an input-field:
--------------------------
one position left : <- or <ctrl-S>
one position right: -> or <ctrl-D>
```

```
Movement between different input-fields:
----------------------------------------
next input-field     : <ret> or <ctrl-X>
preceding input-field: <ESC> or <ctrl-E>
```

The value of a field is internally updated upon leaving the field. Control characters as additional editing-keys are chosen because this is compatible with concepts embedded in packages of CP/M software being in widespread use (e.g. WordStar, DataStar).

Input masks. An input mask consists of a certain number of input-fields which are logically dependent because they form a problem oriented unit. Several input masks for input of the diagram-data have been shown above. With BUSYPLOT one input mask can consist of up to 20 input-fields, thus purposely limiting the amount of information the user can be confronted with in one instant of the dialogue process.

Error handling. Each input character is automatically checked for belonging to the feasible character set of the input-field. When an error is recognized an error message is displayed in the status line (first line of the console). In addition, an acoustic signal is issued. BUSYPLOT demands active user response to undefined input. Error release is accomplished by pressing the <ESC>-key. The cursor moves back to the position where the error was detected, and the user can continue the input process. In addition to this general character based error detecting routine, BUSYPLOT performes content control of input-fields in some cases. This is possible if e.g. the value of a field exceeds a predefined range between minimum and/or maximum limits. In such cases an error message is displayed explaining the type of the error. The user can leave an input-field only if the field value is not recognized to be erroneous.

System messages. While most input shows immediate system response, e.g. the appearance of an input character on the console, or visual processing of images on the graphical display unit, there are several situations where hidden processing is necessary. This is e.g. the case when the system has to carry out calculations, when data are read from a floppy disk, or when internal program paging has to take place. It is good use to inform the user about such unavoidable waiting periods, giving messages about system activities in plain text and contextual explanation from the application user's point of view. This is realized in BUSYPLOT by displaying "system messages" in the status line.

Input helps. To facilitate the data input help informations are displayed in the course of the dialogue. Especially, the usable control characters are displayed, and continuously updated information is given about the feasible alpha-numeric character set of the active input-field.

42. Host

The BUSYPLOT program package is

designed for microcomputers and written in Pascal. With little effort, the available modules of BUSYPLOT can be adapted to a typical (minimal) configuration that fulfills the following requirements:

- Pascal software development environment, and Pascal run-time system supporting overlaying and chaining,
- 64 kB RAM,
- two floppy disk stations (capacity per disk at least 300 kB),
- visual display unit with selectable backgound and foreground colors; character based, low resolution, or high resolution graphics.

A visual display unit supporting only B&W character based visual attributes, like highlighting, reverse video, or character based graphics, can be chosen as well for the (pseudo-) graphic display.

Our actual version of BUSYPLOT is written in PASCAL/Z for the CP/M-80 operating system. The package is overlayed, in addition structured in different chained modules, and consists of some 350 kB source code. The system is running on IMS-8000 CP/M-80-microcomputers using Intelligent Systems' ISC-8001G 8-color low-resolution graphics displays. Further details are outlined in the system documentation /PEINE/.

One reason for choosing a CP/M environment as host for BUSYPLOT has been the perspectives imposed by the abundant software market for office automation tools /FINKE/. Especially, a great deal of reliable packages for data communication and data base management tasks are available at low cost. We intend to use these packages for the further development of the BUSYPLOT approach rather than writing code in a higher level application language.

43. Terminal drivers

For portability, we have tried to isolate hardware dependent functions wherever possible. For the application environment BUSYPLOT is intended to be useful for problems of hardware compatibility are probable to occur in integrating the visual display unit. Thus, we have provided some flexible mechanisms for interfacing the graphical display unit hardware. Terminal features are defined in parameter tables, and certain I/O-drivers are concentrated in a few procedures of the system.

Terminal driver selection can be performed during startup of the program if desired. The package is capable of loading the associated parameter tables during run-time. The parameters describe color-codes, codes for positioning the cursor, display attributes like blinking, the physical viewport on the visual display unit assigned for use in BUSYPLOT in terms of available columns and rows, the resolution of the display, used graphic primitives, etc.. All installed terminals can be included in a possibly increasing selection menu. The associated data are held in files external to BUSYPLOT and only loaded when selected. Especially, this concept allows for protected windowing techniques when BUSYPLOT is used in an integrated environment with co-operating packages.

All hardware dependent parameters are only used in a specific set of elementary display output procedures. Examples for these Pascal embedded primitives are e.g. the procedures CURSOR, BELL, BLINK, CLEARSCREEN, PLOTBLOCK, or PLOTLINE, the names being self-explanatory.
We regard the package being highly portable and configurable for a variety of hardware environments.

44. Data model

Summary. The data model used for complete definition of all BUSYPLOT diagrams is to be evaluated against a variety of concurring aspects. We have tried to compromise upon such contradicting features like: clarity and simplicity, compatibility with existing CP/M file structures in widespread use in many software packages, understandable for endusers, data can be separately manipulated by endusers, storage saving, efficient handling in programs, flexibility, or stability. We do not feel that the suggested solution is the only feasible one.

Datafile. The problem-data are stored in a sequential file. This datafile defines an ordered collection of records each of which is composed of one x-value and five associated y-values. The number of records is not limited and supposed to be problem dependent. A datafile can be assigned to an arbitrary number of BUSYPLOT diagrams (=plotfiles). There is exactly one datafile associated with each BUSYPLOT diagram.

The summarized characteristics of a datafile are:

- sequential data order,
- records separated by <carriage re-

turn>,
- data fields within the records separated by <commas>, and
- records are sorted by x-values.

The symbolized structure of a datafile is shown in Fig. 44-1; an example is given in Fig. 44-2.

```
+-----------------------------------------+
! X1 , Y11 , Y12 , Y13 , Y14 , Y15 <cr> !
! X2 , Y21 , Y22 , Y23 , Y24 , Y25 <cr> !
!  :                                      !
! Xn , Yn1 , Yn2 , Yn3 , Yn4 , Yn5 <cr> !
+-----------------------------------------+
```

Fig. 44-1: Structure of datafile

```
+-------------------------------------+
! 1, 1.0 , 1.7 ,-0.7 , 0.1 , 0 <cr> !
! 2, 1.5 , 1.0 , 0.5 , 0.2 , 0 <cr> !
! 3, 1.5 , 0.8 , 0.7 , 0.2 , 0 <cr> !
! 4, 1.7 , 1.2 , 0.5 , 0.2 , 0 <cr> !
! 5, 1.3 , 2.0 ,-0.7 , 0.3 , 0 <cr> !
! 6, 1.5 , 2.0 ,-0.5 , 0.1 , 0 <cr> !
! 7, 1.7 , 0.6 , 1.1 , 0.2 , 0 <cr> !
! 8, 1.5 , 2.5 ,-1.0 , 0.1 , 0 <cr> !
! 9, 1.4 , 1.1 , 0.3 , 0.1 , 0 <cr> !
+-------------------------------------+
```

Fig. 44-2: Example for datafile (see diagram 31-6)

As the example shows, each record always contains the full set of possible data entries. Empty y-lists are indicated by zero fills.

Plotfile. A plotfile contains the collection of diagram-data describing the visual and graphical properties of a specific BUSYPLOT diagram as shown above. Like the datafile it has a sequential order, the records are separated by <carriage return> and the data fields by <comma>. Each plotfile defines one and only one BUSYPLOT diagram. There is a 1:1 mapping between plotfiles and diagrams. There is exactly one datafile associated with a plotfile.

```
+------------------------------------------------------------------+
! 1 , field value 1 , field value 2 , ... , field value 20 <cr> !
! 2 , field value 1 , field value 2 , ... , field value 20 <cr> !
! 3 , field value 1 , field value 2 , ... , field value 20 <cr> !
! 4 , field value 1 , field value 2 , ... , field value 20 <cr> !
! 5 , field value 1 , field value 2 , ... , field value 20 <cr> !
+------------------------------------------------------------------+
```

Fig. 44-3: Structure of plotfile

Each plotfile consists of five records, each of them defined by the values entered in the associated input mask. The first field of a record indicates the sequence number of the mask. Since one mask can enclose up to 20 distinct input-fields a record of a plotfile can contain the maximum number of 20 items. Unused fields are filled with <question mark>.

The symbolized structure of a plotfile is shown in Fig. 44-3; an example is presented in Fig. 44-4.

```
+--------------------------------------------------------------------+
! 1,D,1,10,S,3,-5,5,-5,5,-5,5,-5,5,-5,5,?,?,?,?,? <cr>              !
! 2,5,8,7,1,P,4,*,P,2,0,B,3,+,B,5,.,B,7,X,? <cr>                    !
! 3,CompanyXYZ,Products,Mio.$,Turnover,Costs,Profit,Subvention,     !
!    ?,J,*,*,*,*,*,*,*,*,*,* <cr>                                   !
! 4,EXAMPLE,A,6,3,3,1,-1.0,0.5,?,?,?,?,?,?,?,?,?,?,? <cr>           !
! 5,6,10,2,6,8,7,10,3,3,0,0,?,?,?,?,?,?,?,?,? <cr>                  !
+--------------------------------------------------------------------+
```

Fig. 44-4: Example of a plotfile (see diagram 31-6)

The relation principle between diagrams, plotfiles, and datafiles are summarized in Fig. 44-5. The collection of datafiles forms a data base out of which graphical patterns can be extracted in a flexible way. Each datafile again is to be regarded as a database as well. Given a specific datafile, arbitrary combinations of y-lists and/or arbitrary sections of the available range of x-values can be presented in various diagrams.

```
   +---------+  +---------+     +---------+
  /  plot- /  / plot-   /     /  plot- /
 / file A /  / file B /      / file Z /
+---------+ +---------+     +---------+
     !           !               !        (plotfile) : (diagram)
     V           V               V              1 : 1
+----------+ +----------+     +----------+
!diagram A! !diagram B!  ... !diagram Z!
+----------+ +----------+     +----------+
     ^           ^               ^        (datafile) : (diagram)
     !           !               !              1 : n
     +-----------+-------...-----+
                 !
         +-------------------+
        /   data base of   /
       /    datafiles     /
      +-------------------+
```

Fig. 44-5: Relation between diagrams, plotfiles, and datafiles

Due to the simple formal structure, both, datafiles and plotfiles can be manipulated separately using e.g. a text editor or a system for handling formatted data (like DataStar). Especially, data in datafiles can be altered, or a whole datafile can be extended without dificulty.

5. Future development

In addition to streamlining work performed on the functions implemented in the present version VS-1.0 of BUSYPLOT, for the near future we intend to develop an interactive integrated communication environment for BUSYPLOT.

This concept has to support two tasks which are principally available in the CP/M-based BUSYPLOT environment for the time being. But they are not accessible in an integrated way. One task is to handle the communication process with remote data bases. The other task is to improve the means to manipulate the locally available data base and to graphically retrieve the contained information. Especially, it is necessary to implement mechanisms for simultaneously handling diagram sets rather than diagrams sequentially.

References

Finke, W.:
Gestaltung von Bueroinformationssystemen mit Mikrocomputern der CP/M-Familie. In: Bueroinformations- und -kommunikationssysteme. Ed. by H.R. Hansen. Berlin-Heidelberg-New York (Springer) 1982, pp.

GrafTalk:
GrafTalk. User's Manual and Reference Manual. West Redding CT (Redding Group Inc.) 1982.

GRID Systems Corporation.
2535 Garcia Avenue. Mountain View, CA 94043, USA.

IGS:
Intelligent Graphics System. User's Manual. 999371. Norcross GA (Intelligent Systems Corp.) Oct. 1982.

Nastansky, L.:
Business Graphics. In: Bueroinformations- und -kommunikationssysteme. Ed. by H.R. Hansen. Berlin-Heidelberg-New York (Springer) 1982, pp. 119-134.

Nastansky, L., and B. Bernartz:
Menuegenerator. In: Software Ergonomie. Proc. German Chapter of the ACM, to appear March 1983.

Peine, H.:
BUSYPLOT: System description. 255 p.
BUSYPLOT: Program documentation. 181 p.
BUSYPLOT: User's manual. 66 p.
Working Papers. Wirtschaftsinformatik, Universitaet Paderborn. Ed. by L. Nastansky. Paderborn 1982 (only in German available).

Robertson, P.J.:
A Guide to Using Color on Alphanumeric Displays. Technical Report. IBM U.K. Laboratories Limited. White Plains NY (IBM) June 1980.

Vinberg, A.:
Computer Graphics and the Business Executive - The New Management Team. In: IEEE Computer Graphics and Applications, 1 (1981) 1, pp. 57-71.

Williams, G.:
The Lisa Computer System. In: Byte, Vol. 8 (1983) 2, pp. 33-50.

Prof. Dr. Ludwig Nastansky
Hildegunde Peine, cand.rer.oec.
Dep. Business Data Processing

FB-5 Universitaet Paderborn
Warburger Str. 100
D-4790 Paderborn / W.Germany
(05251) 60-2808

Session G3:

FAULT TOLERANT HARDWARE

Chairwoman: M. G. Sami
Politecnico di Milano
Milano (Italy)

In the area of fault-tolerant computing, distributed systems are seen as generating - at the same time - powerful facilities and relevant problems. While a multiprocessor structure promises capacity of self-test, error confinement and reconfiguration almost as a natural peformance, problems of synchronization, information exchange, shared access to resources introduce new (and possibly fatal) error sources.

In past Euromicro Symposia, fault-tolerance in distributed systems has been discussed from various points of view, but mostly considering diagnosis and reconfiguration at system level. In this session, the main problem of robust inter-processor communications is considered from two different angles, in the two papers presented. In fact, detection of errors during information exchanges is basic for guaranteeing that no error propagation will occurr through the whole network, with fatal results.

The paper "Taskspecific assignment of redundancy in the fault-tolerant multicomputer system FUTURE" takes a software-implemented approach to fault-tolerance of distributed systems (it may be recalled that such an approach has been introduced with the SIFT system). A very interesting characteristic of the FUTURE proposal is association of reliability classes with different classes of tasks, suitably defined by the application programmer; fault-tolerance functions (e.g. redundancy handling, error detection, voting etc.) are then handled by system software, overlaying the operating system proper. The solution chosen allows the application programmer control of the fault-tolerance performances, without requiring him to actually program the corresponding actions. Message transport is easily recognized as a critical point in a multiprocessor structure; therefore, the solution to communication supports has been particularly studied in order to guarantee robust message transfers among processors.

Robust communications are again the main subject in the second paper, "Fault-tolerant retrying parallel communications, with application to microprocessor bus". Reference is made to a standard parallel bus for multimicroprocessor systems (already presented at Euromicro 82); the problem considered is quite interesting in that robust communications have usually been studied for serial links, where a number of proposals (typically involving coding and suitable protocol organizations) have been made, but not for parallel links. Actually, possible error causes are quite different and therefore totally different approaches have to be considered. The solution proposed in this paper strives to meet requirements created by a reasonable fault model with a fairly simple hardware organization, suitable also for implementation with an LSI chip. No relevant complexity is added to the bus (coding adopted is quite simple) and the modified form of "retrying" chosen keeps the basic protocol also very simple; thus, cost/performance ratio obtained is very favorable.

MICROCOMPUTERS: Developments in Industry, Business and Education
D.R. Wilson and C.J. van Spronsen (eds.) / © EUROMICRO, 1983
Elsevier Science Publishers B.V. (North-Holland)

FAULT-TOLERANT RETRYING PARALLEL COMMUNICATIONS, WITH APPLICATION TO MICROPROCESSOR BUS

G. Danese, D. Dotti

Dipartimento di Informatica e Sistemistica
Università di Pavia, Italy

Parallel data communications are widely adopted in computing systems, when physical distances are limited. In order to give fault-tolerance properties to the transmission, means for detecting faults can be provided leaving to a retry the task of adjusting the received data. This work describes an algorithm capable of identifying fault positions with a single retry operation, irrespectively of whether they are fix or fluctuate; furthermore an application to a standard microprocessor bus is illustrated, where only one bit error per bus line group is assumed.
Operating principles are based on error detecting and correcting codes, properly adapted to the particular application; a self-correcting code is made up of the initially transmitted data and of the contents of the retry message: however it is different from the most common ones, because independent errors are admitted on both sections of the code. Tables of the proposed correcting codes are also given.

1. INTRODUCTION

Parallel communication links are frequently preferred for connecting digital computing systems, whenever distances are small enough to make parallel wiring convenient, as compared to serial; more economical interfacing, faster exchange rate and simpler transmitting and receiving procedures result from this choice, mainly because parallel-to-serial and serial-to-parallel conversions are no more needed.

Not only this situation arises with reference to point-to-point communication, but also when more than two digital units spare the same physical link for data exchange, i.e. when parallel busses are implemented: microprocessors, in particular, need this kind of data transmission, in order to achieve operating efficiency.

Parallel communications are seldom provided with hardware means for detecting possible faults taking place with physical links, as opposite to serial communications, where parity bits, or even more complex coding procedures take care of detecting, or even correcting transmission errors.

Reason for that is the small distances covered by the parallel links, which should make faults less probable; however, sticking at ground or at power supply, or bridging among wires, can take place also in parallel links, so giving rise to incorrect data exchanges or even to system collapses in particular when a microprocessor bus is affected by them.

Security in data transmission can be achieved using techniques of redundancy in space as well as redundancy in time: the former makes the system more expensive, the latter less efficient.

A practical trade-off can be obtained by devoting the former technique to detection purposes, and attributing to the latter the task of correcting the message: a retry protocol has thus to be defined, and is often adopted for serial communications. However, owing to the particular features of the fault that may take place in parallel links, a simple re-transmission of the same bit pattern would be unlikely correctly received at the second trial; proposals for more effective retry have been advanced [2,3], in which bit complementation allows to overcome faults arising from wire stuck-at.

Purpose of this paper is to propose a new retry procedure, capable of correcting communication faults, for permanent and transient failures, without a-priori assumption about the nature of the failure itself: only a restriction in the number of faults per transmission is assumed, without imposing that the same ones take place during the retry.

Main feature of our proposal is to retain the information contents of the original received bit pattern, so as to make information carried by the retry complementary to that.

In other words, the standard transmission only includes means for detecting the fault, whilst the retry, if needed, is added to complete a special case of self-correcting code, capable of recovering faults possibly present in both received messages.
Section 2 describes the main lines of the algorithm; section 3 gives details about the construction of the Correcting Code; sections 4 and 5 describe software and hardware implementation of a point-to-point link, based on the proposed algorithm; section 6 adapts the hardware implementation to a standard bus in-

terface, oriented to the M3BUS; conclusions are drawn in section 7.

2. DESCRIPTION OF THE ALGORITHM

A realistic fault set must be defined, in order to properly design every fault-tolerant device or algorithm; as for a first implementation of the proposed fault-tolerant transmission procedure, a fault set where only one bit can be incorrect at reception is adopted: more general situations can be similarly treated, as for instance in section 6. Of course one bit error has to be admitted also within the second information transmitted, if needed.

Like other retry procedures, information initially transmitted contains means for detecting single bit errors; however the proposed algorithm differs from more common ones, in what concerns the first received information which is retained, instead of being rejected as completely unreliable. In fact, the wrong bit may be identified by computing a correcting code both at the transmitting station from the correct information and at the receiving station from the received information, and comparing them, after the former code has been communicated through the standard link to the receiver.

Let us introduce now some useful definitions,

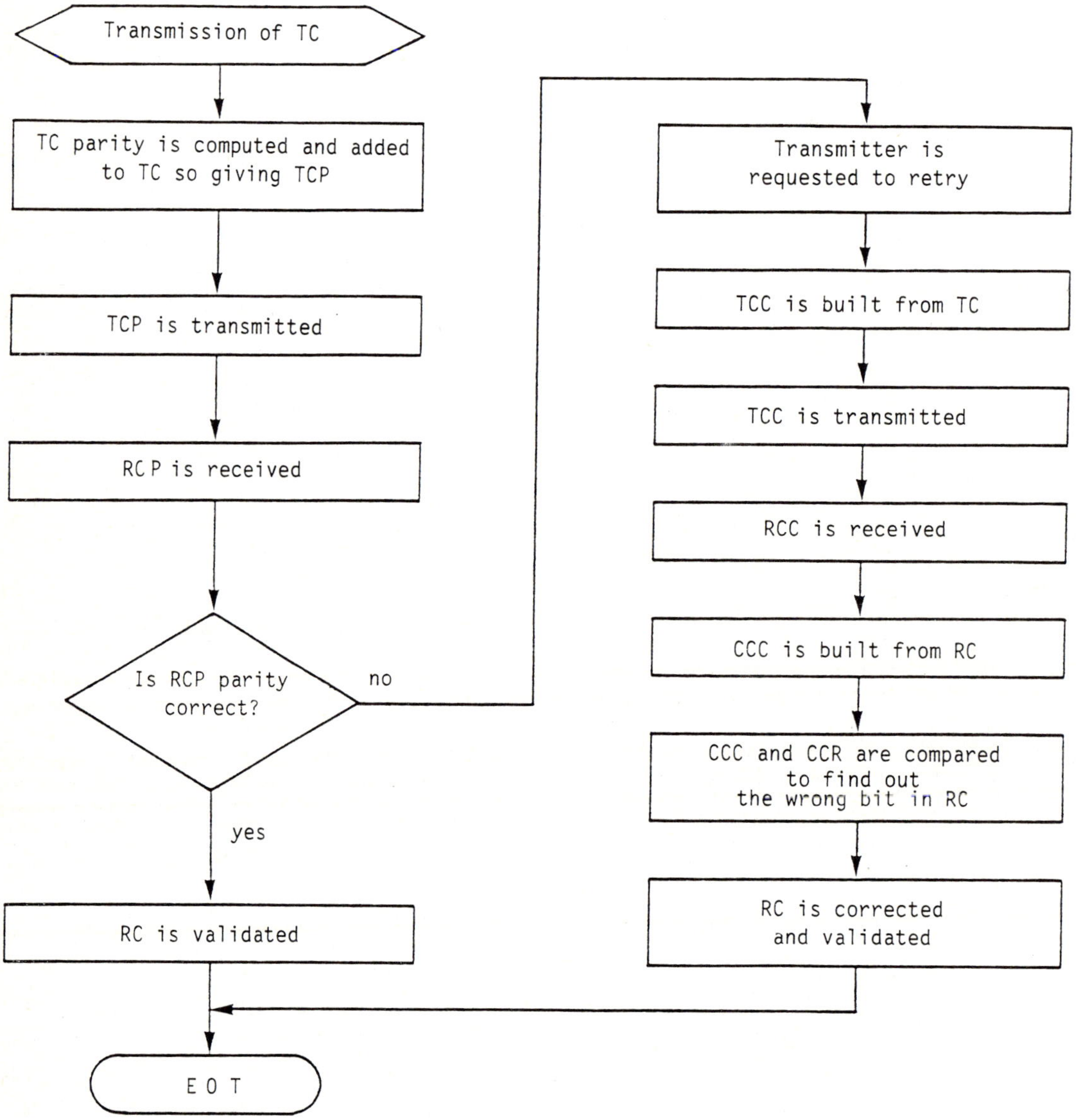

Figure 1 - Flow chart of the algorithm proposed.

to be recalled throughout the description:
- TC is the transmitted code;
- TCP is the transmitted code, plus information for detecting single bit errors;
- RC is the received code possibly differing from TC in one bit position;
- RCP is the received TCP; it may contain one bit error; however an incorrect RCP does not necessarily imply incorrect RC, since the wrong bit may be placed in the error detecting information;
- TCC is the correcting code, as transmitted;
- RCC is the received version of TCC, also possibly incorrect in one bit position;
- CCC is the correcting code, computed from RC at the receiving station, to be compared with RCC.

The flow diagram of the procedure is depicted in Fig. 1 and is self-explanatory.

As concerns the lengths in bits of the defined codes, the following remarks can be drawn:
- TC length "n" is a design datum;
- TCP contains a checking code; however since it only detects single bit errors, it may be a simple parity bit: thus TCP length is n+1;
- RC and RCP are respectively composed of n and n+1 bits;
- TCC, the correcting code computed from TC, has length "m" depending on n, but not equal to it, in general; criteria for determining m are given below; however, in order to allow the transmission of TCC on the same link as TCP, m should be less or equal to n+1;
- RCC and CCC have the same length m as TCC.

3. BUILDING THE CORRECTING CODE

The correcting code is such that the sequence of length n+m composed of TC and TCC is capable of reconstructing the original pattern even if two bit changes are operated.

It differs from ordinary self-correcting codes in that no more than one change can appear within the first n bits nor within the last m; this corresponds to a reduction in code complexity, therefore in the length m.

In terms of Hamming distance [1], i.e. the number of bit positions where codes differ, capability of correcting double faults requires that the allowed codes, n+m long, are distant from each other by at least 5 units, whereas capability of correcting simple faults both in the first n and in the second m bits allows a distance of 3 units between codes, provided that all differences lay within the first or within the second group of bits.
Purpose of the correcting code is to retrieve the position of the possible change in the first n bits; however informations concerning a further change in the last m bits are of interest to the secondary purpose of diagnosing the status of the physical link.

Building the correcting code means finding a function R(X), with variable X and function R consisting of bit vectors, which produces TCC from TC and CCC from RC.

To that purpose, the following considerations can be made:
- in order to evenly manage errors consisting of changes from 0 to 1 and viceversa, function Y=R(X) operates exclusive-or's of some of the X bits to give the Y bits;
- thus function R(X) may be represented by a binary matrix M, n by m in size, that allows to choose the bits of X to be exclusive-ored in order to give each bit of Y. This operation corresponds to an ordinary matrix by vector multiplication, if only the least significant bit of the resulting vector is taken into account for obtaining vector Y;
- a kind of distributive property holds for R(X),

$$R(X1 \oplus X2) = R(X1) \oplus R(X2) \qquad (1)$$

  where the symbol $\oplus$ indicates bit by bit exclusive-or of the operands. This property derives from the way function R(X) is defined, i.e. as a multiple exclusive-or;
- as a consequence of the preceding property, if no error is assumed for the retry (RCC=TCC), the exclusive-or between RCC and CCC equals the function R(X) when X is either completely composed of 0's or has at most one 1: the first situation arises when the transmission error stays in the parity bit. Thus the above exclusive-or is either a set of 0's or one of the columns of M: in the former case RC is correct, in the latter the column of M so identified gives the bit to be corrected in RC;
- since in reality RCC may differ from TCC for one bit, retrieval of the wrong bit can be accomplished by comparing the above exclusive-or to each column of M and to a zero column, looking for a match or for a distance of 1. Unambiguous identification demands for the existence of at least 3 1's in each column of M, and for a distance of at least 3 between columns.

The above considerations allow to establish minimum requirements for the function R(X), and then for the matrix M which implements R(X); in particular, the last point allows to state that:

$$2^m \geq (m+1)(n+1) \qquad (2)$$

In fact, it requires that n+1 m-long columns (recall that zero column is included) find place in a binary m-dimensional space, each one together with a set of other m columns distant from them by 1.

The above restriction is necessary, but not sufficient in general. Definite results have been obtained tentatively searching for the maximum number p of codes having minimum distance of 3 as a function of m; Table I shows the obtained results, together with those derived from Eq. 2, posing

$$p_t = n+1$$

Then Table II shows the p-1 codes, different from zero, chosen for each given value of m.

m	p	p_t
3	2	2
4	2	3
5	4	6
6	7	9
7	16	16

Table I

m=3

1
1
1

m=4

1
1
1
0

m=5

1	0	1
1	0	1
1	1	0
0	1	1
0	1	1

m=6

1	0	1	1	0	1
1	0	0	1	1	0
1	1	0	0	1	1
0	1	0	1	0	1
0	1	1	1	1	0
0	0	1	0	1	1

m=7

1	1	1	0	0	0	0	1	1	1	1	0	0	0	1
1	0	0	1	0	0	1	0	1	1	0	1	1	0	1
1	0	0	0	1	1	0	1	0	0	1	1	1	0	1
0	1	0	1	0	1	0	1	0	1	0	1	0	1	1
0	1	0	0	1	0	1	0	1	0	1	1	0	1	1
0	0	1	1	1	0	0	1	1	0	0	0	1	1	1
0	0	1	0	0	1	1	0	0	1	1	0	1	1	1

Table II

Since n must be smaller than p, from Table I it turns out that the restriction of Eq. 1 implies a minimum value for n:

$$n \geq 5$$

At last matrix M can be built, choosing from Table II an m value greater or equal to that giving at least n codes and not greater than n+1; and assuming as columns for M n codes from Table II.

4. SOFTWARE IMPLEMENTATION OF THE ALGORITHM

Flow diagram of Fig. 1 may be subdivided into two flow diagrams to be implemented in transmitting and receiving stations.

No major problem arises, when developing the software needed, but the main characteristics of parallel interfaces, that is speed and simplicity, are practically lost. However the authors developed an assembler program on a small microcomputer system based on Zilog Z80A, Philips PM4300, in order to fully ascertain the correcting properties of the suggested algorithm.

5. HARDWARE IMPLEMENTATION OF THE ALGORITHM

The described algorithm lends itself to simple implementation of hardware interfaces; broad application could suggest the integration of the functions in a customized LSI device.

Only a random logic implementation is however described in this section, which illustrates the limited complexity of the hardware needed.

Fig. 2 shows the block diagram of the hardware function needed for carrying out the procedure previously described, both for the transmitting and the receiving station.

zeroing is in turn achieved by proper control of the Inverse Code Generator block.

If the parity check detects a fault, a retry is asked to the Hanshake and Control Logic of the Transmitting Station.

Data TC are thus processed by the Correcting Code Generator, originating TCC, that is applied to the Physical Link through multiplexer MUX.

At the Receiving Station, Register B stores the received RCC, and supplies it to one input of the Comparing EX-OR; in the meanwhile,

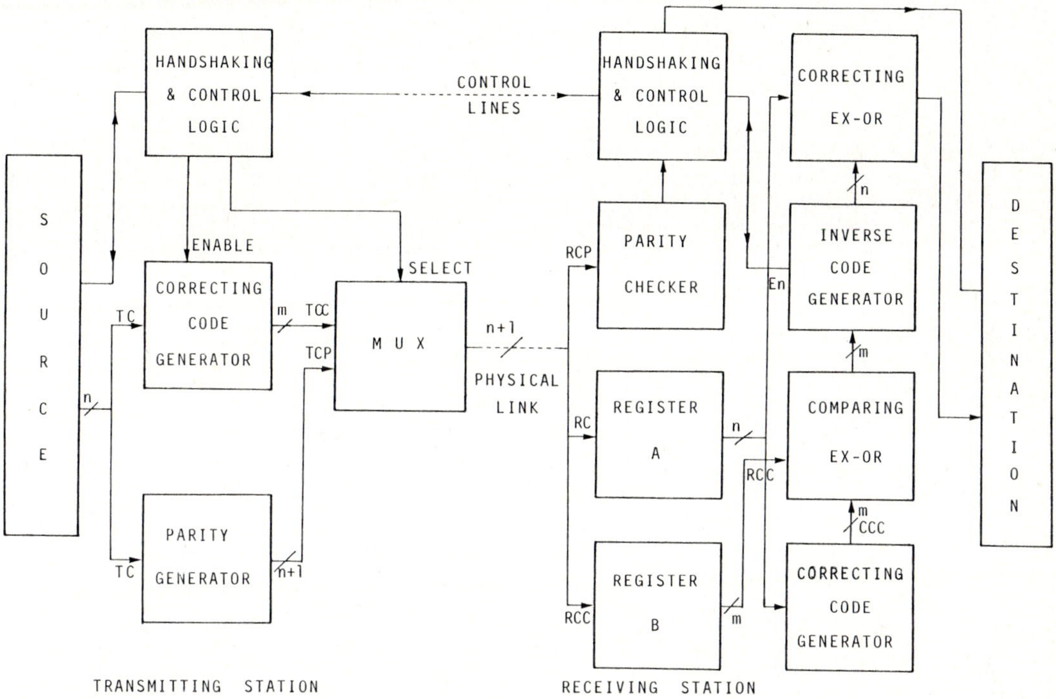

Figure 2 - Block diagram for a hardware implementation of the algorithm; data flow from Source to Destination through a parallel physical link of n+1 lines, plus a suitable number of control lines.

At the transmitting station, data TC are supplied by Source to the Parity Generator, which adds one parity bit (no matter whether even or odd) so giving the n+1 bits of TCP; Handshaking and Control Logic block selects this input for the Physical Link through the multiplexer MUX, and starts a handshake exchange with the Receiving Station.

At the Receiving Station a similar module routes the data supplied by the Physical Link to Register A, and verifies the correctness of the n+1 bits of RCP through the Parity Checker; if the check is positive, data stored in Register A are sent to Destination, through Correcting Ex-Or, an exclusive-or whose other input is zeroed, so that data pass unchanged:

Register A has supplied RC to a Correcting Code Generator, true copy of that of the Transmitting Station, which makes CCC available to the other input of the Comparing EX-OR. Comparison output points out differing bits, and the Inverse Code Generator finds out the wrong bit in RC, supplying a single 1 to the Correcting EX-OR; this function is accomplished comparing the bit set of the input to each column of matrix M, until a match is found, at least within a distance of 1. If no match is observed, Handshaking and Control Logic block is adviced that a non-recoverable fault has happened, probably due to double transmission error in the Physical Link.

The whole transmission procedure described can be managed by the Handshaking and Control Logic blocks, without intervention of Source and Destination; the only consequence of a retry for the latters is thus a longer pause time, waiting for the end of transmission signal from the formers.

A few words may be spent about the implementation by means of random logic.

Parity Generator, multiplexer, registers, exclusive-or's and Parity Checker may be obviously implemented employing commercial MSI products.

As regard Handshaking and Control Logics, their complexity does not greatly exceed that of conventional networks charged to handshake parallel communication: only the retry request capability has to be added.

At last, Correcting Code Generators and Inverse Code Generator may be implemented with PLA's or PROM's; note that the latter, having m+1 input and n+1 output bits:

- acts on m bits in inverse way, with respect to the Correcting Code Generator, so giving n of the output bits;
- is controlled by the m+1-th input, which can put to zero every outputs;
- has an n+1-th output, which signals no match found.

6. APPLICATIONS TO MICROPROCESSOR BUS

Fault-tolerance in microprocessor systems is a goal widely looked for; to that purpose, bus check is one of the most important way to detect failures, arising both from the bus itself and from the devices connected to it [4,5].

Secure bus communication clearly is an important attribute for approaching fault-tolerance, and the proposed method offers a solution to bus security.

As regards the particular bus considered for applying the retry procedures described, the M3BUS developed at the Politecnico di Torino [6] has been chosen, which closely resembles the IEEE-896 proposal, at least as far as it is known.

Reasons for the choice are the following:

- 16 bit microprocessors are employed in medium to large systems, where the added complexity of a fault-tolerant bus interface is likely to the easily embodied;
- multiplexed bus allows more economical implementation, since the same hardware is

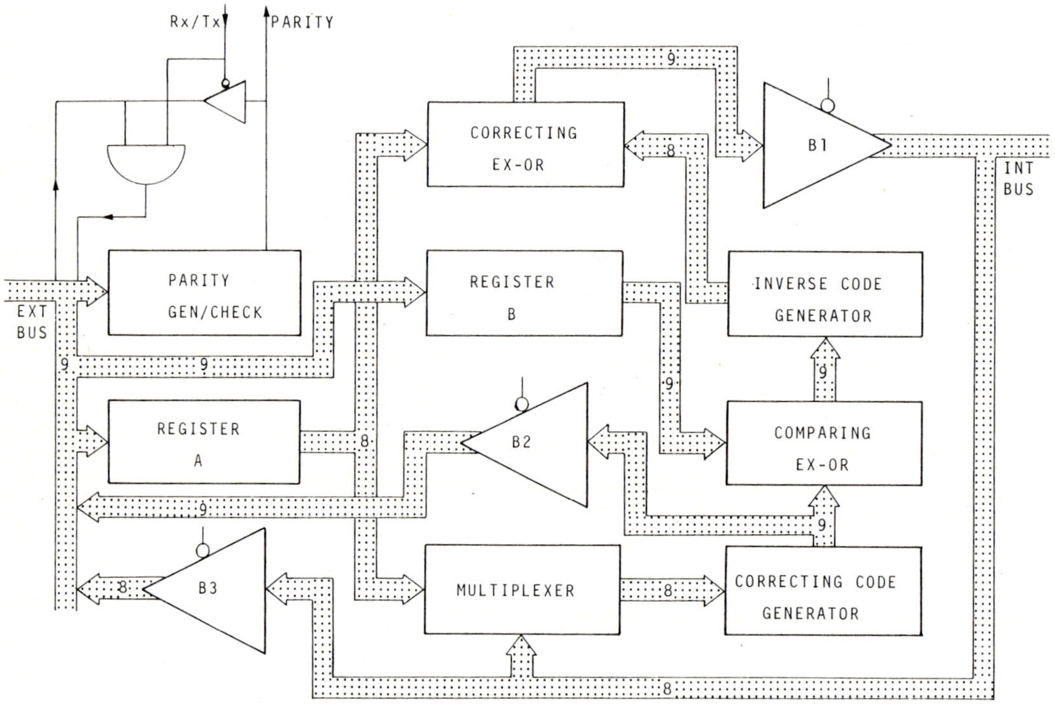

Figure 3 - Block diagram of a bus interface fit to securely manage 8 information lines plus parity. Handshaking and Control Block has been omitted, for clarity sake, together with control lines to functional blocks. Triangles represent line drivers, properly enable during Reception (B1), Transmission (B3) and Retry (B2). A parity generator/checker is included, whose function is altered by Rx/Tx signal, switching from Transmit to Receive Mode and viceversa.

time-shared by data, addresses, etc.;
- handshaking protocols, are a standard feature of that bus;
- a three processor system using the M3BUS will be soon available to us, in order to develop a wider research program on fault-tolerant computing.

Main informations are carried by 30 lines, INF00 - INF29, in M3BUS; clearly the proposed interface is well suited for controlling the information lines, while proper duplication could assure security to the control lines.

As regards the fault set assumptions, multiple error detecting/correcting codes have been considered [7].

However, after short analysis, they have been descarded, due to the high number of extra bus lines that would be required in order to detect errors arising during the first data transmission; from coding theory [1], it turns out that the detection of a couple of error in an n bit code demands q extra bits, with q satisfying the inequality:

$$2^{q-1} > n+q \qquad (3)$$

For n equal to 16, a practical value for a microprocessor bus, Eq. 3 gives a minimum value of 6. Therefore in order to keep bus size as limited as possible, recalling that three parity lines are already provided by the standard M3BUS, it has been chosen to separately treat three groups of 8 of the principal information lines, assigning to each group a parity line, like it is suggested by the standard itself.

This choice is congruent with a fault set assumption with only one bit error per line group; however, for making this assumption more likely, it is suggested to compose the group with alternate lines of the physical bus; this way, a single accident taking place in one of the bus connectors has lower probability to generate more than one fault on the same line group.

Fig. 3 shows an implementation instance for the interface to be placed on each card connected to the M3BUS; it includes the functions of the transmitting and of the receiving station of fig. 2: remark that duplication of parity control and of correcting code generation has been avoided, by proper switching of data paths between transmission and reception phases.

7. CONCLUSIONS

A new method for monitoring and correcting parallel data transmission has been described, together with suggestions for implementing a hardware interface capable of adapting the exposed principles to a microprocessor bus.

The main feature of this interface is to assure a correct data communication also when one bit is incorrectly received in any position of the parallel link, possibly requiring only one retry; permanent and transient faults are admitted.

Future developments of the work include the study of the optimal redundancy for the control lines needed for handshaking and for communicating the retry requests.

REFERENCES:

[1] Hamming, R.W., Coding and Information Theory (Integrated Computer Systems, Santa Monica, California 1978).

[2] Reynolds, D.A., Metre, G., Fault Detection Capabilities of Alternating Logic, IEEE Transactions on Computers, Vol. C-27 (Feb. 1978) 106.

[3] Shedletsky, J.J., Error Correction by Alternate Data Retry. IEEE Transactions on Computers, Vol. C-27 (Feb. 1978) 106.

[4] Danese, G., Dotti, D., Monici, M., Sartori, M., Caratteristiche funzionali e strutturali dell'FBI (FAST BUS INSPECTOR) AICA Annual Conference, Pavia, september '81.

[5] Danese, G., Dotti, D., Fabbiani, M., Minozzi, C.A., Monici, M., Fast Bus Inspector for 16 bit M3BUS MUMICRO internal Report (1982.

[6] Del Corso, D., Maddaleno, F., Extension of Bus Protocols: a Technique for Modular Upgrade of Processing Systems, 8 Symposium on Microprocessing and Microprogramming, Euromicro '82.

[7] Kaneda, S., Fujiwara, E., Single Byte Error Correcting Double Byte Error Detecting Codes for Memory Systems, IEEE Transactions on Computer, Vol. C-31 (July 1982) 596.

MICROCOMPUTERS: Developments in Industry, Business and Education
D.R. Wilson and C.J. van Spronsen (eds.) /© EUROMICRO, 1983
Elsevier Science Publishers B.V. (North-Holland)

Taskspecific assignment of redundancy in the fault-tolerant multicomputer system FUTURE

G. Faerber F. Demmelmeier

Lehrstuhl fuer Prozessrechner,
Technische Universitaet Muenchen
West Germany

Keywords: Fault Tolerance, Multimicrocomputer System, Process Automation, Redundancy, Modula-2

FUTURE a **F**ault-tolerant and **U**ser friendly multicomputer system with **T**askspecific **U**tilization of **RE**dundancy is introduced. This system allows assignment of specific reliability classes to application tasks ranging from TMR to conventional. The application programmer does not have to deal with fault-tolerance functions, he has just to determine the reliability class. The fault-tolerance is implemented in software using Modula-2 as programming language and off-the-shelf microcomputers (LSI-11), a powerful non-retro-active message transport system and a higly reliable input/output system.

1. Taskspecific Fault Tolerance

In most applications - e.g. in process automation - computer systems have to handle multiple tasks in a quasi-simultaneous manner. In conventional singleprocessor systems a multitasking operating system divides the one real processor into as many pseudoprocessors as tasks to be performed.

Using N real processors in a multiprocessor system allows the distribution of the tasks between these processors:

If processor i carries t tasks, a total of

$$M = \sum_{i=1}^{N} t_i$$

pseudoprocessors are available. The only condition to be met is that the dynamic load indroduced by the tasks can be handled according to the time requirements.

Using redundant pseudoprocessors to implement single tasks /1/, each task may then be equipped according to its individual requirement for reliability and availability. Figure 1 shows in a simplified form the funcitional state of a task:

- The dotted circles describe the functional state of a task as observed from outside (functional or failed).

- The initial state within the outer dotted circle defines the degree of redundancy the task is equipped with: It is called the "task class" in FUTURE.

- As well as dynamic redundancy (standby tasks, only the code is provided: left side of the outer dotted circle) static redundancy may also be assigned (multiple execution) and comparing/voting on results: upper part of the dotted circle).

- The task state may degrade if a processor fails according to the restoration/reconfiguration strategy; after correction the original state may be restored.

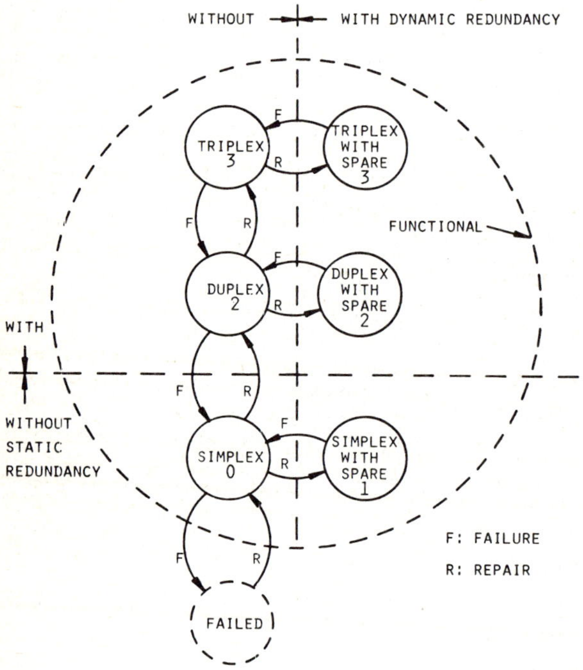

FIG 1: FUNCTIONAL TASK STATES

In FUTURE 4 task classes (class 0 - class 3) are defined as indicated in Figure 1, whereby class 3 tasks tolerate one hardware failure at a time. Table 1 shows some of the characteristic features of each class. It is abvious that class 2 and class 3 tasks detect transient and permanent failures by comparing/voting results; class 3 tasks are also able (single error provided) to continue without interruption: Reconfiguration can be delayed until the task allows it.

	SIMPLEX		DUPLEX		TRIPLEX	
TASKS ACTIVE/STANDBY	1/0	1/1	2/0	2/1	3/0	3/1
TASK - CLASS	0	1	2	2	3	3
REDUNDANCY (STATIC/DYNAMIC)	NO	D	S	S+D	S	S+D
LOAD	1	1	2	2	3	3
DETECTION OF PERMANENT FAULTS	(DIAGNOSTICS)		YES		YES	
DETECTION OF TRANSIENT FAULTS	NO		YES		YES	
EXTERNAL EFFECTS OF FAULTS	YES	YES	NO	NO	NO	NO
SYSTEMINTERUPTION AFTER FAULTS	YES	SHORT	SHORT	SHORT	NO	NO

TABLE 1: CHARACTERISTIC FEATURES OF THE FUTURE-TASK-CLASSES

For the dynamic redundancy it must be either possible to restart the task in case of a failure, or an additional checkpoint strategy has to be installed. The results of comparing and voting are used for error detection and diagnosis.

Figure 2 gives an example for N = 6 processors an M tasks. All hatched boxes constitute a pseudoprocessor that is installed in the real processor i for executing tasks. Diagonal hatching indicates active tasks that create dynamic load for the processor, vertical hatching shows stand-by tasks that require only memory space for their code. In case of a processor-failure (a column disappers) all active tasks have to be reassigned to other processors where the corresponding stand-by tasks reside (reconfiguration). The figure also shows an important restriction: Redundant tasks have to be assigned to distinct processors.

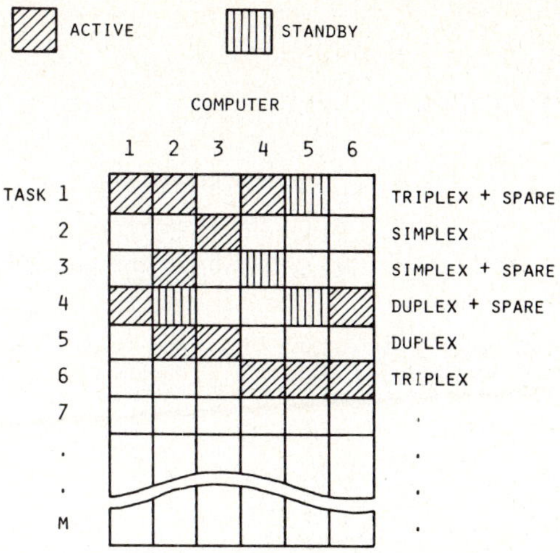

FIG 2: <u>ASSIGNMENT OF REDUNDANT TASKS</u>

It is impossible to charge the application rogrammer with all the redundancy handling, oting, error detection etc. These functions are

- independent of the individual applications and
- very sensitive to design errors.

They therefore belong to the system software: The fault-tolerance has to be hidden from the application programmer. The only interface he has to observe is attaching a "task-class-number" to his task. The creation of multiple tasks, their distribution in the multicomputer system, all comparing/voting etc. has to be done by either the programming system (statically) or the runtime system (dynamically).

2. Architecture of FUTURE

2.1 Hardware-Architecture

In fault-tolerant computer systems a main problem always is to decide which instance should

- detect an isolate faults and
- manage data restoration and system reconfiguration.

Often new modules are introduced for these supervisory functions

- the question has to then be solved which instance now supervises the supervisor (and so on).

It seems to be especially important to avoid this hierarchy of supervisors and to replace it by a cyclic solution: The same hardware that executes tasks must also realize the functions mentioned above. Their implementation may be done in software which is supported by certain hardware-features.

The concept of software implemented fault tolerance has been analyzed intensivly in the SIFT-project /2,3,4/: The hardware-architecture of FUTURE therefore is similar to SIFT. The smallest replaceable unit (SRU) is a complete computer that is based on a standard microprocessor: It consists of processor, memory, I/O-control and a private part of a message transport system which interconnects the computers to a multicomputer system.

Only a complete computer provides enough capability to execute tasks and to implement the required fault-tolerance functions. It is natural to use this level of complexity for one SRU. Additionally VLSI-technology will enforce the use of ever growing complexities as smallest independent parts of a system.

Figure 3 shows the basic hardware architecture. The computers communicate using a message transport system: It has to be constructed in a way that inhibits the propagation of a hardware fault from one computer to the others. It is implemented in FUTURE by write-only-busses that are assigned individually to each computer - with N computers N busses have to be provided. All computers can hear what has been sent (broadcasted) on each bus: The coupling of receivers can be meade completely passive (e.g. by optical couplers), and each receiver may decide on its own whether it accepts data from a computer or not.

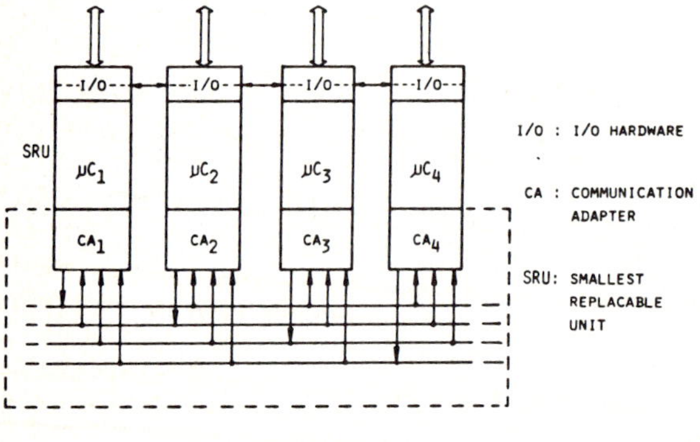

FIG 3: MULTICOMPUTERSYSTEM INCLUDING THE MESSAGE TRANSPORTSYSTEM WITH PRIVATE WRITE-ONLY BUSSES

The performance of the message transport system (MTS) is very important for the fault-tolerance functions, since the following types of informations have to be exchanged:

- There is intertask communication like in other multicomputer systems (the common reason for computer inter-connections).

- Data have to be exchanged to be able to compare or vote decentrally. The more data are compared the earlier faults may be detected: The throughput of the transport system should be sufficient.

- For diagnostic purposes the computers have to check their partners, to transmit their diagnostic results and to decide on faulty computers as close together in time as possible.

These requirements show the importance of a powerful MTS, and in FUTURE each computer broadcasts with a bit rate of 16 Mbit/s.

It is obvious that an interface as commonly used will not be able to reach that data stream: Consider a configuration with 8 computers each transmitting with 2 Mbytes/s: No bus-system will be able to carry these data rates.

Therfore the concept of a "distributed global memory" has been conceptualized: Each receiver has its own dualport memory, the second port being accessible via the computer bus - therefore only the computer's accesses define the bus load. Figure 4 shows the memory-layout: Writing data in a selected address space results in a transmission of address and data which are written into the corresponding memory in each system - the data are accessible globally. Additional hardware allows to wait for the receipt of a selected message (or a combination of messages, e.g. for voting purposes). Data communication is hidden because it is handled like memory write accesses, transmission errors are handled like parity errors in memory. The communication system is very well suited

- to distribute state information and
- to transmit messages.

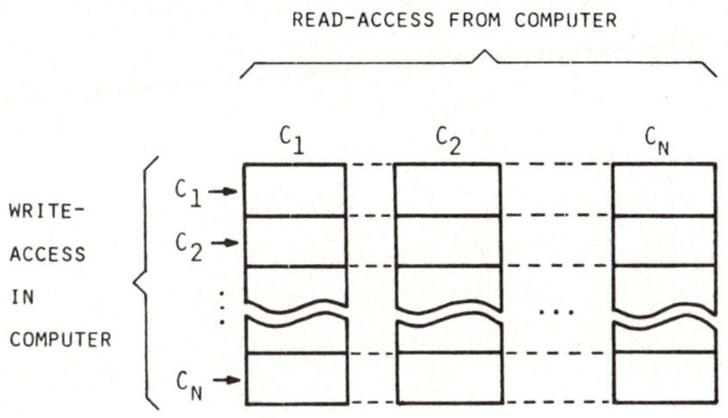

FIG 4: DISTRIBUTED GLOBAL MEMORY

One of the most difficult problems in fault-tolerant computers is the integration of processinput/output (I/O). Especially for instrumentation in process automation it is optimal to install also sensors and actuators redundantly (because its failure rate often is much higher than for electronics) and to attach it to 2 computers each; however since the computer architect normally has no influence on instrumentation, for FUTURE another alternative has been selected: Very small modules using single chip-micro-computers and housing only a few I/O-points are connected redundantly to 2 or more computers - the modules being very reliable (because they are small) and restricting any failure to a local area /5/.

2.2 Software architecture

The operating system is divided into the F-level and B-level (Fig. 5): On F-level (FUTURE-level) the fault-tolerance mechanisms are implemented. The F-level is supported by the B-level (basic system level) which provides a real time operating system /6/ and is based upon the hardware of one microcomputer together with the components belonging to the message transport system and the input/output system. The upper level of the program system is formed by application programs (A-level).

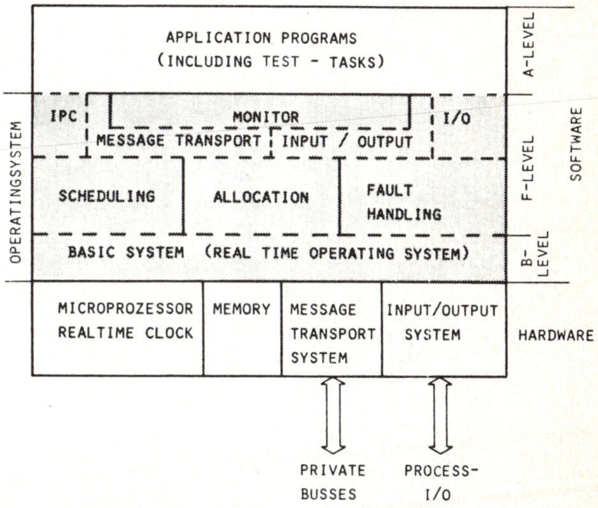

IPC : INTERPROCESS COMMUNICATION

I/O : PROCESS INPUT/OUTPUT

FIG 5: FUTURE OPERATING SYSTEM

Main parts of the F-level programs are

- allocation,
- scheduling,
- message transport system (MTS),
- process input/output system (IOS),

- fault handling and
- monitoring.

MTS and IOS are transparent for the user, all other system services are unaccessible for application programs. The interface between application and system programs is the task control block (see Fig. 6) which is associated with every application task. Besides taskname, description of code and data areas the task control block contains information about the reliability class of the task, where the corresponding co-tasks are activated and system table-links. These data can be read and modified by operating system programs.

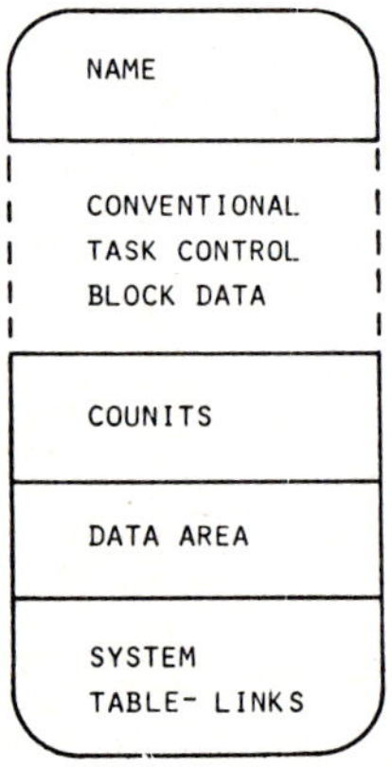

FIG 6: TASK CONTROL BLOCK

The fault detection mechanism is included in the MTS and consists of voting and comparing functions. Voting or comparing are called automatically for class 3 or class 2 tasks respectively, when an intertask communication (send/receive) occurs or in case of process I/O.

o Allocation

The object of the static program-memory assignment is flexibility with respect to system reconfiguration under consideration of the task reliability classes. Precondition for full reconfigurability of class 3 and class 2 tasks is that the code resides in all memories to avoid long transfer times.

Allocation starts with distribution of programs which are bound to specific function carriers (e.g. test tasks). Then class 3 and class 2 tasks are distributed to guarantee that co-tasks run on different microcomputers. The remaining class 1 and class 0 tasks are attached so that a balanced load of the computers is reached.

o Scheduling

Co-tasks of reliability class 2 or 3 should run with maximal degree of synchronism. This is necessary to avoid long delays between these co-tasks during compare or vote respectively. Scheduling is based upon a round robin technique with time slices and global adjustment of the queues. Information of the queue tables is distributed system wide when a time slice ends. Arguments for a global round robin strategy are as follows:

- High degree of fairness between computing tasks is achievable and
- Different run time requirements are resolved in a fair manner.

Time slices are generated by means of (local) real time clocks. At termination or interruption of application tasks the (local) operating system gains control and the queues according to the different task states are reordered. The control is transferred to the global part of the operating system for information exchange between the microcomputers. After sending its own queue information and receiving that of the other computers the scheduling algorithm starts. The result is a set of i tasks which run on the N microcomputers during the next time slice. This information is voted during the mutual exchange and the computers are synchronized.

o Message transport, process input/output

The MTS as well as the IOS have an interface to the application programmer for interprocess communication (IPC) and process input/output (I/O). The user does not have to deal with fault- tolerance functions, he only issues a send/receive or an input/output directive, the decision whether a local or global action including comparing or voting is necessary is made by the operating system.

IPC and I/O are "natural" points at which co-tasks are synchronized via vote or compare functions and thereby the fault detection mechanism is initiated. Synchronization and time out control (for deadlock avoidance) are hardware supported (message transport hardware) as well as the control of process input/output /5/.

o Monitoring

In the runtime-version the monitor has to collect and prepare information for the service staff and is responsible for the automatic restart of repaired modules. During implementation and system test the monitor plays a very important role in proving the proper operation of the fault detection and recovery mechanism by means of supervising, displaying and manipulation system tables.

o Fault handling

Fault handling is responsible for fault recovery. It is divided into two parts, the data restoration and the system reconfiguration. Data restoration is initiated, when a transient failure is detected, a system reconfiguration starts in case of a permanent failure. Fault handling is discussed in the next section.

Complexity of the system software plays an important role for the construction of a system in which fault-tolerance is based on software. A software fault is a design error. FUTURE is designed to tolerate hardware failures but cannot tolerate design errors, neither in hardware nor in software. To minimize the probability of the presence of a design error we use off-the-shelf hardware as much as possible and the high level language Modula-2 /7/ for system programming. Modula-2 is a real time language, supports modular programming of complex problems, has excellent methods for defining dedicated data and program structures and allows the access to hardware components without leaving the high language level.

3. System behaviour

3.1 System interactions

The system interactions are shown in Fig. 7. Once the application programs are developed (programming language is also Modula-2), the task classes are assigned by means of the task-builder and the system is initialized. After this "static" part the control is transferred to the operating system. After code allocation the scheduler assigns the appropriate application tasks to the processors. In a fault-free environment the application tasks are scheduled according to the scheduling algorithm and have access to MTS and IOS for interprocess communication and process input/output respectively.

All system tasks have access to the system tables in order to modify them according to their demands. The monitor watches the system tables, records the significant changes and is allowed to modify their contents to inject "failures" in order

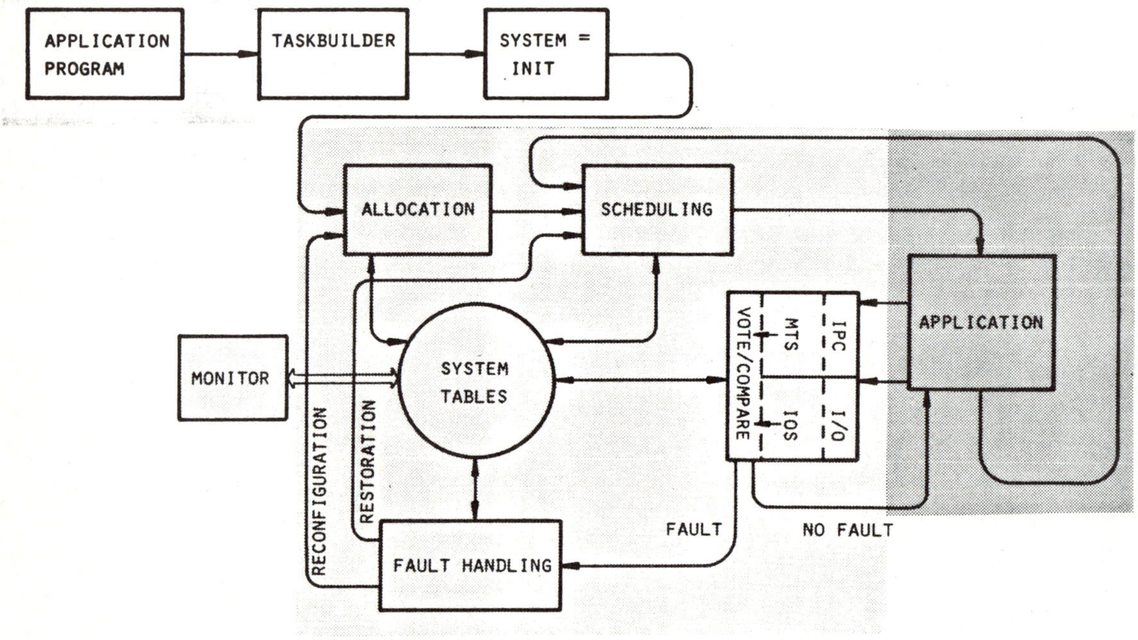

FIG 7: SYSTEM INTERACTIONS

If the presence of a fault is detected via voting for comparing in class 3 or class 2 tasks the fault handling is initiated.

Fault recovery depends on the failure type. A transient failure which is assumed for the first detection of a fault within one smallest replacable unit, leads to a database restoration of the involved task. In case of a permanent failure, on the other hand, a system reconfiguration is necessary to reconfigure out the faulty unit. After a restoration the scheduler becomes active immediately whereas a reconfiguration needs a new allocation.

to test and verify the fault tolerance mechanism.

FUTURE is conveived for process control, that means class 3 tasks may neither fail nor produce wrong results with respect to the process. A diagnosed hardware failure has an immediate effect on the IOS which transmits the (voted) results to the process. The defect unit has to be withdrawn immediately from the competence of issuing process signals. After finishing the actual process output handled by an intact unit, a data restoration or system reconfiguration starts.

3.2 Fault recovery

Recovery from a transient failure which in general leaves permanently disturbed data takes place by restoring the data of the affected tasks. Fig. 8 shows a situation with faulty data in co-task A. The fault handling selects microcomputer 1 to transfer the fault-free data via MTS to microcomputer 3 and reestablish data consistency for task A. After updating the related system tables the original degree of fault tolerance is restored. Now the system can again tolerate one further failure.

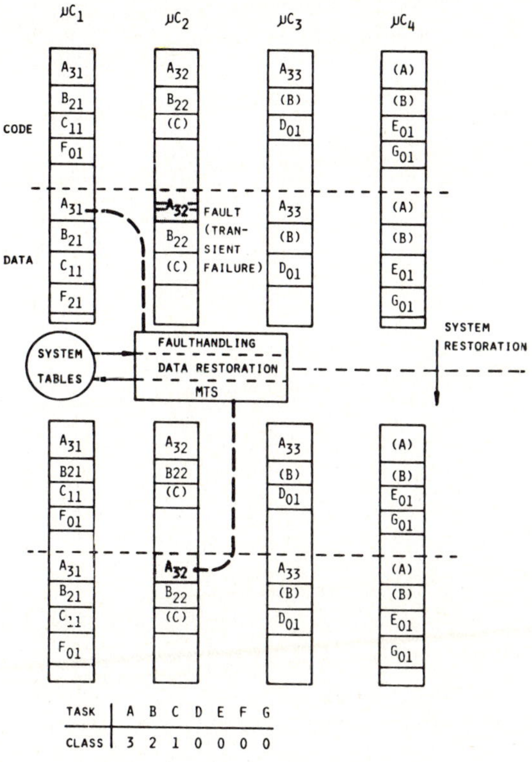

FIG 8: DATA RESTORATION

A second fault in the same SRU within a specific time limit or the report of a permanent failure from the IOS /5/ has as consequence a system reconfiguration.

All affected tasks and cotasks respectively are redistributed to new function carriers, either to a spare unit or to active units.

If a spare unit is available, the actual data of class 3 tasks are transmitted and the code is assumed to be resident at the spare.

Redistribution to an active unit is shown in Fig. 9. Detecting a fault during an IPC or an I/O of task A the voter activates the fault handling. According to the history of microcomputer 1 a permanent failure is diagnosed and after completion of the running I/O function a reconfiguration is initiated.

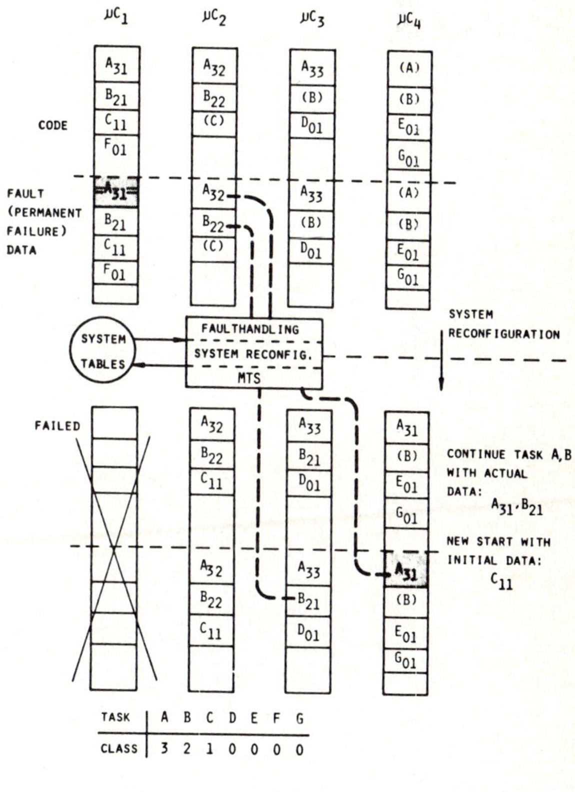

FIG 9: SYSTEM RECONFIGURATION

The fault handling freezes all activities

in microcomputers 2 to 4 and selects microcomputer 2 for updating data of co-tasks A_{31} and B_{21} in microcomputer 4 and 3 respectively. Allocation is started afterward to allow activation of co-tasks A_{31} and B_{21} in the microcomputers 4 and 3 respectively. The updated system tables are input to the scheduler.

The fault history of the system is traced by the global part of the fault handling and is further processed by the monitor as mentioned above. After repair and restart, microcomputer 1 is ready to be used as a spare for a proceeding system reconfiguration.

4. Conclusion

FUTURE tolerates in general one failure at a time. Fault diagnosis is initiated automatically in the case of IPC and I/O of an application task. The rate of diagnostic points as well as the amount of hardware randomly involved in the diagnostic depends on the application task. To increase the confidence in the status of the hardware, i.e. to minimize the problem of lurking errors, test tasks are established. These tasks run on application level whereby some hardware support in the IOS is available.

Reliable test strategies are very important but are not of primary interest in the FUTURE system. Supported by the FUTURE fault detection mechanism, relativly simple and less complex test procedures are possible which run on application program level.

A prototype of FUTURE is under construction and is based on LSI-11 microcomputers extended by message transport and process input/output hardware. Implementation and programming language is Modula-2. The prototype is operable.

Literature

/1/ Faerber, G.
Fault-tolerant computer systems for process automation.
Process Automation, No.2, 1982, pp. 85-92.

/2/ Weinstock, C.B.
SIFT: System design and implementation.
Proc. FTCS-10, Kyoto, Oct. 1-3 1980, pp. 75-77.

/3/ Wensley, J.H., Lamport, L., Green, M.W., Levitt, K.N., Melliar-Smith, P.M., Weinstock, C.B., Shostak, R.E., Goldberg, J.,
SIFT: Design and analysis of a fault-tolerant computer for aircraft control.
Proc. IEEE, Vol. 66, No. 10. Oct. 1978, S. 1240-1255.

/4/ Wensley, J.H., Levitt, K.N. Green, M.W., Goldberg, J., Neumann, P.G.
Design of a fault-tolerant airborne digital computer.
Report SRI project 1406, Stanford Research Institute, Oct. 1973.

/5/ Endl, H., Ries, W.
A strategy for fault-tolerant process input/ output.
Interner Bericht, Lehrstuhl fuer Prozessrechner 1983.

/6/ Maier, G.
MODEB: A real time operating system kernel written in the high level language Modula-2.
Preprints of the 3. IFAC/IFIP Symposium (Software for Computer Control)
5-8 Oct.1982, Madrid, pp. 15-21

/7/ Wirth, N.
Programming in Modula-2.
Springer Verlag Berlin, 1982.

Session H1:

HIGH LEVEL LANGUAGE ARCHITECTURES

Chairman: J. Tiberghien
Free University Brussels
Brussels (Belgium)

The first computer programs did reflect all the hardware particularities of the machines that executed them. They were written in 'machine language'. Soon 'High Level Languages' (HLL) were introduced to alleviate the burden on programmers. Hardware particularities were hidden in compilers or interpreters. The use of these languages increased tremendously the productivity of programmers, but it also revealed some important limitations:

- In the compilation process important information such as the names of the variables, is discarded, so that it becomes extremely hard to relate execution errors to the source code.
- Compilers being fairly complex, sometimes subtle errors can creep into the translation process making program debugging really intricate.
- Compilations, that are not seen by computer users as productive activity, can absorb a significant amount of computer resources.
- Machine code being often much less compact than high level code, the memory space needed to execute compiled programs is often considered excessive.

When instead of being compiled, high level languages are being interpreted, most of the above drawbacks disappear, but the execution speed is reduced by a factor of 10 to 100, making interpreting unsuitable for larger programs. Difficulties associated with high level languages have been related to the 'Semantic gap'[1], that is, the large difference between the semantics of the high level statements, and the machine instructions to be executed by the hardware.

In the first chapter of his book 'Advances in Computer Architectures' Glen Myers [2] analyses very accurately the different undesirable properties of the classical Von Neumann Computers, in the context of their use in HLL environments. In subsequent chapters he reviews several proposed improvements to the Von Neumann Architecture in order to reduce significantly the semantic gap. Most of these improvements result in a significant increase in the complexity of the hardware, but due to the emergence of VLSI technology, such an increase seems to be much more affordable than it used to be.

Many of the improvements reported by Myers are questioned by Ditzel and Patterson [3] who suggest that increased hardware complexity at the processor level is probably not the optimal way to exploit the opportunities of VLSI technology in order to improve the execution of HLL programs. By designing a very simple but still powerful miroprocessor, called RISC (Reduced Instruction Set Computer) [4] Patterson has given some experimental evidence of the correctness of his point of view.

Whether increasingly complex, or simplex processor architectures are the best answer for improved overall system performance in an HLL programming environment, remains an open question. The three papers to be presented in this session are certainly valuable constructions to the debate.

References

[1] V.O. GAGLIARDI
'Report of Workshop 4 - Software Related Advances in Computer Hardware'
Proceedings of a symposium on the high cost of software.
Stanford Research Institute, 1973.

[2] GLENFORD J. MYERS
Advances in Computer Architecture.
John Wiley and Sons, 1978.

[3] DAVID R. DIZEL, DAVID A. PATTERSON
Retrospective on high-level language computer architecture.
Proceedings of the 7th annual symposium on Computer Architecture (IEEE/ACM), 1980

[4] JOHN K. FODERARD, KORBIN S. VAN DYKE, DAVID A. PATTERSON
Running Riscs
VLSI Design, Sept.-Oct., 1982.

[5] ROBERT P. COLWELL, CHARLES Y. HITCHCOCK, E. DOUGLAS JENSEN
Peering through the Risc/Cisc Fog.
Computer Architecture News,
Vol II, Nr 1, March 1983.

MICROCOMPUTERS: Developments in Industry, Business and Education
D.R. Wilson and C.J. van Spronsen (eds.) / © EUROMICRO, 1983
Elsevier Science Publishers B.V. (North-Holland)

HIGH-SPEED EXECUTION OF FORTH AND PASCAL PROGRAMS ON A HIGH-LEVEL LANGUAGE MACHINE

Yukio Kaneda, Koichi Wada and Sadao Maekawa

Faculty of Engineering, Kobe University
Kobe, Japan

This paper presents a microprogram-controlled high-level language machine system which can execute both Forth and Pascal programs efficiently and in high-speed.
To improve the efficiency and speed of execution, this machine is composed of a high-speed memory for variables, a two-bank structured hardware stack, a multiplier, and others. User programs are compiled into micro object codes.
As a result of benchmark test, it has been confirmed that this system can execute about 200 times faster than Z80 microcomputer.

1. INTRODUCTION

Pascal(1) is a very popular programming language and has world-wide user community. Forth(2)(3) is not so known as Pascal, but has a fast-growing number of users in control and other fields. Programs written in these languages are easy to understand and somewhat compact. However, their execution time is ten to hundred times longer than the programs written in an assembly language. Low speed is a fatal defect in applications when a rapid execution is required.

We have developed a microprogram-controlled high-level language oriented machine. This machine is organized from microprocessor slices(AM2903), two hardware stacks, and specially designed electric circuits. We succeeded in realizing high speed execution of Forth and Pascal programs.

In this paper we describe the machine architecture, how to realize the Forth and Pascal machine on it, the Forth and Pascal compilers that translate programs into microcodes, and the system evaluations.

2. ORGANIZATION OF THE MACHINE

Figure 1 shows the organization of the system. The microprocessor Z80 and the microprogram controlled high-level language engine(HLL engine) are interconnected through the Z80's I/O port. The HLL engine has three registers which are accessed by the Z80, and called command register(CMR), word address register(WAR), and output data register(ODR). The Z80 controls the HLL engine with the CMR(i.e. makes it run or halt). The WAR is used for communicating a micro address to start execution. The HLL engine transfers results of culculation to Z80 through the ODR. A data memory of 64k words(16-bit word) is shared by both processors. Figure 2 shows the architecture of the HLL engine. There exist three internal buses, R-bus and S-bus as source buses, and Y-bus as destination bus, each of 16-bit wide. The HLL engine consists of five modules:

(1) Computer Control Unit (CCU)
CCU has a microprogram sequencer and 32k words(32-bit word) writable control storage(WCS) for storing microcodes. Depending on a kind of hardware module(e.g. ALU or by-path controller or data memory) to be activated, cycle time for an operation varies. However, an expected execution cycle time of microinstructions is about 200n seconds. A one-level pipeline provides a high-speed microinstruction fetch.

(2) Arithmetic-and-Logic Unit (ALU)
The ALU has 4 microprocessor slices (4-bit slice, AM2903) and one multiplier(MPY-16HJ, TRW Co.). The AM2903 is designed as a high speed cascadable element intended for using as microprogramable processors. The device consists of a 16-word register file, a high speed arithmetic-and-logic unit, and other circuitry. The MPY-16HJ is a 16bit-by-16bit parallel array multiplier with a typical multiplication time of 100n seconds.

(3) Hardware Stacks
The HLL engine is a stack oriented machine having two hardware stacks installed. One is a parameter stack which contains operands of arithmetic-and-logic operations, and the other one is a return stack which contains return addresses of nested

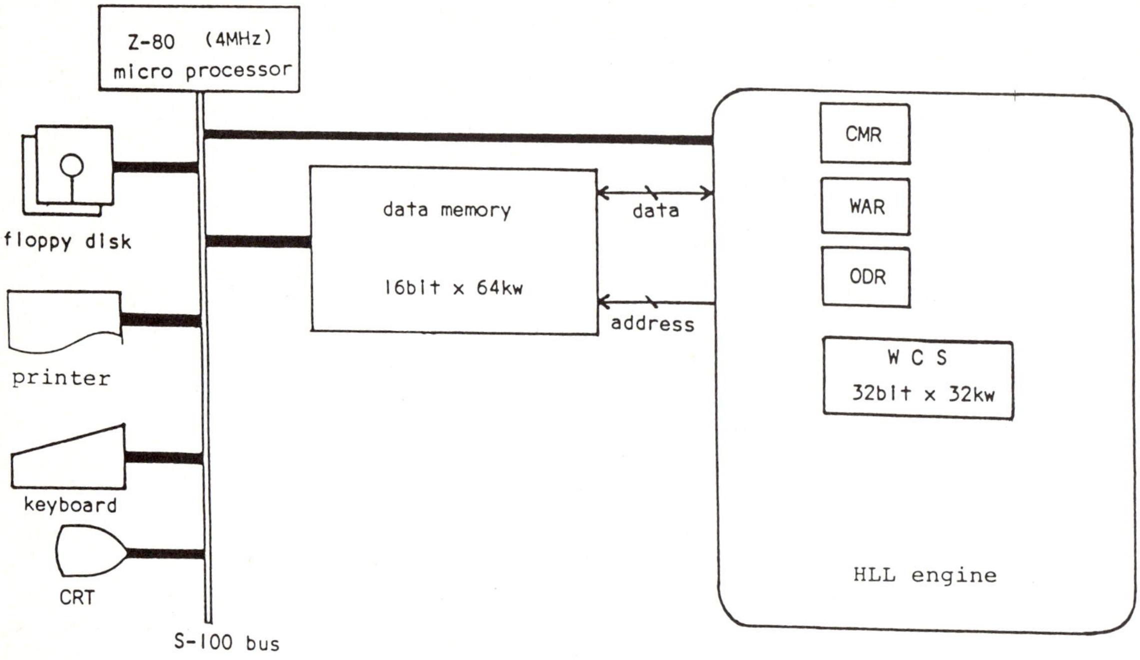

Figure 1 : Organization of the system.

function-calls and control values of do-loops. These two stacks play very important roles in realizing high speed executions. Particularly, the parameter stack comprises two high-speed memory banks. Hence, the top and second items can be simultaniously popped off and sent to the ALU. Thus, the ALU operations for the top two stack items can be done in one microprogram cycle. The parameter stack has 8k 16-bit word capacity organized into two banks of 4k words each. The capacity of the return stack is 4k words(16-bit).

(4) Variable Storage
The variable storage with 4k 16-bit word capacity, is a high-speed temporary memory for predefined variables to which high-rate access are expected. The variable storage can be accessed four times as fast as the data memory.

(5) By-path Controller
This is a shortcut path from S- or R-buses to the Y-bus. In many programs, data transfer operations between stack items are often used. Thus, rapid transfer is indispensable to the HLL engine. Data transfer can be done by the ALU, however, this by-path controller reduces transfer time to half.

3. FORTH MACHINE

Forth system is formed from a large number of functions called word. A Forth word corresponds to a subroutine or procedure in other languages, and Forth dictionary is a collection of Forth words. A defined Forth word is translated and modified to be an entry of Forth dictionary. Each entry consists of a header part and a body part. The header part is formed from identifiers and a link field. A link field is an address pointer to a header part of predefined word for constructing Forth dictionary. A body is the main part for performing the defined function.

Forth system uses two push-down stacks: a parameter stack and a return stack. The use and names of these two stacks in the HLL engine have been conformed to those of Forth system.

All Forth words for I/O processing and compilation are installed in the Z80,

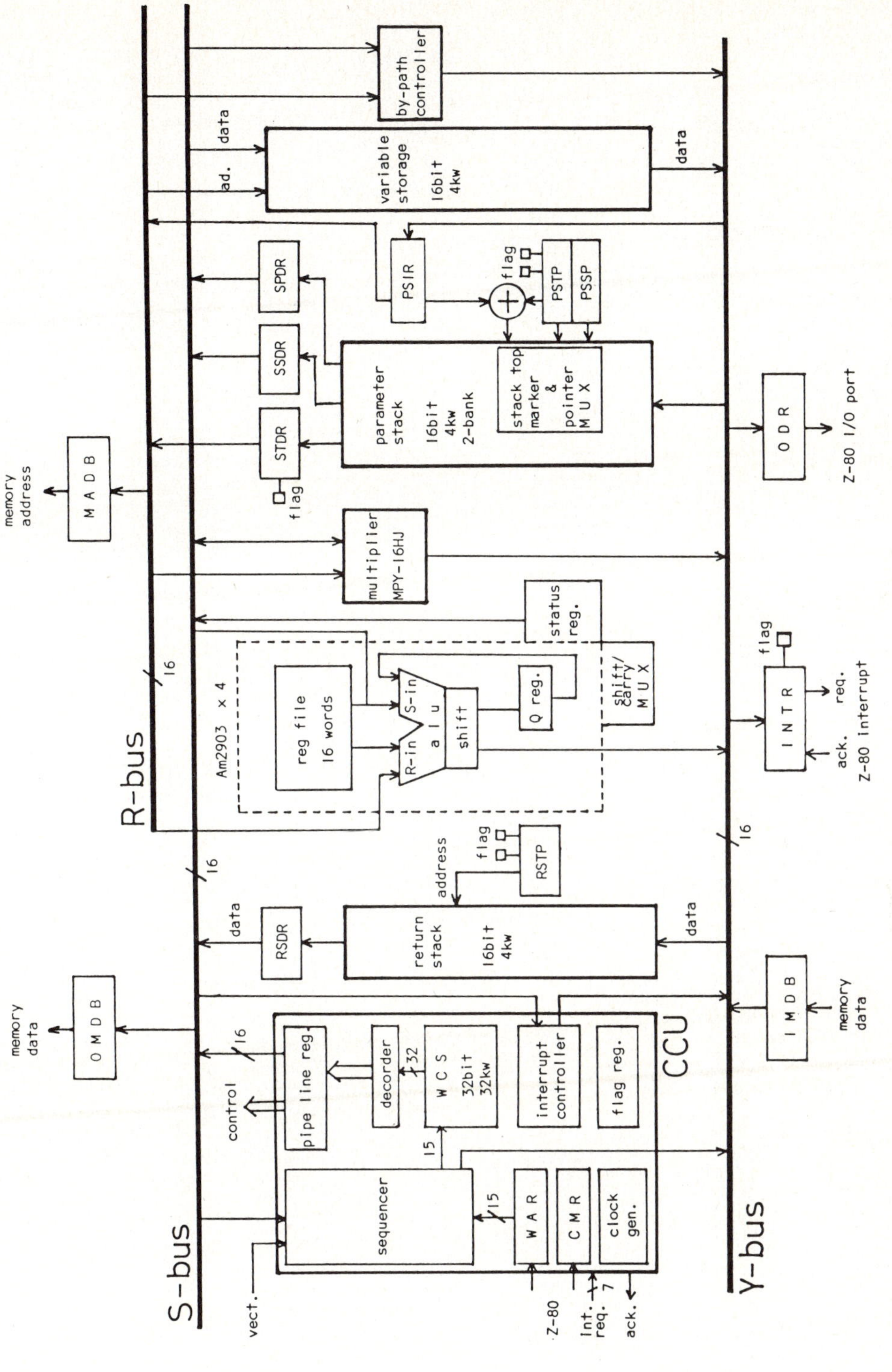

Figure 2 : Hardware structure of HLL engine.

and all other words including user-defined ones are installed in the HLL engine. A defined Forth word is compiled into microcodes and stored in WCS as an entry of the Forth dictionary. In general, a body part of an entry is composed of several address pointers to the body part of refered words. However, in this system, the address pointers are replaced by subroutine-call microinstructions.

Hereupon, the frequent calling sequences to basic Forth words are not negligible overhead. Hence, for generating more efficient object codes, a new compiler is developed. In this optimized compiler, references to these basic words are replaced by direct embedding of microcode sequences. When put into the compiled object codes, these sequences act as the word being refered to. By introducing this technique, the compiler reduces execution time to half.

4. PASCAL MACHINE

In the case of UCSD-Pascal systems, a Pascal source program is translated into an intermediate code called Pseudo-code(P-code) which is an instruction set of Pseudo-machine(P-machine). The P-machine is basically a stack oriented computer and has several pointers and registers in it. Some of these pointers are as follows:

SP : Stack pointer-a pointer to the top of the evaluation stack. The stack plays an important role in execution of the Pascal program.
MP : Most recent Procedure-a pointer for accessing local variables.
BASE : BASE procedure-a pointer for accessing global variables.

4.1 Correspondence between the P-machine and the HLL engine

The Pascal machine is an emulated P-machine on the HLL engine by following methods:

(a) The P-code machine's stack to which more than 60% of operations access, is assigned to the parameter stack. Thus, plenty of main memory references are reduced.
(b) The pointers of the P-code machine such as instruction counter(IC), MP, and BASE are allocated to ALU registers.
(c) Data segments equipped by the compiler are divided into two groups and allocated to the variable storage and the data memory.

4.2 Compiler

Pascal source programs are tranlated into micro object codes by the Z80 and executed by the HLL engine. The translation is done in the following two steps:

Step1. The Pascal compiler first read and analyze a source program to be executed. Then, it generates Pseudo-code sequences as object codes. This compiler is on the basis of Pascal-S(4) compiler. however, it is modified for optimization as follows.
 i). To improve the efficiency of controlling for-loop iterations, new P-codes are added, which can control the return stack in the HLL engine. This reduces a large number of data references in main memory.
 ii). Storing to array-type variables are improved in effiency. This is achieved by adjourning code generation for the address parts of arrays, in which the elements of arrays are stored. This is due to the relation between the parameter stack and the internal buses in the HLL engine.

Let P^+-code denote the new extended Pseudo-code generated by the compiler mentioned above.

Step2. Finally, the P^+-code compiler translates a P^+-code program into a microcode object program. By replacing a P^+-code instructions to associated microcode sequences, the P^+-code compiler translates a P^+-code object into a microcode object that is equivalent to the original one.

Almost all of the P-code instructions are replaced by 2 to 4 microinstructions.

5. SYSTEM EVALUATION BY THE BENCHMARK PROGRAMS

We used the two bench mark programs listed in Appendix 1. Table 1 shows the execution time of the required programs on different machines. Benchmark programs are as follows:

(1) Sorting:

Data 1,2,...,1000 stored in the variable storage are sorted into reverse order. Sorting algorithm is an exchange sorting method shown in Appendix 1(a). The Forth machine on the HLL engine executes the Forth program about 92 times faster than the Z80 poly-FORTH system, and in the case of pascal, 198 times faster than the Z80 UCSD-Pascal system. Then, on this Forth machine, a Forth program can be executed at almost the same speed as the Fortran program on a ACOS-900 system(a large scale computer of NEC). This Forth program is nicely fitted to the architecture of Forth machine on the HLL engine. Thus, the Forth machine is about four times faster than Pascal machine on this program.

(2) Sieve of Eratosthenes algolithm to compute all prime numbers from 0 to 8190:

The program in Gilbreath's paper(5) is refered to. In this program, the Forth machine executes about 56 times faster than the Z80 poly-FORTH system. On the Pascal machine, the Pascal program runs about 102 times faster than the UCSD-Pascal system on the Z80.

Let the utilization ratio denote the percentage of total micro steps at which a hardware module in the HLL engine is activated. Table 2 shows the utilization ratio of the parameter stack, return stack, and by-path controller. The top item of the parameter stack is read at nearly 37.1 to 47.4 percent of total steps. It is noteworthy that the utilization ratio for the reference to the second item on the parameter stack is as high as 20.6 to 30.3 percent. This shows that the two-bank structured parameter stack is very effective.

The utilization ratio of the return stack is 1.9 to 22.2 percent. In the case of Pascal, it is shown that the frequency of use is comparatively lower. This is why the benchmark programs written in Pascal language consist of a single procedure and few calls of built-in functions. As to controls of iteration or accesses of loop indices, processing with a return

Table 1 : Comparison of benchmark programs running on various machines.

Language and Machine	Sorting		Prime numbers	
	Execute(sec.)	Ratio	Execute(sec.)	Ratio
Forth (Forth machine)	2.71	1.00	1.5	1.00
Pascal (Pascal machine)	8.6	3.17	2.3	1.53
UCSD-Pascal version 1.5 (Z-80)	1705.6	629.37	233.9	155.93
UCSD-Pascal (Pascal micro-engine)	---	---	63.0	42.00
poly-FORTH (LSI-11)	237.7	87.71	79.4	52.93
poly-FORTH (Z-80)	248.3	91.62	84.4	56.27
BD Software C (Z-80)	251.6	92.84	50.2	33.47
Fortran (ACOS-900)	3.20	1.18	0.74	0.49

Table 2 : Utilization ratio of hardware modules.

(%)

operation			Sorting Forth machine	Sorting Pascal machine	Prime numbers Forth machine	Prime numbers Pascal machine
Parameter stack	top	read operation	37.1	41.3	38.4	47.4
		write operation	44.5	70.0	45.7	75.8
	second	read operation	22.2	30.0	20.6	30.3
Return stack	read operation		22.2	17.5	16.2	6.3
	write operation		7.4	8.8	10.1	1.9
By-path controller			44.5	53.9	36.4	43.9

stack is much more efficient than with a main memory.

The by-path controller is activated at 36.4 to 53.9 percent, and thus, this module is very effective and requisite.

6. CONCLUSION

This paper presented a specially designed microprogram controlled high-level language machine. User programs are compiled into microinstructions. New compilers which generate optimized micro object codes were developed. Two benchmark programs were coded by Forth and Pascal, compiled, and executed. The execution times were measured, and these values are presented in Table 1. These values show that the our machine is very fast. Our findings are summarized below:

1. The organization of HLL engine is adaptable to Forth system and Pseudo-machine in Pascal system without great effort.
2. The two-bank structured hardware stack which can be popped off top and second items simultaniously is very effient for high speed program execution.
3. The return stack and its relation with the internal buses play important roles in iteration control and reference of loop indices.
4. High speed data transfer by the by-path controller is very effective.

REFERENCES

(1) Shillington, K.A. and Ackland, G.M.: UCSD-Pascal Version 1.5 (Institute for Information Systems, 1978).
(2) Ewing, M.S.: THE CALTECH FORTH MANUAL Second Edition, A Technical Report of the OWENS VALLEY OBSERVATORY (1978).
(3) Moore, C.H., The Evolution of FORTH, an Unusual Language, BYTE, BYTE Publications Inc., Vol.6, No.8 (1981).
(4) Barron, D.W.: Pascal-The Language and its Implementation, John wiley & Sons Ltd, (1981).
(5) Gilbreath J., A High-Level Language Benchmark, BYTE, BYTE Publications Inc., (sept. 1981) 180-198.

Appendix 1 : Implementation of the benchmark programs written in Forth and Pascal language.

(a) Sorting by simple exchange.

i) Forth program.

```
DECI
: PUTDATA 1001 1 DO I DUP !V LOOP ;
: SORT 2 SETPSIR 1000 1 DO
         I DUP @V 1001 I 1+ DO
             I @V OVER OVER < IF SWAP I !V DUP (PICK) !V
                              ELSE DROP
                              THEN
                            LOOP
             2DROP      LOOP ;
```

ii) Pascal program.

```
program SORTING;

  type list = array [1..1000] of integer;
  var  idata : list;
       i,j,k,l,m,work : integer;

   begin
     for i:=1 to 1000 do idata[i]:=i;
     for m:=1 to 999 do
       begin k:=m+1;
         for j:=k to 1000 do
           if idata[m] < idata[j] then
              begin  work:=idata[m];
                     idata[m]:=idata[j];
                     idata[j]:=work
              end
       end
   end.
```

(b) Eratosthenes Sieve prime number program.

i) Forth program.

```
DECI
:  SIZE 8191 ;   : FLAGS 32768 ; ( FLAGS = 8000H )
:  FILL ROT ROT OVER + SWAP DO DUP I !D LOOP DROP ;
:  DO-PRIME
   FLAGS SIZE 1 FILL
   0 SIZE 0
     DO  FLAGS I + @D
        IF I DUP + 3 + DUP I +
           BEGIN DUP SIZE <
           IF 0 OVER FLAGS +
           !D OVER + 0 ELSE 1 THEN END
           2DROP 1+
        THEN
     LOOP ;
```

ii) Pascal program.

```
program PRIME;

const
  size =8190;

var
  flags : array[0..size] of boolean;
  i,prime,k,count,iter : integer;

begin
writeln('10 iteration');
for iter := 1 to 10 do begin
        count :=0;
        fillchar(flags,sizeof(flags),true);
        for i := 0 to size do
                if flags[i] then begin
                        prime := i+i+3;
                        k := i + prime;
                        while k <= size do begin
                                flags[k] := false;
                                k := k + prime
                                end;
                        count := count + 1
                        { writeln(prime) }
                        end;
        end;
writeln(count,' primes')
end.
```

MICROCOMPUTERS: Developments in Industry, Business and Education
D.R. Wilson and C.J. van Spronsen (eds.) / ©EUROMICRO, 1983
Elsevier Science Publishers B.V. (North-Holland)

HLL CONTROL STATEMENTS IMPLEMENTATION THROUGH EXTENSIVE MODULAR MICROPROGRAMMING

M.S. Tudruj, R.F. Gajda

Institute of Computer Science
Polish Academy of Sciences
P.O.Box 22, 00-901 Warsaw, Poland

A new microprogrammable computer architecture is proposed oriented towards the structured implementation of programs written in high level languages. The architecture is based on a two-microprogrammed control unit computer, whose microinstructions have high-level modular control primitives provided for sequencing purposes. These primitives define a specific microinstruction internal language of the computer. Two microprogram stores are contained in the computer for separate storage and then execution of two kinds of microcode modules - concerned with the implementation of the control and data processing elements of the source HLL programs. The PASCAL language is used as the examplary high level language. A complier has been assumed for the computer which translates PASCAL programs directly at the microprogram module level. The general method of the implementation of the PASCAL language statements and the detailed implementation of the PASCAL control statements for structured programming in the proposed computer is presented in the paper.

INTRODUCTION

The constantly progressing VLSI technology makes many computer architectural concepts which ten years ago would seem to be non realistic, to become practically implementable today. This is especially true in the domain of fitting computer logic organization and architecture to software functions being performed. Perhaps we are not yet in the position to define the quantity and features of the hardware used in a given customized computer uniquely by its application functions, but there are evidences of moving fast in this direction.

One of the means frequently used in the design of computers oriented towards solving unconventional software implementation problems is the technique of microprogramming. This technique has significantly progressed during the last ten years and in particular microinstruction sequencing functions have been considerably developed. The capabilities of these functions in many cases are more powerful than those of addressing functions at the instruction level. This is specially true in the environment of modular microprogramming [1,2,3].

In this paper an initial idea of a microprogrammed computer unit is presented designed to perform modular microprograms which constitute the object code of programs written in a procedural high level language. The object modular microprograms are organized in a structured way, in two separate control memories belonging to the two cooperating control subunits of the proposed computer. A subset of the PASCAL language has been used as the exemplary language. Its control statements have been limited to those necessary for structured programming. The implementation of control statements of the subset of the PASCAL language has been based on the modularity oriented compound microinstruction sequencing functions presented by the authors in papers [3,4,5].

The paper is composed of two parts. The first one presents the general method of the implementation of the PASCAL programs and the organization of the proposed microprogrammed computer unit. In the second, the detailed implementation of the PASCAL control statements is presented based on the proposed computer unit and its sequencing functions. The implementation of the data processing expressions is not presented in the paper. Neither the detailed compilation method of the PASCAL programs to the microprogram level is discussed as having been approached in the literature [6].

1. GENERAL ASSUMPTIONS AND THE EXECUTIVE COMPUTER UNIT

The general strategy to perform a program written in a high level language is to translate it to an intermediate language which is accepted by a given computer. Generally, this language is the machine code of the computer. In microprogrammed computers, instructions of the machine code are interpreted by sequences of microinstructions. In fact, this is the second stage of the transition process. We assume in the paper the translation of high level language program to the machine code is eliminated and so programs are translated directly to microprograms. The similar strategy is used in such microprogram automatic generation systems [6] where algorithms of microprograms are given in high level languages.

In the design presented in this paper efficient microinstruction sequencing functions are used at the object microprogram level, which enable extensive modularity in microprogramming. Correspondingly, the object microcode execution computer unit has a particular internal structure which permits a separate implementation of the object microprograms corresponding to the control and data processing elements of source programs. The preliminary concept of the execution unit can be easily developed enhancing the parallelism of its functionning by providing multiple internal functional subunits.

Before the proposed computer unit is presented, let us recall the outline of the syntax of the PASCAL programs and then give some basic information concerning the required compilation process to the microprogram level. To describe the syntax, the Backus notation will be used with the following additions: {<syntactic object>} - denotes an iteration of the object (in partic. an omission), {<syntactic object>} = <empty>| <syntactic object> - denotes at most a single occurence of the object.

The outline of the syntax of the program in the PASCAL language is the following:

```
<program> ::= program <identifier> (<program
              parameters>) ; <block>.
<block> ::= <declaration part><instruction part>
<declaration part> ::= [<lebel declaration>]
                       [<constant definition>]
                       {<procedure declaration>|
                        <function declaration>}
<instruction part> ::= begin <instruction>{;<in-
                       struction>} end
<procedure declaration> ::= procedure <identifier>
                            [<parameter part>];
                            <block>
<function declaration> ::= function <identifier>
                           [<parameter part>] :
                           <result type> : <block>
<parameter part> ::= (<formal parameter section>
                     {; formal parameter
                     section>})
```

The meaning of the syntactic objects which have been used but not fully described in the outline above is identical to that given in [8].

The compilation of a high level language program to microprograms in our case is close to a typical compilation process of a program written in a high level language, except that some spacial features of the object microprogram code are assumed.

First of all the strongly modular character of the object microprograms has been assumed. The compilation results in the generation of microprogram modules of two kinds: the control modules and the executive modules. These two kinds of modules have been introduced as a natural consequence of the coexistence of control and data processing (executive) elements in statements of high level language programs. The control modules are intended to implement the control features of programs which appear for example in such statements as if, case, procedure calls... etc. The executive modules implement arithmetic and logical expressions as well as other kinds of expressions. The microinstructions used to build microcode modules of the two kinds have different formats and so they are stored and executed in separate control subunits. This permits some concurrency of actions in the whole computer unit.

Secondly, it has been assumed that in the compilation process the object microprogram level microinstructions are bound together using compound sequencing functions oriented on efficient implementation of complicated control constructs. The sequencing functions are used by the compiler to build microcode modules and then to provide links between the modules. The sequencing primitives, together with corresponding operational primitives of microinstructions constitute an object microcode language designed for structured microprogrammed implementation of source high level language. This language contains high level means for the control description in microprograms and is directly acceptable by the proposed hardware unit. However, only the control description aspect of the language will be presented in the paper.

The general scheme of the proposed computer unit is presented in fig 1. We have two microprogrammed control subunits US I and US II and the operational subunit in this computer unit.

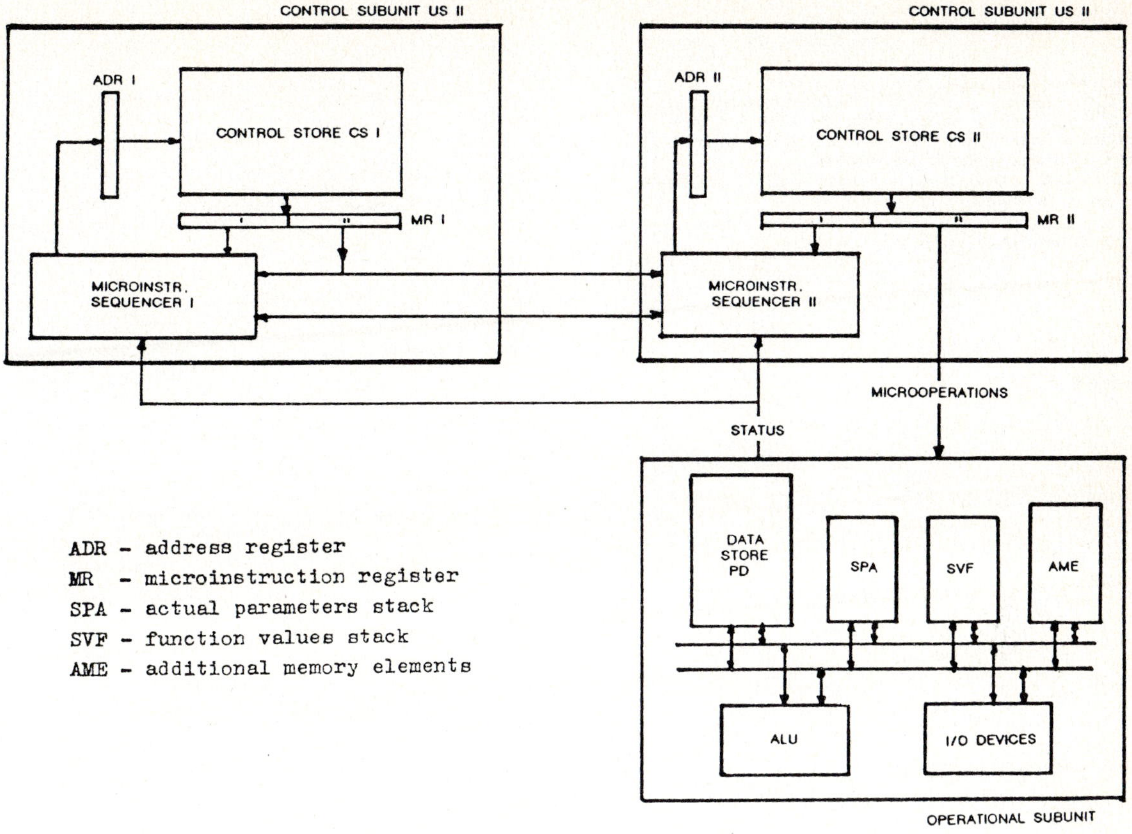

Fig.1. General structure of the proposed computer unit.

The structure of both control subunits is similar. Each of them contains a control store, a control store address register, a microinstruction register and a microinstruction sequencer. In the control store CS I of the US I subunit the control modules are stored while the control store CS II of the US II subunit stores the executive modules.

The microinstruction sequencers contained in the US I and US II subunits have addressing functions which permit very efficient implementation of compound control structures in microprograms, both at the microinstruction and microcode module levels. The general schemes of these functions are shown in fig 2 . These functions and the internal organization if the corresponding microinstruction sequencer have been described in detail in earlier papers [3,4,5] of the authors. However, in sequencers contained in the computer system proposed in this paper some additional circuitry is provided used to synchronize the functionning of both control subunits.

The US I subunit is superior in the system. It initializes the work of the US II subunit and assures the proper sequence of actions of both subunits. The US I subunit begins the work of the whole computer unit by fetching a microinstruction of the control store CS I.

The microinstruction word stored in the CS I consists of two parts:

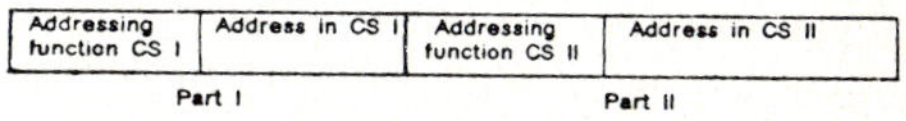

Part I of the microinstruction is used to define the address of the next microinstruction in the CS I control store. It specifies the addressing function

Microinstruction Sequencing Functions

Notations:

α, β, A, A , - addresses in the control store,
C, C_i, C_x, - vectors of computer status information,
BC - the code defining the branching operation and the computer status vector C which has to be analysed and used to perform the branching,
UNCOND or UNC, COND or CD - unconditional or conditional mode of the sequencing function,
φ⊗C - the address φ modified with the value of the computer status vector C_i, i =1, 2, ..., n.

Basic Sequencing Functions

Microinstruction Level

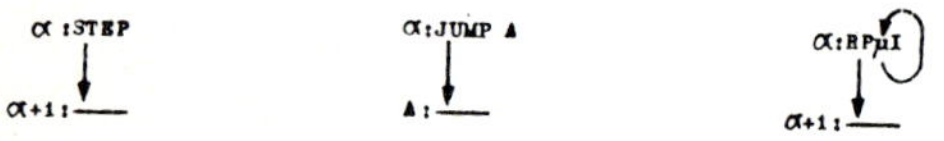

Microcode Module Level

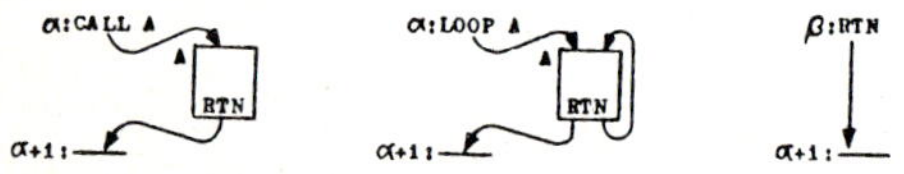

Compound Sequencing Functions

Microinstruction Level

Microcode Module Level

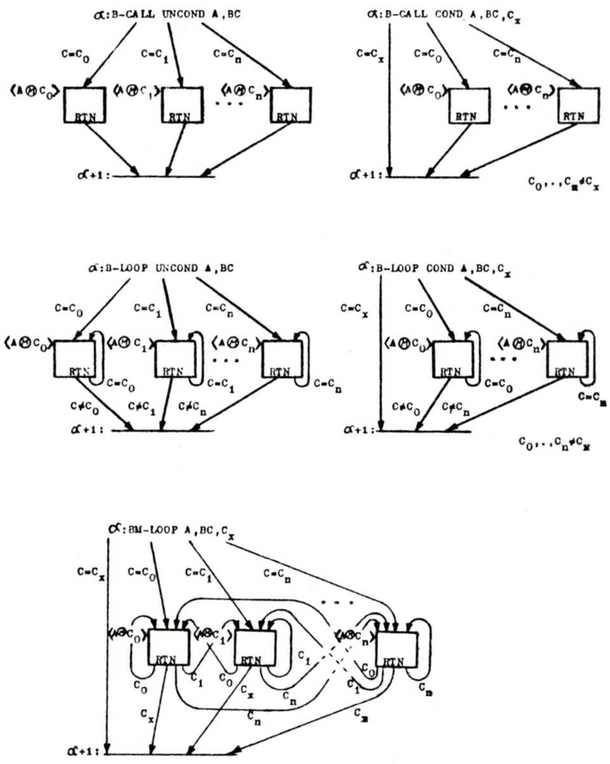

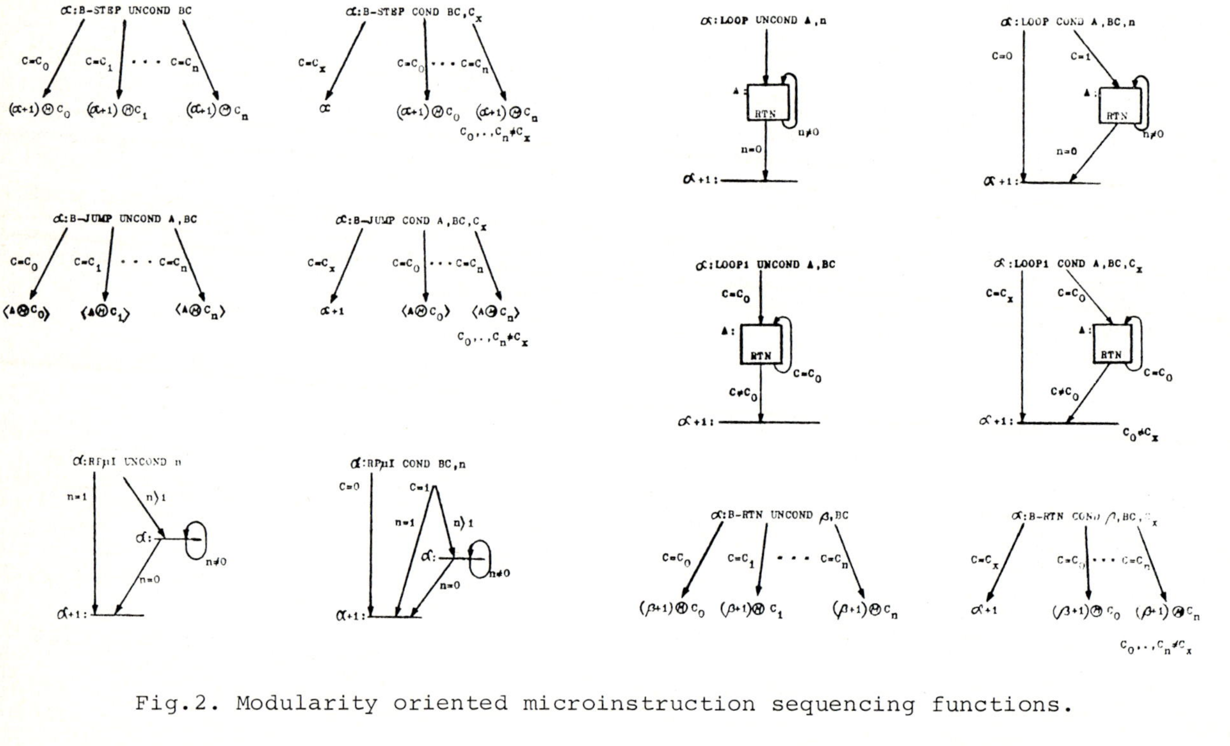

Fig.2. Modularity oriented microinstruction sequencing functions.

that is to be performed in the microinstruction sequencer I and it contains the potential address of the next microinstruction. Part II is used to activate the US II control subunit by calls of executive modules stored in the control store CS II. The address contained in this part is the address of the first microinstruction in such a module. If US II is not activated (NOP function code in part II of the microinstruction), then, the sequencer in US I calculates the address of the next microinstruction and goes to its execution. If US II has been activated, then, US I continues its work until the CS I address calculation process requires an information on the computer status worked out by an executive module from CS II or a microinstruction has been read from CS I which contains in its part II a sequencing function code calling a module from CS II. In both cases the US I subunit enters the waiting state. This state is abandoned when the return operation has been performed from a module executed by CS II. After leaving the waiting state, US I completes the operation defined by part I of its current microinstruction.

The microinstruction words stored in the CS II consist also of two parts:

Addressing function CS II	Address in CS II	Bits controlling the operational subunit
Part I		Part II

Part I is used for generation of next microinstruction addresses in the CS II control store. Part II specifies all operations which control the operational subunit. It can contain the data store address if needed. The modules executed from the CS II control store are used to evaluate different kinds of expressions, to manipulate on control variables in the control statements, to maintain actual and formal parameters of functions and procedures and also for other purposes concerned with data processing in source programs. The words in CS II are significantly longer than the words in CS I.

The operational subunit contains the ALU, the data store, stacks and some additional memory elements. The data store is used to store values of variables and constants which are declared and described in the declarative part of program blocks. This store is loaded with values of constants in the compilation phase and with actual values of variables during the execution of microprogram modules. The operational subunit generates the computer status vector STATUS which is used for the implementation of conditional branchings in microprograms in US I and US II. The stacks have been named according to their usage in the compilation phase. The actual parameters stack (SPA) is used by the compiler to assure the communication between procedures of the source program. The function value stack (SVF) is used to store the function values before their usage in the program. The data store (PD) can be addressed directly from a microinstruction, from the stack of actual parameters of from other additional storing elements (AME). The operational unit assures also the communication of the proposed computer unit with input/output devices.

2. THE IMPLEMENTATION OF THE PASCAL LANGUAGE CONTROL STATEMENTS

In this chapter the microprogrammed implementation of control statements of the PASCAL language will be presented, which will make the functionning of the proposed executive computer unit more clear. We will follow some rules in presenting implementations of practicular statements. Each description begins with the general formula of a given statement. Then object microinstruction modules are presented and next the communication between these modules is described. If W, A denote: a PASCAL language expression and statement, then, <W>, <A> denote the addresses of the microcode modules implementing W, A respectively. Sometimes, when not confusing, <W>, <A> will denote microcode modules themselves. Microcode modules will be presented as sequences of symbolic microinstructions in control stores CS I and CS II. Parts I and II will be distinguished in microinstructions, containing mnemonics of addressing functions used, according to those shown in fig 1. In the example below (Fig.3) a module begins with a microinstruction at the address α in CS I. In part I of this microinstruction, a call of a module from the address <A> in CS I and in part II a call of a module from the address <B> in CS II are encoded. The calls of modules <A> and <B> are performed in parallel. Both modules are ended with simple return operation code RTN. The return from the module <A> will be performed to the address α+1 in CS I. The return from the module <B> will be done to the control store CS I as described in the previous chapter.

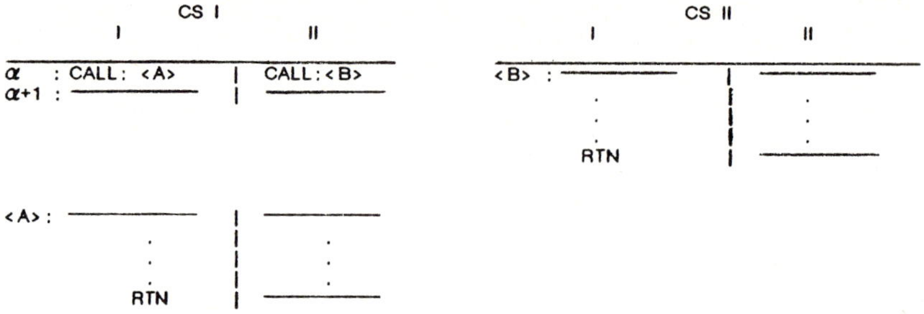

Fig.3. An example.

2.1 The assignment statement

Z := W ;

where Z is the variable to which the value of the statement W is assigned.

2.1.1 W is a simple expression

We asume here that there are no control statements embedded in W. The implementation of the assignment statement in this case (Fig. 4) needs one microinstruction in CS I and one executive module in CS II. The microinstruction from the address α in CS I activates the control unit US II. The executive module is performed from the address <W> which calculates the value of W. The value is assigned to variable Z. In the same time the US I generates the address of next microinstruction for CS I and fetches its new microinstruction. When the RTN code is found by US II the return is performed to the actual location in CS I.

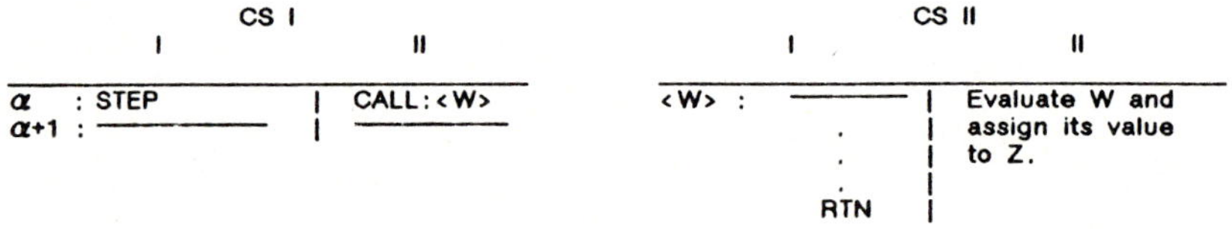

Fig.4. The assignment statement.

2.1.2 W has some control statements embedded

In this case CS I contains microinstructions implementing control for the statement W and CS II contains corresponding executive modules concerned with data processing inside W and next, concerned with an assignement of the value of W to Z. The CS I and CS II contents have been composed by the compiler using frame implementations described in the paper below.

2.2 The conditional statement <u>if</u>

<u>if</u> WL <u>then</u> A1 <u>else</u> A2 ;

The implementation (Fig.5) requires at least one microinstruction and two control modules in CS I and one execution module in CS II. The conditional statement <u>if</u> is implemented with the use of B-CALL sequencing function which, depending on the logical condition value of WL, calls a module from the addres <A1> or <A2> in CS I. The value of the logical expression WL is calculated by the executive module from <WL> in CS II and the execution of the function B-CALL is suspended until this value is known. The modules from <A1> and <A2> implement control which is defined by corresponding fragments A1 and A2 of the source program. When the module from <A1> or <A2> is completed the return is performed to the address α+1 in CS I.

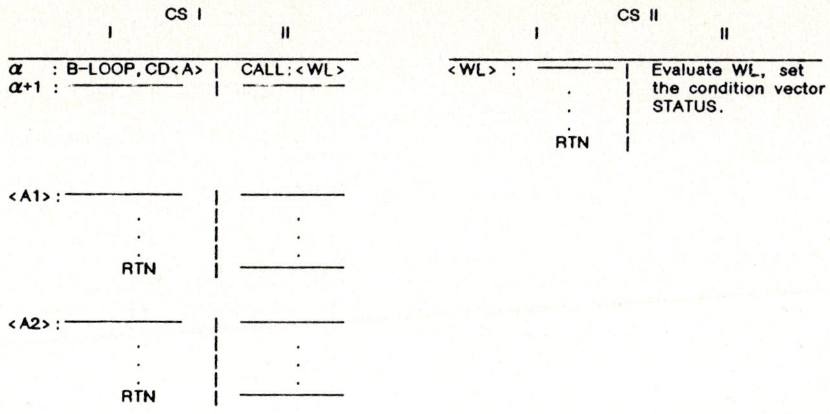

Fig.5. The if statement.

2.3 The case statement

```
case  W of
   L1 : A1;
   L2 : A2;
      :
      :
   Ln : An;
end;
```

where L1,L2,...,Ln are the choice labels which are constants of the type equal to the type of expression W.

The implementation (Fig.6) requires at least one microinstruction and n control modules in CS I and one executive module in CS II. The addresses <A1>,...,<An> are effective addresses for the B-CALL function which result from the modification of the address <A> with the use of computer status conditions vector STATUS. The vector STATUS is set up by the executive module <W> in CS II. The modules <A1>,...,<An> implement the control for statements of the source program that follow labels L1...Ln.

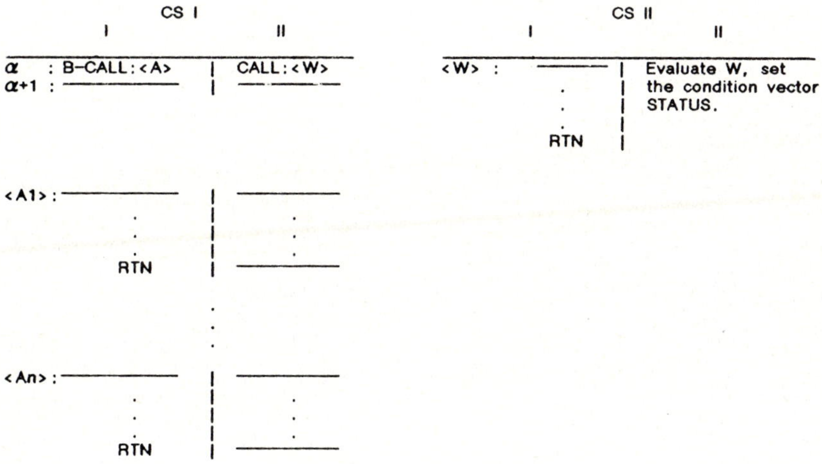

Fig.6. The case statement.

2.4. The program loop statements

2.4.1 for ZK := WP to WK do A ;
or for ZK := WP downto WK do A ;

where WP, WK are initial and terminal values of the control variable ZK, respectively.

The implementation (Fig.7) requires at least one microinstruction and one control module in CS I and two executive modules in CS II. The module <WP> begins with calculating the initial value of the control variable ZK. Then the microcode submodule <WL> is executed which sets up the conditions vector STATUS according to the result of the comparison between values of ZK and WK. If WK>ZK for the instruction of the type to or WK>ZK for the instruction of the type downto, then the control subunit US I calls the module <A> in CS I to implement the body of the loop.

In modules called by the LOOP-type function the return function code RTN is interpreted in a special way. This function is then treated as conditional and dependently on the STATUS vector it renews the execution of a module or causes the normal return. The execution of the RTN function waits for the vector STATUS being set up by the executive module from <WN> in CS II. This module sets up the control variable ZK and then calls the <WL> module, which prepares the STATUS vector. After the return from the<WL> module, the US I subunit performs the RTN function and dependently on the STATUS vector it repeats the module from <A> or returns to the microinstruction $\alpha+1$ in CS I.

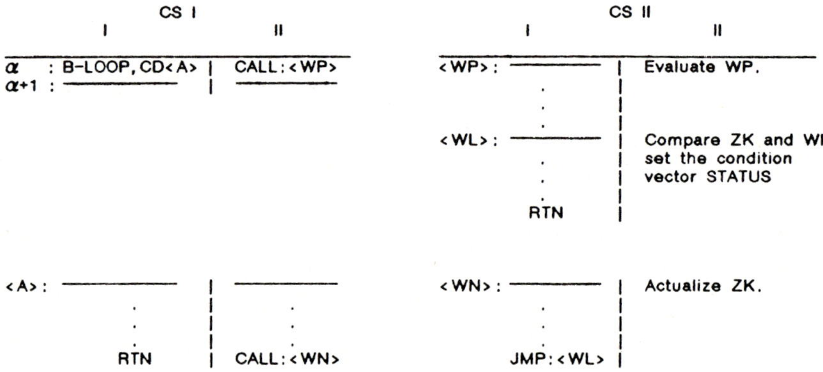

Fig.7. The for statement.

2.4.2 while WL do A ;

The implementation of this statement (Fig.8) requires at least one microinstruction and one control module in CS I and one executive module in CS II. The implementation of the while statement is similar to that of the statement for. First the executive module <WL> is called from CS II. It calculates the value of the logical expression WL and then sets up the STATUS vector accordingly. The execution of the B-LOOP,CD : <A> function in CS I is suspended until a new value of the vector STATUS is delivered. Depending on this value, there is a call of a module <A> in CS I performed, which implements the control for A. The RTN function in the module <A> is preceeded by an additional call of the executive module <WL>, which sets a new of STATUS according to the current value of the expression WL.

Then the RTN function code at the end of the A module is interpreted according to the current STATUS value as the return to the beginning pf <A> or the return to the $\alpha+1$ address in CS I.

2.4.3 repeat A until WL ;

The implementation (Fig.9) requires at least one microinstruction and one control module in CS I and one executive module in CS II. In the implementation of this kind of the loop statement the first microinstruction executed contains the LOOP1 function code which first causes an unconditional call of a module <A> and then organizes an loop over this module with the conditional return. The module <A> implements the control for the statement A and then calls a corresponding executive module from CS II (not shown in the picture above) which evaluates the value for A. Before leaving the module <A>, the executive module <WL> is called, which evaluates the logical expression WL and sets up the STATUS vector correspondingly. The STATUS value is used by the LOOP1 function to interpret property the RTN code at the end of the <A> module.

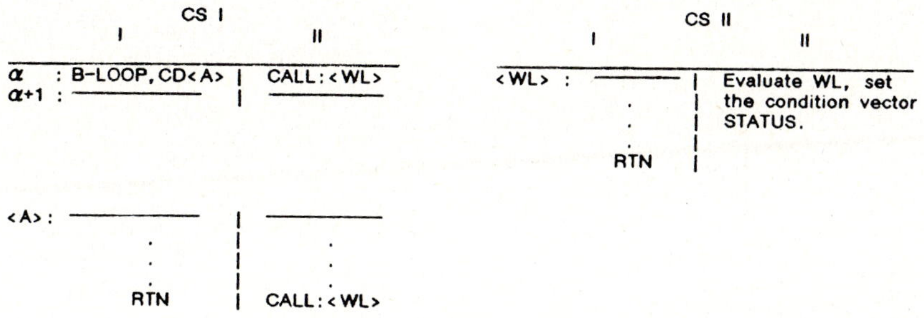

Fig.8. The <u>while</u> statement.

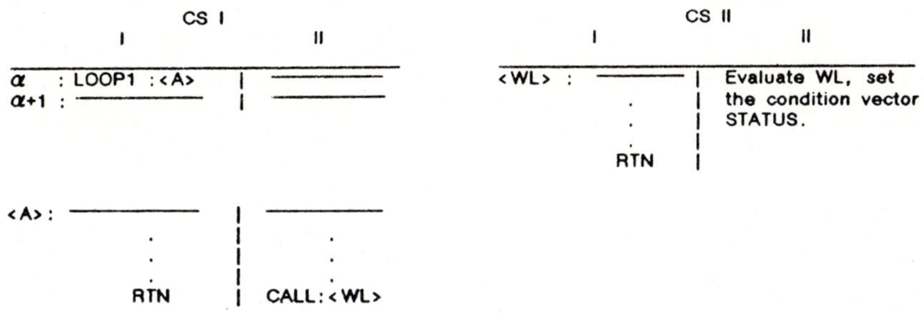

Fig.9. The <u>repeat</u> statement.

2.5 The procedure call statement

NAME (pa1 , pa2, ... , pan);

where NAME is the procedure name and pa1, pa2, ..., pan are the actual parameters of the procedure NAME.

The actual parameters of a procedure in the PASCAL language can be: constants, variables, expressions, procedure and function identifiers. Let us assume for simplicity that all the procedure and function names included into an actual parameters list correspond to the procedures and functions which have been directly declared in the declarative part of a program. Let us also assume that all procedures and functions in our programs are non recursive.

The implementation of the procedure call statement (Fig.10) requires at least one microinstruction and one control module in CS I and three executive modules in CS II. The compiler, having met the procedure declaration in the source program, generates the control module <NAME> in CS I and the executive modules <PF>, <PA> and <P> in CS II. The compiler reserves location in data store PD for all variables in the list of formal parameters and for all variables declared in the procedure NAME. Then after having met the call of the procedure in the program it generates the executive module <PA>.

The implementation of the procedure call begins with a microinstruction at the address α in CS I. First the module <PA> is called from CS I which evaluates expressions included into the actual parameter list and sends to the actual parameters stack SPA an information on the actual parameters for the procedure NAME (for constants and variables the information constitute addresses to the PD store and for procedure and function names it constitutes addresses to the microcode modules in CS I). After comming back from the module <PA> the control module <NAME> is executed, called in the meanwhile from

CS I. This module implements control for the body of the procedure NAME. The execution of this module begins by calling the executive module <PF> which assigns actual parameter values to formal parameters of the procedure. For parameters transferred by value, values of actual parameters are written into locations in PD reserved for formal parameters. For parameters transferred by variables all executive modules called by the module <NAME> act directly on actual parameters using addresses stored in the SPA stack. The return from the module <NAME> is preceeded by calling the executive module <P>, which clears out in SPA the information about the actual parameters.

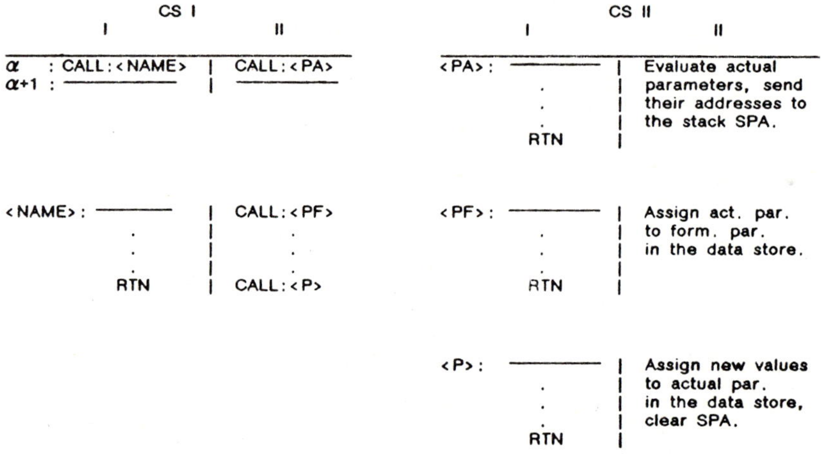

Fig.10. The procedure call statement.

2.6. The function call statement

A function is called in the source programs by giving the name of the function in expressions and statements. Let us discuss the implementation of the function call statement using the following example:

W := FN(pa1, pa2, ..., pan) + W1 ;

where FN is the function name, pa1, pa2, ..., pan are the actual parameters of the function FN and W1 is a simple arithmetic expression.

The compiler will organize the implementation of this statement in the way given below (Fig. 11). The implementation of the above statement requires the generation of at least the following modules: the control module <FN> and executive modules <PA>, <PF>, <P>, <W>. The module FN implements the control for the body of the function FN. The goals of the modules <PA>, <PF>, <P> are very similar to the goals of the corresponding modules described in the previous section of the paper, but the module <P> additionally stores the value of the function FN in the stack of function values SVF. The module <W> evaluates the balue of expression W1, adds it to the value of the function FN taken from the stack SVF and assigns the result of this calculation to W. The value of the function FN is calculated before module <W> is called.

The calculation is started by calling the executive module <PA> from CS II and the control <FN> from CS II. The execution method is similar to the execution of the procedure call statement taking into account the remarks given above. After the return from the <FN> module the <W> module is executed which ends the implementation of the statement given above.

3. CONCLUSIONS

An implementation of control statements of the PASCAL language has been presented in the paper based on the usage of specially proposed computer executive unit organized with two modular microprogramming oriented control units. The proposed executive computer has two control stores for separate storing modular micro-

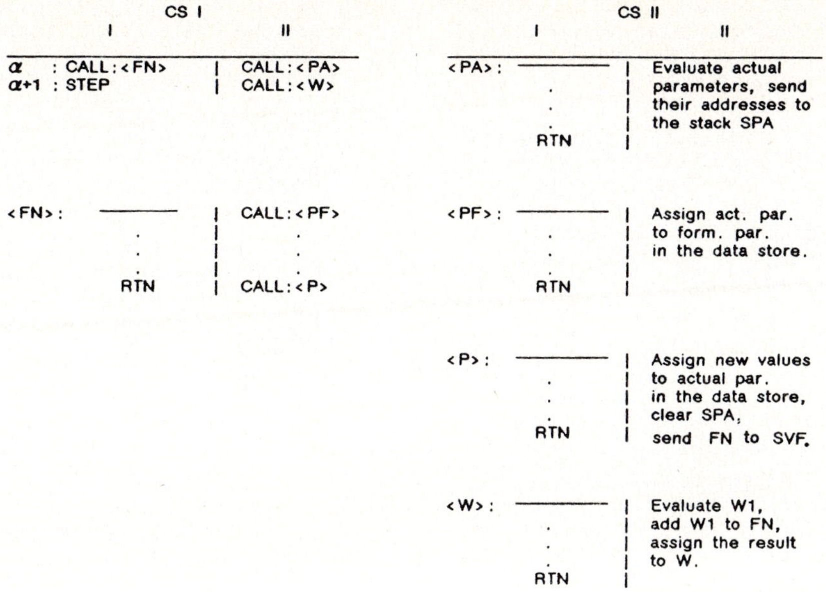

Fig.11. The function call statement.

programs implementing the control and data processing elements of the source high level language programs.

The main interest of the authors concerned the implementation of the control in high level language programs and so the implementation of arithmetical, logical and other kinds of expressions of the PASCAL language has been only scetched in the paper. The structure of the operational subunit of the proposed computer is then only exemplary and will be further developed in practice to enable more parallelism in its functionning (multiple functional subunits for anticipated evaluation of alternative expressions, special functional subunits for evaluation of logical conditions and similar).

The scope of the PASCAL control statements discussed in the paper has been limitted to that necessary for structuring of the source programs. However, an analysis made by the authors but not presented in the paper, enable them to state that, with slight modifications of the applied hardware, the full set of control statements belonging to the PASCAL and to other similar languages can be implemented (ex. ALGOL 60).

The following conclusions can be formulated on the basis of the experience achieved in the design presented in the paper:

- the compound modularity oriented microinstruction sequencing functions enable an structured implementation of the high level language control statements, giving an efficiency in execution time and memory space,

- a separate implementation of control and data processing elements of the source program permits to fit the hardware to the character of these elements and exploits the possible parallelism of execution,

- two control stores provided to store object microprograms give an economy in the usage of memory space, because different formats of words are required,

- the structured implementation of high level statements is easier to be performed and tested by a man and a computer.

4. REFERENCES

[1] Jones,L.H., Instructions Sequencing in Microprogrammed Computer, AFIPS 1975, Proceedings.

[2] Marczynski,R.W., Tudruj,M.S., Microprogrammed Control Units - Towards Modularity in Microprogramming, 2-nd EUROMICRO Symp., Proceedings, Venice, October 1976.

[3] Tudruj,M.S., Gajda,R.F., The Modular Firmware Architecture Through the Stack/Register Based Address Modification, IFIP Working Conf. on Firmware Design, Microprogramming and Restructurable Hardware, Proceedings, Linz, Austria, April/May 1980.

[4] Tudruj,M.S., Gajda,R.F., The Modularity Oriented Microinstruction Sequencer for Microprogrammable Mini- and Microcomputers, MIMI 80 Conf., Proceedings, Budapest, September 1980.

[5] Tudruj,M.S., Gajda,R.F., On the Implementation of Compound Microinstruction Sequencing Functions in Microprogrammed Control Units, Int. Autumn School on Microprocessors, Proceedings, Jachranka, Poland, October 1980.

[6] Davidson,S., Shriver,B.D., Firmware Engineering: An Extensive Upate, IFIP Working Conf. on Firmware Design, Microprogramming and Restructurable Hardware, Proceedings, Linz. Austria, April/May 1980.

[7] Proceedings of the International Workshop on High-Level Language Architecture, Florida, May 1980.

[8] Wirth,N., Jensen,K., PASCAL User Manual and Report, Springer-Verlag, New York, 1975.

[9] Conway,R., Gries,D., Zimmerman,E.C., A Primer on PASCAL, Winthrop Publisher Inc., 1976.

MICROCOMPUTERS: Developments in Industry, Business and Education
D.R. Wilson and C.J. van Spronsen (eds.) / ©EUROMICRO, 1983
Elsevier Science Publishers B.V. (North-Holland)

MICROPROGRAMMED INTERPRETATION OF AN INTERMEDIATE CODE

S. Zöld

Central Research Institute for Physics
of the Hungarian Academy of Sciences
(on leave from the Research Institute for Telecommunication)
Budapest, Hungary

The paper reports on a research project for designing and implementing a microprogrammed intermediate code interpreter. The instruction set has been defined on the basis of the intermediate form of a Pascal compiler. The executed code is a binary P-code.

The interpreter runs on a processor dedicated to P-code interpretation, and which is attached to the EMU11 minicomputer. A compact description is given of the P-code program, the instruction set, some characteristics of the dedicated processor and the structure of the interpreter.

Some conclusions drawn during the implementation are also given. The project proves that microprogramming of an interpreter is a realistic and efficient way to implement programming language oriented instruction sets.

1. INTRODUCTION

Technological development has led to changes in hardware and software. The originally high hardware costs have decreased and software costs have escalated. The growing importance of the software components of computing ystems mean not only more requirements egarding the software development and aintenance methodologies, but also in connection with the design of computer architectures.

In the recent literature several authors [8,5,21], have examined this question minutely, so here we do not go into detail. It has been stated that most of the presently manufactured computers have architectures which are not very advantageous for the production of the required great quantity of complex software nor for the production of efficient and reliable computing systems. The main reason for this is the existence of a semantic gap between the concepts of the programming languages and the concepts realized by the computer arhictects designing the instruction sets. Some consequences of the semantic gap are for example the lower reliability of the systems, relatively larger program sizes, the complexity of the compilation process, etc. These deficiencies can be avoided only partially for a given architecture since the improvement leads to a loss of efficiency, as for example if the compiler generates code for carrying out runtime checks for safety. The real solution to the semantic gap problem is in defining and implementing new architectures, where the decisions are made with top-down reasoning and not on the basis of the execution speed (number of instructions per second) as the only criterion [5,21].

Architectures designed to take into consideration the requirements of programming languages can be divided into different classes [1,5,11]. From the wide spectrum one possibility is the approach of the so called indirect-execution [1] or language-oriented [5] architecture. In this case the code to be executed is produced by a not too complex compilation procedure, the machine code is of medium complexity and resembles the original language constructs.

Tanenbaum [6], Harris [13], and Jones [14,15] report on how instruction sets corresponding to the requirements of structured programming languages have been produced. These authors exploited certain characteristics of the block structured languages (e.g. locality of references, certain language constructs) and the defined instruction sets ensure good execution properties.

Virtual machines defined for programming languages are dealt with in the literature; these virtual machines were designed not in order to produce a real machine but as a means of implementing and enhancing the portability of compilers [9,12,19]. The efforts to establish universal intermediate codes for compilers are also of importance because they represent examples of multi-language approaches [10].

There are papers disclosing implementation goals and experiences of projects for implementating Pascal machines. Bishop [18] emphasizes the structured features and the importance of runtime checks. Hall's paper [22] shows the possibility of implementing an intermediate code via microprogramming; the paper gives some performance characteristics, although the comparison was made with a machine language interpreter.

The compilation of high level languages is usually done in several steps. This process can be divided into two main phases: the analysis phase and the synthesis phase. The interface between these phases is defined by the so-called intermediate form, which can be defined as a low level symbolic language or as a binary code (intermediate code) [10,19]. In the case of the Pascal language this code is called the P-code.

A programming language can be implemented two different ways, viz. on the one hand both the analysis and synthesis phase can be realized or, on the other, the second phase of the compiler can be substituted by an interpreter whose interface - a virtual machine - corresponds to the intermediate code.

Both of the solutions have their own advantages and disadvantages. The interpreter ensures quicker introduction and higher portability of a language and its compiler, but the execution speed is lower compared with the full code generation.

Microprogramming is a systematic and flexible way of designing and implementing computers, and is very good method for solving many problems in computer engineering. An example of this is the migration of functions in order to produce more efficient systems, or systems with better structural characteristics. Microprogramming also seems to be an applicable means of investigating the possibilities of closing the semantic gap. We therefore decided to undertake an experiment to establish a language-oriented architecture by implementing a microprogrammed interpreter. As a first step the short term plan is the implementation of a Pascal oriented instruction set.

The instruction set (hereinafter referred to as the P-code insturction set) supported by the microprogrammed interpreter has been defined on the basis of the intermediate form produced by a Pascal compiler [23] and is similar to the well known intermediate code and virtual machine instruction definitions, see, for example, [9,19,10].

In Section 2 we describe the compilation and structure of P-code programs; Section 3 contains an overview of the organization of data regions used by the interpreter; Section 4 deals with the P-code instruction set; some important characteristics of the P-code processor are described in Section 5. Section 6 gives a short overview of the structure of the microprogrammed interpretet and Section 7 provides conclusions drawn during the implementation.

2. THE P-CODE PROGRAM AND ITS STRUCTURE

The P-code program is produced by a two pass compilation procedure. The first pass carries out the syntactic analysis of the source program, and produces the postfix representation of its syntax tree. The second pass uses the postfix format program representation and with a simple code generation outputs the executable P-code.

The compiler allows independent compilation of procedures. In this way the executable P-code program consists of a main module and one or more separately compiled modules corresponding to the external procedures declared in the main module. The standard procedures of arithmetic functions are an example of external procedures needed in Pascal programs.

A binary P-code module consists of three different segments. The first contains descriptive imformation: the sizes of the segments, the table of entry points of procedures of the given module, and the list of external modules called from the module. The second is called the code segment: it is built up from the executable P-code instructions; its internal structure reflects that of the source program, it contains subprograms corresponding to the procedures, functions and to the main program. The third segment produced by the compiler is the constant segment containing the constant (read only) data of the program such as number constants, constant structures, characters strings, the case value sequences for the CASE OF statements and the branch address table for the Indexed Branch (BRX) instructions.

(See the Appendix containing the list of the P-code instruction set).

3. THE ORGANIZATION OF DATA REGIONS USED DURING INTERPRETATION

Two different kinds of data regions are used in the interpretation. (See Fig.1) The first contains the compiler generated code segments and data segments. The P-code program to be executed can be built up from several independently produced compilation modules. This means that both the constant region and code region may hold several constant segments and code segments, corresponding to the number of compilation modules. The information required for handling the modules is stored in the Module Directory reserved in the operative memory. Each entry of the Module Directory contains the base and limit addresses of code and constant segments. The base and limit addresses of the actually executed module are held in the registers Code_Orig, Code_Lim, Const_Orig and Const_Lim. These registers are loaded by the Call_External_Procedure instruction. The register Instruction_Pointer points to the actually executed P-code instruction. The validity of the contents of this register is compared with the limits of the module.

The second kind of data region is allocated at execution time. One of these regions holds the activation records of procedures and some administrative information. The Module Directory is allocated at the beginning of the region, it is pointed by the Process_Base register.
In this region further sections are allocated in a stack-like way at the execution of procedure calls. The address of the top of the region is in the Activation_Record_Top register. There is a local data segment and a parameter segment in the activation record of each called but not terminated procedure. In this region the interpreter also stores procedure call data e.g. return address, lexical level difference of calling and called procedure, linking information, etc.

The address calculating routine of the interpreter uses a 16 element register vector to calculate the addresses of variables allocated in local data segments.

The evaluation stack is allocated in a separate region. Register Stack_Top is used to access the items in the stack. The stack is used for address calculation and expression evaluation so data of several types can be stored in it, e.g. different types of values, variable descriptors, procedure descriptors. Each item pushed contains a tag field identifying the item. Although the handling of tag fields causes some loss of efficiency, this is balanced by the possibility for extensive execution time checks and improved reliability. There are three more special registers for the management of dynamically allocated variables, viz. register Free Head indicates the first free memory block, the Head and the Tail registers point respectively to the beginning and the end of the chain of allocated variables. Register Level always contains the lexical level of the actual procedure.

The interpreter uses four different internal data formats: byte (8 bits), halfword (16 bits), word (32 bits) and double-word (64 bits). Each of these formats is used to represent several data types. The following table shows the correspondence among data format, P-level data type, and the data type of the Pascal language:

Data format	P-level data type	Pascal data type
Byte (B)	Boolean	Boolean
	Natural number (N)	Scalar type Subrange type Character
Halfword (H)	Long natural (LN)	Scalar type Subrange type
	Integer number (I)	Integer
	Bit set (S)	Set type
Word (W)	Long Integer (LI)	Long integer
	Floating point number (F)	Real
	Pointer (P)	Pointer
Double Word (D)	Long floating number (LF)	Long real
	Long bit set (LS)	Long set

In the present version of the interpreter the load and store instructions - with two exceptions - are defined according to the data formats: the other instructions - depending on type - are defined according to P-level data types.

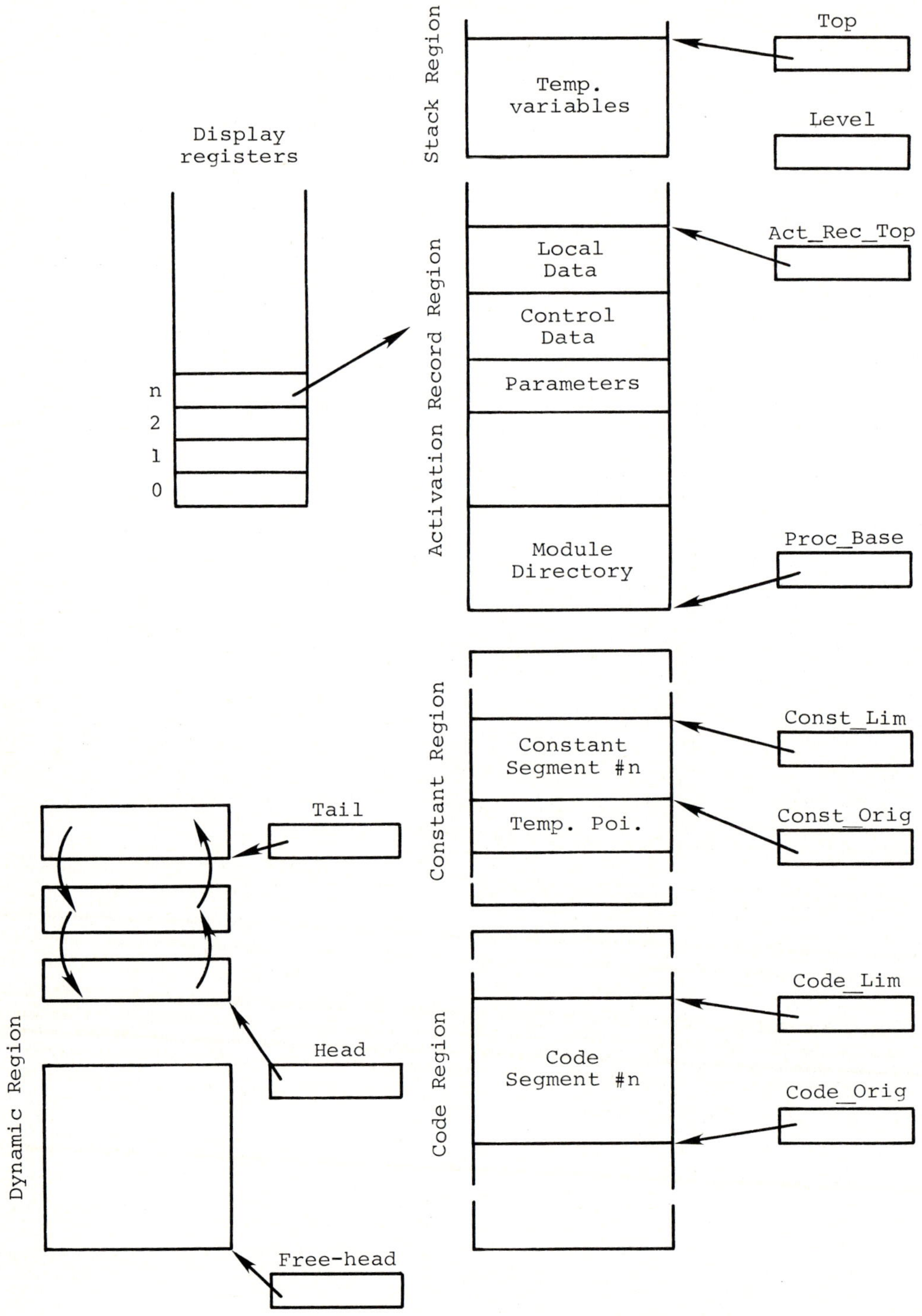

Figure 1. The organization of data regions used by the interpreter

4. THE P-CODE INSTRUCTION SET

For defining the instruction set we have chosen the intermediate form of a Pascal compiler [23] as a starting point. The intermediate form is the postfix representation of the syntax tree of the program, where the nodes correspond to the syntactic units of the language and variables. The defined instruction set is stack oriented, the instructions - with a few exceptions - correspond to the nodes of the syntax tree.

During the definition we gave priority to:

- the choice of a stack oriented instruction set with zero address and one-address instructions because of the simplicity of the required interpreter, and of the code generation.
- exploiting the possibilities of the processor by having the interpreter support several precisions of some of the data types (e.g. integer - long integer, sets with 16 and 64 members).
- ensuring higher efficiency, to some of the decisions to be made and processing to be done by the compiler by deciding for example, to have a larger set of instructions but fewer runtime decisions.
- implementing an interpreter with extensive (though incomplete) execution time checks for the sake of reliability. Therefore, the instructions and operands on the stack have to retain all the information required for checking.
- the instruction set being as general as possible, i.e. in some cases we have to find a good trade-off between the faster monolithic solution, and the slower ones consisting of several primitives. As a good example we mention here the problem of the instructions corresponding to the CASE OF statement [9,20].

The P-code instructions are of several formats, most of them are one byte long; the remaining instructions are 2 to 9 bytes in lenght. Another view point for grouping the instructions is the number of arguments used on stack. Most of the instructions use two items of the stack, but the ITER instruction generated for the FOR TO statement works with four.

Here we give only a short overview of the instructions groups. The grouping is perhaps slightly arbitrary, instructions carrying out roughly similar functions are collected into a group. The instruction groups are:

- Data movement instructions:

  There exist instructions for moving data between the evaluation stack and any other data region. The address of the operand is included in the instruction itself or in the topmost element of the stack.

- Arithmetic instructions:

  This group consists of the ordinary arithmetic operations, increment, decrement and some types of conversion instructions.

- Relational, compare instructions:

  There are relational operations for each data type except the Booleans. The relational operations of sets test the equality or non-equality of sets, whether one of the operands is a subset or a proper subset of the other. The interpretation of character array relations: the elements are compared one by one, the equality - nonequality test is straight-forward, in the other cases the relation between the first non-equal pair defines the result. The remaining instructions of this group select minimal or maximal values of the operands, and carry out oddness and set inclusion tests.

- Logical operations.
- Set and bitfield manipulation instructions:

  Two different sizes of sets, 16 and 64 bits, can be handled by the instructions. In addition to the usual set operations the instructions of bitfield manipulation also belong to this group.

- Address calculation and data structure handling instructions:

  Three of the instructions serve for loading to the stack descriptors of variables or constants reserved in the local data segment, parameter segment or constant segment. The descriptor of a variable consists of a segment indicator, lexical level of declaration, length and address. Two instructions (LRCD, INDX) serve for accessing components of arrays and records. These instructions push to the stack a descriptor calculated from the contents of the topmost element of the stack and the information field of the

instruction (description of the whole structure and identification of the component, respectively). There is an instruction for calculating and loading descriptors indirectly (LIND), here the value of the variable (a reference) defined by the topmost element of the stack and the contents of the information field of the instruction are used to build a new descriptor. Instruction LREF calculates and loads an absolute address (reference) from the information contained on the top of the stack.
The three remaining instructions of this group (RTP, LTP, FTP) are used to realize the WITH DO statement. These instructions use the area reserved in the constant segment, and they store there a vector of pointers. RTP reserves and fills in, FTP frees an element of the vector, LTP pushes to the stack the pointer identified by the information field of the instruction. In order to clarify the role of address calculation and load instruction, the transformation of the top element of the stack are shown in Fig.2. Three different types of information can be found on the top of the stack: the value of a variable, the descriptor of a variable (sometimes called the name of the variable), and the reference to a variable (a descriptor containing an absolute address). The top of the stack is either transformed by the address calculations, or a new element is loaded there by means of the previous top element.

- Execution flow control instructions:

  The first subgroup consists of the instructions for procedure call, entry and return. The call instructions have two different forms. The Call_Internal Procedure activates procedures contained in the same module. This instruction contains the lexical level and address of the called procedure. The Call_External_Procedure instruction activates a procedure declared as external one, and contained in another compilation module. This instruction contains the sequence number of the target module and its procedure, in addition to the lexical level. The external call microprogram carries out the changing of base and limit registers. The Procedure_Entry instruction executes the same algorithm after both types of calls, allocates space for local variables, and loads registers. The Procedure_Return instruction deallocates the local data space, restores the contents of display registers (if necessary) and in the case of returning from an external procedure loads the base and limit registers. There exists a third kind of call instruction, it activates system functions such as, for example, storage management and I/O handling.

  The ordinary unconditional - conditional instructions form the second subgroup, they are used to implement the conditional and some of the loop statements.
  The last subgroup contains instructions used to realize CASE OF and FOR TO/DOWNTO statements.
  Instruction ITER organizes an iterative cycle with the help of the four top elements of the stack. Instructions Select_Case, Case_Sequence, Case_Range are used for one possible and the Indexed_Branch instruction is used for another kind of implementation of CASE OF. The first solution is advantageous for sparse, the other for continuous sequence of case selection values.

5. THE PROCESSOR FOR INTERPRETING THE P-CODE

The interpreter runs on the P-code processor built up from bit slice components, with microinstructions of 64 bits, and with horizontal organization. The processor contains 16x64 bit wide registers and a 16 element register array whose width is 16 bits. The register array can be accessed by means of an index register. The hardware organization permits the use of any processor of width 16, 32 or 64 bits. Some of the registers are used for special purposes (see Section 3 and Fig.1.) others are used as working registers. The indexed registers are used to support the lexical level based addressing.

The P-code processor is attached to the EMU11 [7,16] computer as an orthogonal extension. EMU11 emulates a member of the PDP11[1] family, it is equipped with writable control store and has good microprogram development facilities (see Fig.3.) The microprogram of EMU11 is extended with routines responsible for communication between the two processors. The core memory and I/O devices are accessible to the P processor only through the EMU11 by means of these extension routines.

Loading of the P-code programs is carried out by machine code program executed on EMU11. The runtime support

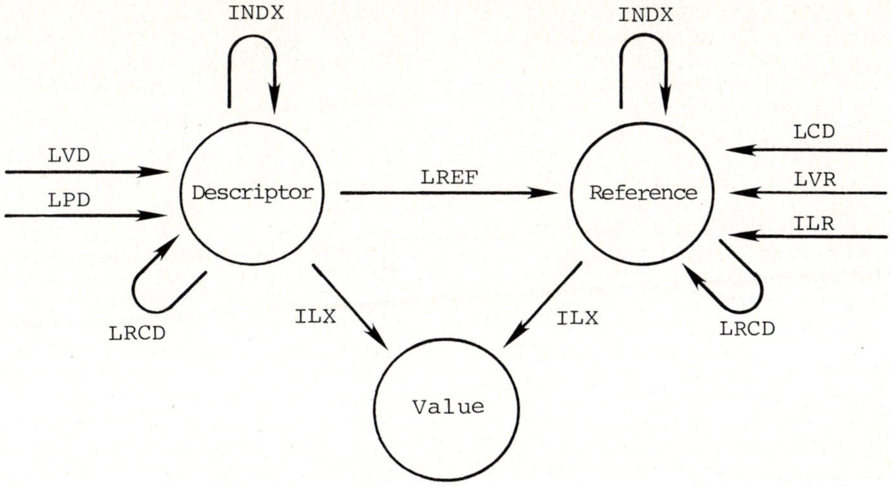

Figure 2. Transformation of the stack top

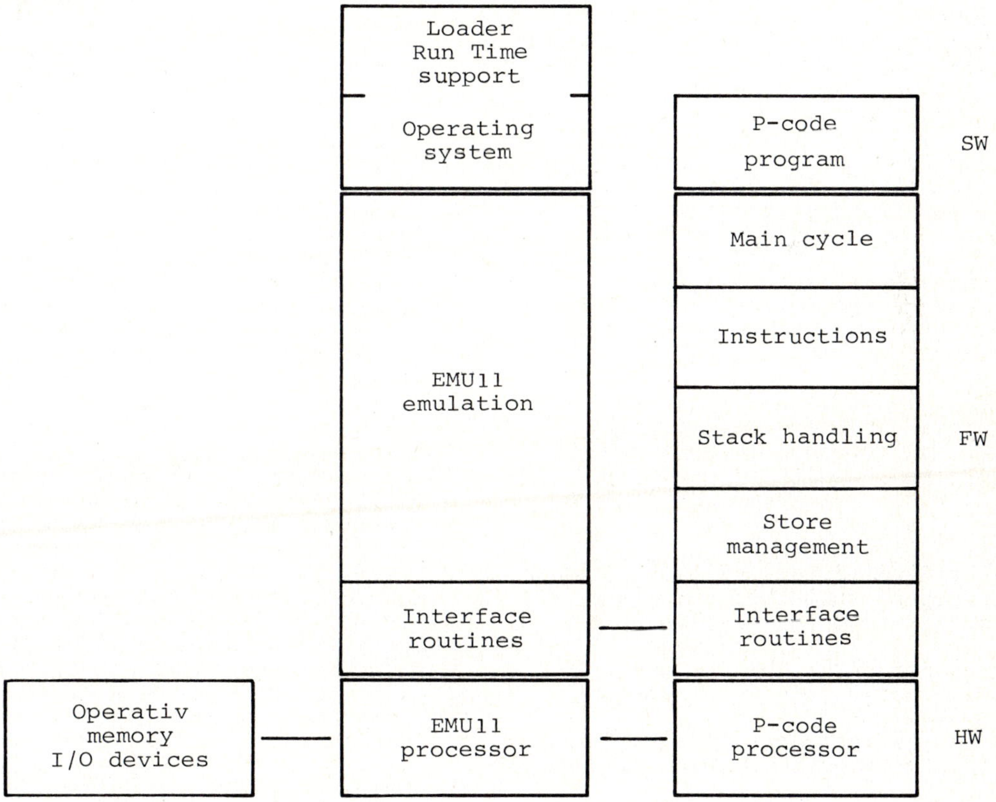

Figure 3. Structure of the system

needed for I/O operation is also provided by the EMU11 machine code program and the operating system.

Detailed information about the P-code processor is given in ref.[25].

6. STRUCTURE OF THE INTERPRETER

The interpreter itself is divided into five functional parts that constitute five separate hierarchical levels (See Fig. 3.) The first part - it can be regarded as the "main program" of the interpreter - is responsible for isntruction decoding, microroutine selection and error condition handling. The interpreter has two entry points, one of which is used for initializing execution of a P-code program. In this case the processor receives parameters from the loader program. The other entry point is used for restarting the interpreter after a system function I/O operations, interrupt handling carried out in EMU11.

The second functional part is built up from the set of microroutines realizing the algorithms of P-code instructions. These routines use the services of the three lower levels.

The third functional part handles the evaluation stack, including the push and pop functions of the four data formats.

The fourth level is responsible for the management of the operative store used by the P-code program (allocation, deallocation of dynamic variables).

The lowest level of the interpreter communicates with the microprogram of EMU11, it is responsible for reading and writing data. This level consists of routines which carry out services such as:

- loading data (bytes, halfwords, words, doublewords) from data regions into the registers of the P-code processor
- storing data from the registers of the P-code processor into data regions,
- loading the instructions into the instruction register before decoding,
- activating the machine code runtime support routines in EMU11 using a trap-like mechanism
- auxiliary services for functions not realized in hardware (e.g. byte swap, some kinds of register-to-register transfers).

Further details of the design of the interpreter are described elsewhere [24].

7. CONCLUSION

Some design aspects of a microprogrammed intermediate code interpreter are described. During the implementation of this interpreter we drew the following conclusions:

The adaptable width of the P-code processor is very convenient for the implementation of operations of programming languages because it allows the efficient manipulation of several formats of the same data type.

The extensive use of procedure and function call statements is one of the most important characteristics of structured programming methods. Therefore the number of executed procedure call statements (and corresponding machine instructions) represents a relatively high percentage of the total number of executed statement. Migrating the actions of procedure call into the microprogram (in the form of fewer instructions) enhances significantly the system performance.

The micro-programmed algorithm of instructions allows efficient execution of runtime checks, which results in a higher level of reliability, easier implementation of new languages and compilers, and last but not least allows easier implementation of the interpreter and P-code generator.

In the design and implementation we have used concepts of structured programming. The application of the said concepts has decreased the time required and has decreased the effect of hardware problems, hardware changes on the design of the interpreter and on the progress of the implementation.

Our final conclusion is that if the facilities of microprogram development are good, the implementation of a microprogrammed interpreter can be carried out in a reasonable time.

ACKNOWLEDGEMENT
I would like to express my thanks to F.Vajda, my thesis supervisor, and to my colleagues G.Ambrozy, who was responsible for the microprogram development facilities, and to J. Miskolczi and I. Szabo who designed the P-code processor hardware.

APPENDIX

TABLE OF P-CODE INSTRUCTIONS

Mnemonic	Operand type	Name
LCx	B,H,W,D,R	Load Constant Value
LIx	B,H,W,D	Load Immediate Value
LVx	B,H,W,D,R	Load Variable
LPx	B,H,W,D,R	Load Parameter
ILx	B,H,W,D,R	Indirect Load Value
SVx	B,H,W,D,R	Store Variable
SPx	B,H,W,D,R	Store Parameter
MVB	B	Move Bytes
ABSx	I,LI,F,LF	Load Absolute Value
NEGx	I,LI,F,LF	Negative Value
ADDx	I,LI,F,LF	Add
SUBx	I,LI,F,LF	Subtract
MULx	I,LI,F,LF	Multiply
DIVx	I,LI,F,LF	Divide
MODx	I,LI,F,LF	Modulo
SQRx	I,LI,F,LF	Square
INCRx	N,LN,I,LI	Increment
DECRx	N,LN,I,LI	Decrement
FLOTx	I,LI	Convert to Floating
TRNCx	F,LF	Convert from Floating
RNDx	F,LF	Convert from Floating
EQx	N,LN,I,LI,F LF,S,V	Equal Relation
NEx	N,LN,I,LI,F, LF, S,V	Non Equal
LTx	N,LN,I,LI,F, LF,S,V	Less
LEx	N,LN,I,LI,F, LF,S,V	Less or Equal
GTx	N,LN,I,LI,F, LF,S,V	Greater
GEx	N,LN,I,LI,F, LF,S,V	Greater or Equal
MAXx	N,LN,I,LI,F, LF	Select Maximum
MINx	N,LN,I,LI,F, LF	Select Minimum
ODDx	I,LI	Check Oddness
INx	S,LS	Set Membership Test
NOT	L	Not
EQ	L	Equivalence
EOR	L	Exlusive Or
IMP	L	Implication
RIMP	L	Reverse Implication
NIMP	L	Negated Implication
NRIMP	L	Negated Reverse Implication
OR	L	Or
AND	L	And
GNSx	S,LS	Generate Singleton Set
ISMx	S,LS	Insert Set Member
EXCLx	S,LS	Exclude Set Member
CMPLx	S,LS	Complement
UNIOx	S,LS	Union
INTRx	S,LS	Intersection
DIFFx	S,LS	Difference
LMTx	S,LS	Leading Member Test
ISFLDx	S,LS	Isolate Field
TFLDx	S,LS	Transfer Field
LVD		Load Variable Descriptor

Mnemonic	Operand type	Name
LPD		Load Parameter Descriptor
LCD		Load Constant Descriptor
LRCD		Load Record Component Descriptor
LIND		Indirect Load Descriptor
INDX		Load Indexed Descriptor
LREF		Calculate Reference
RTP		Reserve Temporary Pointer
LTP		Load Temporary Pointer
FTP		Free Temporary Pointer
CIP		Call Internal Procedure
CEP		Call External Procedure
CSF		Call System Function
ENT		Enter Procedure
RET		Return from Procedure
BRU		Unconditional Branch
BRT		Branch if True
BRF		Branch if False
BRX		Indexed Branch
SELC		Select Case
CLSQ		Case Label Sequence
CLR		Case Label Range
ITER		Iteration Cycle

REFERENCES

[1] E.I. Organic: Computer System Organization The B5700/6700 Series (Academic Press, 1973)

[2] Y.Chou: High Level Language Computer Architecture (Academic Press, 1975)

[3] K.Jensen, N.Wirth: Pascal User Manual and Report (Springer Verlag, 1978)

[4] J.B.Dennis, et al.: Research Directions in Computer Architecture MIT/LCS/TM-114, 1978 AD A061222

[5] G.J.Myers: Advances in Computer Architecture (John Wiley, 1978)

[6] A.S.Tanenbaum, Implication of Structured Programming for Machine Architecture CACM Vol. 21. No.3. (March 1978) 237-246.

[7] G.Ambrozy, et al.: Development of a Microprocessor System by means of a PDP-8E Minicomputer Euromicro Journal, 4, (1978) 92-103.

[8] R.W.Doran: Computer Architecture: A Structured Approach (Academic Press, 1979)

[9] V.Santhanam, A Hardware Independent Virtual Architecture for Pascal Conf. Proc. AFIPS NCC (1979) 637-648.

[10] R.L.Sites, D.R.Perkins, Universal P-code Definition UCSD-CS-79/037 PB298577 (July 1979)

[11] M.J.Flynn: Directions and Issues in Architecture and Language IEEE Computer (October 1980) 5-22

[12] L.J.Groves, W.J.Rogers, The Design of a Virtual Machine for ADA ACM SIGPLAN Notices (1980)

[13] N.R.Harris, A Directly Executable Language Suitable for Bit Slice Implementation International Workshop on HLL Computer Architecture Fort Lauderdale (May 1980) 40-43

[14] J.Jones, Towards a HLL Oriented Microprocessor Instruction Set Euromicro Journal 6, (1980) 158-160 Dept. of Computer Science, Trinity College, Dublin (October, 1980)

[16] F.Vajda, G.Ambrozy, J.Miskolczi, EMU: A Bit-Sliced Microprocessor Based Emulator, in: M.Sami, L.Thompson, L.Mezzalira (eds.), (North-Holland, Amsterdam 1980), Microprocessor Systems: Software Firmware, Hardware

[17] N.Wirth: MODULA-2 Eidgenössische Technische Hochschule Institute für Informatik, Zürich Report No.36 (1980).

[18] J.Bishop: A Pascal Machine? in: D.W.Barron (ed.), Pascal - The Language and its Implementation (John Wiley, 1981)

[19] K.V.Nori, U.Amman, K.Jensen, H.H.Nageli, Ch.Jacobi, Pascal-P Implementation Notes in: D.W.Barron (ed.) Pascal The Language and its Implementation (John Wiley, 1981)

[20] A.Sale, The Implementation of Case Statements in Pascal Software - Practice and Experience Vol. 11. (1981) 929-942

[21] W.A.Wulf, Compilers and Computer Architecture IEEE Computer (July 1981) 41-47.

[22] J.A.Hall, A Microprogrammed P-Code Interpreter for the Data General Eclipse S/130 Minicomputer Software-Practice and Experience Vol. 12 (1982) 755-765.

[23] J.Barr: NBS Pascal User's Guide (RT11 version) Department of Computer Science University of Montana Missoula, Montana 59812

[24] S.Zöld, The Structure of a Microprogrammed Interpreter Central Research Institute for Physics of the Hungarian Academy of Sciences (1983)

[25] J.Miskolczi, I, Szabo, The Floating Point Processor of the TPA1134/EMU Central Research Institute for Physics of the Hungarian Academy of Sciences (1983)

[1] Registered trade mark of Digital Equipment Corporation

Session H2: COMPUTING STRUCTURES

Chairman: Bogdan Lent
Grossenbacher Elektronik AG
St. Gallen (Switzerland)

Exploration of the existing parallelism in computational algorithms laid the foundations of coupled multiple processing units. The design motivations as summarized by Reed and Schwetman in /1/:

- cost/performance
- throughput
- resource sharing
- reliability measures
- serviceability
- availability

brought about the whole spectrum of different processing elements interconnections policies and implementations. These logically founded interconnections and computational abilities of interconnected multiple processing elements form together the Computing Structure.

So far we have not differentiated between the hardware, respectively the software implementations: the area covers both of them ambivalently with a natural trend towards higher hardware integration. This results in spatial separation of highly sophisticated processing elements. The research and development highlights three major focal points:

- interconnection topology evaluation
- processing elements features enhancements
- data routing strategies.

Noise immunity and interconnection channel capacity are intentionally not listed here. They are extensively dealt with within the researches on the computer networks.

INTERCONNECTION TOPOLOGY

The topology of interconnections varies from single channel centralised to fully independent direct links between each processing element. The first one although apparently cost-appealing, saturates quickly with an increase of the individual channel loading e.g.:

- minicomputers: 3-7 processing e. /2,3/
- microcomputers: 2-5 /4,5/

There has been no reported attempt at building the ring data flow machine based on a single communication channel.

Equally discarded by the computing structures researchers is complete interconnectivity of N elements. The number $\binom{N}{2}$ links is hardly efficiently managable.

According to Maekawa /6/ the optimal interconnectivity distance P between any two processing elements yields $P = \log_2 N$ while the interconnection degree stays at m = 3. Highly interesting in this context is the result obtained by the Kartashevs for their Reconfigurable Tree Structure: $P = 3(2 \log_2 N - 1)$ with asymetrical interconnectivity 1 x 2. The result conforms to the conclusions of Umeyama et al. /7/. The logical tree structures are under further investigation at Utah University also (Sharp in /8/). Other works are referred to in the referencies given by the Kartashevs and Winter as well as in /1,6,7/.

Winter's Cube Type Interconnection CTD is deduced by Maekawa /6/ as a redundant resolution into 2 x 2 shuffle of a perfect cube. The CTD average shortest path length is $3(\log_2 N - 1)/2 + 1/N$. Numerous researches view the 2 x 2 shuffle as a promising compromise between the design criteria quoted above. Currently under way are also researches at MIT, Purdue and other Universities, as indicated by Dennis, McMillen and Siegel in /8/ and references of Winter and Auguin.

The correlation of shuffle interconnection and Single Instruction Multiple Data machine, as the one presented below by Auguin, is more than only accidental. The practical usability certified by Auguin is strongly supported by Umeyama /7/ and theoretically the shuffle and SIMD machine design is evaluated by Smith and Siegel in /9/.

Numerous efforts on various topologies for SIMD and MIMD machines are reported. Enslow /10/ distinguishes,besides the bus and multiport topologies, the crossbar switch as the separate third category. The reference to crossbar switch with suitable evaluation is given later by Winter. The most complete survey originates however from Anderson and Jensen in /11/.

PROCESSING ELEMENTS

The computing structures researches on the processing elements features enhancements involve, most of all, the interconnectivity interface feasibility, although, indirectly, the functional behaviour of processing elements is of concern as well. As it goes beyond the scope of this session to analyse the individual designs with regards to the functionality, we restrict ourselves to the statement that the structures developed aim at interconnection of:

- von Neuman processing elements
- SIMD machines processing elements
- data flow processing elements.

The interface feasibility tends towards either

- integrated processing elements, or
- interconnection switch.

Elegant and efficient interface proposed by the Kartashevs falls into the first group. The dynamic reconfigurability maintains the fast node pass-through time partially due to the programmable hardware register design, partially because of simple routing code. Other designs admit static or preprogrammed interconnections as proposed at Westfield (Sharp in /8/) or TU Budapest.

The most popular approach introduces the interconnection switch. Implemented are 1 x n /8,12/, n x 1 /12,8/, n x k (Jajszczyk in /1/) and n x n switches, particularly 2 x 2 (Auguin, Dennis in /8/). The 3 x 3 switch is proposed below by Winter. Certain attempts have been taken towards the synthesis of any size switch from elementary switch

(Jajszczyk in /1/, Dennis and Swan in /8/). A Successful integrated circuit 2 x 2 component for such a network has been developed by Dennis's MIT group. This trend is presented below by Winter. Because of its general applicability the interconnection component is likely to become established as a structure builder.

ROUTING STRATEGIES

The following categories may be distinguished:

- self-carrying routing codes
- centralised stored routing
- centralised command-driven routing

The routing codes accompanying the data transfers are an inherent mark of distributed equally privileged systems. The decisions regarding the destination are taken in the nodes. The expandability and technical feasibility of geographical displacement of the interconnected processing elements introduced this routing into the computer network systems. The routing code adopted influences significantly the node decision time. Special attention to this aspect is given by the Kartashevs: their algorithm brings the data transfer time and routing code size to a minimum. The computing structure operating on such an asynchronous data exchange is generally called packet exchange architecture (Dennis in /8/).

The approach exercised frequently by data flow machine designers is based on a coupling of an interconnection network with a host mainframe computer. The routing is established for a given task prior to the system operation through the appropriate control setting. The raw data then flow through the structure correspondingly to the functional algorithm data relations. Both Winter and Auguin develop their machines according to this principle. It proves its efficiency in the fixed base structure under heavy interconnection channel loading, which is the case with the data flow machines.

The routing, dynamically alterable during execution of the Route-command is an upgraded centralised routing. It introduses however the control information into the routed data structures. The most advanced researches deploying this type routing are reported by Treleaven et al. /2/ on their demand-driven machine.

Summarizing: the following papers are deep insights par excellence into most aspects of the computing structures. Individual evaluations are tutorial and complete, resulting in valuable contributions to the domain of the computing structures.

REFERENCES

/1/ A.Agrawala, U.Herzog edit. "Special Issue on Performance Evaluation of Multiple Processor Systems" IEEE TC, C-32, 1/1983.

/2/ C.Sauer, K.M.Chandy "Parametric Modelling of Multi Miniprocessor Systems" IBM RR RC 5978 (*25 936)

/3/ D.P.Bhandarkar "Analysis of Memory Interference in Multiprocessors" IEEE TC, C-24, 9/1975.

/4/ M.A.Marsan, F.Gregoretti "Memory

Interference Models for a Multi-Microprocessor System with a Shared Bus and a Single External Common Memory" Microprocessing & Microprogramming v.7 2/1981.

/5/ K.T.Fung,H.C.Torng "On the Analysis of Memory Conflicts and Bus Contention in Multiple Microprocessor Systems" IEEE TC, C-27, 1/1979

/6/ H.Maekawa "Optimal Processor Interconnection Topologies" 0149-7111 IEEE 1981.

/7/ S.Umeyama et al. "New Processor Interconnection Strategies for a large Multi-Processor System" Microprocessing & Microprogramming 10/1982.

/8/ Contributions to "Computer Architecture Symposium" 80CH1494-4C IEEE 1980.

/9/ S.D.Smith, H.J.Siegel "Recirculating, Pipelined & Multistage SIMD Interconnection Network" Intl Conf. on Parallel Processing 1978.

/10/P.H.Enslow JR "Multiprocessor Organisation- a Survey" ACM Computing Surveys v9 1/1977.

/11/G.A.Anderson, E.D.Jensen "Computer Interconnection Structures: Taxonomy, Characteristics and Examples" Computing Surveys v7 4/1975.

/12/P.C.Treleaven et al. "Combining Data Flow and Control Flow Computing" The Computer Journal V25 2/1982.

MICROCOMPUTERS: Developments in Industry, Business and Education
D.R. Wilson and C.J. van Spronsen (eds.) / © EUROMICRO, 1983
Elsevier Science Publishers B.V. (North-Holland)

RECONFIGURABLE BINARY TREES: ORGANIZATION OF EFFICIENT INTERNODE COMMUNICATIONS

Svetlana P. Kartashev (University of Nebraska, Lincoln, USA) and
Steven I. Kartashev (Dynamic Computer Architecture, Inc., Lincoln, Nebraska)

This paper discusses efficient routing algorithms for multicomputer networks organized as *reconfigurable binary trees*. The routing algorithms introduced allow organization of very fast node to node communications, $N_s \rightarrow N_d$ where N_s is an arbitrary source node, N_d is an arbitrary destination node. Communication techniques are optimal from both viewpoints: the total bit size of routing information code, BS(RI), that routes the message among various transit nodes of the communication path and the total time of communication. It is shown that $BS(RI) \leq \log_2 K + 2 \log_2 \log_2 K$, where K is the total number of nodes in a reconfigurable binary tree. Further, since each transit node N selects its either right or left successor in the communication path from the root via simple logical operation that takes the time of one gate delay, the total time, CD, of the $N_s \rightarrow N_d$ communication approaches the theoretical minimum.

1. INTRODUCTION

Binary tree is a very popular implementation for a distributed computing system in which each tree node is implemented as a separate and autonomous computational node [1,2,3], since the tree structure describes a variety of control and computational algorithms. Especially important is the use of binary trees in distributed data bases, since most of the file accesses algorithms are based on queries organized as a binary tree [4]. Trees have two types of nodes: *leaves* and *non-leaves*, where a leaf is understood as a node of the lowest level, i=0, and a non-leaf node has level $i \geq 1$, where $i \leq n$ for the n-level tree. In this tree, the node of the highest (n) level is called *the root*.

A multicomputer network that reconfigures into trees as well as other useful structures (stars and rings) can be organized if its nodes identified with computer elements, CE, are interconnected with the memory-processor bus (or DC-bus) described in [5,6]. To organize a data broadcast among a pair of nodes N and N* interconnected with the DC bus, it is sufficient for network node N to generate the position code or address of N*; this will be denoted as transition $N \rightarrow N^*$. For trees to minimize the time of reconfiguration requires that the direction of succession $N \rightarrow N^*$ be maintained from the leaves to the root(s). This will transform trees into *single successors structures* since each node N will have only one successor in this structure. To generate a reconfigurable binary tree, assume that each tree node N is provided with a special shift-register of length n which stores its position code N, where n is the size of the code (Fig. 1). Suppose that in the given network structure to be assumed, node N should be connected with node N* via PE-PE*, PE-ME*, ME-ME*, or ME-PE* data path. Then for each type of communication between N and N*, node N generates position code N* using a left-shifted shift-register that generates N* as follows:

$$N^* = 1[N]_0 + B \qquad (1)$$

where $1[N]_0$ is one bit non-circular shift of N to the left and B is an n-bit reconfiguration constant brought with the reconfiguration instruction to *all network nodes that are requested for reconfiguration* (Fig. 2). Reconfiguration constant B will be called *bias* and the shift-register of Fig. 1 is called a *shift-register with the variable bias* (SRVB). Since to generate a binary tree, SRVB must always perform non-circular shift $1[N]_0$, subscript 0 will be omitted in this paper. We will call (1) the *reconfiguration equation* assuming that it is valid only during reconfiguration into a new tree. During regular node to node communications, both transitions $N \rightarrow N^*$ and $N^* \rightarrow N$ will be maintained. In Fig. 1, the network of eight nodes receiving bias B=101 reconfigures into the 3-level with the root R=011. Since there are 2^n different biases, it is possible to generate 2^n different trees with these techniques.

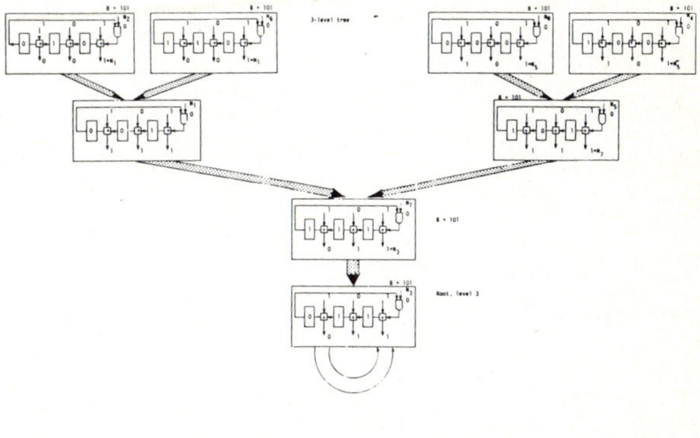

Figure 1: Generation of a binary tree with the use of shift-registers SRVB receiving bias B = 101

In any reconfigurable binary tree, organization of efficient communication among tree nodes presents a major problem because during reconfiguration, positions of tree nodes change. Therefore, to route a communication message from a source node, N_s, to a destination node, N_d, requires to store the position codes of all transit nodes of the $N_s \to N_d$ communication path. This routing information RI can be either stored in a communication message CM or distributed among transit nodes so that each transit node stores the position code of its successor in the $N_s \to N_d$ communication path. Both these alternatives are infeasible since they lead to a large bit size of the RI-code and a long time of internode communication associated with the large size of RI.

This paper is dedicated to solution of communication problem in a reconfigurable binary tree. Two types of communications are considered: 1) Bidirectional node-root communications (node $\to$ root, and root $\to$ node), and 2) Node-node communications. Communication algorithms that are presented allow a dramatic reduction in both the total bit size of the RI code and the overall time of communication. The following upper bound on bit size of RI is obtained: BS(RI $\leq \log_2 K + 2 \log_2 \log_2 K$, where K is the total number of tree nodes.

The relationship of this paper with other work in the area is as follows: First, by introducing original routing algorithms for distributed reconfigurable computing systems organized as binary trees, it is connected with other works on reorganizations and reconfigurations discussed in [8-13]. Second, by using the shift-register theory to develop reconfigurations of binary trees, it is connected with the literature on shift-register sequences [14-19]. Third, by discussing distributed computing systems organized as binary trees, it is associated with [1-4].

2. SYNTHESIS OF THE ROOT AND OTHER NODES OF RECONFIGURABLE BINARY TREE

To form efficient routing algorithms, it is necessary to develop a simple synthesis technique aimed at finding the root, R, without actual construction of a reconfigurable binary tree. For this purpose, the bias structure is defined for a non-circular shift-registers SRVB as follows: Given bias $B = GP_1 + \ldots + GP_t$ where GP_i $(i = 1, \ldots, t)$ is its ones position otherwise called *generating position*. Let $a_1, a_2, \ldots, a_t$ be *bias distances* defined as follows: $GP_{i+1} = a_i[GP_i]$, i.e., a_i shows the number of left-hand shifts between GP_i and GP_{i+1}, where i changes from 1 to t-1. For GP_t, $a_t[GP_t] = 0$, since we are having a non-circular shift (Fig. 2). For each generating position, GP_i, let us form a mod 2 sum of all left j-bit shifts of GP_i ranging from $j = 0$ to $j = a_i-1$, where a_i is the bias distance such that $a_i[GP_i] = GP_{i+1}$. Denote this sum as $BL(GP_i) = GP_i + 1[GP_i] + \ldots + (a_{i-1})[GP_i]$. With the introduction of BL-sums, we can establish the theorem that constructs the root.

Theorem 1. For a binary tree generated by SRVB receiving bias $B = GP_1 + GP_2 + \ldots + GP_t$, let GP_1, GP_3, GP_5, ..., GP_k be odd generating positions of the bias, where k = t, if t is odd and k = t-1 if t is even. Form BL sums for odd generating positions of the bias as $BL(GP_1)$,

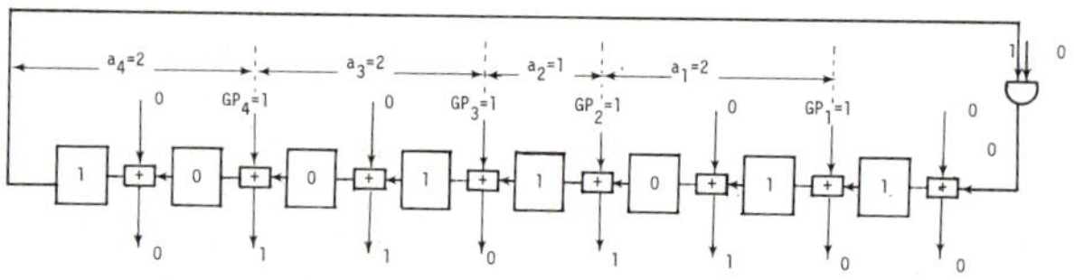

Figure 2: Bias structure

$BL(GP_3)$, ..., $BL(GP_k)$. Then the root R is:

$$R = BL(GP_1) + BL(GP_3) + \ldots + BL(GP_k)$$

Example: Let us form the root R for the bias B = 01011010 (Fig. 2).

Here $GP_1=2$, $GP_2=8$, $GP_3=16$, $GP_4=64$;

and $a_1=2$, $a_2=1$, $a_3=2$, $a_4=2$

$BL(GP_1) = GP_1 + (a_1-1)[GP_1]=00000110$; $BL(GP_2)= GP_2$; $BL(GP_3)=GP_3 + (a_3-1)[GP_3]=00110000$; $BL(GP_4 = GP_4 + (a_4-1)[GP_4]=11000000$

Therefore, the root, R, is: $R=BL(GP_1) + BL(GP_3 = 00110110$. Indeed, R is succeeded by the following node: $N^* = 1[R] + B = 01101100 + 01011010 = 00110110$ which coincides with the node R.

As we have seen, the technique for constructing the root is very simple and can be easily performed either by a programmer or inside each node N using simple circuits that contain two shifters interconnected together with the mod 2 counter that generates two outputs, even and odd. Once the node N has formed the position code for the root R, it can form the position codes for all other nodes with which node N wishes to communicate using the following synthesis procedure. Our objective is to construct a tree node of level $j = 0, 1, \ldots, n$. To establish this result, let us introduce the notion of *recursive sum*, RS_i (k), where $k \leq i$, $i \geq 0$.

Basis: RS_0 (0) = 0, i = 0, k = 0

Inductive Step: $RS_i(k) = X_i + RS_m(k-1)$ where $k \leq i$, $X_i = 2^{n-i}$, and $m < i$
Therefore, if SRVB stores RS_i (k), its position b_{n-i} is always 1, and (k-1) is the total number of other more significant ones positions (Fig.3). For instance, $RS_3(3) = X_1 + X_2 + X_3$ can be represented as follows via this definition:

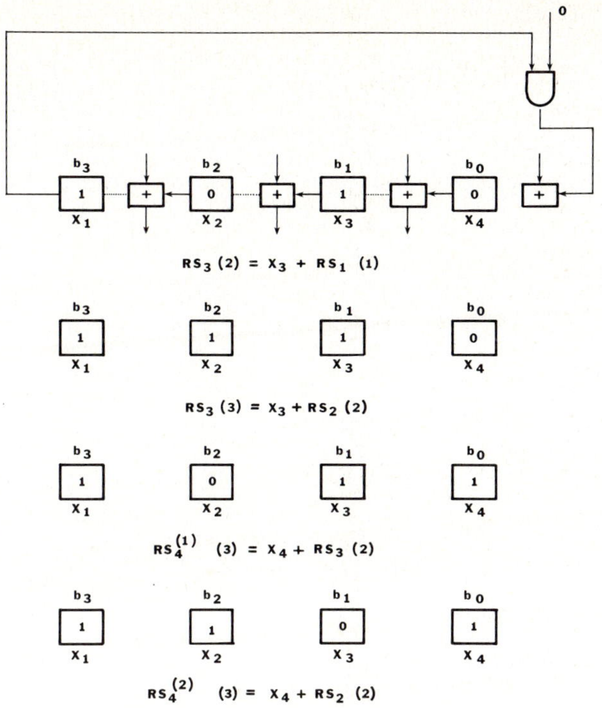

Figure 3: Recursive sums

RS_3 (3) = X_3 + RS_2 (2); RS_2 (2) = X_2 + RS_1 (1) RS_1 (1) = X_1. For a recursive sum, RS_i (k) = X_i + RS_m (k-1), X_i will be called a *level variable*. As shown below in Theorem 2, level variable X_i = 1 uniquely specifies all tree nodes of level n-i.

Theorem 2. In a reconfigurable binary tree formed with bias B, any tree node, N(n-i) of level n-i (i = 0, 1, ..., n) can be found as follows: N(n-i) = R + RS_i (k) where k $\leqslant$ i, R is the root, and RS_i (k) is a recursive sum with level variable X_i.

Example: Given bias B = 1011011. Let us construct all the nodes of levels n-i = 7, 6, 5, and 4. Here n = 7. Thus the root is of level 7: R = BL(GP_1) + BL(GP_3) + BL(GP_5) and GP_1 = 1, GP_3 = 8, and GP_5 = 64; BL(GP_1) = GP_1, BL(GP_3) = GP_3, and BL(GP_5) = GP_5; thus, R = 1001001. Indeed the successor N* of R is N* = 1[R] + B = 1[1001001] + 1011011 = 0010010 + 1011011 = 1001001 = R = X_1 + X_4 + X_7. The node of level 6 is: N(n-1) = R + RS_1 (1) = R + X_1 = 0001001 = X_4 + X_7. This node is succeeded by the root because N* = 1[N(6)] + B = 0010010 + 1011011 = 1001001 = R. There are two nodes of level n-2 = 5: N_1(5) = R + RS_2(1) = R + X_2 = 1101001, and N_2(5) = R + RS_2(2) = R + X_1 + X_2 = X_2 + X_4 + X_7 = 0101001. Indeed, N_1(5) is succeeded by N* = 1[N_2(5)] + B = 1010010 + 1011011 = 0001001 = N(6) = 9. Likewise, N_2(5) is succeeded by N* = 1[N_2(5)] + B = 1010010 + 1011011 = 0001001 = 9, etc. Similarly, one can construct all the other nodes of this tree.

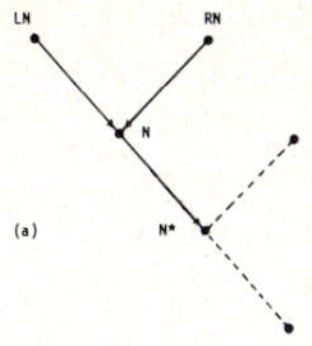

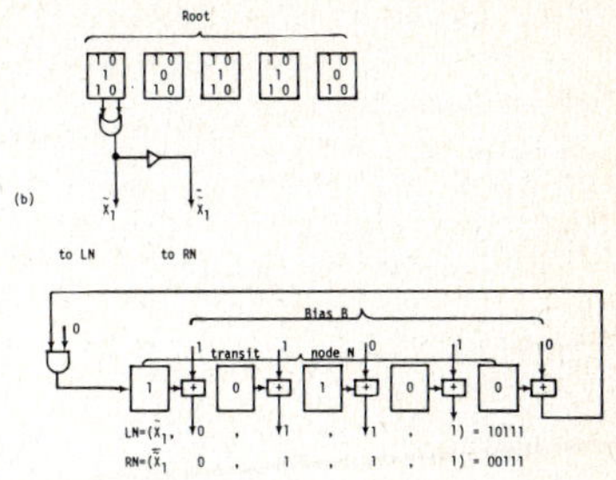

Figure 4(a): Node N and its closest neighbors

Figure 4(b): Generation in N of LN and RN codes

3. GENERATION INSIDE NODE N OF THE POSITION CODES FOR ALL ITS IMMEDIATE NEIGHBORS

Node N has the following immediate neighbors in a reconfigurable binary tree: left node LN, right node, RN, and the immediate successor N* (Fig.4a). Node N must be provided with the hardware circuits that allow automatic generation of LN, RN and N* since availability of codes N*, LN and RN inside a given node N allows dynamic establishment of transfer modes in all the connecting elements that connect N with its closest neighbors. For the N $\rightarrow$ N* broadcast, (MSE_N-MSE_{N*})-pair of connecting elements belongs to node N. Their transfer nodes are established by node N dynamically with the use of N and N* codes (Fig. 5). Similarly, for N $\rightarrow$ LN or N $\rightarrow$ RN, the pair of connecting elements is either MSE_N-MSE_{LN} belonging to node LN or MSE_N-MSE_{RN} belonging to node RN. Their dynamic transfer nodes are established by node N during message transit through N with the use of codes N, LN or N, RN respectively. However, to provide any node N with the power to generate LN and RN inside, we have to fix their positions in reconfigurable binary tree with respect to the root R. Assume that LN > RN. Since LN and RN are on the same level, to establish the order among each LN and RN in each level of the tree, we have to order the recursive sums. Assume that two recursive sums RS_i and RS_j are ordered as follows:

P1. RS_i > RS_j if X_i > Xj where $X_i = 2^{n-i}$, $X_j = 2^{n-j}$ and

P2. RS_i > RS_i' if RS_i + X_i > RS_i' + X_i

Accordingly, the root R = R + RS_0 = R + 0 is the most significant node in the tree. Thus, for each pair LN and RN, R > LN > RN. Then, we can use the following techniques to generate LN and RN inside each node N: N = 1[LN] + B = 1[RN] + B, where 1[...] is 1-bit shift to the left. Thus, 1[LN] = 1[RN] or RN = LN + X_1 since one bit shift of X_1 to the left is 0, i.e., 1[X_1] = 0 and 1[LN + X_1] = 1[LN] + 1[X_1] = 1[LN]. Therefore, since LN > RN, LN = R + RS_i; RN = R + RS_i + X_1. Thus, two nodes LN and RN differ only in position X_1. Since LN > RN, node LN has the same meaning of X_1 variable as X_1 of the root R. The right node RN always has its X_1 variable reversed, i.e., opposite the one of the root (Fig.4b). Thus, LN

$= \tilde{X}_1 (R) + 1^{-1}[N+B]$ where $1^{-1}[\ldots]$ is non-circular shift to the right and $\tilde{X}_1 (R)$ is the meaning of the most significant variable in the node LN. Similarly, since $1[RN] = N+B$, $RN = \tilde{X}_1 (R) + 1^{-1}[N+B]$. Therefore, each transit node N can generate inside all the codes N*, LN and RN of its closest neighbors in the tree via simple logical operations of left and right shift and mod 2 addition.

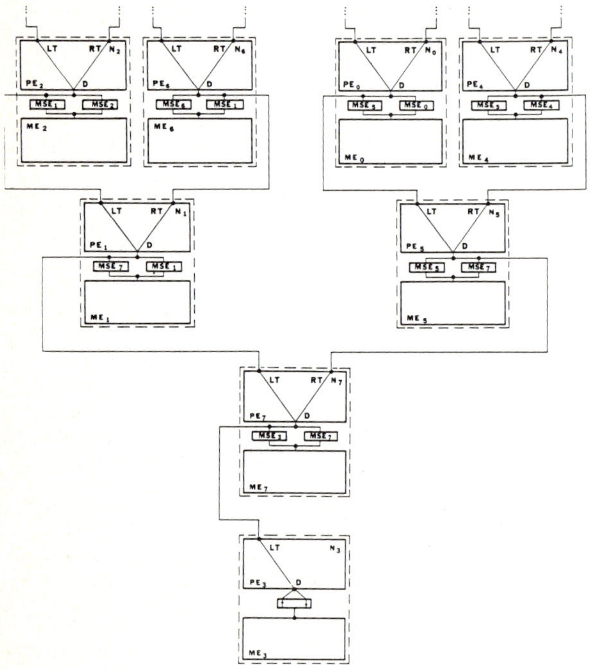

Figure 5: Interconnection diagram of a reconfigurable binary tree

4. INDIVIDUAL COMMUNICATIONS

Below, we will introduce communication algorithms which allow efficient internode communications. Two types of communication will be considered: 1) Node-Root communication, and 2) Node-Node communication.

4.1. Node-Root Communications

There are two types of node-root communication: a) node → root and b) root → node.

4.1.1. *NODE TO ROOT COMMUNICATION, $N_S \rightarrow R$*

For the $N_S \rightarrow R$ communication, N_S is the source, R is the destination; N_S generates communication message CM that stores the position code of the root, R, defined in Theorem 1. In passing this message, each transit node, N, compares R with its own position code, N. If N = R, the message reaches the destination. If N ≠ R, it is passed top down from one of the top terminal (LT or RT) to the only one D-terminal (Fig.5).

4.1.2. *ROOT-NODE COMMUNICATION, $R \rightarrow N_d$*

For this case, the message is generated by the root, i.e., R is the source, N_d is the destination. Message, CM, stores a so-called address code of N_d defined as follows: By the *address code*, AC_N of the node N, we define such a binary word which contains all the routing information that allows a communication message to reach node N from the root via the minimal communication path (i.e., the one which includes each node of the tree only once). Below, we define a procedure which allows one to obtain the address code, AC of node N_d. As was specified by Theorem 2, node N_d of level (n-i) is defined as follows: $N_d = R+RS_i$, where RS_i is the recursive sum. The reconfiguration 1-successor of N_d is the node of the next more significant level, n-(i-1), defined via recursive sum RS_{i-1} which is a one-bit shift to the left of the original recursive sum RS_i that specifies node N_d. Similarly, it is easy to show that the reconfiguration 2-successor of node N_d in the communication path with the root is specified by recursive sum RS_{i-2} which is 2-bit shift of RS_i: $RS_{i-2} = 2[RS_i]$, where RS_i specifies node N. Since the destination node N_d is on the level (n-i), it is connected with the root by the minimal path having i other nodes, where consecutive nodes in this path are specified by consecutive shifts of the recursive sum RS_i that identifies given node N_d: $1[RS_i]$, $2[RS_i]$, ..., $i[RS_i]$. Therefore, consecutive variables X_i, X_{i-1}, X_{i-2}, ..., $\tilde{X}_1$ that are present in RS_i where $X_i = 1$ and $\tilde{X}_j = 0$ or 1 are responsible for the entire route selection from one level to the next in the minimal communication path from the root R

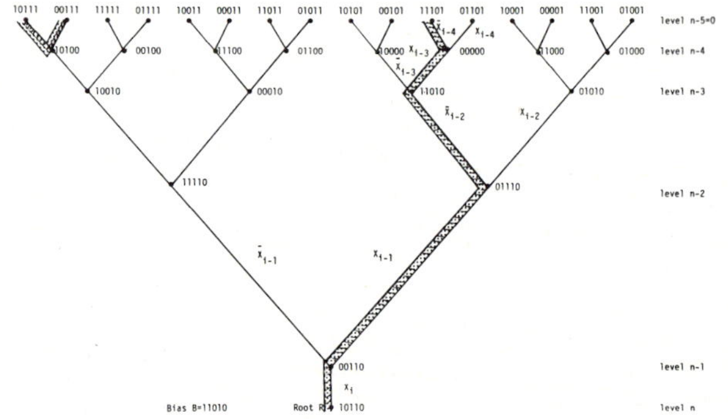

Figure 6. Binary tree generated by bias B = 11010 and having root R = 10110

to the destination node N_d (Fig.6). As follows, $X_i = 1$ selects the route from level n to level n-1; $\tilde{X}_{i-1}$ selects the route from level n-1 to level n-2; ...; $\tilde{X}_1$ selects the route from level n-(i-1) to the least significant level n-i of communication path to the leaves. Therefore, the recursive sum $RS_i = R+N_d$ contains all the routing information necessary to forward the message issued by the root to the destination node N_d. Namely, the address code AC_d may be obtained from $RS_i = N_d+R$ by moving its bit X_i to the bit 1 of AC; $\tilde{X}_{i-1}$ has to be moved to bit 2, ..., $\tilde{X}_1$ to bit i of AC (Fig.7(a)). This simple logical operation will be called *rotate* or symbolically, AC = rot(RS_i). However, to reduce the routing algorithm to execution of a simple logical operation in each transit node, we will stipulate that each node of level n-j will store a so-called *complemented level value*, CL (Fig.7(b)) of the size $\log_2 n = \log_2 \log_2 K$ that shows the bit of the address code that must be selected for finding the route from the given node to the next node

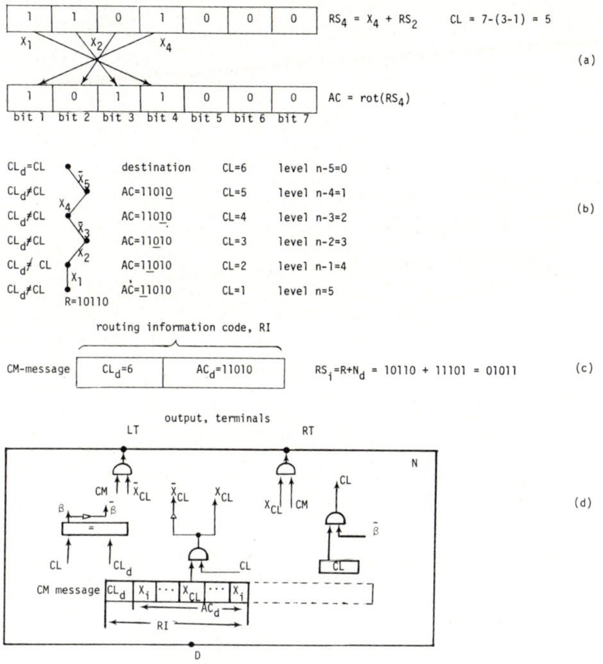

Figure 7(a): Significance of rotation operation

Figure 7(b): Transit of the CM message for $R \rightarrow N_d$ communication

Figure 7(c): Formation of the routing information code, RI

in the path. To find CL, each node N finds its individual recursive sum as RS_i = R+N, then shifts RS_i to the LSB until LSB = 1 and counts the number of shifts k; CL = n-(k-1), where n is the number of levels in the tree.

Example: For the tree of Fig. 6 having root R = 10110, let us find the route from the root R to the node N_d = 11101 of level n-5 = 5-5 = 0.

First, we find recursive sum $RS_i = R+N_d$ = 10110 + 11101 = 01011. Rotation of RS_i gives the following address code AC_d = 11010. The following CL values are stored in the nodes of this tree. Level n: RS_0 = 0; k = n; CL = n-(k-1) = 1, (Fig. 7(b)). Level n-1: $RS_1 = X_1$; k = n-1 = 4; CL = n-(k-1) = 5-3 = 2, etc. The root forms communication message shown in Fig. 7(c); it selects the first bit of AC ($X_1 \equiv 1$) and forwards the message to the node N(n-1) of level n-1 (Fig. 7(b)). This node stores CL = 2. Thus, it selects bit 2 of AC. Since X_2 = 1, CM is forwarded to the RN of level n-2, etc.

4.2. Node-Node Communication, $N_s \rightarrow N_d$

The node-to-node communication is more general case of $N_s \rightarrow R$ and $R \rightarrow N_d$ communications considered above where N_s is the source node, N_d is the destination node. Indeed, for any $N_s \rightarrow N_d$ communication, the task of an optimal routing technique is to find a so-called *the closest intermediate root*, CIR, which is understood as the tree node that connects N_s and N_d with the minimal communication path $N_s \rightarrow$ CIR, CIR $\rightarrow N_d$ (Fig.8), i.e., for $N_s \rightarrow$ R, R $\rightarrow N_d$, CIR = R.

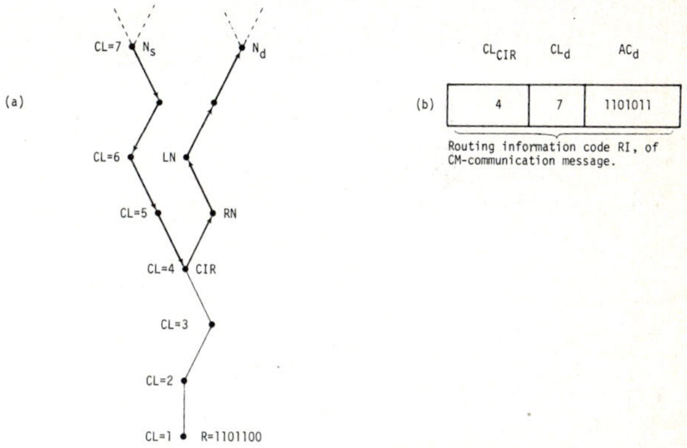

Figure 8: The $N_s \rightarrow N_d$ communication
(a) the $N_s \rightarrow N_d$ communication
(b) routing information code

4.2.1. *CLOSEST INTERMEDIATE ROOT*

To find the minimal $N_s \rightarrow N_d$ communication path, we have to find first, the closest intermediate root, CIR. Since CIR is on the subpath that connects the root, R, with both N_s and N_d (Fig.8), the address code, AC_{CIR} of the CIR is a left prefix of the two address codes, AC_s and AC_d. The number of bits in AC_{CIR} can be determined as follows: First, we find MS = $AC_s + AC_d$, and the number of *consecutive most significant zeros* in MS. This will give us the number of bits in the common left prefix of both AC_s and AC_d or the bit size of AC_{CIR}.

Example: Let us find AC_{CIR} and CL_{CIR} for N_s and N_d given by the following position codes: N_s = 1111111, N_d = 1000111. Assume that these are tree nodes in a binary tree having root R = 1101100 and bias B = 0110100 (Fig.8). First, we find AC_s and AC_d. To do so, we have to find $RS(N_s)$ and $RS(N_d)$: $RS(N_s) = N_s+R$ = 1111111 + 1101100 = 0010011: $RS(N_d) = N_d+R$ = 1000111 + 1101100 = 0101011.

Address code of N_s is found by rotation of $RS(N_s)$: $AC_s = rot(RS(N_s)) = 1100100$. Similarly, $AC_d = rot(RS(N_d)) = 1101010$. Let us find $MS = AC_s + AC_d = 1100100 + 1101010 = \underbrace{000}_{LO}1110$. In the MS, the number of consecutive most significant zeros, LO = 3. Therefore, $AC_{CIR} = 110$ and $CL_{CIR} = LO+1 = 3+1 = 4$. Position code of CIR can be found by rotating first its address code to obtain its recursive sum: $RS(CIR) = rot(AC_{CIR}) = 011$. Thereafter, the CIR position code is $CIR = R+RS(CIR) = 1101100 + 0110000 = 1011100$.

4.2.2. *$N_s \to N_d$ COMMUNICATION PATH*

To reach destination node N_d, the source node N_s has to form communication message that contains the following routing information code: $RI = CL_{CIR}\ CL_d\ AC_d$. (See Fig.8(b)) where CL_{CIR} is the complemented level value for CIR-node; CL_d is the complemented level value for destination node, N_d, and AC_d is the address code for N_d. All these values can be found using the techniques presented above. Each communication path from N_s to N_d includes two subpaths $N_s \to CIR$, and $CIR \to N_d$, where $N_s \to CIR$ is in the direction of TOR (towards the root R) and $CIR \to N_d$ is in the direction of TOL (towards the leaves) (Fig. 8(a)).

Example: For the $N_s \to N_d$ communication path of Fig.8(a)), the routing information code, RI of communication message is shown in Fig.8(b)). As seen $CL_{CIR} = 4$, $CL_d = 7$ and $AC_d = 1101011$. For the broadcast to-the-root $N_s \to CIR$, the message reaches CIR having CL = 4 (Fig.6). Thereafter, it starts the transfer to the leaves, $CIR \to N_d$. In each transit node $N(CL_N \neq CL_d)$, the CL_N-th bit of the address code AC_d brought with the message specifies the next node in the path (LN or RN) (Fig.7d). For the CIR-node, $CL_{CIR} = 4$. Therefore, the 4-th bit of the $AC_d = 1101011$ shows what node of the tree follows the CIR-node (Fig. 8). Since $X_4=1$, CIR is followed by the right node RN. In the RN node, $CL_{RN} = 5$ and $X_5=0$ in $AC_d = 1101011$. Thus, RN is followed by the left node, LN, of the path, etc. The destination is achieved in the node N having $CL_N = CL_d$. Since it is a leaf node, it is final destination and no direction bit of AC is required.

As follows for the $N_s \to N_d$ communication, the bit size of the routing information code, RI is upperbounded as follows: $BS(RI) \leq n + 2\log_2 n = \log_2 K + 2\log_2\log_2 K$ where n is the number of tree levels and K is the number of tree nodes.

CONCLUSIONS

In this paper, we discussed efficient communication algorithms for multicomputer networks organized as reconfigurable binary trees. The algorithms that were introduced allow organization of optimal node to node communications, $N_s \to N_d$ where N_s is an arbitrary source node N_d is an arbitrary destination node. Communication between N_s and N_d is organized via the minimal communication path that contains the minimal number of nodes, i.e., the destination node N_d is achieved in such a way that each transit node of the communication path is included only once in the path $N_s \to N_d$. Communication techniques introduced are optimal from both viewpoints: the total bit size of the routing information code, BS(RI), that routes the message among various transit nodes of the communication path and the total time of communication, CD. It is shown that $BS(RI) \leq \log_2 K + 2\log_2\log_2 K$, where K is the total number of nodes in a binary tree.

REFERENCES

1. A. Despain and D. Patterson, "X-Tree: A Tree Structured Multi-Processor Computer Architecture", *Proceedings Fifth Annual Symposium on Computer Architecture*, 1978, pp. 144-150.

2. Y. Paxer and M. Bozygit, "Variable Topology Multicomputer", *Proceedings of the Second Euromicro Symposium on Microprocessing and Microprogramming*, Venice, 1976, pp. 141-149.

3. L. D. Wittie and A. M. van Tilborg, "MICROS, A Distributed Operating System for MICRONET, A Reconfigurable Network Computer", *IEEE Transactions on Computers*, Vol. C-29, December, 1980, pp. 2233-1144.

4. David J. Dewitt and Dina Friedland, "Exploiting Parallelism for the Performance Enhancement of Non-numeric Applications", *The AFIPS Conference Proceedings*, Vol. 51, 1982, National Computer Conference, pp. 207-216.

5. S. I. Kartashev and S. P. Kartashev, "Problems of Designing Supersystems with Dynamic Architectures", *IEEE Transactions on Computers*, Vol. C-29, December, 1980, pp. 1114-1132.

6. C. Davis, S. P. Kartashev, and S. I. Kartashev, "Reconfigurable Multicomputer Networks for Very Fast Real-time Applications", 1982 *AFIPS Conference Proceedings*, Vol. 51, AFIPS Press, pp. 167-185.

7. S. P. Kartashev and S. I. Kartashev, "Reconfiguration of Dynamic Architecture into Multicomputer Networks", *Proceedings of the 1981 International Conference on Parallel Processing*, August 25-28, 1981, Belleaire, Michigan, pp. 133-141.

8. H. Garcia-Molina, "Elections in a Distributed Computing System", *IEEE Transactions on Computers*, January, 1982, Vol. C-31, No. 1, pp. 48-60.

9. H. Garcia-Molina, "Performance of Update Algorithms for Replicated Data in a Distributed Database", *Department of Computer Science, Stanford University, Stanford, Ca., Rep.* STAN-CS-79-744, June 1979.

10. L. Lamport, "The Implementation of Reliable Distributed Systems", *Computer Networks*, Vol. 2, pp. 95-114, 1978.

11. B. W. Lampson and H. E. Sturgis, "Crash Recovery in a Distributed Data Storage System", *Xerox, PARC, Rep.*, 1979.

12. D. A. Menasce, G. J. Popeck and R. R. Muntz, "A Locking Protocol for Resource Coordination in Distributed Databases", *ACM Transactions on Database Systems*, Vol. 5, pp. 103-138, June 1980.

13. R. J. McMillen and H. J. Siegel, "Routing Schemes for the Augmented Data Manipulator Network in an MIMD System", *IEEE Transactions on Computers*, Vol. C-31, December, 1982, pp. 1202-1214.

14. B. Elspas, "The Theory of Autonomous Linear Sequential Networks", *IRE Transactions on Circuit Theory*, January, 1959, pp. 45-60.

15. N. Zierler, "Linear Recurring Sequencer", *J. SIAM*, 7(1), 1965, pp. 31-48.

16. W. H. Kautz (Ed.), *Linear Sequential Switching Circuits*, Holden-Day, 1965.

17. S. W. Golomb, *Shift Register Sequences*, Holden-Day, 1967.

18. T. L. Booth, *Sequential Machines and Automata Theory*, 1967.

19. S. P. Kartashev, "Theory and Implementation of p-Multiple Sequential Machines", *IEEE Transactions on Computers*, May, 1974, pp. 500-523.

20. S. P. Kartashev, "State Assignment for Realizing Modular Input-free Sequential Logical Networks Without Inverters", *Journal of Computer and System Sciences*, Vol. 7, No. 5, October, 1973, 522-542.

MICROCOMPUTERS: Developments in Industry, Business and Education
D.R. Wilson and C.J. van Spronsen (eds.) / ©EUROMICRO, 1983
Elsevier Science Publishers B.V. (North-Holland)

A CUBE TYPE DISTRIBUTED INTERCONNECTION OF MICROCOMPUTING ELEMENTS

S C Winter

Polytechnic of Central London, School of Engineering & Science
115 New Cavendish Street, London W1M 8JS

The Cube-Type DICE (Distributed Interconnection of Computing Elements), a novel multiprocessor having a data-driven execution mechanism is described, and some vital deterministic characteristics, relating to its implementation cost, communication properties and 'algorithm mappability' (the ability to execute parallel algorithms) are discussed. Potential applications of the multiprocessor are general-purpose numerical computation and signal processing.

1. INTRODUCTION

The binary n-cube multistage switching network (MSN) has found many applications in the design of large SIMD parallel processors [1]. The MSN has $N = 2^n$ inputs and N outputs (typically connecting processing-to-processing element, or processing element-to-memory) and consists of n switching stages, each stage comprising $N/_2$ 2 x 2 switching elements. (Fig. 1.1).

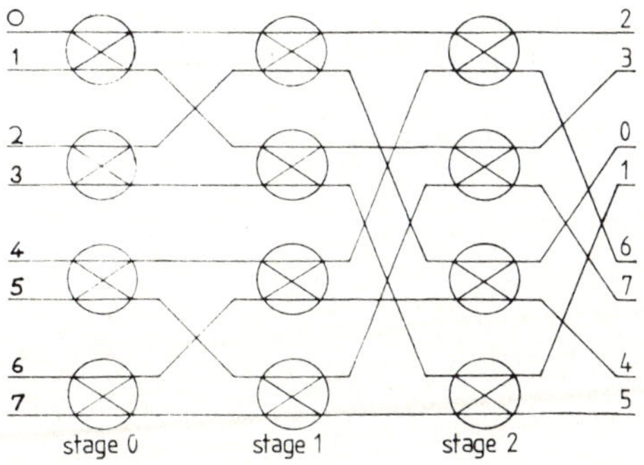

Figure 1.1 Cube-type Multistage Switching Network (N = 8) Implementing a Cube_1 Function

Each switching element has 2 states: straight or exchange (broadcast and merge states are permitted in some systems). The exchange state implements a cube_0 function on a 1-bit input address; that is, input 0 maps into output 1, and vice versa.

The binary cube functions (operating on an n-bit binary address domain) are defined as

$$\text{cube}_i : B^n \longrightarrow B^n$$

$$: b_{n-1} \ldots b_{i+1} b_i b_{i-1} \ldots b_0$$

$$\longmapsto b_{n-1} \ldots b_{i+1} \overline{b_i} {}^n{}_{i-1} \ldots b_0$$

In the STARAN flip network [2], a single control signal is applied to each stage, setting every switching element to the same state. The network is illustrated in Fig. 1.2. If stage i is set to exchange, with every other stage set to straight, the switching network implements a cube_i function on its N inputs. (This situation is illustrated in Fig. 1.3 for i = 1). Other systems, such as the Indirect Binary n-cube Network [3] and the Omega network [4] use individual switch control, increasing the connectivity from

$$\frac{2n}{N!} \text{ to } \frac{2(nN/2)}{N!}$$

The major attraction of the MSN is that it has a low-cost (in comparison with a full N x N crossbar) yet still has a reasonable connectivity [1]. Furthermore, the designers of synchronous SIMD machines were aware that its regularity was particularly appropriate to solving certain types of problem: the FFT, for example, is well-suited to this switching architecture.

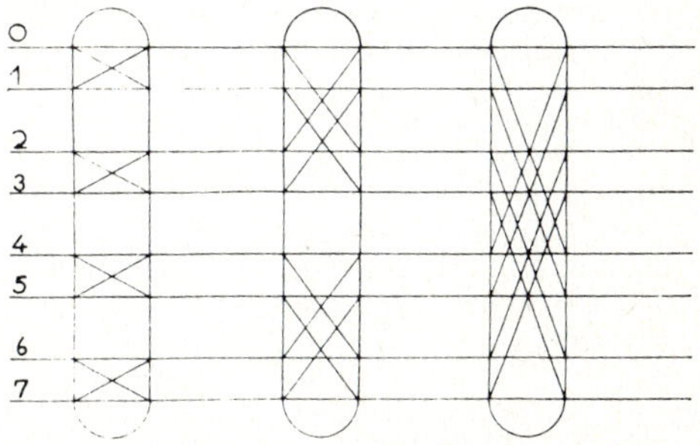

Figure 1.2 Stage Controlled MSN

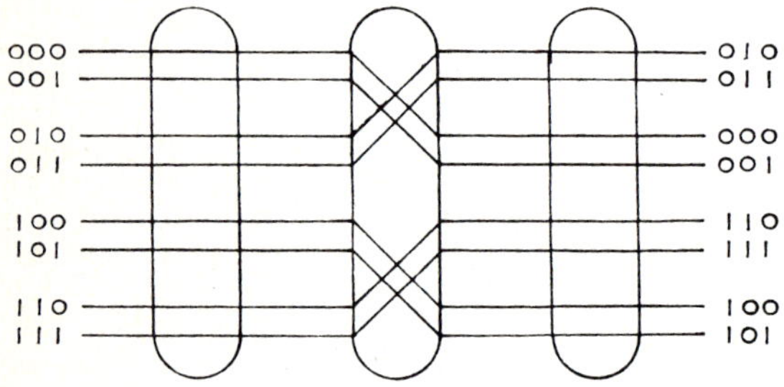

Figure 1.3 MSN Executing a Cube_1 Function

The cube-type MSNs discussed above are a relatively inexpensive method of implementing binary hypercubes, since each cube_i function connects the vertices of the hypercube along the ith axis.

Hypercubes of width r and dimension n ('r-ary n-cubes') form the basis of a more general class of cube-type interconnection structures presented in [5, 15]. A disadvantage of fully connected hypercubes is that the number of inter-processing element links increases linearly with n.

2. A CUBE-TYPE DISTRIBUTED INTERCONNECTION OF COMPUTING ELEMENTS (DICE)

The cube-type DICE (or CTD) is a multi-processor configuration bearing a superficial resemblance to a cube-type MSN. It differs from the MSN in a number of significant ways, however:

i) The computing elements are attached directly onto the 2 x 2 switching elements.

ii) The network contains m distinct stages of 2^m switching/computing elements.

iii) The 2 ends of the network are connected, either together, or to other identical networks, to form a segmented cylindrical structure.

The smallest m x 2^m matrix of elements in the structure is called a facet of rank m. A CTD may be expanded by increasing its rank, by inserting facets of identical rank into the band, or both.

The rank of a CTD is the rank of its component facets; the number of facets it contains is called its replication.

The unreplicated CTD shown in Fig. 2.1 has rank 3; the CTD in Fig. 2.2 has rank 2 and replication 3.

The communication properties of CTDs are generally favoured by minimising the number of facets (in comparing Figs. 2.1 and 2.2, for example, it is seen that the average path-length is undoubtedly longer in the latter case) and multi-facetted units are not thought to be serious contenders for hardware implementation, except in highly restrictive circumstances (for example, if the system must contain 16 processing elements). In the sequel, a CTD is assumed to contain only one facet, unless explicitly stated to the contrary.

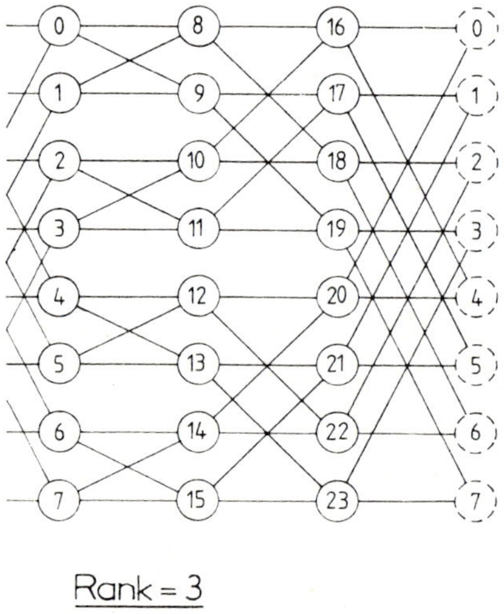

Fig. 2.1 Cube-Type DICE

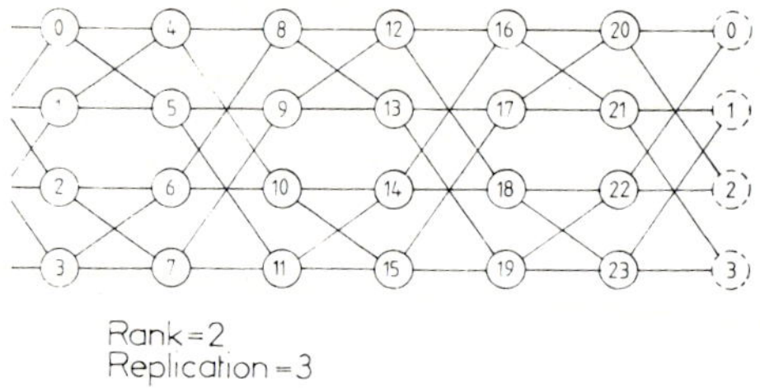

Fig. 2.2 Cube-Type DICE

A CTD of rank m, where $m = 2^{\ell}$ for some ℓ, is said to be regular with inner rank ℓ. Fig. 2.3 shows a regular CTD with inner rank 2.

The switching/computing elements are called processing elements (or more simply, nodes, or cells). The simplified cell model shown in Fig. 2.4 forms the basis for the later discussions. The switching section, or port is represented as a 3 x 3 crossbar having 6 legitimate states. Traffic through the port is generally buffered, and bidirectional, although

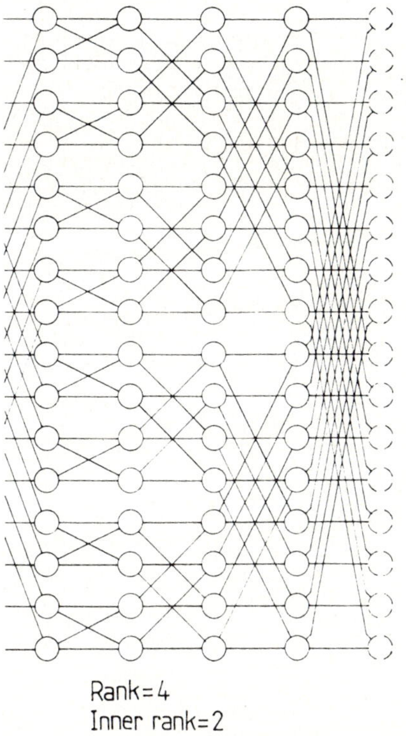

Fig. 2.3 Regular Cube-Type DICE

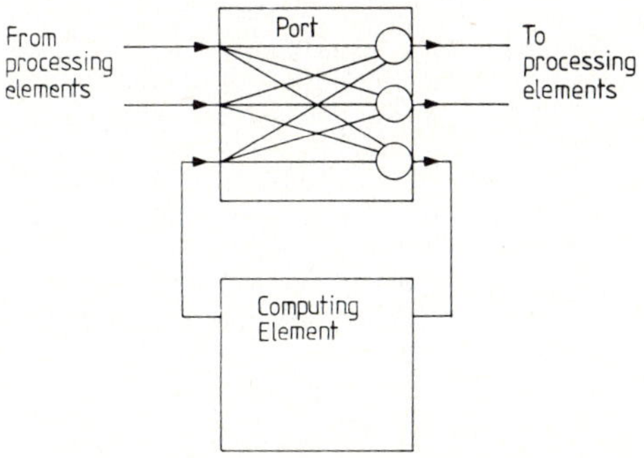

Fig. 2.4 A Simplified Processing Element Model

for a dataflow execution mechanism unidirectional flow is more likely (as shown in Fig. 2.4). The port is autonomous, or at worst, controlled by its attached computing element.

The DICE described reflects an underlying binary hypercube structure of dimension M + 1. Each PE connects to exactly four others. More general DICE corresponding to arbitrary hypercubes of width r may be defined, in which each PE is connected to 2r PEs. The interconnection strategy is described in [16].

3. SOME DETERMINISTIC PROPERTIES OF A CUBE-TYPE DICE

In this section, the Cube-type DICE is compared with certain other communication networks, notably the Cube-type MSN. The following properties are investigated: the cost of implementing the network; cell reachability and related communications properties; and algorithm mappability i.e. the ability of the CTD to execute certain regular and irregular algorithms.

It will be shown that the CTD is relatively cheap to implement, yet its communication and algorithm-mapping properties remain impressive.

3.1 Implementation Costs

The cost of communications hardware in an $M = m.2^m$ unreplicated CTD is compared with the cost of an MxM Cube-type MSN, since the interconnection of M processors is involved in each case. The number of switches in the MSN is $N = \frac{M}{2} \log_2 M$; for a physically realisible MSN, therefore, we require that $m = 2^{\ell}$ for some ℓ i.e. the corresponding CTD must be regular. Under this assumption, $N = (\ell+m)2^{\ell+m-1}$. Figure 3.1 shows the first few regular values of M, and corresponding values of N.

inner rank ℓ	0	1	2	3	4
rank $m = 2^{\ell}$	1	2	4	8	12
ports in a regular CTD $M = m.2^{m}$	2	8	64	2048	1,048,576
switches in a MSN $N = (\ell+m)2^{\ell+m-1}$	1	12	192	11264	10,485,760
$2^{m}(\ell+1)$	2	8	48	1024	327,680

Fig. 3.1 Showing the number of: (a) cells in a regular CTD; and (b) switches in an MSN required to interconnect an equivalent number of processors, for several inner rank values

The usual assumption will be made that a pxq crossbar costs K.p.q., where K is a proportional constant.

The cost of an MSN, comprising N 2x2 crossbars is thus 4KN or

$$4K\ (\ell+m)2^{\ell+m-1};$$

the cost of a CTD, comprising M 3x3 crossbars (refer to previous section) is 9KM or $9K2^{\ell+m}$. For $M \geq 64$, the CTD is always cheaper than the MSN, the cost ratio (CTD/MSN) being $9/(2[\ell+m])$, or $9/(2\log_2 M)$.

In comparing the CTD with a full MxM crossbar (costing M^2K), it is seen that the breakeven cost occurs just above M = 8, but again, for M > 64, the CTD is cheaper by a factor (CTD/crossbar) of $9/(2^{\ell+m})$, or 9/M.

The 3 cost curves (CTD, MSN and Crossbar) are shown in greater detail in Fig. 3.2.

The cost advantage of MSN's over crossbars is well known (see for example [1]). In a CTD, the cost is reduced below the MSN cost by a factor o $(\log_2 M)$. This reduction is significant, even for moderately configured multiprocessors: for M = 2048 for example, the cost is halved, as can be seen from Figure 3.2.

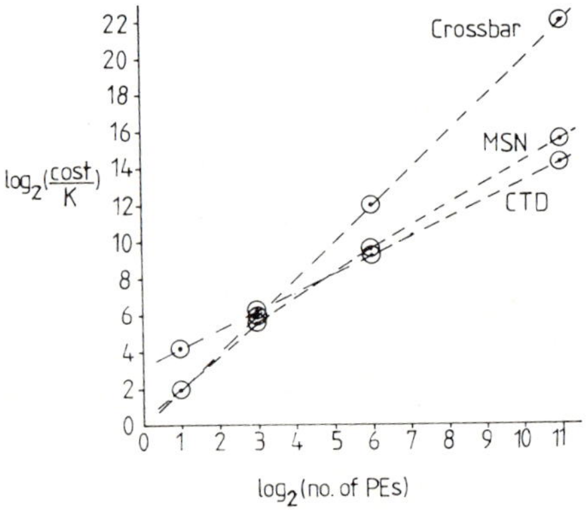

Fig. 3.2 Relative Implementation Costs

The price paid for reducing the hardware cost is to increase the average path-length through the network. This effect is discussed in detail in 3.2.

3.2 Cell Reachability and Communication Properties

It is clear that for all CTDs with consistent unidirectional data flow (i.e. in which the data flow through each port is unidirectional, as shown in Fig. 2.4, and consistent with respect to every stage), a cell may be reached from any other cell in less than 2 complete passes through the network; or, in the case of unreplicated CTDs, in no more than 2m-1 inter-cell links, where an inter-cell link (i.c.l.) is an uninterrupted path between 2 adjacent cell ports, and m is the rank of the network.

It is shown in the Appendix that the average shortest path length connecting 2 cells in an unreplicated unidirectional binary CTD is $3(m-1)/2 + 2^{-m}$.

In contrast, the path length in an MSN, in terms of inter-switch links, is constant, and given by the length of the network i.e.

$$P_{MSN} = \log_2 M - 1$$

Under the usual regularity assumption:

$$P_{MSN} \doteq \ell + m - 1$$

(The PE-to-MSN links are ignored in this measure, as were the port-to-computing element links in the CTD calculation).

P_{MSN} and P_{CTD} are plotted in Fig. 3.3.

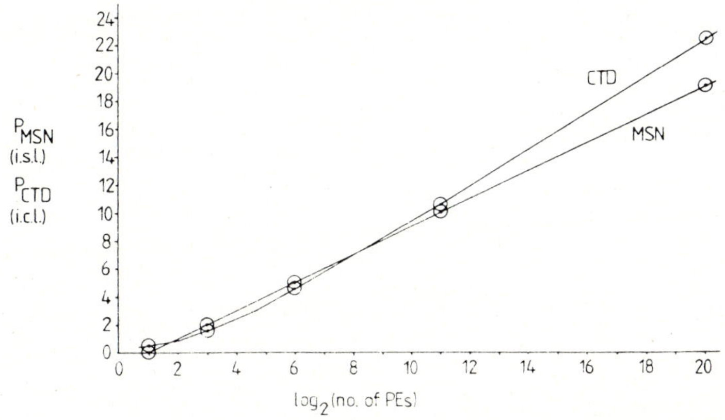

Fig. 3.3 Average Shortest Path Lengths in MSN and CTD - organised multiprocessors

As M increases the CTD is outperformed by the MSN, in terms of path length, when it is assumed that a cell in a CTD is likely to communicate with every cell in the network equally.

In practice, however, it is more likely for CTD cells to communicate most often with their immediate neighbours. This is particularly true if the programs are controlled by a data flow execution mechanism.

The number of unique cells n_ℓ in a regular CTD, which are reachable in ℓ+m-1 i.c.ℓ.'s or less is given by

$$n_\ell = \sum_{i=o}^{m-1} 2^i + \sum_{i=o}^{\ell-1} (2^m - 2^i)$$

$$= 2^m(\ell+1) - 2^\ell$$

$$\cong 2^m(\ell+1) \text{ for } \ell > 2$$

(the first few values are tabulated in Fig.3.1)

The absolute value of n_ℓ is not small even for small ℓ, and it is possible for a compiler, in minimising path lengths, to arrange that the arguments required by instructions in a cell rarely travel further than the fixed path length of the corresponding MSN. This mapping problem becomes easier as m increases, since n_ℓ increases exponentially with m.

The parameters simultaneity, connectivity and broadcast scope [1] arise with line-switched MSNs, and are not a particularly useful measure of performance for the CTD, which uses a packet-switched communication technique.

3.3 Algorithm Mappability

In this section, the ability of an CTD to efficiently execute algorithms, both regular and irregular, is examined.

3.3.1 Regular Algorithms

The algorithm chosen to represent this class of problem is a very common signal processing 'primitive': the FFT. This algorithm is essentially a succession of paired or 'butterfly' computations on 2 inputs u and v, viz:

$$y_r = u_r + v_r W^r$$
$$\bar{y}_r = u_r - v_r W^r \qquad - (3.1)$$

where W^r is a complex rotation.

The full computation for an 8-pt FFT is shown in Fig. 3.4. Readers are referred to [5] for further details.

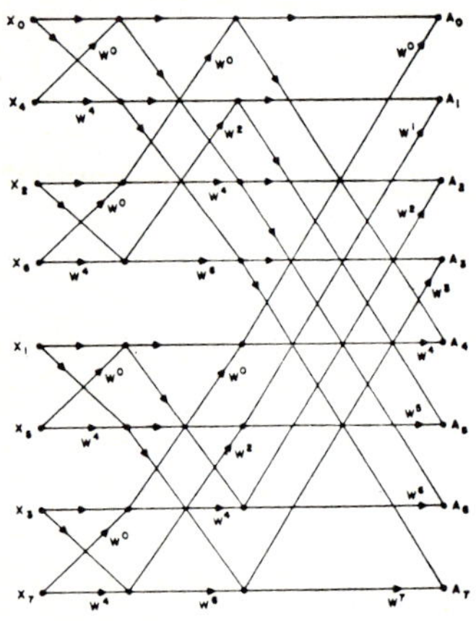

Fig. 3.4 An 8-pt FFT

The performance of an M-element CTD will be compared primarily with that of a Cube-type MSN connected to M processors.

A comparison of Figs. 3.4 and 1.2 shows that the MSN concurrent algorithm to compute an M-point FFT is conveniently implemented in a stage-controlled i.e. lock-step manner. That is to say, every node of Fig. 3.4 lying on a horizontal arc is mapped onto one processing element (time of course, runs sequentially along the arc); with the top arc (connecting input X_o to output A_o in Fig. 3.4) mapped onto processor 0, the second arc (connecting X_4 to A_1 in Fig. 3.4) mapped onto processor 1, and so on.

The sequential algorithm in processor j is:

```
begin
  for i: = o to m-1
      butterfly (i,j)
 end
```

where procedure butterfly (i,j) implements one of the 2 operations defined by (3.1) viz:

```
procedure butterfly (i,j);
begin
 if i = o
   then
    begin
      read (input1) {from external I/O};
      input2 : = input1
    end
   else
    begin
     read (input1, input2,) {from MSN}
    end;
  result: = fij (input1, input2)
                        {eqn (4.1)} ;
if i = m-1
then
  write (result) {to external I/O}
else
 begin
```

```
    wait {for straight interconnection} ;

    write (result) {to MSN} ;

    wait {for cube_i interconnection} ;

    write (result) {to MSN}

  end

end;
```

Let notation butterfly (i) represent the vector of 2^m algorithms butterfly (i, j); j = o, ... 2^m-1

It is clear from Figs. 2.1 or 2.3 that the m.2^m - element CTD is well-suited to solving the 2^m - point FFT i.e. the m algorithm vectors butterfly (i); i = o, ..., m-1 are mapped onto the m stages or 'columns' of the CTD:

butterfly (i) $\longrightarrow$ stage (i)

In computing a single FFT, processor utilization is only 1/m, but by pipelining m FFTs through the machine simultaneously, utilization is increased by 100%. (Note that by renumbering the cells, an FFT may begin at any stage of the CTD. An example of re-numbering is shown in Fig. 3.5). The pipeline may be loaded serially (in time) or in parallel.

In the pipelined node, the throughput of an m.2^m - cell CTD may be reasonably compared

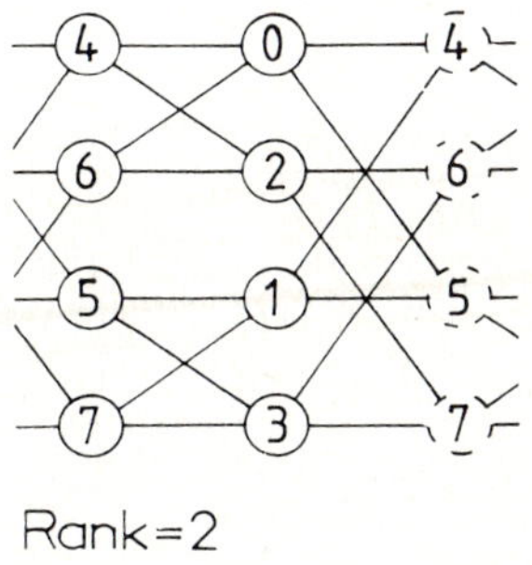

Fig. 3.5 Cube-Type DICE - Renumbered to start at second stage

with that of m MSNs (each connected to 2^m processors), computing 2^m-point FFTS in parallel. Then, the only difference between the completion times per FFT for the two systems is the communication time: for the CTD this is m i.c.l.s (inter-cell links); for the MSN it is m^2 i.s.l.s (inter-switch links): this difference may be significant if computation time is relatively short.

An M-cell CTD is somewhat less ideally suited to the computation of an M-point FFT. In the first place, the FFT requires that M = 2^n for some n. Thus, it would be helpful if the CTD were regular. Secondly, although the 1st m algorithms {butterfly (i); i = o, ..., m-1} are easily computed by partitioning the FFT into m segments of 2^m points, and pipelining the smaller problems through the CTD, the remaining ℓ algorithms { butterfly (i); i = m, ..., m+ℓ-1} are generally achieved by ad hoc methods. This problem is currently being investigated. It is interesting to note, however, that the proportion of inefficient steps in the algorithm, $\ell/(\ell+2^\ell)$, tends to zero as $\ell \to \infty$. This curve is shown in Fig. 3.6.

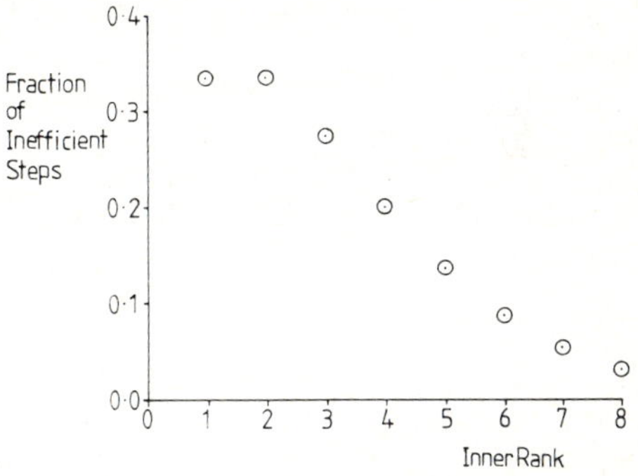

Fig. 3.6 Proportion of inefficient FFT steps on a regular CTD

3.3.2 Irregular Algorithms

All algorithms ultimately may be reduced to an equivalent data flow graph which in turn may be mapped directly onto the CTD multiprocessor. An example of such a mapping, for simple assignment, is shown in Fig. 3.7 (the example first appeared in [6]).

Note that multi-link paths are a feature of the mapping; this technique, made possible by the packet-switched communications network, is sufficient to realise p-input, q-output flow-graph nodes for all p and q.

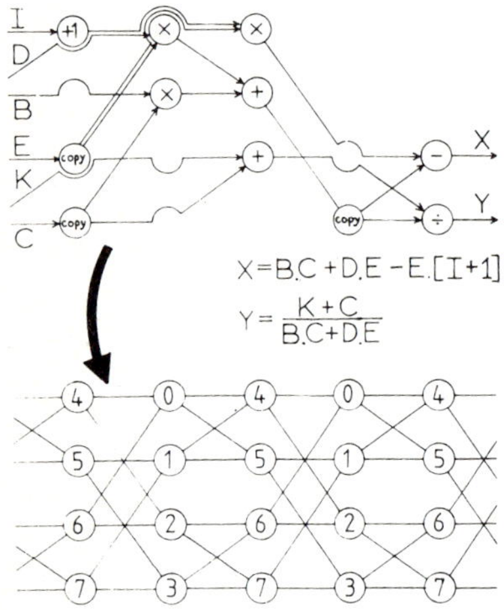

Fig. 3.7 Mapping an Assignment Flowgraph onto an 8-element CTD

Data flowgraphs may be constructed for other language features: the primitives to realise loops, branches, conditional-clauses and subroutines are well-known (see for example [7, 9, 10]; Ada-like tasks may be constructed as subgraphs, with appropriate synchronization primitives. The advantage of the dataflow model is that the inherent parallelism is exhibited in terms of a given set of primitive operations. The choice of primitive operations may be a hardware design decision. Alternatively, the set of primitives may be flexible (micro-, or macro-programmable), allowing the programmer to specify an optional set for a given application type. Research into the full implications of dataflow operation is continuing at PCL and will be reported in due course.

Many researchers believe that the binary tree is a sound basic structure for multiprocessors; X-tree [11] and Hypertree [12] are typical machines employing a binary tree, whose advantageous message switching parameters have been reported in [13]. It should be noted that the CTD is a virtual tree inasmuch as it incorporates an unlimited number of (overlaid) binary trees, which wrap around the network to limitless depth.

In simulation experiments conducted recently at PCL, the performance of the CTD in computing inner products was found to be markedly superior to that of certain other well-known configurations such as shared bus, and hierarchical trees. The results, obtained on MULTISIM, a multiprocessor simulation package, are described in [14].

4. CONCLUSIONS

To achieve high performance, the architecture of a multiprocessor must be directed by 2 major criteria: exploitation of intrinsic algorithm parallelism; and elimination of hardware bottlenecks by distribution of resources. A commercial design should also take account of the benefits to be derived from the use of VLSI technology; that is to say, the design should be incrementally expandable, via replication of the processing elements, yet avoid concomitant software reconstruction.

It is known [7] that the dataflow operational model realises the inherent parallelism of an algorithm expressed in a high-level language in terms of a given set of machine primitives. To reflect this property, the Cube-Type Distributed Interconnection of Computing Elements (Cube-Type DICE, or CTD) has autonomous processing elements controlled by the arrival of data arguments or tokens at its inputs.

Many existing multiprocessors or dataflow machines suffer from poor resource matching, which, under high load, results in congestion at one or more of the major functional subsystems, and ultimately limits the performance of the machine. In the CTD, all the major resources are evenly distributed: the number of independent buses is linearly related to the number of processing elements (PEs); and as well as control units, local memory, and inter-PE communication ports, every PE contains powerful arithmetic and input/output facilities. There are no shared or global resources (other than a host or share computer interface).

To satisfy the VLSI constraint, every cell (PE) in the CTD is identical, and thus replicatable; the topology is regular, yet incrementally expandable. Finally, every cell has a fixed number of immediate neighbours, independent of the scale of the network, thus limiting the number of physical pinouts per cell.

It has been shown that the cost of implementing communication in a CTD is linearly related to M, the number of PEs in the system, and is thus cheaper than an equivalent MSN (multistage switching network), even for relatively small configurations.

Although average path-lengths in the CTD are slightly longer than the MSN when all possible paths are considered (the CTD has an average path-length of $\frac{3}{2}(2^{\ell}-1)$ compared with the (constant) path-length $\ell+2^{\ell}-1$ for an MSN (ℓ is the CTD's inner rank)) in practice the compiler may take advantage of locality of communication and guarantee that the majority of path-lengths in the CTD are in fact less than $\ell+2^{\ell}-1$.

The CTD is well-suited to a dataflow mode of operation and is thus capable of handling most irregular algorithms with acceptable efficiency. This is partly due to the inherent binary-tree structure. Simulation experiments at PCL have also indicated that the CTD can handle regular problems (the calculation of inner-products) extremely well; and an algorithm has been presented for a 2^m-point FFT ($m=2^{\ell}$) which when pipelined through the network is at least as fast as a comparable MSN-based system. M-point FFTs are slightly less efficient however.

Finally, as a virtual tree machine, the CTD is naturally well suited to the execution of recursive, divide-and-conquer parallel algorithms.

5. REFERENCES

[1] Siegel, H J, McMillen, R J and Mueller P T "A Survey of Interconnection Methods for Reconfigurable Parallel Processing Systems" Nat Computer Conf 1979, p 529-542.

[2] Batcher, K E "The flip network in STARAN" 1976 Int'l Conf on Parallel Processing, Aug 1976, pp 65-71.

[3] Pease, M C "The Indirect Binary n-Cube Multiprocessor Array" IEEE Trans Comput Vol C-26, No 5, May 1977 pp 458-473.

[4] Lawrie, D "Access and alignment of data in an array processor" IEEE Trans on Comput Vol C-24, No 12, Dec 1975, pp 1145-1155.

[5] Cochran W T et al "What is the Fast Fourier Transform?" IEEE Trans Audio Electro acoust, Vol AU-15,pp 45-55, June 1967.

[6] Gurd,J and Watson, I "Data driven system for high speed parallel computing - Part 1 Structuring software for parallel execution" Computer Design, June 1980.

[7] Veen, A H "Reconciling data flow machines and conventional languages", Conpar 81, Lecture Notes in Computer Science No 111, Springer-Verlag, 1981, pp 127-140.

[8] Wittie, L D "Communication structures for large networks of microcomputers" IEEE Trans on Comput. Vol C-30, No 4 April 1981.

[9] Davis, A L and Keller, R M "Data Flow Program Graphs" IEEE Computer, Feb 1982, pp 26-41.

[10] Gurd, J R, Glavert J R W, and Kirkham C C "Generation of Dataflow Graphical Object Code for the LAPSE Programming Language" CONPAR '81, Lecture Notes in Computer Science No 111, Springer-Verlag, 1981, pp 155-168.

[11] Despain, A and Patterson D "X-tree: A structured multiprocessor computer architecture" Proc IEEE 5th Annual Symp Comput Arch, Apr 1978, pp 144-151.

[12] Goodman, J R "Hypertree: A Multiprocessor Interconnection Topology" IEEE Trans on Computers, Vol C-30, No 12, Dec 1981, pp 923-933.

[13] Horowitz, E and Alexandro Z "The Binary Tree as an Interconnection Network: Applications to Multiprocessor Systems and VLSI" IEEE Trans Computers, Vol C-30, No 4, April 1981, pp 247-253.

[14] Kwong, W C "Simulation of an Abstract Multiprocessor System" Project Report PCL, July 1982.

[15] Bhat, K V S "On the properties of arbitrary hypercubes" Comp & Maths with Appls. Vol 8, No 5, p 339, 1982.

[16] Burton, F W and Sleep, M R " Communication in a distributed implementation of an applicative languages" ICS 81, East Anglia, 1981.

6. APPENDIX

Lemma The average shortest path length connecting 2 cells in an unreplicated unidirectional binary CTD is $3(m-1)/2 + 2^{-m}$.

Proof It is easily seen that on the first pass through the network the reachable set contains those cells on the binary tree of depth m-1 whose root is the source cell. All remaining cells are subsequently reachable by a second pass of the network. Thus, including the possibility of connecting a cell to itself (with zero path length) and assuming all cells have equal likelihood of connection, the shortest path length P_{CTD} is given by

$$P_{CTD} = \frac{1}{2^m.m} [\sum_{i=o}^{m-1} 2^i.1 + \sum_{i=o}^{m-1} (2^m-2^i), (m+i)]$$

$$= \frac{1}{2^m.m} [\sum_{i=o}^{m-1} (2^m.(m+i) - 2^i.m)]$$

It may be shown (by induction)

that $\sum_{i=o}^{m-1} 2^i = 2^m-1$

and that $\sum_{i=o}^{m-1} i = \frac{(m-1)m}{2}$

Thus

$$P_{CTD} = \frac{1}{2^m.m} [2^m (m^2 + \frac{(m-1)m)}{2} - (2^m-1)m]$$

This equation simplifies to

$$P_{CTD} = \frac{3}{2} (m-1) + 2^{-m}$$

MICROCOMPUTERS: Developments in Industry, Business and Education
D.R. Wilson and C.J. van Spronsen (eds.) / ©EUROMICRO, 1983
Elsevier Science Publishers B.V. (North-Holland)

OPSILA : AN ADVANCED SIMD FOR NUMERICAL ANALYSIS AND SIGNAL PROCESSING

M. Auguin*, F. Larbey**

*LASSY (Laboratoire de Signaux et Systèmes). Equipe de Recherche Associée au CNRS. Université de Nice-41 Bd. Napoleon III-06041 Nice - Cedex
**SINTRA - ALCATEL - 26 rue Malakoff - 92600 ASNIERES

In this paper, we describe a SIMD architecture OPSILA which includes recent concepts in parallel computation : high bandwith interconnection network, operating modes which allow to take into account several levels of parallelism :
- Single instruction stream (SIMD) executed by the processing elements (PE) on multiple data, one data per PE.
- Single program executed independently by all the PE on multiple data (SPMD).
- Multiple instruction stream executed in lockstep mode by PE on multiple data.
We give an evaluation of the performances of OPSILA concerning three application and we compare these, as far as possible, with the performance of commercialized vector computers.

1. INTRODUCTION

Numerous applications require lower and lower execution times especially in such areas as image processing, numerical analysis, signal processing. A peculiarity of these applications is that parallelism can be easily exhibited, namely numerous vector operations have to be performed. Moreover VLSI technologies permit the designing of large scale parallel systems with an incessantly decreasing hardware cost. Experiences with computers like ILLIAC IV, PHOENIX in the 1970's suggest what new capabilities a SIMD computer should have today.

A SIMD system is better suited to the previous applications than a MIMD multiprocessor because these applications require frequent data exchanges between computing elements. In a MIMD system inter-processor synchronizations must be carried out for each exchange which leads to a loss of efficiency. A SIMD computer is synchronous thus all communications of data between processing elements are carried out during the same cycles. As a time shared bus is a bottle-neck for this kind of computer, we consider more efficient structures to interconnect the processing elements.

2. AIMS AND LIMITATIONS

Our aim is to design a SIMD architecture OPSILA which includes recent concepts in parallel computation (operations on vectors) : high bandwith interconnection network, operating modes which allow to take into account several levels of parallelism 1 :

- Single Instruction stream (SIMD) executed by the processing elements (PE) on Multiple Data, one data per PE.

- Single Program executed independently by all the PE on Multiple Data (SPMD).

- Multiple instruction stream executed in lockstep mode by PE on multiple data.

A conventional assembly language is developped to program the overall system which allows the different operating modes to be used. OPSILA is designed in order to evaluate the performances of a SIMD computer on applications below mentionned. To be significant, performances must be measured on actual applications. Thus a sufficient memory space (1 Mega byte memory) and about 10 MIPS computation speed are required. The hardware of OPSILA is composed of about fifty boards with less than about ten different kinds. The system is designed with commercialized components.

3. ORGANIZATION AND ARCHITECTURE

The implementation is split into two sets : the operative part and the control part. The operative part contains an interconnection network, 16 couples composed of a processing element (PE) and a memory bank (BM). The control part is subdivided into a network controller (CR) and a master control unit (UC) (see figure 1). The overall system is attached to a host computer which manages slow peripherals and provides programming software facilities.

3.1 Processing element (PE)

The processing element is carried out by a 16 bits ALU (AMD 29116) which has 32 16-bit registers, a 16-bit barrel shifter, a priority encoder. In order to speed up floating-point operations and some address calculus, a 16x16-bit multiplier and a hardware adressing system are introduced.

The processing element contains a local microsequencer using a 64-bit width microprogram RAM. The clock period of the PE is 200 ns. The major originality is that the PE can operate in two modes (the overall operating mode of OPSILA is described in section 4).

3.2 Memory Bank (BM) and I/O bus

A memory bank is associated with each PE. It constitutes the main memory of PE. The set of the 16 BM forms the main data memory of OPSILA. The main memory can also contain program segments associated with operating mode P (SPMD). Each BM contains 64 Kwords of 16 bits, adressable by two I/O multiplexed ports. A port is attached to the PE, the other allows all the BM to be connected on a fast I/O bus. The memory boards are made with a 16 K x 1 bit CMOS static RAM with an access time less than 100 ns. With these boards OPSILA has a maximum bulk of main memory of 1,5 Megabytes.

3.3 Interconnection network (RI)

~~Only~~ interconnection networks give sufficient flexibility and efficiency required by interprocessor communications in a SIMD computer [2,3] . The OPSILA's interconnection network is a bidirectionnal Omega network of 16 input busses and 16 output busses. The Omega network is composed of 4 stages of 8 switches and can perform permutations on a 16-data vector (see figure 2). A switch can take 6 states (figure 3), four states are used for permutations and 2 states for diffusions from one input to all the outputs. The Omega network carries out a large number of the permutations required for vector processing [4] . The other permutations are carried out on a Benes network [5] emulated by routing data two times in the Omega network. An Omega permutation is accomplished in 200 ns and a Benes permutation is accomplished in 600 ns.

3.4 Network controller (CR)

The network controller has to set up the switches of the interconnection network in order to perform the permutations requested by the master control unit [7,8]. The CR takes into account two kinds of permutations. The first set contains permutations explicity defined at compilation time. The swith setting is computed before execution and is memorized by the CR. During the execution the network controller gets its instructions from the master control unit in order to execute one of these permutations. The second set contains five families of permutations [7]. At compilation time, only the family name is requested. The values of parameters specifying the permutation are necessary at execution time. These families are describe on figure 4. Diffusions are handled as permutations of the second set.

Except for diffusions, the CR can execute the reverse of all the permutations by routing data back in the network. The setting of the switches is effective 200 ns after the permutation is specified.

3.5 Master control unit (UC)

The master control unit has the functions of a classical control unit of a monoprocessor :

- program managing,
- instruction fetching, decoding and controlling the operative part composed in OPSILA of PEs and RI.

Particularly, UC contains the SIMD program memory. The UC instructions, PE instructions and RI controls are stored in this program memory. UC contains also a descriptor memory (like the BSP computer [9]) of vector objects that is to say the caracteristics, type and implementation mode of each vector (or matrix). In order to control program execution, a fast 16-bit ALU is added to the UC, which allows the loop indexes to be controlled. UC receives from each PE a condition bit used for sequencing the instructions and sending a mask vector. UC carries out the synchronizations between PEs and with the RI during the execution. At last, when performing an instruction on a long vector, UC changes this instruction into a sequence of vector instructions with a length equal to the PE number.

4. OPERATING MODES AND DATA STORAGE

The different operating modes of OPSILA have to take into account the different levels of parallelism in applications. Three parallelism levels can be mixed : data level, instruction level and program module level. OPSILA may operate in either the I mode (single instruction multiple data) or the P mode (single program multiple date).

4.1 - I mode operation

UC sends the PE instructions by a mono-directional 16-bit bus. An asynchronous protocol allows the PEs to synchronize after the execution of the instructions the duration of which depends on the data. The instruction flow is not delayed by this protocol ; a single instruction per PE cycle flow can be sustained. In this operating mode the PEs have no program counter, they do not fetch their instructions.

The SIMD mode does not allow the conditional branch instructions to be performed such as IF-THEN-ELSF or CASE. In order to overcome these difficulties two capabilities are added to the I mode : PE masking and CASE instruction.

4.1.1 - Masking operation

Masking operates as in ILLIAC IV [10] . This possibility allows different branches to be carried out in sequence within a data dependent instruction stream (see figure 5). Thus UC sends to PE a MASQ instruction and a 16-bit vector (1 bit per PE). When the bit is set, the PE is enable to operate. Unfortunately, this method may be inefficient. To improve the efficiency of OPSILA, a CASE instruction (similar to the CASE instruction of Actus language [11] of the Phoenix project [1])is used.

4.1.2 - CASE operation

The CASE instruction allows the user to perform independent arithmitic operations on different PEs depending on the value contained in an internal PE register. UC sends, with the CASE instruction, a base address and a register number. Each PE adds the register value to the base address. The result is the adress in the BM of the instruction to be performed (figure 6).

A repetitive use of the CASE instruction allows the performing of independant instruction streams corresponding with conditional branch instructions. This operating mode is a SIMD mode because PEs do not manage program counter and after execution of an CASE instruction they await the next instruction from UC.

4.2 - P-mode operation

A good efficiency is obtained when operating under P-mode on massively parallel problems which are hardly or not at all vectorisable (like Monte-Carlo simulations and programs involving massive "scatter-gather" operations cf.§ 6.3). The program module to be executed under the P-mode is duplicated in each BM. UC initiates the P-mode by sending the start P-mode instruction with a program entry address. Then PEs operate as independent mono-processors until they perform the return I mode instruction. During this runing mode, PEs cannot exchange data, and some SIMD adressing modes are not usable. Thus data exchanges necessitate returning to I-mode.

The P-mode allows the N PEs to work on the above applications as N scalar units, when pipeline computers only use their scalar unit [12]. If the extent of parallelism of the problem is sufficient with respect to the number of PEs, the work load is statistically distributed among the PEs and a good average efficiency of the overall system is obtained.

4.3 Data organization

The efficiency of a SIMD computer depends on its parallel data access potentiality. Thus we use a storage method of matrices allowing parallel access in rows, columns and diagonals [10,13]. An element a_{ij} of a matrix A is stored in one of the $N=2^n$ BM. The BM number is $x = ui + vj \bmod N$, $u,v \in \mathbb{N}$.

Two storage schemes in a BM have been designed

- an helicoidal scheme stores the element a_{ij} at address

$$i\left(1 + \frac{M-1}{N}\right) + \frac{j}{N}$$

M is the number of rows of the A matrix

- a scheme taking into account FORTRAN conventions stores the element a_{ij} at address $\frac{i + (M-1)j}{N}$ in BM $x = i + Mj \bmod N$.

The parallel accesses enabled by this storage method according to the respective values of u and v, are given in the following table :

v \ u	even	odd
even	not allowed	columns diagonals
odd	rows diagonals	rows columns

A storing example is given in figure 7.

This storage method allows accesses to a sequence of elements defined by :

$$\{a_{i+nk,\ j+mk}\} \quad k \in K$$

where k is an index varying from 0 to (N-1) and $n, m \in \mathbb{Z}$

We access to :

- a row if m=1 and n=0
- a column if n=1 and m=0
- a main diagonal if n=1 and m=-1
- the other diagonals if n=1 and m=-1

Summing up, a 16-element vector object is described by the following parameters :

n,m	:	acces mode
u,v	:	storing scheme
i,j	:	the first element to access

In the case of a helicoidal storing scheme, each PE performs the following address computation [14] :

$$(i + n\,[x-(ui + vj)]_{\bmod N})\left(1 + \frac{M-1}{N}\right) + \frac{j+m\,[x-(ui + vj)]\bmod N}{N}$$

A similar equation is obtained with the compatible FORTRAN storing scheme.

If $n, m \in \{0,1,-1\}$, address generations are easily computed. A specialized hardware is added to each PE. The parameters describing vector objects are stored in a descriptor memory of UC.

Notice that the accessed elements are scrambled thus the alignment of data necessitates a $\lambda^{(n)}_{s,t}$ permutation with :

$$s = (un+vm)^{-1} \bmod N \text{ and } t = (ui+vj)(un+vm)^{-1} \bmod N.$$

A specialized operator of the UC performs these computations.

Some instructions are only enabled in P-mode processing. Particularly, these instructions manage the program counter and the stack pointer.

It is important to notice that UC and PEs can process independently while there is no data exchange between these units.

5. SOFTWARE

There are two instruction classes as in Phoenix [1] :

- master control unit instructions
- processing element instructions

The UC instructions set contains the classical instruction of a fast 16-bit processor added with special instructions for managing the different system units. For instance, the instructions associated with the control of the interconnection network. In assembly language the UC instructions are designated with the prefixe U. Likewise the UC registers are noted RUi.

From a user point of view the PE is composed of a set of 8x32-bit general purpose registers. The registers can contain the following operand types : 16-bit integer, 32-bit integer, 32-bit floating point number. Some special registers allows communications with the other units of OPSILA : a UC communication register and a RI communication register. The program counter and the stack pointer are only available in P-mode. A status register contains the classical condition bits, a mask bit and an operating mode bit. The instruction set of the PE is composed of arithmetic an logic instructions (simple and double length), floating point instructions and special I and P mode data movement instructions.

For instance :

PRML Rs,Rd — Permutation by the network of the double length data contained in Rs register and stored after permutation in the Rd register.

FHE A(RU1,RU2),ROW,Rd — Parallel helicoïdal acces (16 elements) of the row of matrix A from element (RU1,RU2) and storage in Rd register.

SMP Ext — The PEs are initiated by P-mode processing. The program entry address is contained in Ext.

CASE Rd,Ext — Each PE execute the instruction at address Ext + Rd stored in its BM.

MASQ RUM — PEi is desabled following the state of the ith bit of the UC register RUM.

6. APPLICATION STUDY

We consider three simple problems of signal processing and numerical analysis : matrix multiplication, FFT and multiplication of a sparse matrix by a full vector. In order to obtain the optimum performance from any computer it is necessary to tailor the algorithm to suit the architecture of the computer. This is particularly true for parallel computers [15] .

6.1 Matrix multiplication

Several parallel algorithms for matrix multiplication have been proposed [16-17] . We consider in this paper the "middle product" method :

$$c(i,*) = \sum_{k=0}^{m-1} a(i,k)*b(k,*) \qquad o \leqslant i \leqslant n-1$$

The algorithm taking into account the architecture of OPSILA is the following :

```
begin {the dimensions of matrices a,b and c are
respectively nxm, mxp, nxp}
 for i := 0 to n-1 do
   for l := 0 to p-16 step 16 do
   c(i,*l) := 0{* l describes a parallel access
               of 16 consecutive elements of
               the ith row of matrix c from
               element (i,l)}
    for k := 0 to m-1 do
    c(i,*l) := c(i,*l) + a(i,k) * b(k,*l)
    end {for k}
   end {for l}
   if l = p then disable the last 16-p+l PEs ;
 {this section is used when p is not a multiple
                                          of 16}
   c(i,*l) := 0
    for k := 0 to m-1 do
    c(i,*l)  := c(i,*l) + a(i,k) * b(k,*l)
    end {for k}
   end  {if}
 end {for i}
end
```

The assembly code of the internal loop of the algorithm is the following :

```
  LOOPK : UDIF RU4        setting the network in
                          diffusion from input RU4.
                          The initial value of RU4
                          is zero
FHEL A(RU1,RU2),ROW,R2    the A matrix is stored
                          with a helicoïdal scheme
PRML R1,R1                routing (R1)--> R1 through RI : diffusion of (R1)
                          from RU4th PE to all R1
                          registers
FHEL B(RU3,RU2),ROW,R2
MULF R1,R2                a(i,k) * b(k,*l)--> R2
ADDF R2,R0                c(i,*l)+a(i,k)*b(k,*l)->R0
UINC RU3                  k := k+1
UMOVE RU3,RU4             RU6 contains 000F. RU4
                          contains the number of
                          the PE diffusing a(i,k+1)
UAND RU6,RU4
UCPR RU3,RU5              comparaison of k and m-1
UBGE LOOPK                jump to LOOPK if k <= m-1
```

A performance evaluation is developped in the next section.

6.2 Fast fourier transform

Different approaches of the parallel FFT have been proposed [18-19-20] . The algorithm developped in this paper is the classical form of the in-place FFT. The architecture of OPSILA allows the FFT with a maximum parallelism to be processed.

Let x be M-elements complex vector stored as illustrated in figure 8.
Figure 9 shows a radix-2 complex FFT on a M=16 point vector.

It is important to note that with 4 PEs, the processing steps for i 0 and i=1 are local to each PE. For the last log2 N steps, the interconnection network must perform cyclic shift by segment [7,21] : permutation $\delta^{(n)}_{j,k}$

The parallel FFT of a $M=2^m$ data vector on OPSILA is the following :

<u>begin</u> The process starts with 16 classical FFT localy executed in each PE under I-mode. This process continues until i = log2 ((M/N)-1). After this inter-processor communications are necessary. Only this last part is presented here. The complete algorithm is developped in [22]

window := N/2 ; {window is a 16 data vector containing 16 times the value N/2}

<u>for</u> i := 0 <u>to</u> log2 (N)-1
    i1 := n-i-1 {N=2**n} ; index := AND (widow, numpe) {numpe is a vector such that the ith element is equal to i-1} ;

    index := SHFT (index,-i) {index is an index vector introduced for adressing the x values in each PE} ; index 1 := AND (window, NOT (numpe)) ; index 1 := SHFT (index 1, -i)

    <u>for</u> j := 0 <u>to</u> M-2 * N <u>step</u> 2 * N

        a := $\delta^{(n)}_{i,2**i1}$ (x(*j + index 1)) ; c:=w(i)*a ;

        x(*j+ index 1) := $\delta^{-1}_{i,2**i1}$ (x(*j+index)-c) ;

        x(*j + index) := x(*j + index) + c

    <u>end</u>

    window := window/2

<u>end</u>

<u>end</u>

At the end of the process a "bit reversal" permutation $\rho^{(m)}$ is necessary for unscrambling the result vector. This permutation is processed by combining permutations $\beta^{(4)}_{j,1,m,k}$ and $\rho^{(4)}$ carried out by RI [23].
The setting of the switches associated with the permutation forms a pre-established permutation in the network [8] .

6.3 Sparse matrix multiplication

This problem necessitates massive executions of "gather" instructions that is to say, accessing to a data vector through an index vector. A sequence of "gather" instructions is not vectorisable on pure pipelined machine such as CRAY-1.

Let a (M,M) be a sparse matrix so that if a (i,j) is not zero then this value is stored in BM j mod N as illustrated in figure 10.

We consider that the y vector, resulting from the multiplication of the sparse matrix and the full vector x is also a full vector.

Each PE computes under P-mode contributions of N components of the y vector. This process is locally performed in each PE without intercommunications. Then the summations of the contributions are computed under I-mode by adding the components of R matrix (of dimensions NxN) obtained under P-mode diagonal by diagonal :

$$R(i,i):=R(i,i)+R([i+k]_{\mathrm{mod}\ N},[i,k]_{\mathrm{mod}\ N});\ i=0,..,N-1$$

The summations are accomplished in N-1 steps : k=1,...,N-1.

After summations the main diagonal of R contains N components of the y vector. These values are stored in BMs without permutation. The complete process is repeated until the entire x vector is analysed.

7. PERFORMANCES

We give an evaluation of the performances of OPSILA concerning the three applications previously presented. We compare these, as far as possible, with the performances of commercialized vector computers.

In each case, we compare efficiency of with efficiency of commercialized pipelined computers AP120B, CRAY-1 and CYBER 205. The efficiency is the ratio for an application of the measured performance to the theoric performance.

7.1 Matrix multiplication

The storage scheme (u=0, v=1) used to map the matrices in BM avoid data permutations thus a better performance is obtained. The behaviour of OPSILA according to the matrix dimensions is plotted in figure 11.

If the matrix dimensions are 64x64 the efficiency of OPSILA is 86 %. For the same dimensions the CRAY-1S, CYBER 205 (2 pipes) and AP120B (with fast memory) efficiencies are respectively 86 %, 13,5 % and 36 % [9]. The execution time of OPSILA is 302 ms. A PDP 11-34 runs in about 18s the same application.

7.2 Fast fourier transform

The execution time of complex FFT of a 1024 point vector measured on OPSILA is 35 ms.

The time required to perform the "bit reversal" permutation is negligible in comparaison with the overall calculation time. The performance corresponds to an efficiency of 75 %. The CRAY-1S, AP120B and CYBER 205 have respectively an efficiency of 32 %, 88 % and 31 % [9].

7.3 Sparse matrix multiplication

Each acces to matrix elements requires the execution of a "gather" operation. The maximum performance of the CRAY-1S on "gather" operations is about 12 Mflop/S [9] which is the maximum performance of the scalar unit of the CRAY-1S. The efficiency of the CRAY-1S is about 10 %. The P-mode of OPSILA allows several "gather" operations to be performed independantly and locally in each PE.

If non-zero values of the matrix are uniformly distributed among BM, the efficiency of OPSILA applied to a 1024 x 1024 matrix with 64 non-zero values per row is 58 %.

8. CONCLUSION

An efficient SIMD architecture is introduced for signal processing and numerical analysis. This parallel processor consists of sixteen processing elements and their memory banks, an interconnection network and a master control unit.

Each 16-bit processing element can operate under two modes :

The I-mode (SIMD) is efficient on vector computation and,

The P-mode (SPMD) allows good performances on massive parallel scalar processing. The Omega-Benes interconnection network provides powerful data manipulations during inter-processor exchanges. In order to perform efficient matrix computation a storage method allowing parallel accesses to rows, columns, and diagonals is implemented.

The overall system is programmed with a conventional assembly language which allows an easy use of the two operating modes of OPSILA.

The study of basic applications (matrix multiplication, FFT, multiplication of a sparse matrix by a full vector) shows OPSILA has a good efficiency where pipelined computers are also efficient (matrix multiplication, FFT) and has better performances on applications which do not fit to pipelined computers.(sparse matrix processing).

All the hardware capabilities of OPSILA are designed without defining special purpose component. Obviously the introduction of specialized chips (i.e. floating-point operations), would greatly enhance the performances but a new balance of the efficiency of the units must therefore be defined.

REFERENCES :

[1] G. Feierbach, D.K Stevenson, The Phoenix array processing system, Parts I and II, (November 1978).

[2] C.Wu - T. Feng, The reverse-exchange interconnection network, IEEE T.C Vol.C29, pp 801-811, (September 1980).

[3] H.J. Siegel, Interconnection networks for SIMD machines, IEEE computer 12(6) 57-65, (1979).

[4] D.H Lawrie, Access and alignment of data in an array-processor, IEEE T.C Vol. C26 N° 5 pp. 548-578 (1977).

[5] V.E Benes, Mathematical theory of connection networks and telephone traffic, N.Y Academic (1968).

[6] J. Lenfant, S. Tahe, Permuting Data with the omega network, RADC, rapport final (Novembre 1978).

[7] J. Lenfant, Parallel permutation of data : a Benes control algorithm, IEEE, T.C, Vol.C27, N° 7, pp. 637-647 (July 1978).

[8] M. Gouget, Etude et realisation d'un réseau de permutation Oméga-Bénès et de sa commande Thèse doc. Ing. Université de Nice (Juillet 1982).

[9] R.W. Hockney, C.R. Jesshope, Parallel computers, Adam Hilger (1981).

[10] G.H. Barnes and al, The ILLIAC IV Computer, IEEE T.C Vol. C17, N° 8 (Aug. 1968).

[11] R.H. Perrot, A language for array and vector processors, ACM Trans. Prog. Lang. Syst. 1 117-95 (1979).

[12] I.S Duff, The solution of sparse linear equations on vector computers, Symposium on vector processors and scientific computation, Rome, 3-5 (March 1982).

[13] J. Lenfant, Les mémoires parallèles, convention de recherche IRIA-SESORI 78-200 (Juin 78).

[14] M. Auguin, OPSILA : un opérateur vectoriel à réseau d'interconnection, Rapport de recherche RR 82-7, LASSY, Université de Nice (1982).

[15] Infotech State of the Art Report : Supercomputers, Vol. 1 ed. C.R Jesshope, R.W. Hockney Infotech Intl. Ltd, pp. 181-187.

[16] W.J. Stewart, Transfers of data on a parallel computer, Vol. 1, RADC AFSOR - 78-3699 (1978).

[17] M.C Pease, An adaptation of the fast Fourier

transform for parallel processing, J. Assoc. Comput., Mach 15 252-64 (1968).

[18] H.S. Stone, Parallel processing with the perfect shuffle, IEEE Trans. Computers, C-20 153-61 (1971).

[19] C. Temperton, Fast Fourier transforms and Poisson solvers on the CRAY-1, Infotech State of the Art Report : Supercomputers Vol. 2 ed. C.R. Jesshope.

[20] L.N. Bhuyan, D.P. Agrawal, Applications of SIMD computer in signal processing, National Computer Conference, pp. 135-142 (1982).

[21] M. Auguin, Réalisation de la FFT sur OPSILA, Rapport de recherche to be published. LASSY, Université de Nice (1983).

[22] M. Auguin, Réalisation de la permutation $\rho^{(n)}$ sur 2^p processeurs, Rapport de recherche RR 83-1, LASSY, Université de Nice (1983).

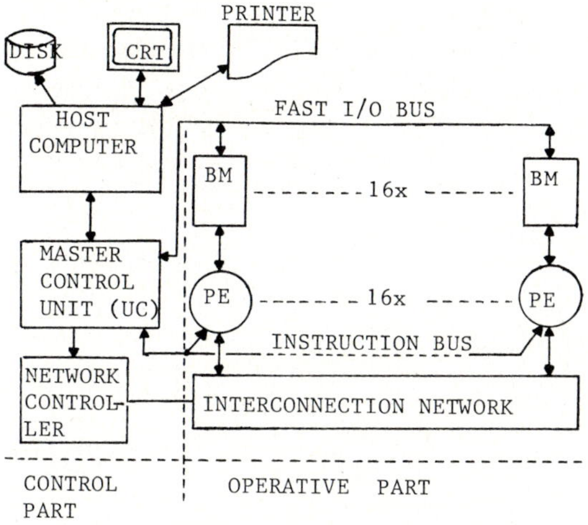

Fig.1- OPSILA overview.

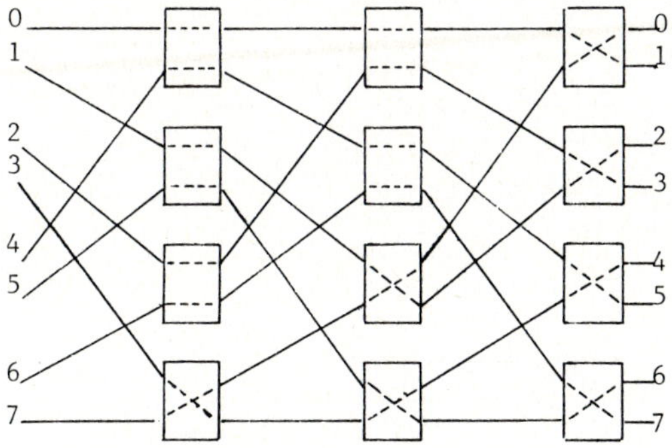

Fig.2- An omega interconnection network setting with a $\lambda^{(3)}_{1,1}$ making a one position circular shift.

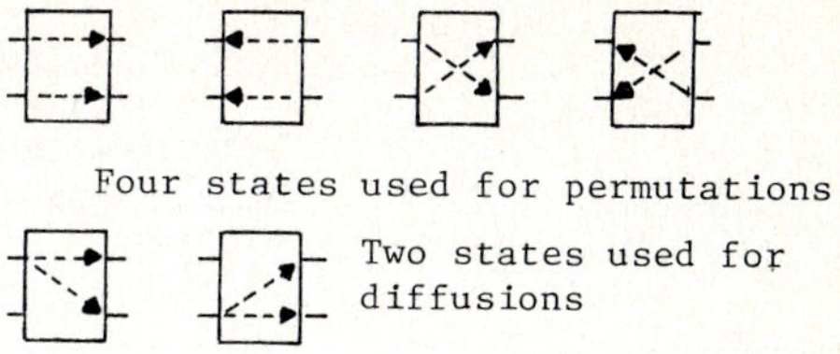

Fig.3- The six states of the elementary switch (CE).

FAMILY	DEFINITION	NETWORK
$\lambda^{(n)}_{jk}$	$x \rightarrow jx+k \bmod 2^n$; j odd; $0<j<2^n$; $0<k\leq 2^n$	OMEGA
$\beta^{(n)}_{jlmk}$	$x=(б_4,б_3,б_2,б_1) \rightarrow$ $(б_4,б_1,б_2,б_3)\oplus k$ $б_4$: j bits substring of x $б_3$: l bits substring of x $б_2$: m bits substring of x $0\leq j,l,m\leq n$; $j+l+m\leq n$; $0<k\leq 2^n$	BENES
$\partial^{(n)}_{jk}$	$x=(\hat{a}_2,\hat{a}_1) \rightarrow (\hat{a}_2,\hat{a}_1+k \bmod 2^{n-j})$ $\hat{a}_2$: j bits subtring of x $0\leq j\leq n$; $0\leq k<2^{n-j}$	OMEGA
$I^{(n)}_p$	if $x<p$ $x \rightarrow x$ if $x = 2^n-1$ $x \rightarrow p$ if $p\leq x<2^n-1$ $x \rightarrow x+1$ $0\leq p<2^n$	OMEGA
$S^{(n)}_{jkC}$	$S^{(n)}_{jkC} = \lambda^{(n)}_{jk}$ o $T^{(n)}_C$ C is a 2^n bit vector ; j odd ; $0<j<2^n$; $0\leq k<2^n$ 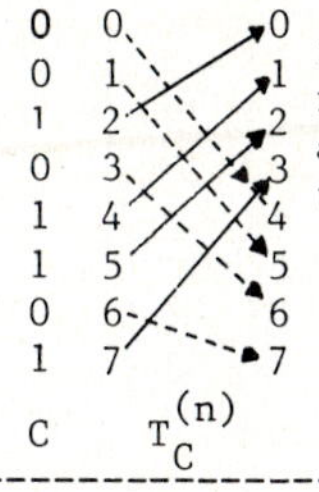 inputs related to all bits true in C	BENES

Fig.4- Families of permutations.

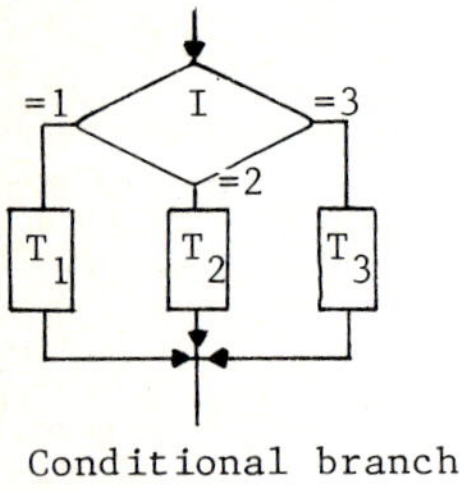

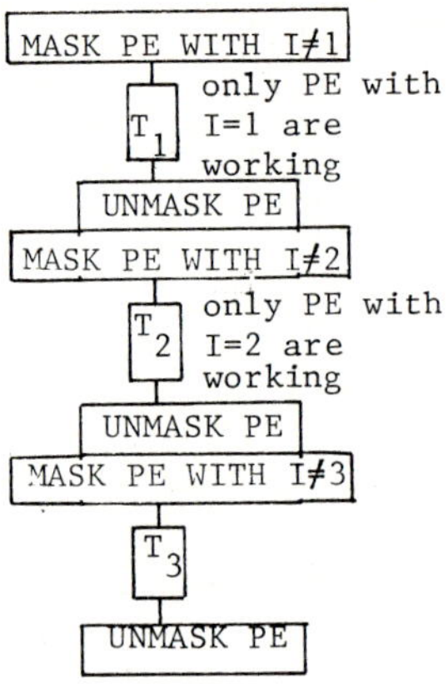

Fig.5- Masking principle.

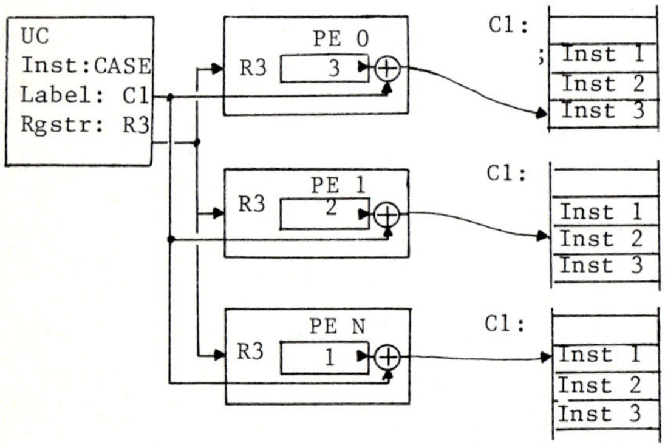

Fig.6- CASE principle.

0	1	2	3
a_{00}	a_{01}	a_{02}	a_{03}
a_{04}	a_{05}	a_{06}	-
a_{13}	a_{10}	a_{11}	a_{12}
-	a_{14}	a_{15}	a_{16}
a_{22}	a_{23}	a_{20}	a_{21}
a_{26}	-	a_{24}	a_{25}
a_{31}	a_{32}	a_{33}	a_{30}
a_{35}	a_{36}	-	a_{34}

Fig.7- A(4,7) stored with a helicoidal scheme.

0	1	2	3
x_0	x_1	x_2	x_3
x_4	x_5	x_6	x_7
x_8	x_9	x_{10}	x_{11}
x_{12}	x_{13}	x_{14}	x_{15}

Fig.8- FFT vector organization for a four processor SIMD.

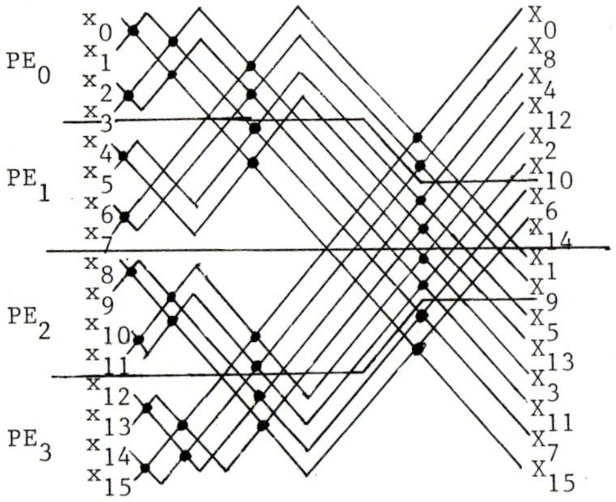

Fig.9- 16 points radix-2 FFT with a 4 processor SIMD.

	0	1	2	3
a:	a_{00}	a_{05}	a_{02}	a_{13}
	a_{10}	a_{09}	a_{06}	a_{17}
	a_{34}	a_{11}	a_{12}	a_{23}
	a_{41}	a_{21}	a_{26}	a_{33}
	-	a_{49}	a_{36}	-
x:	x_0	x_1	x_2	x_3
	x_4	x_5	x_6	x_7
	x_8	x_9	-	-
R:	$a_{00}x_0$	$a_{05}x_5$ + $a_{09}x_9$	$a_{02}x_2$ + $a_{06}x_6$	0
	$a_{10}x_0$	$a_{11}x_1$	$a_{12}x_2$	$a_{13}x_3$ + $a_{17}x_7$
	0	$a_{21}x_1$	$a_{16}x_6$	$a_{23}x_3$
	$a_{34}x_4$	0	$a_{36}x_6$	$a_{33}x_3$

Fig.10- Multiplication of a sparse matrix and a full vector.

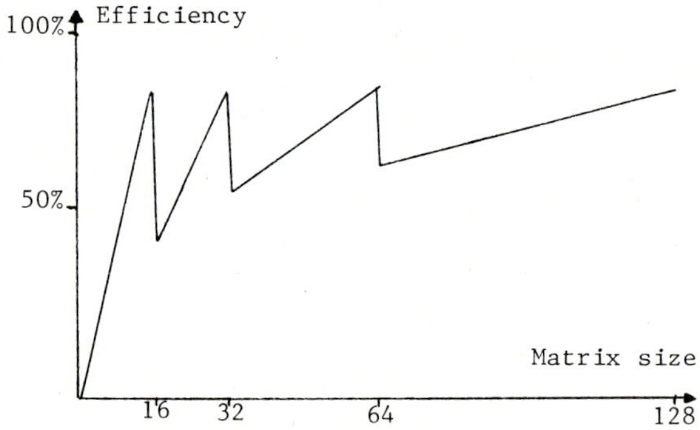

Fig.11- Matrix multiplication

Session I1:

HARDWARE DESIGN METHODS

Chairman: H. Schumny
Physikalisch Techn. Bundesanstalt
Braunschweig (F.R.G.)

Traditional hardware design methods use the Boolean algebra as a tool in order to formalize a problem and to find algorithms matching the available NANDs, NORs etc. In the second phase the number of components have to be minimised by using for instance graphical methods (e.g. a Karnaugh-Veitch diagram). Two actual consequences of modern microelectronics obstruct the traditional engineer's work or even make it nearly impossible: the exponentially increasing complexity of components and systems, and the fact that more and more functional units are programmable. Traditional methods, therefore, can, but must not, result in a clear and structured design with a minimum of errors.

At academia and industrial laboratories, a great deal of time and effort has been spent on defining a design methodology which both meets the technological facts and makes the computing power accessible to the designing engineer or scientist. Specific demands for such a methodology may include:

- to provide a convenient design definition tool,
- to provide a mathematical basis upon which analytical investigations (such as reliability, fault-tolerance) may be carried out,
- to allow the definition, detection, and resolution of specific problems,
- to provide agreement between user requirements and physical realization.

This can first result in a structured and controlled design methodology applicable to fixed function components. The next step might be a change to programmable components and devices, such as processors, I/O adaptors, special controllers.

The Euromicro '82 symposium (Haifa/Antwerp) presented two papers in the Hardware Design Methods section. One of it entitled "On the design of digital systems" (Peels) underlined the need for a high level of design and description methodology. The other paper "Availability analysis of fault-tolerant microcomputer systems with periodic preventive replacement" (Lombardi/Davies) dealt with methods of system modelling, availability valuation, and cost analysis in order to build up defined fault-tolerant systems.

The three papers of this year's session deal with design methodology, formal description, computer aided design, VLSI design, asynchronous machines, real-time applications. The aspects all three papers have in common is the use of special software systems as designer's tools. But intentions and implementations are quite different things.

The first paper "Hardware specification and description" is a continuation of last year's presentation "On the design of digital systems". The author defines a PLA structure to be the basic building block for simulations, and he also defines abstention from irrelevant details of a certain level as a main tool for handling the complexity of programming systems. The function of a basic building block can be described with a structured program written in a standard language. In this implementation, APL has been used to obtain an exact description at each design level.

The second paper deals with "The description of board level components for computer-aided design of microprocessor application systems". A software model for board level components is used which provides access to a data base by a special navigation or menue technique. The three stages of a session have been named Interview, Design and Report. Another aspect mentioned is the so-called resource concept: "An application is described as <u>requiring</u> certain resources, while components <u>are described</u> as <u>providing</u> certain resources."

The third paper discusses "Hardware and software tools for asynchronous systems synthesis with microprocessors" which have been implemented in Pascal. The systematic specification is based on state diagrams, software utilities are described for specification and implementation. A direct memory access functional block with a large number of input variables serves as a demonstration object.

At present, methods and implementations differ and intentions are manifold. Presentations and discussions of ideas and results may help to develop a uniform methodology for the design of complex and programmable hardware.

MICROCOMPUTERS: Developments in Industry, Business and Education
D.R. Wilson and C.J. van Spronsen (eds.) / ©EUROMICRO, 1983
Elsevier Science Publishers B.V. (North-Holland)

HARDWARE SPECIFICATION AND DESCRIPTION

A.J.H.M. Peels, G.J.M. Smit

Twente University of Technology
Department of Computing Science
P.O. Box 217, 7500 AE Enschede
The Netherlands

Abstract: Nowadays, complex digital systems are composed of programmable components as the basic hardware building blocks. A hierarchical design and description methodology is presented which handles complexity of the overall design process by deferring detail to the appropriate level of abstraction and bridges the gap between the user requirements, as defined in the architecture, and the ultimate realization in such a way that every step in the design process can be controlled and verified.

Key Words and Phrases: design methodology, specification, formal description, programmable components, simulation.

C.R. Categories: B.5.2, B.6.3, B.7.1, C.0.

1. Introduction

Advances in semiconductor technology have provided the capability to place complex digital systems on single silicon chips, like microprocessors, input/output devices, timers and interrupt controllers. The complexity of the new VLSI components is at least one order of magnitude higher than the previous used MSI or LSI elements. Even more complex devices such as graphical display controllers and disk controllers have been realized in silicon.

Today and in the near future, these VLSI components are the basic building blocks for the designer of digital systems. A wide variety of digital systems can be composed with these components and used in an even wider field of applications.

The functions of these devices is not fixed but depends on the program that controls it. The programmability gives these components a great deal of flexibility, so they can be used in many different applications. A strong interaction between the systemprogrammer and the hardware designer is required in the design of a system with these programmable components. The systemprogrammer has to know what functions can be performed by the hardware and how he can control the hardware. The hardware designer has to know which functions are required by the software.

To handle the complexity of these systems a structured and controlled design methodology is essential. The traditional designs of digital systems use gates like NAND, NOR, or AND and simple MSI components as basic logical elements [Ref. 1]. The complexity of the new VLSI components is considerably increased compared to the basic elements of the traditional designs [Ref. 6]. At the realization level the logical components have changed from fixed function components to programmable components such as microprocessors and input/output devices.

The traditional design methodology for designing digital systems must be extended in the design of systems with the new programmable components. For instance, the traditional simulation and minimalisation techniques cannot longer be used. In this paper a methodology is presented for designing and describing digital systems with the new programmable building blocks. The main tool for handling the complexity of the new systems is to abstract from irrelevant details of a certain level (information hiding).

In the proposed methodology several levels of abstraction are distinguished. During the design process, the designer works in one of the abstraction levels, with the functions of that level. In this design level he will not be bothered with the details of a lower abstraction level. So, the designer can work out the design in a hierarchical manner, only going down to the details of a lower level when it is really required to study the system design in that detail. The designer works in the level of abstraction most appropriate for the task under consideration. A systemprogrammer for instance will not longer be confronted with for that level unimportant technological details of the components, but will only use an abstract specification model of the hardware. The hardware designer however will be interested in more details of the logical implementation of the components, he will need a, preferably formal, description of the component.

With the proposed methodology we hope to achieve a straightforward, flexible and controlled design and verification process which establishes clear and structured designs with fewer errors. The introduction of abstraction levels in the design process allows a design to be verified at every level of abstraction as for instance by simulation. This means that design errors can be detected and consequently corrected in an early stage of the design process.

2. Design Methodology

The objective of digital system design is to map the user requirements onto a physical realization. The ultimate physical realization of the digital system has to perform the behaviour specified by the user as well as satisfy any constraints imposed upon it. An acceptable trade off must be achieved with respect to a set of pre-defined design goals or objectives.

A hierarchical design and description methodology is developed at our University which handles complexity by deferring detail to the appropriate level of abstraction and bridges the gap between the user requirements and the ultimate physical realization in such a way that every step in the design process can be controlled and verified. A formal notation is a valuable tool to achieve the latter objectives.

Architecture

The requirements generated by the user describe the functional behaviour of the digital system. The system designer or architect transforms the user requirements into a functional specification or architecture. In essence, a mapping of input variables on output variables is specified without reflecting any internal structure.

Implementation

The next phase in the design process is the implementation phase. The functional specification is to be mapped onto functional units, available as hardware building blocks. These functional units are configured in such a way that they constitute the specified architecture. Many configurations are possible to embody the functional specification. Therefore, it is said that the architecture is detailed to an initial implementation, thus deciding which algorithm is used for the architecture.

The functional units incorporated in digital systems nowadays are programmable. Examples of such hardware building blocks are microprocessors, parallel input/output interfaces, timers and synchronous/asynchronous receiver/transmitter devices. The use of these components in the initial implementation phase requires their abstract function [Ref. 7], for it is at this stage that one wishes to evaluate alternative configurations, thereby obtaining an indication of the cost/performance ratio.

The difference between the abstract function of a component and its functional behaviour evolves from [Ref. 4]. The formal descriptions of these components in the programming language APLDL -standard APL extended with control structures [Ref. 2]- give their functional behaviour. However, the descriptions reflect much low level information concerning interconnection signals of the component. These details can be omitted as is shown in [Ref. 5] resulting in an abstract function of a hardware building block. At this level, a distinction is made between the function of a component and its interconnections.

The initial implementation is refined to a configuration of interconnected hardware building blocks and their control. Once an interconnection pattern is defined, the possibility exists to change the datapath dynamically. This is a consequence of the fact that components are programmable and therefore not committed to a single operation but to a range of operations. Adaptability to a different operation is controlled by the programming capabilities of a component.

Now it is necessary to consider how a function communicates with its environment. The input/output signals concerning the interconnection of a function must be defined. Ultimately, a logic level description of the interconnection pattern is obtained, considering the idealized logic levels with the values zero and one.

Realization

The realization is concerned with the physical structure that embodies the implementation. The physical components performing the logical functions require that the user has knowledge of electronic aspects such as electric voltage, current or power, and component operation times.

Furthermore, interconnection of components implies decisions in placement of components and routing of wires.

3. Hardware Building Blocks

General Internal Structure

The introduction has shown that the basic building blocks for the design of digital systems today and in the near future are programmable VLSI components such as microprocessors, PIOs, timers and USARTs. A general chip structure can be derived from these components by analyzing the fundamentals of operation. This analysis yields a general structure according to which programmable components can be compared. The internal structure of this general chip consists of an operation unit, a set of input and output registers and a control unit.

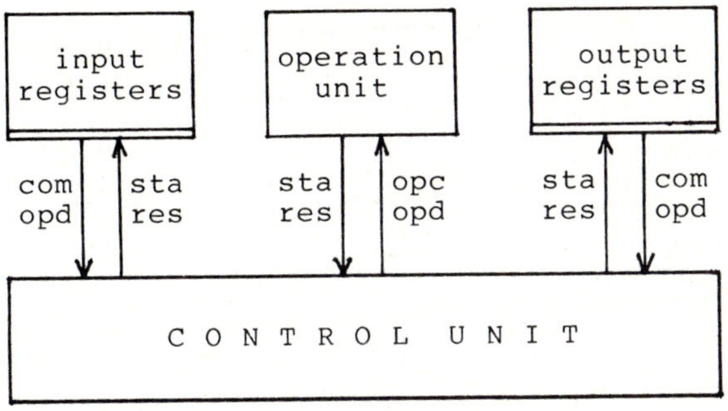

com: command
opd: operands
opc: opcode
sta: status
res: result

Figure 1. Generalized Internal Structure.

Operations performed on the registers are controlled by the control unit. The control unit may consist of an instruction unit and a program memory. The internal program residing in the program memory interprets the commands in the registers and takes care of the data flow in the registers and the operation unit. The internal programs are stored in memory on the chip. Internal programs can be executed after a command has been given. The results of an operation are stored in a register. Taking into account the input/output interconnections with other components consisting of the communication at the so called central processing unit side and the communication at the device side, reveals the general chip structure, as described in [Ref. 3], and presented in figure 2.

General Chip Structure

The interconnection at the central processing unit side with the CPU consists of the address bus, the data bus and the control bus. The device side contains an external data bus which may be controlled by a handshake procedure. So external data can be exchanged between the CPU and the peripheral device.

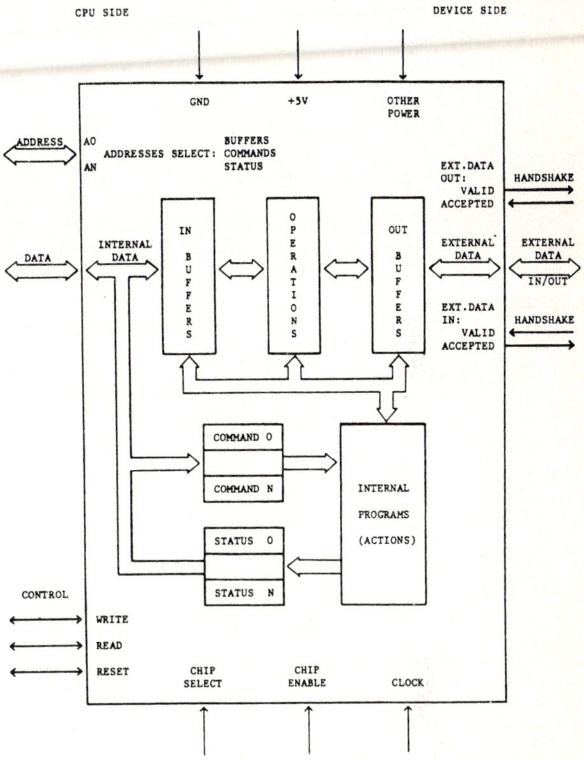

Figure 2. Model of a Generalized Chip Structure.

Notation

A standard procedural programming language (like APL or PASCAL) can be used for the specification, description and simulation of hardware building blocks. The advantage of using a standard language is that the description can be executed on a computer and consequently simulated. One does not have to write a new interpreter or compiler for specifying or describing the hardware modules.

When using these standard programming languages without special techniques for the simulation of a system with one or more hardware components, the sequence of the statements in the simulation program becomes essentially important for the function to be performed at a low abstraction level. The reason why this sequence of statements is so important is that operations in a component, from their nature act in parallel and are not atomic. If more than one component is simulated, all the operations of these components work in parallel. To handle the complexity of parallellism, a simple synchronization mechanism, the logical clock, is introduced at a lower level of abstraction.

Basic Model for a Hardware Building Block

To this extent, a basic model is introduced as well as a technique for simulating such a model. In general, it can be shown that any synchronous digital system can be built with a structure consisting of: a combinatorial part, a sequential part and a feedback part. This structure is called the basic structure for a hardware building block, which has a considerable resemblance with the well-known PLA device (programmable logic array).

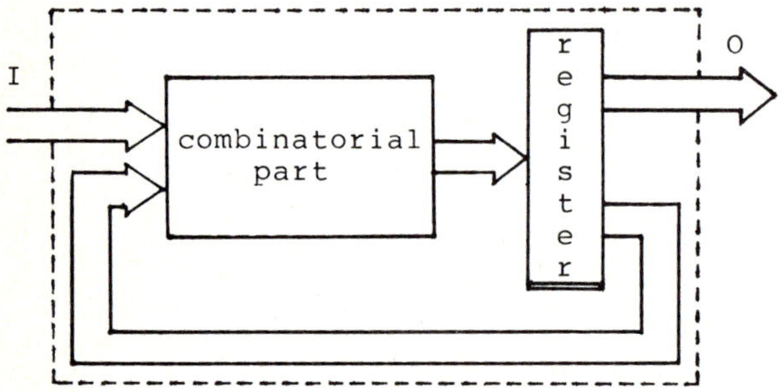

Figure 3. Basic Model for a Hardware Building Block.

This structure is the basis for our simulation technique which uses the contents of the register. With regards to the basic model it is assumed that:

- the input of the combinatorial block must be synchronous with the clock, or in other words the inputs must be a direct output of a clocked memory element,
- there is a fixed relationship between the propagation delay of the combinatorial block and the clock frequency,

$$T_{prop} < \frac{1}{F_{max}}$$

T_{prop} = propagation delay of the combinatorial block

F_{max} = maximum clock frequency

Note: in this formula the influence of set up time and clock-skew is not considered for reasons of simplicity,

- the basic model consists of at least one memory element, otherwise a pure combinatorial structure is obtained,
- the combinatorial part may not consist of any memory element (contradictio in terminis),
- the registers only change at a predetermined edge of the clockpulse.

With regards to these constraints the basic model has some useful advantages:

- the structure can be split-up into one or more subsystems (decomposition),
- two or more models may be integrated to constitute one bigger model,
- if the size of the model is not too big, it may be realized on one VLSI chip. The speed of the combinatorial part may be a serious constraint, if the model is very big and a high speed is required,
- the function of the model can be described with a 'structured' program written in a standard programming language,
- the model can be easily simulated due to the invariant logical function of the model in case the clock speed is slowed down,
- there is no place for time related elements as RC-networks and one-shots in the model,
- the state of the model only changes at the clock transitions.

From the definition of the model it is seen that the state of the structure at a certain point in time is determined by the contents of the registers. The preceding property is used for the simulation of a system.

4. Specification and Formal Description

Specifications should be precise and unambiguous, resulting in an exact and complete description at each level in the design process.

That this is not a trivial remark is shown by our research and effort to derive formal specifications of hardware component descriptions. Microprocessors (Intel 8080 and 8085), ROM and RAM (2716 and 2114), timer (8253) as well as serial and parallel input/output devices (8251 and 8255) have been considered [Ref. 4]. A list is generated for each component showing the difficulties one encounters in trying to establish a formal description. One invariably discovers that the manual of the manufacturer suffers from incompleteness and ambiguities.

Naturally, additional information can be obtained by measurements at the hardware component which is to be described. Besides the fact that this is a time-consuming operation, such a description is also susceptible to production changes by the manufacturer or by second-source manufacturers.

In general, the effort to establish precise and formal specifications at each level in the design process is underestimated. The ideal situation would be that the manufacturer gives a formal specification of the component.

A relation exists between specification and verification. A formal specification simplifies the verification process.

Numerous techniques are used to generate formal descriptions of specifications. The most well-known notational tools are natural language, graphical representation, state-machine methods and formal language.

Here, the programming language APL is used in order to obtain an exact description at each design level. The description is executable on a computer what also allows it to be used as a simulation language for the design method. So, specification and verification are closely related.

Architecture

The functional specification reflecting the user requirements is generated by the architect. It should not give any internal structure of the digital system. The behaviour of the system or in other words what the system does, is of importance, not how it is done, for this belongs to the domain of implementation. Two description principles exist at this level: the assertive and generative description [Ref. 8].

The **assertive** description principle essentially defines the mapping of input variables on output variables. The relation how the output variables are obtained for a given set of input variables is not given. This means that no internal structure is reflected. The assertive description may be very extensive, for complex components.

Examples of the assertive description principle are timing diagrams, input/output sequence tables and truth tables.

The **generative** description principle defines how the input variables are transformed to the output variables. The transformation mechanism is described. This implies an internal structure for the system under consideration. However, giving one possible implementation does not necessarily restrict the freedom of the designer.

Examples of the generative description principle are graphical representation and state-machines.

Because the assertive description reflects no internal structure of the system, whereas the generative description suggests an implementation, one would suppose that the assertive description is the best technique.

However, the transformation mechanism shows the relation between input and output variables and therefore it is best understood and consequently most frequently used as the basis for the specification of a system. The description technique for the specification is therefore mostly the generative description principle. Furthermore, the generative description can be used for demonstration and, if a notation is used that is executable on a computer, a simulation of the description is possible, thereby verifying and eventually revealing misconceptions of the specification.

Implementation

Abstract functions of hardware components, or abstract components, are used at this level as previously stated.

Such an abstract function reflects the operation of a component, not how the operation is performed. As is shown in [Ref. 5], the abstract function for parallel communication is given by a matrix which can also be used as a specification model, giving a data flow specification. A general model for parallel input/output operations, resembling a data bus multiplexer, gives the specifications for the number of buses, their width and operation direction. Furthermore, a data transfer control mechanism for each bus must be defined.

The distinct types are uni- and bi-directional data transfer and for each direct I/O, strobed I/O and I/O with handshake signals, resulting in six possible control mechanisms.

An example of four multiplexed buses is given in the specification model:

SPECIFICATION MATRIX

Dataflow	Input	8	Ø	5	8
	Output	8	7	Ø	Ø
Control	Type	2	Ø	1	1

The data transfer control mechanisms are bi-directional with handshake signals (coded as mode 2), uni-directional with handshake signals (mode 1) and direct I/O (mode 0).

Generalized Chip Structure

So, a specification of **what** the function performs is given. The abstracted function is refined by considering its input/output operations, for the communication at the logic level with other components. The component is described according to the concept of a generalized chip structure as described in [Ref. 3].

The description assumes idealized components, at the pins of which the values zero and one occur. The pins of the package form the possibility to communicate with other components. The pins are usually associated with a name (variable). The digital values of these names is where the description reacts on [Ref. 4].

The relation between the abstract specification model and physical component can be given by a translation mechanism. The translation mechanism is implemented by using the programming language APL, thereby obtaining an automatic generative tool which generates the number of components needed, the control words and port assignments. For example, for the Intel 8255, the previous given operations specification model results in:

```
SPECIFICATION MATRIX SPEC:
  8   0   5   8
  8   7   0   0
  2   0   1   1

*** INTEL 8255 NUMBER: 1

SPECIFICATION MATRIX ALLOC:
  8   5   0   0
  8   0   0   0
  2   1   0   0

PORT ASSIGNMENT:
  A   B  NOT NOT

CONTROL WORD (D7D0):
  1 1 X X X 1 1 X

*** INTEL 8255 NUMBER: 2

SPECIFICATION MATRIX ALLOC:
  8   0   0   0
  0   7   0   0
  1   0   0   0

PORT ASSIGNMENT:
  A   B  NOT NOT

CONTROL WORD (D7D0):
  1 0 1 1 X 0 0 X

NOTE: X=DON'T CARE
```

The formal description of the Intel 8255 now shows the function it performs, taking into account the digital values of the interconnections.

An example of such a description is given for port A of the Intel 8255 interface in the appendix and is taken from [Ref. 4]. At this moment, automatic mapping on other parallel input/output components can be performed. Besides the Intel 8255, translation mechanisms for the Signetics 2655, Motorola 6820 and Zilog 8420 are implemented.

Logical clock

The formal description of the 8255 [Ref. 4] shows the logical function the component performs. However, this description does not consider the time it takes to perform a certain operation. Furthermore, this description technique only allows one action at a time. A physical component can perform more than one action at the same time and every action has its characteristic timing.

The execution time of an action is defined by two events, indicating either begin and end or begin and duration or duration and end of an action.

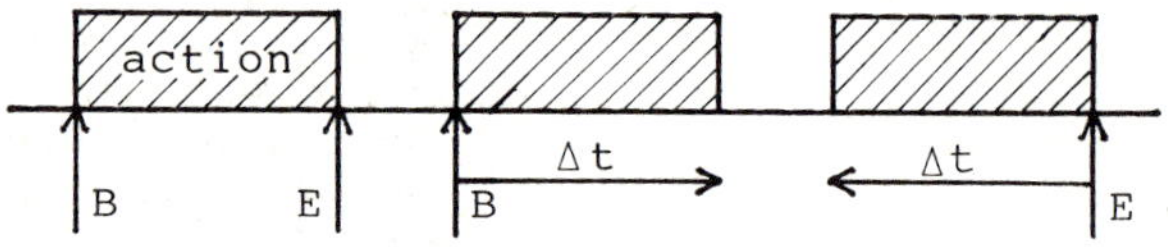

Figure 4. Action Definition.

In signaling conventions, an action is composed of either two transitions or a transition and time interval. This clearly shows two aspects of time, being a sequence reference, indicating the subsequent event occurrences along a time axis and a time reference, reflecting the physical time between two subsequent events and needed for the establishment of actions.

The following description technique takes the logical clock into account and assumes that the actions establish between two clock pulses. The definition of the basic model (section 2) shows that the state of the model at a certain point in time is determined by the contents of the register. This property is used for the simulation of a system.

In general a synchronous digital system can be built up with one or more basic models, each with their own clock or with a common clock. Every model consists of a combinatorial part and a sequential part (one or more registers). Consider a system, that can be decomposed into three sub-systems. This system can be described with the following program.

```
process SYSTEM

   combinatorial-part-sub-system 1
   combinatorial-part-sub-system 2
   combinatorial-part-sub-system 3
   .
   .
   CLOCK
   .
   .
end process
```

In simulation all combinatorial parts of the sub-system are computed first. In the sub-program CLOCK the registers of the sub-systems get new values, which are computed in the combinatorial part. The sequence of the combinatorial parts and the clock part is not important anymore.

The state of the system only changes in the CLOCK module. If the various sub-systems have a different clock, an algorithm has to be added to the module CLOCK, to specify in what sequence and how often a certain clock has to be executed. The algorithm thus reflects the relationship between the various clocks of the sub-systems.

Here, a process is called synchronous if the memory elements only change value at a predetermined edge of the clock. This definition means that processes that have different internal clocks, must be seen as asynchronous processes. Signals that travel from one process to another asynchronous process must be considered carefully. These signals cannot be used as input for a basic model, because they violate the constraints, viz. the inputs of a combinatorial part must be synchronous. It is necessary to synchronize the input signals first. This is for instance possible with the following construction.

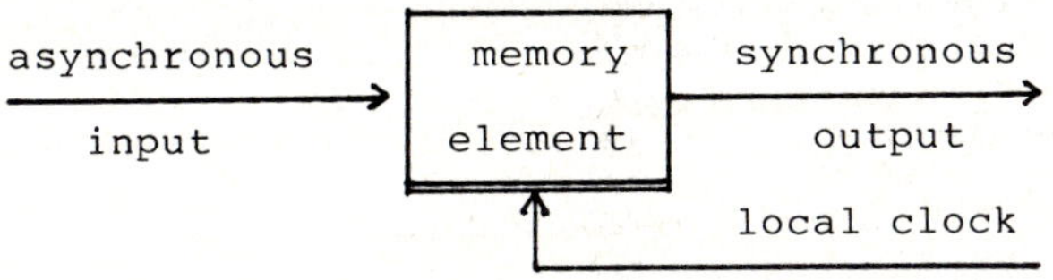

Figure 5. Synchronization of Inputs.

A disadvantage of synchronization is that the input is delayed for at most one clock cycle. If data is sent from one process to another asynchronous process a technique of handshaking must be used to allow correct communication.

Example

The operation of port A and the control word register of the Intel 8255 is used to illustrate the preceding description technique. Due to space limitations, the mode 0 and mode 1 operations of port A are given, being respectively uni-directional direct I/O and uni-directional I/0 with handshake signals. The associated control signals, provided by port C, are also described. Port B operation is similar to port A operation and therefore omitted.

The registers used in the description are: PORTA, port A register; PORTC, port C register for the control signals associated with port A operation; PORTCW, the control word register; D0D7, the data bus buffer; LSTRDA and LSTWRA, registers to store the value of respectively NRD and NWR (negative logic for RD and WR) for one clock pulse.

The contents of the registers do not change in the combinatorial functions. Instead of changing the register values, a temporary variable is computed, which has the same name concatenated with the prefix I, e.g. IPORTA, IPORTC, ID0D7 and ILSTRDA. These temporary variables are occasionally used at the right side of the assignment statements to avoid very long expressions, e.g. the expression:

```
ID0D7←(PA0PA7∧(AM0IN∧RDA))∨(PORTA∧(AM1IN∧RDA))
∨(D0D7∧(~(AM0IN∧RDA))∧~(AM1IN∧RDA))
```

is broken down to the expressions in line 22 and 28 of the function A. The registers are only changed (logical clock) after having computed all the combinatorial functions. The functions used in the example clearly show that only simple logical expressions are used, so these functions can be easily implemented in hardware. A logical description of the component like [Ref. 4] has been used as a starting point. It can be shown that this description can be transformed to the basic model.

```
     ∇  INTEL8255
[1]     CW
[2]     A
[3]     C
[4]    ⍝ LOGICAL CLOCK
[5]     PORTCW←IPORTCW
[6]     PORTA←IPORTA
[7]     PORTC←IPORTC
[8]     PA0PA7←IPA0PA7
[9]     PC0PC7←IPC0PC7
[10]    D0D7←ID0D7
[11]    LSTRDA←ILSTRDA
[12]    LSTWRA←ILSTWRA
     ∇
```

```
     ∇  CW
[1]    ⍝ CONTROL WORD REGISTER OPERATION
[2]    ⍝ RESET
[3]     IPORTCW←((1 1 0 1 1 0 0 1)∧RESET)∨(PORTCW∧
       ~RESET)
[4]    ⍝ WRITE
[5]     WR←(~RESET)∧CHIPSELECT∧NRD∧~NWR
[6]    ⍝ WRITE CONTROL WORD REGISTER
[7]     WRCW←WR∧A0∧A1
[8]    ⍝ MODE CONTROL WORD
[9]     MODE←D0D7[7]
[10]   ⍝ INPUT CONTROL WORD REGISTER
[11]    IPORTCW←(D0D7∧(WRCW∧MODE))∨(IPORTCW∧~(WRCW
       ∧MODE))
     ∇
```

```
     ∇ A
[1]    ⍝ PORT A OPERATION
[2]    ⍝ RESET
[3]     IPORTA←((8ρ0)∧RESET)∨(PORTA∧~RESET)
[4]    ⍝ READ OR WRITE
[5]     RD←(~RESET)∧CHIPSELECT∧(~NRD)∧NWR
[6]     WR←(~RESET)∧CHIPSELECT∧NRD∧~NWR
[7]    ⍝ READ OR WRITE PORT A
[8]     RDA←RD∧(~A0)∧~A1
[9]     WRA←WR∧(~A0)∧~A1
[10]   ⍝ BUFFER READ AND WRITE
[11]    ILSTRDA←RDA
[12]    ILSTWRA←WRA
[13]   ⍝ MODE
[14]    AM0←∧/PORTCW[5 6]= 0 0
[15]    AM1←∧/PORTCW[5 6]= 1 0
[16]   ⍝ PORT A INPUT OR OUTPUT
[17]    AM0IN←AM0∧PORTCW[4]
[18]    AM0OUT←AM0∧~PORTCW[4]
[19]    AM1IN←AM1∧PORTCW[4]
[20]    AM1OUT←AM1∧~PORTCW[4]
[21]   ⍝ MODE 0 INPUT
[22]    ID0D7←(PA0PA7∧(AM0IN∧RDA))∨(D0D7∧~(AM0IN∧
       RDA))
[23]   ⍝ MODE 0 OUTPUT
[24]    IPORTA←(D0D7∧(AM0OUT∧WRA))∨(IPORTA∧~(
       AM0OUT∧WRA))
[25]    IPA0PA7←(D0D7∧(AM0OUT∧WRA))∨(PA0PA7∧~(
       AM0OUT∧WRA))
[26]   ⍝ MODE 1 INPUT
[27]    IPORTA←(PA0PA7∧(AM1IN∧~PC0PC7[4]))∨(IPORTA
       ∧~(AM1IN∧~PC0PC7[4]))
[28]    ID0D7←(PORTA∧(AM1IN∧RDA))∨(ID0D7∧~(AM1IN∧
       RDA))
[29]   ⍝ MODE 1 OUTPUT
[30]    IPORTA←(D0D7∧(AM1OUT∧WRA))∨(IPORTA∧~(
       AM1OUT∧WRA))
[31]    IPA0PA7←(PORTA∧AM1OUT)∨(IPA0PA7∧~AM1OUT)
     ∇
```

```
     ∇ C
[1]    ⍝ PORT C OPERATION
[2]    ⍝ RESET
[3]     IPORTC←((8ρ0)∧RESET)∨(PORTC∧~RESET)
[4]     IPC0PC7←PC0PC7
[5]    ⍝ .
[6]    ⍝ PORT A MODE 1 INPUT
[7]     SIBFA←AM1IN∧~PC0PC7[4]
[8]     RIBFA←AM1IN∧PC0PC7[4]∧LSTRDA∧~RDA
[9]     SINTRA←AM1IN∧INTEA∧PC0PC7[4]∧PC0PC7[5]∧(~
       LSTRDA)∧~RDA
[10]    RINTRA←AM1IN∧(~LSTRDA)∧RDA
[11]   ⍝ SET AND RESET IBF
[12]    IPORTC[5]←(1∧SIBFA)∨(IPORTC[5]∧~SIBFA)
[13]    IPC0PC7[5]←(1∧SIBFA)∨(PC0PC7[5]∧~SIBFA)
[14]    IPORTC[5]←(0∧RIBFA)∨(IPORTC[5]∧~RIBFA)
[15]    IPC0PC7[5]←(0∧RIBFA)∨(IPC0PC7[5]∧~RIBFA)
[16]   ⍝ SET AND RESET INTR
[17]    IPORTC[3]←(1∧SINTRA)∨(IPORTC[3]∧~SINTRA)
[18]    IPC0PC7[3]←(1∧SINTRA)∨(IPC0PC7[3]∧~SINTRA)
[19]    IPORTC[3]←(0∧RINTRA)∨(IPORTC[3]∧~RINTRA)
[20]    IPC0PC7[3]←(0∧RINTRA)∨(IPC0PC7[3]∧~RINTRA)
[21]   ⍝
[22]   ⍝ PORT A MODE 1 OUTPUT
[23]    SNOBFA←AM1OUT∧PC0PC7[6]∧LSTWRA∧~WRA
[24]    RNOBFA←AM1OUT∧~PC0PC7[6]
[25]    SINTRA←AM1OUT∧INTEA∧PC0PC7[6]∧PC0PC7[7]∧~
       WRA
[26]    RINTRA←AM1OUT∧LSTWRA∧~WRA
[27]   ⍝ SET AND RESET OBF
[28]    IPORTC[7]←(0∧SNOBFA)∨(IPORTC[7]∧~SNOBFA)
[29]    IPC0PC7[7]←(0∧SNOBFA)∨(IPC0PC7[7]∧~SNOBFA)
[30]    IPORTC[7]←(1∧RNOBFA)∨(IPORTC[7]∧~RNOBFA)
[31]    IPC0PC7[7]←(1∧RNOBFA)∨(IPC0PC7[7]∧~RNOBFA)
[32]   ⍝ SET AND RESET INTR
[33]    IPORTC[3]←(1∧SINTRA)∨(IPORTC[3]∧~SINTRA)
[34]    IPC0PC7[3]←(1∧SINTRA)∨(IPC0PC7[3]∧~SINTRA)
[35]    IPORTC[3]←(0∧RINTRA)∨(IPORTC[3]∧~RINTRA)
[36]    IPC0PC7[3]←(0∧RINTRA)∨(IPC0PC7[3]∧~RINTRA)
[37]   ⍝ .
     ∇
```

5. Conclusions

It is shown that digital systems with programmable components as basic building blocks can be designed with the proposed design methodology, which handles the complexity of these systems by deferring detail to the appropriate level of abstraction. Every step of the design process can be controlled and verified, description and simulation techniques are extensively used. At a high level of abstraction the systemprogrammer uses a formal functional description. At a low level the hardware designer uses a description technique which is closely related to the physical hardware and uses a logic clock for synchronization. By example it is shown that in the design process the functions of a certain abstraction level can be, automatically or simply manually, mapped onto the functions of a lower abstraction level.

Acknowledgements

We are indebted to Norbert Janssen and Wop Nawijn, who significantly contributed to the final preparation of this document. A preliminary version of their text processing system, consisting of a text-syntax based format generator which generates the input for a TEX based algorithm for text formatting, was used to bring about this paper.

6. References

1. Blaauw, G.A.: 'Digital System Implementation', Prentice Hall, Englewood Cliffs, N.J., U.S.A., 1976.

2. Blaauw, G.A., Duijvestijn, A.J.W., Ledeboer, A.: 'An APL Design Language', IBM Laboratory, Uithoorn, the Netherlands, 1979.

3. Peels, A.J.H.M.: 'A Model of a Generalized Chip Structure', Microprocesssing and Microprogramming, Volume 9, Number 5, 1982.

4. Peels, A.J.H.M.: 'A Formal Description of the Intel 8253, 8255, 2114, 2716, 8080 and 8085', Twente University of Technology, Department of Informatics, Enschede, the Netherlands, 1981 and 1982.

5. Peels, A.J.H.M.: 'The Translation of an Abstract Specification Model for the Intel 8255', Twente University of Technology, Department of Informatics, Enschede, the Netherlands, 1982.

6. Peels, A.J.H.M.: 'On the Design of Digital Systems', Proceedings Eighth Symposium on Microprocessing and Microprogramming, Euromicro, Haifa, Israel, 1982.

7. Peels, A.J.H.M.: 'Programmable Components in Digital System Design', Unpublished Paper.

8. Vissers, C.A.: 'Interface - Definition, Design and Description of the Relation of Digital System Parts', Doctoral Thesis, Twente University of Technology, Enschede, the Netherlands, 1977.

7. Appendix

```
     ∇ CPUSIDE
[1]    ⍝ OPERATION AT THE CPU SIDE
[2]    →CASE ADDRESS
[3]      ⍝ PORT A ADDRESSED
[4]    C0:PORTAINPUTOUTPUT
[5]      →ENDCASE
[6]      ⍝ PORT B ADDRESSED
[7]    C1:PORTBINPUTOUTPUT
[8]      →ENDCASE
[9]      ⍝ PORT C ADDRESSED
[10]   C2:PORTCINPUTOUTPUT
[11]     →ENDCASE
[12]     ⍝ CONTROL WORD REGISTER ADDRESSED
[13]   C3:LOADCONTROLWORD
[14]   ENDCASE:
     ∇
     ∇ OUT←ADDRESS
[1]    OUT←2⊥A1,A0
     ∇
```

```
     ∇ PORTAINPUTOUTPUT
[1]    ⍝ DETERMINE MODE OF PORT A
[2]    →CASE GROUPAMODE
[3]    C0:PORTAM0
[4]      →ENDCASE
[5]    C1:PORTAM1
[6]      →ENDCASE
[7]    C2:PORTAM2
[8]    ENDCASE:
     ∇
```

```
     ∇ PORTAM0
[1]    ⍝ DETERMINE FUNCTION OF PORT A IN MODE 0
[2]    →IF FUNCTIONPORTA∧(NRD=0)∧NWR=1
[3]    THEN:PORTAM0IN
[4]    ENDIF:
[5]    →IF1(~FUNCTIONPORTA)∧(NRD=1)∧NWR=0
[6]    THEN1:PORTAM0OUT
[7]    ENDIF1:
     ∇
```

```
     ∇ PORTAM0IN
[1]    ⍝ PORT A MODE 0 INPUT
[2]    ⍝ NRD=0 AND NWR=1
[3]    D0D7←PA0PA7
[4]    WAIT 'NRD=1'
     ∇
```

```
     ∇ PORTAM0OUT
[1]    ⍝ PORT A MODE 0 OUTPUT
[2]    ⍝ NRD=1 AND NWR=0
[3]    PORTA←D0D7
[4]    WAIT 'NWR=1'
[5]    PA0PA7←PORTA
     ∇
```

```
    ∇ PORTAM1
[1]   ⍝ DETERMINE FUNCTION OF PORT A IN MODE 1
[2]    INTRA←PORTC[3]←PC0PC7[3]
[3]    →IF FUNCTIONPORTA
[4]   THEN:NSTBA←PORTC[4]←PC0PC7[4]
[5]        IBFA←PORTC[5]←PC0PC7[5]
[6]        →ENDIF
[7]   ELSE:NACKA←PORTC[6]←PC0PC7[6]
[8]        NOBFA←PORTC[7]←PC0PC7[7]
[9]   ENDIF:
[10]  REPEAT:→IF1 1=∨/CONDPORTAM1
[11]      THEN1:
[12]          →CASE CONDPORTAM1⍳1
[13]        C0:PORTAM1IN1
[14]            →ENDCASE
[15]        C1:PORTAM1IN2
[16]            →ENDCASE
[17]        C2:PORTAM1OUT1
[18]            →ENDCASE
[19]        C3:PORTAM1OUT2
[20]        ENDCASE:
[21]      ENDIF1:
[22]   →UNTIL 0=∨/CONDPORTAM1
[23]   →IF2 FUNCTIONPORTA
[24]  THEN2:PC0PC7[3 4 5]←PORTC[3 4 5]←INTRA,
     NSTBA,IBFA
[25]       →ENDIF2
[26]  ELSE2:PC0PC7[3 6 7]←PORTC[3 6 7]←INTRA,
     NACKA,NOBFA
[27]  ENDIF2:
    ∇
```

```
    ∇ OUT←CONDPORTAM1
[1]    →IF FUNCTIONPORTA
[2]   THEN:OUT←(NSTBA=0),((NRD=0)∧NWR=1),0,0
[3]        →ENDIF
[4]   ELSE:OUT←0,0,((NRD=1)∧NWR=0),NACKA=0
[5]   ENDIF:
[6]    →IF1 CHIPSELECT=0
[7]   THEN1:OUT[1 2]←0
[8]   ENDIF1:
    ∇
```

```
    ∇ PORTAM1IN1
[1]   ⍝ PORT A MODE 1 INPUT DEVICE TO PORT A
[2]   ⍝ NSTBA=0
[3]    PORTA←PA0PA7
[4]    IBFA←1
[5]    WAIT 'NSTBA=1'
[6]    →IF INTEA
[7]   THEN:INTRA←1
[8]   ENDIF:
    ∇
    ∇ PORTAM1IN2
[1]   ⍝ PORT A MODE 1 INPUT PORT A TO D0D7
[2]   ⍝ NRD=0 AND NWR=1
[3]    INTRA←0
[4]    D0D7←PORTA
[5]    WAIT 'NRD=1'
[6]    IBFA←0
    ∇
```

```
    ∇ PORTAM1OUT1
[1]   ⍝ PORT A MODE 1 OUTPUT D0D7 TO PORT A
[2]   ⍝ NRD=1 AND NWR=0
[3]    PORTA←D0D7
[4]    WAIT 'NWR=1'
[5]    INTRA←0
[6]    PA0PA7←PORTA
[7]    NOBFA←0
    ∇
    ∇ PORTAM1OUT2
[1]   ⍝ PORT A MODE 1 OUTPUT PORT A TO DEVICE
[2]   ⍝ NACKA=0
[3]    NOBFA←1
[4]    WAIT 'NACKA=1'
[5]    →IF INTEA=1
[6]   THEN:INTRA←1
[7]   ENDIF:
    ∇
```

MICROCOMPUTERS: Developments in Industry, Business and Education
D.R. Wilson and C.J. van Spronsen (eds.) / ©EUROMICRO, 1983
Elsevier Science Publishers B.V. (North-Holland)

THE DESCRIPTION OF BOARD LEVEL COMPONENTS FOR COMPUTER-AIDED DESIGN OF MICROPROCESSOR APPLICATION SYSTEMS

J. A. Bowen

Department of Computer Science, University of Reading,
Reading RG6 2AX, United Kingdom

A program which automates the configuration of microprocessor application systems using pre-designed boards is briefly described. This program has access to a database of pre-designed boards. The model used by this database to represent such board level components is described. Particular emphasis is given in this paper to the method of describing the functionality of a board. The designer program uses experience to guide its design decisions. Part of this experience is reflected in value judgements about the effectiveness of various boards in the database. This aspect of a board's description is also mentioned.

Design of microprocessor applications

A microprocessor application can be described in terms of the following attributes:

* hardware requirements
* software requirements
* design constraints

The hardware requirements are a list of the types and quantities of processor, memory and interface needed by the application. The software requirements consist of the transformations that must be applied by the processor(s) to the data in the memory and at the interfaces. The design constraints specify the allowable limits for development time and cost, production cost, power consumption, physical size and so on, and their relative importance.

A design solution for a microprocessor application is a configuration of hardware and software elements which provides the hardware and software requirements of the application. An acceptable design solution is one which provides these requirements and which also satisfies the limits imposed by the design constraints. The optimum solution is that which satisfies these limits with the widest weighted margin (using the relative importance of the design constraints as weighting factors).

A designer of microprocessor application systems has available to him a range of hardware and software components. These components have certain capabilities, for example the ability to store data or the ability to transform data from one format to another. The designer's task is to choose the set of hardware and software components which provides the corresponding needs of the application at minimum cost.

There are two main approaches to hardware design for microprocessor applications: special boards can be designed using device level components (ICs, resistors, and so on) or a set of pre-designed boards can be configured [1]. It is possible, of course, to use both approaches at once: a set of pre-designed boards can be used in conjunction with some new boards specially designed to provide functions not previously available.

In a manner analogous to hardware design, software design can be conducted at the instruction level, at the routine level or using a combination of instruction level and routine level components.

Hardware design using board level components

MAPLE is a computer-aided design system for microprocessor applications. It is intended that MAPLE will, eventually, be able to design hardware using both board and device level components and to assist in the design of software using routine level components. At present, however, MAPLE is limited to hardware design using board level components. Although MAPLE is presently primarily concerned with hardware design it does attempt to facilitate software development by choosing a design based on a processor device for which good development support is available in the laboratory.

Each MAPLE run has three stages: INTERVIEW, DESIGN and REPORT. During the interview stage, MAPLE learns the hardware resources needed by the application and the design constraints that apply (Figure 1). During the design stage, MAPLE uses its knowledge to design a system which provides the resources and satisfies the constraints. During the report stage, MAPLE issues a design report which includes the original specification, as well as a complete set of documentation for the design.

```
            MAPLE
            =====

Microprocessor Applications Expert
==================================

INTERVIEW:
=========

Your user identity number? 2
Your password?
Please classify your project? Local Network Interface
Your project's title? CHIMP

Interface Requirements:
======================
Do you want any serial interfaces?YES
Do you want asynchronous serial interfaces?YES
   Do you want selectable baud rate?YES
      Baud Rate Selection: programmable?NO
                           strappable?YES
      Required Baud Rates: 110?NO 300?YES
         600?NO 1200?NO 9600?YES Other?NO
   External Interface:RS-232C? YES
   Do you want modem control? NO
   Do you want selectable character size? NO
      Character size required:7data+OddParity+2stop?NO
                              7data+EvenParity+2stop?YES
   How many resources of this type do you want?1

Do you want any more asynchronous serial interfaces?NO
Do you want any bit-oriented synchronous serial interfaces?YES
   Do you want selectable protocol?NO
      Required protocol:SDLC?NO HDLC?YES
   External Interface:RS-232C?NO RS-422?YES
   How many resources of this type do you want?1

Do you want any more bit-oriented synchronous serial
interfaces?NO
Do you want any parallel interfaces?NO
Do you want any analogue interfaces?NO
Do you want any other type of interface?NO

Memory Requirements:
===================
Do you want any erasable programmable read-only memory?YES
  How many bytes?3k
Do you want any battery-backed random-access memory?NO
Do you want any volatile random-access memory? YES
  How many bytes?1k

Processor Requirements:
======================
Data word size: 8 bit?YES

Other Requirements:
==================
Do you need a real-time clock?NO
Do you have any other requirements?NO

Design Constraints:
==================
Power consumption limit (watts)?2        Importance of this limit [0-5]?2
Development Time limit  (days)?30        Importance of this limit [0-5]?4
Development Cost limit (pounds)?2000     Importance of this limit [0-5]?3
Production Cost limit (pounds)?75        Importance of this limit [0-5]?5

Expected production:
===================
How many do you expect to make?100

Development Support Required:
============================
     High-level language support?NO
     Assembly language support?YES
     In-circuit Emulation?YES


INTERVIEW SUMMARY
=================

     (the results of the interview are summarised here)

Is this correct?YES

DESIGN:
======
Mono-board computers are on file
Boards compatible with the following buses are on file:
  S-100 Bus, Multibus, Green Bus II, RBug-09 Bus
Do you want to limit the design search to any families of boards?YES
  Do you want to consider Mono-board computers?YES
  Do you want to consider these buses: S-100 BUS?NO Multibus?NO
            Green Bus II?YES RBug-09 Bus?YES

Your hardware requirements can be satisfied by a set of
2 Green Bus boards.
Your design constraints cannot be satisfied:
    The best design requires 4 watts
    Will you accept this?YES

REPORT:
======
```

Figure 1: A typical MAPLE consultation.

An important element of an automated system for the design of microprocessor applications is some method of describing application needs and component features which facilitates the matching of these needs and features. MAPLE's approach is the resource concept. An application is described as requiring certain resources, while components are described as providing certain resources. MAPLE's schema for resources is flexible and completely user-definable: MAPLE can learn about new types of resources. Initially, however, a MAPLE installation knows about processor resources, memory resources and the more common types of interface resource. The resource concept, by providing a common basis for describing application needs and component features, facilitates one important sub-task of the design problem: recognition of which components are potentially useful for a given application.

The application's resource requirements, as learned during the interview stage, are a set of descriptions, each description being a sequence of descriptors. The hardware requirements of the system under consideration in Figure 1 are shown in Table 1.

```
Application: CHIMP
===========
  No. of resource types: 5

    Resource Type 1:
      Description: interface, serial, asynchronous,
                   strappable baud rate, 300 baud, 9600 baud,
                   RS-232C, 7data+EvenParity+2stop
      No. required: 1

    Resource Type 2:
      Description: interface, serial, synchronous,
                   bit-oriented, HDLC, RS-422
      No. required: 1

    Resource Type 3:
      Description: memory, read-only, programmable,
                   erasable
      No. required: 3072

    Resource Type 4:
      Description: memory, random-access, volatile
      No. required: 1024

    Resource Type 5:
      Description: processor, 8 bit
      No. required: 1
```

Table 1: The hardware resources required by the application in Figure 1.

MAPLE refers to several databases when making its design decisions. One of these, called BOARDS, contains information about board level components (i.e. pre-designed boards) known to the system. These boards are organised into families. Within each family MAPLE tries to generate design solutions by matching the resource requirements of the application with the resource provisions of the boards in the family. A design solution is a combination of compatible boards which provides the resources required by the application.

Each entry in the BOARDS database contains information about the hardware attributes of the board and a description of the resources provided by the board. The program which updates the BOARDS database is driven by a decision tree containing a schema for resources. This same tree drives MAPLE's interviewer sub-program. This ensures compatibility of resource description between an application's requirements as defined during an interview and the entries in the BOARDS database. This schema tree is flexible and user-definable. As new types of resource occur the schema can be modified. Boards containing these new types of resource can then be stored in the database. Applications requiring these new types of resource can then be processed.

Board Descriptions

Each board in the BOARDS database is described in the following terms:

```
  * list-of-families
  * bus-master-board/bus-slave-board
  * has-processor-resource/has-not-processor-
                                     resource
      if has-processor-resource then
          * name-of-the-processor-device
  * list-of-clock-speeds
  * house-made-board/bought-in-board
      if house-made-board then
          * basic-board-layout
          * assembly-time
      if bought-in-board then
          * list-of-manufacturers
          * list-of-prices
          * total-power-consumption-of-basic-
                                     board
  * backplane-bus-loading
  * backplane-bus-driving-capability
  * physical-dimensions (length, width, depth
                                and weight)
  * range-of-operating-temperatures
  * list-of-resource-sectors
```

The field called list-of-resource-sectors is concerned with describing the functional resources provided by the board. The other fields describe the hardware attributes of the board: compatibility, layout, physical dimensions, and so on. The hardware description will now be discussed briefly, and the functional description will be considered in more detail in a later section.

Mono-board computers (stand-alone boards which cannot be connected to a backplane) are not compatible with any family of boards and their list-of-families will, consequently, be empty. Other boards are compatible with some family or other of boards, for example, the Multibus family or the VME bus family. Most boards belong to only one family. Some boards, however, may be compatible with several families and this possibility is catered for by allowing a board to have a list-of-families. Bus "standards" and families are not synonymous. A tightly specified bus, such as Multibus, forms the basis of a coherent family of boards. A less tightly specified bus may form the basis of several over-lapping families. For example, boards based on the STD bus have to be divided into at least two families. One family comprises boards which are compatible with processors from the Intel family and the Z80. A second family consists of boards that are compatible with the 6800-type processors. Some boards, such as memory boards, may belong to both families [2].

Boards can be either masters or slaves of the backplane bus. Each family places a limit on the number of bus-master boards that can be configured, and MAPLE avoids configurations which exceed these limits.

Some bus-masters provide a processor resource to execute application programs. Other bus-masters do not provide a processor resource, for example, interface boards with DMA capability. If a board has-processor-resource then the name-of-the-processor-device used to implement this processor resource is noted. MAPLE's databases contain information about the development facilities (cross-assemblers and -compilers, in circuit emulators and so on) available in the application design laboratory. During the design stage of a consultation MAPLE chooses a solution based on a processor device for which good development facilities are available.

MAPLE, at present, only configures uni-processor systems. It is assumed that the backplane clock is generated by the cpu-board. Each board has a list of the backplane clock-speeds with which it is compatible. For a cpu-board, this is a list of the backplane clock speeds which it can generate. For any other type of board, it is a list of the backplane clock speeds which it can accept.

The boards known to MAPLE are classed as being either house-made (that is designed by and assembled to the specifications of the laboratory), or bought-in (that is boards whose design and assembly are not under the control of the laboratory). These two classes of board are treated slightly differently. The basic-board-layout of a house-made board (the devices used to construct the board, the positions and orientations of these devices and the pin-connections between them) is noted and can be documented during the REPORT stage of a consultation. The devices used to construct house-made boards are all documented in another of MAPLE's databases, the DEVICES database. During a consultation MAPLE can calculate the power consumption of a house-made board by summing the power consumed by the constituent devices. The time in man-hours needed to assemble a house-made board is also noted. This means that MAPLE can, by using the current cost of a man-hour and the costs of the constituent devices, calculate the cost of a house-made board. Bought-in boards, on the other hand, are treated essentially as "black-boxes". No attempt is made to document the basic layout of a bought-in board. A list of the companies manufacturing the board, a set of prices (different batch sizes and different vendors) and the total-power-consumption of the board are noted.

The above remarks refer to a basic board, that is the basic configuration of the board. Most boards, whether bought-in or house-made, can accept certain standard predefined modifications, for example the addition of extra devices, to provide different combinations of resources. These modifications are documented, for both house-made and bought-in boards, as part of the description of a board's resource provisions.

There is a limit to the number of boards that can be configured in an application system. MAPLE is able to avoid exceeding this limit because it knows the backplane-bus-loading and backplane-bus-driving-capability characteristics of each board in its database.

MAPLE does not yet consider the design constraints that may be imposed by limitations on physical size and exacting operating-conditions. Provision is made for this, however, by storing the physical-dimensions and range-of-operating-temperatures of each board.

Functional Description

The functional description of a board is a description of the resources that are provided by the board. Many boards provide optional resources. Some boards require external provision of certain resources in order to function correctly. In order to represent these various possibilities a fairly complex structure is required. This structure is called the list-of-resource-sectors. The rest of this paper is concerned with describing this structure.

MAPLE has several classes of user. Users who wish only to avail of MAPLE's expertise and experience in designing application hardware need not be aware of the complexity of the list-of-resource-sectors structure. Only those users who introduce new boards to the database need appreciate the description structure which is outlined in the rest of this paper.

Briefly, for the purposes of describing the resources provided, each board is said to have one or more resource-sectors. Resource-sectors can accommodate different resource-bundles.

A resource-bundle is an indivisible collection of resource-provisions. A resource-provision is the hardware implementation of a resource-bunch. A resource-bunch is a contiguous collection of resources all of the same type.

Consider a board which provides a cpu, an asynchronous interface, a ROM-based monitor, and a memory socket capable of holding either a 4K EPROM device or a 2K RAM device. This board would be described as having two resource-sectors (Table 2). The memory socket constitutes one resource-sector. It is able to accommodate either of two resource-bundles. Each of these resource-bundles contains only one resource-provision: the first bundle provides 4K of EPROM; the second bundle provides 2K of RAM. The rest of the board constitutes the second resource-sector. This resource-sector accommodates one fixed resource-bundle. This bundle contains three resource-provisions: cpu, asynchronous interface, ROM-based monitor.

These concepts will now be considered in more detail. Each resource-sector is described as follows:

* list-of-swoppable-bundles
* comes-empty/does-not-come-empty

Into each resource-sector it is possible to plug different resource-bundles. On many boards a combination of memory sockets would, for example, be regarded as a resource-sector. Into this sector different resource-bundles could be plugged. These resource-bundles would, typically, provide different combinations and amounts of RAM and EPROM. On a basic board it is possible that a resource sector comes-empty, or it may contain some default resource bundle which has to be removed before plugging in one of the alternative bundles in the list-of-swoppable-bundles.

Each member of the list-of-swoppable-bundles is an item of type resource-bundle. A resource-bundle is described as follows:

* list-of-resource-provisions
* list-of-extra-devices
  if house-made-board then
    * list-of-strappings
* time-to-modify-basic-board
* list-of-resource-requirements

As implied by their names, the list-of-resource-provisions, the list-of-extra-devices and the list-of-strappings are lists of items of type resource-provision, extra-device and strapping, respectively. The list-of-resource-provisions describes the resources that are provided by the resource-bundle. The list-of-extra-devices specifies the devices that must be plugged into the resource-sector in order to implement this resource-bundle. The list-of-strappings describes the pin-strappings that must be made to accommodate these extra devices. The time-to-modify-basic-board estimates the number of man-hours required to modify the basic board in order to accommodate this resource-bundle; this information is needed to enable the cost of the modified board to be calculated.

Most resource-bundles are self-sufficient in that they do not require, for their correct operation, external provision of any other resources. There are, however, some resource-bundles that do require external provision of resources: for example a dynamic memory board may require external provision of memory refresh, or a processor board that contained no ROM would require that a start-up ROM be provided by some other board. To cope with this type of situation, MAPLE allows a resource-bundle to have a list-of-resource-requirements. In any configuration using this resource-bundle these resource requirements must be provided by other bundles.

A resource-provision is described as follows:

* resource-bunch
* memory-address-block
* i/o-address-block
* interrupt-address-block
* value-judgements
* software-driver-routines
* time-taken-to-design-and-implement

The resource-bunch field comprises two-subfields: resource-description and number-provided. The resource-description is a sequence of descriptors describing the type of resource provided, while number-provided states how many resources of this type are provided by the resource-provision.

A resource-provision is a concrete instance of an abstract resource-bunch. This concrete realization must be further defined. The address-blocks occupied by the resource-provision must be specified. Three types of address space are allowed: memory, input/output and interrupt. A resource-provision may occupy some or all these types of address space. For example, on a board based on a simple backplane bus a memory resource would only occupy memory address space, but on a Multibus board a memory resource may occupy both memory and input/output address space [3].

MAPLE uses feedback from previous applications to guide its design decision-making. Part of this experience consists of value-judgements on the resource-provisions offered by the boards in the database. A resource-bunch is an abstract and, therefore, ideal entity. The value-judgements attached to a resource-provision are measures of how well it meets this ideal.

If a resource-provision requires a software-driver-routine, MAPLE accumulates experience of the routines used to drive the resource-

```
FUNCTIONAL DESCRIPTION:
======================

This is a CPU-board based on the MC6809.
No. of resource sectors: 2.

Resource Sector #1:
==================
    Sector comes empty.           No. of bundles: 2.

        Bundle #1:      No. of provisions: 1.
        =========
            Provision #1:
            ============
                Description: memory, read-only,
                             programmable, erasable.
                No. provided: 4096.

        Bundle #2:      No. of provisions: 1.
        =========
            Provision #1:
            ============
                Description: memory, random-access,
                             volatile.
                No. provided: 2048.

Resource Sector #2:
==================
    Sector does not come empty.   No. of bundles: 1.

        Bundle #1:      No. of provisions: 3.
        =========
            Provision #1:
            ============
                Description: processor, 8 bit.
                No. provided: 1.

            Provision #2:
            ============
                Description: interface, serial, asynchronous,
                             strappable baud rate, 9600 baud,
                             1200 baud, 300 baud, RS-232C,
                             programmable char size,
                             7data+EvenParity+2stop,
                             7data+OddParity+2stop.
                No. provided: 1.

            Provision #3:
            ============
                Description: memory, read-only,
                             fixed-contents, monitor.
                No. provided: 1.
```

Table 2: Extract from a board description, showing only the resource descriptions and their organization into provisions, bundles and sectors.

provision in past applications and this information is also used to guide MAPLE's design decisions.

If known, MAPLE stores the time-taken-to-design-and-implement the resource-provision; this information is used to estimate how long it would take to design and implement similar resource-provisions.

As mentioned earlier, it may be necessary to modify the basic hardware of a board in order to provide one of the optional resource-bundles. These modifications may simply involve the insertion of different devices into some of the sockets on the board, or they may also involve some pin strapping. MAPLE only documents these pin-strappings for house-made boards: strappings for bought-in boards are documented in the manufacturer's literature.

MAPLE documents the device changes required to implement an optional resource-bundle, by listing the extra-devices required. Extra-devices are described as follows:

```
*  device-name
   if house-made-board then
         *  position-of-socket
```

They are handled slightly differently for bought-in and house-made boards. On bought-in boards no attempt is made to document the positioning of an extra-device. On house-made boards an extra-device is positioned by referring to the socket on the basic-board-layout into which it must be inserted.

The future

MAPLE's model for board level components facilitates a form of design reasoning similar to the general model of design reasoning proposed by Freeman and Newell [4]. It is intended to develop a similar model and line of reasoning for design using device level components.

REFERENCES

[1] Roop, G.C., Cummings, W.C. and Burckle, R., Designing with compact boards as components, Computer Design vol 21 no. 3 (1982) 175-178.

[2] Elsmore, T., Standard bus for 8-bit microprocessor systems, Microprocessors and Microsystems vol 6 no 9 (1982) 455-465.

[3] Barthmaier, J., Intel Multibus Interfacing (Intel Corporation, application note AP-28A, 1979).

[4] Freeman, P. and Newell, A., A Model for Functional Reasoning in Design, in Proceedings, International Joint Conference on Artificial Intelligence II, 621-640.

MICROCOMPUTERS: Developments in Industry, Business and Education
D.R. Wilson and C.J. van Spronsen (eds.) / ©EUROMICRO, 1983
Elsevier Science Publishers B.V. (North-Holland)

HARDWARE AND SOFTWARE TOOLS FOR ASYNCHRONOUS SYSTEMS SYNTHESIS WITH MICROPROCESSORS

Enrique Mandado and Perfecto Mariño

Department of Automatic and Electronic Engineering, Industrial Engineering
University, Vigo, Spain

This paper describes a method of asynchronous systems design, defined through input variable edges.
Specifications of the system are made first by a sequential diagram. From this diagram algebraic equations are systematically obtained. This equations are introduced in a microcomputer through a PASCAL program called SPECIFICATION. Another program translates the equations into a machine language program for a specified microprocessor.
A multiprocessor structure has been developed to achieve systematic system implementation. Finally two LSI DMA circuits especially designed for binary variable inputs and outputs are proposed.

1. INTRODUCTION

The asynchronous systems synthesis method, defined through input variable edges [1], [2], [3], allows systematic specification through an operations flowchart. Implementation by means of a microcomputer system, achives systematic design.

Recent developments in integrated technologies mark a trend in hardware-software tradeoff towards hardware superiority.

This paper presents a multiprocessor structure with a two port access RAM memory and a DMA processor. This one is implemented with two LSI integrated circuits in order to achieve a modular and systematic hardware design (Fig. 1).

To translate the asynchronous system performance specifications into a program that manages the above mentioned circuits, we implement PASCAL language programs that systematize the design.

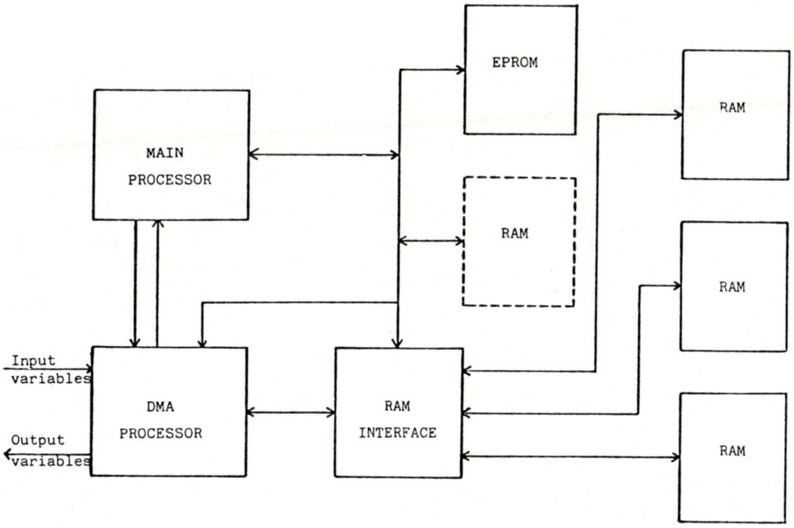

Fig. 1. Multiprocessor block diagram

The asynchronous sequential systems synthesis with a microcomputer implies a large number of input variables connections across different channels. By other hand, input channels number can change largely for different applications. This situation makes the input programmable peripheral circuits unappropiated for this application by two reasons:

a) complexity to select a large number of input-output circuits.
b) need of executing an input-output sweep program.

The program contained into the EPROM memory must only simulate the asynchronous sistem flowchart.

The proposed synthesis of control asynchronous systems with microprocessors, covers therefore the following design looks:

a) Software:

- Aid programs for asynchronous system specification in a standard way. (SPECIFICATION program).
- Aid programs to implement the program that performs the asynchronous system flowchart and its writing into an EPROM memory (SIMULATOR program).

b) Hardware:

- A multiprocessor architecture system. (Fig. 1)
- Proposal of LSI integrated circuits for DMA real time performance.

2. SYNTHESIS AID PROGRAMS

Programs to which the designer is in dialogue during synthesis are written in PASCAL. This language has been chosen by its structurated modularity and adresses memory access capability features.

The asynchronous system specification is made by means of a program called SPECIFICATION, that allows an interactive handling with the designer. To answer to interactive program questions, the transition capacities and flowchart states must be written in a specific way. This one is related with the asynchronous sistems design method defined through input variable edges.

This method characterises transitions between states by means of transition capacity C_{IJ}. When this binary variable reaches logic one value, the asynchronous system goes from E_I to E_J (Fig. 2a). The different equations for transition capacity are displayed in Fig. 2b. The meaning of the symbols that appears in those equations are the following:

x_i : input variable.
X_β : vector including all input variables.
X^i_β : vector without the input variable x_i.
X'_β : vector including a certain number of input variables.
$x_i\updownarrow$: change of input variable x_i.
$X_\alpha\updownarrow$: change of an input vector.

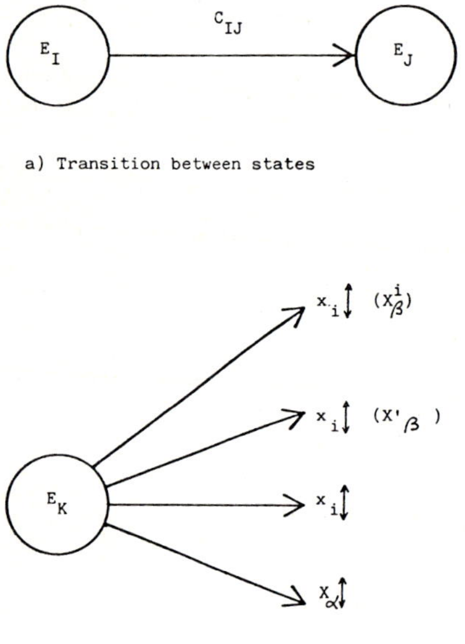

Fig. 2. Asynchronous system flowchart symbols.

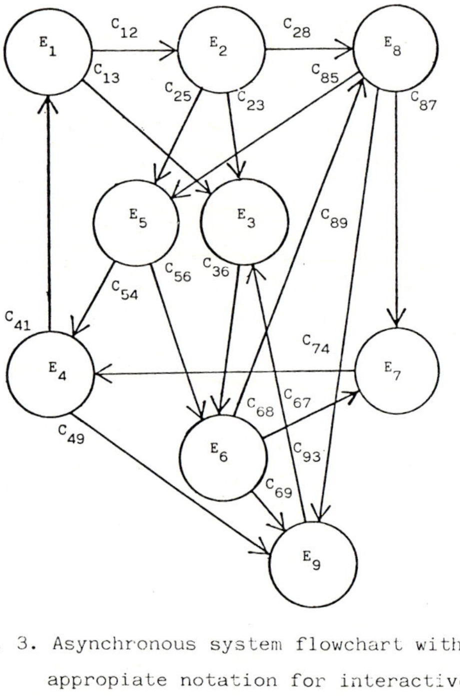

Fig. 3. Asynchronous system flowchart with appropiate notation for interactive program.

Fig. 3 shows an asynchronous system flowchart whose states (9), transition capacities (18) and input variables (4) have been arbitrary chosen. The logic equations of flowchart transition capacities are:

$$C_{12} = x_1\downarrow \; (X^1_\beta) \quad ; \quad X^1_\beta = x_3\, x_4\, \overline{x}_2$$
$$C_{13} = x_3\uparrow \; (X^3_\gamma) \quad ; \quad X^3_\gamma = \overline{x}_1\, x_2\, \overline{x}_4$$
$$C_{23} = x_3\uparrow \; (X'_\alpha) \quad ; \quad X'_\alpha = \overline{x}_2\, x_1$$
$$C_{25} = x_3\downarrow \; (X'_\delta) \quad ; \quad X'_\delta = \overline{x}_4$$
$$C_{28} = X'_\varepsilon\uparrow \quad ; \quad X'_\varepsilon = \overline{x}_1\, x_4$$
$$C_{36} = x_2\downarrow \; (X'_\psi) \quad ; \quad X'_\psi = x_3\, \overline{x}_2$$
$$C_{41} = x_2\uparrow \; (X'_\eta) \quad ; \quad X'_\eta = \overline{x}_1$$
$$C_{49} = x_4\uparrow \; (X^4_\mu) \quad ; \quad X^4_\mu = x_2\, x_3\, \overline{x}_1$$
$$C_{54} = X'_\sigma\downarrow \quad ; \quad X'_\sigma = x_1\, x_4$$
$$C_{56} = x_1\uparrow \; (X'_\lambda) \quad ; \quad X'_\lambda = \overline{x}_4\, x_2$$
$$C_{67} = x_2\uparrow \; (X'_k) \quad ; \quad X'_k = x_1$$
$$C_{69} = x_2\uparrow \; (X'_\tau) \quad ; \quad X'_\tau = x_3\, \overline{x}_1$$
$$C_{68} = x_2\downarrow$$
$$C_{74} = x_4\downarrow \; (X'_\psi)$$
$$C_{89} = x_3\uparrow \; (X^1_\beta)$$
$$C_{87} = X'_\theta\downarrow \quad ; \quad X'_\theta = \overline{x}_4\, x_1$$
$$C_{85} = x_2\uparrow \; (X'_\theta)$$
$$C_{93} = x_4\downarrow \; (X^4_\omega) \quad ; \quad X^4_\omega = \overline{x}_3\, x_1\, x_2$$

The interactive SPECIFICATION program uses integers to characterise the input variables and its assignment is free. States are ordered through integer indexes assigned from the departure state E_1 until the last state E_9 (Figure 3). Level or edge characterized input variables are adapted to the possibilities of CRT information display and keyboard input system. For this purpose, the following equivalences are used:

SYMBOL	EQUIVALENCE
$\uparrow$	>
$\downarrow$	<
x_i	i+
$\overline{x}_i$	i-

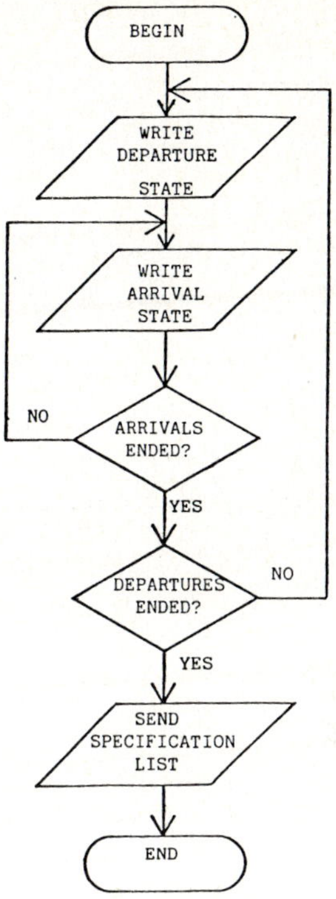

Fig. 4. SPECIFICATION interactive program flowchart.

Table 1 shows transition capacity equations obtained as a printer output of SPECIFICACTION program (Fig. 4).

In each state the program asks to the designer for its arrival states, and correspondent transition capacities. Once the arrival states for a determined state are finished, the process is repeated over the next state. When the flowchart last state is reached, SPECIFICATION program sends the asynchronous system specification list to the printer. Table 1 shows the list obtained for the example in Figure 3. This document allows debug operations before the designer goes ahead in the asynchronous system synthesis. Table 2 presents the list of a SPECIFICATION program simplified version.

The asynchronous system design next step is to write within an EPROM memory the simulation program that executes its flowchart. This program is obtained through the transition capacities equations from the previous step by another PASCAL translator program.

3. ASYNCHRONOUS SYSTEM SIMULATION PROGRAM

The proposed multiprocessor structure (Figure 1) performs asynchronous system simulation and other differents tasks, simultáneously with DMA binary input and output variables.

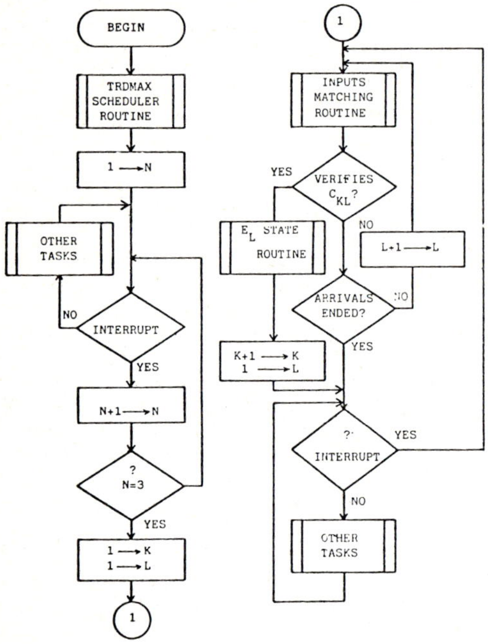

Fig. 5. MAIN PROCESSOR program flowchart.

RAM memories are conventional ones and an interface system converts them into two port RAM memories. The whole memory is divided into three sections. At the same time that the MAIN PROCESSOR reads or writes two sections, the other one is accessed by the DMA PROCESSOR. When a DMA cycle ends, several actions occur:

a) A new DMA cycle begins with a different RAM.

b) The MAIN PROCESSOR is interrupted and the simulation routine (INPUTS MATCHING ROUTINE) begins (Fig. 5).

The different RAM sections are sequentially accesed by the MAIN PROCESSOR and the DMA PROCESSOR. This sequential access is managed by the DMA PROCESSOR and the MAIN PROCESSOR always sees the same memory locations. The result is that the proposed hardware solution simplifies asynchronous system simulation program and makes possible the design of very complex real time controllers.

Fig. 5 shows the MAIN PROCESSOR program flowchart. It starts with a DMA PROCESSOR initiation routine (TRDMAX SCHEDULER ROUTINE). The asynchronous system simulation begins after two DMA cycles (detected by two interrupt requests) and is alternated with other tasks.

Table 1

```
********************************************************************************
*                              SPECIFICATION LIST                              *
********************************************************************************

--------------------------------------------------------------------------------

  1       DEPARTURE STATE = E  1        ARRIVAL STATES  =   2,   3,

     1      C  1.  2 = 1<(3+,4+,2-)
     2      C  1.  3 = 3>(1-,2+,4-)

--------------------------------------------------------------------------------

  2       DEPARTURE STATE = E  2        ARRIVAL STATES  =   3,   5,   8,

     3      C  2.  3 = 3>(2-,1+)
     4      C  2.  5 = 3<(4-)
     5      C  2.  8 = >(1-,4+)

--------------------------------------------------------------------------------

  3       DEPARTURE STATE = E  3        ARRIVAL STATES  =   6,

     6      C  3.  6 = 2<(3+,2-)

--------------------------------------------------------------------------------

  4       DEPARTURE STATE = E  4        ARRIVAL STATES  =   1,   9,

     7      C  4.  1 = 2>(1-)
     8      C  4.  9 = 4>(2+,3+,1-)

--------------------------------------------------------------------------------

  5       DEPARTURE STATE = E  5        ARRIVAL STATES  =   4,   6,

     9      C  5.  4 = <(1+,4+)
    10      C  5.  6 = 1>(4-,2+)

--------------------------------------------------------------------------------
```

```
6       DEPARTURE STATE = E  6        ARRIVAL STATES  =   7,   8,   9,

  11      C  6.  7 = 2)(1+)
  12      C  6.  8 = (2()
  13      C  6.  9 = 2)(3+,1-)

--------------------------------------------------------------------------------

 7      DEPARTURE STATE = E  7        ARRIVAL STATES  =   4,

  14      C  7.  4 = 4((3+,2-)

--------------------------------------------------------------------------------

8       DEPARTURE STATE = E  8        ARRIVAL STATES  =   5,   7,   9,

  15      C  8.  5 = 2)(4-,1+)
  16      C  8.  7 = ((4-,1+)
  17      C  8.  9 = 3)(3+,4+,2-)

--------------------------------------------------------------------------------

 9      DEPARTURE STATE = E  9        ARRIVAL STATES  =   3,

  18      C  9.  3 = 4((3-,1+,2+)

*******************************************************************************
*                          DIAGRAM STATES TOTAL NUMBER    9                  *
*                             EQUATIONS TOTAL NUMBER    18                   *
*******************************************************************************
```

Table 2

```
PROGRAM  SPECIFICATION  ;
(*LISTS THE  FLOWCHART TRANSITION CAPACITIES EQUATIONS*)

TYPE
  MARGEN = 1..100 ;
  NUMEST = ARRAY [MARGEN] OF INTEGER ;
  LISNUM = ARRAY [MARGEN,MARGEN]  OF INTEGER ;
  LISCAP = ARRAY [MARGEN,MARGEN] OF CHAR ;

VAR
  CORREGIR : BOOLEAN ;
  I,J,K,EO,ED : INTEGER ;
  TOTDES,ESTORIG,LISTDEST,CODALFA : NUMEST ;
  TABDES : LISNUM ;
  TABCAP : LISCAP ;


PROCEDURE LEEOR ( VAR ORIGEN:INTEGER ) ;
(*TAKES DEPARTURE STATES AND CHECKS THE LAST*)
BEGIN
   IF CORREGIR THEN WRITELN (PRINTER , '-----LEEOR BEGINNING---') ;
   WRITELN ('TYPE DEPARTURE STATE NUMBER') ;
   WRITELN ;
   READLN (ORIGEN) ;

   IF ORIGEN (= 0  THEN
       BEGIN          (*CHECKS FLOWCHART END*)
          WRITELN ('FLOWCHART IS FINISHED ?') ;
          WRITELN ('YES:TYPE 0 . NO: TYPE ITS NUMBER') ;
          WRITELN ;
          READLN (ORIGEN)
       END ;

    IF CORREGIR THEN WRITELN (PRINTER , '*LEEOR END*') ;
    WRITELN (PRINTER)
END  ;

PROCEDURE LEEDES ( VAR DESTINO:INTEGER ) ;
(*TAKES ARRIVAL STATES AND CHECKS THE LAST*)
BEGIN
    IF CORREGIR THEN WRITELN (PRINTER , '((LEEDES BEGINNING))') ;
    WRITELN ;
    WRITELN ('TYPE ARRIVAL STATE NUMBER') ;
    READLN (DESTINO) ;

    IF DESTINO (=  0 THEN
       BEGIN        (*CHECKS THE LAST ARRIVAL STATE*)
```

```
                    WRITELN ('ARRIVAL STATES ARE FINISHED ?') ;
                    WRITELN ('YES : TYPE 0 , NO : TYPE ITS NUMBER') ;
                    WRITELN ;
                    READLN (DESTINO)
                 END ;

    IF CORREGIR THEN WRITELN (PRINTER , '*LEEDES END*') ;
    WRITELN (PRINTER)
END ;

PROCEDURE LEECAP (ECUACION:INTEGER) ;
(*TAKES EVERY ARRIVAL STATE TRANSITION CAPACITY*)
     CONST
        BLANCO = ' ' ;
        PARENT = ')' ;
     VAR
        COD : CHAR ;
        I   : INTEGER ;
BEGIN
   IF CORREGIR THEN WRITELN (PRINTER , '*LEECAP BEGINNING*') ;

   WRITELN ('TYPE TRANSITION CAPACITY   C', EO:2 , '.' , ED:2 ,
                  '  THROUGH INTEGERS AND SIGNS ') ;
   WRITELN ('FIRST EDGE VARIABLE AND THEN LEVEL VARIABLES BETWEEN ROUND ' ,
                                    ' BRACKETS ') ;
   WRITELN ;
   COD := BLANCO ;
   WHILE (COD = BLANCO) DO READ (COD) ;
   I := 1 ;

   REPEAT
      TABCAP[ECUACION , I] := COD ;
      READ (COD) ;
      I := I + 1
   UNTIL COD = PARENT ;

   TABCAP [ECUACION , I]  :=  COD ;
   CODALFA [ECUACION] := I ;
   IF CORREGIR THEN WRITELN (PRINTER , '*LEECAP END*') ;
   WRITELN (PRINTER)
END ;

PROCEDURE LISTADO (TOR , TEC : INTEGER ) ;
(*LISTS ALL TRANSITION CAPACITIES FOR EVERY DEPARTURE STATE*)
   VAR
       M,N,P,R : INTEGER ;
BEGIN
   IF CORREGIR THEN WRITELN (PRINTER , '*LISTADO BEGINNING*') ;
   WRITELN (PRINTER) ;
   WRITELN (PRINTER , '****************************************************' ,
                      '***************************' ) ;
   WRITELN (PRINTER , '*                              SPECIFICATION LIST     ' ,
                      '                            *' ) ;
   WRITELN (PRINTER , '****************************************************' ,
                      '***************************' ) ;
   WRITELN (PRINTER) ;
   P := 1 ;

   FOR M := 1  TO  TOR  DO
      BEGIN       (*DEPARTURE STATE LINE*)
         WRITELN (PRINTER , '----------------------------------------------' ,
                            '--------------------------------' ) ;
         WRITELN (PRINTER) ;
         WRITE   (PRINTER , M:3 , '       DEPARTURE STATE = E' ,  ESTORIG[M]:3 ,
                        '            ARRIVAL STATES  = ' ) ;
         FOR N := 1 TO TOTDES[M] DO WRITE (PRINTER , TABDES[M,N]:3 ,', ' ) ;
         WRITELN (PRINTER) ;
         WRITELN (PRINTER) ;
         FOR N := 1  TO TOTDES[M] DO
            BEGIN
               WRITE   (PRINTER , '    ' , P:3 , '      C' , ESTORIG[M]:3 , '.' ,
                        TABDES[M,N]:3  , ' = ' ) ;
               FOR R := 1 TO CODALFA[P] DO WRITE (PRINTER,TABCAP[P,R]) ;
               P := P+1 ;
               WRITELN (PRINTER)
            END ;

         WRITELN (PRINTER)
      END ;

   WRITELN (PRINTER , '****************************************************' ,
                      '***************************' ) ;
   WRITELN (PRINTER , '*                          DIAGRAM STATES TOTAL NUMBER  ' ,
                      TOR:3 ,     '                          *' ) ;
   WRITELN (PRINTER , '*                              EQUATIONS TOTAL NUMBER   ' ,
                      TEC:3 ,     '                          *' ) ;
   WRITELN (PRINTER , '****************************************************' ,
                      '***************************' ) ;
```

```
   WRITELN (PRINTER) ;
   IF CORREGIR THEN WRITELN (PRINTER , '*LISTADO END*')
END ;

BEGIN                    (*MAIN PROGRAM*)

   CORREGIR := FALSE;
   IF CORREGIR THEN WRITELN ( PRINTER , '= SPECIFICATION  PROGRAM =' ) ;
   I := 1 ;
   K := 1 ;
   LEEOR (EO) ;

   WHILE  EO ) 0  DO

      BEGIN
         ESTORIG[I] := EO ;
         J := 1 ;
         LEEDES(ED) ;

         WHILE ED ) 0  DO
          BEGIN
            TABDES[I,J] := ED ;
            LISTDEST[K] := ED ;
            LEECAP(K) ;
            K := K + 1 ;
            J := J + 1 ;
            LEEDES(ED)
          END ;

         J := J - 1 ;
         TOTDES[I] := J ;
         I := I + 1 ;
         LEEOR (EO)
      END ;

   K := K - 1 ;
   I := I - 1 ;
   LISTADO (I , K) ;
   IF CORREGIR THEN WRITELN (PRINTER , '= SPECIFICATION END=')
END .
```

4. MULTIPROCESSOR ARCHITECTURE HARDWARE

The proposed asyncronous system synthesis implements the hardware specified in Figure 1 by means of conventional and specially developed - integrated circuits. MAIN PROCESSOR, EPROM and RAM blocks are conventional microprocessor and memories respectively. The other circuits are described in the following paragraphs.

DMA controllers have been implemented in LSI circuits but only for a few parallel ports [4],[5]. An asynchronous system has a lot of inputs and outputs so special DMA circuits are neccesary.

4.1 LSI INTEGRATED CIRCUITS FOR DMA PROCESSOR IMPLEMENTATION

The two principal operations of the DMA processor are:

a) Distributed input and output of binary variables.
b) Control of RAM memories for simultaneous input-output and process execution.

These two operations are implemented in different circuits because pin number restraints. Capacity of these circuits is limited, but they are bit-slice in order to acheive any capacity. The ADMAX circuit (Fig. 6) implements distributed input and output and TRDMAX circuit (Fig. 7) generates control signals.

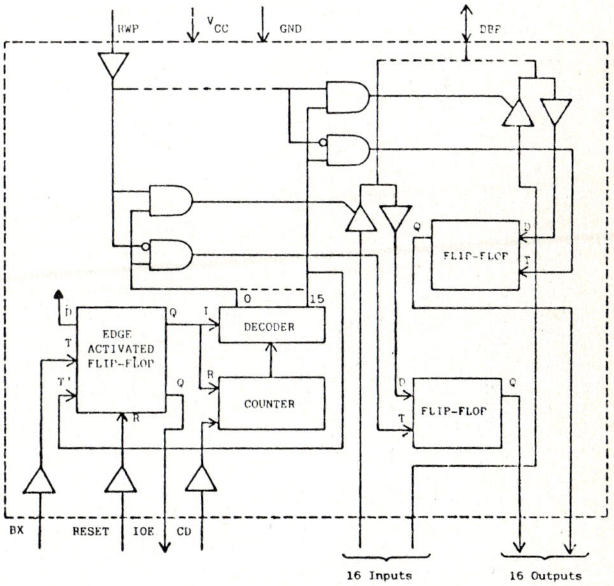

Fig. 6. ADMAX integrated circuit for DMA PROCESSOR.

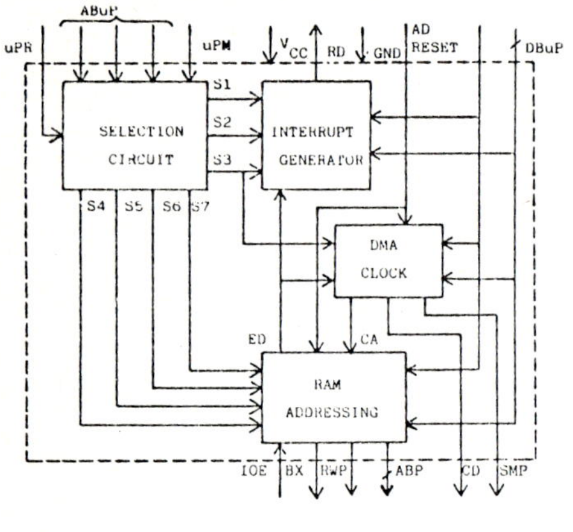

Fig. 7. TRDMAX integrated circuit block diagram

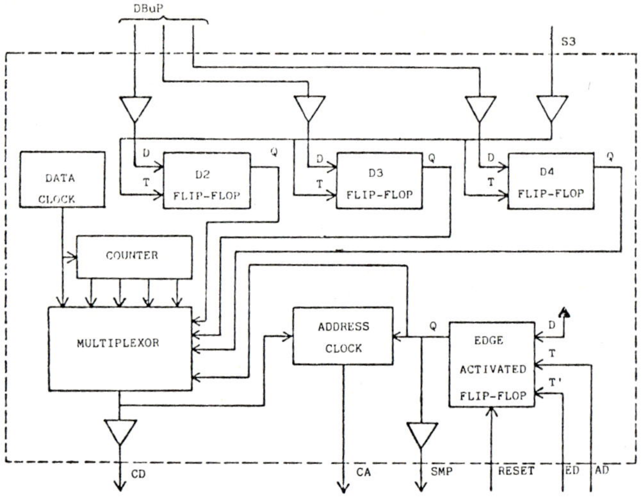

Fig. 9. TRDMAX DMA CLOCK section circuit.

ADMAX has sixteen bits input output capacity tied to the RAM INTERFACE through a single pin (DBP). The BX, CD and RWP pins are transference control inputs generated by the TRDMAX circuit. Connection of the IOE output to the BX input of the next ADMAX circuit allows input-output capacity extension. When an active edge is applied to the BX input, the counter is enabled and an input or output sweep is made under CD pulses in accordance with RWP input binary value. When the sweep finish, IOE output changes and the counter is reset. The IOE output of the last ADMAX is connected to the TRDMAX IOE input to point out the DMA input-output cycle end.

TRDMAX block diagram is shown in figure 7. TRDMAX may be programmed by the MAIN PROCESSOR through address and data buses (ABuP and DBuP input pins). Synchronization between the DMA PROCESSOR and the MAIN PROCESSOR is provided by the AD input and the RD output pins. The TRDMAX generates the RAM INTERFACE address bus through ABP output pins, as well as the ADMAX control signals BX, CD and RWP.

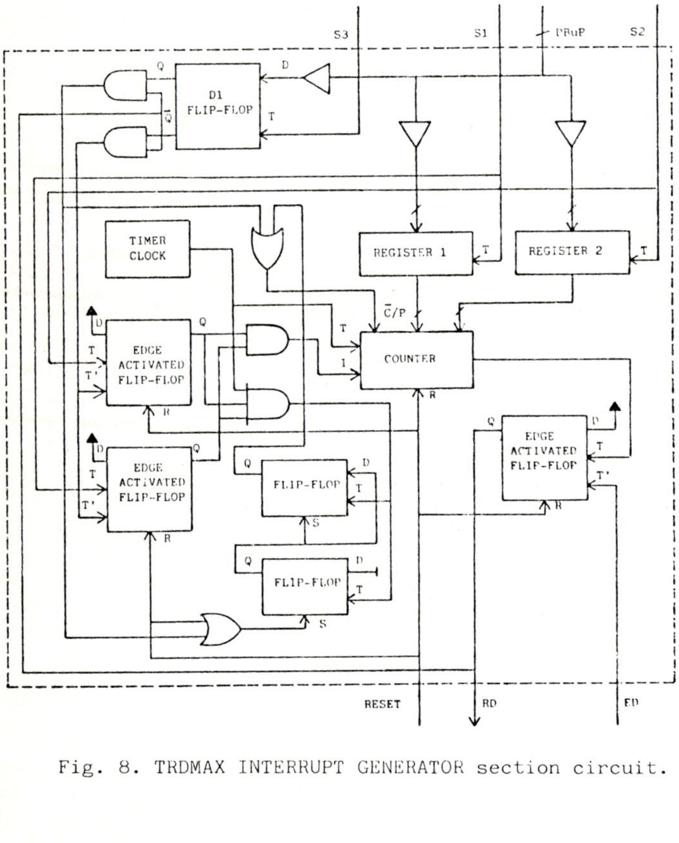

Fig. 8. TRDMAX INTERRUPT GENERATOR section circuit.

Figures 8, 9 and 10 describe TRDMAX block sections.

The INTERRUPT GENERATOR section (Fig. 8) generates an interrupt (RD output signal) when a DMA cycle ends (ED input signal). Programmable interrupt timing is optional and provided by two registers (REGISTER1 and REGISTER2).

Synchronization between DMA PROCESSOR data and address buses (DBP of ADMAX and ABP of TRDMAX) is performed by the DMA CLOCK section (Figure 9). The SMP output signal is connected to the correspondent RAM INTERFACE input (Figure 13) in order to rotate the RAM sections assignment. Different DMA sweep frequencies may be programmed by means of flip-flops D2, D3 and D4.

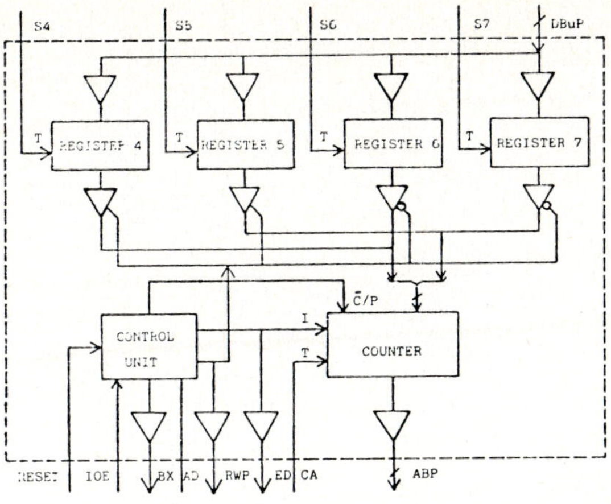

Fig. 10. TRDMAX RAM ADDRESSING section circuit.

Figure 10 presents the TRDMAX RAM ADDRESSING section. Four registers (REGISTER4 to REGISTER7) provide initial adresses for input and output variable. The CONTROL UNIT is a synchronous sequential system and generates all DMA control signals. The RWP output signal is connectted to the RWP ADMAX and RAM INTERFACE inputs to select read or write operations.

Figure 11 shows a DMA PROCESSOR system with eigth ADMAX and one TRDMAX. The TRDMAX CD, BX and RWP outputs are connected to the equivalent inputs of all ADMAX. TRDMAX and MAIN PROCESSOR are synchronized by RD and AD signals. The DMA PROCESSOR data bus (DBP) is provided by the ADMAX circuits. TRDMAX provides the DMA PROCESSOR address bus (ABP).

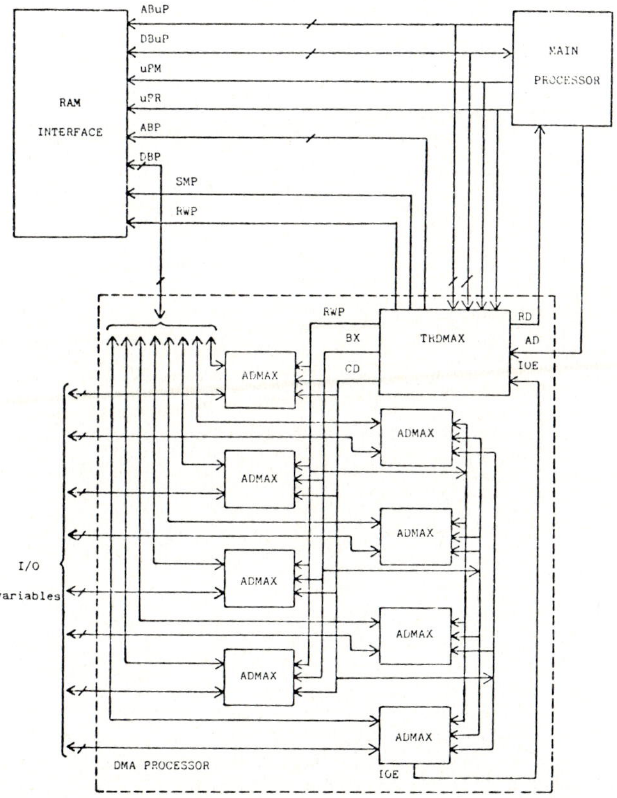

Fig. 11. DMA PROCESSOR scheme and multiprocessor connection.

Fig. 12 shows a DMA PROCESSOR with input and output variables extension.

4.2 RAM INTERFACE CIRCUITS

Figure 11 displays all Multiprocessor buses and its control signals. RAM INTERFACE block (Fig. 1) allows memory partition between both processors.

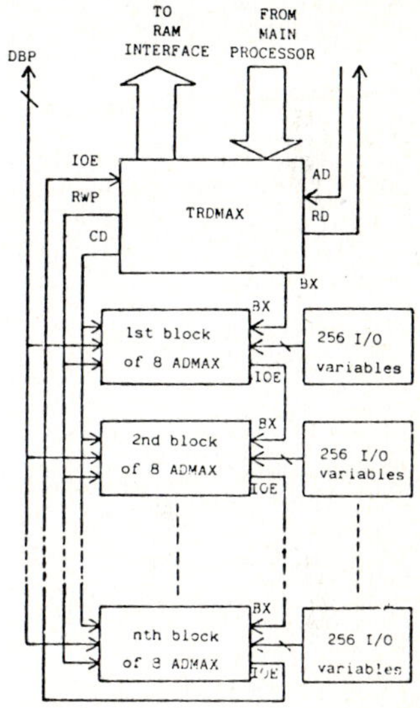

Fig. 12. DMA PROCESSOR with I/O variables number extension.

Figure 13 shows the RAM INTERFACE circuits that control the RAM buses (ABRAM, DBRAM) switching between DMA PROCESSOR and MAIN PROCESSOR. A counter makes a continous RAM buses rotation by means of SMP signal.

The DMA PROCESSOR BUS SELECTION circuits of Figure 13 are described in Figure 14. Three-state ports allow RAM memory access when SP or uS signals are activated. The RP or uR signal select between read and write operations.

5. CONCLUSION

The proposed solution allows simultaneous input-output operations and process program execution. It is specially useful when the MAIN PROCESSOR not only simulates an asynchronous system but also executes another complex control task.

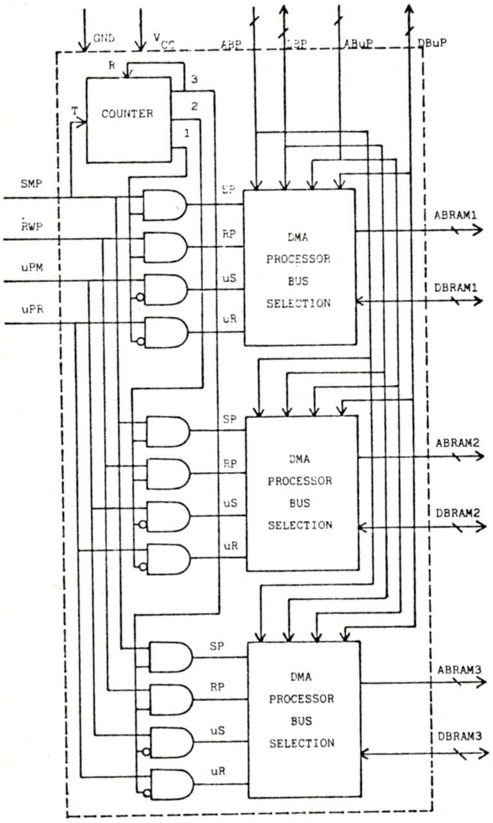

Fig. 13. RAM INTERFACE circuit.

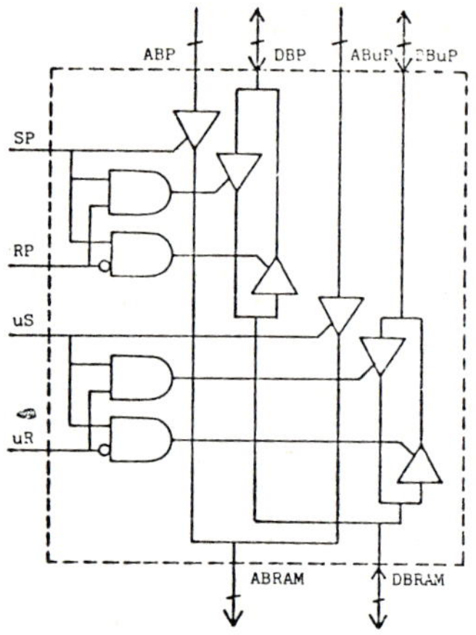

Fig. 14. DMA PROCESSOR BUS SELECTION circuit.

REFERENCES

1 E.Mandado, New systematic methods of electronic asynchronous automata synthesis, Ph. D. Thesis, Polytechnic University of Barcelona (May 1976).

2 J. R. Smith Jr. and C. H. Roth Jr., Analysis and sinthesis of asynchronous sequential networks using edge-sensitive flip-flops, IEEE Trans. Computers, vol. C-20, 8 (1971).

3 H. Y. Chuang and Santanu Das, Synthesis of multiple-input change asynchronous machines using controlled excitation and flip-flops, IEEE Trans Computers, vol. C-22, 12 (1973).

4 John Mick and James Brick, Bit-slice microprocessor design, 239-256 (McGraw-Hill, 1980)

5 Texas Instruments engineering staff, 16 Bits microprocessor system, 11.1-11.11 (Mc Graw-Hill, 1982).

MICROCOMPUTERS: Developments in Industry, Business and Education
D.R. Wilson and C.J. van Spronsen (eds.) / ©EUROMICRO, 1983
Elsevier Science Publishers B.V. (North-Holland)

THE DESIGN AND PERFORMANCE OF A REAL-TIME MICROCOMPUTER OPERATING SYSTEM

John G. Vaughan and Joseph E. Higgins

Computer Science Department, University College, Cork, Ireland

The paper describes the design of a real-time operating system with a two-level scheduling mechanism. Processes with critical constraints on execution completion are serviced preferentially in the foreground. In the background, processes without a deadline are serviced when no foreground work is available. Foreground-background communications are implemented with a restricted version of the Controlled Data Set, called a Window. Processor utilization and response time are studied. Performance curves and surfaces are presented, and conclusions are drawn regarding the influence of process time quantum and active process load on system operation.

1. INTRODUCTION

The most important activity performed by microcomputers employed in industrial control systems is that of responding to asynchronous events having hard real-time deadlines. Such a microcomputer system must also ensure that the process outputs and inputs occur at preselected times. Usually, there is a fine tolerance specification on the I/O instant. Other responsibilities of a real-time microcomputer system may include less time-critical activities such as the printing of status reports and responding to operator queries. This latter consideration implies that it is desirable for a real-time operating system (RTOS) to contain a facility for supporting non-time-critical tasks without degrading the level of service provided to real-time functions.

Real-time scheduling algorithms have been investigated by several authors [1-3]. Liu and Layland [1] examined fixed and dynamic priority schemes. In particular they showed that a fixed priority plan with rate-monotonic priority assignment is optimal among fixed priority rules. However, this Intelligent Fixed Priority (IFP) algorithm, as it is called by Serlin [2], has a least upper bound on its processor utilization factor of approximately seventy percent. This means that a feasible IFP assignment may be found for all process sets whose processor utilization factor is below this bound. However, it is only if a suitable relationship exists between process repetition rates that utilization above the 70% bound can be attained. Liu and Layland also showed that if a dynamic priority scheme is used, called the Deadline Driven Scheduling Algorithm, the least upper bound on processor utilization factor becomes 100%. This algorithm is referred to as Relative Urgency (RU) by Serlin. It is due to these results that the RU dynamic priority scheme has been chosen for time-critical process scheduling in the operating system presented in this paper.

A previous study [4] has examined online RTOS performance and evaluated the adverse effects on the controlled system of employing a non-preemptive process scheduling policy. Our current research is motivated by the work of several authors in the field of operating systems control [5-9]. Kritzinger *et al* [7] proposed a reference-model parameter adaptive control system which adjusts the operating system of a time-sharing installation to respond optimally to any significant change in workload composition. The system contains a seven-level queueing network with no preemption at level 1 and variable, increasing timeslice lengths from levels 2 to 7. The authors express the opinion that "the timeslice lengths ... are important system control parameters". Geck [8] examines an operating system feedback control scheme in which, *inter alia*, load is decreased by suspending processes and increased by resuming suspended processes in order to maintain a desirable system performance. Serazzi [9] identifies levels at which controls may be exerted within the operating system. One of these levels uses CPU quantum length as a control variable for minimizing overhead due to CPU switching.

This paper describes the design of a real-time operating system in which surplus CPU time is granted to non-deadline oriented tasks. Processor utilization and response time are used as indices in system performance evaluation. Variation in these indices is examined as the process load and the CPU quantum length are altered. The system is shown to have good response time characteristics. Performance surfaces are plotted in an attempt to identify local and absolute optimal operating points.

2. SYSTEM OVERVIEW

The principal objective of the RTOS is to support deadline-oriented servicing of time-critical processes (TCPs). It seems desirable to permit the performance of some non-time-critical activities, while ensuring that the presence of non-TCPs will not degrade the level of service provided to TCPs. Accordingly, a two-level scheduling scheme is proposed such that all TCPs are foreground-resident and all non-TCPs reside in the background. Foreground processes are serviced in preference to background processes.

In the foreground, because many TCPs will require to be initiated at specific time intervals, a time-scheduling queue is provided. Scheduled processes are attached to a READY queue. The TCP scheduling queues are illustrated in Fig. 1(a). In order to implement deadline servicing, process descriptor fields allow for priority ordering on the TCP READY queue.

In the background, only a READY queue is provided as shown in Fig. 1(b). A dynamic priority scheme allows for preferential service without indefinite postponement. Time-scheduling may be implemented by synchronization with foreground processes.

The RTOS is designed to operate on any microcomputer which has two interval timers and a multilevel priority interrupt controller. Although systems to date have been implemented for 8080 or 8085 processors, most modules are written in PL/M and are portable to any microcomputer system which supports a compiler for that language. The RTOS as presented here consists of an uninterruptable kernel, system processes assisting kernel operation, and a real-time interprocess communications layer.

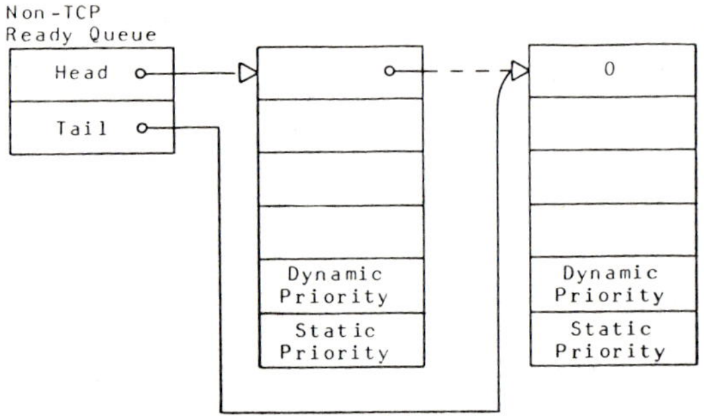

FIGURE 1(b) Background Scheduling Queue

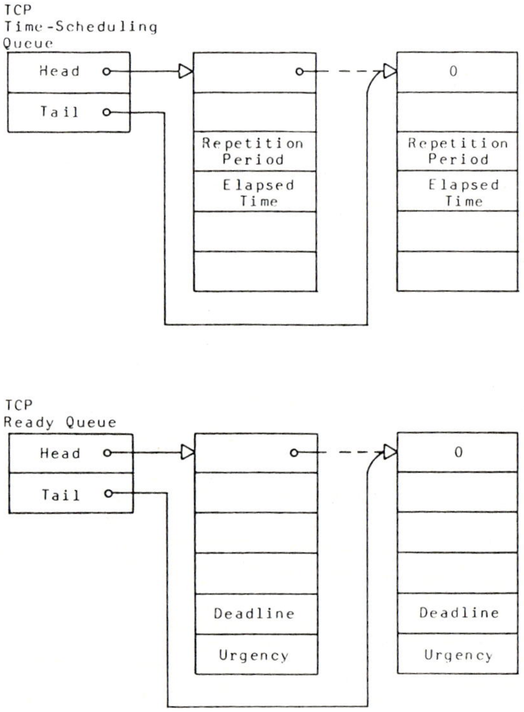

FIGURE 1(a) Foreground Scheduling Queues

3. THE KERNEL

The kernel comprises an interrupt handler, a low-level scheduler for time-critical processes, a dispatcher and synchronization primitives. The interaction of a time-critical process with these system components is shown in Fig. 2.

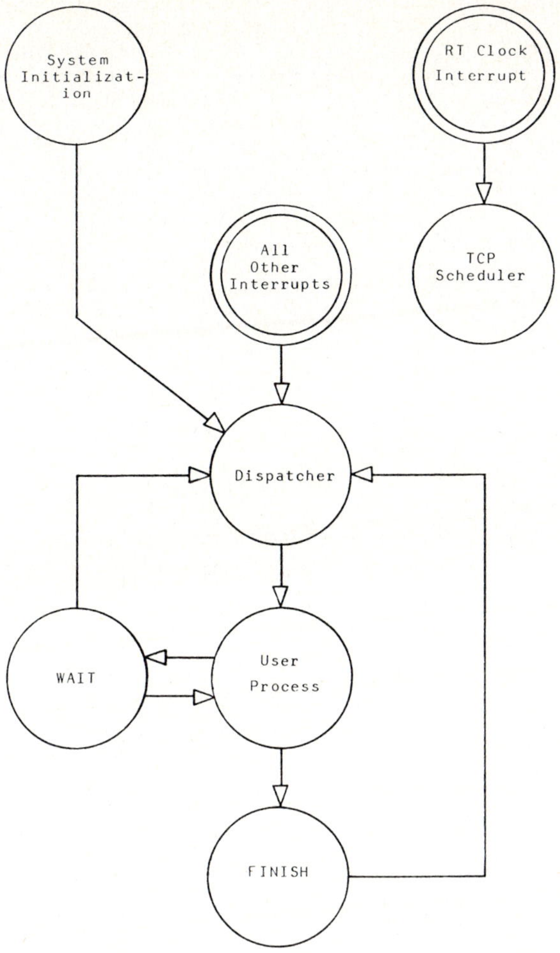

FIGURE 2 Process-Kernel Interaction

3.1 SYNCHRONIZATION AND INTERRUPT HANDLING

The basic synchronization and mutual exclusion facility provided by the RTOS is in the form of semaphores and the primitive operations Wait and Signal. Semaphores are implemented as a data structure having an integer field and a FIFO queue for blocked processes.

This synchronization facility supports event scheduling. A process to be scheduled by an external event executes a Wait on a special interrupt semaphore. The RTOS kernel's interrupt handler responds to an external interrupt by signalling the unique semaphore associated with that interrupt. As well as this, the real-time clock interrupt causes the time-critical process low-level scheduler to execute before handing control back to the current process. All other interrupts - including that associated with time-quantum expiry - initiate the execution of the dispatcher, with the possible result of a context switch.

3.2 DISPATCHING

The dispatcher's function is to select the next process to run on the processor. First, it searches the TCP READY queue. If several processes exist on this queue, the highest priority process is selected for dispatch. If no processes are found, the non-TCP queue is scanned. A null process is included in the non-TCP queue so that the dispatcher is guaranteed to find a process in the READY state. Multiple processes at the highest encountered priority level are serviced in round-robin fashion.

3.3 SCHEDULING AND THE PRIORITY STRUCTURE

A distinct priority mechanism and low-level scheduler is provided for both the foreground and background processes.

In the foreground, TCP descriptors contain two scheduling fields, REPETITION-PERIOD and ELAPSED-TIME and two priority fields, DEADLINE and URGENCY. The kernel-contained foreground scheduler, initiated at regular intervals by a real-time clock interrupt, increments the elapsed-time of all foreground processes on the ready queue. Processes on the scheduling queue for which elapsed-time equals repetition-period are transferred to the ready queue. Simultaneously, the elapsed-time of these processes is set to zero and the process' urgency is set equal to its deadline. Increasing process priority is indicated to the dispatcher by a decreasing process urgency value.

In the background, non-time-critical process descriptors contain two priority fields, STATIC-PRIORITY and DYNAMIC-PRIORITY. The background scheduler is run as a time-critical system process outside the kernel. If the dispatcher has examined the background queue since the previous execution of the scheduler, the scheduler increments the dynamic priority of every background process. Increasing process priority is indicated by increasing value of dynamic-priority. When a background process is dispatched, its dynamic-priority is reset to equal its static-priority.

The purpose of the foreground-background system organization is to ensure that preferential service is given to real-time processes, while allowing any surplus processor time to be expended on less urgent functions, thus obtaining maximum benefit from available processing power. Relative urgency scheduling in the foreground enables real-time process deadlines to be met. The background dynamic priority scheme allows priority ordering of non-time-critical processes while ensuring that no process will have to wait indefinitely for service if the background queue is receiving frequent CPU attention. Overall, the preemptive approach to process scheduling encourages rapid response to asynchronous events.

4. THE COMMUNICATIONS LAYER

4.1 FOREGROUND-BACKGROUND COMMUNICATION

Owing to the system philosophy of having status report processes and perhaps data entry processes located on the background queue, a mechanism must be established whereby system parameter values may be communicated between foreground and background. Synchronization of operations on a buffer shared between a background and foreground process will cause an unacceptable degradation in the foreground process' speed while it Waits for the background process to execute. Provision of an interlevel conventional message-passing facility with operations send, wait and accept results in two problems. First, messages are received in FIFO order, so the receiving processes obtain the earliest copy of transmitted data. Second, synchronization on the return of used buffers will cause speed degradation.

4.2 WINDOWS

It is highly desirable that when interlevel communication occurs, neither the sender nor the receiver should be delayed. Also, the receiver should obtain the latest copy of transmitted data. To enable interlevel data transfer having these characteristics, a logical interface called a WINDOW is presented to applications processes. The system contains two windows, the FOREGROUND-WINDOW and the BACKGROUND-WINDOW. Data produced by a foreground process may be displayed on the FOREGROUND-WINDOW from which it may be copied by a background process. Similarly, data produced by a background process may be displayed on the BACKGROUND-WINDOW. Processes access the windows via procedures GAZE and DISPLAY. Data is transmitted in units of one buffer, the length of which is set at system initialization. The system expects that only four processes in all will be engaged in window access, one for transmission and reception at each scheduling level. This expectation is enforced by the use of queueing semaphores to restrict access to each window. Pseudocode for GAZE and DISPLAY appears as follows:-

```
GAZE : Procedure (Localbufferaddress)
If calling process is a TCP then
 Begin
 WAIT (Queueing-Semaphore-Gaze-BW);
 Copy data from BACKGROUND-WINDOW into
                              Localbuffer;
 SIGNAL (Queueing-Semaphore-Gaze-BW)
 End
Else
 Begin
 WAIT (Queueing-Semaphore-Gaze-FW);
 Copy data from FOREGROUND-WINDOW into
                              Localbuffer;
 SIGNAL (Queueing-Semaphore-Gaze-FW)
 End
End  GAZE
```

```
DISPLAY : Procedure (Localbufferaddress)
If calling process is a TCP then
 Begin
 WAIT (Queueing-Semaphore-Display-FW);
 Copy data from Localbuffer into
                  FOREGROUND-WINDOW;
 SIGNAL (Queueing-Semaphore-Display-FW)
 End
Else
 Begin
 WAIT (Queueing-Semaphore-Display-BW);
 Copy data from Localbuffer into
                  BACKGROUND-WINDOW;
 SIGNAL (Queueing-Semaphore-Display-BW)
 End
End  DISPLAY
```

4.3 IMPLEMENTATION OF WINDOWS

Windows are implemented in the system using the concept of a Controlled Data Set developed by Sorenson [10,11]. A controlled data set (CDS) is a buffer management structure in which each buffer may pass through four states as shown in Fig. 3. A CDS of n buffers is initialized with n-1 buffers in the AVAILABLE state and one buffer in the COMPLETED state. When a process wishes to send data to the CDS, a buffer is moved from the AVAILABLE to the RECEIVING state, where the process loads it with data. When the buffer is full, it is moved to the COMPLETED state.

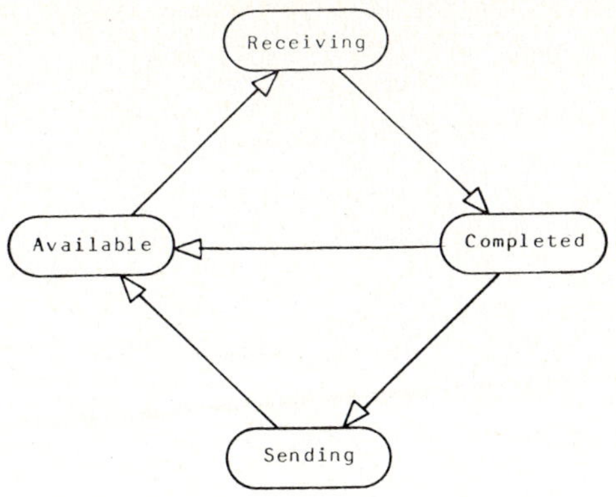

FIGURE 3 Controlled Data Set State Diagram

The buffer previously occupying the COMPLETED state is moved either to the AVAILABLE state if no process is reading from it, or to the SENDING state if one or more reading processes already exist.

When a process attempts to read data from the CDS, it accesses the buffer in the COMPLETED state. A use-count on the buffer is incremented. While the read operation is in progress, the buffer may be moved to the SENDING state due to the arrival of a newly-filled buffer from the RECEIVING state, but this does not affect the reading process. When the read operation has finished, the usecount on the CDS buffer is decremented. If the usecount is nonzero, the buffer remains in its present state. If the usecount is zero and the buffer is in the COMPLETED state, it remains there. A SENDING state buffer whose usecount is zero is moved to the AVAILABLE state.

The Controlled Data Set enables a sending process and a receiving process to communicate without delay. If there are n senders and m receivers, the total number of buffers necessary within the CDS is n+m+1. In order to conserve storage in a microcomputer system, the Windows are implemented as controlled data sets which are each restricted to access by one sender and one receiver.

4.4 IMPLEMENTATION OF CONTROLLED DATA SETS

Within this RTOS, a controlled data set is represented by the data structure shown in Fig. 4. The structure contains head and tail pointers for a list of buffers in the AVAILABLE state and a pointer to the single buffer in the COMPLETED state. Semaphores used to resolve access conflicts on the AVAILABLE and COMPLETED states are linked to the structure, and a 'Buffersize' field

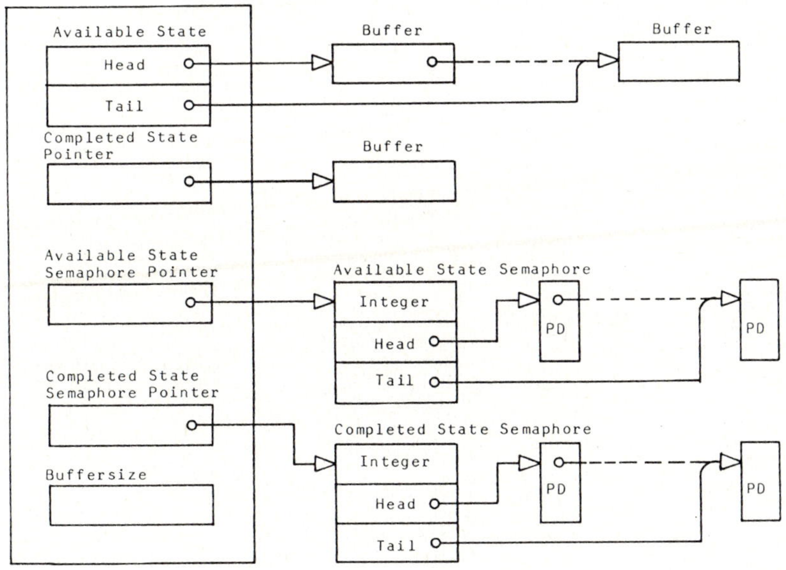

FIGURE 4 Physical Representation of a Controlled Data Set

specifies the size of the buffers which are manipulated by CDS operations. Four reentrant CDS access procedures are defined, namely:

GETBUFFER : Called by a process wishing to send data to the CDS. GETBUFFER returns the address of a RECEIVING buffer which may be accessed by the calling process alone.

BUFFERFULL : When a sending process has filled its RECEIVING buffer, it calls BUFFERFULL to pass the up-to-date buffer to the completed state.

GETDATA : A process wishing to receive data from a CDS calls this procedure. GETDATA returns the address of the buffer in the COMPLETED state. The receiving process then copies this data into a local buffer.

DATAFINISH : A receiving process calls DATAFINISH when it has copied all required data from the buffer returned by GETDATA. DATAFINISH decrements the buffer's usecount and moves the buffer to the AVAILABLE state if appropriate.

Because two processes may simultaneously attempt to access the AVAILABLE state queue by means of GETBUFFER and DATAFINISH, it is necessary to provide for mutual exclusion with an available state semaphore. Similarly, the completed state semaphore protects the COMPLETED state pointer from corruption.

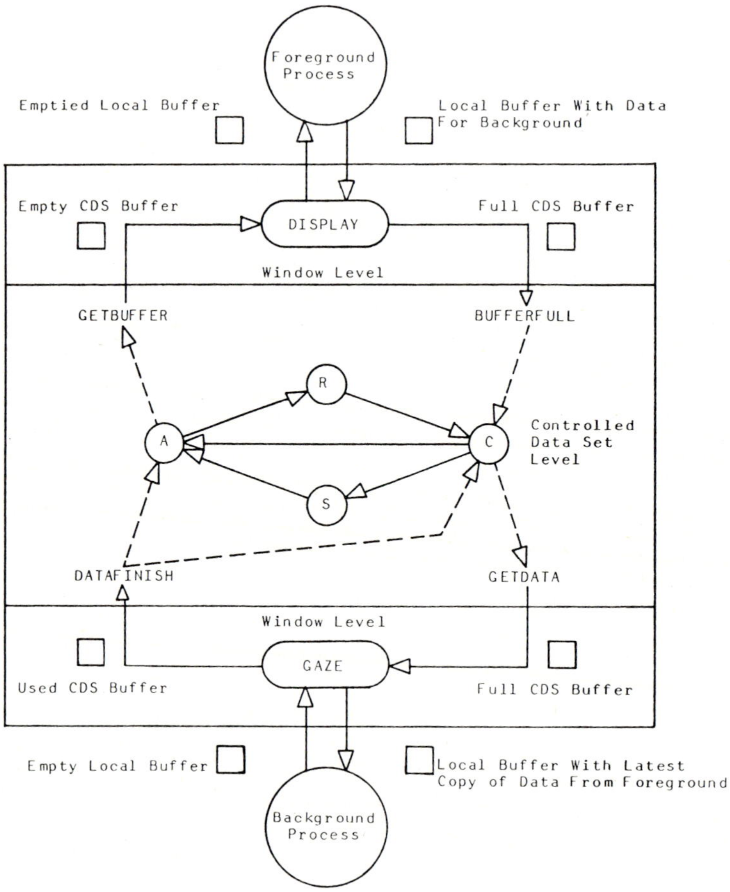

FIGURE 5 Process Interaction Through The Foreground Window

The interaction of processes through the foreground window is shown in Fig. 5. GAZE and DISPLAY calls from user processes are transformed into appropriate controlled data set management procedure calls. The required semaphore operations are transparent to the calling process. Since controlled data sets are implemented outside the kernel, the effect of window management overhead on interrupt response is minimal.

5. PERFORMANCE EVALUATION

RTOS performance tests were oriented towards quantifying effects on processor utilization and response time due to changes in process service time, process load (i.e. number of active processes) and CPU quantum size.

In order to measure processor utilization, sets of processes with equal repetition period, T, and service time, τ, were run under the RTOS. A desired repetition period of 50 ms was arbitrarily assigned to each process. The circulation time, C, of processes was measured as being the time between two successive process executions. The processor utilization, ρ, is calculated as

$$\rho = \frac{n\tau}{C}$$

where n is the number of processes in the process set. The circulation times for a range of service times, number of processes and timeslice values were experimentally determined by an automatic measurement system. The results were averaged over 50 readings per point. The worst case coefficient of variation was 0.1, with the vast majority of readings having a coefficient of variation better than 0.03. The resulting utilizations are plotted in Fig. 6.

Fig. 6(a) shows utilization as a function of number of processes for varying service times and a timeslice of 20 ms. In general, as the number of processes is increased, ρ rises sharply to a peak over a period where full processing capability is not demanded. After peak utilization is reached, ρ decreases steadily due to the overhead incurred by searching the system queues. As service time is increased, processor utilization increases, and the number of processes giving rise to peak utilization decreases.

Fig. 6(b) again shows the effect of increasing the number of active processes on the processor utilization. The service time is constant at 15 ms and results are plotted for a range of

Figure 6(a)

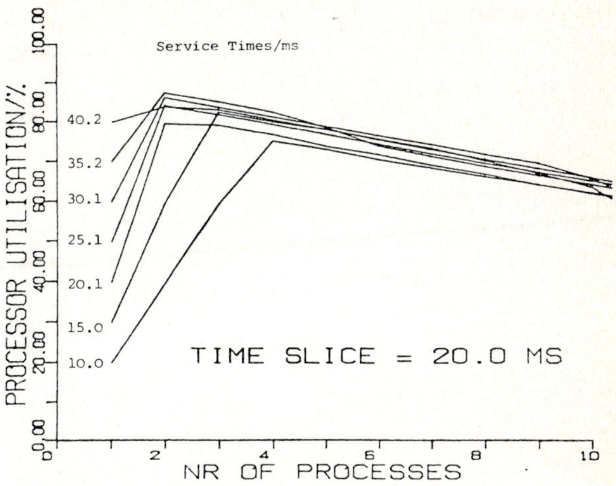

Figure 6(b)

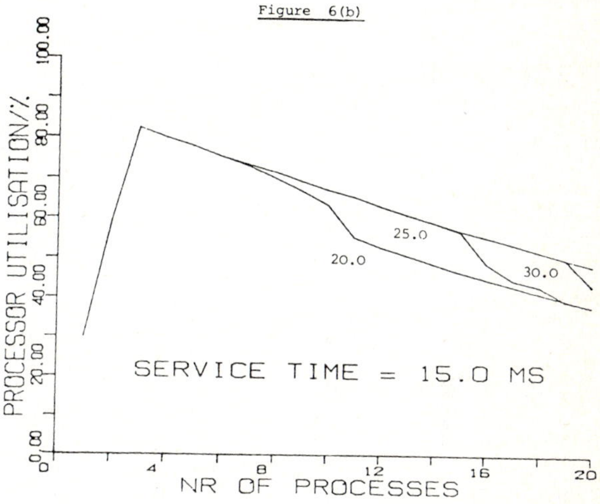

timeslice values. For a 20 ms timeslice, utilization begins to fall off more rapidly when the number of processes exceeds seven. This is due to TCP scheduler execution time increasing with number of processes and reducing the effective quantum size available to the running process. Eventually, process execution extends over a timeslice, resulting in a sudden increase in overhead and a decrease in utilization. Clearly, as the time quantum is increased the likelihood of an overlap is reduced until from 35 ms upwards, no sudden decrease in processor utilization is apparent within the scope of the graph. Fig. 6(c) shows the same results in three dimensions for a service time of 20.1 ms. Fig. 6(d) is a plot of proc-

Figure 6(c)

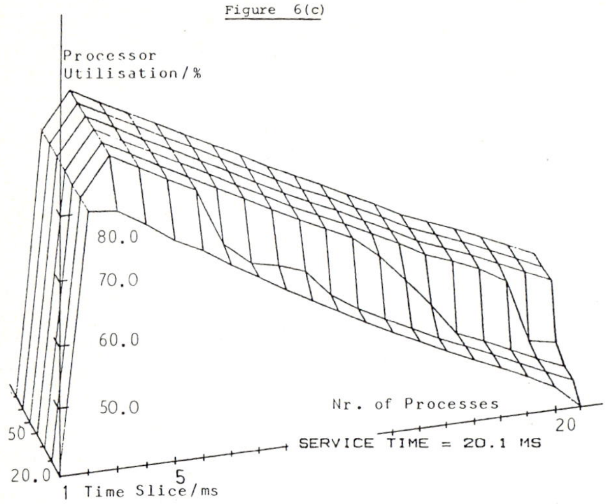

Figure 6(d)

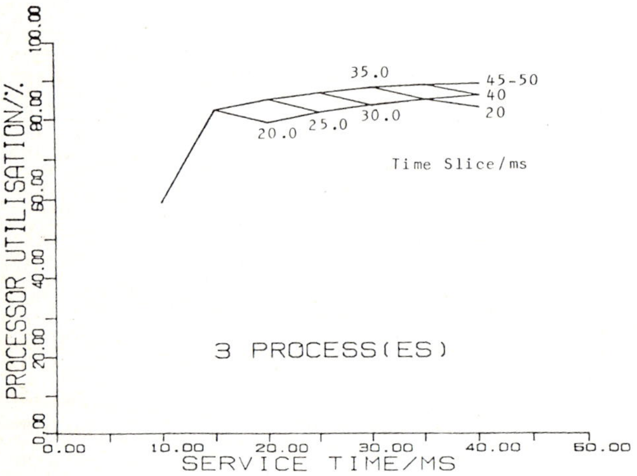

essor utilization against service time for three processes and a range of timeslices. Again, the detrimental effects of timeslice overlap and the remedy of increasing the time quantum are apparent.

In order to quantify RTOS response time performance, a time-critical process was made to Wait on an interrupt semaphore. The deadline for the interrupt service process was 1 s, and for all other processes was 2 s, the relative values being of greater importance than the absolute deadlines. The measurement system recorded the interval between the occurrence of the external interrupt and the execution of the servicing process while varying process load and timeslice as for the utilization measurements. The response times are plotted in Fig. 7. Fig 7(a) illustrates variation in response time with number of processes for various service times and a fixed timeslice of 15.0 ms.

Figure 7(a)

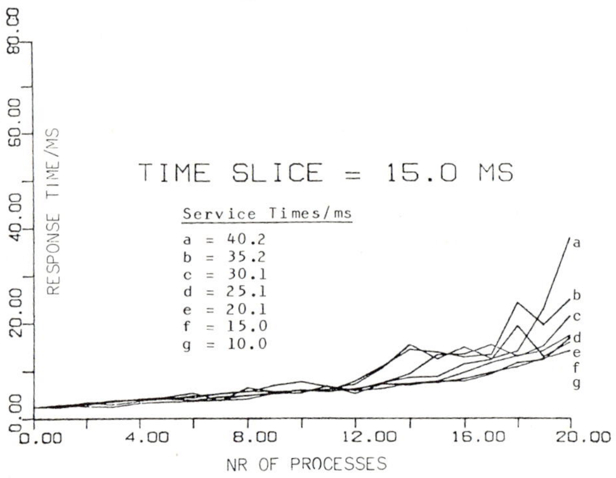

Figure 7(b)

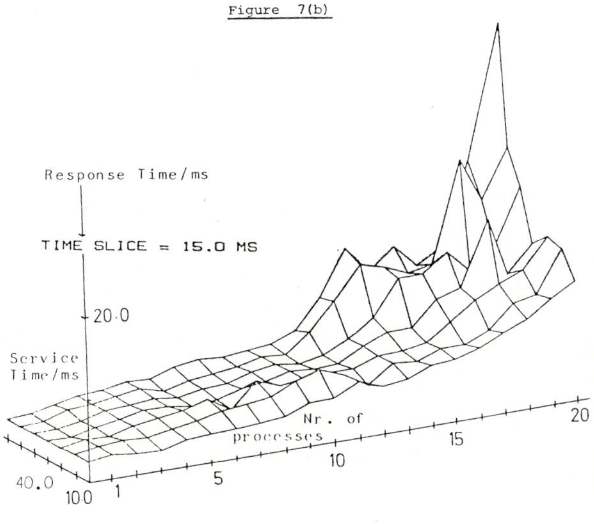

For up to twelve processes, response times increase gradually from 2.4 ms to approximately 8 ms, the slight increase being due to increasing scheduling and dispatching overhead. As the number of processes rises to twenty, however, response time rises more rapidly and becomes less predictable. This is caused by an overlap in priorities between the interrupt service process and other processes which have been waiting a long time for service due to the considerable load on the system. This appears more dramatically in Fig. 7(b), which plots response time against service time and number of processes.

Figure 7(c)

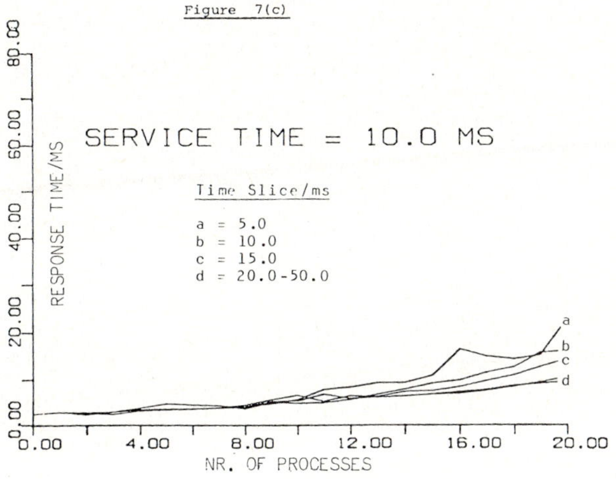

Figure 7(d)

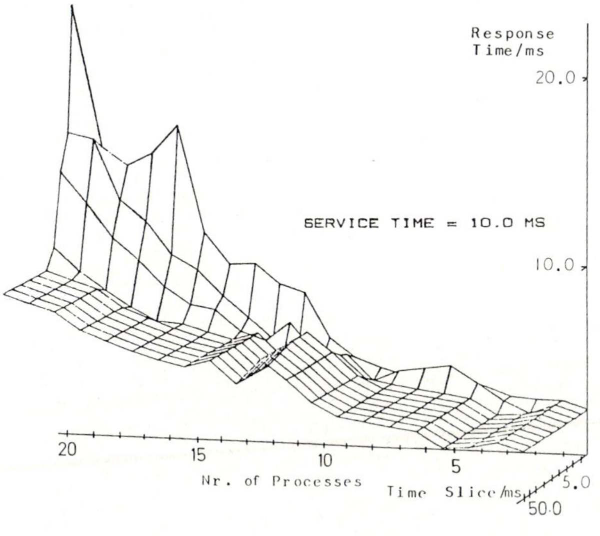

For large system load, response time degradation is clearly shown. In Figs. 7(c) and 7(d), response time is plotted as a function of number of processes and timeslice length for constant service time. With low timeslice values, and more than twelve processes, process switching overhead causes some non-interrupt processes to be delayed long enough for their priorities to overtake the priority of the interrupt process, causing a sudden increase in response time. As timeslice is increased, this problem disappears since more processes execute completely within the quantum and overhead is reduced.

6. CONCLUSIONS

This paper has presented a design for a real-time operating system which runs on single-processor microcomputer systems. The RTOS uses a foreground/background scheduling scheme in which processes with hard deadlines are serviced preferentially in the foreground. System performance in the foreground has been experimentally evaluated and results have been presented. Good response times have been achieved in a reasonably loaded system. Processor utilization has been shown to vary largely as a function of the number of active processes in the system. It is evident that the number of active processes could be manipulated to maintain optimum processor utilization. This is hardly practical in a real-time single-processor system. However, in a multiple-CPU environment, achievement of processor utilization optima could be used as a motivation for task distribution rather than suspension.

In terms of both processor utilization and response time, it appears that, for the RTOS presented here, variation of CPU time quantum will not cause the system to converge towards a local or absolute optimum operating point. Indeed, the overall system performance improves as the timeslice is increased, leading to the conclusion that at least in respect of the time-critical portion of the system, it seems inadvisable to employ time-quantum assignment. However, the timeslicing scheme is necessary for correct operation of the background queue. Also, time quantum assignment may be used to estimate process service times which must be known if load distribution in a multi-CPU system is to be realised.

7. REFERENCES

[1] Liu, C.L. and Layland, J.W., Scheduling Algorithms for Multiprogrammin a Hard-Real-Time Environment, JACM. 20, No.1 (1973) 46-61.

[2] Serlin, O., Scheduling of Time-Critical Processes, Proceedings AFIPS Spring Joint Computer Conference (1972), 925-932.

[3] Leinbaugh, D.W., Guaranteed Response Times in a Hard-Real-Time Environment, IEEE Trans. Soft. Eng. Vol. SE-6, No.1 (January 1980) 85-91.

[4] Vaughan, J.G., Barry, M.E., Higgins, J.E. and Murphy, J.M.D., Real-Time Operating System Performance in the Control of a Chopper-Fed DC Motor, Conference on Microelectronics in Power Electronics and Electrical Drives, Darmstadt, West Germany, (October 1982) 103-110.

[5] Blevins, P.R. and Ramamoorthy, C.V., Aspects of a Dynamically Adaptive Operating System, IEEE Trans. Computers, Vol. C-25, No.7 (July 1976) 713-725.

[6] Badel, M. and Leroudier, J., Adaptive Multiprogramming Systems Can Exist, Proceedings of the International Conference on Performance of Computer Installations, ICPCI '78 (June 1978) (North-Holland 1978).

[7] Kritzinger, P.S., Krjesinski, A.E. and Teunissen, P., Design of a Control System for a Timesharing Computer System, *ibid*, 103-114.

[8] Geck, A., Performance Improvement by Feedback Control of the Operating System, Proceedings of the 4th International Symposium on Modelling and Performance Evaluation of Computer Systems, (North-Holland, 1979) 459-471.

[9] Serazzi, G., The Dynamic Behaviour of Computer Systems, in D. Ferrari and M. Spadoni (Eds): Experimental Computer Performance Evaluation, (North-Holland, 1980, ISBN 0-444-86129-7) 127-163.

[10] Sorenson, P.G., Interprocess Communication in Real-Time Systems, OpSys. Review, Vol. 7, No.4 (October 1973) 1-7.

[11] Sorenson, P.G. and Hamacher, V.C., A Real-Time System Design Methodology, INFOR, Vol. 13, No.1 (February 1975) 1-18.

MICROCOMPUTERS: Developments in Industry, Business and Education
D.R. Wilson and C.J. van Spronsen (eds.) / ©EUROMICRO, 1983
Elsevier Science Publishers B.V. (North-Holland)

LTOS STATE TABLE CREATION PROCEDURES FOR LTMuP

E.L. Zapata and J. Mira

Department Electronics. Faculty of Physics
University of Santiago de Compostela
Spain

This paper describes the various procedures by means of which LTOS, the operating system of the lesion tolerant multi-microprocessor system LTMuP, enables each processor to set up a fault-free area of RAM in which to create its personal picture of the state of the LTMuP system. This fault-free area may lie in any RAM unit, the only restriction being that no two processors may create their tables in the same unit. However, since the LTMuP processor units each contain a local RAM, they initially try to set their tables up in a fault-free area of this local memory so as to cut down the frequency with which they need to access shared resources. The table is, of course, re-locatable. Its creation is the primary objetive of LTOS.

1. INTRODUCTION

A crucial aspect of any operating system (OS) for a system with distributed architecture is the coordination of the various processors, which may have different visions of the hardware configuration of the system. Such coordination may be achieved in at least two. One approach is for the processors jointly to define an area of common memory in which the configuration map of the system is written, and thereafter to cooperate in any decision to modify the map. This is the method adopted in Pluribus (Katsuki, D. et al., 1978) and MuTEAM (Grandoni, F. et al, 1981), among other systems. A second approach is to forego the use of centralized resource control tables accessible to various processors and for each processor to define an area of private memory in which it writes its own vision of the system. This is the strategy adopted in MICRONET systems (Witie, L.D. 1979) and by ourselves in LTMuP (Zapata, E.L. 1983; Mira et al, 1983).

OS controlling multiprocessor systems are generally cooperative and distributed and responsible for the control of shared resources, which together with recovery from hardware and/or software faults is the main function of any distributed architecture system. Means of carrying out this function have been described in the work of E.M. Clarke and C.N. Nikolaou (1982) who have developed dynamical reconfiguration strategies in multiprocessor systems with shared memory subject to possible faults, and in that of F.B. Schneider and R.D. Schichting (1981). The latter, however, assume that shared resources are infallible, and structure their OS as a cyclic collection of procedures.

LTMuP is a cooperative architecture system with various processors and shared multigate memory accessible to them all. Which may in this way be considered as "anonymous" subscribers. Given an input vector, each processor can execute any job residing in shared memory. LTOS, the OS controlling LTMuP, is made up of a series of procedures, many of them running in parallel, which are structured in six phases: initialization, state table definition, election of a coordinator, resource checking, resource evaluation, and applications. Each phase is self-sufficient, i.e. each involves mechanims detecting faults in interprocessor communications.
Many aspects of LTMuP and LTOS have been published already (Mira, J. et al, 1981; 1982; 1983; Zapata, E.L. 1983), and we will not repeat them here in detail. They are summarized in Tables I and II. The present paper is concerned exclusively with hard- and/or software aspects necessary for understanding the procedures by which each processor sets up its state table.

	CHARACTERISTICS OF LTMuP
1	Modularity: identical 8-bit microprocessors, each with its own clock controlling the resources corrently present in the module.
2	Volatile local memory.
3	Direct inter-processor communication subject to possible faults.
4	Generation and reception by each processor of NMI, IRQ and HALT interrupts to or from all other processors.
5	Shared multigate memory (RAM and EPROM) subject to possible faults.
6	I/O units interfacing between the system and the external world (physical effectors and sensors with A/D or D/A conversion if necessary, printer, TV, monitor, etc.).
7	Access to the shared resource units (I/O, EPROM, RAM) by means of a bus switching program.

Table I. Characteristics of the LTMuP system.

	CHARACTERISTICS OF LTOS
1	Resides in the local EPROM of each processor unit.
2	Controls a shared multigate resource structure in which shared resources belong to an addres space paged in 56 Kbyte blocks.
3	Provides direct communication between processor modules, with provision for recovery from faults (since processors have independent clocks, communication between them requires a protocol involving acknowledgement of the receipt of messages).
4	Tolerates permanent hardware faults in shared resources and processor units, the detection of a fault triggering the execution of routines to isolate and identify the fault and when possible, transfer to another unit the work of the faulty one.
5	Enables any processor module to be HALTed and disconnected from the shared resources assigned to it prior to being HALTed.
6	Enables the system to be reconfigured by means of flexible re-assignation of resources.
7	Protects against local faults with global effects on the system.
8	Creates in each processor a relocatable (and therefore fault-tolerant) stack and state table area.
9	Consists of segmented procedures, each of which is accompanied by an identification code and the number of bytes of RAM it needs for temporary storage of data.
10	Enables a processor which deems itself to be isolated because no instructions have been received from any other processor to appropriate for itself areas of shared RAM, EPROM and I/O and beging execution of the user tasks stored in the EPROM.
11	Treats all faults detected as permanent, no provision being made for intermittent faults.

Table II. Characteristics of LTOS.

DIRECT INTERPROCESSOR COMMUNICATIONS AND ALLOCATION OF SHARED RESOURCE CONTROL SWITCH ADDRESSES

The direct interprocessor communications subsystem (DICS) is made up of a set of I/O (MC-6821 PIAs) connected pairwise by flat cable as in fig. 1, which also shows the addresses assigned to each ship. Although this interconnexion scheme increases the cable density of the system it facilitates isolation of faults and simplifies interprocessor communications, since the use of a bus would require extra logic to control traffic along it. Any ECPU (extended CPU; there are three in the system actually constructed) can generate NMI, IRQ or HALT interrupts in any other via the DICS by programming the control registers of the

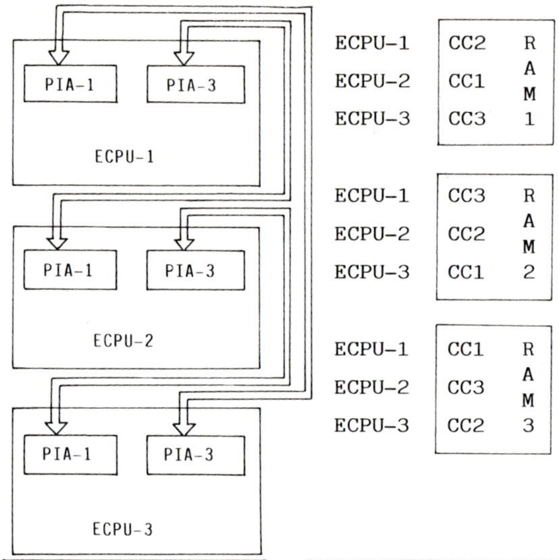

C.C.	Addresses
CC1	E3C0
CC2	E3C1
CC3	E3C2

I/O Chip	Addresses
PIA-1	E3BC-E3BF
PIA-3	E3B8-E3BB
Halts-1	E3B0
Halts-3	E3B1

Fig. 1. Direct Interprocessor Communications.

Fig. 2. Allocation of RAM Control Switch Addresses.

I/O chips involved.

LTOS has direct access capacity for up to 3.5 Mbytes of shared multigate memory paged in 56 Kbyte blocks, though the RAM units actually used in the current implementation are three 8 Kbyte blocks each containing the addresses 0000-1FFF (hex). In each processor these pages are distinguished by the control switches giving access to them maving different addresses assigned to them, and the address of a given control switch is different for each processor (see fig. 2). For example, if the three ECPUs each wish to access their RAM-2, they will each CLR CC2, but these identical operations will give rise to their each accessing a different page of RAM. Access to the other shared resource units is on exactly the same plan.

STACK AND STATE TABLE AREAS

LTOS is responsible for detecting, isolating and identifying permanent faults in the system and for subsequently reconfiguring the LTMuP modules. These functions mean that tables must be created to contain descriptions of the current state of the system at any moment, and since these tables are essential to the operation of a distributed structure they themselves must be protected from faults. In some other systems (e.g. Luque, E. et al, 1979) this is achieved by providing "fault-proof" hardware in the shape of two or more copies of the same area of memory. This method is relatively safe, but the redundant hardware means a considerable rise in the cost of the system, and LTMuP units are not equipped with it. It is therefore LTOS which is responsible for finding a fault-free area of RAM in which to locate stack and state table, and for protecting these by means of re-location procedures. Indeed, the preservation of the stack and state table is the primary objective of LTOS.

Since each ECPU is provided with an area of local RAM, that is where it first attempts to locate its stack and state table, so as to reduce the frequency with which it has to access shared resources. If the local RAM is unusuable, then shared RAM may be used, the only restriction being that no two processors may set their tables up in the same page of shared RAM. The shared RAM page initially approached is the processor's RAM-2, i.e. the page whose control switch address is E3C1. If RAM-2 is also unavailable, RAM-1 and RAM-3 are approached, and if these cannot be used either, and the table-less processor has direct communication with the others, then it waits for one of them to send it instructions. If it lacks direct communication with the other processors, then it will probably be HALTed by them and disconnected from the shared resources it might access.

Each processor has exclusive control over the definition of stack and state table in its local RAM, but before trying to set them up in shared RAM it must dialogue with the other ECPUs. For the purposes of this dialogue, and for its own internal use too, each processor possesses a state flag declaring whether, and where, it has its table. Fig. 3 illustrates the search for a suitable fault-free area in RAM and the value of the state flag for each contingency.

It is a platitude that the hardware characteristics of a system limit the possibilities of its operating system. In the present case the fact that the microprocessors used in LTMuP possess but six registers means that none is available for permanent use as a pointer to the state table. To overcome this difficulty the state table has been linked to the stack. Once a fault-free 256 byte area of local or shared RAM has been found, the stack pointer (SP) is set to n+30, where n is the lowest address in the fault-free area. The state table begins at n+40. Its position relative to SP is therefore affected by all the assembly language instructions that modify the latter: PSH (SP = SP - 1), PUL (SP = SP + 1), JSR ó BSR (SP = SP - 2), RTS (SP = SP + 2), SWI (SP = SP - 7), and RTI (SP = SP + 7). WAI is not included in the above list because the state

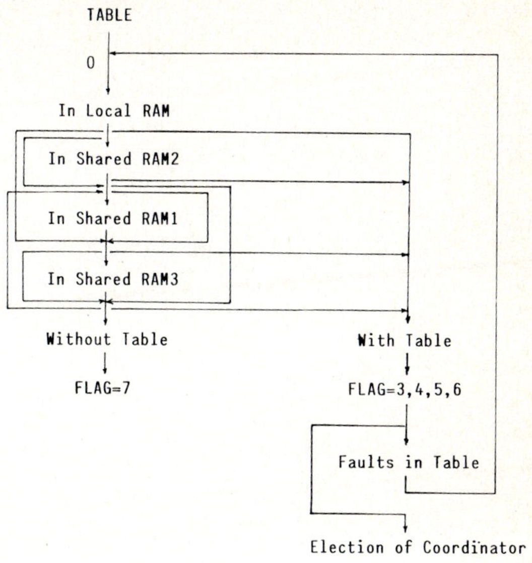

Fig. 3. Exploration of RAM to set up stack/state table.

table is inaccessible after execution of WAI, which halts the system until an interrupt is received.

Access to the state table is via the software interrupt SWI, which leads to the routine whose flowchart is shown in fig. 4. The input parameters of this routine are held in SP; in accumulator A, which is set negative to read the table, and to write in it holds the positive value to be written; and in accumulator B, which holds the position relative to SP + 17 of the location to be accessed, i.e. location = SP + 17 + B. To access the ith position of the table from an Nth level subroutine, PSH and PUL having been used n and p times respectively, the value that B must hold is giben by

$$B = i + 2N + n - p$$

For example, to read the tenth position of the table and subtract 2 from it from a level 2 subroutine when one PUL and three PSH instructions have been used, the following assembly language instructions would be used:

```
LDAA  #$80   A set negative to read
LDAB  #16    B=10+(2x2)+3-1
SWI           10,1     A
SUBA  #2     A=A-2: A positive to write
SWI          A    10,T
```

THE PROCESSOR STATES

Before defining areas of RAM in which to locate their stacks and state tables, the processors enter into direct communication with each other so as to establish their own states and that

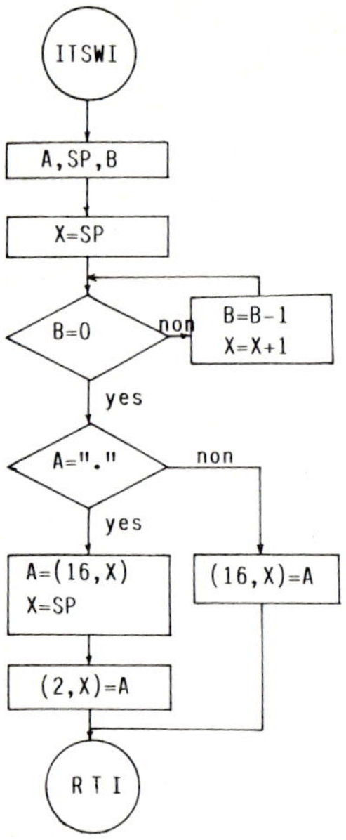

Fig. 4. Accesing the state table.

of the DICS. In this and subsequent dialogues each processor considers itself as ECPU-2 (Zapata, 1983). After terminating the initialization phase, each processor marks time for a short fixed period so as to allow the others to complete initialization too. The first processor to exit from this delay commences the dialogue, and becomes its putative acting coordinator, by sending NMIs out on the DICS to the other ECPUs.

The NMIs used on the DICS are accompanied by a code determining the response. Like the others that sent out by the putative acting coordinator to initiate dialogue, NMI-(11), requires in the first place that is receipt be aknowledged. After sending NMI-(11)s to the other two processors, the putative acting coordinator therefore polls its I/O chips a certain number of times, and, depending on the results, enters one of three procedures, DI11, TXAYB and TX1Y1. DI11 is entered if not direct communication has been established with any other ECPU, and iniatiates an attempt to set up indirect communication via shared resources. TXAYB and TX1Y1 are entered if direct communication has been established with respectively one or both of the other ECPUs.

TXAYB and TX1Y1 continue investigating the state of the DICS by means of further coded NMIs requiring one of the other processors to test its direct communications with the third. NMI-(22) tells the receiver that the sender has direct communications with the third ECPU, NMI-(33) that it has not. The interrupt sent to the third ECPU if NMI-(22) has been received is another NMI-(22), and NMI-(44) if NMI-(33) has been received. The origins and emanings of the four coded interrupts used in the state table definition phase of LTOS are therefore as in Table III.

On receiving a coded interrupt, NMI-(KK), an ECPU's first response is to acknowledge receipt by sending back an acknowledgement signal plus the code KK. If an NMI is received accompanied by a faulty code, the receiver tries to return to the procedure it was executing when it was

INTERRUPT	SENT BY	INFORMATION RE. SENDER	ACTION TAKEN ON RECEIPT (apart from acknowledgement)	ACTION TAKEN BY ACTING COORDINATOR ON RECEIVING REPORT
NMI-(11)	Any processor whose post-initialization delay has ended without being interrupted	Sender is acting coordinator	Await further instructions	———
NMI-(22)	Acting coordinator in TX1Y1	Sender enjoys direct communications with third ECPU	Send NMI-(22) to third ECPU and report result back. If communication is established, enter DD22. If not, enter DI11.	If successful communication is reported, acting coordinator enters DD22. If not, a.c. enters DIRX2Y and tells third ECPU to enter DIR2XY.
	Any processor receiving NMI-(22) from acting coordinator.	Ditto	Enter DD22	———
NMI-(33)	Acting coordinator in TXAYB	Sender has no direct communications with third ECPU	Send NMI-(44) to third ECPU and report result back. If communication is established, enter DIRX2Y. If not, enter DI11.	If successful communication is reported, acting coordinator enters DIR2XY. If not DIR2XD.
NMI-(44)	Any processor receiving NMI-(33)	Sender enjoys direct communications with third ECPU	Await counter-acknowledgement If received, enter DIR2XY. If not, enter DI11.	———

Table III. Coded interrupts, their origin and effects.

interrupted. If direct communication with the acting coordinator breaks down, investigation of the DICS will be re-initiated.

As a result of the investigation of the DICS, each of the processors enters one five state table definition procedures: DI11, DIR2XD, DIR2XY, DIRX2Y and DD22. DI11 is entered by a processor when the only direct communication in the system is between that processor and one other; DIR2XY is entered by ECPU-2 when ECPU-2 has direct communication with ECPU-X, and ECPU-X with ECPU-Y, but ECPU-2 has no direct communication with ECPU-Y; DIRX2Y is entered by ECPU-2 when there is direct communication between ECPU-2 and both ECPU-X and ECPU-Y, but not between the latter two; and DD22 is entered by all processors when all parts of the DICS are functioning correctly. Figure 5 shows the relationships between the eight states of the system when the processors are distinguished one from another; the states of the processors themselves; and the four effective states of the system when symmetry is taken into account.

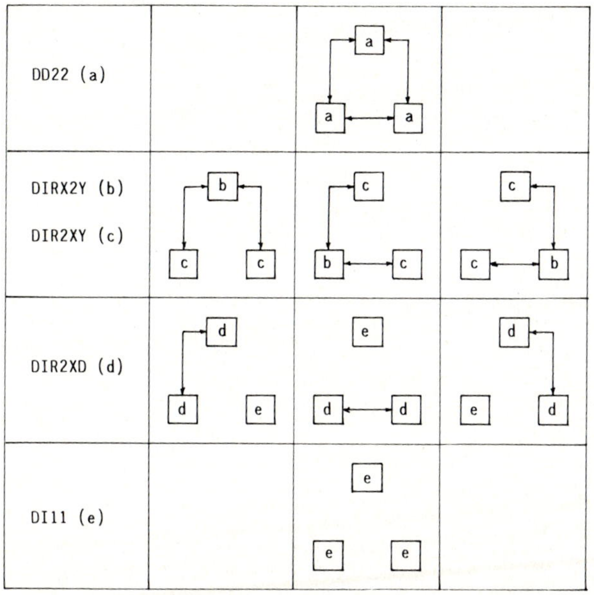

Fig. 5. DICS States.

If any lack of direct communication is detected between two processors, it is first assumed that the fault lies in the DICS, and the process of redefinition of the system is initiated by a jump to appropriate procedure, which may be one of the five listed above or TXAYB. Later the processors themselves are checked. All five state table definition procedures are self-sufficient, i.e. each possesses both means of defining a stack/state table area and means of detecting faults in the DICS. LTOS can therefore react appropriately to faults whatever the state of the DICS.

STATE TABLE DEFINITION PROCEDURES

All the state table definition procedures converge on one of three possible routines depending on the state of the system. A procedure in DI11 must remain there and organize indirect communication with the others via the shared resources, if it can; a processor with direct communication but which has been unable to set up a stack/state table enters FLAG7; and a communicated processor with a stack/table proceeds to the next LTOS phase by entering COORD, the procedure to elect one of the processors as coordinator.

DIR2XD (fig. 6)

In this procedure the stack and state table can only be set up by ECPU-2 in local RAM, in RAM-2 or in the RAM-2 of the processor with which there is direct communication. The RAM-2 of the isolated processor is ignored until dialogue with that processor is attempted via the shared resources. Setting up the stack/table in the RAM-2 of the other communicated processor can only be done if that processor has not itself put its stack/table there. For this reason, and as a routine check on their intercommunication, the two communicated processors periodically keep each other informed of their current state flag values, and if no such message is received after a certain waiting time, communication is assumed to have failed and DI11 is entered. If it has been possible to set up a stack/table (state flag 3,4,5, or 6), the state of the system is stored in the table and COORD entered. If not, and communication is maintained, then FLAG7 is entered.

DIR2XY and DIRX2Y

As with DIR2XD, (figs. 7 and 8) has no initial need to listen to the other with which it is communicated (which we shall call the intermediary), but will nevertheless periodically keep the other informed as to its own state. However, if the attempt to create its stack/table in local RAM or RAM-2 fails, it must ender D2XY and await the intermediary's instructions as to which of the other shared RAM pages to explore. Once its stack/table has been set up, a processor in DIR2XY continues to exchange information with the intermediary until the state of the whole system has been written in its state table. It then exits to COORD.

The intermediary in this process executes DIRX2Y, shown in figs. 9-11. If the intermediary is unable to set up this stack/table in local RAM or RAM-2, it waits until the other processors have attained state flag values of 2,3 or 4, but has priority as regards the use of any shared RAM left over. In routine X2Y it tells the other ECPUs to wait until its own

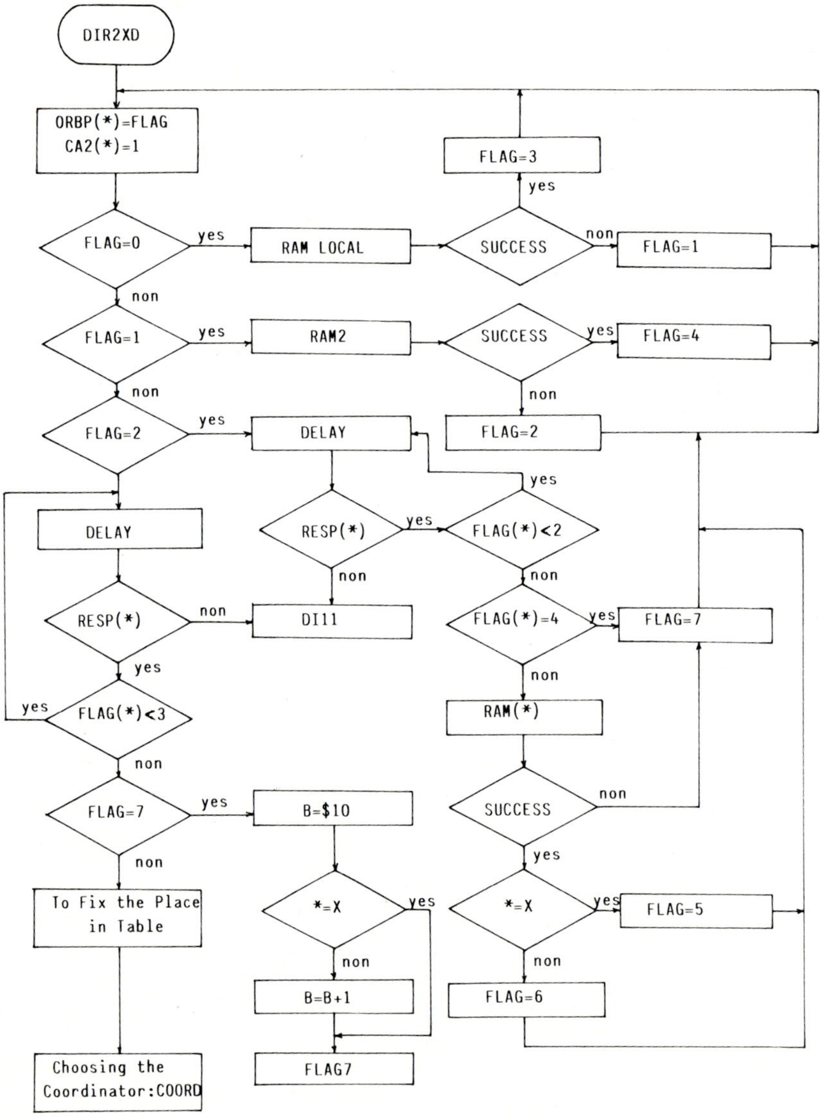

Fig. 6. Procedure DIR2XD. ORBP is an I/O chip output register and CA2 its control signal line.

exploration has finished, after which, in CAIXY and X27Y, it controls which pages of shared RAM the other processors may explore, should they require to do so. Once the intermediary has learnt the state of the other processors, it passes this information on so that they can all write up their tables. It then exits to COORD.

DD22 (fig. 12)

The first action of a processor in DD22 which retains communication with the other two but has been unable to set up its stack/table in local RAM or RAM-2 is to wait until it receives word from the other processors that they too have either finished exploring RAM (with state flag values other than 2) or (with state flag value 2) have unsuccessfully explored their local RAM and RAM-2s without so far having either set up a stack/table elsewhere or given up trying. When this information is received the processor enters D222D, D22*D or DX2YD according to whether both, one or neither of the other processors has a state flag value of 2. All three of these routines eventually lead to D37D, in which the state of the whole system is written in the state table, if this exists.

In D222D (fig. 14) each processor first tries to use its RAM-1, and if that fails, RAM-3

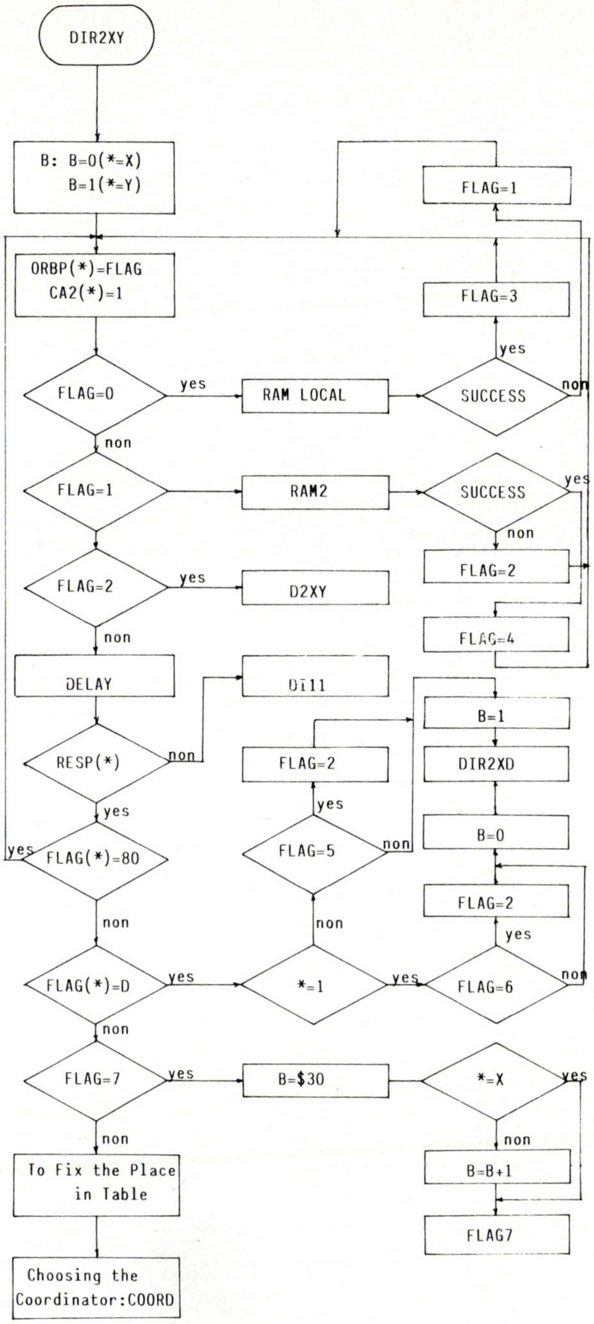

Fig. 7. PROCEDURE DIR2XY. Reception of a value of 80 for FLAG(*) is an instruction to wait. Reception of a value of D re-routes the receivers to DIR2XD.

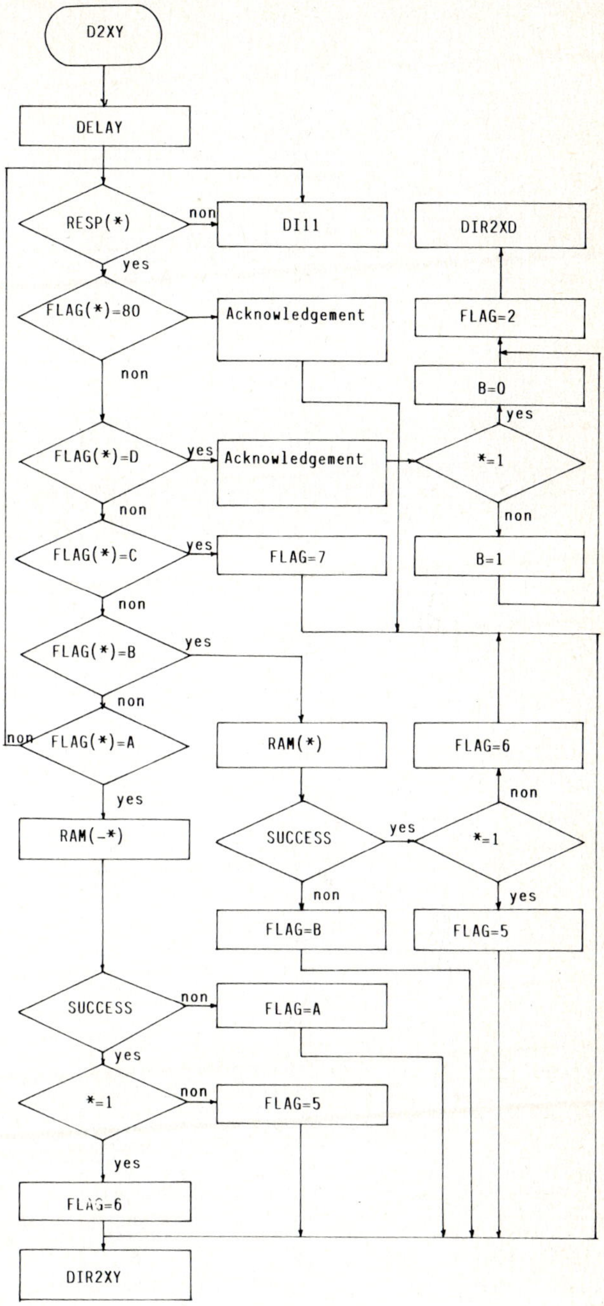

Fig. 8. PROCEDURE DIR2XY (D2XY).

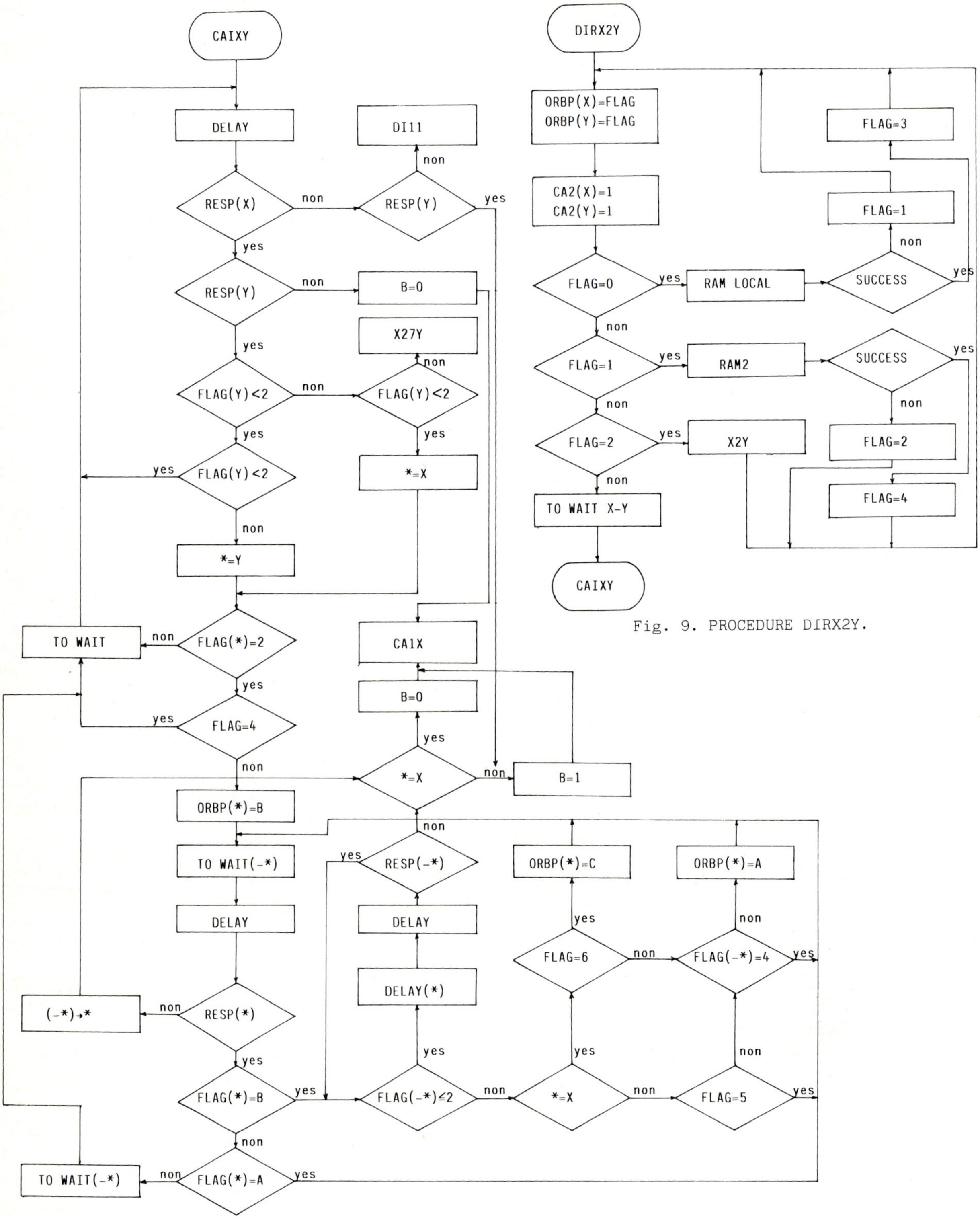

Fig. 9. PROCEDURE DIRX2Y.

Fig. 10. PROCEDURE DIRX2Y (CAIXY). If there is a communications failure, CAIX re-reoutes the intermediary to DIR2XD and tells the other communicated processor to do the same.

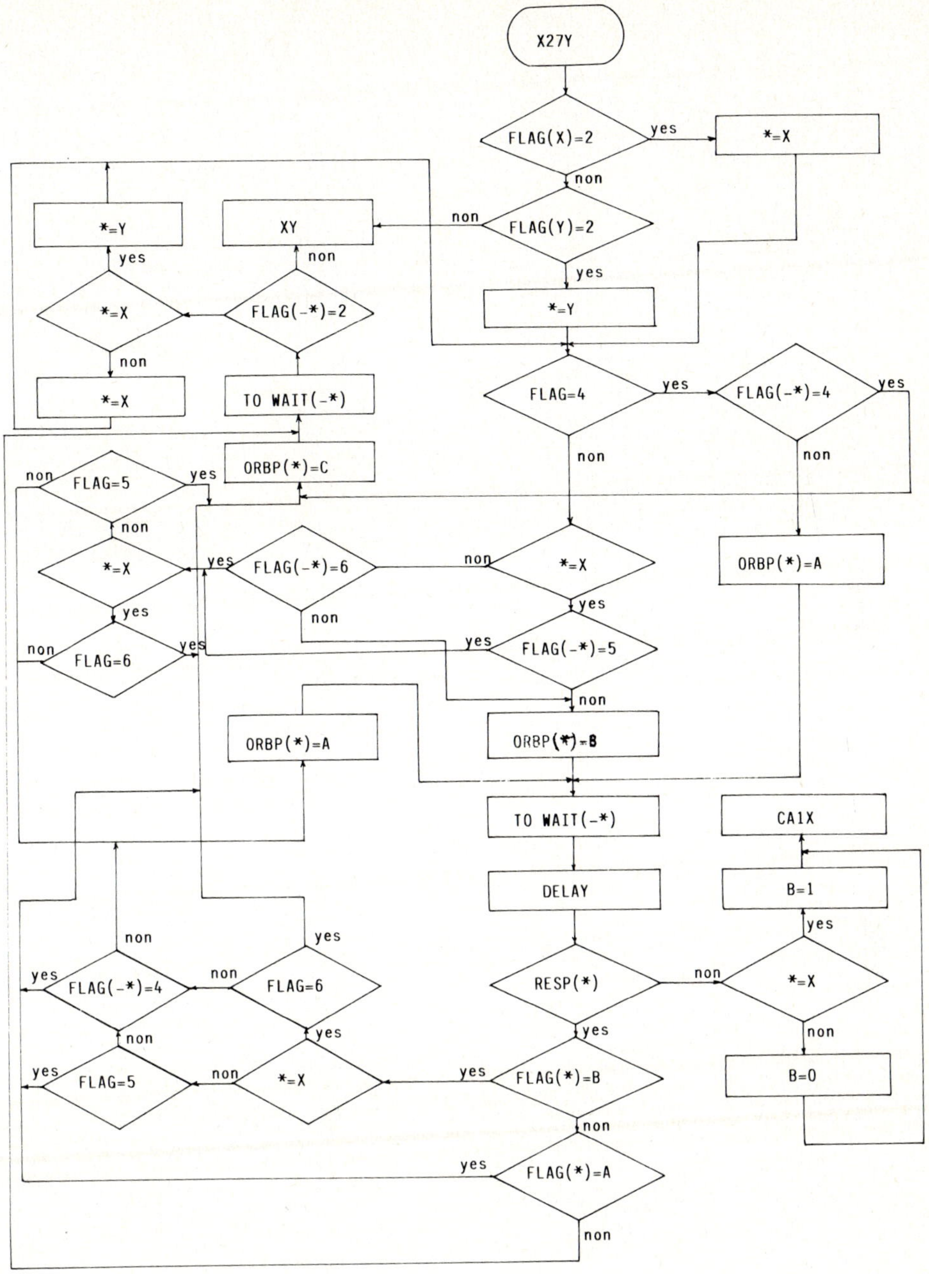

Fig. 11. PROCEDURE DIRX2Y (X2Y). XY exits to COORD.

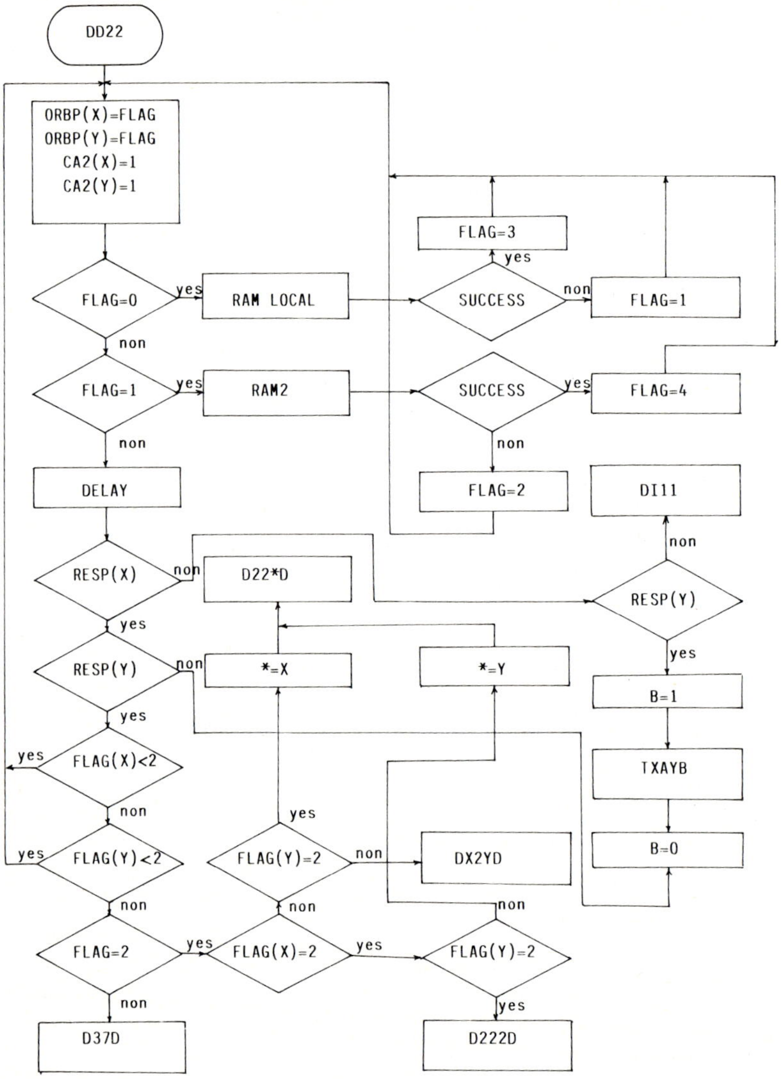

Fig. 12. PROCEDURE DD22.

(if ECPU-1 has left it free). In D22*D (fig.15) the two processors with state flag values of 2 first explore each other's RAM-2, so long as it has not been appropriated by the third ECPU for its stack/table. If either of them is successful in setting up its stack/table there, it enters D37D. If one is successful but not the other, the latter enters DX2YD. If neither is successful, they explore the third RAM page and, whatever the result of this exploration, exit to D37D. In DX2YD (fig. 13), the processor that has yet to complete exploration of the RAM tries to set up its stack/ table in RAM-1 or RAM-3, if these are free.

If D37D is reached without a stack/table having been set up, i.e. with state flag value 7, then exit is made to a FLAG7 procedure. Otherwise, COORD is entered after the state table has been written up.

CONCLUSION

Establishing a fault-free area for the relocatable state table of a processor forming part of a multiprocessor system is a complex process requiring a lot of time if the exchange of information between processors is to be guaranteed. However, we believe that the distributed software solution described here for a system like LTMuP, whose initial version comprises just three processors, if safer than the usual hardware methods.

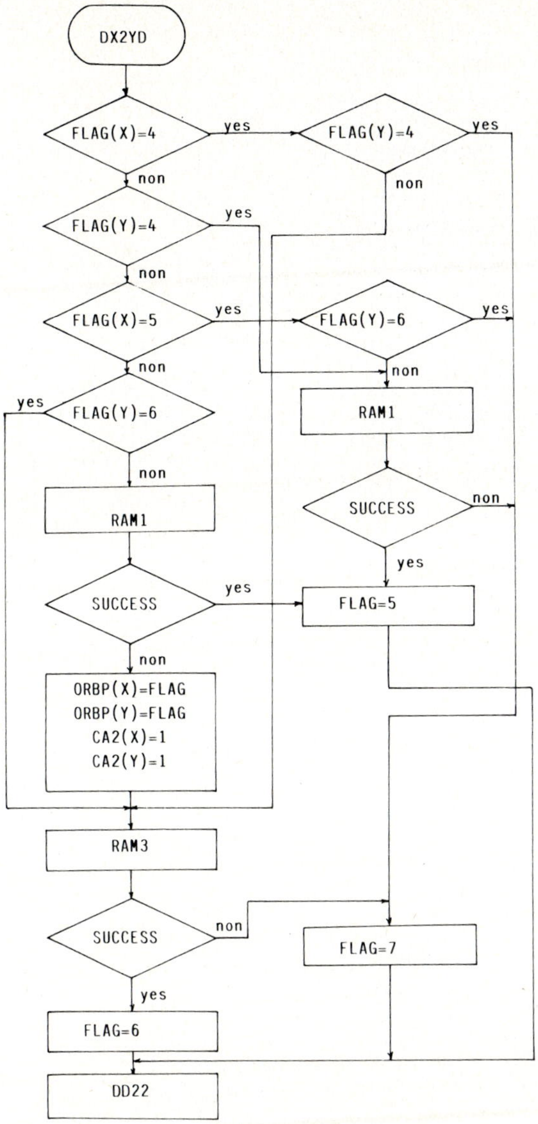

Fig. 13. PROCEDURE DD22 (DX2YD)

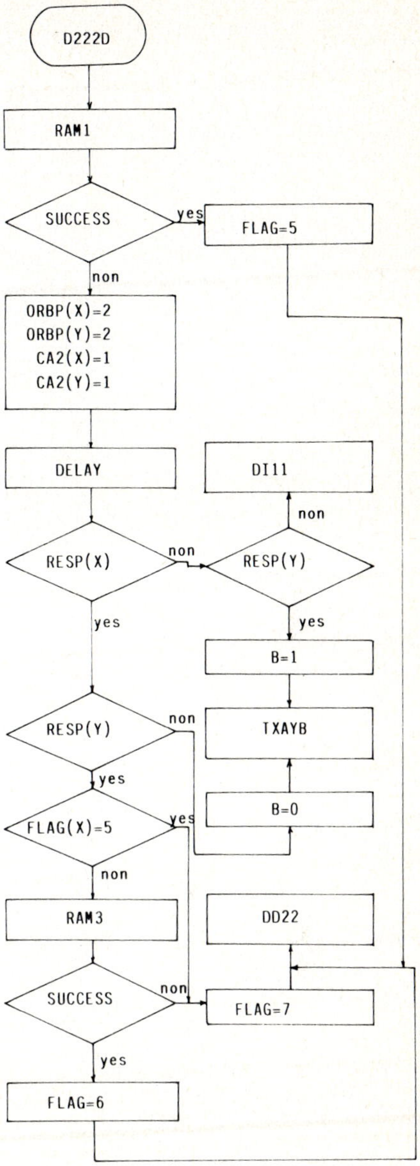

Fig. 14. PROCEDURE DD22 (D222D).

ACKNOWLEDGEMENT

The authors wish to acknowledge the support of the spanish Comision Asesora de Investigación Científica y Técnica under grants ref. 3803/79 and 995/82.

REFERENCES

1 Clarke, E.M. and Nikolaou, C.N. "Distributed Reconfiguration Strategies for Fault-Tolerant Multiprocessor Systems". Trans on Computers (1982), 8:773-784.

2 Grandoni, R. et al. "The MuTEAM System: General Guidelines". 11th Conference on Fault-Tolerant for Computer Systems (1981) 15-29.

3 Katsuki et al "PLURIBUS- An Operational Fault-Tolerant Multiprocessor". Proc. of the IEEE, 10 (1978), 1146-1159.

4 Luque, E., Bautista, A. and Ruz, J.J. "Memoria Tolerante a Fallos con Capacidad de Recuperación de Contenidos". IV Congreso Informática. Madrid, Oct. 1979, 1284-1293.

5 Mira, J., Delgado, A.E., Zapata, E.L. and Cabello, D. "On the Lesion Tolerance Problem for Cooperative Processes". in L. Richter (ed.), Implementing Functions: 55-63 (Amsterdam, North-Holland, 1981).

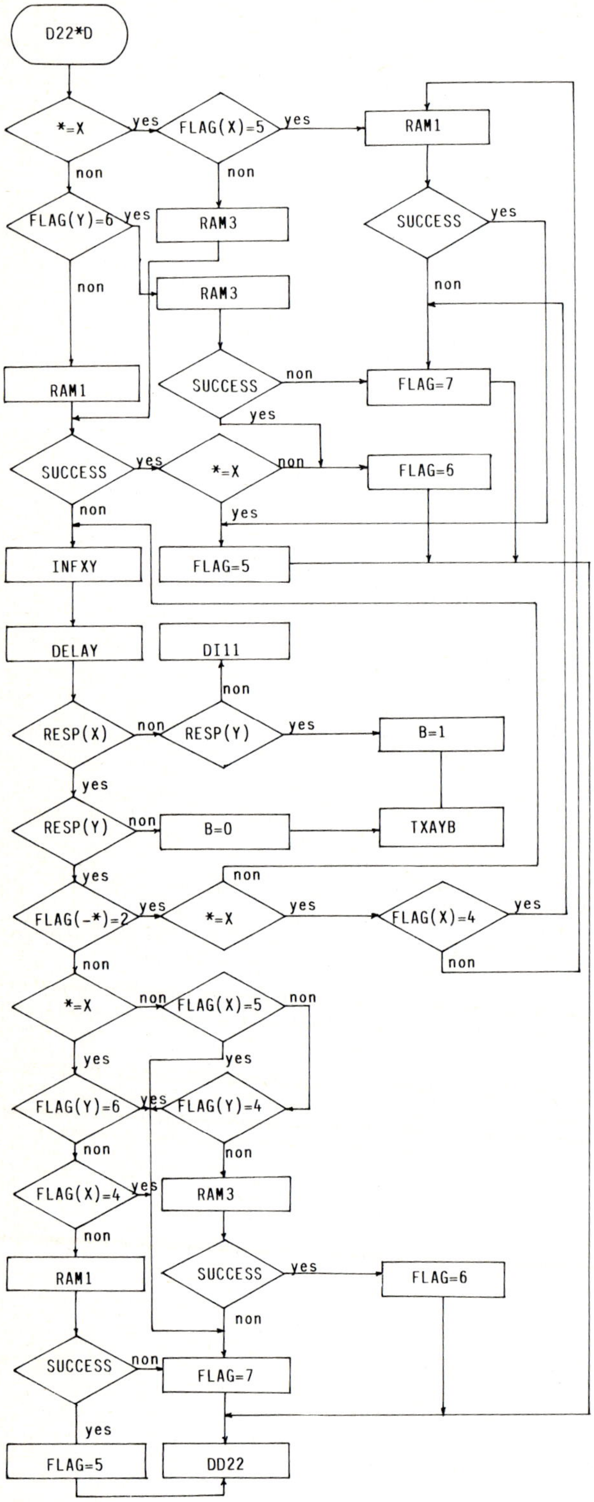

Fig. 15. PROCEDURE DD22 (D22*D)

6 Mira, J., Delgado, A.E., Zapata, E.L. and Cabello, D. "LTOS: A Lesion TOlerant Operative System". 3th IFAC/IFIC Congress, Software for Computer Control. 1982. 9-13.

7 Mira, J., Zapata, E.L., Delgado, A.E. and Cabello, D. "LTMuP and LTOS, A Distributed Cooperative Multimicroprocessor system that Tolerates Physical Damage". 27 Annual Meeting of the Society for General Systems Research (1983). (To be published).

8 Schneider, F.B. and Schlichling, R.D. "Towards Fault-Tolerant Process Control Software". 11th Conference on Fault-Tolerant for Computer Systems (1981), 48-51.

9 Wittie, L.D. "A Distributed Operating System for a Reconfigurable Network Computer". Proc. 1st Inter. Conference on Distributed Computing System (1979), 669-678.

10 Zapata, E.L. "LTMuP, Un Sistema Multimicroprocesador Cooperativo que Tolera la Lesión Física". Ph. D. Department of Electronics Univ. of Santiago de Compostela, (May 1983).

MICROCOMPUTERS: Developments in Industry, Business and Education
D.R. Wilson and C.J. van Spronsen (eds.) / ©EUROMICRO, 1983
Elsevier Science Publishers B.V. (North-Holland)

AN APPLICATION OF COROUTINES TO QUASI-PARALLEL PROGRAMMING

Petro Istavrinos

Siemens AG, ZTI SYS 133,
Muenchen, Germany

This paper describes an application of Edison oriented concurrent statements and synchronization mechanisms. The implementation on a single processor systems was based on coroutines as a tool for quasi-parallel programming. A delay function is introduced, which enhances performance on single processor systems, while retaining the simplicity of Edison.

1. INTRODUCTION

Coroutines were first introduced in 1963 / 8 / and have been utilized for different problems. Our application was the programming of a printer-server. Five MDSs (Microcomputer Development Systems) and three printers can be connected to the server. The hardware consists of an 8086-board, 256 kbyte ram, and the peripheral interface board. One main design requirement was to work without interrupts.

To the MDS the printer-server acts as a very fast printer. The connection between the printer-server and the MDS is just a printer-cable. So the operating system of the MDS had not to be changed.

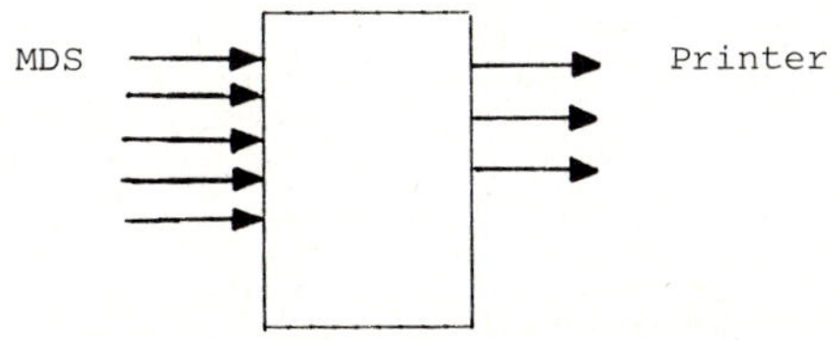

Figure 1: The Printer-Server

The task of the printer-server is to buffer the byte stream from the MDS and, if there is any printer available, start printing simultaneously. All printers and MDSs should be served in parallel.

The organisation of concurrent processes on a computer system requires some programming tools, which support the design of reliable and easy to maintain programs. We were inspired by Brinch Hansen's programming language Edison / 1 /. It offers some features for concurrency and synchronization, whereby the main concern is to achieve simplicity.

2. EDISON CONCEPT

In Edison concurrent processes can appear and disappear dynamically - but only at the same time / 2 /. They have the syntactical form of procedures.

The main mechanism to synchronize concurrent processes is the 'when' statement. The Edison report / 1 / describes it as follows:

"A when statement consists of a conditional statements list known as a synchronized statement. This is a mechanism which can be used to give concurrent processes exclusive access to common variables when their values satisfy certain conditions.

A process executes a when statement in two phases:

1. Synchronizing phase:

The process is delayed until no other process is executing the critical phase of a when statement.

2. Critical phase:

The synchronized statement is executed as described in Section 15.4. If the statement lists are skipped the process returns to the synchronizing phase; otherwise the execution of the when statement is terminated."

Section 15.4 / 1 / describes the execution of conditional statements (if statements). The boolean expressions in the conditional statements list are evaluated one at a time in the order written until one yields the value true or until all have been found to yield the value false. In the latter case, none of the statement lists are executed and the statement lists are said to be skipped; otherwise the statement list following the boolean expression with the value true is executed.

The 'when' statement has the effect that its boolean expressions are evaluated repeatedly until one condition is satisfied. Execution then proceeds with the statement list following and the 'when' statement is terminated.

3. IMPLEMENTATION

Coroutines were implemented as a basic tool for quasi-parallel programming / 3 , 4 / by means of predefined procedures. Because seperate compilation is possible with the ISIS operating system / 5 /, this was the simplest way to realize coroutines. These procedures can be linked to both Pascal and PL/M programs for the 8086 environment.

Coroutines transfer control to each other in a symmetric way. A coroutine continues execution until it suspends itself by transferring control to another coroutine. The supended coroutine can only be reactivated, when one of the other coroutines transfers control back to it. Processing then resumes at the statement following the point of suspension. If coroutines are interleaved with each other appropriately, they can be used to simulate parallel processes.

Our implementation allows multiple activation of a piece of code describing a coroutine and coroutines accept parameters at the moment of initialization. Since coroutines behave like processes, each coroutine has exclusive access to its own private stack.

The implementation of the coroutines was guided by the paper of Kriz and Sandmayr / 4 /. Adopting their concept to the Intel implementation of procedures written in Pascal / 6 / or PL/M / 7 /, some changes were necessary due to a different stack organization. Also some very simple routines for heap management were implenented to organize memory allocation for the coroutines.

The predefined procedures perform the following tasks:

- procedure COROUTINES (var CID: CORID);
  Initialization of the runtime package for coroutines. The initializing (main) program is also considered to be a coroutine. CID is an identification returned for the coroutine represented by the main program.

- procedure ALLOCATE (var CID: CORID; SL: INTEGER);
  Allocation of a private stack for a new coroutine. The stack length required is given as parameter SL. The variable parameter CID returns the identification of the new coroutine.

- procedure NEWCOR (PL: INTEGER);
  PL is the length of the parameter block of the coroutine. NEWCOR copies the context of the procedure describing the coroutine to the coroutine's private stack and prepare it for subsequent activation of the coroutine. It returns control to the initializing program. A call to this routine must be the first statement of the procedure describing the coroutine.

- procedure ENDCOR (CID: CORID);
  Terminates the active coroutine, deallocates its stack and transfers control to the coroutine identified by CID.

- procedure TRANSFER (CID: CORID);
  Transfers control to the coroutine CID. The activated coroutine continues with the statement following its last call of NEWCOR or TRANSFER.

Based on the coroutine concept a simple process scheduling mechanism was realized. Here we were inspired by the Edison philosophy / 1, 2 /.

'When' statements were imitated by loops and if statements. As the printer-server is a single processor system it executes one process at a time, so no problems occur with several processes trying to evaluate scheduling conditions simultaneously. The processes are executed in cyclical order. A process leaves the processor, when it attempts to execute a 'when' statement in which the boolean expressions yield the value false / 2 /.

With this basic tools at hand, programming of the printer-server was simplified considerably. For each printer and each MDS a process was generated. The MDS process handles the byte stream from 'his' MDS, while the printer process handles the output to 'his' printer. The input is stored in buffers, which can be linked together to form queues. When a printer is available its printer-process gets access to the buffer-queue and starts printing by sending the bytes to the output port. The free storage buffers are managed by a separate module. Altogether eight processes are running on the system.

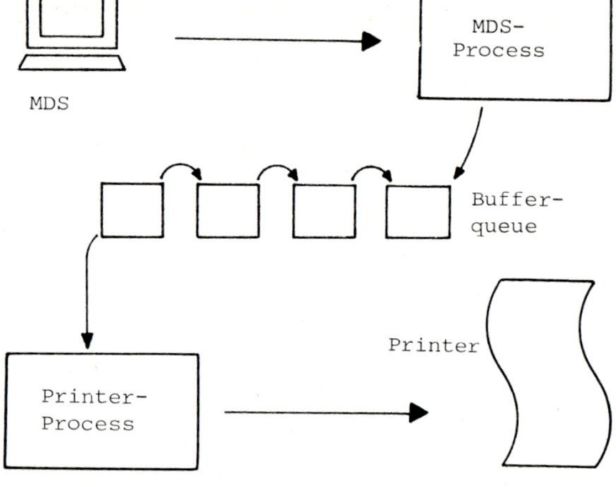

Figure 2: MDS-Process and Printer-Process.

3. EXTENSIONS

After debugging the system we ran some tests. Although the system could handle parallel input and output, the performance still seemed to be improvable. The wait-time for printing at the MDS was shortended only by the factor 1.8.

On the older MDSs (Series II) the wait-time is shorter than on the new ones (Series III). The reason is that the MDS hardware (Series III) behaves different. After sending one byte to the printer output port, the hardware waits one millisecond before attempting to send the next byte.

The second reason was in our software system. When the active input process did not get a byte, the system switched to the next process. The period of time until the actual MDS process gained control over the processor again, was rather long. The switching through all the seven other processes and the evaluation of the different conditions in the 'when' statements requested too much time. So the MDS process was too slow in taking over the bytes delivered by the MDS.

One solution would have been to give up the simple scheduling scheme and to implement a wait and signal mechanism. This solution would have requested considerable changes in the software. Therefore another solution was taken by introducing a delay function and just a second queue for the delayed processes.

The delay function, after delaying the process for a constant time, returns the boolean value false and can be used in any expression. For example in a 'when' statement:

```
when sense (channel, ready)  do
     c = input(port)
else delay do skip
end
```

Execution of the delay function has the effect that the running process is appended to the delay queue and its wake-up-time (actual time plus constant) is stored in its process descriptor. Whenever now process switching occurs the delay queue is checked. If the delay queue is not empty, the wake-up-time of the first process in the delay queue is compared to the actual system time. In case its wake-up-time is reached, the process is removed from the queue and activated.

The execution of the above 'when' statement has the same logical result as its execution without the else clause. The difference is that the processor is not blocked by reevaluating the boolean expression. Instead the process, after checking the condition and yielding the value false, is suspended for a certain time (for example 800 ms). When activated, it will check the condition again. This relieves the processor from unnecessary work, but has no effect to the user.

The else delay clause is used only in those parts of the program, where the processes have to deal with longer time breaks, so for example after an end-of-file.

The implementation of the delay function posed no problems, because a timer was available in our printer-server and was already in use for time-out conditions. The delay time being a constant implies that sorting of the delay queue is not necessary. The delayed process is just appended to the end of the delay queue.

The new version works very satisfying. The wait-time after a print command on a MDS is now five times shorter than without the printer-server. The delay function increased the performance of the implementation while retaining the simplicity and clearness of the Edison concept.

4. CONCLUSION

The application of the Edison concept for concurrency eases the task to manage small and medium scale programs considerably. Its easy to understand mechanisms support development and maintenance of such programs. With coroutines as basic tool for quasi-parallel programming different process scheduling mechanisms can explicitly be programmed depending on the application / 3 /. In our case the Edison scheduling primitive, which was designed for multiprocessor systems, was enhanced by the delay function to gain efficiency on a single processor system, too.

REFERENCES

/ 1 / P. Brinch Hansen: 'Edison - a Multiprocessor Language', Software - Practice and Experience, 11, 325-361 (1981)

/ 2 / P. Brinch Hansen: 'The Desing of Edison', Software - Practice and Experience, 11, 363-396 (1981)

/ 3 / N. Wirth: MODULA-2 Institut für Informatik, ETH Zürich, 36, 1980

/ 4 / J. Kriz and H. Sandmayr: 'Extension of Pascal by Coroutines and its Application to Quasi-parallel Programming and Simulation', Software - Practice and Experience, 10, 773-789 (1980)

/ 5 / IAPX 86, 88 FAMILY UTILITIES USER'S GUIDE
Intel Corporation, 1980

/ 6 / PASCAL-86 USER'S GUIDE
Intel Corporation, 1981

/ 7 / PL/M-86 USER'S GUIDE
Intel Corporation, 1981

/ 8 / Melvin, E. Conway:
'Design of a Separable Transition-Diagramm Compiler',
Communications of the ACM,
Vol. 6, Nr. 7, 396-408 (1963)

Session J1:

IMPLEMENTING ARCHITECTURE VIA FIRMWARE

Chairman: F. Vajda
Central Research Institute
for Physics
Budapest (Hungary)

Microprogramming has made a considerable progress both in techniques and applications since the basic idea was proposed by Wilkes in 1951. In the first decade computer scientists discovered microprogramming and published their findings. Then it was rediscovered by computer specialist and was applied in computer systems'implementation. Later it has been learned by a lot of people who had to use and program bit-sliced microprocessors. Recently, microprogramming has also been discovered as an important means of microelectronics for VLSI chip implementation [1].

With the growth in microprogramming came the requirement for better microprogram production techniques considering all the phases of microprogram development in stages of system life-cycle: design, specification, construction techniques, verification, testing, debugging and maintenance [2].

On its recent symposiums Euromicro devoted many sessions to the actual problems of microprogramming. Perhaps, just a list of the microprogram-oriented session titles of the last five years gives an impression of the problems covered:

- Microprogramming Languages [3], [6]
- Computer Architecture [3]
- Tools for Microprogram Developments [4]
- Performance Improvements by Microcode [4]
- User Microprogramming [5]
- Microprogrammable Machines [5]
- Firmware Environment [5]
- Microcode Generation [6]
- Migration of Functions [6]
- Firmware Development Systems [6]
- Firmware Engineering [7]

The 30th anniversary of microprogramming was commemorated by a special issue of Microprocessing and Microprogramming, the Euromicro Journal [8].

In the recent design of computers, microprogramming has become the standard techniques for implementing architecture due to the advantages of its systematic methodology and its flexibility in defining problem oriented virtual machines in real hardware.

Another area called tuning of computer architecture is still in its early stage but is expected to gain tremendously in the future. Tuning a computer architecture means an approach of matching the language and the computer architecture to the application problem. There are different methods for solving this problem applying manual, heuristic tuning, static or dynamic analysis.

In the paper of M.De Blasi and G.Turco a real-time tuning mechanism is proposed. In the suggested solution the tuning is a new phase of an interpreter so the execution is optimized during each single run. The model and implementation criteria are analysed and a learning algorithm composed by its two phase of measurement and intervention is described.

The second paper ("The Synthesis of a Microprogrammable PCB Router Architecture") by B.Hansen proposes a novel solution for the layout design of a Printed Circuit Board. It uses the well-known Lee algorithm but discusses the synthesis of a microprogrammable architecture for implementing a new routing CAD system by converting the algorithm into firmware. The tuning procedure and useful hints for the final implementation are also given. At least two order of performance improvement is expected to achieved compared to the conventional software based solution.

In the paper of P.Dembinski and M. Pawlowski a new algorithm for microprogram compaction is presented. A major area of contemporary research in microprogramming is the definition and implementation of methods for microcode parallelization which results in less microprogram execution time and/or control store size. The correctness of the algorithm proposed in the paper is justified and illustrated by many examples.

I am convinced that this session dealing with different interesting problems of microprogrammed architectures will be useful for the participiants in the long series of Euromicro symposium sessions devoted to microprogramming and firmware engineering.

REFERENCES

[1] F.Vajda: Recent Developments in the Applications of Microprogramming, Report of the Central Research Institute for Physics of the Hungarian Academy of Sciences, KFKI-1982-18 (1982).

[2] S.Davidson,B.D.Shriver: Firmware Engineering: An Extensive Update, in G.Chroust, J.R.Mühlbacher (eds.): Firmware, Microprogramming and Restructurable Hardware (North Holland, Amsterdam, 1980) 1-40.

[3] H.W.Lawson, Jr., H.Berndt, G. Hermanson (eds.): Large Scale Integration: Technology, Application and Impacts (North Holland, Amsterdam, 1978)

[4] J.Tiberghien, G.Carlstedt, J.Lewi (eds.): Microprocessors and their Applications (North Holland, Amsterdam, 1979)

[5] M.Sami, L.Thompson, L.Mezzalira (eds.): Microprocessor Systems: Software, Firmware and Hardware (North Holland, Amsterdam, 1980)

[6] L.Richter, P.Le Beux, G.Chroust, G.Noguez (eds.): Implementing Functions: Microprocessors and Firmware (North Holland, Amsterdam, 1981).

[7] C.J. van Spronsen, L.Richter (eds.): Microsystem: Architecture, Integration and Use (North Holland, Amsterdam, 1982).

[8] Microprocessing and Microprogramming (The Euromicro Journal) 8 (Oct. Nov. Dec. 1981).

MICROCOMPUTERS: Developments in Industry, Business and Education
D.R. Wilson and C.J. van Spronsen (eds.) / ©EUROMICRO, 1983
Elsevier Science Publishers B.V. (North-Holland)

REAL-TIME TUNING OF COMPUTER ARCHITECTURE

Mario De Blasi and Giovanni Turco

Istituto di Scienze dell'Informazione
Università di Bari, Italy

A tuning mechanism of computer architecture which constantly follows the variations of the execution profile, optimizing the execution times during each single run, is proposed. In this context, the tuning becomes a new phase of the interpreter, in addition to the fetch and execute phases. Model and implementation criteria on microprogrammable computers are all described, and the problems arising are discussed.

KEYWORDS: Automating tuning, Vertical migration, Real-time tuning, Dynamic microprogramming, Self-modifying algorithms.

1. INTRODUCTION

Tuning of computer architecture, or matching the machine language to the application problem by means of vertical migration from higher levels to the microprogramming one, has evolved from manual techniques to automatic synthesis of microprograms.

The <u>automatic</u> tuning originated with the classic work of Abd-Alla and Karlgaard /1/, who based the entire process on statistics gained in a phase of program execution tracing (<u>heuristic</u> tuning).

Extensions and improvements of this method were developed by El-Ayat and Howard /2/, and by Abd-Alla and Moffet /3/.

A different approach, based on analysis of static programs by the compiler, which produces the new architecture and the code compiled in the language of this machine, is due to Rauscher and Agrawala /4/. This method is independent from any machine, has a low time overhead, and it also takes account of expected execution frequencies, computed at compile time using a Markow model of program behaviour.

A more rigorous analytical methodology, which also introduces a dynamic analysis phase, is due to Luque and Ripoll /5/.

The essential merits of the above methods are the elimination of human work, in particular in this field, which requires high human skill and competence on the physical structure of the machine. The figures on time performance improvements, obtainable by all the methods described, were highly encouraging, and, in some cases (see /1/), competitive with those reported in implementations of manual tuning.

On the basis of these results we believe that it is not unrealistic to think of going towards a full automation of the tuning process.

It is true that optimization of a global situation is generally difficult and can lead to solutions which are not specifically optimal. However it is worth while examining the present state of tuning methods in order to deduce the main points that must still be overcome.

First of all, none of the above methods is completely "transparent" to the user: the tuned system is to be obtained in one or more runs, which are set up specifically for this aim, and precede the real runs. Thus they are automatic but not transparent.

Secondly, the tuning is based on a particular profile of the program execution, with particular sets of data. This is the critique that Rauscher and Agrawala make of the heuristic methods /4/, but their method is based on estimates made at compile time, less specific, but more unreliable than measures taken at run time.
This problem was also clear to El-Ayat and Howard /2/, who, after tuning the architecture, undertook a period of observation to verify if the new architecture matched the applicative program successfully or if it was necessary to re-tune it. Similarly, in the analytical method of Luque and Ripoll /5/, the dynamic analysis is made by running the program for several sets of data and averaging the frequencies obtained.

The profile of the program can not only change with different data, but can also vary during the course of the same run: this is, perhaps, the main point lacking in every method based on preliminary runs or on the static analysis of the program.

Thus, the third bias of all the methods described is that the tuned architecture risks being a compromise which optimizes the time of execution in a given period of time, and lowers the performance in other periods of the same run.

From these considerations, we conclude that an "ideal" tuning mechanism has to possess the following characteristics:

a) it has to be transparent and in operation for every program to be run by the computer;
b) it has to be adaptive, i.e. it must follow the execution profile constantly;
c) it has to be equally effective in stationary, quasi-stationary and non-stationary environments.

To achieve these goals, it is necessary that the tuning process be continuous and in real-time with program execution, and not an isolated activity preceeding the production runs.

The sum of the above requirements, of course, sets serious time constraints on the implementation, which do not guarantee success in a short time. In this paper, various problems are pinpointed and a preliminary solution is proposed.

2. THE ABSTRACT TUNING MACHINE

In /6/ is shown that a computer which is capable of tuning its own architecture to external environment (programs and data), can be represented as a two-algorithm system (Fig.1).

The first one is the usual operative algorithm, whose function is to transform the input words which come from main memory.

The second algorithm, called the control, monitoring or learning algorithm, acts on the first by changing the operating mode of the same.

The model described pertains to the more general self-modifying algorithm theory /7/.

The object of learning is, in the tuning, an increasing of the operative algorithm speed in interpreting a particular program.

The model is applicable both to manual and automatic tuning, the variations being in whether or not man is included in the tuning process control.

However, following the considerations made in Sect.1, we have to adopt a more restrictive definition. We will say that the object of learning in the tuning is a gradual increasing in the operative algorithm speed while interpreting each program.

That is, the tuning process control has to be, as we outlined, continuous ('while'), adaptive and transparent ('each'). Moreover, we also intend for 'each program' the same program in each of its executions.

To fulfill these requirements, also taking into account that in this case the skill is to run the program more speedly, it is necessary (but not sufficient) that the learning algorithm interacts with the operative one without burdening its execution. In particular, we have to maintain a

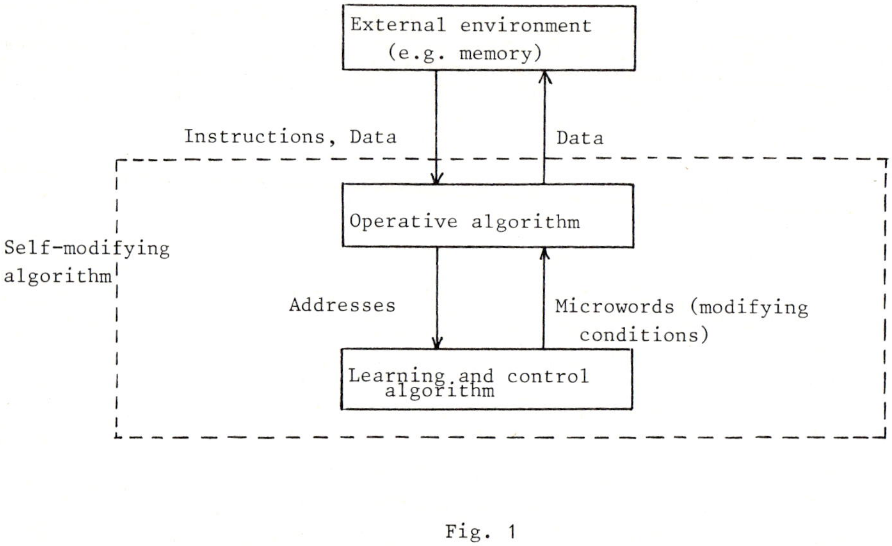

Fig. 1

strict hierarchy in the levels of machines in Fig.1, i.e.: a) the language of the learning algorithm must be at a lower level than the 'operative' language; b) direct connections between the control algorithm and the external environment (main memory), are to be kept weak, i.e. statistically infrequent.

It is noteworthy that the rules a) and b), that are always followed for the sake of efficiency in every tuning methodology, are mandatory in the real-time tuning.

In real-time tuning, two phases alternate which each other for the overall duration of the program execution: a measurement phase and an intervention phase.
The measurements must be applied even to the optimized code to compare it with the other sections of code. The resources of the operative algorithm are finited and, therefore, are to be managed dynamically. Thus, the code which is not yet optimized competes for the use of resources with the code already optimized, that uses these resources.
The intervention phase is applied whenever a new section of code has to be optimized and must take the place of a section previously optimized, which is less active than the first one.

Lastly, precautions are to be taken against interventions that risk becoming too frequent, as happens in the case of non-stationary processes.

In any case, the measurements have an incidence much higher than interventions: therefore, any operation which can be transferred from the measurement phase to the intervention phase, has to be located.

Let us now see how these general rules have been applied in an implementation that we have developed on an HP 1000 system.

3. IMPLEMENTING A TUNING MACHINE

3.1 Analysis of the resources

The resources commonly available on the microprogramming level for vertical migration, are:

a) the dynamic microprogramming memory;
b) the opcodes and entry points to dynamic microprogramming memory, usable for the new instructions ("extended" instructions);
c) the scratchpad registers or local store;
d) the main memory.

a) Dynamic microprogramming memory. Using this resource, one can apply traditional dynamic memory management techniques. This implies periodical recompacting of stored microcode, its relocation, loading and relocation of new microcode.

In this operation the first bottleneck of a tuning machine is located, for which it can be useful to resort to less "sensitive" techniques.

To this end, we introduce the concept of environment, as the set of critical areas in which the program spends the greatest part of its time and has, instant for instant, possession of the resources of the microprogramming level available for vertical migration. It can vary during a run, as detected from a decreased global activity and, then and only then, the environment as a whole will be substituted in dynamic microprogramming memory.

The instantaneous activity is measured by counting, over a given period of time, the number of executions of extended instructions. It can then be compared to the "initial" activity of the environment, which is measured immediately after the filling up of the dynamic microprogramming memory.

b) Opcodes and entry points. Usually, the code to be migrated is replaced by an extended instruction followed by a "jump" instruction to the section subsequent to the code itself.

Thus, for every portion of code to optimize, it is necessary to dedicate a new operation code. This code corresponds to an entry point in a jump table in the dynamic microprogramming memory. Even these resources, opcodes and entry points, are limited and their exhaustion can stop the filling of the dynamic microprogramming memory. Again, a decreasing activity of the present environment will restart the tuning by loading the new environment.

c) Scratchpad registers. Ordinarily, scratchpad registers of the microprogramming level are locally used by microprograms which fetch and execute the single instructions.

The tuning machine, on the contrary, has need of registers of a global type in respect to each single instruction.

These registers have to contain:
1) counters for measuring the activity of the most recent critical areas (we measure loop activities);
2) identifiers (i.e. addresses in the main memory) of the same areas;
3) the counter for environment activity;
4) control variables.

In HP 1000, a number of scratchpad registers is used only by floating point instructions. They are usable, then, as quasi-global registers if at least one register not used for other purposes is available. Using this register as a control register, it is possible to store the quantities of interest in the other registers, until a floating point instruction is encountered. At this time, these registers are saved in the main memory and made available to the floating point instruction. At return from this instruction, the registers are restored when needed.

d) Main memory. As indicated in Sect.1, the connections with the main memory are to be as weak as possible. The use is then limited to: 1) save locations for scratchpad registers; and 2) a table of critical area descriptors.

The saving and restoring of scratchpad registers is effected, as indicated in c), only in executing floating point instructions.

The critical areas table look-up is more frequent. This happens at every entrance in loops whose descriptors are not in scratchpad registers. After the first iteration, loop descriptors are loaded in scratchpads and used here until the appearance of a new loop.

To diminish the number of accesses in main memory for loop-table look-up, as many scratchpads as possible have to be used to contain descriptors of recent loops. Moreover, a filtering of the loops is advisable before deciding to search for them in scratchpads and in the loop-table. For example, it is not useful to microprogram loops which are too short or too long. Other criteria of non-microprogrammability, such as the existence of jump-out or jump-to-subroutine instructions within the loops, are too expensive to be considered in this phase. They are to be deferred to the much less frequent subsequent phase of intervention, when the loop will have overcome the threshold for its optimization.

3.2 The learning algorithm

The learning algorithm is composed, as seen in Sect.2, of two phases, one of measurement and the other of intervention.

3.2.1 Measurement phase

Both the activity of the loops which are not yet optimized and the activity of the environment are measured. The measurement phase uses, as seen in Sect. 3.1, a group of scratchpad registers which it shares with the floating point instructions. Another register, not used by any instruction, not even by the floating point, has been dedicated to the control of the sharing. These registers have been reported in Table 1.

Table 1

SP12	=	Scratchpad controlling the sharing of SP6-SP10: -1 : the scratchpads are assigned to the learning algorithm; else: the scratchpads have been assigned to the floating point instructions.
SP8	=	Identifier (address of the last instruction) of the most recent loop.
SP7	=	Counter of loop iterations, whose identifier is in SP8.
SP6	=	Pointer to loop-table descriptor whose identifier is in SP8.
SP9	=	Identifier of the most recent non-microprogrammable loop.
SP10	=	Counter of executions of extended instructions.

Moreover, two other registers, local to each instruction, are of interest to us. They are SP1, which contains the operand address at the exit of the fetch phase, and P, the Program Counter. In "jump-back" instructions which, as already known, identify the loops, these two registers have the meaning given in Table 2.

Table 2

SP1	=	Address of the first instruction of the loop.
P-1	=	Address of the last instruction of the loop (instruction of jump-back).

Once a jump-back instruction is detected, a test on SP12 reveals if the scratchpads have been assigned to the floating point. In this case, they are restored from the main memory.

Then, the identifier of the most recent loop, SP8, is compared to P-1, the address of the jump-back instruction. If it is the same loop, the maximum efficiency is reached, and SP7, the corresponding loop-counter, is incremented.

Another situation of high efficiency is given if the loop coincides with the most-recent non-microprogrammable loop (scratchpad SP9). In this case, the control leaves the learning algorithm and passes directly to the execute phase of the instruction.

If the entering loop does not coincide with the preceeding one, it is examined on its length, given by:

length = P - SP1

A loop which is too short or too long leaves the learning phase.

If the loop is accepted, it is searched for in the loop-table in order to load the scratchpads with its descriptors. If it is not in the table, a new descriptor is entered.

If the loop is in the table and it is tagged as non-microprogrammable, its identifier is loaded in SP9.

The environment activity, i.e. the activity of the loops which are already optimized, is measured by-passing the search in the loop-table. This is obtained by inserting a microinstruction which increments the counter SP10 in each microprogram interpreting an extended instruction.

Lastly, the event which switches the control from the measurement phase to the intervention phase is the overcoming of a threshold by the loop-counter.

The value to assign to this variable depends essentially on the overhead of the intervention phase. From one intervention to the next it is necessary at least to recover this time, so that the interventions do not have to be too frequent.

Another process, which will be analized in the next Section, is indirectly influenced by this threshold: the environment renewal process. The latter depends on the activity of the environment, but the examination of the renewal conditions is triggered off by every loop that overcomes the threshold.

Thus, low values of threshold can not only make too frequent interventions, but also risk starting environment renewals on the basis of an occasional temporary decreased activity.

3.2.2 Intervention phase

The loop, whose counter has overcome the threshold, competes for the use of the resources with the environment, i.e. with the loops which have got their possession.

If there are sufficient resources, the loop can be microprogrammed, if it is not already, and relocated and loaded in the dynamic microprogramming memory.

If the dynamic microprogramming memory or the entry points are exhausted, what we have called a <u>race</u> starts. That is the counter SP10 is cleared for measuring the environment activity until the next occurrence of threshold overcoming by the same or another loop. At this point, the environment activity is compared to the initial activity of the environment and, if it were much less than this, the race would be won by the external environment, that will begin its loading in the dynamic microprogramming memory at the place of the present environment.

This operation implies the restoring in the program of the first two instructions of each loop pertaining to the environment, which were stored in the loop-table descriptors.

If the environment activity is still high, then the race is left open and SP10 is cleared again for a new confrontation of the environment activity with the external loop activities. This process continues for the entire run.

4. CONCLUSIONS

The real-time tuning process, seen as an activity which is an integral part of the interpreter in the same manner as the fetch and execute phases, has been shown to be possible.

After all, the interpreting of machine language instructions is the job that computers carry out most frequently. And in this skill they can gain experience quickly, during a small fraction of the single runs.

It is not necessary to resort to new physical architecture to reach this goal: the microprogrammable computer is the one which furnishes the two levels for the self-improvement required.

However, various problems still exist essentially because of the need for using the main memory. The table look-up for the search of the loop-descriptors is undoubtedly the major source of inefficiency.

Another problem is in the dynamic microprogramming memory management strategy. For the high overhead exhibited by the intervention phase, we have conceived a slowly responsive technique, based on the environment concept, but prompter and faster interventions are advisable.

REFERENCES

/1/ Abd-Alla, A.M. and Karlgaard, D.C., Heuristic synthesis of microprogrammed computer architecture, IEEE Trans. on Comp. C-23 (1974) 802-807.

/2/ El-Ayat and Howard, J.A., Algorithms for a self-tuning microprogrammed computer, Proc. 10th IEEE Annu. Workshop Microprogramming (1977) 85-91.

/3/ Abd-Alla, A.M. and Moffett, L.H., On-line architecture tuning using microcapture, Proc. 3rd Annu. IEEE Symp. Computer Architecture (1976) 165-171.

/4/ Rauscher, T.G. and Agrawala, A.K., Dynamic problem-oriented redefinition of computer architecture via microprogramming, IEEE Trans. on Computers C-27 (1978) 1006-1014.

/5/ Luque, E. and Ripoll, A., Microprogramming: a tool for vertical migration, Microprocessing and Microprogramming 8 (1981) 219-227.

/6/ De Blasi, M., Degli Antoni, G. and Marino, D., Investigations on self-improvement techniques in microprogrammable digital systems, Proc. Annu. AICA Symp. (1980) 295-303.

/7/ Glushkov, V.M., Introduction to Cybernetics (Academic Press, 1966).

MICROCOMPUTERS: Developments in Industry, Business and Education
D.R. Wilson and C.J. van Spronsen (eds.) / ©EUROMICRO, 1983
Elsevier Science Publishers B.V. (North-Holland)

THE SYNTHESIS OF A MICROPROGRAMMABLE PCS ROUTER ARCHITECTURE

by Birgit Hansen

Dept. of Automation Technology
Technological Institute
2630 Tastrup
Denmark.

The design of a distributed modularly autonomous microprogrammmable Printed Circuit Board tracking system is discussed which provides a general purpose computing facility with many in-built special purpose processors to speed up critical paths in the routing process whilst allowing non-critical routing activities to executed by an ALU.
The Lee algorithm with cost functions to guide the router on the PCB surfaces is presented to provide an understanding of the system architecture based on the AMD2903 bitslice processor. The paper discusses the optimisation strategy employed to convert the software implementation of the algorithm to a suboptimal, but near optimal, firmware multiprocessor implementation.
Finally, the performance of the PCB routing system is shown to be at least 2 orders of magnitude better than conventional mainframe or minicomputer solutions running the Lee algorithm with cost functions.

The Computer Aided Design problem to be addressed in this paper is the layout of the wiring of a Printed Circuit Board (PCB), which continues to be a real engineering problem. The methods developed may well be applicable to Uncommitted Logic Arrays (ULA) or even Large Scale Integration (LSI) layout solutions. In a manual layout the designer must place components and interconnection paths in such positions that the wiring diagram is fully represented in one or several planes with no two connections crossing on the same plane. The difficulty for the designer lies in the effect each connection may have on any connection to be laid down in the future and this problem has not become easier with increased interconnection complexity.

The PCB layout problem has so far been solved by the employment of digital computers running one or several algorithms or heuristic solutions in sequence to perform the layout of a PCB as well as producing Numerically Controlled machine tapes and other output formats for the routed board for use in the manufacturing phase. This essentially software approach has proved expensive in terms of time, and hence money, for large complex boards without obtaining completely routed boards in all but the simpler cases. More sophisticated algorithms and heuristic solutions or improvements to existing ones frequently increase the number of routed interconnections by more than 1 percent, however, with adverse effect on computer time and computer memory requirements.

In recent years with the phenomenal decrease in the price of microelectronic components, problems that hitherto had been solved exclusively in software have the realistic potential of being more hardware oriented without losing the flexibility inherent in software implementations. One well established example is hardware floating point arithmetic units added to conventional computers. This trend together with the long turn around time of computer layouts led to the proposal for a dedicated microprogrammable PCB hardware router.

This paper discusses the process of synthesising a microprogrammable architecture to implement a flexible high performance PCB routing system based on the Lee algorithm. The principles and methods employed to convert the algorithm, normally implemented in software, into a suboptimal, but near optimal, firmware implementation is discussed with less emphasis on the final implementation details resulting from the tuning process.

The following section provides a description of the Lee router employing cost functions to enhance the router performance. This is followed by a high level system specification relating the described algorithmic statements to equivalent logical hardware modules forming the basis of the architecture. Finally, a detailed description of the manual tuning process is given resulting in the final design of which an overview is given.

The Lee Algorithm.

An algorithm or heuristic rationale should be relatively simple, general and preferably exhaustive in order to be implemented in a tailored architecture. For these reasons a maze-runner, the Lee algorithm (Lee /7/), with a multitude of different cost functions (Hansen /4/, Hoel/5/, Rubin /9/, Rubin /10/ and Allen /2/) is selected. The Lee algorithm in its simplest form will now be discussed.

	1						
1	A	X	X	X			
	1						
		Z					
		Z		B			
		Z					

Fig. 1a

	2	1	2				
2	1	A	X	X	X		
	2	1	2				
		2	Z				
			Z		B		
			Z				

Fig. 1b

3	2	1	2	3	4	5	6
2	1	A	X	X	X	6	
3	2	1	2	3	4	5	6
4	3	2	Z	4	5	6	
5	4	3	Z	5	B		
6	5	4	Z	6			
	6	5	4				
		6	5	6			

Fig. 1c

		A	X	X	X		
		1	2	3	4		
			Z	4	5		
			Z	5	B		
			Z				

Fig. 1d

Fig. 1a-d Example of Wave Front Growth.

Figs. 1a-d show how a path is constructed to join point "A" to point "B" avoiding the obstacles "XXX" and "ZZZ" on 4, 2-dimensional matrixes:
1.Elements orthogonally adjacent to point "A", if not containing an obstacle, are assigned the value "1" to indicate their orthogonal distance from "A".
2. Likewise, elements orthogonally adjacent to those marked with "1" are assigned a value equal to the sum of their orthogonal distance from elements marked "1" plus the value in the element marked "1". The result is "2" which is their orthogonal distances from "A".
3. This process is continued until the "wave front" reaches element "B" which terminates the expansion.
4. One of the shortest paths is selected by marking elements in numerically descending order from "B" to "A"; at least one such path exists in this example and hence a route is found.

This is the simplest manner in which the Lee algorithm works. The numbers used for marking represent the resource usage or "cost". In the example given, the differential cost of jacent element is unity. In general, the differential cost covers a range of values and is a function of the "terrain" which determines how the growth proceeds.

It is presupposed that a PCB has a limited number of resources available such as the size of the board, number of vias permitted, preferred directions etc. Different incremental costs are imposed on these resources and their combinations to guide the router on a particular layer and through the board to other layers to complete a net. If a non-unity cost is imposed for traversing a surface the cost of reaching the target cell is no longer equivalent to a minimal length path, but to a minimal cost path. The amount by which the marking number increases from one cell to an adjacent cell is the differential cost or the cost function.

The Lee algorithm with cost functions is described in fig. 2 in Pascal like notation and was programmed in Pascal on a PDP 11/60 minicomputer. The main body of the Lee Algorithm (the leftmost WHILE statement) using several stacks to store cell coordinates for later expansion will now be discussed. The unloaded coordinates from the stack are passed to the address generator which produces the neighbouring X-Y-Z addresses for the 3 dimensional map which contains the entire state of the PCB routing surfaces. The data processor marks a neighbouring cell if it is unmarked or if the mark previously given to this is higher than the sum of the expansion cell cost and the cost of entering the neighbour cell. The resultant mark placed in the neighbour cell equals the expansion cell cost plus the cost of entering the neighbour cell. The cost is also used to control the stack switch enabling the marked cell to be loaded into the store which is "cost" stores away from the current expansion store (in reality implemented with pointers). The algorithm terminates when the target has been reached or when all stacks are empty. The latter means that no path exists. The retrace algorithm is very simple and will not be discussed further here.

```
program Lee algorithm;
BEGIN
clear all stacks;
mark all non-obstacle cells with 'unoccupied';
place obstacles "XXX" and "ZZZ" in map;
set current expansion count to zero;
load coordinates of point "A" into stack;
WHILE  stack not empty OR target not found
DO  BEGIN
    WHILE stack not empty
    DO  BEGIN
        unload next coordinates from stack;
        load coord. into neighbour address generator;
        FOR all neighbours
        DO  BEGIN
            generate next neighbour address;
            IF neighbour cell unmarked
            OR neighbour contents
               >current expansion count + cost
            THEN  BEGIN
                  mark neighbour cell with
                  'current expansion count+cost';
                  load marked cell coord. into
                  stack(current expansion count+cost);
                  END
            END
        END
    END;
FOR i=0 TO stack(max. number)
DO copy contents of stack (i+1) to stack(i);
reset current expansion stack(0);
increment current expansion count
END.
```

Fig. 2. The Lee Algorithm with Cost Functions.

Synthesis of the Architecture.

The PCB layout system is required to implement the router specification as efficiently as possible in terms of memory requirements and time taken to route a PCB. It is also required to provide a flexible, i.e. programmable, environment in order to provide a research vehicle for experimentation with different types of routers using raster scan graphics.

The PCB hardware router is specified to be capable of routing 2 layer multipoint (max. 64) nets or 4 layer 2 point nets on a 1K*1K resolution image map employing the above described Lee algorithm with user defined cost functions. The router must be capable of supporting 45 degree lines as well as the storage of complete track information enabling deletion or movement of entire nets iteratively during the routing process.

The identification of each high level logical module based on the simulation results of the multipoint Lee algorithm with programmable cost functions allows a logically distributed multiprocessor structure to be created which expresses a high degree of parallelism with each module performing one or several tasks in parallel. The system is shown in fig. 3 and contains the following modules:

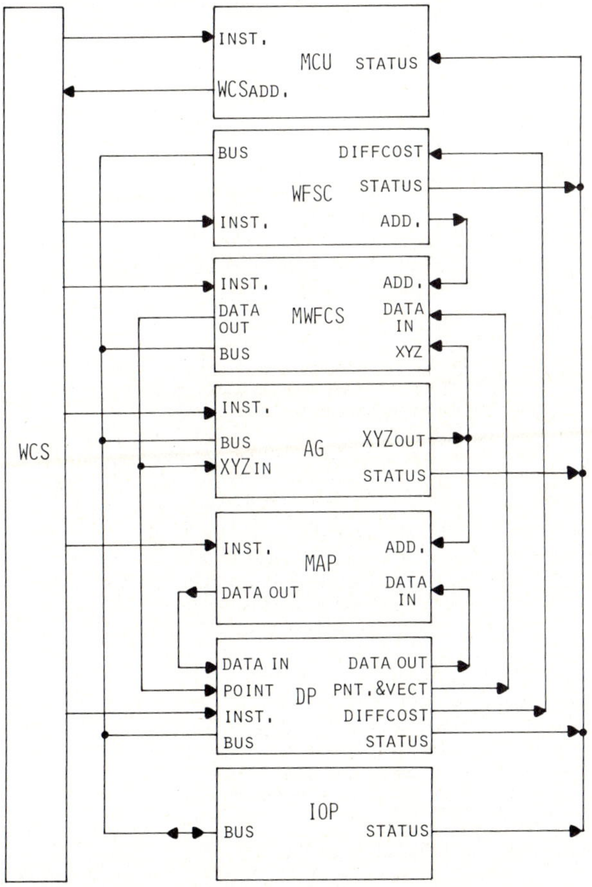

Fig. 3 PCB Router Modules.

1. The Data Processor (DP) performs all the processing of the data selected from the 3 dimensional map. On entering a cell during expansion the total cost of a path is computed and stored in the cell whereas on retrace the track data is stored defining the final path. The differential cost is also used by the Wave Front Store Control unit. During multipoint expansion the point numbers from the 3 dimensional map and the Multiple Wave Front Coordinate Store are compared to determine whether a "hit" has occured.
2. The Address Generator (AG) generates all addresses to access the desired cell in the 3 dimensional map i.e. the X-Y-Z coordinates. It also determines whether the address is within the defined board limits.
3. The Multiple Wave Front Coordinate Store (MWFCS) temporarily stores the quintuple (X,Y,Z,cost vector,point number) for possible later expansion. X-Y-Z contributes the 3D address of the marked cell and the cost vector indicates the direction of entry into the cell and may be used to reduce the number of expansions as no track is allowed to change direction by more than 90 degrees in any cell. The point number is stored to allow point number comparison during multipoint expansion.
4. The multiple Wave Front Store Control unit (WFSC) controls the reading from (the current expansion store) and the writing to any of the specified stores in the MWFCS (using the differential cost from the DP).
5. The 3 dimensional map (MAP) contains the image of the PCB routing surfaces e.g. if a track is present in the form of encoded directional data, if a the cell is marked the cost of the cell in modulo arithmetic.
6. The Microprogram Control Unit (MCU) controls the actions of all the above modules from the status received from these.
7. The Writable Control Store (WCS) holds the microprogram to be executed by the MCU.
8. The Input-Output Processor (IOP) provides the external communication to the router system via a bidirectional bus and supplies data to it during initialisation and enables data to be output during debugging and subsequent to routing completion.
9. The Graphics Unit allows the routing image contained in the MAP to be viewed on a graphics monitor (not shown in fig. 3).

The router modules receive all instructions from the WCS. This in turn is controlled by the MCU which upon testing of the status bits produces the next microprogram address. The MWFCS provides the unloaded cell address to the AG and corresponding data to the DP (the cost vector and point number). The AG then produces the neighbour cell MAP address whose content is processed by the DP. The necessary data of a marked cell is passed to the MWFCS for later expansion.

Manual Tuning of the Architecture.

Numerous techniques may be employed to achieve program execution performance improvements. A completely hardwired solution may lack the flexibility afforded by a software solution with its adverse execution time and programming demands. A firmware solution i.e. a microprogrammed implementation enables reconfiguration of the data and control structures to suit the required high speed routing environment. A microprogrammed architecture combines several microoperations or instructions into one new instruction thus paralleling the execution of these and may reduce main memory accessing. Interpretation phases may be eliminated, operand fetching reduced and all data paths used as extensively as possible to maximise parallel processing. Memory referencing, processor execution, status setting, testing and control may be overlapped to improve performance.

The instruction execution can be optimised by eliminating redundant or negated actions, microcode motion or direct use of multiway-branching. Pipelining of the architecture to exhibit either timestationary or data-stationary controls further enhances the performance. A Writable Control Store rather than a Read-Only Memory allows the data structure to be reconfigured statically or dynamically. Each processor should be examined carefully to assess whether a special purpose implementation and/or whether a more general purpose ALU type of solution is required. With a tuned microprogramming instruction set the user may program the router at the conceptual level divorced from low level implementation detail thus simplifying the design of router algorithms and reducing the cost and complexity of programming. A microprogram instruction set is not a macro requiring interpretation, rather it is a mnemonic which is assigned to a specific field of the microword which is used to control all the modules of the machine simultaneously. Thus the routing machine is a stand-alone system controlled by a sequence of microwords, each consisting of many microprogram instructions.

The synthesis phase of the tuning process is concerned with the generation of a problem oriented architecture based upon program execution under a general purpose computer architecture. The specialised architecture is synthesised iteratively, one instruction at a time, until an instruction set is formed with minimal expected execution time. The instruction set is changed through redesign of previously used programs or synthesis of new programs that realise the individual instructions. The general architecture instructions within each loop can be decomposed into microoperations, each of which is decomposable into a set of executable microorders. By concatenating all microinstructions within each high frequency program loop and then optimising the resultant stream of microoperations, a new instruction is defined that is dependent upon user application and which is optimal for these constraints. Thus by reducing the number of instructions in critical loops, execution time is reduced as a result of eliminating many interpretation cycles. The memory requirements are reduced due to the fewer program instructions to be stored and the combined execution phase requires less time than the sum of the individual execution phases due to microoperation elimination and overlapping. At each iteration an execution profile is gathered which is used to improve the execution performance. When only marginal improvements occur between iterations the synthesis process is considered to be completed and a tuned architecture defined. The following contains the procedure which was carried out in order to tune the PCB router architecture to its optimum performance applying the above optimisation strategies.

To achieve a high speed implementation with processing capability a microprogrammed architecture was envisaged employing bitslice processors to provide at least one order of magnitude increase in speed over a microprocessor based implementation. The Advanced Micro Devices (AMD) bitslice ALU (AMD2903) was selected as it provides the necessary facilities with a well structured instruction set. The inner microprogram loops of the Lee algorithm with cost functions were provisionally considered for the AMD2903 ALU to implement the DP, AG and WFSC units together with the AMD recommended Microcomputer Control Unit architecture (AMD handbook /1/ page 2-128) using the AMD2909 sequencer and the AMD29811A Next Address Control unit with a status input selector in order to estimate the following:

1) the number of microinstructions required to execute each inner loop,
2) the frequency with which each inner loop is executed and hence the percentage time spent on each activity,
3) the critical paths to determine the possibility of pipelining, parallel processing, concurrent processing and/or the application of special purpose units to speed up critical activities,
4) to determine from the above if and where unnecessarily time consuming overheads exist and ways to reduce these by the addition of special purpose features where applicable,
5) the microprogram memory length and width.

The innermost loops (the leftmost WHILE statement in fig. 2) of a 2 point net were then written, but not implemented as no appropriate simulator was available. A 1K*1K MAP was assumed. The 2 point net whose source and target points form the diagonal of a 256 by 256 square is placed in the middle of the routing MAP requiring 256 wave fronts to join the source and target points using 9 expansion vectors (8 adjacent to the expanding cell and 1 to reach the other layers). The number of "retrace" and stack "rotate" instructions are included completing the algorithm and its effect on the proposed hardware architecture.

Results of the Manual Tuning Process.

The results of the microprogramming exercises for the 2 point net is given in table 1 which shows all activities executed sequentially with one ALU. The DP requires an average of 9.3 instructions (including the reading from and the writing to the MAP) to execute an expansion vector which is the average number of instructions per vector to execute 5 unoccupied cells and 4 occupied cells each of which require a different number of instructions. This is equivalent to 65% of the total activity. The corresponding number of instructions is 5 for "load", 6 for "unload" and 6 for "address". It is noticed that the "rotate" and "retrace" operations contribute insignificantly to the total number of instructions. The highest frequency loops consist of the "expand" and "address" functions. These occur 9 times during the expansion of the 9 vectors whereas "load" occurs 5 times and "unload" once during this period.

inner loop	ALU no. of instructions	% of total no. of instructions
rotate	1,536	0.001
unload	20,889,600	15.70
address	8,355,600	6.28
expand	87,050,880	65.44
load	16,711,680	12.56
retrace	11,264	0.01
TOTAL	133,020,790	100.00

Table 1. Sequential instruction execution with one ALU bit-slice processor implementing all data module functions.

inner loop	DP-RAM no. of instructions	% of total no. of instructions
rotate	1,536	0.002
unload	20,889,600	28.21
address	8,355,600	11.28
expand	28,080,929	37.92
load	16,711,680	22.57
retrace	11,264	0.02
TOTAL	74,050,849	100.00

Table 2. Sequential instruction execution with DP look-up tables and ALU bitslice processors to implement the AG and the WFSC units.

inner loop	ALU no. of instructions	% of total no. of instructions
rotate	1,536	0.001
unload	20,899,600	19.35
parallel exp	87,050,880	80.64
retrace	11,264	0.01
TOTAL	107,953,270	100.00

Table 3. Pipelined parallel instruction execution with bit-slice ALUs to implement the DP, AG and WFSC units.

inner loop	DP-RAM no. of instructions	% of total no. of instructions
rotate	1,536	0.003
unload	20,889,600	38.93
parallel expansion	32,761,083	61.05
retrace	11,264	0.02
Total	53,663,483	100.00

Table 4. Pipelined parallel instruction execution with DP look-up tables and bitslice ALUs to implement the AG and WFSC units.

The expansion process may be condensed using special purpose processors in the form of RAM "loop-up" tables to perform the many instructions executed in sequence by the ALU processor in one instruction cycle regardless of whether an occupied or unoccupied cell is entered. The results of employing RAM look-up tables in the DP processor is shown in table 2 for the routing of a 2 point net with all other activities unchanged. This is seen to reduce the "expand" activity to 38% of the total sum of instructions.

Paralleling the frequently occuring activities of "expand", "load" and "address" (where the DP, AG and WFSC units each require one ALU) with all other activities being performed in sequence as previously, further enhances the performance (speed) of the machine. These parallel activities must be piped such that the AG generates the next address associated with vector v, while the DP retrieves and processes the data belonging to vector v-1 and the WFSC loads the address of the cell expanded during vector v-2 into the MWFCS if required. If each of these activities can be executed in parallel and implemented to ensure similar electrical path lengths the speed of the machine may be increased considerably.

The results of the parallel implementation is shown in table 3. The parallel ALU implementation spends 87% of the time on the expansion phase although the overall number of microinstructions required to complete a net has been reduced significantly compared with the purely sequential implementation. However, employing special purpose RAM look-up tables in the DP as shown in fig. 4 reduces the proportion of the time spent on expansion even further and requires the lowest number of microinstructions in order to complete a net as well as ensuring that each parallel activity requires a similar, but as yet unequal number of microinstructions.

To continue the performance matching and minimisation of each parallel activity, if possible to 1 microinstruction each, further pipelining is proposed in which MAP data is piped before entering and exiting the DP respectively. This reduces the special purpose DP expansion processing time and the reading and writing of MAP data to 1 instruction each. The AG requires 6 instructions or 3 instructions per X and Y generation 1) to generate the actual address and 2) to check if the generated address is within the board limits, taking up 2 instructions. However, if the address comparisons are performed in 1 instruction simultaneously with the actual address generations only 1 microinstruction is required per address generator unit. Furthermore, the control of the MWFCS with a paged addressing scheme can be implemented with a 2 tier bit-slice processor configuration requiring only 1 microinstruction for any one of the WFSC activities with a a pipe between the WFSC and MWFCS units.

To increase the speed of the routing machine further the fetching of instruction I+1

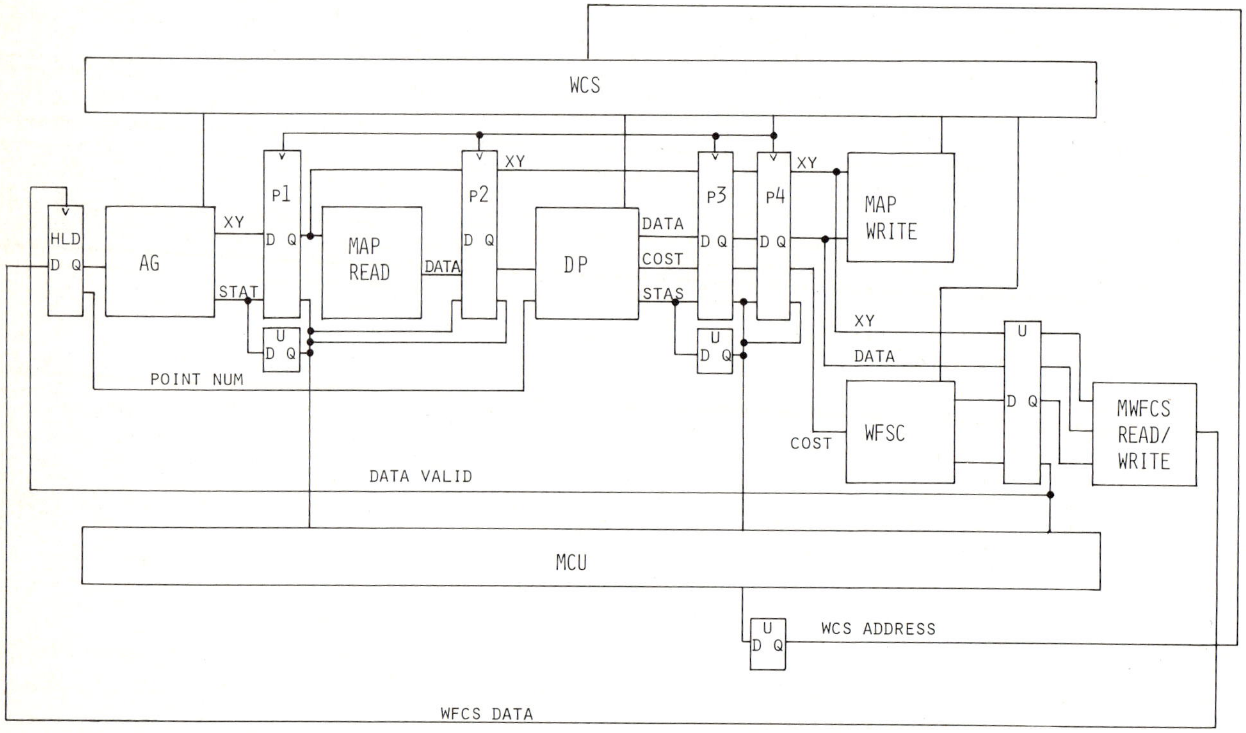

Fig. 4 PCB Router Pipe Flow.

can be overlapped with the execution of instruction I thus improving the speed of the overall system by a factor of approximately 2. If the status produced by the execution of instruction I is sampled at the end of this instruction it will be available for testing during the execution of instruction I+1. During this instruction the next instruction, I+2, is generated based on the status available i.e. the status generated by instruction I. This infers that the decisions made by the MCU will be 2 instructions behind the available data thus requiring appropriate piping of all data in order that correct processing may take place without loss of vital data. However, as the AG, MAP, DP and WFSC units with the MWFCS are piped already due to their staggered operation, 2 additional pipes, P3 and P4, must be included as shown in fig. 4. The "hold" register (HLD) which provides input to the DP and the AG constitutes a set-up register for the unloaded data from the MWFCS.

To allow subroutine calls with parallel testing of up to 8 status bits to be executed without affecting the data in the pipes these must be frozen until normal program flow resumes. To test status generated by the DP and the WFSC units during subroutine calls while the pipe is frozen, a second unconditionally clocked status pipe (marked "U" on fig. 4) is required. The WFSC status bits are set as appropriate during processing and reset once the selected status bit has been serviced.

The data pipe now operates as follows: during instruction I 1) the AG output contains the X-Y-Z address generated, 2) pipe 1 holds the X-Y-Z address generated in instruction I-1, 3) the MAP is addressed from pipe 1 to retrieve the contents for all layers during I-1, 4) the DP processes the contents of the X-Y-Z data fetched from the MAP during instruction I-2, 5) pipe 3 holds the modified data and status produced by the DP in instruction I-3, 6) pipe 4 holds the data and status produced during instruction I-4. To allow the MCU to determine the resultant control flow based on the status in pipe 3 the data must pass through a 4th pipe before the instruction to steer the data can be made available.

The total microprogram length including the outer loops of the general Lee algorithm was estimated to be approximately 0.25K words. The microprogram wordwidth required to cater for seperate AGs, the DP and the WFSC all implemented using AMD2903 bitslice processors together with the recommended MCU requires minimally 200 bits. To enable the microprogram to be incorporated in a 128 bit wide WCS, methods of reducing the microword width had to be considered without reducing the speed or flexibility of the machine. This requires special purpose processors for each unit tailored to the application to reduce the number of general purpose bitslice processors.

The architecture displaying parallel constructions, in which the major part of the execution time is spent, has been tuned to a first approximation where each of the frequently occuring instructions such as "expand", "address" and "load" has been reduced to 1 microinstruction. Each module now requires careful examination, not in isolation but in conjunction with the other modules before the final design emerges. From this a mnemonic instruction set can be formulated which in turn enables the MCU addressing modes to be defined and all low level control to be derived.

The fine tuning of each of the router modules continues to ensure similar electrical path lengths in all pipes to enable the machine to operate as efficiently as possible. This process will not be discussed further here as the level of detail would be too involved in this paper (the entire system implementation is described by the author in /4/). However, an overview of the resulting functional design is given together with the estimated performance of the system showing the importance of tuning the architecture in order to achieve enhanced system performance.

Functional Description of Modules.

In the final implementation the Data Processor consists of 2, 4 bit AMD2903 bitslice processors employed to do infrequently occuring functions such as initialisation of all modules with known data or complex data processing. The RAM look-up tables generate the differential cost of entering a neighbouring cell as well as the total path cost during expansion based on the selected "least-cost-path" strategy. During the retrace phase the look-up tables provide the encoded track data enabling entire nets to be moved or deleted when required as each routed cell is associated with one and only one net. Likewise, part of the status information (i.e. if the target is reached, if a cell is already marked etc.) is also generated by the look-up tables. A suitable partitioning of the logically independent entities ensures a minimum memory configuration of two 1K*8 bit, one 1K*4bit and two 4K*1 bit RAMs. The point number comparisons are performed by random logic.

The identical X and Y Address Generators consist of 10 bit adders which are capable of incrementing, decrementing or passing the current address on to the MAP. A comparator ensures that each AG is within the limits of the board held in appropriate registers. The Z dimension of the address is implemented using a modulo 3 incremental adder to enable the Z-direction to be traversed when required.

The Wave Front Store Control unit is used to compute the address of the store in the MWFCS into which a marked cell is loaded. This is achieved in one microinstruction in 2 stages with a 2 level hierarchy of processors implemented with AMD2903 bitslice processors. The first level consists of an ALU performing the addition of the differential cost from the DP and the number of the current expansion store. The resultant value is used to address the "line store" ALU which together with the "page address" and the "page pointer" ALU provides the required MWFCS address.

The final Microprogram Control Unit design is very different from the MCU architecture suggested by AMD and is capable of parallel selection and testing of 1 out of 16 groups of 8 bit status words with a multitude of different addressing modes for efficient microprogramming of the selected router algorithm.

The MCU consists of a fast 16 bit adder working in conjunction with a 16 bit word deep stack, a single port RAM providing 16 index registers and an offset register for relative addressing. The address inputs to the stack consist of the current address register. The A inputs to the adder consists of the selected status, the relative, the offset address input or a "zero" input and the B inputs are the current address or the selected index address.

This configuration provides the system with the following addressing modes: incremental, repeat until, indexed, relative, direct branch and return in addition to register load instructions.

The incremental addressing mode enables the current address incremented by one to become the next address allowing contiguous program locations to be executed and so provides the function of a program counter. The repeat until addressing mode enables the same instruction to be executed a specified number of times. There are 2 indexed addressing modes: priority indexed and vector indexed. Priority indexed addressing enables the highest priority status bit set in conjunction with the selected index address to provide an indexed address which is the starting address of the corresponding service routine. Lower priority status servicing routines may then be executed in turn according to priority. The first address of all service routines associated with a specific index register and hence a specific selection of status inputs reside in sequential locations. A direct jump instruction allows any subsequent addresses to be executed elsewhere in the program memory. The vector indexed addressing mode is particularly suited to enable initiation of the next sequence of cost vectors during expansion and retrace by supplying the adder with the vector from the WCS and the selected index address to provide the direct or indirect starting address of the next sequence of cost vectors. Both indexed addressing modes allow "call" and "jump" instructions to be executed.

The MAP contains all the data required for the routing of a PCB with up to 4 layers on a 1K by 1K board area. The layer dependent data contains either the marking state or track data (6 bits/layer). The layer independent data consists of location dependent cost functions (wirespreading metrics) and encodes whether a cell is a source cell, a via or component restricted area etc. This requires a 1K*1K by 32 bit memory.

The MWFCS must as a minimum store the X-Y-Z coordinates of the marked cells (12 bits). However, if the point number (6 bits) associated with each cell (for multipoint expansion) is stored in the MWFCS then all cell entries with a given point number can be manipulated directly by the DP without being fetched from the MAP thus reducing processing overheads. Furthermore, if the 4 bit cost vector, used by the DP to enter the marked cell whose coordinates were stored in the MWFCS, is stored then it can be used by the MCU to point to the next appropriate sequence of directionally dependent expansion vectors to reduce the number of expansion vectors per stored cell. Norman /8/ shows that a stack length of 16K words is required for the selected board size thus requiring a stack of 16K by 32 bits.

The necessary microprogram word width for the defined architecture is 105 bits. However, the assignment of fields to the WCS is such that a minimum of 34-way headers is required for the implementation of each board resulting in a non-contiguous usage of the WCS word.

The size, speed and control of the MWFCS, MAP and WCS memories are almost identical. This resulted in a modular 8K by 32 bit design of the memory boards to enable the same design to be used for all data bases. Thus the MWFCS and the MAP each require 2 boards and the WCS 4 memory boards.

The system is currently being implemented in the Electrical Engineering Dept. at Bristol University, England, under the supervision of Prof. E.L. Dagless.

Expected Performance.

The PCB router is expected to operate at 3 (IBM) Million Instructions Per Second (MIPS) which provides a higher yield than many mainframe solutions such as the ICL/2960 and the ICL/2976 with 0.65 and 1.95 MIPS respectively; minicomputers normally fall below this limit. A measure in terms of MIPS does not allow the designed routing machine to be compared to best advantage due to its inherent parallelism and the absence of overheads caused by the virtual memory management and housekeeping system present in conventional mainframe or minicomputer solutions. An assessment of the number of instructions, which a conventional machine would require to perform a Lee expansion of all neighbour cells using cost functions excluding all overheads caused by the operating system such as disc transfers, interpretation phases etc., may be performed with reference to the initial provisional microprograms written for a conventional computer architecture using AMD2903 bitslice processors. This requires 168 instructions to expand a cell into its 9 neighbouring cells, 5 of which will be marked or remarked. The equivalent number of instructions for the tuned router is 14. Normalising the 168 expansion instructions for the ICL/2960 and the ICL/2976 mainframe computers to 3 MIPS gives 775 and 258 instructions respectively. Thus the tuned architecture shows a 19-55 fold inrease in speed over the above mainframe solutions which is due purely to the parallel processing of the modules. However, because the architecture is tuned to the routing problem requiring no secondary storage (virtual memory) accesses and no overheads in order to read the cell content from the MAP and cell coordinates from the MWFCS the actual increase in speed is estimated to be 2 orders of magnitude or more, equivalent to 300 MIPS or more.

Conclusion.

The development of the router architecture using appropriate optimisation strategies in order to achieve a highly tuned routing environment in which to achieve performance improvement has been discussed. It provides a general purpose computing facility with many in-built special purpose processsors to speed up critical paths in the routing process whilst allowing non-critical routing activities to be executed by an ALU. It achieves 2 or more orders of magnitude increase in speed over conventional software based systems due to its optimum or near optimum pipelined parallel implementation of all critical paths together with the lack of overheads. It provides a highly programmable and tuned architecture with a tailored microprogram instruction set (not discussed) permitting programming at the conceptual level thus reducing programming costs and thereby provides the opportunity to explore a variety of routers.

The tailored hardware architecture with its orders of magnitude increase in speed provides the opportunity to achieve a higher success rate as iteration of the routing process is feasible even for large complex boards. Iteration allows back-tracking and movement of tracks to achieve a higher success rate in conjunction with a variety of cost function strategies whose parameters may be determined from iteration to iteration providing the desired feedback. It is important to achieve a high success rate (at least 95% of all paths should be completed automatically) in the layout process as it is of little consequence if the router is fast but yields inferior results without the possibility of upgrading the routing strategy to improve performance i.e. the provision of a programmable system to allow modification of old and the creation of new algorithms. Examples of such very fast but inflexible custom designed VLSI routers are Carroll /3/ and Iosupovicz /6/.

The hardware router has as its prime application the routing of PCBs. However, the data structures may readily support the routing of custom designed chips which require a similar but not identical routing strategy to accommodate different technologies. It is envisaged that the generated architecture may be used in processes which require a "quantity" to be connected or moved efficiently (least-cost-path) to its destination without causing undue disturbance to other "quantitites". Examples of such activities include the routing of messages in computer networks, the routing or timetabling of avionic and terrestial traffic, the routing of telephone calls etc.; the architecture may also be suitable for many image processing applications. The router architecture may thus provide the inspiration towards other specialised and highly tuned architectures in related as well as unrelated fields.

Acknowledgements.

I would like to thank Prof. E.L. Dagless for his invaluable support and encouragements throughout the project and a special thanks to my colleague Mr. R. Norman for his constructive critisism and involvement in the PCB project.

References.

1. Advanced Micro Devices Handbook on the 2900 series bitslice processors.

2. Allen J.R. A Topologically Adaptable Cellular Router" Proc. Design Automation Conf., June 1976, pp161-167.

3. Carroll C.R. "A Smart Memory Array Processor for Two Layer Path Finding" Proc. of the Second Caltech. Conf. on Very Large Scale Integration, Computer Science Dept., Calif. Institute of Technology, Jan. 1981.

4. Hansen B. "A Programmable Hardware Router" Ph.D. thesis, University of Manchester Institute of Science and Technology, Jan. 1982.

5. Hoel J.H. "Some Variations of Lee's Algorithm" IEEE Trans. on Comp., vol. c-25, no.1, Jan. 1976, pp19-24.

6. Iosupovicz A. "Design of an Interactive Array Maze Router" Proc. International Conf. on Circuits and Computers, Oct. 1980, pp908-911.

7. Lee C.Y. "An Algorithm for Path Connections and Its Applications" IRE Trans. on Electronic Computers, vol. ed-10, pp346-365.

8. Norman R. "Programmable Hardware For Routing Algorithm Data Structures" M.Sc. Thesis, University of Mancester Institute of Science and Technology, Jan. 1982.

9. Rubin F. "The Lee Path Connection Algorithm" IEEE Trans. on Comp., c-23, no. 9, Sep. 1974, pp907-914.

10 Rubin F. "A Comparison of Wire Spreading Metrics for Printed Circuit Routing" Journal of Design Automation and Fault Tolerant Computing, 1978, pp231-239.

MICROCOMPUTERS: Developments in Industry, Business and Education
D.R. Wilson and C.J. van Spronsen (eds.) / ©EUROMICRO, 1983
Elsevier Science Publishers B.V. (North-Holland)

A NEW APPROACH TO THE MICROPROGRAM COMPACTION

Piotr Dembiński

Institute of Computer Science
Polish Academy of Sciences
Warsaw, Poland

Marek Pawłowski

Institute of Computer Science
Warsaw Technical University
Warsaw, Poland

A new algorithm of microprogram compaction (parallelisation) is presented. The algorithm can be performed at different microprogramming levels. It takes into account the overall flow structure of microprograms, branching and executive microoperations are equally treated, and conditional microoperations are admissible. It is based on a repeatedly performed microprogram transformation, applicability of which is dynamically tested for consistency with machine dependent constraints resulting from specific realizations (execution conflicts, microinstruction formats, etc.). The correctness of the proposed algorithm is justified and the estimation of its results is given.

1. INTRODUCTION

Much of the work has been done on microparallelism as one of the important aspects of microprogram optimization, i.e., of an effort to minimize the microprogram execution time and/or the microprogram memory size. Surveys [1] and [3] present the optimization techniques developed in mid-seventies. All so far proposed compaction (parallelisation) algorithms are "local" in that they deal with the straight-line segments of a microprogram (for example, [2], [13] and [9] in which comparison of "local" algorithms is done). Some efforts to overcome this locality have been made in [4] and [12] or [15] (in a broader context) but the basic idea of microprogram partition into straight-line segments has remained. This is also true if one looks at papers concerning more general problem of searching for the optimizing microcompilers (like, e.g., [10,11,14, 15]) in which the microprogram (or rather microcode) compaction is only a fragment of the task. With such anapproach the problem seems to be solved ([5]). It is, however, important to notice that the obtained that way parallelism is far from maximal (in most cases) if measured by the number of horizontal microinstructions in the target microprogram. This measure seems to be adequate at least if the execution time is the prevailing optimization factor (and we believe it is). The microprograms in Fig. 2.4 - 2.7 serve as examples. Those of Fig. 2.5 - 2.7 are all horizontal solutions equivalent to the vertical microprogram in Fig. 2.4. Even in the "worst" case (Fig.2.6, when conditional microoperations are prohibited) the result is almost twice better than this which could be achieved by any of the "local" algorithms. (One can argue that conditional microoperations require additional time to stabilize the control signals. However, in the overall evaluation of the execution time the (cumulative) delay caused by conditional microoperations is much less than this gained by reducing the number of steps in computations).

The compaction (parallelisation) algorithm proposed in this paper is based on principle that branching microoperations are equally treated with those "normally" called executive, and conditional microoperations are not, at least from the begining, excluded. The "locality" exploited in this algorithm is of a different sort than that described above. It consists in performing a "local" transformation on the microprogram statements. The transformation is proved to preserve "global" microprogram properties and is defined in machine independent terms. On the other hand, the <u>applicability</u> of the transformation is dynamically checked with respect to constraints which serve to express different machine dependent features. That way the algorithm may be applied at different levels and viewed as an automatic aid in the correct design of microprogrammed hardware. We consider this to be an important property.

In order to clarify the presentation we have decided to deal with RTL microprograms and we have simplified the algorithm itself. The more general approach is given in [8] and a theoretical basis in [7](the algorithm, in fact, is a byproduct of a system of microprogram transformations defined in [7] and thought of as an aid in the design and verification of microprograms).

At last, it should be explained that, although some kind of notation is adopted from [6], the results are not language-dependent and could be easily formulated by purely algebraic means.

2. BASIC NOTIONS AND NOTATION

We are going to define a simple microprogramming language ML(BMO) over a given set of basic or available microoperations. From among microprograms in ML(BMO) vertical microprograms are distinguished. On the other hand the set **C** of, so called, machine derived constraints serve to describe restrictions resulting from specific realizations (like execution conflicts, microinstruction formats, etc,). The optimization goal, as assumed in this paper, is then to find, for a given vertical microprogram, a semantically equivalent (in a strong sense since the underlying algorithm is not supposed to be changed) one in ML(BMO) with possibly minimal number of horizontal microstatements and satisfying the constraints in **C** .

The two sets BMO and **C** establish the level of microprogramming since they define, in a sense, how many of the implementation details are taken into account. The optimization procedure should work independently of the choice of BMO and/or **C** , i.e., independently from microprogramming level as postulated in the introduction.

If **C** = ∅ then, intuitively speaking, the situation is described as if none of the possible digital systems was determined and realization decisions were to be taken with respect to the microprograms constructed (and optimized) in ML(BMO) . Another extreme situation assumes that **C** characterizes one particular digital system the designed microprograms are to be implemented. Between these two there are many itermediate situations, e.g., when the data part of a digital system is known and its control part is to be designed. In any case it is reasonable to postulate that any existing or designed system under consideration is able to execute every basic microoperation from BMO in one clock cycle (otherwise they were not basic for it). This means that vertical microprograms in ML(BMO) are realizable whatever **C** is to be considered, and, on the other hand, any nonempty set **C** exclude some horizontal microprograms from ML(BMO) .

All this means that any constraint in **C** has to be formulated as a decidable property about horizontal microstatements of programs in ML(BMO). It is a separate (and sometimes difficult) question how to characterize that way desirable features of digital systems but, in any approach, there is no other possibility to prove the proposed compaction algorithm correct. In the Example 2.1 we demonstrate the problem and its solution. Example 2.1 illustrates all the notions introduced in this section.

Basic microoperations are divided into basic functional microoperations (bfmo) written in the form of a simple assignment

$$X := F(X_1,\dots,X_n)$$

(e.g., X:= ADD(X,Y), X:= SHR(X) or sometimes X := X+Y , etc.), and basic branching microoperations (bbmo) written in the form

$$Q(X_1,\dots,X_n)$$

(e.g., LESS(X,Y), EQUAL(X,0) or X=0, etc.), where:

- F and Q denote primitive operation and predicate respectively,
- X on the left hand side of the assignment is a (destination) variable

- $X_1,\ldots,X_n$ are (source) variables or constants (variables may be indexed)

We assume basic microoperations have their well defined meaning. This meaning obviously depend on the level of description considered. Having in mind the RT level, the variables denote memory elements and their values range over sets of binary words of an appropriate length, and the primitive operations are defined in these sets.

From bbmos we can form *(branching) conditions* by means of boolean connectives: −(NOT), (OR), (AND).

From bfmos and conditions we can form *functional conditional microoperations* written

$$X := \{E_1/Q_1,\ldots,E_n/Q_n\} \qquad (2.1)$$

with $X := E_i$ and Q_i being a bfmo and a condition respectively, $i = 1,\ldots,n$. For a given valuation of variables occurring in the above conditional microoperation, $X := E_i$ is performed if Q_i is satisfied, and, if none of the conditions is satisfied, X remains unchanged.

We say that the conditional microoperation is *deterministic* if $Q_i \wedge Q_j \equiv 0$, for all $1 \leq i \neq j \leq n$.

We write $X := E/Q$ instead of $X := \{E/Q\}$ and a bfmo $X := E$ can be identified with the conditional microoperation $X := E/1$.

By a *costatement* (co) we understand a finite list (set) of functional microoprations (basic or conditional). Any coastatement is interpreted to perform all its microoperations simulaneously and therefore its microoperations are assumed to have distinct destination variables. A costatement is *deterministic* if all its microoperations are deterministic.

Finally, by a *microprogram* we mean a list of *labeled microstatements* headed by the

$$\underline{\text{start}}\ L \qquad (2.2)$$

form which indicates the statement labeled by L with which the program begins its computation. Any (labeled) microstatement has one of the following four forms:

$$L : \text{co}\ \underline{\text{exit}}\ Q_1.L_1,\ldots,Q_n.L_n \qquad (2.3)$$

$$L : Q_1.L_1,\ldots,Q_n.L_n \qquad (2.4)$$

$$L : \text{co}\ \underline{\text{exit}}\ L_1 \qquad (2.5)$$

$$L : \qquad (2.6)$$

where $L,L_1,\ldots,L_n$ are labels, co is a costatement, $Q_1,\ldots,Q_n$ are branching conditions. The statement of the form (2.6) is called *halting statement*.

Graphical representations of the above statements are given in Fig.2.1.

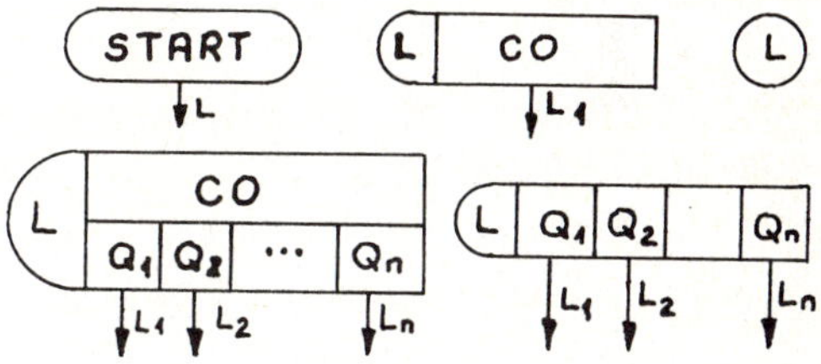

Fig.2.1

Examples of flow-charts representation of microprograms are provided by Fig. 2.4 - 2.7.

A microprogram is called *vertical* iff all its non halting statements are those in the form (2.4) or (2.5), with $n=2$, $Q_2 = \overline{Q}_1$ and Q_1 being bbmo in the case (2.4), and co consisting of a single bfmo in the case (2.5). Any other microprogram is called *horizontal*.

Any microstatement simultaneously computes not only functional microoperations of its costatement but also all its branching conditions. This means that although a destination variable may have its value changed by a functional microoperation within the costatement, any of the branching condition which refers to that variable is computed with respect to the initial value of the variable.

This interpretation mirrors the fact that microstatements are thought of as describing the effect of parallel computation in one clock cycle of a digital system under consideration.

A microstatement is called deterministic if its costatement is deterministic and its branching conditions are pairwise disjoint. Any vertical microprogram is, by definition, deterministic.

Microprograms are semantically characterized by their input-output functions. The (partial) function is defined for a valuation v of the program variables, and yields a valuation v′ iff there is a computation beginning with the start statement and the initial valuation v, and ending in a halting statement of the program with the final valuation v′.

Microprograms are said to be semantically equivalent iff their input-output functions are identical.

Example 2.1.

Consider the following set BMO = BFMO ∪ BBMO of basic microoperations:

```
BFMO = { LB := DIN;   LB := SHL(LB,LB[7]);
         LB := LB;
         CS := 0;     CS := SHL(CS,CD[3]);
         CS := CS;    CS := ADD(CS,3);
         CD := 0;     CD := SHL(CD,CJ[3]);
         CD := CD;    CD := ADD(CD,3);
         CJ := 0;     CJ := SHL(CJ,LB[7]);
         CJ := CJ;    CJ := ADD(CJ,3);
         LP := LP;    LP := INC(LP);
         LP := 8;      L := L;
          L := 13;     L := INC(L) }

BBMO = { B(CJ) > 4; B(CD) > 4; B(CS) > 4;
         B(L) = 13; B(L) = 14; B(L) = 15;
         B(LP) = 15 }
```

It is easy to check that block diagrams in Fig.2.2 and Fig.2.3 describe two, adequate to the given BMO, realizations of the data part of a digital system, i.e., every microoperation in BMO can be realized in one clock cycle. The realizations give, however, different possibilities in parallel execution of these microoperations (this is characterized in details below).

Fig.2.4 presents a vertical microprogram in ML(BMO) (conversion of 8 bit numbers in NB code into 3 digit decimal numbers in BCD code), while three different horizontal versions (in ML(BMO)) of the same algorithm are given in Fig. 2.5 - 2.7. All three could be performed in the execution unit of Fig.2.2 (assuming an appropriate control unit) but only the third one (Fig.2.7) in the unit presented in Fig.2.3. This is due to the different execution (or path) conflicts generated by the two units. From microprogramming point of view it is not important what causes a conflict but what microinstructions are prohibited because of the conflicts, and this has to be expressed by a constraint in $\mathbb{C}$. This means that we need to define precisely what we understand by a microstatement in ML(BMO) free of the execution conflict resulting from the given execution part of a digital system. We are going to show how the property is to be formulated provided the set CBM of all pairs of conflicting basic microoperations (for that unit) is given. CBM_1 and CBM_2 below are examples of such sets for the units of Fig2.2 and Fig.2.3 respectively.

```
CBM1={CS := ADD(CS,3), CD := ADD(CD,3);
      CS := ADD(CS,3), CJ := ADD(CJ,3);
      CD := ADD(CD,3), CJ := ADD(CJ,3);}

CBM2={CS := ADD(CS,3), CD := ADD(CD,3);
      CS := ADD(CD,3), CJ := ADD(CJ,3);
      CD := ADD(CD,3), CJ := ADD(CJ,3);
      CS := ADD(CS,3), B(CD) > 4;
      CS := ADD(CS,3), B(CJ) > 4;
      CD := ADD(CD,3), B(CS) > 4;
      CD := ADD(CD,3), B(CJ) > 4;
      CJ := ADD(CJ,3), B(CS) > 4;
      CJ := ADD(CJ,3), B(CD) > 4;
      B(CS) > 4, B(CD) > 4;
      B(CS) > 4, B(CJ) > 4;
      B(CD) > 4, B(CJ) > 4 }
```

We define:

1. a branching condition composed of bbmos $Q_1,\dots,Q_n$ is free of (execution) conflict if no pair (Q_i,Q_j) is in CBM,

2. two conflict-free conditions composed of $Q_1,\dots,Q_n$ and $P_1,\dots,P_m$ bbmos respectively are not in conflict if no pair (Q_i,P_j) is in CBM,

3. a free of conflict condition composed of $Q_1,\dots,Q_n$ bbmos and a bfmo

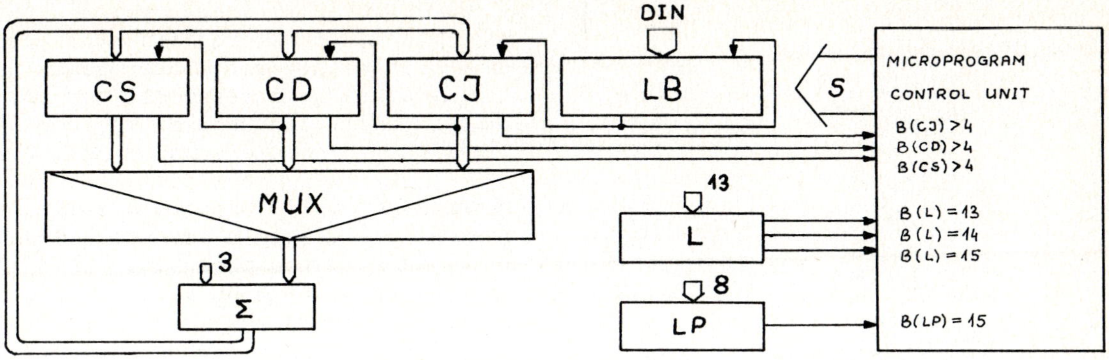

Fig.2.2.

X := E are not in conflict if no pair $(Q_i, X := E)$ is in CBM,

4. a conditional microoperation $X := \{E_1/Q_1, \ldots, E_n/Q_n\}$ is free of conflict if $Q_1, \ldots, Q_n$ are free of conflict conditions, and for every $i,j=1,\ldots,n$ neither Q_i, Q_j nor $Q_i, X := E_i$ are in conflict,

5. two conditional microoperations $X := \{E_1/Q_1, \ldots, E_n/Q_n\}$ and $Y := \{F_1/P_1, \ldots, F_m/P_m\}$, each one free of of conflict itself, are not in conflict if (Q_i, P_j), $(Q_i, Y := F_j)$ and $(X := E_i, P_j)$ are not in conflict, and, if $(X := E_i, Y := F_j)$ are in CBM (are in conflict) then $Q_i \wedge P_j \equiv 0$, $i=1,\ldots,n$, $j=1,\ldots,m$.

6. a fre of conflict condition Q and a free of conflict conditional microoperation $X := \{E_1/P_1, \ldots, E_m/P_m\}$ are not in conflict if neither (Q, P_i) nor $(Q, X := E_i)$ is in conflict,

7. a statement

$$L : X_1 := E_1, \ldots, X_n := E_n \ \underline{\text{exit}} \ Q_1 . L_1, \ldots, Q_m . L_m$$

is free of conflict if for every $i,j=1,\ldots,n$ and $k,l=1,\ldots,m$, $(X_i := E_i, X_j := E_j)$, (Q_k, Q_l) and $(Q_k, X_i := E_i)$ are not in conflict.

Denote by C_1 the above defined constraint. This complex inductively defined property would be time consuming if checked directly. But due to the way the optimization procedure is defined, only

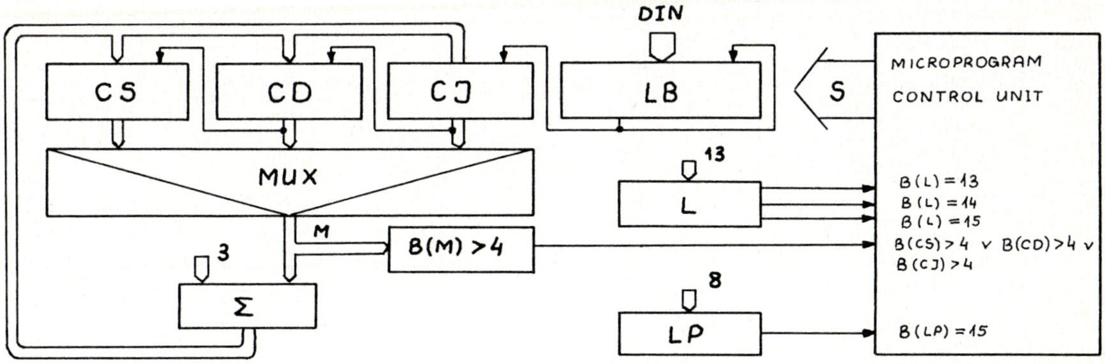

Fig.2.3

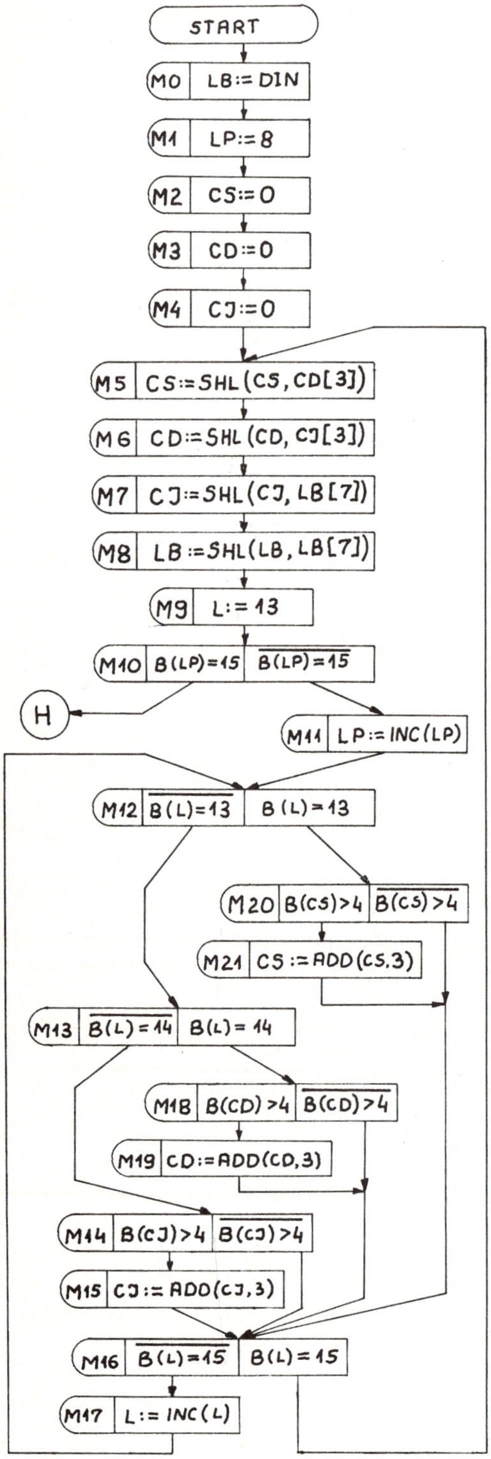

Fig.2.4.

a much less complex property has to be verified to be ensured that the procedure do not introduce conflicts (Lemma 3.1). On the other hand it is obvious that any vertical microinstruction is free of conflict.

Another source of constraints may be the control part. We may have no decoder of conditional microoperations and this feature translates into the simple property which says that no conditional microoperation is allowed in microstatements. Denote this constraint by C_2 . We may have another constraint limiting the number of conditions in conditional microoperations and/or branching conditions in the exit part of statements. Denote by C_3 such a constraint which do not allow more than, for instance, 4-way branching. The same field in a specific microinstruction format may control more than one execution block which means that some basic microoperations may not be executed in parallel despite the fact that they are not in execution conflict. New pairs may be then added to the CBM set. It seems that these examples suffice to convince the reader that with more or less difficulty the realization features can be expressed as decidable properties of microprogram statements.

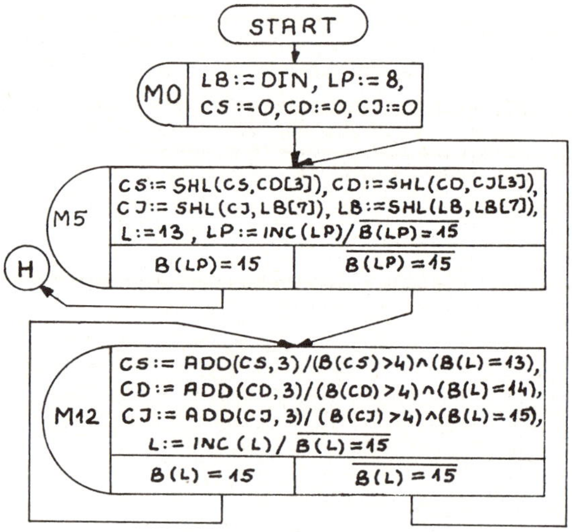

Fig.2.5

In the working example of this paper, if CBM_1 is taken into account (execution

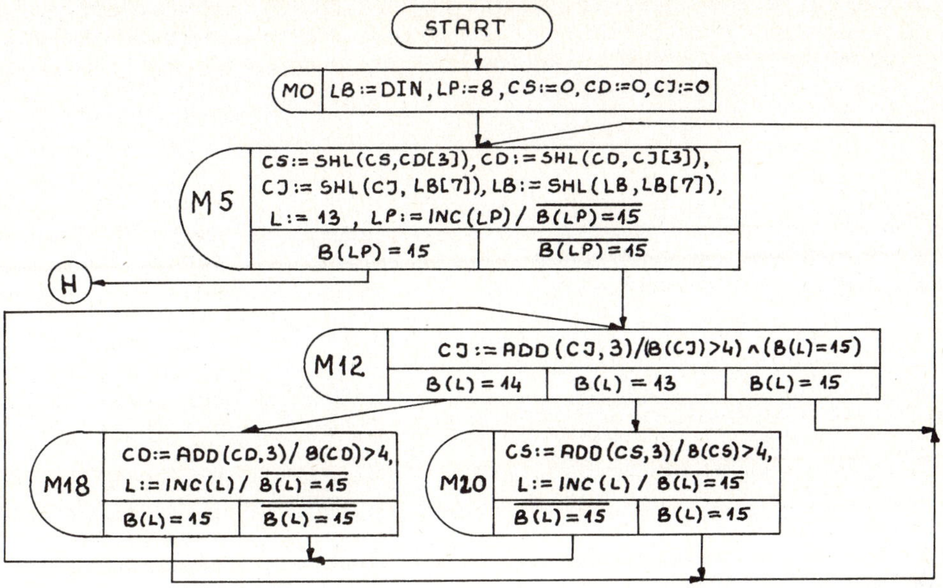

Fig.2.6.

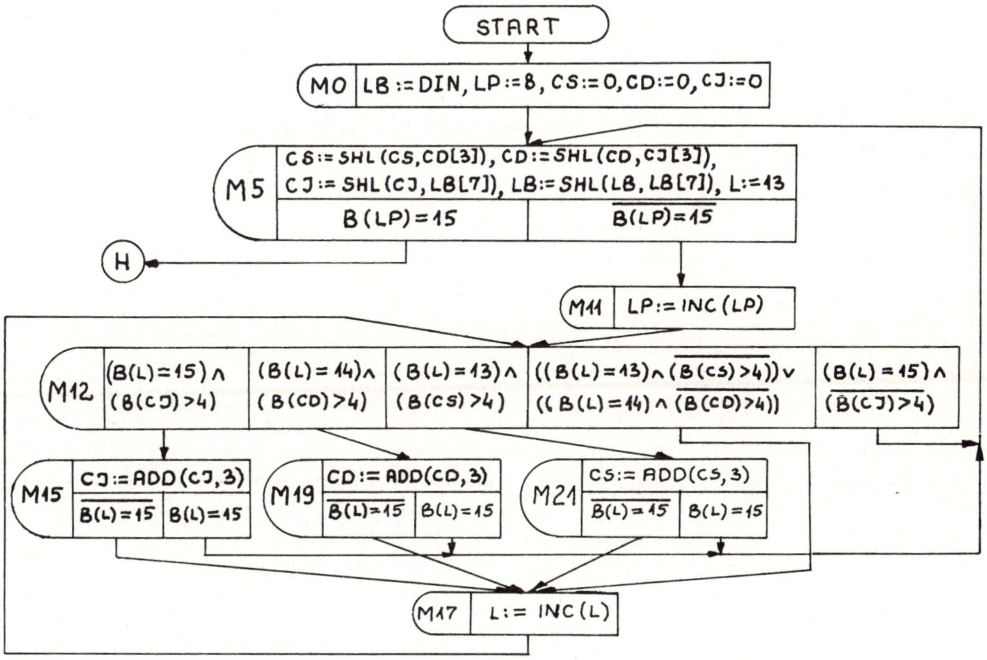

Fig.2.7.

unit of Fig.2.2) and $\mathbf{C} = \{C_1\}$, then all examplary horizontal microprograms are admissible. If $\mathbf{C} = \{C_1, C_2\}$ only this of Fig.2.6 is allowed, and with $\mathbf{C} = \{C_1, C_2, C_3\}$ none of them. If CBM_2 is considered and $\mathbf{C} = \{C_1\}$ then only microprogram in Fig.2.7 satisfies the constraint.

It is the task of the following two sections to show that all these microprograms are outputs of the optimization procedure performed, with various sets of constraints, on the vertical microprogram in Fig.2.4.

3. RESULTS

In this section we introduce the main transformation (and some auxiliary ones) the compaction algorithm is based on.

Let $X := \{E_1/Q_1, \ldots, E_n/Q_n\}$ be a conditional microoperation and Q a condition. By $X := \{E_1/Q_1, \ldots, E_n/Q_n\}/Q$ we understand the conditional microoperation

$$X := \{E_1/Q \wedge Q_1, \ldots, E_n/Q \wedge Q_n\}$$

If co is a costatement and Q a condition then co/Q denotes the costatement in which every microoperation becomes conditional with respect to Q.

Denote by var(L) the set of all variables occurring in the microstatement labeled by L. Let $X := E$ and Q be a bfmo and a bbmo respectively. Consider the following sequence of statements:

$$\begin{array}{l} L : X := E \ \underline{\text{exit}}\ M \\ M : \text{co}\ \underline{\text{exit}}\ Q_1.M_1, \ldots, Q_m.M_m \end{array} \qquad (3.1)$$

or

$$\begin{array}{l} L : Q.M,\ \overline{Q}.N \\ M : \text{co}_1\ \underline{\text{exit}}\ Q_1.M_1, \ldots, Q_m.M_m \\ N : \text{co}_2\ \underline{\text{exit}}\ P_1.N_1, \ldots, P_n.N_n \end{array} \qquad (3.2)$$

By FOLD(L;M) we mean the transformation which:

1. exchanges the statement L in (3.1) for

   $$L : X := E,\ \text{co}\ \underline{\text{exit}}\ Q_1.M_1, \ldots, Q_m.M_m \qquad (3.3)$$

   provided $X \notin \text{var}(M)$; otherwise FOLD(L;M) is not defined,

2. exchanges the statement L in (3.2) for

   $$L : \text{co}_1/Q\ \underline{\text{exit}}\ Q \wedge Q_1.M_1, \ldots, Q \wedge Q_m.M_m \qquad (3.4)$$

   (FOLD(L;N) is a symmetrical transformation)

By FOLD(L;M,N) we mean the transformation which exchanges the statement L in (3.2) for

$$L : \text{co}'\ \underline{\text{exit}}\ Q \wedge Q_1.M_1, \ldots, Q \wedge Q_m.M_m, \overline{Q} \wedge P_1.N_1, \ldots, \overline{Q} \wedge P_n.N_n \qquad (3.5)$$

where co′ is defined as follows:

if $X := E \in \text{co}_1 - \text{co}_2$ then $X := E/Q \in \text{co}'$

if $X := E \in \text{co}_2 - \text{co}_1$ then $X := E/\overline{Q} \in \text{co}'$

if $X := E \in \text{co}_1 \cap \text{co}_2$ then $X := E \in \text{co}'$

if $X := E \in \text{co}_1$ and $X := F \in \text{co}_2$ and $E \neq F$ then $X := \{E/Q, F/\overline{Q}\}$ co′

(if, in the last case, one or both microoperations are conditional, then the inner brackets should be omitted).

FOLD(L;M), FOLD(L;N) and FOLD(L;M,N) are always defined for (3.2).

THEOREM 3.1. If a FOLD transformation is defined and applied to the statements in the form (3.1) or (3.2) occurring in a deterministic program **P**, then the resulting program **P**′ is deterministic and semantically equivalent to **P**.

The proof of the theorem, in more general formulation, can be found in [7]. A simple example of FOLD transformation is given in Fig.3.1.

Note, that after a FOLD transformation was performed the statement M (or N, or both) may become isolated (i.e., without any entrance to it from another statement) and therefore can be removed without altering the semantics of the program in which it occurs. Next, the new statement L may have two exits to the same statement L′, say Q.L′ and P.L′, then, since determinism of the statement is preserved, these two can be merged into one $Q \vee P.L'$. Similary, two components E/Q and E/P of the same conditional microoperation can be merged into $E/Q \vee P$. Finally, some of the conditions in the new L statement may be simplified by the known logical rules (like $Q \wedge \overline{Q} \equiv 0$ or $Q \wedge (P \vee R) \equiv (Q \wedge P) \vee (Q \wedge R)$) and then "false" components can be deleted.

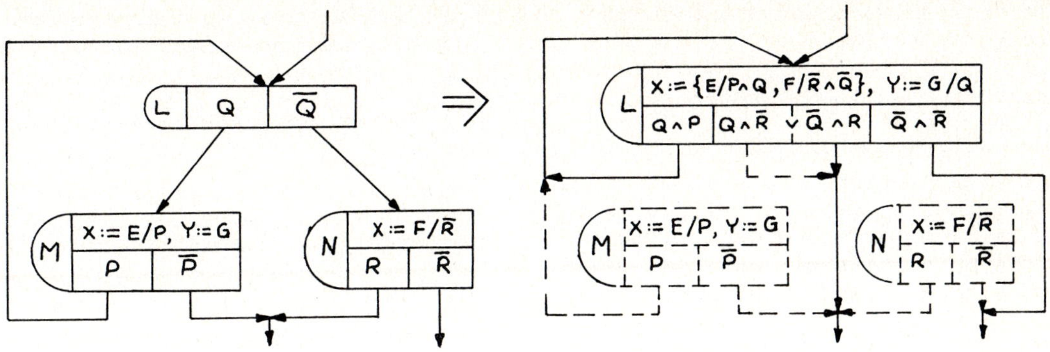

Fig.3.1.

In view of the above, we intoduce the convention which says that each FOLD transformation is immediately followed by the "local" simplification procedure SIMPLIFY which does the described operations. That way the FOLD(L;M,N) transformation presented in Fig.3.1 would result in the right hand side diagram with all dotted components removed.

Consider the situation described in the Example 2.1, when the free of conflict statement has been defined (constraint C_1). We say that a bfmo X := E (bbmo Q) is not in conflict with a free of conflict statement

M : co exit $Q_1.M_1,\dots,Q_m.M_m$,

if X := E (Q) is not in conflict with co and with each Q_i of the branching conditions.

LEMMA 3.1.

1. If the statement M in (3.1) is free of conflict, X := E is not in conflict with M, and $X \notin var(M)$, then the statement (3.3) is free of conflict.

2. If the statement M in (3.2) is free of conflict and Q is not in conflict with M then the statement (3.4) is free of conflict.

3. If the statements M and N are free of conflict, every two conditions P and R, such that P occurs in M and R occurs in N, are not in conflict, and Q is not in conflict with M and N, then the statement (3.5) is free of conflict.

Let **C** be a set of constraints. We say that FOLD(L;M) or FOLD(L;M,N) is <u>C-applicable</u> if the resulting L statement satisfies all constraints in **C** .

It is now visible that Lemma 3.1 gives sufficient conditions for the C_1-applicability of the FOLD transformations. Verification of these conditions requires only some checks in the set CBM and is much simpler than the verification based on the definition of the constraint C_1 (see Example 2.1, in particular no.5 of this definition).

One can easily check that if M or N in (3.1) or (3.2) has an entrance to itself (i.e., M (N) occurs in the exit part of the statement M (N)) then the FOLD(L;M) or FOLD(L;M,N) transformation can not remove this statement (i.e., the SIMPLIFY procedure following the FOLD one). The transformation is then called <u>reductive</u> if M (M or N) has no enrance to itself.

A reductive and **C**-applicable FOLD transformation is called <u>(generally) applicable</u>.

It is easy to predict that we are basing our compaction algorithm on the repeating use of the applicable FOLD transformations. It is not irrelevant to the result, however, what sequence of transformations is chosen. The order of application is similary important. Another difficulty arises when two microinstructions are in a loop which means that there is no clear order of execution. In the next section we present a solution to all these problems.

4. THE COMPACTION ALGORITHM

The compaction algorithm, for a given vertical microprogram **P** and a set of machine derived constraints **C**, consists of the following four major steps the content of which is explained in detail below:

STEP 1: Find a minimal partition of **P** into closed and free of storage resource conflicts subsets (cfsc subsets)

STEP 2: For each cfsc-subset **I** in the minimal partition of **P** obtained in the STEP 1, find a loop-free reduct of the graph G(**I**)

STEP 3: For each loop-free reduct obtained in the STEP 2, form the sequence of FOLD transformations

STEP 4: For each sequence T of FOLD transformations obtained in the STEP 3, perform the ADJUST(T,**C**) procedure.

Roughly speaking, the first three steps in this algorithm produce such sequences of FOLD transformations as if there were no constraints, and the order in sequences is this one which guarantees maximal reduction. In the fourth step these sequences are performed and dynamically adjusted to satisfy the constraints in the set **C**.

STEP 1

Let G(**P**) denote the graph described in the obvious way by the microprogram **P**. We shall identify the graph nodes with labels. Consider now a vertical microprogram **P** to be optimized. Let $M \in G(\mathbf{P})$. A subset (subprogram) **I** of **P** is called M-closed iff

1. $M \in G(\mathbf{I})$
2. if $L \neq M$ is in G(**I**) then, for all $L' \in G(\mathbf{P})$ such that (L′,L) is an arc in G(**P**), $L' \in G(\mathbf{I})$
3. if $L \in G(\mathbf{I})$ then L is not a halting statement in **P**.

The condition 2 roughly says that the only entrances to the subprogram **I** are through the statement M.

A path in a graph is called direct iff it is repetition-free.

A M-closed subset **I** of **P** is called free of storage resource conflicts (cfsc subset) iff for each direct path $L_1,\dots L_k$ in G(**I**), such that $L_1=M$, if X := E is the bfmo of the statement labeled by L_i $(1 \leq i < k)$ then $X \notin var(L_j)$ for $i < j \leq k$.

By a partition of **P** into cfsc-subsets we mean any partition of the nonhalting statements of **P** into such subsets. A minimal partition of **P** is this with the minimal number of the subsets

From the above definitions one can see that a minimal partition of **P** always exists and can be effectively determined. There may exist, however, more than one minimal partition. This nondeterminism can have some bearing on the microprogram reduction. This will be explained later on.

Example:

For the microprogram in Fig.2.4 one can give the following two minimal partitions:

1. $\mathbf{I}_1 = \{M0 - M4\}$, $\mathbf{I}_2 = \{M5 - M11\}$, $\mathbf{I}_3 = \{M12 - M17\}$
2. $\mathbf{I}_1 = \{M0 - M4\}$, $\mathbf{I}_2 = \{M5 - M10\}$, $\mathbf{I}_3 = \{M11 - M17\}$

STEP 2

Consider a cfsc-subset **I**. Remove from the graph G(**I**) a number of arcs in such a way as to get a loop-free graph without isolated nodes. Any such graph which results from G(**I**) by the minimal number of removals will be called the loop-free reduct of G(**I**) ($lfr_{G(\mathbf{I})}$).

Example:

$\mathbf{I}_3 = \{M12 - M17\}$ is a cfsc-subset of the microprogram in Fig.2.4. $G(\mathbf{I}_3)$ is presented in Fig.4.1, and its loop-free reduct results by removing the dotted arc (M17,M12).

Again, there may exist more than one loop-free reduct. It is irrelevant for the algorithm which one is chosen.

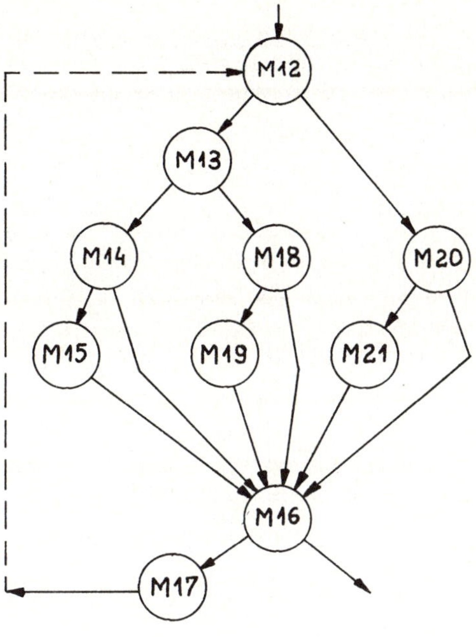

Fig.4.1.

STEP 3

For each inner node L in $lfr_{G(\mathbf{I})}$, (i.e., having at least one direct successor in $lfr_{G(\mathbf{I})}$, define the transformation

FOLD(L;M) or FOLD(L;M,N) (4.1)

where M (or M and N) are direct successors of L in the graph $lfr_{G(\mathbf{I})}$.

Every such transformation is well defined since **I** is free of storage resource conflicts.

Assume the number of the above transformations to be $n > 1$. Let us order them into a sequence which satisfies the following property:

- The transformation FOLD(L;M) (or FOLD(L;M,N)) may stand i-th in the sequence if M (M and N) is (are) either final node(s) in $lfr_{G(\mathbf{I})}$ (i.e., without any direct successor in the loop-free reduct) or the transformation(s) FOLD(M;..) (FOLD(M;..) and FOLD(N;..)) stand(s) earlier in the sequence.

This property says that the compacting transformations are performed "bottom-up" within each cfsc-subset of **P** . This guarantees the maximal reduction since none of the transformations may now introduce a storage resource conflict.

Example:

For the $lfr_{G(\mathbf{I})}$ of Fig.4.1 the following sequence of transformations satisfies the order property:

FOLD(M16;M17), FOLD(M15;M16),
FOLD(M14;M15,M16), FOLD(M19;M16),
FOLD(M18;M19,M16), FOLD(M21;M16),
FOLD(M20;M21,M16), FOLD(M13;M14,M18),
FOLD(M12;M13,M20)

STEP 4

Let $T = T_1,\dots,T_n$ be a sequence of FOLD transformations defined in the STEP 3, and **C** a set of constraints.

ADJUST(T,**C**) is the following program (recall that "T_i is applicable" means T_i is reductive and **C**-applicable" - see Sec.3):

<u>For</u> i=1 <u>to</u> n <u>do</u>
  <u>if</u> T_i is applicable
  <u>then</u> <u>do</u> T_i
  <u>else</u> <u>case</u>
  T_i=FOLD(L;M,N) and
  FOLD(L;M) is applicable: <u>do</u> FOLD(L;M);

  T_i=FOLD(L;M,N) and
  FOLD(L;N) is applicable: <u>do</u> FOLD(L;N);

  otherwise : <u>skip</u>
  <u>end</u>

Example:

Let us apply the procedure ADJUST to the sequence defined in the example of the STEP 3, with the set of constraints:

A. $\mathbf{C} = \{C_1,C_2\}$ where C_1 is based on CBM_1

B. $\mathbf{C} = \{C_1\}$ where C_1 is based on CBM_2

This would result in performance, on the microprogram in Fig.2.4, of the following two sequences of transformations respectively:

A. FOLD(M15;M16), FOLD(M19;M16), FOLD(M21;M16), FOLD(M13;M14,M18), FOLD(M12;M13,M20)

B. FOLD(M16;M17), FOLD(M15;M16), FOLD(M14;M15,M16), FOLD(M19;M16), FOLD(M18;M19,M16), FOLD(M21;M16), FOLD(M20;M21,M16), FOLD(M13;M14), FOLD(M12;M13)

Now, one can easily check that each of the horizontal microprograms in Fig.2.5 - 2.7 is the result of applying the compaction algorithm to the vertical microprogram of Fig.2.4:

- the microprogram in Fig.2.5 when $\mathbf{C} = \emptyset$
- the microprogram in Fig.2.6 when $\mathbf{C} = \{C_1, C_2\}$ and C_1 is based on CBM_1
- the microprogram in Fig.2.7 when $\mathbf{C} = \{C_1\}$ but C_1 is based on CBM_2

Few words should be devoted to the nondeterminism appearing in the algorithm. The one which may have some bearing on the microprogram reduction is that occurring in the STEP 1 . It is explained below in detail. All others may only and insignificantly alter the form of the resulting microprogram.

Let $\mathbf{I}$ be a cfsc-subset of a vertical microprogram $\mathbf{P}$. In order to get a loop-free reduct of $G(\mathbf{I})$ one has to remove a number of arcs from the graph. The number of loops $l(\mathbf{I})$ is then identified by those removed arcs which have different target nodes. In other words, two arcs, say (L,M) and (K,M) , identify the same loop. It is easy to notice that if $l(\mathbf{I}) = 0$ and $\mathbf{C} = \emptyset$, then the compaction algorithm reduces the statements of $\mathbf{I}$ to a single one. On the other hand, none of the FOLD transformation can isolate a statement which has an entrance from itself (that is why we do not perform nonreductive transformations). The conclusion is that the algo rithm (if $\mathbf{C} = \emptyset$) reduces the number of microstatements in $\mathbf{I}$ to

$$l(\mathbf{I})+a \text{ , where } a=0 \text{ or } a=1 \text{ ,} \qquad (4.2)$$

and $a = 1$ if there is an initial loop-free fragment in $G(\mathbf{I})$.

Now, let $\mathbf{I}_1,\ldots,\mathbf{I}_k$ and $\mathbf{J}_1,\ldots,\mathbf{J}_k$ be two minimal partitions of $\mathbf{P}$. It is easy to show that

$$\sum_{i=1}^{k} l(\mathbf{I}_i) = \sum_{i=1}^{k} l(\mathbf{J}_i) \qquad (4.3)$$

Denote the number by $LB(\mathbf{P})$. The (4.2) and (4.3) mean that in the best case the algorithm (with $\mathbf{C} = \emptyset$) reduces the number of microstatements in $\mathbf{P}$ to $LB(\mathbf{P})$ and in the worst case to $LB(\mathbf{P}) + k$. $LB(\mathbf{P})$ is therefore the lower bound for the performance of the algorithm with an arbitrary $\mathbf{C}$. The upper bound is obviously the number of microstatements in $\mathbf{P}$ since verticality itself can be the postulated constraint.

5. CONCLUSIONS

We have formulated a method of microprogram compaction (parallelization) which has the following main properties:

- It takes into account the overall structure of microprograms allowing for, precisely defined, manipulations with branching and/or conditional microoperations. This leads to much better (in most cases) results, if measured by the number of reduced (or obtained) microstatements, than any other method based on microprogram partition into straight-line segments optimized separately.

- The method clearly separates machine independent features from those realization derived constraints. This makes possible to treat the optimization (compaction) procedure as an automatic aid in (microprogrammed) hardware design at different stages of this design.

- The correctness of the obtained horizontal microprogram with respect to its vertical specification and machine constraints is guaranteed. It forces to define the constraints in terms of microstatement properties (which may occur not a simple problem) but one cannot avoid this difficulty if the correctness problem is to be treated seriously.

At last we have to add that the FOLD transformation could be defined with weaker assumptions concerning independance of storage resources. This leads to the situation when some basic microoperations one starts with in the input vertical microprogram may be replaced by others. This interesting aspect requires however, some additional mechanism checking for equivalence (and existance) of available microoperations. Some theoretical considerations and examples of such transformations are given in [7] and [8].

REFERENCES

[1] Agerwala, T., Microprogram Optimization: A Survey, IEEE Trans. on Comp., vol. C-25, 10 (1976)

[2] Dasgupta, S., Tartar , J., The Identification of Maximal parallelism in Straight-line Microprograms, IEEE Trans. on Comp., vol. C-25, 10 (1976)

[3] Dasgupta, S., The Organization of Microprogram Stores, ACM Computing Surveys, vol. 11, 1 (1979)

[4] Dasgupta, S., Parallelism in Loop Free Microprograms, Proc. IFIP 77, Gilchriot, B. (ed.)(North-Holland, Amsterdam, 1977)

[5] Davidson, S., Shriver, B.D., Firmware Engineering: An Extensive Update, Chroust, G. and Mubacher, J. (eds.), Proc. IFIP TC-10 Conf. Microprogramming, Firmware and Restructable Hardware

[6] Dembiński, P., Budkowski, S., Verification, Design and Description Oriented Microprogramming Language, in Lawson, H.W., Berndt, H. and Hermanson, G. (eds.), Proc. Euromicro 78 (North-Holland, Amsterdam, 1978)

[7] Dembiński, P., Microprogram Transformations, ICS PAS Report (September 1982)

[8] Dembiński, P., On Automated Design of Compact Microprograms, to appear

[9] Mallet, P.W., Methods of Compacting Microprograms, Ph.D. Thesis, Dept. of Comp. Sc., Univ. of Southwestern Louisiana (1978)

[10] Mezalama, M., Prinetto, P. and Filippi, G., Microcode Compaction via Microblock Definition, Proc. 15th Annual Workshop on Microprog.(1982)

[11] Poe, M.D., Measurment and Manipulation of Potential Parallelism in Microcode, Proc. Euromicro 81 (North Holland, Amsterdam, 1981)

[12] Tokoro, M., Takizuka, T., Tamura,E. and Yamaura, F., A Technique of Global Optimization of Microprograms, Proc. 11th Annual Workshop on Microprogramming (1978)

[13] Tsuchiya, M., Gonzalez, M., Toward Optimization of Horizontal Microprograms, IEEE Trans. on Comp., vol. C-25, 10 (1976)

[14] Vegdahl, S.R., Phase Coupling and Constant Generation in an Optimizing Microcode Compiler, Proc. 15th Annual Workshop on Microprogramming (1982)

[15] Wood, G., Computer Aided Design of Microprograms, Ph. D. Thesis, Univ. of Edinburgh (1979)

Session J2:

HUMAN FACTORS

Chairman: B. Myhrhaug
Tandberg Data A/S
Oslo (Norway)

Whenever a human and a computer acts together, there will be human factors involved. The topic of this session is thus very large.

In the call for paper for this conference, we wrote as an outline of the contents of this session:

"The human interface to a microprocessor system will typically be on more than one level: the hardware defines the physical characteristics of the user interface. The operational aspects are a combination of what the hardware is, and how the software uses this hardware".

Amond the specifically mentioned areas of interest were: Novel input/output devices and methods; User guidance in systems training and use; Data and command presentation; User friendly systems. Much to our surprise, we did not receive any papers devoted mainly to these topics.

We did, however, receive quite interesting papers on other human factors in computing.

The first paper, by F.G. Duncan is entitled "Substitutes for speech: experience of applications of artificial voice production in microprocessorbased systems for the disabled", and deals with how handicapped people can be aided by microcomputers to overcome serious disabilities. This is truly an interesting and fascinating area where I would expect an increasing amount of research to be done in the future.

The second paper is also from the United Kingdom, by P. Turner and J. Hall. It also deals with using microcomputers for the disabled, but concentrates more on the educational aspects. It is entitled "The liberating microchip... the computer as access to communication, independence and dignity".

Taking human factors into account when using microcomputers for <u>any</u> application will indeed make the microchip "the liberator" in many ways.

MICROCOMPUTERS: Developments in Industry, Business and Education
D.R. Wilson and C.J. van Spronsen (eds.) / ©EUROMICRO, 1983
Elsevier Science Publishers B.V. (North-Holland)

SUBSTITUTES FOR SPEECH

F.G. Duncan

University of Bristol
Computer Science Department
Bristol, England

Two projects in which microcomputers and voice synthesizers are applied to the needs of the physically disabled are described and discussed. Personal information systems for the blind require personalised software but can make use of available components. Communication aids for the speech-impaired also require tailored software and in addition, because of the diversity of other accompanying disabilities, personalised hardware, specifically in the area of the "man-machine interface".

1. INTRODUCTION

The man-machine interface is widely recognised as a major area of concern in information processing. This recognition is comparatively recent; many of us can remember a time when it would have been improper even to think of adapting a computer to merely human needs. We were expected, and we were on the whole content, to meet the computer on its own terms. We would make an appointment with it at its own convenience, as if we were to pay homage to a feudal lord or to consult an eminent surgeon. And by the time arranged for the audience we would have prepared our text in the language and form required by it - punched cards in binary, or, even worse, in COBOL. Communication with a computer is less formal now. We keep personal computers on our desks. These relatively undemanding machines are there when they are wanted, and no trouble when they are not. Some of them are designed to be friendly, even helpful; they will, for example, remind us what they can do next and how we may indicate our choice. If we have good eyesight, good fingers, and a fairly functional brain, we can hardly ask for more. These machines, if used in moderation, impose less strain upon their users than do many other well established aids to modern living.

The conventional computer terminal, or the personal computer with VDU and printer, makes, however, no concessions to the operator who through physical disability cannot use a standard typewriter keyboard or read the characters on a screen. There are, for example, many blind people - some of them already creative and productive programmers - who would like to be able to use computers on equal terms with their sighted colleagues. Devices giving permanent or transient Braille output exist which can operate in parallel with the printer or screen. They are very expensive. More recently, speech synthesizers have become available which, suitably interfaced, allow whatever is put out to the screen or printer also to be "spoken" and repeated as necessary. This is, in principle, an easy and inexpensive adaptation which has been successfully implemented in many cases. It is particularly regrettable that some otherwise satisfactory microprocessor systems have been so put together that the addition of a standard serial interface is extremely difficult, sometimes impossible, without information from the manufacturers which is not forthcoming. The urgent need of provisions for blind operators has led some very ingenious people to embark on elaborate schemes which should be quite unnecessary as, for example, using a video camera to reconstitute information which already exists in the required form somewhere on a printed circuit board inside the computer or terminal.

Some of us are professional computer scientists. The vast majority of people are not, nor indeed are the vast majority of present-day computer users. Most people - and even computer scientists for part of their time - use computers only as a means to an end. The idea of a personal computer implies a machine that will serve its user's own ends. If the user suffers from some form of disability, why should not those ends include the overcoming of the consequences of that disability? Well, of course, for some people with some forms of disability they already do. New products of technology adapted as computer peripherals are needed to serve those with other, often more distressing, forms of disability. Synthetic speech devices have been available for some time and some progress has been made in using them to ease the everyday problems of two groups of the disabled - the blind and the speech-impaired.

2. A SYNTHETIC SPEECH APPLICATION FOR A BLIND PERSON.

The blind computer operator with the Braille or synthetic speech terminal as mentioned in the introduction can no doubt work as effectively as his sighted colleagues, or as he himself would have done had he not been blind. But even computer operators do other things beside work. The modified terminal helps the man to work well - can it help him in his other activities too? And if so, can it help another blind person, who is not a computer operator, in his everyday activities? The answer obviously is that it can, but with some quite severe limitations. The use of any computer requires the application of a degree of specialised skill which not everyone can acquire easily, and it is in most cases impracticable for the machine to be taken everywhere where it might be of use. There is undoubtedly great scope for devices exploiting current technology and designed to be used with the minimum of training and made as compact and portable as possible.

Work over the past year or so with a blind colleague who has not the slightest interest in computers or computing as such has been a very stimulating and salutary experience. Our first idea was to attach an inexpensive voice synthesizer to an existing microcomputer and try out a few simple information processing programs. His first requests were for an audible note-book, diary, bank statement, and telephone directory with perhaps a dictionary as well. All of these are difficult or cumbersome in Braille or with an ordinary cassette recorder.

Our first major problem was that the experimental system was not portable - it was mains-operated, and bulky with awkwardly shaped components. Other people carry their diaries and notebooks around with them. If the project were to result in a useful device, that device would have to be battery-operated and small and light enough for its user to want to carry it.

The second major problem surprised us at the time, but in retrospect it should have been anticipated. The programs were being written under a rather friendly operating system. Consequently our user had to become familiar with the system's friendly and helpful ways. He found them tiresome, even exasperating. He complained that the machine kept repeating information; he wanted to be told less, and to be told it less often. "Make it smaller, and make it talk less, particularly about itself. Most important, make it cheap enough for me to have one of my own." We think we can meet all these requirements; in the mean time our friend has declined offers of other equipment on loan - he, very reasonably, does not wish to become dependent on something which will tie him to one place, or which will have to be given up at a later date.

The device on which we are working and which we hope will be suitable for permanent use will have the following specification:

1. Overall size no bigger than a portable typewriter and certainly lighter. Integral weatherproof case with carrying handle. Internal rechargeable battery. (Battery charger as separate unit.)
2. Standard layout, standard size typewriter keyboard with embossed tops for control keys.
3. No built-in visual output device, but interface and socket for connection to standard serial devices such as printers.
4. Built-in voice synthesizer giving word output - for example, Votrax SC-01 controlled by microprocessor programmed for translation from English text. The synthesizer to be replaceable.
5. Built-in speaker and pair of headphone sockets.
6. Internal microprocessor system comprising Z80 8-bit processor, EPROM and RAM in 2K or 4K packages, interfaces to keyboard and synthesizer, external interface, microdisc unit and associated control circuitry.

The human factors indicating this specification include the following:

1. The device must be conveniently portable, and usable where there is no mains supply.
2. The user is already proficient with the standard typewriter, and should not be required to adapt to a non-standard input device.
3. The user wishes to produce documents such as letters and scientific papers for publication. The necessary printer is too large and too heavy to be incorporated into a portable device.

4,5. The speech output must be able to generate plain language and also be able to spell out words and formulae. The speaker is needed for ordinary use. Headphones will be helpful in noisy surroundings, or in ensuring privacy. The inexpensive addition of a second headphone socket will allow another person simultaneous access to the device.

6. An eight-bit processor is right for this application, and the Z80 is the most convenient of those available. (This human factor concerns the designer and programmer.) A random-access disc is preferable to a sequential-access tape. The application requires a fairly large storage capacity.

The software is to consist of a single sectionalised program, with detachable and replaceable sections for the talking diary, talking note-book, and so on. A more "advanced" section would provide word-procassing facilities, including printing. The device is of course compatible with other systems; whether software will be written to take advantage of this will depend on the development of the user's interests and wishes.

Copies of this device will no doubt be of use to other blind persons, not all of whom, however, will wish to use the software of the prototype. The development of variations to the software, a major project in itself, would ideally be carried out by programmers who were also users of the device.

The man-machine interface in this application is from a technical point of view relatively straightforward. It uses a standard input device. The speech output is intended primarily for the user himself, who is likely to be satisfied if it is reasonably intelligible and not too monotonous or irritating. (In this connection it may be of interest that we find a device whose synthetic voice output has a superimposed periodic variation of pitch and speed very irritating indeed. The flat robot-like speech of a less complicated synthesizer is much more tolerable.) It is of course the software - what it does and how it is controlled by the user - which determines the acceptability and usefulness of the device as a whole. It is vital that the potential user should be involved in its specification and design - without this help the sighted programmer cannot hope to succeed in producing something which will be willingly used.

3. AN APPLICATION FOR THE SPEECH-IMPAIRED.

A type of disability other than blindness which the voice synthesizer may help to relieve is of course speech-loss or speech- impairment. Here the balance of considerations is very different, and often very difficult to resolve.

We are concerned in a project to provide an "artificial voice" device for each one of a number of people nominated by the speech therapists of Frenchay Hospital, Bristol, as representing a cross-section of those who are thought to be able to benefit thereby. This is a considerably more delicate and complicated problem than that of designing a personal information system for the blind colleague. That machine could be designed to take full advantage of its user's unimpaired ability to type, to hear, and to use language. Speech-impairment is rarely an isolated disability. None of our group has simply lost the ability to use his or her voice. Each one suffers from a combination of disabilities, and all are different. They have, moreover, different expectations of an artificial voice. One is happy to take his machine to the shop around the corner; he doesn't mind showing it off, and he doesn't care what it sounds like as long as it is understood, after repetition if necessary. Another will come to terms, reluctantly, with the machine only when it produces a voice as clear and euphonious and feminine as the voice she has lost and when it is small enough to be concealed. The one will settle for anything that can be made to talk; the other demands a vocal prosthesis of high quality. Their two attitudes are in fact not so extreme - the one hopes for something better and the other accepts the need for compromise with the available technology. There is, however, an important difference within the group between those who see the machine as a useful object (like a wheel-chair) and those who see it eventually as a substitute for part of themselves (like an artificial limb). In every case the user's expectations must be considered in the design of the machine and its facilities.

It is not possible here to describe all of our users and their machines, although brief sketches of a few will be given. It must be emphasised that this paper is written from the point of view of a computer scientist and so can give only a layman's perception of the medical and therapeutic aspects of the project.

Initial impressions based almost entirely on a potential user's apparent physical ability and disability can be very misleading. At a first meeting it may be possible to decide what kind of keyboard or other input device may be suitable, but it takes time and collaboration both with the user and with the therapists concerned to decide exactly what hardware to put together and what kind of software facilities to implement.

None of our users and potential users can operate a standard typewriter keyboard with all ten fingers. Most can use one hand with difficulty; one - the youngest - can use neither hands nor feet and must rely instead on a device operated by head movements. Some can formulate expressions in words and spell these words out; some have great difficulty with language and can do little more than select short messages from a pre-arranged set. The former can make use of a keyboard with the full alphabet; the latter need a keyboard labelled with pictures or symbols. Amongst those who can use the full alphabet there is a wide range of abilities. Some are limited to the formation of very simple sequences of words, and work very slowly; others are so garrulous that the machine can hardly keep up with them. In every case, however, there is one principle to be observed; the user must feel that the machine is right for him and that he has complete control over it. It is a mistake to provide facilities which are beyond the user's needs and capabilities. To be right, the software must be sufficient to cope with the user's current level of expertise with the machine and very little more. At the same time, if he is making progress, the software must be capable of development and keep half a step ahead. The artificial voice machine is essentially an intimately personal device, and at least as much care is required in fitting it to its user and keeping it fitted as is commonly given to such other devices as dentures and artificial limbs.

In the following, single capital letters have been used to distinguish individuals.

A is a middle-aged man who several years ago suffered a stroke which left his right side and arm paralysed and his speech severely impaired. Before the stroke he could use a typewriter; now he can manage one with his left hand only. We made his machine in a case of overall dimensions approximately 225mmx300x100, light enough to be carried in a special satchel supported by a shoulder strap. The keyboard had about 50 keys, arranged as on a typewriter, each about 12mm square and placed very close to one another.

The original software allowed any English text to be typed - though phonetic spelling was to some extent necessary - and spoken and, if necessary, repeated. The user was invited to specify a two-letter abbreviation for each of any number of short messages of his own choosing. His first list contained names of family and friends, and items of food and drink. He was thus enabled to use a limited shorthand. Further software allowed a certain amount of text-editing so that a "speech" could be built up in the RAM phrase by phrase and revised before being spoken either complete or a phrase at a time.

A's experience has shown the need for a number of improvements. Although the size and spacing of the keys was precisely the same as on the printing device he had previously used as a communication aid, because he was so much more eager to express himself quickly with the artificial voice it was found that in attempting to reach high speeds he was often pressing two keys at once and producing gibberish. This problem was overcome by the use of a simple key-guard - a pierced metal plate over the keyboard. The system of abbreviations is very successful. As A had compiled them, he had no difficulty in remembering them. His requests for additions are interesting as a measure of his progress - from original basic needs (e.g. GT for "gin and tonic") to complex social concerns (e.g. DT for "Shall I take the dog out, or will you?"). The text-editing features have been a failure; after early attempts to use them they have been abandoned and are being cut out of the hardware and software. It remains to be seen how other users cope with text-editing. In this case the main problem was the lack of any form of visual display and insufficient audible information as to the state of the text. It is interesting, though, that this is the sort of difficulty which blind users of computers take in their stride.

B suffered brain-damage in a car accident some years ago when he was 18. Apart from the obvious difficulty he has in controlling the movements of his hands, he has poor visual coord-ination and he has lost the ability to read and spell. Instead of an alphabetical keyboard, his machine was provided with a top panel divided into sixteen 50mm squares, the idea being that by pressing the right square he would cause the machine to speak a message like "Can I have a drink?" The squares were originally marked by boldly printed short keywords in the hope that he would learn to associate the keywords and the messages. This was far too hard, and the keywords were soon replaced by pictures. It was still too hard, the problem now being how to find and operate the right square out of sixteen. We tried covering all the squares except two. This helped. Gradually, over several months, more pictures were uncovered until he could achieve fair success with seven or eight. But using the machine was clearly a painful process, combining the mental and visual problem of selection with the visual and mechanical problem of operation. Even with the device fixed at the optimum angle, and with a key-guard to allow the hand to rest on it, the strain was too much. It became clear, too, that the messages were not the most suitable. "Yes" and "No" were quite unnecessary, as were "Please" and "Thank you", and even "Mum" and "Dad"; B has his own very clear way of expressing these words. "Can I have the television on?" could be used only at home where his parents did not need a machine to give them the message. The machine was abandoned after six months. B has certainly been stimulated by this experience, which has helped his other attempts at communication. It is perhaps possible that with a different set of messages the machine might yet have some success. But this is not something that should be forced on anyone, least of all on one with severe disability. A communication aid should help, not impose an additional burden.

F borrowed B's abandoned machine while waiting for his own to be built. At first sight these two young men are very similar, both in wheel-chairs and both having the same sort of difficulty in operating the special panel. But F is the less unfortunate in that he seems to have no problem in deciding which message he wants to use and which square should be pressed. He took to the machine immediately and within half an hour was using it quite successfully, if only to tease his mother. He can now manage a special panel with 42 (=6x7) smaller squares labelled with keywords. His former communication aid was a set of cards divided into small rectangles each containing a short text. At his first encounter with the speech machine, his finger stayed determinedly on a square with the message "Please explain".

C is a lady with motor neurone disease, a long-term patient in hospital. She likes the artificial voice machine, which is very similar to A's but with the keys arranged in a non-standard order at her own request. She doesn't mind at all that the voice is that of a male American robot, although of course she will prefer to have something more feminine when this becomes practicable. Unlike A, she can manage the "text-editing" feature, but in her own way which was not foreseen by the programmer. As she thinks of things she needs, she adds them to the recorded text, and when a visitor comes she plays the list through: "Library book, eggs, stamps,...". As the items arrive so are the corresponding words deleted from the recording. We hope to add a small printing unit; no doubt visitors will then be issued with shopping-lists. The advantage of the voice machine is in lessening the stress on visitors and in increased speed in comparison with the exclusive use of a printer. Difficulties in managing the keyboard are partially overcome by the use of a key-guard and by holding the device at the right angle in the right place.

D is something of a star performer with the artificial voice machine. He is a 12-year old boy unable to use either his arms or his legs, but with a very lively intelligence. He holds a record by being the only user to get the machine to speak a sentence correctly at the first attempt. This was a machine built for another user - E - with a very large keyboard - 500mmx250 - with heavy keys at a pitch of 40mm which he was able to operate with his "unicorn" head-pointer. With a keyboard more suitable for this method of operation - all the keys within a square of side 175mm and beneath a transparent plastic sheet - and lying on the floor, he was using the machine within half an hour to express opinions as well as communicate information. He was, moreover, using spelling accurately modified for correct pronunciation. He seems likely to make very good use of his machine - he has already told us "This is ace for me" - and he will no doubt offer much critical advice. His machine will probably undergo more development in both hardware and software than any of the others. It will be particularly important to attempt to achieve coordination with the other equipment which he uses, or at the very least to avoid conflict with it. As always, collaboration with teachers and therapists is essential.

E, whose machine hs already been mentioned, is a young man of 19 who suffered severe brain damage in an accident 18 months ago. He has ambitions as a writer, but he cannot use a pen or cope with any ordinary keyboard as his hand movements are heavy and awkward. The keyboard made for him is covered with a metal plate pierced with 20mm holes at 40mm intervals. This allows his hand to rest across the keys without actuating them while a finger can press one key through the appropriate hole. The plate is covered by a flexible and waterproof sheet on which the key-legends are printed in symbols 25mm high. Poor vision is another side-effect of the brain damage. E seems very glad to have his artificial voice, but his progress with it must inevitably be slower than D's. Limited text-editing has been provided, but it is too early to say how it will be used.

The foregoing notes will, it is hoped, give some idea of the human factors entering into one particular project for the disabled. These notes are by no means exhaustive but the problems mentioned are reasonably representative of those encountered. In applications of this kind the needs of the individual user are the dominant factor in the design of the man-machine interface.

4. SOME TECHNICAL CONSIDERATIONS.

The object of the project outlined above may be restated concisely as follows. It is to enable each of a number of very different individuals to exploit as fully as possible the voice synthesizer as an aid to communication.

Technically, this means designing, building and providing with suitable software, as many different machines. How much can these machines have in common? Superficially, very little - we have had to use four different cases, three different types of keys, five different arrangements of the keyboard. Internally, however, the machines show very little difference, such differences as there are showing convergence towards a uniform design which in retrospect would have served well in every one of the machines. Three different battery arrangements have been used - this is largely a question of the shape and size of the available space. The power supply design has evolved towards two alternative forms. The development of the microcomputer and voice synthesizer system shows that in future it will be possible to use one printed circuit board allowing differences in the complements of storage and interface devices. Storage has been based on the very convenient and mutually interchangeable 2K-byte EPROM and static RAM; the printed circuit board will allow for the equally convenient 4K versions. The different keyboards and key arrange-ments are dealt with by a common interface controlled however by different scanning routines using different look-up tables held in EPROM. Provision for optional additional interfaces will allow each machine to be developed in accordance with its user's requirements. Some wish to use a printer, some a television screen, and some wish to use the device as an input to a computer. In addition, some machines may be required to control other equipment.

There was very little difficulty in deciding to use the Z80 processor in all the machines. The application is essentially one for an eight-bit processor, and the Z80 is both convenient and familiar.

The programs required are all different, though of course they have substantial parts in common. It is clearly desirable for each one to be as compact as possible so that the amount of semiconductor storage can be minimised while keeping adequate space for recorded texts. Unnecessary overheads must be avoided; in other words, each program must be a machine-code program which can run by itself without the need for an operating system or interpreter. If we look at all the programs together we see a fairly large set of subroutines and a set of calling programs each of which makes use of a subset of the subroutines. Some of these subsets have several members in common. Among the subroutines are some which deal at the finest level of detail with the signals required to control the input-output devices. Compactness, clarity, simplicity of structure, as well as compatibility, all demand a homogeneity of treatment. The whole software has been written directly at machine-code level. This has avoided the conceptual derangement and awkwardness which a mixture of machine code and high-level language would have induced. The much-publicised and widely accepted myth that machine-code programming is difficult, time-consuming, and inimical to the production of well-structured programs must be refuted. On the contrary, if carried out in a disciplined manner it can lead quickly to very reliable results without the need for elaborate hardware and software development tools.

At each stage in the development of the software, programs and subroutines already written have been refined where possible, taking into account the requirements of each machine. This has allowed two of the machines to be built without RAM. These are for very severely disabled users; their operation is simply to select pre-recorded texts. No information read from the keyboard needs to be stored; the processor has sufficient registers for working space; no stack is needed as the subroutines have been copied "into line". Even so, each of these machines has only one 2K EPROM package.

5. THE ARTIFICIAL VOICE PROJECT IN CONTEXT.

Several "ready-made" or "off-the-peg" artificial voice devices intended for the speech-impaired are commercially available. Thes range from a primitive device which can say only "yes" and "no" (it may have found its way into the wrong market) through devices with varying numbers of pre-set messages to others with unlimited vocabulary using conventional keyboards. Some use synthetic speech; others are based on digital recordings of human speech, with a heavy bias towards the speech of the male North American space scientist. Most, if not all, of them have found users and are to that extent worth while. However, it may be doubted whether all these users are adequately served, and our experience has shown that there are many speech-impaired persons who cannot make use of any of them. The enormous diversity of complex disabilities is such that there seems no possibility of designing a range of devices from a stock of which a suitable machine can be chosen for every speech-impaired person.

There will for many years be a need to design and build new machines. Of course the potential benefits of a personal device have to be blanced against its cost. The cost of the device itself, including its software, can be assessed with some accuracy; if hardware and software are designed systematically on the basis of the accumulated experience of previous work the cost will reduce with time. It is, however, after delivery when the major part of the overall cost will, and should, be incurred. The machine is one component involved in a continuing process directed at improving, or at least maintaining, its user's quality of life. Persistent efforts by the speech therapist and others to ensure that its contribution is positive, and to prevent it becoming negative, will be needed. For their part, those responsible for the machine itself should remain available, in the background, to maintain and improve the device in response to the user's progress.

6. ACKNOWLEDGMENTS.

The work described in this paper is being carried out under contract to the United Kingdom Department of Industry and with the aid of a grant from Bristol City Council.

Most of the design and construction work has been done in the University of Bristol Computer Science Laboratory by Michael Wilkins, Paul Buttner, and Tim Garland of the Computer Science Department.

The artificial voice project originated in a proposal by Mrs Sheila Duncan, physio-therapist, Ham Green Hospital, Bristol, and became possible through the support and encouragement of Dr M.H. Proctor, Department of Industry, and Professor M.H. Rogers, head of the School of Mathematics, University of Bristol. It has been sustained throughout by the professional advice and practical help of Dr Pam Enderby and Mrs Jayne Easton of the Speech Therapy Department, Frenchay Hospital, Bristol. The "guinea pig" volunteers whom they persuaded to take part in the project have all contributed uniquely, and both they and their families have shown remarkable forbearance. Many other friends and colleagues have assisted in various ways.

In connection with other work mentioned here, acknowledgment is due to Mrs Alison Dodd, Royal National Institute for the Blind, and to Dr Bernard Chapman and Dr Arthur Chatters of the University of Bristol, both for specialised information and for helpful advice.

[February 28th 1983; revised May 17th 1983]

MICROCOMPUTERS: Developments in Industry, Business and Education
D.R. Wilson and C.J. van Spronsen (eds.) / ©EUROMICRO, 1983
Elsevier Science Publishers B.V. (North-Holland)

THE LIBERATING MICROCHIP - THE COMPUTER AS ACCESS TO COMMUNICATION, INDEPENDENCE AND DIGNITY

P. Turner
Education Department
London Borough of Haringey
48 Station Road
London N22, UK

J. Hall
LBMS Ltd
22 Newman Street
London W1P 3HB, UK

Improved surgical techniques and changes in medical policy have brought about a very significant increase in the number of grossly and multiply handicapped young people in the community. Until the advent of the cheap, easily-accessible microcomputer, many of these people were destined for a life of frustration and sterile dependency.

This situation has been radically changed. Children whose needs we simply lacked the techniques to meet can now be significantly helped and a degree of independence and dignity made possible that before the advent of the computer would have been completely out of the question. Two case studies are described.

At a more mundane level, ignorance is a fairly serious disability. Statistics published by the UK Department of Education and Science show that one in six pupils fails to achieve fluency in reading and writing.

The computer, with its ability to match quasi-individual, highly-structured programs with the needs of individual pupils can be a teaching tool of enormous power. It is proposed that it should be used as such in mainstream as well as handicappd schools

1 INTRODUCTION

We are not sure what proportion of the European population is denied a satisfactory education; we have however a rather clearer idea of the situation that obtains in Britain.

The Warnock report on Special Educational Need (WAR 78) published in 1978 showed that up to a quarter of the school population manifests special need at some time. The degree of need does however vary considerably. The number with impairments so serious as to be deemed incapable of education in ordinary mainstream schools is approximately two per cent, and of these about half are placed in special schools in consequence of what are euphemistically described as emotional or behavioural difficulties.

We can establish that about one per cent of the school population of the United Kingdom suffers from some kind of clinical condition that denies them access to ordinary public education, and a significant number of them are physically handicapped.

The absolute size of the severely disabled population is unknown as they are virtually an invisible community. The very nature of their handicaps places them in a position of great dependence, and once they leave the educational system they are cared for and contained rather than consulted.

The situation is, furthermore, becoming progressively more serious as the severity of disability found in the special sector of education becomes more grave. There is, in short, a marked increase in the number of grossly and multiply disabled young people being presented to the schools, and subsequently passed into the community.

It would, we think, be helpful to commence by simply and briefly describing the changes that have taken place.

If one had entered a school for the physically handicapped ten or fifteen years ago, it would not in general have looked so very different from any "mainstream" school. One would have been confronted by classes being conducted in which most of the usual subjects were taught to pupils who, in general, differed from the norm only in that they were confined to wheelchairs or were dependent on elbow crutches.

They would have been largely made up of a small but consistent proportion of boys suffering from Muscular Dystrophy, a majority group of Cerebral Palsy cases, some Spina-bifida sufferers, a few residual Polio victims and a residuum of children with brittle bones, chronic arthritis, Haemophilia and assorted disabling conditions.

The degree of intellectual impairment would have been limited and relatively few would have had any difficulty in communicating.

A similar visit in 1983 would show an entirely different population. Changes in medical policy and surgical and general medical technique have transformed the clientelle of such schools. This process has been accellerated by the increasing number of more able pupils placed in mainstream schools. As a result, the general level of disability found in special schools has markedly worsened.

One will still find a small group of boys suffering from Muscular Dystrophy. There will still be a few children with brittle bones and arthritic conditions. It is likely however that the majority of these pupils will have been mainstreamed. Spina-bifida cases have largely disappeared.

Instead of the almost normal classrooms of the sixties one is confronted by small groups of children, often dependent on elaborate standing frames or fibre-glass shells for physical support and a whole battery of aids to give them even rudimentary mobility and communication.

Why has this happened? The reasons are complex and concern the changes in medical policy and methodology mentioned above. Genetic counselling and such techniques as amniocentesis have reduced the number of children being born with well-understood hereditary defects.

Improved primary medical provision has had a similarly benevolent effect and changes in surgical policy and post natal management have significantly affected the incidence of surviving children suffering from Spina bifida.

The obverse side of the coin is the extent to which, as a result of improvements in surgical techniques and life support systems, those babies suffering from very grave congenital defects, birth injuries or grave early childhood infections are likely to survive. There is also a very marked increase in the number of children surviving after sustaining severe cranial damage in road traffic accidents.

As a result, although the absolute number of children in schools for the physically handicapped has not increased, the degree of impairment confronted has become very much more severe. It is likely to be the majority of the pupils who require elaborate aids to enable them to write, interact in any meaningful way with their environment, move or even speak. The advent of the computer has transformed our ability to educate these pupils and the effect upon their subsequent life chances can not yet easily be estimated.

To show how the computer is bringing about these changes we propose to discuss two not untypical cases, who we shall call Rosemary and Catherine, both pupils at Vale School for Physically Handicapped Pupils in the London Borough of Haringey.

2 CASE STUDY 1 - ROSEMARY

Rosemary is a girl who at the age of ten was badly injured when she was struck by a car.

When she first came to the school, she was a total care case. She could not walk, needed care in all physical areas of her daily living, was unable to drink or eat unaided and could not speak or communicate in any way.

Three years later considerable physical improvement had been achieved. Rosemary can now walk very slowly with the aid of a Rolator (a kind of wheeled walking frame), can cope alone with the lavatory, can feed herself and drink from a cup and has quite good use of her left arm.

She remained however extremely frustrated. She is quite intelligent enough to realise that her physical abilities are now going to improve slowly, if at all, and she still cannot readily communicate. Her previously dominant right hand is of very little use to her and writing or typing with her left will improve only with persistent practice. Above all she was constantly infuriated with her inability to speak. She resorted to such strategems as gesture and "air writing" and resolutely refused to have anything to do with such alternative means of communication as Bliss (BLI 8Ø) or Makaton (MAK 8Ø). This refusal was based on her recognition that these systems would give her access only to people who also understand their conventions.

We did not believe that her intelligence had been as severely impaired as the psychological testing indicated. An IQ of 66 did not seem consistent with Rosemary's obvious awareness of what was being said to her and the sensitivity of her response. It should however be said that IQ testing of the physically handicapped is notoriously unreliable.

We knew that the only real way to give her motivation to break through to further progress was in some way to give her some form of speech. We had already been doing some work with specialised interfaces in her school and had available an Apple II computer.

The Head Teacher of the Vale School had been on a visit to the USA (her report is reference HAL 83) and had seen a Votrax Type'n'Talk speech synthesiser which seemed to offer a possible solution to the problem, if appropriate software could be obtained.

We obtained a speech synthesiser from the USA and put together a development system, consisting of:

- Apple II computer and monitor
- Twin disc drives
- Votrax Type'n'Talk with transformer and speaker
- Dot-matrix printer

After some initial teething troubles the system was persuaded to run and some prototype programs were written. Several objectives concerning the use and further development of the programs were defined, and these and the approach taken are discussed in the next section.

The technical problems having been overcome, the next problem was that of introducing Rosemary to the system. At thirteen she remains very conscious of her femininity and it was not clear how she would respond to the robotic monotone of a synthesiser.

She was shown the equipment and it was explained that this was not "her" voice, but simply "a" voice that she could use to express her thoughts.

In the event she proved delighted. Her motivation has been intense, her keyboard skills have improved very rapidly and "her Votrax" shows every sign of being a very powerful teaching tool giving Rosemary the ability to communicate readily. It seems probable that the quality of speech will be improved in the foreseeable future and we can already see how the somewhat cumbersome development system can be replaced by a more portable setup.

A number of other non-communicating pupils are now using similar equipment and we are convinced that we have made a major step forward in improving the quality of life for the severely disabled.

The immediate value of such systems is obvious, but one can see that they have the potential to open up everything from Higher Education to employment for some people.

3 TECHNICAL APPROACH FOR THE VOTRAX SYSTEM

There were a number of important considerations for the development approach at the school, including:

- versatility of equipment and software
- cost and availability
- non-dependence on technical experts for development and experimentation
- system acceptability

The school had chosen the Apple microcomputer as the main development system for several reasons. The system is widely-used, and there are large ranges of both proprietary software such as typing training packages, and useful programs developed by other users that can be borrowed or exchanged. The system is easy to use and the user documentation is good. It has inexpensive colour graphics, important for attention-getting with many of the children who will make use of it. Particularly, it provides easy interfacing of "foreign" devices via standard interfaces and hobby boards.

The equipment, Apple II, Votrax and printer are all readily available and maintainable in the UK. (Although the first Votrax unit was obtained from the USA, subsequent units have been supplied from UK sources). The cost of the equipmant compares very favourably with that of the purpose-built equipment currently used by children in the school.

It was important that the equipment be easily useable by non-technical staff, such as teachers with limited training in computing. This allows easy and quick experimentation and further development of the prototype programs (which usually are initially developed by experienced programmers). The Votrax unit has an RS232C interface, and interprets text strings internally. This means that a teacher who can write a BASIC program to print output can use a Votrax Type'n'Talk.

System acceptability required that the child should have a useful range of facilities for speech, note taking, composition and reference, but that the command set should be small enough to be kept in her head. It also required that the system should be easily adaptable and extensible, and that both child and teacher should accept it as a useful everyday tool, like, for example, a typewriter

The major objectives for the programs developed for Rosemary's use were:

- The system should have a "personality" of its own - should talk to Rosemary as well as for her, so that it would be seen as a tool she used, rather than an extension of herself.

- System messages should be separate from program, to allow change to be made easily. There is even the possibility of using the system in languages other than English, although this would depend on the availability of an appropriate speech synthesiser.

- The programs should be portable between computers (the Votrax unit has an RS232c interface, so can be used with many types of computer).

- The main communication mode should be natural language, but should not preclude pictures

- Rosemary should be able to define her own vocabulary, and not depend completely on predefined menus.

- The programs should be easily extensible by teachers with limited computer experience, so that the system would not depend solely on technical specialists

The first program was fairly primitive, and Rosemary used it for about two weeks, to help define what she wanted and could cope with.

The second program has now been in use for several months, and has proved fairly successful. Another child in the school is using an identical system, the only change to the programs being his name in messsages rather than Rosemary's.

A number of extensions and refinements have been defined during the system's use, and these are due for inclusion during the next school vacation. It is then expected that the system will be fairly stable.

BASIC is the only programming language in wide use among teachers and also allows for portability. The programs are written in almost-standard BASIC (the deviations from standard being: multi-statement lines and some Apple II screen handling).

The main program is carefully structured as a strict hierarchy with no attempt at optimisation (operational performance is not a problem), and the text is separate from the code in three tables:

- Rosemary's working text
- Normal dialogue messages
- Help messages

Anything typed in is taken as working text, unless it is a response to a system question or a command. The facilities provided are invoked by commands in the format ".X" where "X" is a single letter, and Rosemary can have the menu of commands statically displayed at the top of the screen in the format:

```
.L (LAST)     .A (ALL)    .C (CHANGE)
.P (PRINT)    .T (TALK) .......
```

The commands in the current system are:

- .L displays the last sentence input
- .A displays everything in the current working text
- .C allows a sentence to be changed
- .P prints hard copy
- .T turns speech on (coupled with display) and off
- .H turns help messages on and off
- .S saves the current working text on disk
- .R retrieves stored working text from disk
- .X cancels a sentence in working text

The size of working text and the speed of operation can be set by parameters within the program.

It is fairly simple to vary system messages, to modify commands or to add new commands. Some short computing workshops have been run for teachers at the school and several teachers are now gaining confidence and experience in experimentation.

4 CASE STUDY 2 - CATHERINE

Rosemary, despite the severity of her disabilities, is one of the more tractable problems that confronts us. She had pre-existent reading skills, some mobility and enough fine motor control to manage a keyboard. We would now like to turn our attention to Catherine, for whom keyboard access is impossible, and for whom we have been developing some special interfaces.

Catherine typifies a kind of disability that until the advent of the computer was very difficult to help. She is an Athetoid tetraplegic, has no voluntary limb control, no apparent fine motor control, no speech, is in frequent spasm and is apparently totally helpless. We have good reason to believe however that she is of normal or near-normal intelligence.

In addition to this Catherine's disabilities were compounded by the fact that they had existed from birth. She had never enjoyed independent movement, she had no pre-existent skills. There was no foundation on which to build.

When we first encountered Catherine she had been communicating through the medium of Bliss (BLI 80) - a symbolic method involving pictograms - by using a pointer mounted on her head to indicate the concept symbols which were mounted on a chart in front of her. Unfortunately as she got older she got taller and the angular movement of her body became too great for her to control. She lost the ability to communicate easily and as a result was deeply frustrated.

We thought of using a proprietory computer-based communications aid such as MacApple (MAC 81) a product which enables a user to build output, selecting predefined items by moving a cursor around two-dimensional tables and defining additional words and phrases as required. But the problem remained - how could she operate it?

In fact, Catherine had been using for some time an electromechanical product which was similar to the MacApple. This was a large perspex board displaying letters, numerals and punctuation marks, and connected to an electric typewriter. Catherine could, by hitting two large foam-padded rods with her forearms, cause the symbols in a row or column to light up one at a time. When a required symbol was lit, she could strike one of the rods again, and it would be typed. This mode of communication was far too slow for anything like conversation, and because of Catherine's lack of motor control, was error-prone. Error correction required backspacing and overtyping with "X" or "*", which sometimes made for difficult reading. Obviously, a transient display such as a VDU screen would alleviate this problem at least.

None of the conventional switches would work. Catherine simply did not have the residual fine motor control to operate chin switches, grunt switches, paddles, joy sticks or any obvious interface. We then noticed that Catherine's ability to point her eyes was superb. She could watch television while lying on the floor and despite the continuous spasms would keep her eyes focussed on the screen.

We thought initially of using the actual eye pointing but could not achieve this with our existing resources and so went to a second alternative. We realised that Catherine could control her eye blinking, which appears to be not untypical, as this mechanism appears to be so far up the brainstem as to usually be present if life itself is sustained. What is more, if fine motor control exists then we have a trainable skill and with the ability to wink as well as blink can control three switches: the first eye, the second eye and both together.

We concentrated for some time on constructing switches which were operated by light being reflected from an L.E.D. by the open eye but the problems of refraction were proving intractable. It was here that we tried bouncing the beam from the closed eyelid and were agreeably surprised by the result. In the end we compromised on an L.E.D. emitting light at the low end of the visible red spectrum which was in turn reflected and received by a photo-transistor connected to the computer by a cable connected to the circuit board.

The board was in turn mounted in one of the vacant slots in an Apple II and the "Katie" switch used to operate a MacApple program.

One of the developments planned for the next few months is to provide a "Katie" input, as an alternative to keyboard input, for a synthesiser system as used by Rosemary.

5 MICROCOMPUTERS IN SPECIAL EDUCATION

In summary the Micro-computer aided by an array of specialised interfaces can give a range of abilities to the severely disabled.

They can, with the aid of a synthesiser, speak. They can type either on a monitor screen or hard copy and they can, via a simple bolt-on module, exercise a very significant degree of control over their environment.

What is more, special schools are no longer buying aids in a highly specialised and very expensive market geared exclusively to their needs. They can now take advantage of the very much larger, cheaper and highly competitive market for commercial microprocessor equipment.

Computers can, as we showed above, give new independance, new chances and new dignity to this small and desperately deprived group.

6 MICROCOMPUTERS IN MAINSTREAM EDUCATION

We would now like to turn our attention to the second and much larger body of young people who pass through our educational system and derive very little benefit from it. We would argue that for them as well,the computer offers a very real possibility of overcoming their disabilities, for they are basically victims of inadequate educational technique.

It may seem the wildest hyperbole to suggest that basic educational techniques have not significantly changed since the third century B.C. but we believe this statement to be significantly true. Indeed, the third century contributed our more advanced methods, the lecture and subsequent dialogue. Rote learning, learning the words of power by heart was probably known to Neolithic man and was certainly a feature of education in Ancient Egypt.

These two methods are still the core elements used in most academic institutions in the United Kingdom, and so far as we know, in most other countries in the world.

The researches of the behaviourist school of psychologists, notably B. F. Skinner and his associates, made a very significant change in the communication of skills possible and for any linear structure of information Programmed Learning has an enormous potential, although potential is what it largely remains.

Insofar as public education is concerned, Programmed Learning is little used and still less understood. Business may have adopted Skinnerian techniques, the instructional branches of the Armed Forces may have followed suit, but schools and universities are still deeply commited to neo-Platonism.

As a result, in order to obtain any significant benefit from conventional educational institutions, the student must achieve very early fluency in the most complex linguistic skills. Verbal agility must be quickly followed by fluent literacy, and unless this is achieved at a very early age - in the UK typically eleven years - educational opportunity is effectively denied. In a class-based society such as the UK this usually results in higher education being largely confined to those whose upbringing gives them access to the language famimliar to their teachers, teachers who themselves rarely understand how this language is acquired (See BER 61).

As a result in the United Kingdom, and one supposes in most other countries, there exists a very large group of those who have been filtered out of the educational system by their inability to master the increasingly complex language of instruction and form an alienated and increasingly unemployable sub-culture.

The only organisation in the UK that has records over the greater part of the 20th Century is the Army, and these show a steady improvement to 1939, a steep decline during the Second World War, and a steady improvement until the early 1970's.

The figures kept by the English Department of Education and Science show a similar trend although they are susceptible to a more sophisticated analysis which shows that the bottom 17% of the group - the fairly constant group of poor scorers - had shown a slight deterioration in performance towards the end of the period under review. (The test used, the Watts Vernon, was last applied in 1971).

A common sense appraisal of the information would seem to confirm what we as teachers empirically know. Teachers know how to teach people like themselves, using as foundation a shared body of early linguistic experience and cultural expectations. Children from families of semi-skilled and unskilled workers who do not share this experience are rapidly left behind in the process and, without fluent literacy, drown in the sea of written language on which the educational process floats.

There seems little to suggest that conventional teaching techniques will ever significantly change this situation. Teachers generally are not trained to teach skills and even if they were, the sheer magnitude the task would demand a teacher-pupil ratio which is economically unrealistic. The development of linguistic skills demands either an environment which is congenial and a rudimentary programme of teaching, or a programme which is complex, flexible, meticulously structured and rigorously applied.

The first instance is essentially the experience of the children of middle class and aspiring working class parents in Britain. The second is rarely, if ever, achieved or even contemplated in mainstream education. The theoretical background is simply not understood and, even if it were, the practical problems would be quite insurmountable.

The preparation of individual programmes of work and the concomitant one-to-one teaching schedules are quite incompatible with the pupil-teacher ratio existing (and capable of existing) in any forseeable real school. Such a proogramme is also incompatible with existing administrative and curricular structures.

The availability of computers can transform this scenario. Programs can be constructed to relate to the needs of any number of individual pupils, and by sharing materials teachers can effectively create an almost infinite range of programs designed to meet the needs of a very wide range of pupils. These packages do not have to be computer-based. The availability of inexpensive text processing software makes it easy to produce individually tailored texts and work schemes for many children from a single computer.

Given that our present system of education is still geared to the production of a small administrative elite, a larger middle managerial group and a very large body of unskilled and semi-skilled labour, given also that structured economic changes have rendered many of the latter group virtually unemployable, we are now presented with a situation in which we either educate this increasingly alienated group or we face the prospect of simply policing them.

It is not hard to see that the second alternative is unlikely to remain compatible with the preservation of liberal democracy.

7 CONCLUSION

What then are we saying?

We are suggesting that computers can radically transfrom our ability to educate.

At one level we can reach a small group which is grossly disadvantaged and significantly improve the quality of their lives.

The computer can assist the diabled to achieve genuine integration into the wider community. Their potential can be maximised, their inarticulacy minimised and they can quite properly become more independent individuals.

In a very real sense, with the aid of the computer the disabled can become people.

At a second level, we can envisage an even more important if superficially less spectacular change which could help preserve the fragile social stability of Post-Industrial Britain

REFERENCES:

BER 61

"Social Class and Linguistic Development" B. Bernstein, in "Education, Economics and Society" ed. Halsey, Free Press of Glencoe, 1961

BLI 8Ø

"Blissymbols for Use"
Blissymbolics Institute, Toronto, 198Ø

HAL 83

"The Integration of Physically Handicapped Children into Mainstream Schools" M. J. Hall
Report to the Winston Churchill Foundation, 1983

MAC 81

"The MacApple Communicator" P. Poon
Dept. of Electronic and Electrical Engineering, Kings College, London, 1981

MAK 8Ø

"The Makaton Vocabulary Development Project" M. Walker, 198Ø

WAR 79

"Report of the Committee of Enquiry into the Education of Handicapped Children and Young People"
M. Warnock (chair), HMSO 1978

MICROCOMPUTERS: Developments in Industry, Business and Education
D.R. Wilson and C.J. van Spronsen (eds.) / ©EUROMICRO, 1983
Elsevier Science Publishers B.V. (North-Holland)

ARCHITECTURAL AND SOFTWARE CONSIDERATIONS IN VME-BUS BASED MULTIPROCESSOR SYSTEMS

András Palotási, Gyula Turchányi, Paul Verebély

Division Electronics
Computer and Automation Institute of the Hungarian Academy of Sciences
XI. Kende u. 13-17 Budapest 1111 Hungary

The paper describes some considerations for VME-Bus based multiprocessor systems. Different processor, memory and I/O modules were developped to achieve a consistent building block set. Using these building blocks different configurations are planed ranging from local area network couplers to microprocessor based multiprocessor systems and high performance graphics workstations for scientific and computer aided design use. The configurations can be linked together via high speed local area network. State of the art development tools are used to set up a network operating system based on today's portable operating systems.

KEYWORDS: multiprocessor system, VME-Bus, master and slave processors, local area network.

1. INTRODUCTION

The VME-Bus has been proposed at the end of 1981 by several major semiconductor suppliers including Motorola, Mostek, Signetics/Philips and Thomson CSF. The specification defines an interfacing system for use in interconnecting data processing, data storage and input-output peripheral devices. The bus system includes data transfer capability (8, 16 or 32 bit data; 16, 24 or 32 address lines), 7 level priority interrupt system, 4 level data transfer bus arbitration system and utilities. Card size, connectors, blackplane and signal pinout are all defined by the proposal. We will use the basic definitions (Backplane, Slot, Board, Module, Master, Requester, Interrupt Handler, Slave, Interrupter, Controller) as well known terms.

The VME Bus enables the use of both single and multiple masters. Examples will be shown for both cases.

2. GENERAL ARCHITECTURE

The systems discussed are all moderately coupled multiprocessor sytems. By moderately coupled we mean, that each processor - master or slave - has some local resources which will decrease some of the bandwith demands on the global memory. These resources include local stores from which the processor can execute its program.

The general architecture is shown in figure 1. A single 16 bit master processor (VME MCP: Memory Control Processor) is in this system (see chapter 3). Four 8 bit slave processors are connected to the VME Bus (VME Z80 LBC: Local Board Controller). They have all the same architecture as it is explained in Chapter 4. The four processors have different tasks so they have four types of I/O interface extensions. LBC0 has the function of serial line multiplexer, LBC1 is a local area network (COBUS) front-end processor, LBC2 is an intelligent mass storage controller, LBC3 is the heart of a graphic display subsystem.

In single master configurations may be adequate to have a bus controller built onto the master CPU board. We have chosen a separated bus controller module as shown in figure 2. This implematation allows to utilize multiple master CPU modules without conflict or duplication of circuitry. The modul includes a priority arbiter, a power and reset logic with manual and external inputs (second ones are connected to the power supply), a system monitor with a watch-dog timer (a switch selectable bus timeout between 4 and 8192 usec is avaiable). The system monitor enables to display the state of all VME Bus signals on indicators or on a logic state analyzer. A clock generator produces 16 and 4 Mhz signals for all modules. The terminators serve for reflection and ringing reduction and high state pullups for open collector drivers.

As a common resources multiple memory boards are available (figure 3). They provide 512 kbyte of dynamic RAM with parity generation and check and onboard refresh. 8 and 16 bit data transfers are standard, but provision is made for future processors with 32 bit data pathes. The address range is limited to 24 bit (16 Mbyte).

3. PROCESSORS

There are two main tasks which require different types of processors: MCP is dedicated for data, LBC for intelligent I/O processing. Besides differences there is a lot of identical solutions in both types: their onboard peripheral contollers and the external bus

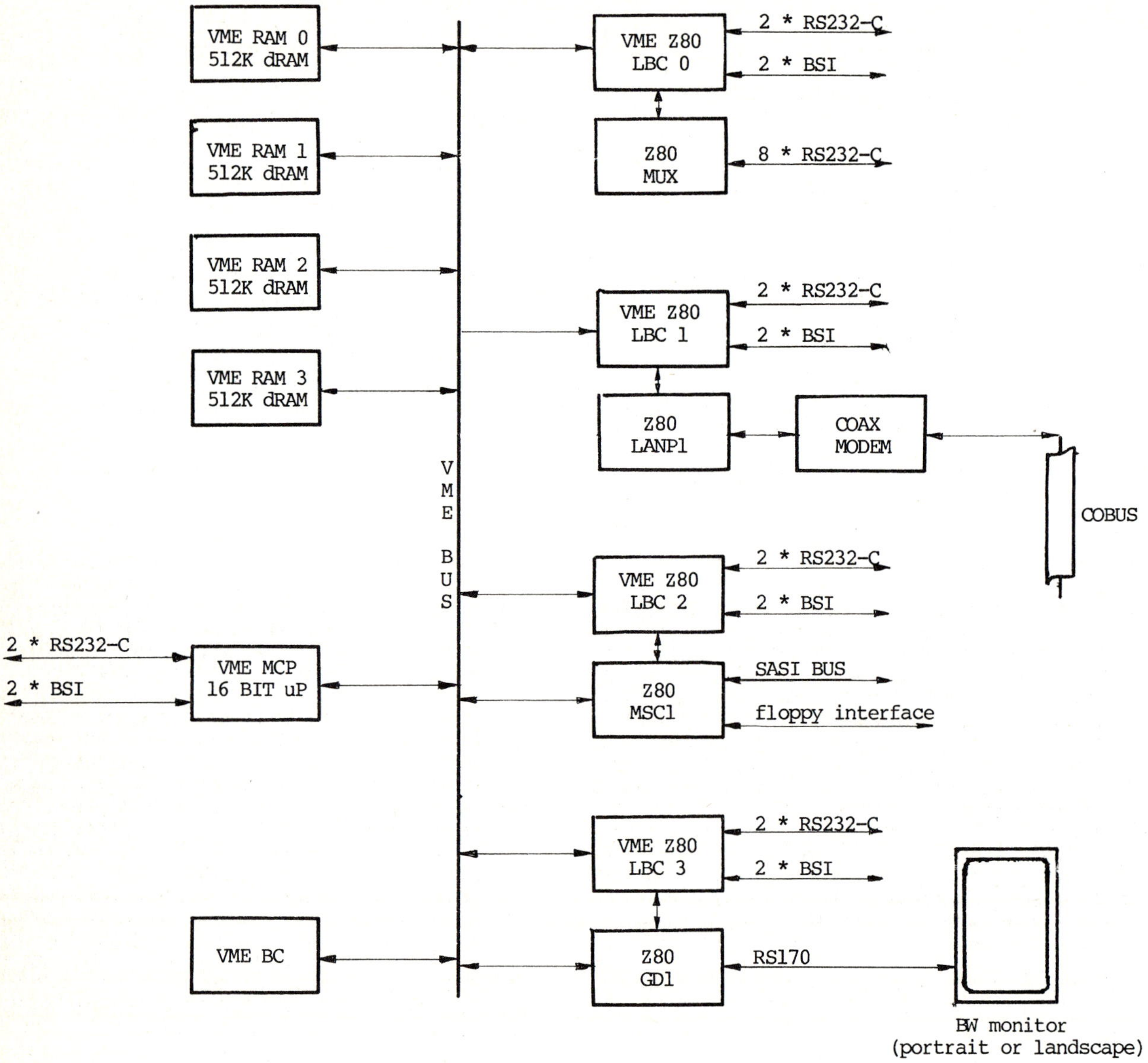

Figure 1 : General architecture

system compatible with one of the most popular microprocessor families, the Zilog Z80, which is produced by several second sources in different countries.

3.1. Master processors

The MCP master processors include a 16 bit microprocessor with hardware memory managment, a floating point extension, 128 kbyte parity RAM and 4-16k EPROM (onboard) (figure 4). The peripherals devices are a Z80 CTC timer, a Z80 PIO with two independent 8 bit parallel ports (BSI), Z80 SIO with two high speed serial lines (RS232C). The I/O ports can be used for debugging, external down-loading, peripheral interfacing (such as CRT display, printer, etc.) The connection to the VME bus is three-fold. A Z80 PIO enables to realize an interrupt requester which can use any of the seven interrupt levels. The level can be changed dinamically under software control for realizing

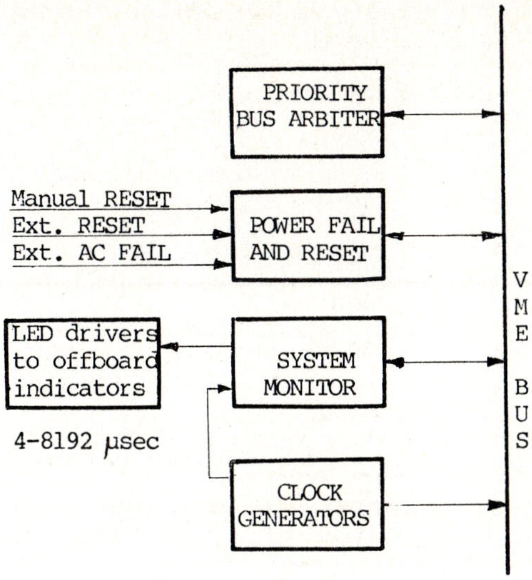

Usage: 1 per VME BUS card cage, mounted in SLOT1

Dimensions: 220mm * 233.4mm, two 50 pole edge connector for offboard indicators

Allocation speed: 100 nsec

Clocks: 16 MHz 50% duty cycle, 4 MHz 25% duty cycle

Indicators: BUS ERROR, SYSTEM FAIL (onboard) Driver for all VME BUS signal indicators (offboard)

Options: PRIORITY BUS ARBITRATION timeout (4-8192 usec)

Figure 2 : VME BUS CONTROLLER (VME BC) SPECIFICATIONS

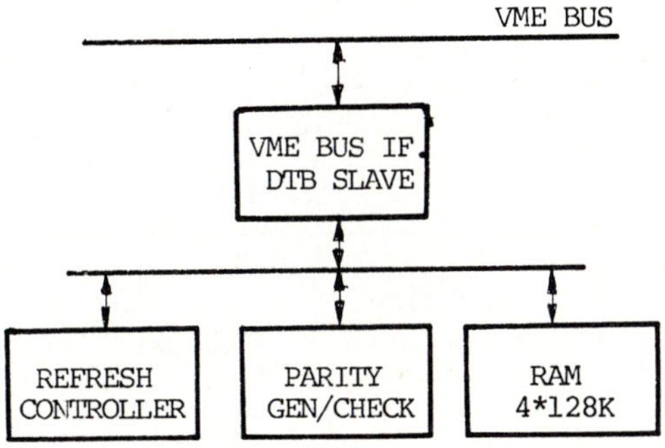

Configuration: DTB SLAVE A(24); D(16)-D(32)

Usage: one or more per VME BUS card cage

Dimensions: 220mm * 233.4mm

Speed: 200 nsec write, 260 ns read, 350 ns cycle time

Error handling: BUS ERROR (BERQ) on parity fail

Options: ADDRESS BLOCK: 512K boundaries, MODE D(32)

Figure 3 : VME RAM SPECIFICATIONS

an interprocessor interrupt system.

The second connection is the interrupt handler capability. An MCP handles only a single interrupt level. Receiving an interrupt signal from the bus at the appopiate level CPU begins to execute an interrupt acknowledge cycle. The Interrupt Handler requests the use of VME Bus on the highest request level (BR3) for a single cycle via the DTB Requester (so in the case of an interrupt the DTB Requester work in the "Release When Done mode). The 8 bit identifier sent by the Interrupt Requester (MCP or LBC) is gated into the CPU during the end of the interrupt acknowledge cycle. (CPU is synchronized to the interrupt handler by its READY signal.)

The third connection is the DTB mastership: the most part of the CPU's address range (except onboard memory) initiates a data transfer on the VME Bus with 16 data and 24 address bits. For data transfers the DTB Requester has to get control of the VME-Bus using low-level bus requests (BR1 or BR0) in "Relase on Request" mode (this means if BR3 and BR2 are not active - there is no interrupt acknoledge or DMA cycle - an MCP can use VME Bus for long data transfers or can release it if another master wants to use it and there is a "hole" in the current master's demand for common memory (the mastership can change let us say every microsecond or less).

The external, Z80 compatible bus of the MCP makes possible to use any peripheral interfaces of the LBCs.

3.2. Slave processors

The slave processors are intelligent peripherals controllers which take over most of the I/O

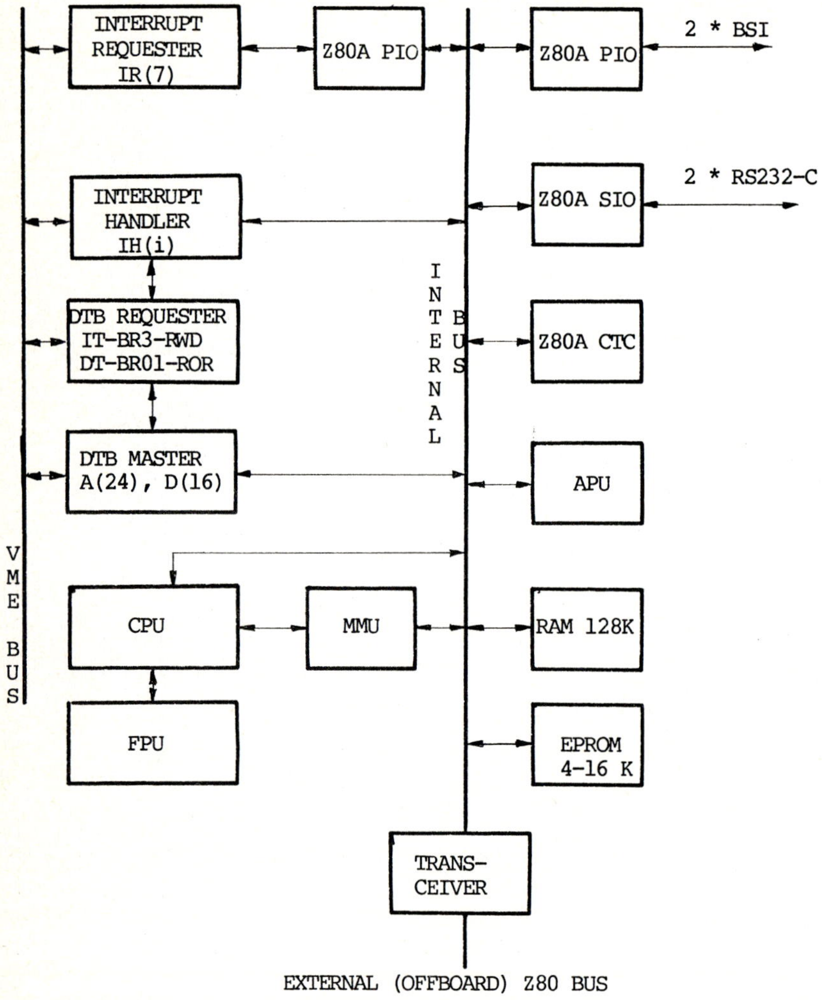

Configuration: DTB MASTER A(24)
D(16)

Usage: Standalone or 1-7 per
VME BUS card cage

Dimensions: 220mm * 233.4mm
two 25 pole Cannon
female (for RS232Cs)
two 26 pole edge
connector (for BSIs)

CPU: 16 bit microprocessor
with memory managment
and floating extension

I/O: Z80A PIO (for BSI)
Z80A SIO (for RS232-C)

MEMORY: 4-16K byte EPROM
(2*28 pin sockets)
128K byte RAM
(with parity)

Options:
DTB REQUESTER
BR3 Relaise when Done
for IT handling
BR0 or 1 Relaise on
Request for DATA trf.
INTERRUPT REQUESTER
any one of 7 levels
(dynamically alterable)
INTERRUPT HANDLER
any one of 7 levels
(static)

Figure 4 : VME MCP SPECIFICATIONS

overhead. They get program and data from the master(s), and upon completion of their tasks they report with interrupts.

To the contrary of many multiprocessor systems, where the peripherals processor "see" the common memory, we realized the Local Board Controllers (figure 5). The LBC's memory (16-64 K of RAM and 2-16 k ROM, which can be mapped off) can be accessed on the VME Bus as ordinary memory (except access time). This memory is not a real dual port memory: it can be reached using a so called "DMA-State Machine" which takes over the Z80 bus (using the Z80 CPU's bus request line) during the VME Bus transfer using the DTB Slave logic. High speed data transfers can be realized between common (or MCP private) and LBC memory using special instructions of MCP or with a DMA device capable for memory-memory transfers. The DMA State Machine has lower priority than LBC's off board DMA controlled peripherals. The DMA State Machine is realized using a pipeline register and PROM resident microprogram.

The Interrupt Requester has the same task and architecture than MCPs' one. Their two BSI type parallel ports, two RS232-C lines and the counter-timer are the same circuits as MCP's ones. The CPU of the LBC is a standard 8-bit Z80.

4. INPUT-OUTPUT INTERFACES

The I/O interfaces are Z80 Bus compatible extensions of the LBC, but they can be connected to the MCPs as well, because of the identical external buses of both types of processors.

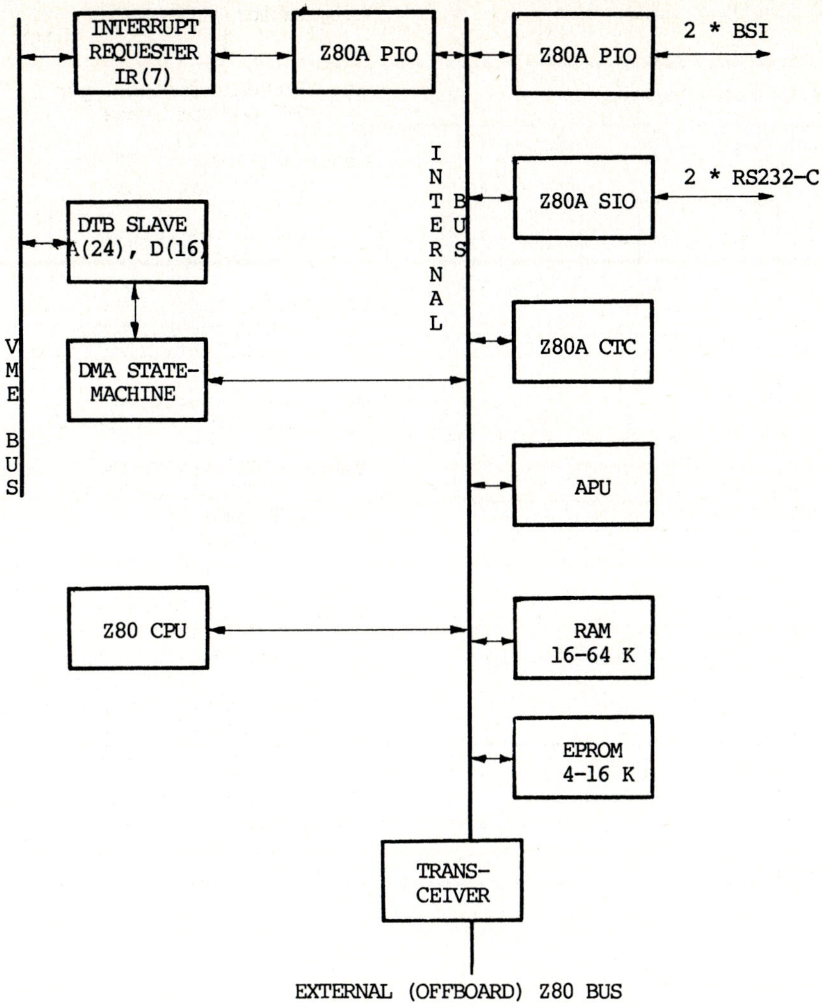

Configuration: DTB MASTER A(24) D(16)

Usage: Standalone or 1-4 per VME BUS card cage

Dimensions: 220mm * 233.4mm
two 25 pole Cannon female (for RS232Cs)
two 26 pole edge connector (for BSIs)

CPU: Z80 at 2.5 MHz or
Z80A at 4MHz or
Z80B at 6MHz

I/O: Z80A(B) PIO (for BSI)
Z80A(B) SIO (for RS232-C)

MEMORY: 4-16K byte EPROM
(2*28 pin sockets)
(can be mapped of)
16-64K byte RAM
(with parity)

Options:
INTERRUPT REQUESTER
any one of 7 levels
(dynamically alterable)

Figure 5 : VME Z80 LBC SPECIFICATIONS

4.1. Z80 MUX (eight channel serial multiplexer)

The Z80 MUX realizes eight RS232-C synchronous/asynchronous lines using 4 interrupt driven SIOs and a CTC as baud rate generator (figure 6). In this case the only task of the LBC software to handle these lines for example to produce eight communication lines with high level protocols up to CCITT X25 or to cooperate with MCP's software to realize an inteligent terminal handler for 8 interactive CRT terminals. In the second example the LBC's software relieves oparating system of I/O activity problems in man-machine interaction.

4.2. LANP1 (local area network processor)

Using LANP1 LBC becomes a communication front-end for the COBUS local area network (figure 7). (The COBUS supports 255 station at 1 Mbit/sec.) LANP1 consists of two Z80 DMA controllers, a Z80 PIO and a 2652 type USART. It also contains the neccesary transceivers for the COBUS interfacing. The LBC-LANP communication front-end realizes minimum four layers of the ISO Open System Interconnection standard. This combination can be used as a standalone product as well: in this case the serial and parallel ports of LBC can be used for interfacing personal computers or simple CRT terminals to the COBUS. The software (up to the virtual terminal protocol) can be placed into LBC's 2-16 Kbyte EPROM.

4.3. Mass Storage Controller

The Mass Storage Controller is also an LBC extension (figure 8) but it can initiate byte or

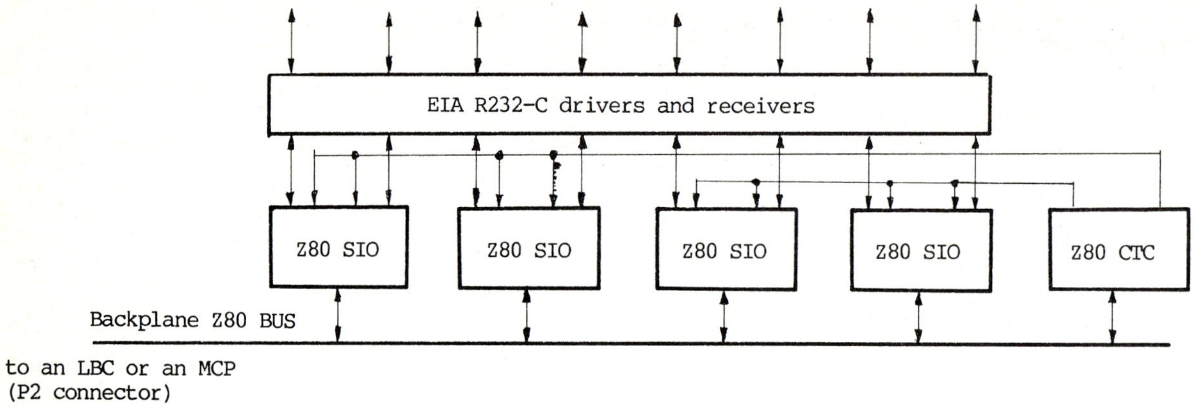

Figure 6: Z80 MUX (8 channel serial multiplexer)

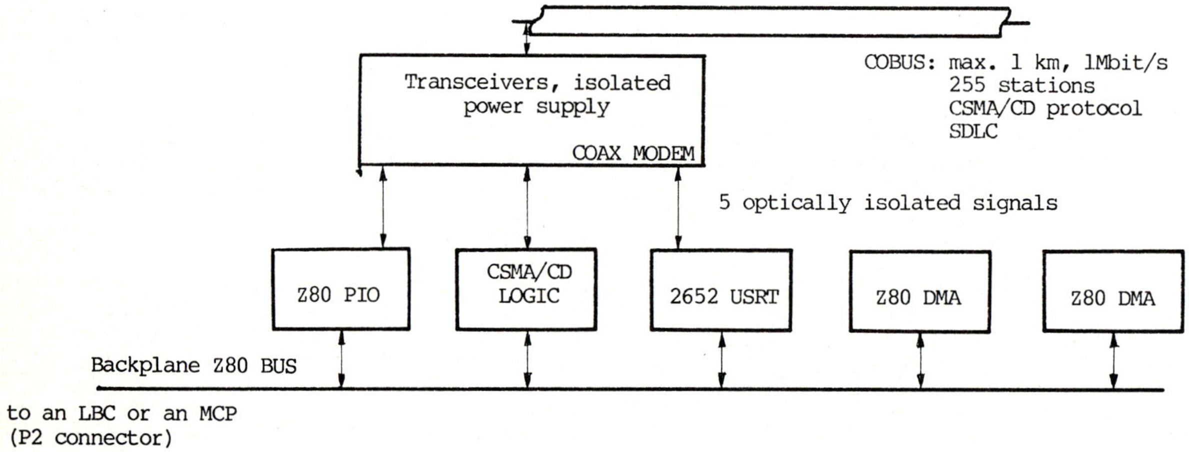

Figure 7: LANP1 (Local Area Network Processor)

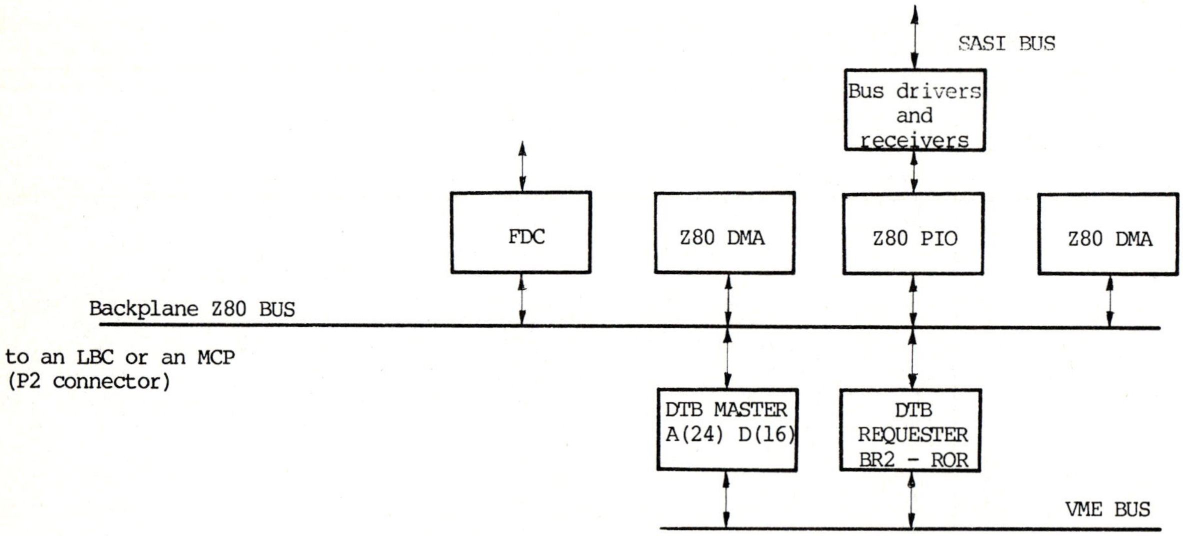

Figure 8: Z80 MSC (Mass Storage Controller)

word type data transfer on the the VME Bus (DTB Master). The associated DTB Requester uses the BR2 level in "Relase on Request" mode. MSC is a DMA type device which interfaces rotating memories therefore it can not wait too long for the VME BUS being free. It has higher priority than the MCP masters, but lower than "single cycle stealer" Interrupt Handlers.

The MSC uses a floppy disk controller with Z80-DMA (single and double density, 5 1/4 or 8 "), and a Z80 PIO with a second Z80-DMA to realize a parallel I/O bus (SASI) for different mass storage devices (disks and magnetic tapes).

4.4 Graphic subsystem

The graphic subsystem (figure 9) attached to the LBC contains a display picture generator (GD1) with a 1024*1024*1 frame-buffer and an RS-170 output for high resolution noninterlaced digital CRTs (1024*768, portrait or landscape monitors). For color monitor it can be expanded with dual port memories (GDEXT; 1024*1024*4 each): they can be accessed on the VME BUS as an ordinary memories in each plane. The other port is used for VIDEO input or output. TEXPRO provides an independent text overlay. The VME BITMOVER makes fast pixel manipulations possible from LBC and uses the VME BUS to get geometrical data to be transformed into pixel information. The GDVLT contains shift registers, look up tables (loadable by the LBC) and D/A converters to generate R,G,B signals (interlaced color monitors up to 1024*1024 can be attached). The interactive graphic input devices (tablet, joystick, keyboard) are connected directly to the LBC.

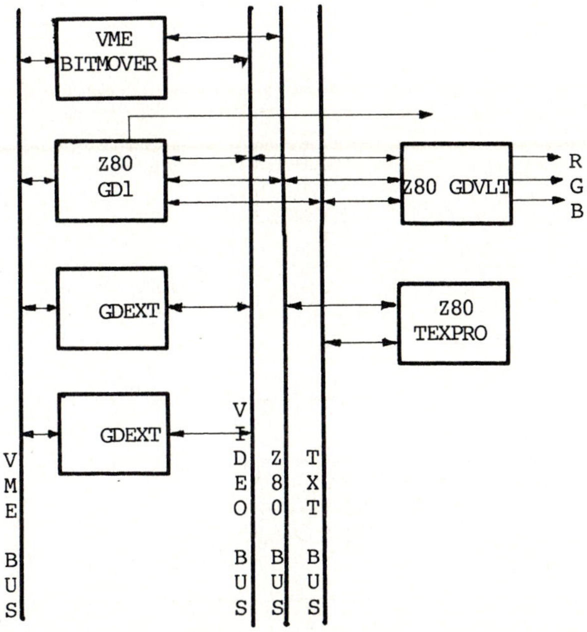

High performance color graphic subsystem
Figure 9

5. Configurations

Most of the configurations can be deducted from general architecture shown in figure 1.

Using LBC1 + LANP1, an intelligent standalone local area network coupler can be built (as it has been discussed in chapter 4; the VME Bus and circuits related to it are not used in this case). An eight user standalone time-sharing system consists of a single MCP + several VME rams + LBC0 + MUX + LBC2 + MSC. A single graphic terminal can be built using LBC3 + GD1 (let us say a TEKTRONIX 4014 emulator). A complete CAD graphic workstation consist of an MCP + four VME RAMs + LBC2 + MSC + LBC3 with the high performance graphic subsystem.

Our VME Bus implementation allows using of maximum 7 masters and 4 slaves. Multiple master configurations are needed first of all by high reliability applications. These include different control tasks such as computer conrol of NC machine tools, air traffic control, computer aided manufacturing, etc.

The other area of interest for multiple (master) processor systems is enlarging the processor throughput when a single processor is not adequate. In this case the tasks - not related to I/O handled by the slaves - are to be distributed beetween the processors. This area includes picture processing, simulation (for instance air traffic controller training system), data base or file server machine, etc..

All configurations listed previously can be organized into a local-area network based system for different purpose (word processing, information system with distributed data bases, office automation, complex CAD/CAM systems, etc.)

6. Software development

A PDP11/40 based cross system has been set up for software development. It includes cross compilers for high level and assembly languages and crosslinker for both microprocessors. Both master and slaves use their RS232-C lines for down-loading crosscompiled programs and they have a PROM resident debug and test system.

A state of the art portable operating system of the single master configuration is being developed. The hardware dependent part is arranged and mostly written in assembly language. There is an interface for other parts of operating system - called roots - described in a high level language in which roots are implemented. This is a real portable system. Making a new implementation only the relatively small, well separated hardware dependent part has to be rewritten.

Examples of roots are time sharing operating system, data base managment, local area network communication, graphics, real time applications.

The operating systems to be linked via the local network will provide a common user interface and acces to common resources such as file store, letter quality printers, plotters etc.. This is called network operating system: none of the users does know whether he has acces to a single processor with local resources only or to any recources attached to the network (except turn around time).

7. Conclusions

A VME Bus and local area network based limited module set allows to get a wide variety of configurations and complex multiworkstation systems. State of the art operating system is provided to utilize both local and network-wide services.

8. References

"VME Bus Specification Manual"
REV. A., Oct 1981, Mostek Corp., Motorola Inc., Signetics/Philips

"Peripherals Controller Technology"
Computer Technology Rewies Spring/Summer 1981 pp. 105-118

"Compare microcomputer-bus to find the bus you need" EDN, June 10, 1981, pp. 141-153

"ZBI: a system bus for the Z8000"
Mini-Micro Systems, June 1980, pp. 67-74

"Extend microcomputer capability via multiprocessing"
EDN April 14, 1982, pp. 175-180

"16-bit families swell with greater integration"
Electronic Design, Oct. 14, 1982, pp. 103-158

SESSION CHAIRMEN ADDRESSES

J. Billingsley
Electrical Engineering Department
Portsmouth Polytechnic
Portsmouth
U.K.

F. de Bruyne
Bell Telephone Mfg. Co.
Francis Wellesplein 1
B2000 Antwerpen
België

J. Calzadilla Daguerre

A.G. Guerra
ETSI Telecommunications
Cuidad Universitaria
Madrid 3
Spain

B. Lent
Grossenbacher Elektr. AG
Oststrasse 25
9006 St. Gallen
Switzerland

J. Molgaard
Elektronikcentralen
Venlighedsvej 4
2970 Horsholm
Denmark

B. Myhrhaug
Tandberg Data
P.O. Box 9
Korsvoll
Oslo 8
Norway

M. Sami
Elecrtronic Department
Piazza L. da Vinci 32
20133 Milano
Italy

H. Schumny
Physikalisch Techn. Bundesanstalt
Bundesallee 100
3300 Braunschweig
F.R. of Germany

T. Skard
Tandberg Data
P.O. Box 9
Korsvoll
Oslo 8
Norway

C.J. van Spronsen
Delft T.H.
P.O. Box 5031
2600 GA Delft
The Netherlands

A.C.G. van Strien
PTT/KMC
Trompstraat 62
2266 KL Leidschendam
The Netherlands

D. Tabak
Elec. Eng. Department
Ben Gurion University
of the Negev
Beer Sheva 84105
Israel

L. Thompson
HSDE Ltd.
Bridge East Road
Welwyn Garden City, Herts AL7 1LR
U.K.

J. Tiberghien
V.U.B.
Pleinlaan 2
1050 Brussels
Belgium

F. Vajda
K.F.K.I.
P.O. Box 49
1525 Budapest
Hungary

H. Vrielink
Philips Research Laboratories
Buildings WB 342
5600 JA Eindhoven
The Netherlands

K. Waldschmidt
Goethe University
Fachbereich 20
P.O. Box 111 932
6000 Frankfurt a/Main 90
F.R. of Germany

J. Wilmink
T.U. Twente
Dept. Inf. Room A306
7500 AE Enschede
The Netherlands

D.R. Wilson
Polytechnic of Central London
115 New Cavendish Street
London W1M 8JS
U.K.

F. Winkelhage
G.M.D.
P.O. Box 1240
5205 St. Augustin
F.R. of Germany

AUTHORS ADDRESSES

J. Aramberri, F. Garijo, L. Gurruchaga,
F. Verdejo
Facultad de Informatica
Apartado 649
San Sebastian, Spain

M. Auguin
LASSY
Equipe de Recherche Associée au CNRS
Université de Nice
42 Bld. Napoléon III
06041 Nice Cedex, France

Dr. Ben Zion Barta
Ministry of Education
State of Israel
51, Disraeli Street
Haifa 34333, Israel

Lawrence W. Bernhard
InterFace Computer GmbH.
Oberföhringer Strasse 24 a/b
D-8000 München 81
F.R. of Germany

Mario De Blasi
Istituto Di Scienze Dell'Informazione
Via Amendola 173
70126 Bari, Italy

J.A. Bowen
Department of Computer Science
University of Reading
Reading RG6 2AX, U.K.

G. Capizzi
CSELT - Sez. Doc. e Inform.
Via G. Reiss Romoli, 274
10148 Torino, Italy

Gianni Conte
Dipartimento di Elettronica
Politecnico di Torino
Corso Duca Degli Abruzzi 24
Torino, Italy

S. Copelli
ARG Spl
Via Strambio 11
20133 Milano, Italy

G. Danese, D. Dotti
Ist. Di Informatica Sistemistica
Dell'Università di Pavia
Strada Nuova 106/C
27100 Pavia, Italy

Jared L. Darlington
Institut für Software-Technologie
Gesellschaft für Mathematik und
Datenverarbeitung mbH, Bonn
P.O. Box 1240
D-5205 St. Augustin 1
F.R. of Germany

Prof. Dr. Piotr Dembinski
Institute of Computer Science
Polish Academy of Sciences
P.O. Box 22
00-901 Warsaw, Poland

F.G. Duncan
University of Bristol
Computer Science Department
School of Mathematics
University Walk
Bristol BS8 1TW, U.K.

G. Faerber, F. Demmelmeier
Lehrstuhl für Proczessrechner
Technische Universität München
Franz-Joseph-Str. 38
D-8000 München 40
F.R. of Germany

Alessandra Ferrero
Dipartimento di Elettronica
Politecnico di Milano
Piazza L. da Vinci, 32
20133 Milano, Italy

R. Fothergill
Director, M.E.P.
Cheviot House, Coachlane Campus
Newcastle upon Tyne NE7 7XA, U.K.

G. Goncalves
Université de Lille
ERA 771, Bâtiment M3
Villeneuve d'ASCQ Cedex
France 59655

Marnix Goossens
Jacques Tiberghien
Free Univ. of Brussels (V.U.B.)
Dept. of Informatics
Pleinlaan 2
B-1050 Brussels, Belgium

Dr. Birgit Hansen
Dept. of Automation Technique
Institute of Technology
2630 Tastrup, Denmark

Yigal Hoffner
Microprocessor Unit
University of Reading
Reading RG6 2AX, U.K.

K. Inchausti and F. Garijo
Facultad de Informatica
Apartado 649
San Sebastian, Spain

Petro Istavrinos
Siemens AG
Otto-Hahn Ring 6
8 München 83, F.R. of Germany

Dr. D.G. Jameson
The Dept. of Medical Physics &
Institute of Nuclear Medicine
The Middlesex Hospital Medical School
Windeyer Building, Cleveland Street
London, W1P 6DB, U.K.

Yukio Kaneda, K. Wada
S. Maekawa
Faculty of Engineering
Kobe University
Rokkodai-cho, Nada-ku
Kobe, Hyogo 657, Japan

J. Karszt, G. Lausen, R. Salz
Institut für Angewandte Informatik
und Formale Beschreibungsverfahren
Universität Karlsruhe
Kollegium am Schloss, Bau IV
D-7500 Karlsruhe, F.R. of Germany

Prof. Svetlana P. Kartachev
Department of Computer Science
Ferguson Hall
Lincoln, Nebraska 68588, U.S.A.

F. Larbey
SINTRA-ALCATEL
74-76, Av. G. Peri
92230 Gennevilliers, France

J. Lewi, K. De Vlaminck,
J. Huens, E. Steegmans
Katholieke Universiteit Leuven
Dept. of Computer Science
Celestijnenlaan 200A
B-3030 Leuven, Belgium

J. De Man, M. Peerlinck,
D. Genin, V. Goovaerts
Bell Telephone Mfg. Co.
Francis Wellesplein, 1
B-2000 Antwerpen, Belgium

Enrique Mandado, Perfecto Mariño
Escuela Tecnica Superior de
Ingenieros Industriales
Universidad de Santiage de Compostela
c/ La Paz, s/n Vigo, Spain

Prof. Dr. Ludwig Nastansky
Hildegunde Peine
Dept. of Business Data Processing
FB-5 Universität Paderborn
Warburgerstrasse 100
D-4790 Paderborn, F.R. of Germany

A. Palotási, G. Turchányi, P. Verébelÿ
Magyar Tudomanyos Akademia
Szamitastechnikai Es Automatizalasi
Kutato Intexete
Budapest VI, Kende U. 13-17, Hungary

A.J.H.M. Peels, G.J.M. Smit
Twente University of Technology
Department of Informatics
P.O. Box 217
7500 AE Enschede, The Netherlands

Professor G.L. Reijns
Delft University of Technology
Dept. of Electrical Engineering
P.O. Box 5031
2600 GA Delft, The Netherlands

C. Robach, G. Michel
Laboratoire d'Informatique
Et. de Mathématiques Appliquées
de Grenoble, BP 68
38402 Saint Martin d'Hères Cedex, France

X. Ruiz del Portal
IKERLAN
Centro de Investigaciones Technologicas
P.o. Jose M.a. Arizmendiarrieta s/n
Apartado 146
Mondragon (Guipuzcoa), Spain

Dr.-Ing. Djamshid Tavangarian
Universität Dortmund
Abteilung Elektrotechnik
Postfach 500500
D-4600 Dortmund 50, F.R. of Germany

M.S. Tudruj, R.F. Gajda
Institute of Computer Science
Polish Academy of Science
00-901 Warsaw, Poland

P. Turner
Haringey Education Service
Education Offices, 48-62 Station Rd.
Wood Green, London W1P 3HB, U.K.

John G. Vaughan
Joseph E. Higgins
Computer Science Department
University College
Cork, Ireland

S.C. Winter
Polytechnic of Central London
School of Engineering and Science
115 New Cavendish Street
London W1M 8JS, U.K.

Prof. E.L. Zapata
Universidad de Santiago
Departamento de Electricidad &
Electronica, Facultad de Ciencias
Santiago De Compostela, Spain

Sandor Zöld
Research Institute for Measurement &
Computing Techniques, KFKI
1121 Budapest, Hungary
XII., Konkoly Thege ut 29-33
Postacim: 1525 Bp. Pf. 49